Social Space: Canadian Perspectives

Social Space: Canadian Perspectives

Edited by
D. I. Davies *and*
Kathleen Herman

new press
Toronto
1971

ISBN 0-88770-113-2 paper bound
0-88770-112-4 cloth bound

Design/Peter Maher

Printed and bound in Canada

new press
84 Sussex Avenue
Toronto 179

Contents

Preface

In some ways this is a presumptuous book. In it we endeavour to apply what we identify as a distinctively Canadian intellectual tradition to the analysis of Canadian society. We deliberately eschewed the conventional categories which sociologists usually use to order their observations in the hope that by posing a different set of questions about Canada we would be forced to look in directions we might not have thought about otherwise. Once we had formulated, as our principal analytical concept, the notion of social space (which derived in some measure from the pioneering work of the late Harold Innis of the University of Toronto) we became increasingly excited about its usefulness in bringing together what seemed at first to be a disparate array of materials from many sources and many intellectual disciplines. Whether or not we have been able to provide the unity and coherence we have sought remains for our readers to decide.

Many people helped in the compilation. First, we wish to thank the Deans of the Faculty of Arts and Science at Queen's University, and in particular Dr. Clint Lougheed, for providing a very substantial grant towards publication. Tom Evans was the ideal library assistant. Our colleagues in the Department of Sociology gave time and shared enthusiasm in launching the project. Dave Godfrey was a critical and encouraging publisher, and Marilyn Field-Marsham a meticulous editorial assistant. New Press as a whole did us proud. Finally, and most importantly, we want to thank the authors who have given permission to include their work in this collection. Many of the selections appear here for the first time.

Ioan Davies

Kathleen Herman

*Queen's University
Kingston, Ontario
September 1971*

Introduction

Space is not only a physical reality, it is also psychological and sociological. In his play, Huis Clos, *Jean-Paul Sartre does not primarily use physical space to establish the contours of human relationships, he's telling us that the restrictions on relationships come from the personalities and modes of interaction of the individuals who find themselves enclosed. 'Hell' is not the walls of the prison, but 'other people'. It is mainly in this sense that the word 'space' is used throughout this reader though with the awareness that 'other people' include collectivities such as business, political parties and religious organizations. But as the example should make clear, relationships are also framed by physical space, one which is marked out by geography and by technology. So in order to understand how we distance ourselves from, or are enclosed with, other people we have to be able to know how social relationships are demarcated by physical, social, cultural and technological factors.*

Some political analysis has emphasized 'closed' and 'open' systems, which might appear to mean the same thing as 'private' and 'public' space. In point of fact, however, these terms refer to different dimensions: space categories refer to social claims while systems categories refer to social structures. Or in other words, systems analysis deals with formal hierarchies of relationships while space categories attempt to account for perceived boundaries of relationships. Thus systems analysis can only stress the interconnecting structural features which make particular frameworks 'open' or 'closed' – the explanation is in the structures; space analysis is concerned with the ways that people see, use and create structures – the explanation is in the perception of interaction. These two approaches are not incompatible, rather they do different things, but it is probably true to say that while systems analysis cannot explain variations – it can only identify similarities and differences – spatial analysis begins to provide a basis for understanding, if not explaining, the specifics of relationships.

This book, then, is about social space, but in a particular sense: it is entirely about Canada, but a Canada which is not seen as testing out theories and frameworks developed elsewhere, but as actively creating its own categories to frame answers to its own problems. The initial task of the reader is therefore to ask what questions have Canadians themselves posed in order to understand their predicament? And in searching for an interpretation it seems clear that there have been three fundamental areas of analysis: the area of dependence-independence; the sphere of communication; and the physical-biological forces of self-realization. In an important sense these areas are interdependent. Canada has always been dependent on other, more prosperous economies and this has had implications for the ways that Canadians have viewed communications and the use of physical and ecological resources. In turn, successions of conquests have provided real problems in the modes of communication between sectors of the population, further complicated by problems of physical distance and ecological determination. Finally physical and ecological space was not simply 'there' to be conquered, the conquest was determined by power relationships and by existing forms of communication. The continuing tradition in Canadian social science research, in political rhetoric, and in journalistic reportage is focused on these problems. How do Canadians take account of the external political and economic control of their society? How do they speak to each other? And how, with the second largest land mass in the world can they actually create something called a society? As Canadian social scientists have long recognized, these issues are crucial for the understanding of Canada and for the development of a critical social science related to its problems, but to date in Canada they have been discussed mainly by people who would not claim to be

sociologists, though this may be because the Canadian social science tradition is essentially interdisciplinary. Outside of Canada, however, similar questions have been central to sociological enquiry. The task of this book is therefore to use this analysis as the basis for a Canadian sociology and also to indicate the ways that non-Canadian sociological theories and methods might be reformulated to take account of the peculiarly Canadian social processes.

In order to do this we have everywhere attempted to move from generalities to specifics, from formal structures to people thinking out their own relationships. The task is not an easy one. With some societies (e.g. Britain, France or China) the definition of what a society is, is largely contained within its own boundaries. Other societies may impinge from time to time, and the country itself may take over other territories with important consequences for its own internal development. But, by and large, it is possible to say that certain institutions and processes are unique to that country: in other words it made itself. With Canada this is not possible. Canada did not make itself – it was made by others. When we talk about family patterns in Canada we are talking about English or Scots or American or French or Ukrainian family patterns; and yet not entirely. The subsequent development of imported institutions makes the character of these different from those of their country of origin. The problem is to be able to specify the interconnecting structures, values and time sequences which give these institutions their specifically Canadian meaning.

In order to be able to do this the book commences with a number of essays which provide the parameters of Canadian social institutions and processes and indicate the Canadian debate on definitions of social space. In each case, the essays present frameworks for viewing aspects of social structure and cultures, though these frameworks do not necessarily coincide with that used for this book as a whole. The importance of these essays is that they present within themselves an integrated picture of the data and the problems that are taken up in the rest of the book.

It is in the second section that the themes of this collection become clearer. The essays here all contribute in some sense to definitions of social space and its connections with physical or ecological space. Lyman's and Scott's essay is a classic definition of social territory, without any specific reference to ecology though drawing its terminology from it. Dorothy Smith provides perhaps the most sensitive essay available on the relationships between physical and social space, concentrating on households and family relationships. Hall, Bernstein and Stebbins provide other and different frameworks for spatial analysis – on communications, education and social networks. All of these essays provide the essential contours for our analysis of Canadian society, and pitch us into the problems of establishing the salient interconnections between physical distances and resources, and public and private spheres of activity. But in themselves they do not provide an indication of how sociology can do more than simply map out the territories. For analysis to be useful it does not only have to specify what relationships are or have been but how they might or should develop. John O'Neill, drawing on a critical American and German sociological tradition, presents a philosophical basis for such a task. His essay provides the cornerstone for the approach adopted in this book.

The next four sections of the book are devoted to exploring the specifics of social relationships in Canada. Section 3 examines the ways that areas which are formally public are redefined in order to exclude sections of the population. This includes discrimination on grounds of sex, race, social class, and languages as well as the procedures by which government policy defines certain policy areas as either private or 'against the public interest'. In this context we commence a debate – taken up again in Section 6 – on whether the 'public interest' reflects majority opinion or the interest of a 'private' group who happen to monopolize the power pyramid of public territory. In all these cases the important questions are not whether public space is controlled by private groups but how and why it is. In Section 4 we provide examples of the ways that people use the private space they have, while in Section 5 we explore some cultural aspects, including ways that people make sense in religious and political terms of their private life styles and the wider society in which they live. From this we move back in Section 6 to some examples of how public territories are monopolized by private groups. This section includes a journalist's assessment of the ways in which a debate within a private circle has become the arena for Quebec, and therefore Canadian national, disputes; an examination of the difficulties facing ethnic groups in entering public territory already monopolized by another group; a classic examination of a 'professional' monopoly in an area of public interest; control by elites of the two main Federal parties; and Joey Smallwood's strategies as Premier of Newfoundland.

This process leaves some people out in the cold – either because they are excluded by existing social structure and cultures from sharing in public territories or because they reject the terms on which they might be included. The important question is not whether they are correct in feeling excluded but what they do when they decide to act on this feeling. Section 7 provides five cases of such exclusion: Indians, French Canadians,

students, radical socialists, and youth. Each of the essays suggests ways in which 'exclusion' is precipitated and how the awareness of exclusion produces certain strategies which might range from attempts at inclusion to a total redefinition of the social structure of the country which provided the terms for exclusion. The fact that people feel deprived of their rights or indifferent to the terms on which they are offered is one of the dilemmas of all modern societies. In Canada, which in its history has provided refuge for people who were excluded from other societies (e.g. the Doukhobors) the dilemma is more than academic.

The final section is therefore devoted to exploring the redefinition of Canadian social relationships and their implications for social order. Central to this task is the role of Quebec and the recent transformations within the province. Richard Ossenberg's review of recent developments provides the essential framework for such an analysis. Alongside Quebec, however, other issues are crucial in the determination of the future profile of Canadian society – reorganizations in higher education, the job-market and technology, international relations, and in civil rights. Altogether the book offers the framework for an assessment of the interconnecting structures of Canadian society, critically examines some of our preconceptions about basic institutions, and suggests lines for further research and theory construction.

Social Space: Canadian Frameworks

Social Space: Canadian Frameworks

The search for a Canadian identity is in large measure a self-conscious effort on the part of Canadians to spell out what it is that makes them different from Americans and, though to a much lesser extent, other peoples of the Western world. Put another way, it is an attempt to define the Canadian 'national character' as this concept is used by anthropologists. Canada, as John Porter has pointed out, is a mosaic of many peoples with many cultural traditions and ethnic identities. Integration has been precarious, national identity elusive. To ask questions about Canadian identity, then, is to ask questions about the nature of Canada itself. In what ways has the unique conjunction of our history and our geography combined to shape our institutions in such a way as to make them unmistakably Canadian? And how, in turn, have these institutions moulded the character and world-view of Canadians?

Social institutions are patterned ways of doing things that persist through time (though not necessarily unchanged), prescribing and constricting people's behavior. Institutions don't just happen; they grow and develop and change in response to the exigencies of living. Some of these exigencies derive from basic human needs – such as the need for food, shelter or protection. Others derive from social needs, the problems a group confronts as it moves through space and time. Education, governance, economic institutions are examples. What kinds of institutions the members of a society develop to cope with their physical and social needs are, in part, a function of their beliefs, values and traditions; in part they are a function of what works. This pragmatic character of institutions implies a time dimension that has been neglected in sociological theories that give priority to structure, integration and order. Such theories, with their emphasis on man as well-socialized role player, ask a different set of questions (and come up with a different set of answers) than do those that view man as a self-conscious, responsive, acting

person who is the creator of his social forms with not only the capability but the responsibility to change them when they are no longer adequate to his needs.

Social institutions define for man his social space. They are at one and the same time enabling and delimiting. They regularize people's behavior, making at least some of it sufficiently predictable so as to make group life possible. If there were no institutional arrangements at all, no norms regulating behavior, there would be no 'social' space. Completely privatized man would be, as C. Wright Mills has reminded us, an 'idiot'. But just as there can be no freedom (and hence no space) in a completely privatized world – if such were possible – so too can there be no freedom, no personal or social space, in a society with institutions that are no longer responsive to the basic needs of its members. Alienation, the feeling that our institutions are not only beyond our understanding and control but dehumanizing as well, can be just as constricting as the self-destroying Hobbesian world of the war of all against all. A humanistic sociology asks such questions as, how and for what reasons did a given institution develop as it did? In what ways does it include some members of the society and exclude others? What are the consequences of such inclusion-exclusion? How are the variously-placed members of the society, both those whose room for movement is slight and those for whom it is great, participating to re-form its institutions to make them more responsive to the needs of all?

The essays in this section illustrate the pragmatic character of some of the major institutions and social arrangements in Canadian society. They provide the time dimension we need to understand how our institutions have taken shape, and they raise questions about the appropriateness of some of them for today. Taken together these essays constitute a sociological mapping of the boundaries that delineate and demarcate the social space of Canadians.

---

1. The Harvest of Lengthening Dependence

Kari Levitt/*McGill University*

Marx claimed that economic institutions were the substructure of society. All else – the family, education, legal and political institutions, as well as all belief systems – were superstructure. Not all social scientists accept Marx's rigid, uni-directional economic determinism, but they do acknowledge there is a fundamental relationship between the economic and other institutions in society. Because this is so, and because Canada's position with respect to the United States has always been a major parameter of Canadian social space, it is appropriate to open this book with a selection that deals with American economic penetration of Canada. This selection by Kari Levitt, a British economist now teaching at McGill, is the final chapter of her book Silent Surrender *in which she documents the extent to which Canadians have let slip away ownership of their natural resources and much of their industry. The boundaries between Canadian and American society, always tenuous, have become even more attenuated. Just how much room Canadians have for deciding their own destiny is no longer very clear.*

After twenty-five years of heavy American direct investment Canada's freedom of action has been progressively restricted to the point where it is doubtful whether it can be regained. The loss of sovereignty is most evident in the matter of 'extra-territoriality'. When the metropolitan government insists on the primacy of its law over subsidiaries located in hinterland countries there is a direct conflict of jurisdiction.[1]

The subsidiary is faced by the question: which law is to be respected, the law of the land in which the firm is located, or the law of the country in which the owners reside? As the authors of the Watkins Report put it: "Confronted with two peaks of sovereignty, it is likely to defer to the higher peak on which its foreign owners reside." In Canada the extra-territorial issue has arisen in three areas of conflicting jurisdiction: export policy, anti-trust legislation, and measures taken by US authorities to protect their balance of payments. In each case, Canadian subsidiaries of US corporations have been obliged, by American law or administrative pressures, to follow practices which are in conflict with pronounced Canadian policy; indeed, in some instances, in conflict with Canadian law.

Although the extension of US anti-trust legislation to Canadian subsidiaries may yet prove to be the most serious aspect of the 'extra-territoriality' issue, public attention has fastened on the export policies of American subsidiaries.[2] The US Trading with the Enemy Act prohibits affiliates and subsidiaries, in which fifty per cent of the stock is American-owned, from engaging in trade with Communist China, North Korea and North Vietnam. Violation of the law invites criminal action against all Americans who are stockholders or directors of the parent company. The law applies even where subsidiaries do not use American materials, components or technology. Although similar legislation with respect to Cuba is slightly less restrictive, US authorities called for 'voluntary compliance' which, in effect, placed administrative pressure from the US Treasury Department on their foreign subsidiaries not to engage in trade with Cuba. These practices are in direct conflict with Canadian trade policy, which is much more liberal. China is becoming an increasingly important customer for Canada. Although the volume of business lost is not known, it is obvious that Canada is losing both cash and legal jurisdiction over the large American-owned segment of her economy by permitting US legislation to govern the export policy of a substantial part of Canadian industry.

In all these situations there are, of course, the inevitable exemptions and special deals. Concesssions are made by the US authorities on a case-by-case basis, when Ottawa can prove that a particular order is of importance to the Canadian economy, or that it cannot be filled by a comparable Canadian-owned company. Once again, we have the pattern of begging favours from the metropolitan power to lift restrictions which violate Canadian sovereignty in the first place.

In commenting on the legal and administrative apparatus set up by the US government to implement their legislation abroad, the Watkins Report concluded that:

> This poses for Canada a basic political problem, namely that for an uncertain future the 'elbow room,' or decision-making power of the Canadian government has been reduced in regard to economic relations involving American subsidiaries. The essence of the extra-territorial issue is not the economic costs . . . but rather the potential loss of control over an important segment of Canadian economic life.[3]

Twenty years of unprecedented intake of American capital, technology, know-how and marketing connections have probably resulted in increased income and employment. Direct American investment has not, however, secured the basis of continued growth. Indeed, there has been a regression in Canada's economic position relative to other equally industrialized countries. The author of a survey of recent trends and patterns of Canadian trade concluded that "Canada's position resembles more closely that of a less developed nation than that of other developed countries."[4]

The golden days of easy export earnings have long passed. The resource boom which fed the income-generating process of the fifties and attracted the heavy inflow of direct investment in secondary manufacturing is largely played out. In the sixties the trend of US direct capital flow is towards expansion of manufacturing facilities in the rich and growing markets of Europe. The honeymoon is over, and the realization is dawning that the heavy intake of direct investment and the consequent loss of economic control has restricted Canada's freedom of action in a highly competitive world economy.

In the key sectors of the Canadian economy, decisions concerning what is to be produced, where it is to be sold, from whom supplies are to be purchased and what funds are to be transferred in the form of interest, dividends, loans, stock-purchases, short-term balances, charges for management, research or advertising services, and so on, are made externally in accordance with considerations of global strategy of foreign corporations. Nor is dependence confined to decisions transmitted through parent-affiliate links. For Canada, freedom of action has been progressively restricted by a proliferation of commitments – both formal and informal – arising from bilateral arrangements with the government of the United States. In this manner the free market is being replaced by internal transfers within multinational corporations. Correspondingly, inter-governmental relationships resemble increasingly those of the old mercantilist systems. Although the country is richer, the Canadian economy is less flexible than it has been in the past. The instruments of public policy are constrained by umpteen commitments made in exchange for 'special favours'.

In the private sector there is little entrepreneurship and technological dynamism. The share of crudely processed materials in exports has not diminished significantly. Imports of manufactured goods as a percentage of domestic production have increased. Technological dependence is greater than ever and unequalled by any other industrialized country. In a world in which competition places a premium on innovation and entrepreneurship, imitative technology is reflected in a high cost structure and lagging productivity. The capital market is distorted in the sense that Canadian savings cannot find attractive equity investments in Canada, while large proportions of savings generated in Canada are not available to other sectors of the economy because they accrue in the form of retained earnings and depreciation allowances of foreign-controlled corporations. The structure of ownership and control is such that there are barriers to the flow of Canadian savings to finance new Canadian enterprise. Technology-oriented industries are firmly in the hands of foreign corporations. As the Watkins Report observes: "Power accrues to nations capable of technological leadership, and technical change is an important source of economic growth."[5]

The Mercantilist Nexus

The facts concerning foreign control of Canadian industry are well known: 60 per cent of manufacturing industry, 75 per cent of petroleum and natural gas and 59 per cent of mining and smelting were foreign controlled in 1963.** The degree of control has increased significantly since 1939, when the corresponding figures for manufacturing and mining were 38 per cent and 42 per cent. As recently as 1954 foreign control in both manufacturing and mining was only 51 per cent.

By contrast, railways have always been and continue to be under Canadian control. Here foreign portfolio capital has diminished from 57 per cent in 1939 to 22 per cent in 1963. The only sector which has experienced a marked reduction in foreign control from 26 per cent in 1926 to the present level of 4

**Eds. The Committee for an Independent Canada reports the following figures for 1967, taken from the *CALURA Report*:
Extent of Foreign Ownership of Canadian Corporations, 1967

Manufacturing Industries	56.7%
Mining Industries	60.0%
Oil and Gas Wells	82.6%
Petroleum Refining	99.9%

(Data from Hansard)
Approximately 80% of foreign-owned industry on average is under American control. Specific industries where American control is particularly high include:

Motor Vehicles and Parts	95.6%
Industrial Electrical Equipmt.	89.6%
Rubber Products	82.9%
Synthetic Textiles	71.5%
Industrial Chemicals	58.9%

per cent is utilities. Canadian control in railways and utilities is public rather than private. Indeed, in 1964, of $34.4 billion Canadian-controlled assets of all corporate non-financial enterprise, over one-third, or $12.2 billion, was in the public sector – almost exclusively railways and utilities (see Table 1).

Public investment in utilities is more than twice the value of railway assets and equals the entire value of Canadian-controlled assets in manufacturing, mining and smelting, and petroleum. It equals also the value of assets of all foreign branch plants in manufacturing. This would indicate that very large

Table 1: Locus of Control of Canadian Industry, 1963

	CONTROLLED IN (Billions of dollars)					CONTROLLED IN (Percentages)				
	Total	*Canada*		*U.S.A.*	*Other*	*Total*	*Canada*		*U.S.A.*	*Other*
		Public	*Private*				*Public*	*Private*		
Manufacturing	13.7	0.1	5.3	6.3	1.9	100	1	39	46	14
Petroleum and natural gas	7.3	–	1.9	4.6	0.8	100	–	26	62	12
Mining and smelting	3.8	0.1	1.5	2.0	0.3	100	–	40	52	7
Railways	5.3	3.7	1.5	0.1	–	100	69	29	2	-
Other utilities	12.2	8.3	3.4	0.4	0.1	100	68	28	4	–
Construction and merchandising	*9.8*	*0.1*	*8.6*	*0.7*	*0.5*	*100*	*1*	*87*	*7*	*5*
TOTAL	52.1	12.2	22.2	14.0	3.6	100	24	42	27	7

Canadian Balance of International Payments, 1963, 1964 and 1965, August 1967, page 80.

sums of capital have been mobilized under Canadian entrepreneurship – where this has taken the form of public enterprise. We should note that a significant amount of these utility investments are provincial rather than federal public assets.

In manufacturing, for reasons previously suggested, foreign capital seeks control rather than participation. There is no significant foreign portfolio investment in Canadian manufacturing. This is not so in the mining industry. Thus, in manufacturing, the percentage of assets owned by foreigners was 54 per cent, whereas the percentage of assets under foreign control was 60 per cent. By contrast, in mining and smelting the foreign ownership percentage (62 per cent) exceeded the foreign control percentage (59 per cent).

Foreign control in general and US control in particular is highest in those industries in which metropolitan taste-formation and technological and product innovation are crucial. These are automobiles (97 per cent), rubber products (97 per cent), chemicals (78 per cent), electrical products (77 per cent) and aircraft (78 per cent). All these industries primarily serve the Canadian domestic market. Industries in which Canadian control predominates are characterized either by small production units, such as sawmills, construction concerns or certain food-processing industries or, as in the case of textiles, by thoroughly dim prospects. Among industries in which there still exists a substantial degree of Canadian control, and where technology does play an important part we find pulp and paper (with 40 per cent foreign control), agricultural machinery (50 per cent), and primary iron and steel (20 per cent). In all three industries Canada established and maintained a technological lead. The production of agricultural implements and primary iron and steel dates from the period of railway construction and the wheat economy. The pulp and paper industry, even where foreign-controlled, is characterized by considerably more autonomy in decision-making than are other foreign-controlled industries. The research conducted by Professor Safarian into 288 Canadian subsidiaries suggests that this may be due to the fact that in this industry Canadian subsidiaries tend to be large compared with their corporate parents.[6] Similar independent behaviour is found in some sectors of mining, particularly where foreign-controlled concerns do not have any corporate parent, as in the case of the Aluminum Company of Canada or International Nickel Company (see Table 2).

Foreign Subsidiaries in Canada

Foreign subsidiaries are strongly entrenched in both resource and in manufacturing industries. Of a total of $17.6 billion invested in foreign controlled enterprises in 1963, $2.3 billion were invested in mining and smelting, $5.4 billion in petroleum and natural gas and $8.2 billion in manufacturing.** Because foreign investment in Canadian resource industries is substantial and concentrated in large concerns, it is widely believed that direct investment in Canada is mainly directed to exports. In fact, the sales of foreign subsidiaries are heavily concentrated in the Canadian domestic market. A study on foreign subsidiaries in Canada published by the Department of Trade and Commerce in 1967 showed that 82 per cent of the output of foreign-controlled companies covered in this survey was sold in Canada. Of total sales of $15.1 billion by subsidiaries and branch plants in 1965, $12.7 billion were domestic sales and only $2.7 billion were exports. These exports represented over one-third of total Canadian exports for 1965 and were almost entirely resource-based. Branch-plant export sales of manufactured goods amounted to a mere $900 million – and these were strongly related to special bilateral deals.[7]

The degree to which intra-company transfers between parents and subsidiaries have replaced market transactions is revealed by the fact that 50 per cent of export sales of subsidiaries were sales to parent companies and 70 per cent of their purchases of imports were procured from parent companies. The percentage of exports made by transfers varied considerably: minerals and primary metal 68 per cent; gas and oil 59 per cent; pulp and paper 40 per cent. Transportation equipment was by far the most important fully-manufactured export: here 68 per cent of export sales were intra-company transfers. In

**Eds. The Committee for an Independent Canada reports that, according to figures from the Dominion Bureau of Statistics, at the end of 1969 foreign investment in Canada (short-and long-term) was estimated to be $46 billion, up from $40.2 billion in 1968.

These figures are not directly comparable to those quoted here by Levitt or to those in Table 2, however.

Table 2: Concentration of Foreign Direct Investment in the Commodity-Producing Sectors, 1963

INDUSTRY	Percentage of capital under foreign control		Total capital in enterprises controlled in:			Percentage of capital controlled in:		
	1954	1963	Canada	U.S.A.	Elsewhere	Canada	U.S.A.	Elsewhere
			(in million of dollars)					
Manufacturing								
Automobiles and parts	95	97	15	558	-	3	97	-
Rubber	93	97	6	195	15	3	90	7
Chemical	75	78	45	295	727	22	54	24
Electrical	77	77	22	161	458	23	66	11
Aircraft	36	78	55	85	113	22	33	45
Agricultural machinery	35	50	104	103	-	50	50	-
Pulp and paper	56	47	1,217	817	279	53	35	12
Textiles	18	20	568	96	49	80	13	7
Beverage	20	17	488	101	-	83	17	-
Primary iron and steel	6	14	752	14	108	86	2	12
Other	-	70	1,790	3,154	944	30	54	16
Total manufacturing	*51*	*60*	*5,451*	*6,308*	*1,895*	*40*	*46*	*14*
Petroleum and natural gas	*69*	*74*	*1,841*	*4,609*	*845*	*26*	*62*	*12*
Mining								
Smelting and refining of non-ferrous ores	-	51	521	545	-	49	51	-
Other mining	-	62	1,038	1,435	270	38	52	10
Total mining	*51*	*59*	*1,559*	*1,980*	*270*	*41*	*52*	*7*
TOTAL OF ALL INDUSTRIES		60	8,851	12,897	3,010	36	52	12

Canadian Balance of International Payments, 1963, 1964 & 1965, August 1967, p. 128.

other manufacturing industries, exports, though small, were also organized primarily through transfers. For example, 91 per cent of the exports of machinery and fabricated metal products were corporate transfers.

Similar corporate links were reported on the import side. Total imports of the surveyed companies accounted for over one-third of all Canadian imports in 1966, and 75 per cent of these were purchased from parent companies. Subsidiaries in the mining and petroleum industries, for example, obtained over 80 per cent of imports from parents, as did machinery and metal fabrication branch plants.

In the branch-plant economy the valuations placed on goods transferred to the parent company affect the distribution of profit between foreign and local residents. Evidently there is here considerable scope for arbitrary valuation of intra-firm transactions. Where the wage bill is small in relation to the capital invested, as is the case in most resource industries, the tax yield on the profits of the subsidiary may be the most important gain which accrues to the host country.[8] The authors of the Watkins Report urge Canadian tax authorities to exercise caution in the granting of special tax treatment or special subsidies to industries which are predominantly foreign-owned, particularly industries which do not generate substantial earnings for Canadian factors of production.[9] While there may be a case for concessions which attract employment creating industry, there is an obvious danger that further transfer of the corporation tax field to the provinces could result in a game of competitive tax concessions from which nobody except foreign capital can gain.

The fact that 70 per cent of the imports of subsidiaries were obtained from parent and affiliated companies substantiates our earlier argument that branch-plant manufacturing in the hinterland is the result of new forms of market competition which transfer tastes, techniques and assembly facilities to the hinterland. This creates a built-in demand for materials, components, capital goods and fully-processed goods for resale. Branch-plant imports are, to some extent, captive sales. Here

the mercantilist nexus does not result in over-valuation of imported inputs – although this may occur – but rather in a backward linkage of product differentiation. Typically, branch-plant technology requires a number of specific inputs which are supplied only by the parent company.

The US Department of Commerce study of 1963 showed that American branch plants located in Canada purchased a far higher proportion of their materials in the form of imports than did similar branch plants in any other major area of the world. For US subsidiaries in Canada, imports amounted to 15.5 per cent of gross sales, compared with 8.8 per cent in Latin America and 4.8 per cent in Europe. It appeared that one reason for the high import content of Canadian branch-plant costs was the large volume of purchases of finished goods for resale.

The ties of the mercantilist nexus were revealed in the year following the devaluation of the Canadian dollar in 1962. While the value of total imports into Canada rose by only 6 per cent, imports purchased by US subsidiaries from parent companies increased by 15 per cent. If we remember that these are substantial (about one-third of all Canadian imports) it is clear that the purchasing policies of the subsidiaries inhibited the substitution of domestic for imported goods, when the latter rose in price as a result of devaluation.

Professor Safarian's study concluded that to the extent that the subsidiary produces items identical to or marginally different from those of the parent there is a built-in incentive to buy from the parent. He found that the smaller the subsidiary in relation to the parent, and the more it tends to assembly-type operations, the higher the proportion of imported purchases.[10] The fact that the Canadian branch-plant economy is characterized by an excessive number of firms, each producing too many product lines, is reflected in the high import content of their purchases. Safarian concluded that: "The only systematic difference between [resident and non-resident firms] in terms of economic performance . . . is with respect to imports. The non-resident owned firm makes relatively more of its purchases abroad."[11] The Watkins Report also found that non-resident-owned firms appear to have a greater orientation towards imports than do resident-owned firms.[12] The study by Wilkinson finds that "imports of secondary manufactures are an increasing function of the extent of foreign ownership of industry."[13] In an interesting argument Wilkinson approaches an explanation which is similar to ours: he suggests that manufacturing subsidiaries will buy from their parents at a price which does not need to cover total fixed costs in the short run. The "short-run," however, is perpetuated "by the continuous development of new products and processes." As a result, the author suggests, foreign owned firms will always tend to buy a larger proportion of imported inputs than will domestically-owned firms.[14]

The most serious consequence of the bias towards imports resulting from branch-plant economy in Canada is the discouraging effect on Canadian entrepreneurship, as we have noted earlier. The more market demand is shaped by metropolitan corporations, the more restricted becomes the area in which independent Canadian enterprise and innovation can operate. The results of this situation are most clearly reflected in current trends in Canada's external trade.

Profile of a Rich, Industrialized, Underdeveloped Economy

In spite of Canada's high income and high degree of industrialization, the country has not shared in the recent world trend towards an increase in the importance of trade in relation to domestic production. In consequence, Canada's trade as a percentage of that of industrial countries dropped from 9.6 per cent in 1953 to 7.2 per cent in 1965 and her commodity terms of trade declined from 101 in 1954 to 97 in 1965. The deterioration in terms of trade for all underdeveloped countries over the same period was from 109 to 97. In developed countries the corresponding improvement in terms of trade was from 96 to 104.[15] The reasons for these trends are to be found in the high proportion of primary or crudely processed materials in Canada's exports and the correspondingly high proportion of finished manufactures in her imports. Canadian exports are heavily concentrated in a few product lines. These are either pure raw materials such as wheat, iron and other metallic ores, petroleum and natural gas, or crudely processed manufactures such as woodpulp, newsprint, lumber, flour, aluminum, copper and metal alloys, and primary iron and steel products.

In a study of 13 industrialized countries of the Western world it was found that end-products accounted for 60 per cent of exports. For Canada the comparable ratio was only 19 per cent. Although there has been an increase of 12 per cent in the share of highly manufactured goods in Canada's exports in the last decade, the increase for other relatively small industrialized countries[16] over the same period was 37 per cent.[17] In 1954 Canada was exceeded only by New Zealand in value of trade per head. By 1964 Canada ranked eighth, exceeded by Belgium, Luxembourg, Holland, Switzerland, Denmark, Norway and Trinidad-Tobago, in that order. In none of these countries, with the exception of the last-mentioned, do crudely processed materials account for as high a percentage of exports as they do in Canada.

Recent trends in Canada's imports are equally suggestive of structural underdevelopment. The share of consumer goods in imports rose from 29 per cent in the mid-fifties to 34 per cent in the mid-sixties, mainly due to increased imports of automobiles and new-technology manufactures. End products increased their share in imports from 50 per cent to 54 per cent over the same decade. The indication is that technological advance of a type that results in new products not produced in Canada,

together with imitative demand by consumers and producers, are an important factor in explaining Canadian import patterns. It should be noted that the heavy inflow of direct investment to Canada's manufacturing industries has coincided with a rise in manufactured imports relative to domestic production. This ratio rose from 18 per cent in 1954 to 21 per cent in 1965, reversing a contrary trend in operation since the mid-1920's.[18] It is well known that world trade in highly manufactured goods is rising more rapidly than trade in industrial raw materials and primary products. Canada appears unable to share in the gains which these trends offer to other industrialized countries.[19]

While there has been an increase in the export of manufactured goods in recent years, this has been strongly related to the implementation of the Defence Production Sharing Agreements of 1959 and the automobile agreements of 1963. The proportion of highly processed exports which fluctuated between 11 per cent and 14 per cent in the 1950's had risen to 19 per cent in 1965. Inedible end products rose from less than 8 per cent of total Canadian exports in 1959-60 to a level of 15 per cent in 1965. Most of the expansion took place in the US market.

While the devaluation of 1962 undoubtedly resulted in some increase in commercial exports, the bilateral arrangements between the governments of Canada and the United States accounted for the greater part of the increase. These special arrangements are a manifestation of increasing corporate and governmental integration between the two countries. The industries directly involved are the automobile, aircraft, electrical, chemical and machinery industries – all heavily controlled by US capital. Increased export sales to the United States have been gained at the expense of economic and political vulnerability.

The Defence Production Sharing Agreements, whereby Canadian firms are permitted to bid on equal terms with US firms for American war contracts, accounted for $260 million of Canada's exports in 1965, or 30 per cent of all Canadian inedible end-product exports to the US. In 1966, US defence contracts placed in Canada had increased to $317 million. Although these sales are small in relation to total Canadian production, the concentration of employment exposes Canadians to the possibility of severe unemployment in given areas in the event of the termination of these agreements. As the Canadian Minister of External Affairs explained: "Think of the impossible position we would be in if the Defence Production Sharing Agreements were abrogated . . . to pull out would be to endanger our economy and safety." It should be noted that the foreign exchange earned by these defence exports is pre-empted by the undertaking of the Canadian government to purchase American war supplies. Thus in 1966 Canadian defence purchases in the US amounted to $332.6 million.

Of greater importance than the defence arrangements are the automobile agreements which lifted exports of cars and parts to the US from a level of $36 million in 1963 to $231 million in 1965 and to $2,428 million in 1968. The *quid pro quo* for these automobile exports, however, has taken the form of increased imports by the automotive corporations involved, and the balance of commodity trade in cars and parts with the US remains in deficit. This deficit rose from $551 million in 1963 to $714 million in 1965, and has since declined to $343 million in 1968.

The expansion of normal commercial sales of highly manufactured goods abroad has thus been extremely modest. This is so in spite of efforts to promote exports, including the provision of export credit, the work of the Export Finance Corporation, the promotional efforts of the Department of Trade and Commerce, and strings on foreign aid which sometimes require 80 to 90 per cent Canadian content.

Table 3: R and D Expenditures as Percentages of Manufacturing Industry Sales, Canada and the United States

	R and D as Percentage of Sales *Intramural and Extramural* [a]	
Industry	Canada 1963	United States 1962
Aircraft	10.09	27.2
Drugs and pharmaceuticals	3.92	4.4
Scientific and professional equipment	3.19	7.1
Electrical products	2.58	7.3
Other chemical products	1.53	3.8
Petroleum and coal products	1.17	0.9
Machinery	1.04	3.2
Pulp and paper	0.72	0.1
Primary metals (non-ferrous)	0.86	0.8
Rubber	1.50	1.4[b]
Primary metals (ferrous)	0.33	0.5
Non-metallic mineral products	0.35	1.1
Textiles	0.26	0.2
Metal fabricating	0.22	0.8
Other manufacturing	0.11[c]	0.4[d]
Food and beverages	0.10	0.2[e]
Other transportation equipment	0.06	2.8
Furniture and fixtures	0.05	0.1
Wood	0.02	0.1
Average, all manufacturing	*0.7*	*2.0*

a Intramural refers to expenditure on R and D within the firm.
Extramural refers to outlays for research and development performed outside the reporting firms, and primarily outside the country.
b Includes plastics.
c Includes tobacco and products, leather, clothing and knitting mills, and miscellaneous manufacturing.
d Covers same industries as in note c, plus printing and publishing.
e Food only.
SOURCES:
Canadian data: Dominion Bureau of Statistics, *Daily Bulletin Supplement* — 3: "Industrial Research and Development Expenditures in Canada 1965," April 12, 1967, Table 2; and *Manufacturing Industries of Canada Section* A, 1963.
US data: Gruber, Mehta, and Vernon, "The R and D Factor in International Trade and International Investment of United States Industries," *Journal of Political Economy*, February, 1967, p.23, Table 1.
Reproduced from Wilkinson, *op. cit.* p. 122.

Research and Development

The difficulties of expanding commercial manufactured exports are compounded by the low level of industrial research and development expenditures in Canada and their high concentration in industries which service the special requirements of the US defence department. Canadian expenditures on research and development are smaller, in relation to its GNP (1.1 per cent) than that of industrial countries of Western Europe – West Germany (1.3 per cent), France (1.5 per cent), the UK (2.2 per cent), and very much smaller than expenditures in the USA (3.1 per cent).

What is more, in Canada 79 per cent of such research is performed by government and only 12 per cent in the business sector compared with the United States where, even though much of the work is done under government contracts, 71 per cent is carried on by industry. Comparable figures for West Germany, France and the United Kingdom are 61 per cent, 48 per cent and 71 per cent.[20] The bulk of industrial research expenses in the US are, however, subsidized by public funds. The situation in Canada was summed up by Dr. Steacie, president of the National Research Council in the following words: "Because of the financial relationship between Canadian and American firms, most Canadian plants are essentially branch plants and research is normally done by the parent organization outside the country. As a result Canadian industry has been largely dependent on research done in the US and Britain."[21]

The most recent survey conducted by the Dominion Bureau of Statistics reported a total of $264 million spent on industrial research and development. Thirteen firms accounted for half of these expenditures and they were heavily concentrated in the electrical, aircraft and chemical industries. The electrical products and aircraft industries accounted for 47 per cent of total research and development expenditure and these same industries received 83 per cent of federal funds granted to industry for research. Four companies alone received 55 per cent of total federal support. We already observed that Canadian government subsidies to industry are heavily directed towards industries in which foreign firms predominate and which are heavily engaged in defence production. The huge utility industry is, by contrast, according to the Dominion Bureau of Statis-

Table 4: Relationship between Research Effort and Export Performance of 19 US Manufacturing Industries

	RESEARCH EFFORT		EXPORT PERFORMANCE	
	Total R & D expenditures as a percentage of sales	*Scientists & Engineers in R & D as a percentage of total employment*	*Exports as a percentage of sales*	*Excess of exports over imports as a percentage of sales*
Transportation equipment	10.0	3.4	5.5	4.1
Electrical machinery	7.3	3.6	4.1	2.9
Instruments	7.1	3.4	6.7	3.2
Chemicals	3.9	4.1	6.2	4.5
Machines (non-electrical)	3.2	1.4	13.3	11.4
Five (above) industries with highest research effort	6.3	3.2	7.2	5.2
Fourteen other U.S. industries	0.5	0.4	1.8	-1.1

SOURCE Gruber, Mehta and Vernon, *op. cit.*

tics' report, entirely self-financing as regards research.

Industrial research in Canada is strongly biased towards applied rather than basic work. The Dominion Bureau of Statistics survey reports that only 356 of 6,367 trained scientists and engineers engaged in R and D in Canadian industry in 1965 were doing basic research.[22] Information compiled by Professor Wilkinson shows the lower levels of R and D expenditures in almost every industry in Canada as compared with the US.

The comparison is interesting because there is evidence of a strong correlation between R and D expenditures on the one hand, and success in the export of manufactured products on the other. Gruber, Mehta and Vernon, following the hypothesis suggested by Professor Vernon in his article on "International Investment and International Trade in the Product Cycle,"[23] offer impressive statistical evidence that American strength in the export of manufactured goods does not lie in a greater abundance of capital, but rather in the ability to develop new products and cost saving processes. Initiatives in R and D thus yield an oligopoly position in supplying foreign markets to countries which have the capacity to innovate. Their results are summed up in Table 4.

In this analysis comprising nineteen industries, the five most research-intensive ones accounted for 89 per cent of total R and D expenditures, 78 per cent of company-financed R and D expenditures, and employed 85 per cent of industrial scientists and engineers. While their sales were only 39 per cent of the total sales of all nineteen industries, they accounted for 72 per cent of the exports. The study debunks a widely held belief that high-technology industries are, to use economists' jargon, capital-intensive, and consequently that countries in which capital is cheap relative to labour enjoy a 'comparative advantage' in such industries. The correlation to this proposition of course is that countries in which capital is relatively scarce should not attempt to develop such industries.

The Gruber-Mehta-Vernon study found that labour costs form a larger percentage of value added in the five most research-intensive industries (24.7 per cent) than in the fourteen others (17.2 per cent). Correspondingly, the capital component of cost measured in terms of depreciation as a percentage of value added is smaller in the five most research-intensive industries (4.3 per cent) than in the other fourteen (5.3 per cent). Net fixed assets as a percentage of value added is also lower in the five leading industries (31 per cent) than in the other fourteen (41 per cent). The picture is completed by the observation of the authors that:

> Industries with comparatively high export sales of products involving scientific and technical aspects in their sales and servicing will have a high propensity to invest in manufacturing subsidiaries in the markets they serve and that in these 'oligopoly industries' therefore, individual firms are likely to consider foreign investments as important forestalling tactics to cut off market pre-emption by others. And they are likely to feel obliged to counter an investment by others with an investment of their own.

While Canadian industry is basically derivative and imitative, there exist the proverbial exceptions. These consist of cases where indigenous Canadian R and D has been a vital factor in gaining export markets. The list is familiar because it is pitifully short. It includes Canadian developments in nuclear power plants, telecommunication systems, the STOL aircraft developed by De Havilland for bush mining and explorational landing fields, the air navigational devices of Canadian Marconi and Computing Devices of Canada, and products pioneered by the Polymer Crown Corporation. The Canadian steel industry, primarily Stelco, has, as previously mentioned, maintained its world-wide reputation for innovation. The list, however short, belies the negative attitude of many experts that Canada is too deficient in technical skills to develop its own products.

A tragic feature of Canada's technological hinterland status is frustration experienced by her scientists, many of whom sooner or later depart in search of more challenging work in the United States. In the words of a Canadian scientist:

> It is well known that many a Canadian scientist in the US would happily return to the land of his birth and early nurture if the same scientific opportunities existed here. But there is the rub–the same opportunities do not exist in Canada; partly this is to be expected from the disparate populations of the two nations, but partly it arises as a concomitant of science in Canada... and our attitudes toward it, are largely fashioned in the US.... It is one thing to learn something from the American way of doing things, but complete integration into the American way stifles development of a distinctive Canadian style and a distinctive Canadian attitude about science, particularly with regard to its cultural values in society.[24]

Another measure of the technological dependence of Canadian industry is the nationality of patent applicants. Here we find that 95 per cent of all patents taken out in Canada over the period of 1957-61 were by foreign applicants, with 65 to 70 per cent by US applicants. This is probably the most remarkable single statistic of technological dependence. The proportion of foreign applicants for patents is much higher for Canada than for any other developed country. Similar figures for other industrial countries were 80 per cent for Belgium, 70 per cent for Scandinavian countries, 59 per cent for France, 47 per cent for the United Kingdom and 32 per cent for West Germany.[25]

The 'Miniature Replica' Effect

The effect of branch-plant economy on the structure of domestic industry is by now well established: too many firms producing too many product lines at high unit cost. When branch plants enter a tariff-protected market in which consumer tastes approximate those of the metropolitan economy we get what Dr. English has named the 'miniature replica' effect.[26] The spill-over of advertising and other corporate overheads related to product-differentiation and promotion make it profitable for foreign companies to assemble or sell a large range of their products in the hinterland. In many instances the international corporation does not enjoy a technical superiority as much as a marketing advantage arising from the familiarity of the consumer with the trade marks and brand names of its products. As Safarian has observed, "the great majority of the companies are a small fraction of the parent in size yet they are producing almost the full range of the identical or slightly modified products of the parent. Not surprisingly their unit costs are in most cases higher than those of the parent on major comparable products."[27] The case best documented is that of the refrigerator industry. Here it has been estimated that the Canadian market of 400,000 per annum could be efficiently served by two plants. In fact there are nine plants, and seven of these are US-controlled branch plants. In 1966 these accounted for 80-85 per cent of refrigerator production, compared with 71 per cent in 1960. These Canadian subsidiaries almost duplicate in number the plants producing refrigerators for the much larger American market. All of them operate well below optimum size.[28]

It is not true that the Canadian domestic market is too small to support a diversified manufacturing industry. Rather the combination of tariff protection and branch-plant organization has resulted in the inefficient production of too many similar products. The manufacturing industry catering to the domestic market, both foreign and locally-controlled, tends to be inefficient. Safarian's original study and the more recent investigations he undertook as a member of the Watkins team found that the nationality of ownership is irrelevant to economic performance. Foreign-controlled subsidiaries are no more efficient than locally-controlled firms. Nor are they less efficient. The evidence suggests that the key to efficiency in Canadian industry lies in rationalization, specialization, and innovation. Economic policies designed to this end would require a reduction of Canadian tariffs, the planned rationalization of select sectors of the manufacturing industry by means which include the takeover of redundant branch plants, and a large increase in research and development expenditures in high-technology industries catering to commercial markets. It requires above all a rejection on the part of Canadians of the branch-plant mentality which breeds a debilitating attitude of complacent incompetence and resignation to perpetual dependence on external initiatives.

Canadian Savings and the Growth of US Subsidiaries

There is a widely held belief that Canada needs foreign investment because the country is 'capital-hungry' and domestic savings are inadequate to finance expansion. While it may be advantageous to borrow portfolio capital, which does not transfer control, there is no conclusive case for the view that foreign direct investment constitutes the only way in which sufficient savings can be mobilized. Nor can a convincing case be made for the view that direct investment is necessary because entrepreneurial opportunities cannot be exploited without it.

In fact the inflow of direct investment funds constitutes a small fraction of total gross national saving in Canada. In 1965 for example, which was a year of relatively heavy foreign direct capital investment, the flow of new funds into Canadian subsidiaries was $500 million, or less than 5 per cent of total Canadian domestic savings, which exceeded $10 billion in that year. Indeed, these new funds are a minor source of finance for expansion by the subsidiaries; the major portion is provided by the re-investment of profit, by depreciation and depletion allowances, and by borrowings from Canadian financial institutions.

Over the years 1957 to 1965, 85 per cent of the funds used to expand US-controlled industry in Canada was provided from Canadian domestic savings. More specifically, US subsidiaries in Canada obtained 73 per cent of their funds from retained earnings and depreciation and a further 12 per cent from other Canadian sources, and only 15 per cent from the United States. While the mining industry received 19 per cent of total funds from the US and the petroleum industry 22 per cent, manufacturing branch plants obtained only 9 per cent from the US throughout the period.[29] In the year 1964, for example, of a total investment of $2,557 million by US subsidiaries in Canada, $1,244 million was financed from retained earnings, $764 million from depreciation allowances, $423 million from Canadian and third-country borrowing and only $126 million from funds from the United States. Of the funds obtained in Canada, only $71 million was issue of equity stock. The Dominion Bureau of Statistics has estimated that, in the nineteen-year period 1946-64, the accumulation of undistributed earnings added $5.2 billion or 40 per cent, to the increase in Canadian external indebtedness.** Well over half of these reinvestments

** Eds. The Committee for an Independent Canada reports, "In the

accrued to manufacturing subsidiaries.[30]

We have estimated that the gross internal savings of foreign-controlled firms constitute about 15 per cent of total annual Canadian domestic savings. The proportion of profit which is ploughed back is much higher in the branch-plant sector than in the rest of the Canadian economy. Thus about one-third of total Canadian retained earnings accrued to foreign-controlled companies. These internal savings are pre-empted for investment in the concerns in which they are generated. If the parent companies do not wish to re-invest subsidiary profits, they can and do transfer funds out of the country. Such funds, whether re-invested or transferred, are not available to finance the expansion of other sectors of the Canadian economy.

The Canadian Department of Trade and Commerce study revealed a similar pattern of financing. In 1965 a total of $1.8 billion was available to foreign-owned subsidiaries for investment expenditures. Of this amount, $1.2 billion was generated within the subsidiaries by retained earnings and depreciation. The remaining $658 million was raised from sources external to the subsidiaries: $274 million in loans from parents; $113 million in equity holdings by parents; $254 million in bank loans and long-term borrowing; and only $37 million in equity holdings by independent shareholders.[31]

The shortage of finance is at least in part the result of branch-plant economy. Contrary to common belief, Canadian savings are not low, nor is the Canadian investor averse to taking risks. Despite lower average incomes in Canada, the rate of personal savings is substantially higher than that in the United States. In 1967 Canadians saved about 9 per cent of disposable after-tax income compared with a rate of 7 per cent in the United States. What is more, the average Canadian is more inclined to invest his savings in equity stock than his US counterpart. Thus interest income forms a larger proportion of total investment income in the United States than in Canada, despite the fact that interest rates are lower there.[32] There appears to be no shortage of demand for equity investments in Canada—only a shortage of available stock.

For these reasons Canadian financial institutions have, in recent years, greatly increased their holdings of foreign equities. As recently as 1960, major Canadian financial institutions held only 10 per cent of their stock portfolios in foreign equities; the proportion had risen to 24 per cent by 1966. The trend was most pronounced in mutual funds which held 17 per cent of equity holdings abroad in 1962, 35 per cent in 1966, and 53 per cent in 1967. Most of the foreign stock portfolios of the major Canadian financial institutions are in industries which are not listed on the Canadian market. Over 40 per cent is invested in office equipment and airline stock, and about 35 per cent in electrical and electronics, drug and cosmetics, automotive, aerospace, photography and rubber stocks. The York University study points out that "if suitable Canadian stock issues do not become available, there is some likelihood that half the equity holdings of these institutions may soon be in foreign equities, a proportion already exceeded by the mutual funds."

While the trend towards internal financing and reliance on banks' trade credit and the bond market is creating a general scarcity of equity issues, the proportion of listed equities which are 'locked in' is substantially higher in Canada (30 per cent), as compared with the United States (10 per cent). The total annual demand for additional equities in Canada has been estimated to be almost double the supply provided through new Canadian issues. The meagre supply of Canadian equities re-

years 1966-69 . . . the net outflow of dividends and interest was $3.6 billion. If you compare this with the net (new) capital imports during those years of $2.5 billion, it is apparent that there was a net *outflow* of funds from Canada of $1.1 billion during those years."

sults from the fact that so many Canadian corporations are private companies, and even where they are public a very substantial portion (40 per cent) of listed Canadian equities are held as direct investments by non-residents.

There is a lack neither of savings nor of opportunities for profitable economic activity. Canada provides the classical case of a rich underdeveloped economy in which the capital market is too narrow to channel local savings into local investments. A substantial volume of trading in Canadian shares takes place on US exchanges and large blocks of Canadian shares are held as direct investments for the purpose of guaranteeing control. While 15 stock exchanges in the United States increased the volume of trading in equities by 171 per cent between 1962 and 1967, the six exchanges in Canada increased trading volume by only 38 per cent. A comparison of the industry-composition of listings of the Toronto Stock Exchange with the New York Stock Exchange underlined the difference between a metropolitan and hinterland economy: 25 per cent of TSE listings represent mining stocks, compared with 3 per cent of New York listings, while very little automobile, chemical, electrical and electronic stock is traded in Toronto.

On the assumption that Canadian financial institutions may find it necessary to invest half their total equity portfolios in foreign equities, the York University study estimated that, by the early 1970's they could hold $5 billion in foreign equities. Not only are the Americans buying up Canadian industry with Canadian savings, but they have in effect mobilized Canadian savings to assist in the expansion of the US based multinational corporations. As Professor Conway suggests:

> The sizable outflows of Canadian institutional and private capital coupled with the substantial direct investment holdings of Canadian equities by non-residents raises questions. If Canadian money must go abroad for suitable equity vehicles while non-resident capital in the form of direct investment creates such vehicles based on viable enterprises in Canada, possibly some additional effort must be made by the investment community towards encouraging a climate where Canadian entrepreneurs and financiers undertake to create more domestic investment vehicles which will attract domestic capital.[33]

Evidently, barriers to the expansion of Canadian enterprise do not lie in a global shortage of savings but rather in the structure of the goods and capital markets which places the independent enterprise at a disadvantage with respect to the branch plants. Frequently the former do not have access to sales outlets because markets are firmly controlled by existing corporations.[34] The capital market places the foreign branch plant at a decisive advantage in obtaining funds. Although it typically relies on internally-generated capital, large expansion can be financed by transfers from parents and affiliates in the form of loans or equity purchase by the parent. Here the small branch plant enjoys a strong advantage *vis-à-vis* the small independent firm.

The Royal Commission on Banking and Finance, 1964, noted that small independent Canadian-owned firms appear to have more difficulty at all times in obtaining long-term finance than do those which are subsidiaries of large and well-financed Canadian or American corporations. It is interesting to note that more than one-third of Canadian-controlled firms with assets under $1 million reporting to a CMA questionnaire reported sources of long-term capital as inadequate. This compares to one out of twenty-nine non-resident firms in the same size category.[35]

The authors of the Watkins Report suggest that the only way Canadian savings seeking equity investment can be channelled into Canadian industry is by incentives that would make all large private companies in Canada offer equity shares. Many, although not all, of these are wholly-owned subsidiaries of foreign corporations, such as British Petroleum, General Motors, General Foods, IBM, Canadian International Paper, and many others. It is doubtful how many of these firms would respond because, as the authors of the Report themselves admit "the commitment of some firms to the wholly-owned subsidiary is too strong to be shaken by any feasible set of incentives."[36] It is estimated that a 25 per cent minority share in all corporations with assets over $25 million or more amount to $3.5 billion or $4.5 billion at a minimum. Even if some of the capital so raised were transferred abroad, there would be an increase in Canadian minority participation, and a reduction in the long-run drain of dividends abroad.

Apart from the fact that US subsidiaries have shown little enthusiasm for selling any part of their equity to Canadians, there remains an obvious need to develop new Canadian-controlled enterprises. To this end the Watkins Report recommended the implementation of the Canada Development Corporation proposed by Walter Gordon years ago. This corporation would be a large quasi-public holding company with entrepreneurial and managerial functions. It might organize and participate in consortia of investors, both domestic and foreign, so that large projects beyond the capacity of a single institution could be undertaken under Canadian control. There would presumably be emphasis on joint ventures, on rental of foreign licences and patents, where necessary, and on arrangements in which controlling interests would remain Canadian.

Other instruments of policy, including those proposed by the authors of the Watkins Report, can be devised without difficulty. The real question is whether there exists the will to regain control over the economy. This is not a question which economists can answer. This fact does not, however, relieve them of the responsibility of asking it.

Political Disintegration

The most bitter harvest of increasing dependence and diminishing control may yet be reaped in the form of the internal political balkanization of Canada and its piecemeal absorption into the American imperial system. The final outcome of a branch-plant society is a merging of value systems and a meshing of corporate and technocratic elites which must ultimately call into question English Canada's willingness to pay the price of continued independence.

The ruling elite which founded Canada a hundred years ago were nationalists. But they were never called upon to pay. There was, in the days of Macdonald's National Policy, no conflict between the pecuniary interests of the dominant classes and their nationalism. Circumstances were such that they could enjoy both wealth and power. Power was exercised within a political framework which granted to the central government wide rights of control over the population. In distinction to the open frontier lawlessness of American democracy, Canada was an ordered, stable, conservative and authoritarian society, based on transplanted British institutions. Canada's constitution was appropriately enacted by the British Parliament, on the initiative of a group of colonial politicians, venerably depicted as the 'Fathers of Confederation', who could evade the necessity of seeking the popular consensus which they could never have obtained. The arrangements were quite compatible with the interests of the bureaucratic clerical elite of French Canada. Between these groups, there was no serious conflict of interest or of outlook. The elite of English Canada was defined by their rejection of American democracy. The elite of French Canada was in effective control of a national community which had been by-passed by the French Revolution. Canada has been, from its foundation in 1867, a conservative society.

Hitched to an east-west spine of trade and investment, the Canadian nation found strength to resist American annexationist pressures in the might of the pound sterling and in British imperial power. For decades Canadian politicians refined the techniques of compromise and survival. Externally, they manoeuvred between the British and the American metropolis. Internally, French-Canadian national survival was guaranteed by the powers exercised by the Catholic Church and the isolation of French Canada from modernizing influences. Members of the French-Canadian elite were integrated into the political structure on the terms of the English-Canadian elite, which controlled the economic structure. There developed over these years, a sense of Canadian national identity, corresponding to the conservative character of the nation under construction. Canadian patriotism *vis-à-vis* the United States was defined in terms of loyalty to the British monarchy.

The passing of time has eliminated Britain as a significant factor in Canadian politics. The problems are more difficult than they were in 1867 and the structures appropriate a hundred years ago are plainly obsolete today. The English-Canadian elite are no longer sure where they are going. Compromise and accommodation are useful political techniques for a small or middle power that knows what it wants, and can navigate the cross-currents created by stronger external powers. But compromise and accommodation as an operating philosophy of a community that does not know what it wants, in a situation in which the current runs powerfully in one direction, can lead only to drift and eventually to disintegration. The performance of Prime Minister Pearson and his administration bears witness.

The crisis of Canada's national existence is expressed in three distinct, but related confrontations: Canada versus the United States; Ottawa versus the provinces; and English Canada versus French Canada. Our theme is the effect of the new mercantilist links with the American empire on each of these conflicts, and the interplay of these relationships on Canada's chances of survival.

It is clearly no longer in the interests of the economically powerful to be nationalists. As George Grant has said: "Most of them made more money by being the representatives of American capitalism and setting up branch plants. . . . Capitalism is, after all, a way of life based on the principle that the most important activity is profit-making. That activity led the wealthy in the direction of continentalism."[37] In the National Policy era Canadian business could enjoy both wealth and power. The former was always primary; power was mainly a means to wealth. If today wealth comes more easily without power, no tears are shed. In the words of E.P. Taylor, "Canadian nationalism? How old-fashioned can you get?"

While economic factors are quick to act on the orientation of the business class, the erosion of the value system, which was formed during the nation-building phase of Canada's history, is a slower process. Although branch-plant industry, branch-plant trade unions, branch-plant culture and branch-plant universities are undermining traditional Canadian values, yet these values persist. Respect for law and order, regard for civil rights, abhorrence of mob rule and gangsterism (whether practised at the bottom or the top of the social scale), and traditional respect for Ottawa as the national government of the country are still deeply felt in English Canada. These are the elements of English-Canadian patriotism and they define the English Canadian, as distinct from the American. This value system is as real as the branch plants. It is the source which nourishes English-Canadian nationalism, and it is reinforced by every action of the United States which violates these values.

Whereas these values were created by the older Canadian elite, which shaped the nation, the existing business class can-not give effective expression to Canadian nationalism because it has been absorbed into the world of corporate empire. It rejected John Diefenbaker because he is a nationalist; it rejected Walter Gordon for the same reason. Grant has observed that the power of the American government to control Canada lies not so much in its ability to exert direct pressure as in the fact that the dominant classes in Canada see themselves at one with continentalism.[38]

The effect of the American corporate presence on relations between central and provincial governments is clear; the linear trans-continental axis, which once integrated the nation under an active and strong central government, has largely disintegrated. The new pattern of north-south trade and investment based on resource-development and branch-plant manufacturing, does not require a strong central government. The central government is left to manage the old infra-structure of communications and commercial institutions carried over from the previous era. However, new public expenditures are typically regional – hydroelectric schemes, highways, schools, hospitals and the like. The system of fiscal redistribution conflicts with the economic interests of the richer and more fortunate provinces. The federal function of providing for the defence of the nation is not sufficiently urgent to offset the shift of so many other functions to the regional level. Furthermore, a considerable part of the prosperity of defence work originates from the United States government, and is strongly regional in its impact on employment and income.

Political fragmentation along regional lines serves the interests of the international corporations. While the Ottawa mandarins ponder how to emasculate the Canada Development Corporation, the provinces have been forced to create their own development agencies. Recent efforts to launch regional development policies at the federal level have produced a bureaucratic structure whose organizational sophistication far out-distances that of the policies which have to date been announced by Ottawa.

In the absence of effective federal initiatives to provide the means of mobilizing and directing Canada's resources towards the elimination of regional disparities, the provinces will reinforce the continentalist trend by joining the competitive scramble for foreign investment. They opposed the rationalization of the fiscal structure proposed by the Carter Commission and the government White Paper on taxation; they pressured the federal government into begging exemption from the US interest equalization tax. They may be expected to oppose each and every measure devised to control the terms on which foreign capital may enter Canada. In the absence of effective leadership by Ottawa they reinforce the continentalism of big business by dismembering the federal structure of Canada.

The relationship between English Canada and Quebec is a special one. Quebec is both a province within Confederation and the *patrie* of the French-Canadian nation. The demand for more autonomy by the province of Quebec thus has a dual character. In part, it resembles demands for increased provincial powers expressed by all the larger provinces, in part, it is the political form in which the desire for self-determination of French Canada expresses itself.

Clearly, there can be no national equality for French Canada without power over economic decisions. In the area of public policy, we thus have the demand for a larger share of revenue, and for a voice in tariff, monetary and immigration policy. For French Canada, more economic power for the government of Quebec is crucial, because the provincial public sector is the only effective lever by which French Canadians can influence decisions affecting their lives. While the English-Canadian elite is rapidly relinquishing economic control to the American corporations, the French-Canadian elite urgently desires entry into private corporate power. Such entry is highly restricted at present, and the situation has been fully documented by John Porter in his book *The Vertical Mosaic*. Yet national equality requires that economic decisions affecting Quebec must be made by French Canadians, not by English-Canadian or American corporations. Nothing less can assure the continued existence of a French-speaking community on the North American continent.

For French Canada, modernization has meant not only dislocation and disruption of settled routines but also incorporation into the industrial system, and the new humiliation of daily dictation by the anglophone. This is as true for the miner, the factory worker, the sales clerk, as it is for the professional and middle classes. Whereas the latter may have an educational advantage in terms of ability to function in the language of those who hold economic power, the humiliation is greater rather than less. Their education and their wider horizons enable them to articulate the frustrations of the French-Canadian community in Canada. The island of anglophone privilege which extends from McGill University and Westmount to the western edge of Montreal and which controls much of the commercial and industrial life of the French-speaking province, acts as a constant abrasive to these frustrations. This experience is unknown to the English Canadian. It is unknown also to the immigrant, who chose to leave his native land to come to North America. In this sense the so-called 'ethnic groups' are assimilated and become an integral part of English Canada.

The experience of linguistic domination also explains the lack of discrimination in French-Canadian resentment between English-Canadian and American domination. It is interesting that public opinion polls constantly show less concern about American domination in Quebec than anywhere else in Canada, and no less a politician than René Lévesque does not appear to fear the consequences of 'liberating' Quebec from the domination by the English-Canadian financial elite with the help of more powerful American capital. What difference, after all, to the French-Canadian worker in Arvida, whether orders are received in English from a foreman employed by a Canadian company like Alcan, or an American company, like Union Carbide?

The French-Canadian middle class is comprised of self-employed professionals, small businessmen and bureaucratically-employed technocrats. No private French-Canadian entrepreneurial group can effectively challenge the powers of the anglophone corporations. The logic leads from nationalism to state entrepreneurship. This was the policy which guided the more radical elements of the Lesage administration during the so-called Quiet Revolution. It was symbolized by the creation of Hydro-Quebec as the first step to a more extensive expansion of the public sector into the resource industries of the province.

In such a confrontation with the corporation, the advantage which French Canada has over English Canada is a more clearly defined sense of national purpose and a greater confidence in its ability to achieve its objective. That objective is to build, in North America, a modern French-speaking society in which the population can enjoy both prosperity and dignity. If this can be achieved in union with English Canada, so much the better. If English Canada makes this impossible, there is every indication that eventually, Quebec will secede. If there is an economic price to be paid for control by French Canadians over the terms on which their daily lives are lived, an increasing minority seems ready to pay it. Nationalism and separatism have struck a chord because the population of Quebec is Québécois in the sense in which no resident of Ontario is Ontarian.

Those who view Quebec separatism as the main threat to Canada's survival, might ask themselves why French Canadians should remain within Confederation when the dominant English-Canadian majority appear to put such a low value on Canada's national independence? What is being offered? To wander hand-in-hand, biculturally and bilingually, into the gravitation orbit of the American empire? Is it any wonder that some Quebeckers believe that separation might offer a better chance for cultural survival in North America? At worst, Quebec would have its own *Roi nègre* to administer the French marches of the Empire, while the Ottawa bureaucrats are presiding over the English marches.

The 'continentalist' orientation is fundamentally destructive of Canadian unity because it rejects the maintenance of a national community as an end in itself. The value system by which a nation is ultimately defined is put up for sale. In every 'cost benefit' calculation concerning the gains and losses from the continued US presence within the Canadian economy there is an implicit price tag on national values and beliefs. The American corporations which reach forward to control the markets they presume to serve homogenize the culture of the inhabitants. Continentalism extends the American melting-pot philosophy into Canada. Bilingualism and biculturalism, even if it were to be translated from a pious wish to reality, is no defence to this process of seduction. By the intake of branch-plant factories and the associated branch-plant culture, national values in the hinterland are shaped in the image of the metropolis. When the process is complete there remains, as Gad Horowitz has suggested, no reason to regain control.

The process is far advanced. What is in question today is the will of English Canada to survive as a distinct national community on the North American continent. If the will is waning, if English Canada is succumbing to a sort of national death-wish in relation to the United States, why should Quebec, and in particular the young people now pouring out of schools and universities, wish to remain junior partners in this sad venture?

Writing in 1960, before the consequences of Canada's branch-plant status were as apparent as they are today, Professor Aitken summed up the dilemma in the following words:

> No one doubts that American investment has accelerated the pace of economic development in Canada; ... but it seems also likely to convert Canada into a hinterland of United States industry.... To each spurt of expansion there is a corresponding shrinkage in Canada's freedom of action, in its self-reliance, and in its ability to chart its own course for the future.[39]

The locus of decision-making has been transferred from Canada, where in the past it was subject to strong direction by the federal government, to the board rooms of huge US corporations, operating on a world scale and each charting its own future under the protection of its metropolitan government. An increasing number of English Canadians (and undoubtedly the majority of her academic economists) do not care who charts the course so long as income continues to grow. An able young English-Canadian economist recently dismissed as 'pernicious' the argument that American corporate control constitutes a constraint on Canadian decision-making, with a reference to Buridan's ass which starved because it could not choose between two piles of hay. "He did achieve the goal of preserving the freedom to choose, but at what a price!" The preservation of freedom, we are told, is a means to an end. As such it should not be elevated to the status of a goal. Not even economists can put a value on a means, so that we are asked to pay a price to achieve something whose worth can never be assessed. Very few of us are willing to pay an infinite price for anything – and certainly not for such poor excuses for a national objective.

Because freedom is priceless, it is worthless. A strange conclusion even for an economist. The logic, of course, is flawless. 'Maîtres chez nous', in French, or in English, is plainly assinine; it is a 'non-goal'. The rational Canadian presumably will not lift his head from the trough for long enough to explore unknown pastures in search of greener grass. He will eat whatever hay is dished up, secure in the knowledge that he is getting the same all-American grub – albeit a somewhat smaller ration.

The attitude of the Quebec technocrats presents a striking contrast. Confident in their ability to chart their own course, French Canadians are asserting their determination to control their economy – including the right to make their own mistakes. In the words of one of Quebec's leading economists:

> French Canadians in Quebec can set themselves concrete objectives, achieve them fully, partially, or even fail to meet them, like any other people.... When a society has been for so long in search of fulfilment and has found it within itself, it is very unlikely that it can be distracted from this purpose.

The dominant Protestant culture of English Canada resists the idea that a nation, like a family, is more than an aggregation of individuals; that it is a community shaped by common cultural and historic experiences. More particularly it does not seem to understand that the experiences shared by English and French Canadians have left a very different imprint on the consciousness of the two national communities. Instead of an outward-looking and self-confident sense of national purpose, English Canada has at times exhibited an angry reaction to the fact that French Canadians do not want equality on the terms set down by the dominant English-Canadian elite. The effort to head off French-Canadian self-assertion with a bilingual federal civil service and French schools in English Canada has little appeal in Quebec, while causing considerable dissension in some areas of English Canada. The refusal of Ottawa to recognize French Canada as a nation, and its insistence on the ten provinces concept of Confederation has led to the balkanization of the country, as the pressures applied by Quebec are used as a lever to escalate the fiscal demands of all the provinces at the expense of effective central government. As René Lévesque put it, there must be more to English Canadian nationalism than just "holding on to Quebec." If there isn't, then "it's cheaper cars and cigarettes for you all, and US citizenship – – along with the fading away of a growing (even though 'branch-plant') economy and its managerial society; and the draft, and present and future Vietnams and a share in the terrific agony the American society is inflicting upon itself."[41]

The refusal of the dominant English-speaking community to recognize explicitly the national aspirations of Quebec is propelling the fragmentation of the country to the point of piecemeal absorption into the American empire. Under these conditions it becomes increasingly difficult to repatriate the locus of decision-making, or to implement the 'new national policies' suggested by Professor Watkins and his associates.

The obstinate refusal of Ottawa to accommodate the demands of Quebec for national equality within a Canadian partnership of two nations is pushing nationalist forces in the French province to seek their own independent hinterland relationship with the United States, on the theory propounded by an economist close to René Lévesque and the Parti Québécois that "we have no choice but to strike our own bargain with American capital." As Peter Regenstreif reported in January 1969, Quebeckers are selling out and Americans, who regard the province as a relatively safe place in comparison with really troubled areas of the world, are buying in. The Quebec economy is becoming ever more Americanized in the process.[42]

One is entitled to doubt the wisdom of exchanging domination by St. James Street for domination by Wall Street and the American corporations. The tragedy, however, is that the root of this dilemma rests in the failure of Ottawa to accommodate the special fiscal needs of Quebec within the framework of a national policy aimed at making all Canadians masters of their own house. The advent of Trudeau promised to rescue the federal government from the all-time low in prestige and power associated with the Diefenbaker and Pearson eras. In spite of the flair of the new prime minister for projecting the image of revitalization, the pattern of subservience to Washington continues. The erosion of Canadian sovereignty and national unity has not been arrested by proclamations of bilingualism and biculturalism and a 'get tough with the provinces' policy.

The ambivalence of English Canada concerning the reality of the nation as a community underlies the difficulties of communication with Quebec. Sadly, this same ambivalence renders English Canada so vulnerable to the disintegrating forces of continentalism. If national purpose is nothing more than a cumulation of individual purpose, and if individual purpose consists essentially of more money, more leisure and more consumer goods, then why trouble about Canada's loss of independence? And yet English Canada is deeply troubled.

The 'foreign investment' issue in Canadian politics will remain unresolved until English Canada redefines its goals as a national community. As Horowitz asked: "Control our economy for what?" That question, in the end, is one which individuals must answer. Dwelling in the web of the new mercantilism of the great corporations, Canadians will have to decide what value they place on living in a human community that they can control and handle. For French Canada that community appears to be Quebec. From the desire to control their environment arises the demand for effective political and economic power.

In English Canada there exists the possibility that the cultural integration into continental American life has proceeded to the point where Canada no longer is a meaningful national community. Yet here there is the possibility that the current reaction among the younger generation against domination by the efficiency-mongers of big business, big government or big anybody may revive the 'conserving' nationalism which derives from the desire to control and shape the conditions of life within a community. Only the emergence of a new value system within English Canada can ensure the continued existence of a nation here.

NOTES

1. In the words of the Watkins Report: "The successful intrusion of foreign law constitutes a direct erosion of the sovereignty of the host country insofar as the legal capacity of the latter to make decisions is challenged or suspended. Insofar as subsidiaries become instruments of policy of the home country rather than the host country, the capacity of the latter to effect decisions, i.e. its political independence is directly reduced." *Foreign Ownership and the Structure of Canadian Industry*, p. 311.

2. For a comprehensive treatment of the Trading with the Enemy Act and US subsidiaries in Canada see J.I.W. Corcoran, "The Trading with the Enemy Act and the Canadian Controlled Corporation," *McGill Law Journal*, Vol. 14, 174-208.

3. *Foreign Ownership*, p. 339.

4. B. W. Wilkinson, *Canada's International Trade: An Analysis of Recent Trends and Patterns*. Canadian Trade Committee, 1968, p. 17.

5. *Foreign Ownership*, p. 35.

6. A. E. Safarian, *Foreign Ownership of Canadian Industry* (Toronto: McGraw Hill Company, 1966).

7. *Foreign-Owned Subsidiaries in Canada*, a report on operations and financing based on information supplied by the larger subsidiary companies. Published by authority of the Hon. Robert H. Winters, Minister of Trade and Commerce, Ottawa, June 1967, pp. 7-15.

8. Consider the case of a foreign firm which enters Canada to develop a new resource. Assume that the technique of production makes intensive use of machinery, which is imported, and uses little labour, and that the output is exported and at prices determined, in part, by the foreign firm; these assumptions are often, though not always, realistic. To the extent that relatively little domestic labour is employed and the resource is exported, benefits will accrue mostly to foreign consumers and foreign factors of production, and Canadian benefits will consist

largely of taxes imposed on foreigners. To the extent that the foreign firm is able, at least for tax purposes, to set the export price, Canadian benefit will further depend on the Canadian tax authorities ensuring that the firm, for whatever reason, does not price low and therefore shift profits and tax liability outside Canada. *Foreign Ownership*, pp. 72-73.

9. *Ibid.*, p. 86.

10. Safarian, *op. cit.*, chapter 5.

11. *Ibid.*, p. 304.

12. *Foreign Ownership*, p. 205.

13. Wilkinson, *op. cit.* p. 150.

14. "The more important become innovations of products and processes, the more consequential becomes this explanation." *Ibid.*, p. 129.

15. International Monetary Fund, *International Financial Statistics*, Supplement to 1966-67 issues; and United Nations *Yearbook of International Trade Statistics*, various years.

16. The small industrial countries here are Austria, Belgium, Luxembourg, Denmark, Netherlands, Norway and Sweden.

17. M. G. Clark, *Canada and World Trade*, Staff Study No. 7, Economic Council of Canada, Ottawa, 1964.

18. Wilkinson, *op cit.*, chapter 3.

19. If Canadian trade follows this pattern (and it promises to do so) then total imports which are heavily concentrated on highly processed commodities will tend to rise more rapidly than will total exports, which are largely raw and crudely processed materials. *Ibid.*, p. 44.

20. See Gruber, Mehta and Vernon, "The R and D Factor in International Trade and International Investment of United States Industries", *Journal of Political Economy*, February 1960 p. 26.

21. Dr. E. W. R. Steacie, president of the National Research Council. Statement to the Royal Commission on Canada's Economic Prospects, quoted in Safarian, *op cit.*, p. 171.

22. DBS Industrial Research and Development Expenditure in Canada, Dec. 1967. See pp. 15 & 16 and 38-40.

23. Raymond Vernon, "International Investment and International Trade in the Product Cycle". *Quarterly Journal of Economics*, May 1966.

24. L. E. H. Trainor, "Americanization of Canada – A Scientist's Viewpoint." (Mimeo).

25. C. Freeman and A. Young, *The Research and Development Efforts in Western Europe, North America and the Soviet Union* (Paris, OECD, 1965). For comment by Watkins and associates, see *Foreign Ownership*, p. 97.

26. H. E. English, "Industrial Structure in Canada's International Competitive Position," The Canadian Trade Committee, Montreal, June 1964.

27. Safarian, *op. cit.*, p. 305.

28. *Foreign Ownership*, pp. 154-55.

29. *Sources of Funds of Direct US Investments in Canadian Manufacturing Mining and Petroleum*

	percentage							average	
	1957	*1958*	*1959*	*1960*	*1961*	*1962*	*1963*	*1964*	*1957 1964*
Funds from the U.S.	26	25	20	21	13	10	8	5	15
Re-invested profit	35	32	39	45	41	43	45	49	42
Depreciation	26	30	30	35	34	32	33	30	31
Funds from Canada	13	14	11	-1	12	15	14	17	12

SOURCE: *U.S. Survey of Current Business*, various issues.

30. DBS, *The Canadian Balance of International Payments: A compendium of statistics from 1946 to 1965.*

31. *Foreign-Owned Subsidiaries in Canada, op. cit.*, section 3.

32. G. R. Conway, "The Supply of, and Demand for, Canadian Equities," A conspectus of the study commissioned from the Faculty of Administrative Shares, York University, by the Toronto Stock Exchange (Toronto, September 1968).

33. *Ibid.*, p. 44.

34. In the primary resource field industries, a guaranteed long-term market in the parent for at least part of the subsidiary's output has often been the critical factor in the decision to exploit the resource, sometimes much more important than the supply of capital or of technology. *Foreign Ownership*, p. 76.

35. Report of the Royal Commission on Banking and Finance, Ottawa, 1964, pp. 87-88.

36. *Foreign Ownership*, pp. 291, 412.

37. George Grant, *Lament for a Nation*, p. 47.

38. *Ibid.*, p. 41.

39. Hugh G. J. Aitken, *American Capital and Canadian Resources*, pp. 112-113, 114.

40. Jacques Parizeau, quoted by René Lévesque in *The Star Weekly Magazine*, Toronto, January 20, 1968.

41. *Ibid.*, Lévesque.

42. Peter Regenstreif, *Montreal Star*, January 18, 1969.

2. The Religious Sect in Canadian Politics

S. D. Clark/*University of Toronto*

The author of this essay has devoted a lifetime of outstanding scholarship predicated upon his belief, expressed elsewhere, that the twin eyes of sociology are history and geography. Using these twin eyes, his well-honed sociological perspective has focused on the interrelations of social institutions in the developing Canadian society. In particular, he has been interested in the ways in which religious and economic institutions have been related to the polity.

In this essay Professor Clark presents three case studies which illustrate how persons on the economic and geographic fringes of society, perceiving their social space constricted by economic, political and religious institutions to which they have been denied full access and which are irresponsive to their needs, turn to innovative sectarian movements as a means of carving out new space for themselves. In so doing, he argues, they set up new boundaries which distance them even more from the rest of society.

Reprinted from *The American Journal of Sociology*, 51:3 (1945), by permission of the author and The University of Chicago Press.

This paper is concerned with the part played by evangelistic religious movements in Canadian politics and, more particularly, with their influence upon the development of liberal political thought in the country. It has been assumed by most students of Canadian church history that the evangelistic religious movements, through the support of radical programmes of political reform, have made substantial contributions to liberal thought. This paper contends that such a view has been based upon a superficial examination of the facts. While it is true that the evangelical churches have at times lent support to the cause of political radicalism, it is questionable whether such support has been nearly as significant as supposed in revealing their political thinking. It is argued here that the political activities of the evangelical churches have not grown out of a deeply embedded political philosophy and that the real contribution to the development of liberal principles of government must be sought not in their activities but rather in the peculiar role of the religious sect out of which the evangelical churches had developed. Discussion of the part played by evangelistic religious movements in politics compels consideration of the political influence of the sect as well as the church.

For the purposes of this paper, it seems best to confine the discussion to three evangelical groups which have played an important role in Canadian politics: the Baptists in Nova Scotia, the Methodists in Upper Canada, and the followers of William Aberhart in Alberta. The contribution of these groups to the cause of political radicalism has been well recognized.

In Nova Scotia the Baptists constituted a distinctive revolutionary force in religious and social life toward the close of the eighteenth century, and early movements of political reform owed much to their indirect and direct support. Similarly, in Upper Canada, the Methodists, in the two decades of political turmoil after the war of 1812-14, strongly supported radical political movements in the country in opposition to the Family Compact; and the close working alliance which grew up between Egerton Ryerson, the acknowledged leader of the Methodist Church, and William Lyon Mackenzie, the leader of the Reform party, was indicative of the increasing active participation of Methodists in politics. The radical political implications of the religious movement in Alberta founded by William Aberhart are obvious: the Social Credit party, with its sweeping programme of monetary reform, grew directly out of Aberhart's Prophetic Bible Institute. Here, very definitely, political revolt was born out of a movement which had grown up on a religious foundation.

A combination of forces led to this alignment of the evangelical churches with radical movements in the country. In the first place, vested interests of denominationalism tended to produce such an alignment. The evangelical churches found themselves opposed by the old, traditional churches closely associated with the state or with ruling parties in the state. The Baptists in Nova Scotia and the Methodists in Upper Canada were compelled to fight church establishment to secure the rights to which they felt themselves entitled as religious denominations, and, in fighting church establishment, they inevitably found themselves fighting all the forces of special privilege and reaction in the country. Somewhat similarly, William Aberhart, in attacking the claims of the powerful and wealthy churches represented in Alberta, many of them with strong creditor interests in the province, found himself launching out in an attack upon those business and political interests which largely supported, and in turn were supported by, these churches. The evangelical church, the moment it became denominationally conscious, very naturally championed the cause of religious freedom in one form or another, and such championship threw it on the side of political radicalism in the country.

Strong social forces as well, however, tended to an identification of the evangelical churches with the cause of political radicalism. Of these, regional-economic interests were by far the most important. Their effect was to strengthen greatly the tendencies deriving from denominational interests.

The political affiliations of the evangelical churches were determined by the kind of area from which they drew their support. The established or traditional churches were the churches of the metropolis. Their most imposing houses of worship were located in the better residential sections of the larger centres of population; their most successful ministers occupied city pulpits. Within governmental centres, in particular, their influence tended to be dominant. They gave expression to the interests of Empire or nation. The evangelical churches, on the other hand, grew up as religious sects on the social fringes of the communi-

ty. Their emergence as new sects represented efforts of scattered or downtrodden folk, neglected by the traditional churches, to develop a form of religious fellowship on their own. It was in outlying areas of the country, or within working-class sections of the city, that sectarian activity flourished.

Thus the separatism of the sect, its efforts to separate itself from the worldly society, became, within the evangelical church, closely related to political separatist movements in the hinterland or in marginal urban areas. The political reaction against the control of the metropolis–the struggle to secure a greater measure of local political autonomy–found support in, and in turn supported, the isolationism of the religious sect. Rebellion in the backlands expressed itself usually in religious as well as in political form; few movements of political independence in history have been unrelated to movements of religious schism. The attempt of Brigham Young in Utah to bring into being a theocratic state largely independent of the federal authority provides possibly the best example on this continent of the combination of sectarian religious and frontier political separatism, but similar forces in Canada led to like forms of political and religious expression.

The struggle of the Baptists in Nova Scotia in the late eighteenth century to secure an independent religious life was simply a part of the much larger struggle of the Nova Scotian outsettlements to resist the domination of Halifax and to free themselves from the restrictions of the British colonial system. The collapse of Congregationalism had followed upon the break of Nova Scotia from New England with the American Revolution, and the rise of the Newlight Baptist movement represented an effort to strengthen the position of the outsettlements which had lost the support of the tie with New England. The aggressive separatism of the new religious sect was not unrelated to the efforts of the town meeting to control local village affairs, to the refusal of local magistrates to convict for offences against unpopular colonial laws, and, during the Revolution, to smuggling and tax evasion, and, after the Revolution, to the conflict between the Assembly and the Council and the growing demand for responsible government.

Similarly, the struggle of Methodism in Upper Canada became closely tied up with efforts of the backwoods farm communities to free themselves from the controls of centralized land-granting, taxing, and road-building authorities. The chief strength of the traditional churches, and especially of the Church of England and Church of Scotland, was in the larger towns and the provincial capital. These churches, represented the official classes of the community–the classes which had a stake in the imperial connection–but made no effective effort to serve the outlying backwoods farm population. Political dissatisfactions of people who, because of their isolation, had little voice in government, found expression in religious separatism. Methodism grew rapidly in outlying sections of the country and supported efforts to secure a greater measure of local independence and colonial autonomy.

The close relation between frontier political and religious sectarian separatism can be seen even more clearly in Alberta in the religious-political movement led by Aberhart. Aberhart's break with the traditional organization of religion forced him into an isolationist position. The dominance of the national churches became closely associated in his eyes, and in the eyes of his followers, with the dominance of the large eastern cities and of the federal authority. On the other hand, the religious separatism of Aberhart's new sect – its attempt to stand apart from the worldly society – became closely associated with the political separatism of such a frontier area as Alberta. It was not difficult for Aberhart to translate the religious exclusiveness of the Prophetic Bible Institute into a political exclusiveness, once he became leader of the Social Credit party. The society of the elect found expression now in political terms. It was not without significance that some of the more prominent members of the Social Credit Government belonged to the Mormon church in southern Alberta. The religious-political experiment in Alberta resembled very closely that tried much earlier in Utah; in both cases, religious separatism sought support in political separatism, and encroachments of the federal authority were viewed as encroachments of the worldly society.

Regional interests which found expression in movements of religious and political separatism were closely related to economic interests. The society of the backlands or of the urban working class area was a debtor society. The religious sect attracted the support not only of the isolated but of the economically dispossessed. It provided a cheap religion in that it did not make heavy financial demands for the support of elaborate places of worship and highly educated clergymen. Furthermore, it provided, in the way of preaching appointments, occupational opportunities for young men (and, in some cases, young women) who did not have the means of securing the training necessary for a professional career. It was the poor fishermen and farmers of Nova Scotia who largely comprised the early following of the Baptist Church. The debt-ridden farmers of the Upper Canadian backwoods communities rallied about the banner of the Methodist itinerant preachers. Aberhart secured his greatest support, both as a religious evangelist and as a political compaigner, in that area of Alberta stretching northeast from Calgary to the Saskatchewan border, the approximate centre of which is the town of Hanna. It was here that the drought was most fully felt.

The message of the religious evangelist as a result became easily translated into economic panaceas of various sorts. Magical remedies were seized upon to solve problems of the economic system just as patent medicines and the prescriptions of the quack are seized upon to deal with bodily ills. Monetary experiments, in particular, have tended to be closely related to religious experiments in the means of salvation. Resort to the use of scrip or to the establishment of special banks served the purpose of strengthening the isolation of the religious group and, at the same time, of offering a solution to the problem of debt. The close relation between sectarian techniques of religious control and monetary techniques of economic and political control has been most evident, of course, in the Social Credit experiment in Alberta; here the Mormon members of the Government in particular had a perfectly good historic example in the use of scrip and the carrying-on of banking operations by the Mormons in Utah. Awareness of monetary solutions of economic problems was less fully developed among the earlier evangelical religious groups in Canada, but the pressures of a rigid credit system in the hands of the merchant class in Nova Scotia and Upper Canada, and the shortage of money, led to economic dissatisfactions which found expression among Baptists and Methodists in demands for economic reforms not unlike those of Social Credit.

The denominational, regional, and economic interests of the evangelical churches were probably most responsible for their support of radical political movements in the community. To some extent, as well, the nature of the evangelical religious appeal in itself may have contributed to a fostering of an attitude of political radicalism. Such an appeal involved a sharp break from traditional theological systems; theological trappings, and an elaborate ritualistic system, were cut through to emphasize the elementary problem of man's relation to his God. At the same time, conversion involved an equally sharp break with his past for the individual. The effect of this was to encourage an untraditional approach to problems of life in general. It was for this reason that followers of new religious sects often became the most active in promoting novel types of economic activity. Something of the experimental attitude was carried over into politics as well.

These considerations suggest the nature of some of the more important factors favouring the alignment of the evangelical churches with radical political forces in the community. It would be a mistake to conclude from this, however, that these churches have invariably lent support to the cause of radicalism. If the political activities of the Baptists in Nova Scotia, the Methodists in Upper Canada, and the followers of William Aberhart in Alberta are examined further, it will be found that these groups, while at times supporting radical political movements, have at other times constituted a distinctive conservative influence in the community. Indeed, in the decisive test of strength between opposing political forces in the country, they have more often thrown their weight on the side of conservatism. This fact has to be recognized before any conclusion can be drawn respecting the relation of the evangelical churches to political thought.

In Nova Scotia, in the second quarter of the nineteenth century, opposition to the non-sectarian educational policy of Joseph Howe, the leader of the Reform party, led the Baptists to shift to the Conservatives in the province. It was a prominent Baptist–J.W. Johnson–who became the leader of the Conservative party, and the votes of the Baptist population were decisive in bringing about the defeat of the Reformers in the election of 1843. Likewise, in Upper Canada, the early alliance between the Methodists and Reformers was sharply broken in 1833, when Egerton Ryerson came out in opposition to William Lyon Mackenzie; and in the election of 1836, and again in the election of 1844, the Methodist vote was at least in part responsible for the Tory victories. Even moderate reform leaders, like the Baldwins, were unable to rely upon Methodist support. In Alberta similar tendencies were evident within the combination erected by Aberhart out of religious and political materials. Aberhart himself never really ceased to be a conservative in political outlook, and the political party which he founded moved steadily in a conservative direction. The radicalism which persisted within the party came very largely from elements which became a part of the political movement after 1935 but which were quite unrelated to the religious movement led by Aberhart. Frontier agrarianism continued to force the party into a radical position, but radical tendencies were sharply checked by the strength of sectarian religious influences.

Factors which at one time favoured the alignment of the evangelical churches with political reform in the community favoured their alignment with conservative forces at another. Denominational vested interests changed in character as the evangelical church became less concerned about the privileges enjoyed by the older, established churches in the community and more concerned about protecting privileges which it itself had secured. The sect grew into the church and, in doing so, found its interests more closely identified with the interests of the traditional churches. Promotion of such objects as education, temperance, and Sabbath observance forced the evangelical church into opposition to religious movements more evangelistically aggressive, and secular movements which threatened the teachings of religion. Baptist Church leaders in Nova Scotia and Methodist Church leaders in Upper Canada increasingly directed their fire against the new religious sects which sprang up in the community, while by 1935 Aberhart in Alberta was feeling very keenly the competition of rival radio evangelists in Calgary. Subsequently his churches in the country were steadily crowded out by churches organized by the new sects. The threat of the loss of some of its members to other religious bodies weakened in the evangelical church an interest in the cause of religious freedom, and only in those churches, such as the Quakers and some of the smaller Baptist groups, where the spirit of the sect remained strong, have liberal principles been adhered to consistently. Denominationalism tended to make the more prosperous evangelical churches increasingly dependent upon the state and the community at large.

At the same time the evangelical churches, in gradually withdrawing from sectarianism, became much more a part of the metropolitan structure. With the migration of their followers, they established themselves in the larger centres of population, and their leaders became much more sympathetic to the views of city residents. Their houses of worship began to rival in elegance those of the older churches, and most of their leading ministers came to occupy city pulpits. Country stations were increasingly neglected, and methods of organization such as itinerancy and street preaching, which had been developed to make possible the serving of people in the country or in working-class districts of the city who could not be reached within regular places of worship, were abandoned. The evangelical churches came to draw most of their financial support from the cities, and from the better residential sections and, consequently, to identify their interests with the interests of the metropolitan population. They became churches of Empire or nation rather than the churches of the social fringe.

Such a development was clearly evident with respect to the Baptists in Nova Scotia and the Methodists in Upper Canada. The considerable influence exerted within the Baptist denomination by the Granville Street Church in Halifax, after its break in 1827 from the Church of England, and the shift of denominational leadership from preachers and laymen attached to churches in the out-settlements to preachers and laymen attached to the church in the capital, were indicative of fundamental changes in the position of the Baptist group. The leadership of Dr. E. A. Crawley in Baptist educational endeavours reflected the greater dependence upon the resources of the metropolis. Likewise, with the Methodists in Upper Canada, the increasing importance of Toronto as a Methodist centre, and the union in 1832 with the English Wesleyan Conference, reflected the closer identification with the political interests of the capital and with the British imperial system. New Methodist leaders emerged with much stronger urban ties, and new techniques, such as the religious journal, developed which strengthened the influence of churches in the larger centres. The change in the character of the Methodist camp meeting from a religious gathering held in the backwoods to a religious gathering held in summer resorts and attracting city people was suggestive of the new Methodist appeal.

At first glance it might seem that the religious-political movement founded by Aberhart in Alberta escaped developments leading to a closer identification with metropolitan interests, but in actual fact it did not. The increasing competition of radio evangelists led Aberhart and his fellow preachers to place less emphasis upon the appeal to country people and to think more in terms of the work of the large city churches in Calgary and Edmonton, while, at the same time, the political party which grew out of the religious movement steadily ceased to be a frontier party and became more interested in building up a national following or, at least, in securing acceptance within the nation at large. Efforts in various parts of the country to secure the election to Parliament of Social Credit members was an indication of the extent of the shift away from the early position of sectarian and provincial separatism.

The change in the position of the evangelical churches in the cities was accompanied by a change in their relation to the wealthier economic classes. Substantial men of business, though not necessarily changing their religious affiliations, began to make financial contributions to these churches on the theory that their teachings made for good citizens and for well-disciplined workers. At the same time, many of the adherents of the evangelical church became rich themselves. The asceticism cultivated within the religious sect tended to success in business enterprise, and religious nonconformists were likely to find their way into mercantile pursuits in particular. Commercialism favoured the sort of qualities developed within the sect,

while, on the other hand, members of the more traditional churches were likely to avoid commerce as something not becoming their social position.

Commercial prosperity thus inevitably resulted in considerable changes in the economic status of the membership of the evangelical churches as over against the membership of the traditional churches. The evangelical churches ceased to be churches of the poor as an increasing number of their members became substantial citizens, and such a shift in social status led to a shift in political attachments. An anxiety to establish a claim to a position of respectability led these churches to repudiate their earlier connections with the socially humble and politically radical. The increasing conservatism of the Baptists in Nova Scotia and the Methodists in Upper Canada can be explained at least in part on these grounds. By the middle of the nineteenth century these churches had many wealthy members. In Alberta the same sort of thing happened, but it was more evident within the Social Credit party than within the Prophetic Bible Institute. In the election of 1944 many prominent Alberta businessmen – and, there is reason to believe, a number of large business firms outside – lent their active support to the party which nine years earlier had advocated a radical programme of monetary reform.

In the end the evangelistic religious appeal also tended to the development of attitudes of conservatism among the followers of the evangelical churches. While such an appeal did promote, on the one hand, a more rationalist approach to the problems of life, it promoted, on the other hand, a narrow intolerance which increasingly found expression in anti-liberal forms of behaviour. Religious sectarianism involved a shift to a more fundamentalist, elementary conception of religion; it represented a reversion to a simpler form of Christianity. Its appeal, therefore, was essentially reactionary in character. New movements within theological thought were strongly resisted by the religious sect, and it was almost inevitable that something of this theological illiberalism would be carried over and become identified with political illiberalism. The feeling developed by the evangelistic religious sect that it possessed the only true means of salvation led to a type of bigotry which found expression in politics as well as in religion. Reliance upon special revelation ruled out discussion as a way of arriving at decisions, and the religious evangelist was likely to prove highly impatient when caught within the checks and balances of democratic political processes.

Consideration of the influences which tended to force the evangelical churches into a conservative position in politics, as over against those influences which tended to force them into a radical position, suggests that the nature of their political alignments at most can only in part be explained in terms of a fundamental political philosophy. Evangelical church leaders displayed considerable capacity to change their minds, and the minds of their followers, to suit circumstances; and it was never possible to predict what political programme they would support at any particular time. They developed no consistent body of political principles.

The explanation for this would seem to lie in the sectarian origin of the evangelical church. Religious sectarianism as such tended to foster an attitude of political indifference. The whole attention of the individual was directed to the state of his (and of his neighbour's) soul. So long as the sect remained truly evangelical in character, it avoided any connection whatsoever with secular groups or associations, remaining wholly otherworldly. This was true of the Baptists in Nova Scotia, of the Methodists in Upper Canada, and of the religious movement led by Aberhart in Alberta, as it has been true of all other sects.

Although the preaching career of Henry Alline, the founder of the Newlight Baptist Church in Nova Scotia, coincided almost exactly with the period of the American Revolutionary

War, he referred to it only twice in his journal, and then quite incidentally. The Newlight movement grew out of the unrest created by the Revolution, but the Newlights carefully avoided any identification with political interests. Their strength as a religious sect largely derived from such non-involvement in politics. Similarly, the Methodists in Upper Canada made their greatest gains just before and after the War of 1812-14, but few Methodist preachers expressed any interest in the controversies growing out of the war or in the subsequent fierce political conflicts. Methodist preachers and Methodist converts subordinated political allegiances to what they considered the much more important allegiance to their God. Likewise, during the period in which Aberhart gained his greatest influence as a religious leader in Alberta, he had no interest whatsoever in politics, and his followers tended to be people who engaged very little in political activities and who were little informed respecting political issues.

The effect of the sectarian religious appeal thus was virtually to disfranchise a considerable section of the population. The religious sectarian in many cases did not vote; if he did vote, he very often took no other interest in public questions. His political allegiances were of a tenuous sort; he made a poor party member because he was seldom prepared to accept the obligations of party loyalty. His religious conscience too often served to justify an attitude of non-co-operation. This resulted in fostering a state of political illiteracy. For the most part, the membership of religious sects was drawn from the least-educated sections of the population, and no attempt was made, within religious teachings, to correct this initial disadvantage in exercising the privileges of citizenship. Rather, ignorance of political matters was considered a virtue of the evangelical-minded person; it was indicative of his complete break from the fellowship of the ungodly and his full participation in the fellowship of the elect. Thus political illiteracy was deliberately promoted by discouraging contact with people outside the group and by discouraging the reading of non-religious publications. Theological commentaries and religious journals, as well as the evangelical sermon, served to weaken efforts of the secular press to build up party loyalties and a political consciousness.

Political indifference gave way to an interest in public issues only when the position of the religious sect was threatened by public policy. It was the leaders who were most alive to the effects of public policy and who, therefore, were most likely to initiate political action to protect the interests of the sect. Indeed, the followers of the religious sect tended to be little more concerned about its interests as a religious denomination than they were about the interests of any secular institution; sectarianism encouraged an attitude of non-denominationalism. The truly saved were members of the spiritual elect, and the preservation of that connection depended upon no formal institutional organization, a common experience of faith being sufficient bond of attachment. The leaders, however – those whose livelihood or prestige depended upon the continued existence of the sect as a religious denomination – became increasingly jealous of its rights and privileges. They built it into a church because their security depended upon the security of denominational attachments. Efforts to strengthen the social position of the church led to the promotion of activities, such as education and temperance, which brought it more closely into contact with other groups. Challenges to such activities compelled the leaders to mobilize their following for collective political action.

It was such vested interests of office which led to the active political participation of the followers of religious sects. Baptist leaders in Nova Scotia, after the turn of the nineteenth century, could not afford to adhere to the position of political neutrality taken earlier by Henry Alline. Attacks upon denominational enterprises which they promoted, in particular a Baptist college, compelled them to interest themselves in matters of politics. If effective political pressure was to be exerted, they had, in addition, to arouse a strong political interest in their followers. Similarly, Methodist leaders in Upper Canada after 1828, in contrast with the earlier Methodist itinerants, found themselves becoming involved in political controversies in support of their denominational claims. Attacks upon Methodist undertakings were in the nature of attacks upon the vested interests of leadership; a denominational college, Sabbath observance, and the cause of temperance were issues which continued to force Methodist leaders into politics in the provincial and municipal as well as the federal field. Aberhart's sudden break into politics can be explained likewise. Increasing competition from rival radio evangelists led him to search for something new in his appeal, and he seized upon the message of Social Credit. Attacks upon his political teachings forced him into politics in their defence. What he did was to convert a religious crusade into a political crusade; political allegiances were forged to take the place of weakening religious allegiances. None of this, of course, was done with a clear consciousness of the effect. Leadership very seldom appreciated the nature of the forces which drove it into certain lines of action, and in no case, perhaps, was this more evident than in the emergence of the Social Credit movement out of the evangelical preaching of Mr. Aberhart.

It was, indeed, one of the paradoxes in the role of the sectarian leader that his evangelical message should lead him, in the end, into political controversy. To arouse concern in the cause of religious salvation – that is to say, to win converts – the evangelical preacher had to resort to the spectacular, and, as the spectacular in religion ceased to be effective in meeting the competition of more aggressive evangelists or of more highly organized religious institutions, the spectacular in politics was sometimes turned to. It was not in any way remarkable that the Rev. T. T. Shields of Toronto, who broke from the main Baptist body on religious fundamentalist grounds, should have sought to maintain the support of his following by discussing in the pulpit highly controversial political issues. Violent attacks upon public men, like the noise of a brass band, create something of a sensation and provide effective advertising. Such attacks, in the end, can only be sustained by pulling the whole following of the church into politics in support of certain lines of action.

The way which the evangelical church was drawn into the field of politics explains its failure to develop any consistent programme of political action. Lacking any clearly defined political principles, opportunism was the most natural determinant of political action on the part of leaders and followers alike. The nature of the evangelistic religious appeal placed the leaders in a particularly powerful position in mobilizing the support of the followers for political action.

The religious evangelist escaped the checks upon leadership secured through an elaborate denominational organization and an accepted ritual. His relationship to the convert was a purely personal one; it was he rather than any formal church which offered the means of salvation. The result was that the religious evangelist came to assume a very considerable dominance over those whom he converted. The democratization of the institution of religion made possible the concentration of authority in one who enjoyed the privilege of divine revelation. When the religious evangelist moved into the political field, he lost little of his charismatic influence. His strong personal authority made it possible to carry his followers with him no matter what political line he might take. No Roman Catholic bishop could, in fact, ever hope to exert the personal influence over his following as was exerted by Joseph Smith, the founder of the Mormon Church, or by Brigham Young, his successor.

Although Ryerson in Upper Canada was never able to command the support of the whole membership of the Wesleyan

Methodist Church, he nevertheless achieved striking success in swinging the Methodist body behind whatever political party he favoured. The Methodists became a powerful pressure group in Canadian politics about the middle of the nineteenth century simply because expediency determined to a considerable extent their actions; they tended to vote in terms of the interests of their denomination without regard to wider public issues, and political solidarity was maintained by effective leadership, at any rate during the period of ascendancy of Egerton Ryerson. Similarly, Aberhart in Alberta could mobilize his following in support of a personally sponsored political programme because of the peculiar type of influence which he had built up as a religious evangelist. It was his boast that he was completely ignorant of economics before his advocacy of Social Credit ideas, but his economic pronouncements were readily accepted because of the claim to divine revelation which he had established as a religious evangelist.

It would be an exaggeration to conclude from this that the influence of the evangelical churches in Canadian political life has been to produce a citizen body politically illiterate or unprincipled, but such a conclusion would contain an element of truth. An indifference to politics which religious sectarianism engendered has checked the growth of political thought, and the weakness of political thought, in turn, in contributing to a political opportunism on the part of evangelical church leaders, has checked the growth of political statesmanship. It is significant that leadership in politics from the Protestant group in the country has come very largely from people with a Scottish Presbyterian or Scottish Baptist background. Denominationalism and religious fundamentalism have exerted too strong a hold upon members of the evangelical churches for them to go far in a career of politics. Much of their energy has been dissipated in support of programmes of moral reform sponsored by religious groups. They have as a result tended to be more successful in municipal or provincial politics, where party organization has been weak and where voting blocs have exerted a much greater influence, than in federal politics. The repeated failure, in Canada as well as in the United States, to build a national party around the prohibition issue was an indication of the limitations of evangelistic religious thinking in politics.

It is questionable, however, whether the political influence exerted by the evangelical church reveals the real contribution of the religious sect to the development of political thought.

That is to say, the contribution of the sect should not be sought in the political activities of the evangelical church, whether those activities were in the way of supporting radical or conservative political movements in the community, but rather it should be sought in the religious influence of the sect as such, before it developed into the evangelical church. Its political contribution lay in its very emphasis upon the separation of the religious from the political. The indifference of the religious sect to politics provided a healthy corrective to tendencies within the church to become greatly occupied with political matters and so entrenched in the political interests of the state. It was in the teachings of religious sectarianism that the threat to liberal principles through the alliance of church and state was most effectively met. The religious sect, by concentrating upon the purely religious message of salvation, escaped the demands of nationalism so evident in times of war. Moreover, by placing the emphasis upon spiritual values in the making of preaching appointments, the sect was freed from social pressures making for the development of a denominational bureaucracy which sought support in the bureaucracy of big business and the state. In Canada the maintenance of a successful federal system in particular has depended upon the strength of forces of decentralization, secured, within religious organization, through the influence of new religious sects.

As the sect has grown into the church, new sects have grown out of the church. Thus the effect of the increasing participation of evangelical church leaders in politics has been offset by secession and the emergence of new sects which have withdrawn completely from political activity. In Nova Scotia the rapid growth of the Freewill Baptist movement after 1820 emphasized the weaknesses of the Baptist Church as a result of its shift away from an evangelical position. The entry of the Methodists in Upper Canada into politics under the leadership of Egerton Ryerson was followed almost immediately by the break of the local preachers and the organization of the Methodist Episcopal Church. In Alberta, likewise, the participation of Aberhart in politics led very quickly to the weakening of his religious influence and to the shift of evangelical leadership to new religious sects. It is this persistence of the sectarian spirit in religious organization which has given religion its dynamic force in society. It has exerted a decisive influence upon determining the relation of the church to the state and thereby upon determining the contribution of religion to political thought.

---

3. Industrialism and Settlement in Western Canada

Harold A. Innis

No one has contributed more to our understanding of the ways in which technology, communication and ecology have been intricately intertwined in the social and economic development of Canada than the late Professor Innis who taught at the University of Toronto for more than a quarter of a century. Whether he focuses upon the fur trade, the fisheries on the Atlantic seaboard, the lumbering industry or, as in this essay, wheat farming on the western prairies he elaborates his thesis that the exploitation (originally through the fur trade) of the vast, open and relatively empty space that was later to become Canada required extensive organization which led to the formation of economic monopolies.

Reprinted from *Problems of Staple Production in Canada*, by Harold A. Innis, published by the Ryerson Press, Toronto. ©1933.

*To protect these monopolies a military policy was needed, and that meant centralized political control, manifest in the activities of the government, the church and the seigniorial system. "No such tendency toward unity of structure in institutions and toward centralized control as found in Canada can be observed in the United States," Innis declares. "The diversity of institutions has made possible the combination of government ownership and private enterprise which has been a further characteristic of Canadian development."**

By the time western Canada was opened up this pattern was well established. The introduction of a single-crop economy

**Edn. Harold A. Innis, *The Fur Trade in Canada*, (revised edition) Toronto, University of Toronto Press, 1956, p. 401

(wheat) was necessitated largely through external economic needs and technological resources, principally those of Britain and the United States. In this selection Innis explains how the pattern of settlement derived from the wheat economy, and the institutions that evolved around it were quite different from those developed elsewhere. The effect of physical space on patterns of community development is vividly drawn. While we have as yet no precise theoretical propositions that would enable us to deduce the relation between physical space and social space, the work of Harold Innis is suggestive of the form those propositions must take.

The papers which have been read before this section, and those published in the *Report of the Commission on Types of Rural Settlement*, 1928, have dealt chiefly with settlements in England and in Europe which had been thoroughly established at the beginning of the so-called Industrial Revolution. These settlements have been profoundly influenced by modern industrialism, but in most cases a continuity of life and organization is evident. This paper purposes dealing with a radically different type of settlement – such as is found especially in western Canada and the new countries – which have had their *raison d'être* in modern industrialism. Although a study of these settlements must proceed from different premises, it is hoped that the final conclusions may prove suggestive to the study of the types of rural settlement which have been of chief interest to this section. Moreover, a study of the influence of modern industrialism, as confined to western Canada, should be of value to the study of settlements in new countries, such as Argentina and Australia. This paper can only attempt a study of the background of the main movements and clear the ground for later more intensive work. It must be content with a survey of the factors peculiar to the spread of industrialism as they are shown in western Canada.

In the first place, an appreciation of the characteristics of modern industrialism is essential. The general trends are well known as to space and time. The conspicuous rise of industrialism in the latter half of the eighteenth century and in the nineteenth century in England, and the spread in the latter half of the nineteenth century, especially to the United States, Germany, and Japan, are matters of common observation. The spread has been of an uneven character and has been affected materially by wars and in turn by the development of the iron and steel industry. The United States became rapidly industrialized after the Civil War, Germany after the Franco-Prussian War, Japan after the Russo-Japanese War. The repercussions of the Great War on the industrial growth of the new countries have been evident on all sides. Important as these sudden spurts of industrialism have been to the new countries, they must not be permitted to obscure the significance of steady and persistent experimentation essential to the evolution in technique of machine industry. The technique involved in the countries which have had the longest experience, as in England, has been modified and improved and borrowed wholesale by the new countries.[1] The painful experiences incidental to earlier inventions have been eliminated, and the results of the experiments are taken over with little difficulty by the new countries. Industrialization of the new countries, given suitable political and social organizations, tends to become cumulative – the United States became industrialized more rapidly than Great Britain, and Canada more rapidly than the United States. The more recently the country has been industrialized, the more rapid tends to become its industrialization.

On the other hand, the cumulative tendency is accompanied by a continuity. The early centres of industrial growth become more directly linked with the new centres. The experience, fixed capital, financial and social organization, and the advantages which facilitated the growth of industrialism are factors which enable the older centres to benefit from the industrial growth of the new centres. Abundant supplies of iron and coal and accessible, all-the-year-round water-transport permit continuous operation, the reduction of overhead costs, and the concentration of industry. The advantages of England as an industrial centre need no description.

The significance of the cumulative tendency of industrialism and of the continuity of industrialism to Canada and the new countries is obvious. Canada has been able to produce on an increasingly large scale, on account of the essential advantages of machine industry, the raw materials for the industrialized countries. She has in turn provided a market for the products of the industrial countries. Her limitations, of iron and coal, and of her seasonal navigation, have made her more dependent on the older industrial countries. The concentration on raw materials is immediately suggested by a reference to wheat, lumber, pulp and paper, minerals, and fish. The rapidity with which production in these commodities has increased since the opening of the present century has depended on extensive borrowing of technique from the United States which had been in part earlier engaged in providing these staples to Great Britain and Europe. It has depended also on the increasingly rapid industrialization of the older countries with the rapid growth of urban population and the increasing demand for supplies of raw material, especially with the exhaustion of old sources.

From the standpoint of this paper we can limit our attention to the study of wheat[2] as produced in western Canada. The Civil War in the United States gave a direct impetus to the iron and steel industry and rapidly hastened the spread of industrialism. In the succeeding decade railroad construction proceeded rapidly and the wheat-producing areas were rapidly extended. In the new areas the technique of production was improved materially, especially in the decade from 1872 to 1882. Immediately after the Civil War the self-rake reaper was in general use. The harvester displaced the self-rake reaper between 1872 and 1875, and the wire binder came in between 1874 and 1878, to be quickly displaced by the twine binder in 1879. The effect of these improvements was shown in a reduction of the number of men required in the peak harvesting season, the saving of grain and the rapid occupation of the north-western states. The self-rake reaper required for one day, cutting eleven acres, two horses and a driver, four or five men to bind and one man to shock. The harvester required two men to bind and one man to drive two horses. The twine binder with a six-foot cut required for twelve acres a day three horses and one man to drive and one or two men to shock. With the introduction of steam-power and especially of the straw-burning engine in 1875 to 1880, harvesting was speeded up materially. With these technical advances, the Homestead Act of 1862 and the uniform system of surveying of quarter-sections of 160 acres and townships of six miles square, the territory was rapidly settled and brought under cultivation. Transport improvements accompanied the improvements of agricultural implements. Steel rails were substituted for iron, canals were enlarged, and larger grain vessels introduced on the Great Lakes, especially from Chicago to Buffalo. Rail competition forced down lake and canal charges; and reduced costs of handling at terminal points, as Chicago, New York and Liverpool, accompanied lower freight rates. Grain elevators were in use in Liverpool towards the end of the decade and were rapidly installed in other centres. Improved marketing accompanied improved transport. After 1874 grain was graded and shipped in bulk, whereas formerly it had been handled chiefly in special lots on consignment. Through these reduced charges it was estimated that the cost of hauling one bushel of wheat from Chicago to New York declined from 1876 to 1881 from thirty-two and one-quarter cents to seventeen and four-tenths cents. Ocean shipping was subject to marked improvement. In 1867-8 the iron steamship was beginning to replace the sailing vessel. Ocean freight rates declined steadily from 1873 to 1891. Indirectly improved ocean-transport favoured the position of hard spring wheat. Fresh meat shipments to Great Britain began about 1875, and the winter wheat sections became more concerned with mixed farming. Hard spring wheat occupied a stronger position, however, through the introduction of new milling processes after 1880-1 – the roller process and the gradual reduction method. After 1875 winter wheat tended to remain stationary and spring wheat to increase rapidly. The higher price of winter wheat gradually disappeared, and by 1889 had vanished entirely.

In the decade from 1872 to 1882, wheat production had increased materially in the United States. England as a consuming country through increasing industrialization became adjusted to this situation. It has been shown that from 1852 to 1872 the price of wheat in England varied inversely with British crops. After 1872 the world crop became a determining factor, and price became the relation between the crop of industrial countries and the world market. The American price of wheat was governed neither by the American volume of wheat nor by the British volume. Wheat had shifted to a world market, and England became more definitely dependent on outside areas for her food supply.

The technical developments in the United States responsible for a rapid increase in the production of wheat and the increasing industrialization of Great Britain were significant factors in the opening up of western Canada. The experience of the United States was taken over and adapted to Canadian territory. In railroad construction Van Horne, Shaughnessy, and others brought to Canada the ripe experience of the United States. Lower costs of production for dynamite facilitated construction through the difficult Precambrian area north of Lake Superior. Railroad cars, rails and general equipment were produced at lower costs through the advantages of American experience and large-scale production. The Canadian Pacific Railway was completed from Winnipeg to Vancouver on the west and to Montreal in the east in a remarkably short period of time – almost one-half of the time provided for in the charter. The country was rapidly surveyed and the territory opened for new settlers, who were brought into the country by extensive advertising on the part of the railway and the government. The industrial equipment of the United States, of Great Britain, and latterly of Canada hastened the production of agricultural implements, of lumber for farm buildings, of fuel, and of food and clothing. In the wave of industrialism of the past century and a half, Canada was in the crest and received the full impetus of the momentum.

The geographical background tended to accentuate the rapid development of industrialism and the rapid borrowing from the United States. In the first place the continental background of the United States was an important factor in the development of large-scale production, mass output and low costs. The level prairies of western Canada facilitated rapid railway construction[3] and rapid occupation by settlers. The relative absence of large trees made possible the rapid breaking up of virgin soil and hastened the production of wheat. The Great Lakes offered a convenient waterway for the shipment of great quantities of wheat to the Atlantic seaboard. Geographical handicaps,[4] occasioned by the location of the mountain-passes which determined the projection of the main line, were of relatively slight importance.

The political background had a similar tendency to accentuate rapid development. The Prairie Provinces and British Columbia were transferred at practically one stroke from the control of the large centralized organization of the Hudson's Bay Company[5] to the government of Canada. It was imperative that western Canada should be developed in the shortest possible time from the standpoint of the prosperity of eastern Canada and from the fear of annexation to the United States. The importance of the unified control of eastern Canada was shown in the substantial subsidies in money, in land, and in other forms to hasten the construction of the Canadian Pacific Railway and the settlement of the west.

The political background affected in turn the financial background and hastened the spread of industrialism. Control of the railway was placed in the hands of a single company in order that construction should be carried out more rapidly and that the country should be settled more effectively. The energies responsible for rapid settlement could be directed with great effectiveness toward the single task of encouraging immigration and developing traffic. Moreover, the impact of the tremendous overhead charges involved in railway construction, especially through the Precambrian area in the east and the Rocky Mountains in the west, and in the heavy peak-load traffic incidental to the export of wheat in the season of open navigation, necessitated the immediate and rapid settlement of the west.

Another important factor in hastening the spread of industrialism in western Canada was the growing efficiency of the price-mechanism. Wheat produced in Canada was sold on a world market in return for a direct cash payment. The numerous transactions involved in the transfer of wheat from the Canadian producer to the English consumer necessitated a high stage of efficiency in the marketing of wheat and in foreign exchange and internal exchange. Canadian banks[6] were rapidly extended from headquarters in the east, and adjustments were made by which wheat could be sent directly from the frontier to the centres of industrialism with the least possible friction. This efficiency assumed improvements of communication, elaboration of banking skill, and a comparatively effective educational system.

The cumulative effects of these factors were shown in the marked and rapid increase in the production and export of wheat.[7] The effects on settlement of this concentration on wheat production may be suggested. Settlers were scattered along the railway lines in a belt generally not exceeding twenty miles[8] on each side of the right-of-way or of a total width of forty miles. Land was occupied which could be broken into cultivation with the least possible difficulty and from which grain could be hauled to the elevators for shipment with the lowest possible costs. Land areas near the railways not suitable to wheat production have been devoted to other products, with the aid of the railway companies, for example, in financing irrigation projects. Rapid production of wheat involved the immigration of virile young men. Farm buildings were rapidly constructed on the quarter-sections with reference to accessibility to field work. Family life and social life were temporarily broken up. Wheat production involved periods of great activity in the sowing and harvesting, and periods of relative inactivity in the winter months and the growing seasons. Long-run fluctuations followed periods of prosperity and depression, depending on prices but chiefly on the weather and on seasonal changes of a long-run character. As a result of these factors, social and community life was seriously handicapped. Village communities transplanted especially from Russia, as with the Doukhobors and the Mennonites, faced obvious difficulties. Schools, churches, and the centres of community life generally grew up very slowly. Urban centres were created in direct relation to the railroads and the convenience of elevators for grain shipment, e.g., approximately eight miles apart with loading platforms four miles. These centres became distributing points for supplies, e.g., agricultural implements, lumber, coal and general merchandise. Larger centres flourished at divisional points located approximately 110 to 130 miles apart, depending on accessibility of water and the efficiency of engines, at which engines and train crews were changed. The largest centres were dependent on the location of branch lines and junction points, of terminal points, and the stimulus to population afforded by government buildings,[9] educational facilities, and wholesale houses. The importance of railroads and government subsidies to the growth of towns has been largely responsible for periods of feverish real-estate speculation and the heavy charges for long street-car lines, electric light lines, gas pipes, telephone lines, and sewerage systems characteristic of the urban centres of western Canada.

With increasing population, industrialism has been partly responsible for an alleviation of the difficulties of slow community growth. Branch lines have been built, giving greater accessibility. The automobile, the telephone and the radio have contributed to a solution of the problems. Better living conditions have followed the improvements of transport and communication. The wheat pool has developed as an evidence of a new solidarity.

It is not the intention of this paper to discuss in detail the effects of industrialism. It is hoped, rather, that an appreciation may be gained of the necessity of a different point of view for the study of settlement in new areas. Important as has been the work of Prof. Gras[10] and his students in the study of metropolitan economy, it is doubtful whether the conclusions can be applied satisfactorily to western Canada. Certainly settlement in western Canada differs fundamentally from settlement in eastern Canada and in the old world.[11]

NOTES
1. See Thorstein Veblen, *Imperial Germany and the Industrial Revolution* (New York, 1918), for the argument on Germany's borrowing, and numerous references in C.R. Fay, *Great Britain from Adam Smith to the Present Time; an Economic and Social Survey* (London, 1928), to the borrowing of the United States. The problems of anthropology which centre about the study of diffusion of culture as shown in C. Wissler, *The Relation of Nature to Man in Aboriginal America* (New York, 1926) and W. F. Ogburn, *Social Change* (London, 1923) are of crucial importance to an understanding of settlement in Western Can-

ada. It is important to note that the advantages of borrowing which arise from the application of mature technique to virgin natural resources are reduced by the tendency for countries to dispose of or dump obsolescent machinery, e.g., agricultural implements, to countries with virgin natural resources and in this way to reduce their own costs of improved equipment.
2. See T. B. Veblen, "Price of Wheat Since 1867," *Journal of Political Economy*, 1, p. 68, also C. W. Peterson, *Wheat* (Calgary, 1930), Ch. lx; J. E. Lattimer, "Labour Requirements in Farming," *Contributions to Canadian Economics*, Vol. II, pp. 14-33; D. A. MacGibbon, *The Canadian Grain Trade* (Toronto, 1932).
3. See W. H. Barneby, *Life and Labour in the Far Far West* (London, 1884) in which six and a half miles is given as a record for one day's construction.
4. The Kicking Horse Pass necessitated the development of less productive soil in the south. The choice of the southern route has been of enormous significance to Canadian economic development.
5. See H. A. Innis, *Fur Trade in Canada* (New Haven, 1930 and Toronto, 1933).
6. See Victor Ross, *A History of the Canadian Bank of Commerce* (Toronto, 1920), especially Vol. II.
7. For statistical evidence the *Canada Year Book* should be consulted. The increase was far beyond the most optimistic estimate of those consulted in James Mavor's *Report to the Board of Trade on the North-West of Canada* (London, 1904). See D. A. MacGibbon, "The Future of the Canadian Export Trade in Wheat," *Contributions to Canadian Economics*, v; also *Agriculture, Climate and Population of the Prairie Provinces of Canada* (Ottawa, 1931).
8. Wheat may be hauled 50 miles to the elevators, particularly with the increasing importance of trucks, but the handicaps are obvious.
9. In Saskatchewan the university is located at Saskatoon, the parliament buildings, the normal school and police headquarters at Regina, the provincial asylum at Weyburn, and the penitentiary at Prince Albert.
10. N. B. Gras, *An Introduction to Economic History* (London, 1922), also M. Hartsough, *The Twin Cities as a Metropolitan Market* (Minneapolis, 1925).
11. The Pioneer Belt project, under the direction of Professor W. A. Mackintosh, has in hand a thorough survey of settlement problems in Western Canada. See *Pioneer Settlement* (New York, 1932) and I. Bowman, *The Pioneer Fringe* (New York, 1932).

---

4. The Canadian Family: Variations and Uniformities

K. Ishwaran/*York University*

The most important decision an individual can make is his choice of parents. (The paradox is, of course, that this is a choice over which he has no control.) The family is the institution that, initially at least, assigns him a place in the stratification system and which, as the principal agent of socialization in the child's earliest years, functions as a filter through which he acquires his awareness of social space, his own and that of others. In learning the society's rules and roles he comes to see that there are boundaries that enclose him and those of his kind while distancing him from others. Though he may change his position on one or more of society's many ranking systems as he moves through the life cycle, this early world view will continue to affect his spatial perceptions. To the extent that this is so, the centrifugal strain towards uniformity which Professor Ishwaran detects within vastly

different family types in Canadian society is not likely ever to be complete. In large measure this essay consists of a summary of the evidence provided by different authors in Professor Ishwaran's reader, The Canadian Family, *Holt, Rinehart and Winston (1971).*

Reprinted by permission of the author. Also published in *Social Process and Institutions: The Canadian Case*, edited by James E. Gallagher and Ronald D. Lambert, Holt, Rinehart and Winston (1971).

It has been widely assumed that there is such a social phenomenon as the 'Western family', a form of social grouping based on descent and marriage, generated by processes of industrialization and urbanization of the type characteristic of the highly complex technological society of the West (Goode, 1963; Shamas and Streib, 1965; Litwak, 1960, 1965). The bulk of the Canadian population is of Western origin, its people are predominantly urban, and its economy is based on a highly developed technological system. It would thus be reasonable to infer, as has been done, that "The *Canadian Family* fits the model of the urban family characteristic of industrial societies. . . . As many post-1945 immigrants have been subject only to urban influences in their countries of origin as well as immediately on settlement in Canada, their families can be expected to resemble the dominant type from the outset" (Jones, 1968:631). Often implicit in such a view is the assumption that the 'American family' comprising parents and their unmarried children, the so-called *nuclear family*, is the prototype of the Western, urban, industrial family, and that Canada simply displays a variant of the type. Canada's small Indian and Eskimo populations are seen as temporary exceptions because, having come under the impact of Western-type industrialization only recently, they are still in a state of transition towards the Western, urban model.

The extent to which the notion of the "the urban family characteristic of industrial (Western) societies" is analytically useful for an understanding of the dynamics of the Canadian situation is a point requiring careful thought, and we briefly return to it after an outline and analysis of the substantive data. The point of immediate concern is that directly opposed to the orientation of Jones and those who agree with him, there is another view the crux of which may be stated as follows:

> There is no one Canadian family. With its distinctive geography and history, Canada is much too heterogeneous to have one or ten or twenty distinctive family types. As the geographical setting, and the social class, religious, ethnic, occupational, and other groupings vary, so too do our families (Elkin, 1968:31).

Clearly, in Elkin's orientation, formulated on the basis of his analysis of the published and unpublished data as of 1964, there is no room for the concept of *the* Canadian family such as the one that Jones adopts and recommends.

The sociology of the Canadian family or families is still in its formative stages. Detailed information regarding environmental, technological, demographic, and socio-cultural factors are simply not available to test either proposition. Examination of the available data rather favours the following hypothesis: *While numerous factors–demographic, environmental, technological, historical and socio-cultural–generate pressures for variation; a different, but related, set of factors–processes of urbanization and industrialization, based on modern technology–produces pressures for uniformity. Consequently, what one actually finds is a whole range of variations continuously under pressure for uniformity.*

This means that particular cases will show the result of this two-way pull from the forces of 'variation' and those of 'uniformity'. The tension is not just between 'tradition' and 'modernity', as one may be tempted to suppose. There are conditions when the two mingle without any tension; and there are others when they do not. The tension is between two sets of processes. One of them pulls towards variation and the other towards uniformity. Both sets are extremely complex and include the various factors mentioned above.

A Matter of Definition

A definitional problem should be settled at the outset. The term 'family' in everyday English is used in at least two different contexts:

(1) it may refer to that grouping comprising 'husband, wife, and unmarried children', technically known as the nuclear family or the elementary family;

(2) it may refer to other groupings that, in addition to (1), include those who are related either through 'blood' or marriage. Technically, 'blood relations' are formed on the principle of descent; and 'relations through marriage' are based on the principle of *affinity*. The two principles together are taken to define *kinship*. Unless otherwise stated, the term family will be used in this report as in everyday English. When it seems necessary to be specific, we shall use terms like 'nuclear family',

'extended family', 'modified extended family', and so on. Briefly, then, following the usage in current English, the term *family* will stand for any grouping that is based on "who is descended from whom" and "who is related to whom through marriage."

One is actually related through descent and affinity to hundreds and thousands of people, but in everyday life, people neither know all their relatives, nor do they think it necessary to do so. Lines and circles are always being drawn so that some people are included, others are not. Moreover, we draw circles within circles for different contexts: some by custom must be included for certain purposes; but others must be included for other purposes. One result of this process of *social selection* of certain relations based on descent and affinity is that the family in common speech varies in *span of inclusion* from society to society, and from context to context within a given society. Thus, the family in some societies may effectively include only the nuclear family and, for certain limited purposes, a few other relatives. On the other hand, a whole island population in the Pacific, like the Tikopia, may constitute a family in the sense of the term as used in everyday English.

A long-term and spatially wide-ranging view of the question of who is, or is not, in the family, is answered on the basis of numerous factors and very complex decisions. Family membership depends on issues such as, the size of the population; the relative number of men and women who may marry and procreate; technology; resources in relation to the total population, but food supplies especially. In other words, the size and the actual composition of kinship groupings, based on descent and affinity, are not just a matter of personal fancy. This applies, too, when it is a question of inter-group relations based on kinship and non-kin principles.

Our clarification of the span of family relations and factors that generate varying spans is an attempt to simplify a complex body of literature on kinship.

The remainder of this paper is divided into three main sections. In the first, we will consider certain general but crucial features of the Canadian population as a whole. The main source of information for this section is to be found in the Canadian census. Although helpful, the data provided by the census are of limited usefulness, because they fail to probe the complexities and subtleties of kinship relations. The second section reviews the more recent research bearing on identifiable Canadian families. Our concluding remarks in the third and last section point to the task ahead for those who wish to achieve a social scientific understanding of Canadian family life.

Ethnicity, Urbanization, and Family

Ethnicity

The census of 1961 presents the ethnic structure of the Canadian population according to 16 categories. It reveals that 43.8 percent of the population were of British extraction, while 30.4 percent were French in origin. Some 25 percent of the population were divided among the remaining fourteen categories.

Since our purpose at this stage is to draw special attention to the *fact* of ethnic diversity in the Canadian people, Table 1 taken from the 1951 census is more telling. The fact of Franco-British numerical predominance obtained in that census, too, but the breakdown of categories was 30 instead of 16.

The figures reported in Table 1 should be treated with caution. The relevant information for the 1961 census was gathered by asking each person, "To what ethnic or cultural group did you or your ancestor (on the male side) belong on coming to this continent?" Elkin has noted that such a method of determining ethnicity ignores the psychological aspect of

Table 1: Origins of Population in 1951 (in thousands)[1]

British	**6,709**
English	3,630
Irish	1,440
Scottish	1,547
Other	92
Other European	**6,872**
Austrian	32
Belgian	35
Czech and Slovak	64
Danish	43
Finnish	44
French	4,319
German	620
Greek	14
Hungarian	60
Icelandic	23
Italian	152
Jewish	182
Lithuanian	16
Netherlands	264
Norwegian	119
Polish	220
Romanian	24
Russian	91
Swedish	98
Ukrainian	395
Yugoslav	21
Other	36
Asiatic	**74**
Chinese	33
Japanese	22
Other	19
Other Origins	**354**
Native Indian and Eskimo	166
Negro	18
Other and not stated	170
Total	**14,009**

1. The figures in the table report origin as traced through the paternal line, largely by language, with no consideration of the maternal line.

actual identification among Canadian-born descendants of immigrants (1968: 44). There is also the problem of the ethnic identity of the children of inter-ethnic marriages. If we do not set our expectations too high, census figures are accurate enough for a broad indication of the ethnic heterogeneity of the Canadian population.

As the 1961 census showed, some 25 percent of the population were fragmented into 14 ethnic categories. The percentage in each was bound to be small, but in terms of our framework, the size of a 'population subsystem' is significant only in relation to the social-forms that are generated. A relatively small ethnic category is not negligible because it is small. The Chinese, who accounted for only 0.2 percent of the population in 1961 are, in terms of the demands of our framework, initially as important as the more formidable numbers of British, French, and so on.

We believe it reasonable to expect, at least initially, that there were at least as many patterns of the family in Canada as there are ethnic categories. So many of Canada's ethnic peoples remain unstudied that we cannot venture to test this assumption. In fact, Elkin comments in his survey of the literature on the family that he will not consider those of British origin because the information is so inadequate even for them. Most of the available knowledge concerning the other ethnic catego-

ries is historical and has very little to say about contemporary family patterns (Elkin, 1968:52-64). The quality of data pertaining to French Canadians, however, has improved recently.

Urban Canadians
According to the census of 1961, any settlement with a population of "1,000 or above" in unincorporated areas and over 5,000 in densely populated incorporated areas qualified as urban (Simmons, 1969:9).

In 1871 about one half of the labour force was engaged in some kind of farming and four fifths of the population lived in rural areas. Since then, the rural population has declined steadily, although the micro-processes adding up this decline have varied from year to year and from area to area in Canada. Off-farm migration has been continuously adding up and continues to this day. It has been estimated, for instance, that "through the nineteen-sixties, 7,000 people will be leaving Saskatchewan farms each year, the majority of whom will be looking for work in the non-agricultural part of the labour force. Many will have to seek such work outside the province, chiefly in Central Canada where the new industrial epoch has its centre of gravity" (Porter, 1970:137-8).

Porter points out the parallel trend towards concentration of agriculture in larger farms and the decline of small family farms, which depended greatly on the family for its labour. The exodus to the city also means a large number of young and untrained additions to the urban labour force. Porter's hypothesis is that these people will enter at the bottom of the urban occupational system (Porter, 1970:140). Most people migrate from farms to cities in search of a 'better life'. Whether or not they are able to achieve their objective is not clear. What may be anticipated, however, is that many of the prerequisites for a better life are relatively inaccessible at the bottom of the urban occupational structure. Just what forms of family life may be emerging among these migrants remains a matter for systematic study. It seems reasonable to suppose that even if they are nuclear families, their location at the bottom of the occupational structure places them in quite a different context from that of other urban nuclear families.

An unincorporated settlement with a population of 1,000 may be as 'urban' as a settlement with a population of 100,000, according to the definition employed by the census. Sociologically, the two are likely to be very different indeed. It is probably misleading to think of both as urban, in the same sense, even if there is a predominance of nuclear families in each. Variation in size of settlements is the result of very complex processes which, in today's world, may include national and even international dimensions. The nuclear family in a small town is likely to occupy a different matrix compared with the apparently similar form appearing in a large city.

Households and Families in the Census
The census of Canada defines "family" as a group comprising "parents and never married children" (1966:609-613). Hence a married person, even if he or she is a member of a parent's household is not regarded as a member. The "household", according to the census, comprises "persons or groups of persons occupying the same dwelling" (1966:605-609). Types of family are classified on the basis of whether or not the head of the household is also the head of the family as defined in the census. In 1966, a large majority of units comprised "parents and never married children." Fully 96 percent maintained their own household, while 4 percent did not have households of their own. The statistical predominance of the nuclear family in the Canadian population is apparent. It is our belief, though, that this is a static and thus inadequate view of the Canadian family for reasons to follow.

The cumulative forces of expanding urbanization and industrialization in Canada, pressing for uniformity of familial forms, operate on a population that is ethnically diverse. Is the outcome a uniform grouping of "parents and never married children" described by the census as the family? Let us assume for a moment that the answer is affirmative; after all, the census does show that most of the households do comprise only "parents and never married children." But what about the inter-relations among census families, on the one hand, and relations among such families and non-kin groups, on the other hand? Are they also of a uniform nature despite ethnic variations and regional differences in terms of demographic, environmental, and technological factors? Moreover, there is the question of location. Major generators of urbanization and industrialization in Canada are not evenly distributed even though the forces of industrialization and urbanization may be expanding into the remotest corners of Canada's vast and environmentally varied surface.

We hold that the factor of ethnicity will remain relevant, though the degree of relevance will of course vary. Ethnicity will interact with urbanization-industrialization in interesting ways. We propose in a rather broad way three types of settings for the analysis of familial forms:

(1) outposts
(2) rural settings
(3) urban settings.

Some of the empirical cases which we shall discuss will be difficult to fit into any one category but they seem to correspond sufficiently with known facts about Canada and so should prove adequate for the purposes of a preliminary inquiry.

We conclude this section with the reminder that it is not our intention to survey all the major instances of variations and uniformities. The purpose is to illustrate the thesis that all actual cases of familial forms and processes that produce them are consequences of the two-way pull between forces of variability and uniformity.

Variations and Uniformities

The Outpost Family

The Canadian Indians, descended from the most ancient inhabitants of North America, have varied greatly among themselves due to their varying ecological niches during aboriginal times; and, despite stereotypes to the contrary, so have the Eskimo. For a considerable period of time, in some cases beginning in the late seventeenth century, the fur trade with Europeans generated significant pressures for uniformity. The indigenous economy in the case of all Eskimos and some Indians was based on hunting, fishing, and gathering. Some 12,000 Eskimos who live in Canada's vast Arctic regions, and some 170,000 Indians who inhabit approximately 2,300 reserves (mostly in the subarctic regions of all the Canadian provinces, except Newfoundland), definitely belong to the outpost. Few Indians and Eskimos, comparatively speaking, live in the larger urban centres. In spite of their outpost settlements, forces of urban, industrial society nevertheless affect the native peoples from a distance, because they are located at the periphery of the expanding administrative frontiers of the Provincial and Federal Governments.

Even so, the standard and range of diversified urban services to be found in the economically significant urban areas are not available at the outpost. Moreover, the traditional skills of hunting are of scant significance to the main centres of urbanization-industrialization in Canada. Consequently, opportunities for direct participation on the part of native peoples are clearly limited. Indeed, a growing segment of the Eskimo-Indi-

an population in the outpost manages to ensure bare survival due to Government welfare measures and additional subsidies. These and other factors collectively cast the outpost into a fairly distinctive role and give rise to pressures for uniformity. These pressures, however, operate within the constraints of forces making for variability.

Contemporary Indian Variations

Although a clear picture will require far more information than is presently available, instances of familial forms produced by the two-way pull of forces towards variability and uniformity can be found. One major variant is to be found among some of the Athabaskan Indians near Whitehorse, capital of the Yukon Territory. Here is an instance of the so-called matrifocal family familiar to students of Negro families in the United States and the family in the Caribbean. The Indians of our concern live either in the mining settlements or in their vicinity. These areas represent outposts of a modern technological society and attract unskilled, semiskilled, and highly skilled people who naturally come from the South and are of European extraction.

The Indian economy of early contact times, based on trapping and hunting, fishing and gathering, is no longer adequate for survival. Traditional resources have been depleted, partly as a result of hunting with guns, a technological innovation introduced in the early stages of culture contact. In addition, the people have become dependent on some of the consumer goods, including foodstuffs, which were introduced by Europeans.

The overall effect is that most Indian men are unable to provide for themselves and their families. Opportunities opened up by the extension of urbanization-industrialization are available only to those with formal education and are highly competitive. Processes of urbanization-industrialization, therefore, have had a debilitating impact on men, excepting those who are able to earn wages by participating at the lower levels of the structure of the white-centred economy.

The process of industrialization-urbanization, however, has had a kind of 'liberating' influence on some Indian women. Indian men have to compete with white men both for jobs and Indian women, but women do not face any direct competition. Native women retain their traditional roles of home-making, child-rearing, and so on. But the new environment is no longer as unpredictable as it was in the past when marriage and survival were closely connected so far as women were concerned. Today, an Indian husband is no longer an asset and often survival is easier without a husband.

Untrained women, unlike untrained men, have better economic opportunities because they can and do work as domestics, in cafés along the Alaskan Highway, and in Whitehorse. Such positions put women in an effective network of communication about job opportunities. This limited but effective *pied à terre* in the white man's world exposes some women to the 'Southern model' of womanhood, particularly through magazines like *True Romance*. Collectively, these factors add up to a different model for being a woman than was possible within the traditional life style.

It is thus clear that industrialization-urbanization has affected Indian men and women in different ways and has created a situation in which, under the circumstances, the women seem to have superior opportunities compared to the men.

Members of a dominant, intrusive culture in general enjoy sexual access to the women of the subordinate culture. Whitehorse and its vicinity are no exception. Many White men, in search of entertainment, good time, and liquor, find them in the Indian villages. Given the new model of womanhood and other factors associated with their status as Indian women, it is apparently not difficult to arrange for social meetings between

White men and Indian girls. But such meetings are not likely to lead to marriage, although in Canada between 1957 and 1967, 4,431 Indian women married non-Indians (details not known) and thus become legally assimilated and lost the rights attached to their Indian status. In any case, marriage is not a probable outcome when White men and Indian women come together under the circumstances described here. What develops is a short-term relationship, especially because few White men are willing to accept publicly any long-term relationship with Indian women who, in their turn, are in no great hurry to abandon their native rights.

Not all women are aware of their new alternative, and certainly not all in the vicinity of Whitehorse have taken advantage of it. Indian men still marry Indian women, although a significant number of both remain unmarried. But some of the women have taken advantage of their new situation so that the pattern of family organization has been affected. The crux of all this is that some Indian women denigrate marriage with Indian men and are willing to accept relationships with the transient white population, relationships which, when they produce children, do not create socially recognized fathers. The result is a basis familial form comprising a mother and her unmarried children. Throughout the woman's lifetime different males may come to be attached to the basic unit through the same processes that produced the matrifocal arrangement in the first place.

A recent study, which reports and analyses the formation of matrifocal families among the Athabaskan-speaking Indians in the Yukon, indicates quite clearly that this new type is related to a complex set of environmental, technological, economic, and cultural factors (Cruickshank, 1971). The explanation does not lie in some simple notion of sex-hungry "loose Indian women" or in anything equally simple. A great deal of research is required before we can say more about the *social* processes that have given rise to the matrifocal family among some of the outpost Indians.

Another study of Canadian Indians in three towns in the Great Slave Lake area in the District of MacKenzie, Northwest Territories, shows that

> For the Indians in all three towns the basic unit of organization revolves around the household and the family. The demands of the ecology and the economy, along with the adjustment made to these by the political system means that there is no push or pull drawing men and women into wider community groupings. Household composition is for the most part that of the nuclear family, i.e., a church married or common law couple with or without children (Cohen, 1970:20).

Cohen further comments that, "The only other permanent group to which the individual belongs is that of his kindred ... besides primary kin, people know and interact with secondary kin in their own community and refer to other kindred" (Cohen, 1970:20). This observation leads one to feel that need for data on actual patterns of interaction in order to be sure that the nuclear family household is as basic as we are told.

Dunning (1971) has studied the kinship system of the Northern Ojibway of northwestern Ontario, and Algonkian-speaking people. Their hunting-trapping territory of 4,800 square miles has not increased in resources between 1876, when the territory was delimited by treaty, and 1955, for which data were available. During the same period, however, the population increased from 55 to 382.

Traditionally, the people lived in small dispersed groups, which were kin-based but *not* nuclear families. Their traditional bilateral cross-cousin marriage system was admirably suited to their ecological niche. The major axis (of their kinship system)

is the separation of offspring of same-sexed and opposite-sexed siblings. The former or parallel relative is defined as blood relative, hence brother or sister. The latter is defined as non-blood relative, hence eligible marriage partners. Hence, the children of those whom *we* would describe as brothers and sisters could intermarry.

Increased population and the outpost condition of modern Canada have combined with kinship principles to produce a new type of community. Traditionally, the community meant a small group, and the major concern in marriage was the choice of partner outside the parallel category of relatives. As a result of increased population and various urban services and welfare measures such as schools, nursing family allowance, old age pension and the decreasing value of the traditional economy, the community is no longer the highly mobile small group in pursuit of game, but a relatively large population aggregate stabilized at Pekangekum Lake. This population aggregate, according to Dunning, seems large enough to provide spouses without looking outside. About half the marriages of the Pekangekum band, in the past, were with members of other communities. But by 1955, almost all the marriages were within the expanded community. Visiting unmarried young men in the cross-category from other communities was suspect because of pressures on trapping land which potential sons-in-law from other communities implied.

Dunning's study, therefore, presents a case of one type of kin-based community, or family in everyday English, being transformed into a larger and new type. There is no indication at present that the nuclear family comprising parents and their unmarried children is becoming a basic, behaviourally notable familial unit in response to the forces of urbanization and industrialization.

Contemporary Eskimo Responses

It is difficult to assert that traditionally the Eskimo lived in a harsher habitat than the subarctic Indian, but insofar as their economies were based on hunting, gathering, and fishing, they shared at least a minimal ecological framework. It is also not easy to be sure that the forces of urbanization and industrialization reached the Eskimo later. But the Eskimo population was drastically depleted due to diseases of European origin and, although food resources provided by the big game may also have decreased (since the introduction of the gun), available data do not permit any general statement about regional and intraregional variations in the population/food ratio in terms of the prevalent and changing technologies. The relevance of these observations is that systematic comparison of Eskimo familial forms in terms of some of the basic generative factors is not possible at present.

The prevalent stereotype in the ethnographic literature is that the traditional Eskimo family is nuclear. A recent study by Damas (1971), however, has shown that while this statement may be true for the Copper Eskimo, the Netsilik and Iglulik Eskimos formed groupings with a patrilineal bias and so tended to comprise father-son and/or brother-brother relations. Hence the last two Eskimo categories were characterized by the extended family, not the nuclear family. Damas also discovered that as one moves from west to east, kinship ties stretch increasingly wider.

Traditionally, the groupings among all Eskimos in Canada were highly fluid. They varied in size from summer to winter and their composition, although generally kin-based, varied in terms of actual occupants of kin-roles who hunted together, lived together in various house types in winter and in tents in summer, ate together, and so on. Some role-occupants overlapped in these and other behavioural contexts, but not in all. In any case, recognition of kinsmen, both generationally and collaterally, was shallow in the sense that beyond the first-cousin level, one could marry anyone; and there was no unilineage, corporate descent group as such, despite the patrilineal bias noticed by Damas among the Netsilik and Iglulik.

It seems fair to state, then, that in general the Eskimo society in most parts of the Canadian Arctic was such as to make it possible for various constellations of people related through descent and affinity to come together for changing subsistence activities in response to the ecology changing through the annual climatic cycle. It is true that the nuclear family was not the only basic grouping in such contexts and, despite a patrilineal bias in household units among Eskimo categories, no lineal groups as such were significant in any other context. It was a 'small group' society and the smallest it could get, as a group, was the nuclear family. Judged by a recent study of the contemporary scene among the Eskimo, our general statement would hold good even today for most who live on the land but would be "an oversimplification for those who live in the settlement" (Vallee, 1971).

Since money is the medium of transaction in the settlement for goods and services, households tend to become independent of each other and each household comes to depend almost entirely on cash income. There are changes, too, that have taken place among Eskimos who earn cash wages and live in settlements. For instance, there seems to be a definite tendency to delay marriages because marriage is no longer closely tied to survival as it was in the traditional environment. The traditional ideal of arranged marriages has not disappeared in the settlement, but it is no longer the clear-cut ideal that it once was.

The ambiguity applies to the ideal of 'male priority' also. In the traditional context, the hunter's needs received primacy and this theme appeared even in cases such as serving the family meal. But in no respect was a woman's role considered less important than a man's role. The general impression one gets from the literature is one of mutual co-operation. Forces of urbanization and industrialization, which generate the settlements, are generally believed to lead to individualism and the breakdown of male authority over women and of parental authority over children. Facts, however, are more complex than such generalizations would lead one to believe. The co-operative character of the husband-wife relationship, rather than the male-primacy aspect of it, appears to be prominent.

Nor did the traditional ways of winning a livelihood encourage a 'permissive society' in the modern sense. The crucial thing was the struggle for survival and only the parents, being older, knew how to explore and exploit the environment. But children traditionally were always loved and welcomed, despite the fact of female infanticide, which must be understood in the context of the belief that there is a part of the spirit which, after physical death, is reincarnated in a new-born child. It may be these attitudes towards children, or other factors of which we are unaware, that prevented the 'breakdown' of parental authority and the emergence of 'individualism.'

It seems that the emphasis in the traditional context was on small groups, if not always on the nuclear family, and the emphasis continues in the emergent setting. Eskimo urbanization has not required the breakdown of complex, large kin-groups because none existed. But urban-industrial forces have created new problems which are not directly familial. Family forms, however, operate in the matrix of these unsolved problems.

A recent report based on comparative data from two Eskimo settlements, Tuktoyaktuk and Coppermine, states the problems and predicts the cumulative results if they remain unsolved. These comments may be relevant to other indigenous populations of the Canadian outpost of industrialization and urbanization,

. . . cut off from purposeful economic activities (because skilled jobs are very scarce and in the outpost are bound to remain so) and living from various kinds of welfare activities, the typical Eskimo community will become more, and not less, of a satellite society. For this is the last and certainly the most important factor in the maintenance of such a society – the lack of meaningful work for adults. Attendant with this will be many other social problems, and one could expect that differing forms of deviancy will develop. If one could develop a picture of what the society will be like, it would have to include a healthy, well-housed, population growing at a very high rate, fed only reasonably well on canned foods, having an enormous amount of leisure time, and little purposeful or gainful activity. To top off this picture, one would add that they would have almost all administration done for them, they would not get sufficient education to compete for the available civil service jobs, nor would they participate in politics. Accordingly, their resentment would increase proportionate to their status as second-rate citizens . . . (Ferguson, 1970:37).

The Rural Family

As one enters the rural segment of the country's ecological structure, one expects the pattern of all aspects of life to become more diversified than in the outpost due to three primary factors:

(1) involvement of a wider range of ethnic peoples, mainly of European origins

(2) a greater range of variation in the agricultural ecology than in the outpost ecology

(3) a more direct interdependence between rural areas and urban centres in various respects, particularly with the Provincial and Federal Governments as they mediate the international economic forces before releasing them upon the rural segment of the economy.

In a highly urbanized country, the rural cannot be all *that* rural. The forces whose complex interplay creates social forms in rural areas are more specialized, diverse, and 'centre-oriented' (towards main centres of urbanization and industrialization). Therefore, rural areas in a country such as Canada present more complex problems of description and analysis than the outpost. And yet, so far as the literature on the rural family in Canada is concerned, the available material is more spotty, if possible, than the available research on the outpost. Ideally, what is required is a sample of studies on rural families at least by their ethnic subdivisions and distance, in terms of channels of communication, from regional and national urban centres. The available information is far from ideal. What we will do, however, is outline four cases which throw some light on the two-way pull of forces in rural Canada as they generate familial forms and relate them to some of the other social forms. The cases are:

(1) the farmers and ranchers in the 'Jasper' region ** of Saskatchewan (Bennett, 1969)

(2) the sectarian family of the Hutterite Brethren who are ethnically of German origin (Peter, 1971)

(3) the Dutch-Canadian rural family

(4) the French Canadian rural family

The 'Jasper Region' Farmers and Ranchers

It is difficult to say how representative studies of farmers and ranchers in the 'Jasper' region of Saskatchewan are representative of rural Canada (Bennett, 1969; Bennett and Kohl, 1971).

** Eds. 'Jasper' is the pseudonym which Bennett, the author of the case study cited, gave to the principal town in the southern Saskatchewan district he was studying.

Although out-migration of young men from 'Jasper' is minimal, the region does pose a number of questions about the mechanics of rural out-migration. Ranchers and farmers figure as two major categories of Canadian ruralities. Out-migration and kinship ties operate for the two types, generated by variations in environmental and other factors, but in quite different ways. Indeed, the data presented by Bennett and Kohl (1971) indicate that the farmers and ranchers represent two different subcultures if the matrices of their nuclear families are taken into consideration.

Succession to a ranch or a farm is strategic in understanding some of the processes that have produced rural familial forms. The crucial fact is that economic support is necessary for entrance into agriculture, so much so that young men are placed in a dependent position. At the time of Bennett's study, ranch prices varied from $15,000 to $600,000. Such sums are usually beyond the initial reach of any young man who wishes to own a ranch, as is the lower price for a farm.

Ranchers, more than farmers, disdain city life and value the 'open-spaces,' independence, and other characteristics that are believed to be associated. Moreover, ranchers usually among the very early settlers (1870-1900), have developed the ideology that the ranch should remain a family enterprise. This means that there is pressure on sons to stay on, both among ranchers and farmers. The ties of the nuclear family are used in both cases to achieve this end, though more among ranchers with higher property values than among farmers. Family ties are used to enlist a son to take over the family enterprise, and each successful enlistment means a relationship of dependence of a young man usually on his father who, if he is a rancher, is likely to delay his retirement as long as health permits. It is customary for a married son to live with his parents and gradually take over the enterprise. Terms are so organized that the son is actually able to obtain full ownership of the property. Farmers, too, attempt the techniques of ranchers. But there is an overriding process in Canada today in which rural properties are consolidating into larger and larger units. Small property-holders are simply unable in many cases to retain their farms, let alone pass it on. The farmer, therefore, has an eye on alternatives, including out-migration for himself or his sons. The 'dependence relationship' is for this reason less certain among farmers' sons than among ranchers' sons.

Most people in the 'Jasper' region, apart from the Canadian Indians and the Hutterite Brethren, are enmeshed in ties through descent and marriage. It seems that the early differences among ethnic peoples of European origins no longer count except as a reminder that those of East European origins came later and had to be satisfied with the land that was left. But the enmeshing network of kin-based relations are not crucially relevant as a 'corporate group' in the context of who gets whose property, when, and how. Such networks may operate more as friendship groups and as a basis for decisions about who can marry whom within the 'Jasper' region. Extended kin-relations are additionally important only in the case where farmers and ranchers retire and live in a house in a town. Their house may become the place where grandsons come to spend their school days, often going back home to the ranch or the farm. Such a 'residential exposure' to the town, made possible through kinship ties, acquaints a new generation with a different range of alternatives from which it will tease out its future.

The position of daughters is quite different from that of sons. Although there are very few exceptions, a daughter is not expected or groomed to succeed either to a farm or a ranch. She can stay on in the community, if one may designate the 'Jasper' area as such, only if she marries locally. The only alternative for her is to out-migrate to cities in search of a husband, job, or both. Education is acknowledged by farmers and ranchers alike to provide the necessary passport for their daughters to move to the urban centres.

When ranch or farm sons are forced to leave 'Jasper' for the urban settlements, they find themselves in many cases at the bottom of the urban labour force categorized as 'unskilled'. Their sisters are likely to find themselves better prepared educationally and in terms of skills for the urban market.

The Hutterite Family

Even with one of the highest birth rates in North America if not in the world, Hutterite husband-wife-children relationships are effectively submerged in the network of relationships that constitute a Hutterite 'local group' or community. Moreover, the community is at once a religious and social entity. It is quite impossible to understand anything significant about the Hutterite family, in the two usages of the term in common English, without taking into account the salient features of the Hutterites as a religious sect organized for survival into communities with very distinctive characteristics. It is necessary to stress this at the outset, otherwise those who subscribe to the view that modernization of the Western-type brings about isolation of the nuclear family are likely to miss the adaptive aspect of the Hutterite family. Since it is so different from the 'urban Western type', there is the understandable temptation to treat it as no more than a curious example of conservatism.

The Hutterites are descended from people of Central Europe and their faith, which they have practised tenaciously for some four centuries, is close to the beliefs of the early Christians. They number approximately 20,000 today, most of them in Alberta and some who have moved recently to Saskatchewan. When they accepted Canada's invitation to colonize the prairies, they did so to evade the military draft in the United States where they had settled between 1871 and 1879. Details of their movement and settlements are provided by Bennett (1967 and 1969) and by Peter (1971). It is sufficient for our purposes to note that the Hutterite Brethren in Canada are descended from eleven German-speaking families from the Austrian Tyrol. These families were among the remnants of a widespread but loosely organized religio-political movement growing out of the peasant rebellions in Central Europe in 1524-25. The Anabaptists of the time believed that the wealthy townsmen and the aristocracy, who were held to be responsible for the heavy taxation on the peasant and the small town tradesmen, had vulgarized Christianity by their greed. They believed that genuine Christianity, with its emphasis on simplicity, austerity, and community-sharing of all material goods as exemplified in early Christian communities, should be restored. The Anabaptists found support for their reaction in the Book of Acts.

The Hutterite Brethren comprise a community first. Everything, including the relationship among husbands, wives, and children, are responsive and subordinate to the perpetuation of the religious community set amidst a secular and alien social environment. They have spurned the temptations of the materialism of Western urbanization-industrialization. Inveterate ruralites, the Hutterites have been committed to the cultivation of their land and have remained aloof, as much as possible, from 'outsiders', a category that includes all non-Hutterites and urban forms of material desire.

The Hutterite community is made up of people who are already related either on the basis of descent or marriage, or both. They have so far managed to work out a design of kin-based relationships which for purposes of marriage excludes relatives up to the first cousin. Each kin-based local group, consisting of ten to thirteen enmeshed nuclear families is organized in such a way that it can operate in varying contexts both as a highly stratified community and as an egalitarian community.

A Hutterite man does not achieve full political membership

in his society until his baptism about the age of twenty. At that time, he achieves the right to vote in the community-assembly and may aspire to a very limited number of offices in the two power-echelons: the 'Executive' and the 'Managerial'. Women, however, are regarded as subordinate to men. They have no voting rights although, as always and everywhere, they may play significant roles through their husbands.

Opportunities are provided for marriageable men and women to meet and it is assumed that 'love' precedes marriage. Supervision of the couple never relaxes, not even after children are born. Married couples are provided with the basics: a house in a system of row-houses, a sewing machine, essential furniture, and so on. A child is looked after by his parents until he is three years old. At this age, the child attends a kindergarten where the norms of the community are inculcated. The child remains in that context during most of his waking hours until his sixth birthday when he graduates to the next school. Schooling typically does not go beyond the eighth grade. The idea behind the educational system is to discourage temptations to explore the secular non-Christian world, well ensured by a deliberately contrived low level of education which would put a Hutterite in the wider urban world (if he desires to explore it) at such an unrewarding level that he would soon realize the benefits of remaining a contributing member of his community. The net effect is that the Brethren comprise a remarkably stable society.

Subordination of women, rejection of higher education, emphasis on kinship to the extent of nearly total submergence of the nuclear family into a viable community-system based on a hierarchic organization, may seem incredibly antiquated to an average Canadian. Such a Canadian may be surprised to know that a Hutterite community farms excellently, is carefully conservationist and produces very much more than the non-Hutterite whites whose land they have been buying.

Despite what may appear as dyed-in-the-wool conservatism, the Brethren have nevertheless embraced all technological innovations related to farming, the only alternative for survival that they have chosen for themselves. In the Hutterites we have an instance of a modernizing people, fully of Western derivation, which spurns urbanization and has opted to remain rural. It is also clear that a husband in their society is no more and no less the 'breadwinner' than his wife. Indeed, it is the whole *community* that works to earn a livelihood and to survive through processes of organization that we have briefly noted. Since the husband is not the unique breadwinner, the Hutterites present a case of Westerners who have roles (husband-wife-unmarried children) which are supposed to characterize the highly technological, urban, Western society, but who articulate these roles into a relatively self-sufficient communal pattern. This pattern departs greatly, not only from the stereotype of the urban Western world, but also from the stereotype of the rural Western world.

The Dutch-Canadian Family

The Dutch settlers of Holland Marsh, a market-garden settlement situated about 40 miles from Toronto, present yet another ethnic family pattern, different still from the patterns found among the Hutterite Brethren and the farmers of the Jasper region. The settlement in Holland Marsh began when, in 1934, eleven Calvinist Dutch farmers arrived and began to transform the swamp into cultivable farm land. Because of its recency, we were able to gather information concerning family relations in the early days (Ishwaran, 1971). Detailed analysis reveals clearly that these relations have changed radically between 1934 and 1970. The year 1950 may be identified as a decisive turning-point.

Most of the settlers arrived as nuclear families which were not interrelated among themselves. Once in Holland Marsh, however, they were all faced with the common task of transforming a swamp and of wresting their livelihood from it. They were not rich settlers, so that they were in no position to hire outside labour. Although they subscribed to a common faith, a Calvinist denomination of Christianity, they were not, like the Hutterites, members of an all-encompassing socio-religious community. Under these circumstances, the only alternative remaining to the pioneers was to help each other in their task of reclamation of the swamp and in their other agricultural activities. The settlers built their church, school, and houses with their own hands. From mutual co-operation founded on common problems of adaptation to a new environment, there developed a community whose units were closely interdependent so much so that on numerous occasions they acted as a community rather than as an assemblage of unrelated nuclear families. Yet they were unrelated nuclear families when they first arrived in Holland Marsh. These ties were further augmented through a great deal of inter-marriage among the original families, yielding in due course a closely-knit society.

But over time, something else happened. In establishing themselves, it became clear that some farmers were proven more successful as entrepreneurs than others. Consequently, the dimension of social class was introduced to a community which had hitherto been undifferentiated in that respect. In the early phase of this process, the more successful farmers sponsored immigrants from the Netherlands and were thus able to employ extra labour. In this way they became at least partially independent of the community in that they were no longer obliged, as they were earlier, to depend on it for their agricultural labour. Slowly and surely, the nuclear families, despite their community and kinship ties, began to undergo experiences which created new intra- and extra-community alignments. These re-alignments meant that there was still a 'community', many of whose members were further interrelated through kinship; but some of its members were less dependent on their community and kinship bonds for the solution of problems.

The change was by no means sudden, though our description may give that impression. In the early years following the end of World War II, mechanization of farm activities advanced rapidly. The farmers who had proved more successful as entrepreneurs in the pre-war days and had, meanwhile, consolidated their position, were able to derive the maximum benefit from mechanization. Partly through later immigration from the Netherlands but largely through their own birth rate, the original 11 families have multiplied to 139 families over a period of 36 years. Many of today's families are still inter-related through marriage and descent, as well as through diverse community ties. But different families have differential command over resources and are thus differently located in relation to opportunities. Such a situation is inherently competitive and competition, both overt and covert, follows the lines that group the people of Holland Marsh into nuclear families. Understandably, some of the wider kinship relations are now in practice basically friendship relations.

The Dutch Canadians of Holland Marsh continue to inter-marry, so that the settlement is still a kin-based community. Rarely do all kinsmen interact as a single organized group. Perhaps the only remaining active aspect of the total community is to be found in the integration afforded by the local church. Those who remain outside the church are readily sorted out as deviants whose social survival in Holland Marsh becomes difficult indeed. The local school is another integrating social entity where the teachers always have been, and still are, Dutch Calvinist. Significantly, however, the English language is the medium used both at school and at church. Church services in Dutch were available only during the first seven years or so; today, it seems that very few children, if any, learn Dutch as a working language. The Dutch Canadians of Holland Marsh, then, manifest the pressure of uniformity in their common use of English. The Dutch-Canadian contribution to variability is produced by their adherence to their religious faith, to a limited extent by the local school, by intermarriage and perhaps by many subtle domestic customs and practices, which intensive investigations may one day reveal. These common characteristics add up enough to maintain their ethnic identity and to enable them to use the community as a frame of reference or category of thought. But they no longer are enough to add up to the circumstances of the pioneering times when the community was not a category, but a group; not a frame of reference, but an actual and complex pattern of interdependence in a variety of contexts of everyday life.

Other factors are affecting the evolution of the Dutch Canadians of Holland Marsh. As population pressure on land increases, smaller farmers find it increasingly difficult to survive. Typical of many rural areas in Canada, out-migration becomes prominent, so that Holland Marsh will likely change again and its Dutch settlers will have to work out new familial forms.

A further, though related factor, is the increasing number of residents, especially among the younger generation, who commute regularly to Toronto, but continue to live in Holland Marsh. This means that Holland Marsh may well become a kind of 'dormitory village'. Toronto's proximity and the fact that English is the only language that the younger generation of Dutch Canadians are learning effectively, may be contributing factors determining the evolution of familial forms during the next decade or so.

We have no evidence that the Dutch-Canadian situation in Holland Marsh is representative of the Dutch-Canadian situation(s) elsewhere in Canada. Only further research will supply these answers.

The French-Canadian Family

The body of data on the French Canadian is richer than that on any other of Canada's thirty or so ethnic peoples. A review of Elkin's (1968:64-71) references, however, establishes that the evidence bearing on family forms in French Canada show only three things:

(1) the presence of a widespread network kinship system
(2) the relevance of strong religious traditions deriving from Roman Catholicism
(3) rather confused statements regarding the impact of urbanization and industrialization of French Canada.

Not only are the data piecemeal, as Elkin's comments on the literature lead one to infer (67-71); but they are confused because French-Canadian sociology of the family has somehow remained relatively insulated from the kinds of theoretical issues raised by research on the family elsewhere in the world.

These observations are necessary in order to underscore the fact that the information available on French-Canadian families does not yet permit clear understanding of the distinction, if any, between rural and urban family structure. Perhaps there are no differences of note; perhaps there are some differences, but not significant ones; perhaps there *are* significant differences. Definitive studies are simply lacking. Our observations may, therefore, apply to rural French Canadians or to urban French Canadians, although in an indeterminate way, some of the things we say may be more relevant to the rural milieu and other things to the urban milieu. Meanwhile, the very distinction between urban and rural, demographically so clear in the census report, continues sociologically as a source of confusion.

When in doubt, perhaps the best approach is to anchor our understanding in historical processes. French pioneers in this country were traders, especially fur traders; and sometimes, as an outgrowth of these activities, they were hunters. Values of agriculture used to be stressed by the French Catholic clergy.

But these clerics themselves were largely of urban origin in France and knew very little of the practical problems of agriculture. They knew less about such matters in a land where resources and opportunities resembled little that existed in seventeenth century France. The clerics lauded the virtues of agriculture and settled communities. But the fact that the settlers, for their part, found it more attractive to be traders and/or hunters, created a situation which lies at the root of the evolution of French-Canadian familial forms.

The upshot of all this was that men were away from their homes for extended periods of time. This freed them from continuous and effective influences of church leaders, with their second-hand ideas about the primary significance of agricultural communities. Their wives and daughters remained at home, constantly exposed to these agrarian homilies. Survival also forced women into agrarian pursuits in one capacity or another. Consequently, women acquired a role and a say in rural French Canada which were more effective in that context than the role and the say of their husbands wandering in the bush.

Families in such a situation were often bound, in other words, to assume a matri-centric structure, a pattern which is hardly a twentieth-century American innovation as some students of the family are prone to assume. The French-Canadian woman, as mother and wife, was the *de facto* head of her household. It must be remembered that a tradition born as part of an adaptive struggle dies hard. It is our contention that the French-Canadian family has always been matri-centric, that women have played a dominant role in the agrarian revolution in post World War II French Canada, and that they have played a most significant part in the processes of urbanization in Quebec. This position is based on recent research by Fortin (1970:224-229) and Moreux (1971).

In a sense, French Canadians, rural or urban, exhibit the standard nuclear family. But the matri-centric emphasis, not a contemporary phenomenon but an aspect of tradition from the earliest times of French settlement in this country, constitutes a difference of some significance compared to other instances of rural families in Canada. The French-Canadian family, as we know it today, exemplifies the continuity between urban and rural in Canada which makes the distinction, elaborated in the census and in monographs based on it, so utterly misleading.

The Urban Family

Variations and uniformities in forms and functions of the family will be represented in this section by the Jews and the Japanese Canadians. Together they constitute a microscopic minority of the Canadian population, so that it may seem odd to base an outline of the urban family on these two ethnic peoples.

There are two reasons for our choice. First, both ethnic categories are urban. Second, the highly complex urban scene requires detailed studies on larger ethnic groups, but these are simply undone. Therefore, some indication of variations and uniformities is all that can be ventured, and the two peoples we have selected serve this limited purpose satisfactorily.

The Jewish Family

Abraham Gradis, a French citizen, was probably the first Jew to settle in Canada. He established a warehouse in Quebec in 1758 and supplied General Montcalm's army. In 1846, nearly a hundred years later, there were only 200 Jews in Canada. Some of them pioneered in transport, particularly shipping, and later, telecommunication. All of them were in nonagricultural occupations. The Jewish population in Canada in 1960 was 250,000 (Latowsky, 1971), but only 2,200 or so were residents on farms (Ausubel, 1969:189). It is not known whether this minority actually practised farming. Clearly, the Jewish population was urban and remains so. In their long history of wandering throughout the world and their experience of discrimination as a minority in lands where they lived, the urban commitment of the Jewish population, until the emergence of the state of Israel, stands out. Their significant participation as tradesmen, professionals, middle-men in commerce and bankers has placed them in roles critical to the modernization of the Western world, including Canada.

Sociologists who regard 'individualism' as a necessary condition for modernization may note that the Jewish family was ideally patriarchal in its structure, very much in the shadow of the Old Testament. The father was considered the final authority in matters of discipline and spiritual training within the family. The woman's role, although highly valued as homemaker and for her transmission of Jewish ethics (as distinguished from religious scholarship which was the male prerogative), was a subordinate one.

The grouping of husband-wife-unmarried children has always been important among the Jews. Indeed, the 613 commandments relate to 3 major sets of Jewish obligations: to study constantly the word of God; to establish a family; and to observe all the social and ritual obligations regulating Jewish behaviour (Latowsky, 1971). Also, religious precepts were taught by parental examples and thus, in this respect, the family and not the synagogue was the primary religious institution. This means that the primary family grouping was as much a religio-ethical grouping as a social grouping. The meagre information available about the early Jewish families in this country closely corresponds with the ideals noted here.

The synagogue was and still is the centre of community life. It functioned as the House of Study and the House of Worship. The primary family and the synagogue were interdependent in inculcating the Jewish ethos and in this context the community and the family were so closely interlinked that in attempting to understand the one, the other must be understood. This is to say that socio-cultural survival of the community depended on the proper performance of the roles in the family and such performance depended on community support.

The long urban and minority status of the Jewish people has contributed to a high valuation of literacy and scholarship. This emphasis on higher education and a tradition in the professions and diversified trade have contributed to a level of prosperity among Canadian Jews. Detailed information is lacking, so that it is difficult to judge the extent to which their articulation with an affluent society has altered intra-family and family-community relationships. But some changes are discernible.

It is evident, now, that the father is no longer vested with the authority and status which were traditionally his. His involvement in the secular world of business and profession has meant a reduced commitment to religious scholarship and spiritual overseeing of his family. The mother's role is still traditional in many respects, but she was never a religious scholar and therefore, in the contemporary Canadian setting, she is unable to substitute for the father's role as a spiritual authority. She is still the chief transmitter of Jewish ethics.

The family is future-oriented and child-oriented. According to Latowsky, who recently concluded an intensive study of Toronto's Jewish population, 'permissive' child-rearing practices, as spelled out in Dr. Spock's manual, are favoured. Details of consequences are not known, but this fact in itself represents a major shift from the historical pattern of child training.

A side-effect of the permissive ethos, one which is reinforced by alternative models available in the wider society, is that there are women who are no longer satisfied with their subordinate role within the family. Many husbands object to their wives taking paid jobs. Accordingly, many women who feel 'trapped' are active members in a profusion of Jewish communal, social philanthropic groups.

Jewish religiosity seems also to be waning in the sense that eighty percent of Latowsky's sample reported infrequent attendance at services of worship. There are, however, many secular activities that revolve around the synagogue. Participation in these activities is most intense. It appears that the synagogue has become for most Jews an embodiment of their Jewish cultural identity, based not so much on Judaism but on what may be described as 'Jewishness'. Interest in the religious component of Judaism springs, in large part, from the belief that 'Jewish identity' cannot survive without an emphasis on Judaism as a faith.

The emergence of Israel has provided many younger Jews with an alternative approach to the survival of their identity. Survival is reinforced by the fact that Jews still find most of their relatives and friends among their own ethnic people. Marriages to non-Jews remain low, although the rate has been increasing in those urban centres where Jews are very small in number.

The Jewish family is an example of the urban family which possesses the structure of a nuclear family. Although the matrix of this family has been changing, there is still a great deal about it which cannot be understood without continuous reference to the Jewish community, kinship, and friendship.

The Japanese Family

There were some Japanese in Canada prior to 1890 but the largest number arrived between 1890 and 1924. Thus, the first generation (Issei) may be expected to have brought with them the traditional family pattern of the Meiji era (1868-1911). By 1960 the children of the first generation and the second generation (Nisei) ranged between 30 and 55 years of age. The third generation (Sansei) generally appeared after World War II and were well into their schooling in the sixties. Although much remains unknown concerning the evolution of the Japanese-Canadian family, some interesting leads can be found in a study by Maykovich (1971). She compared familial changes in rural Japan, in a ward in Tokyo, and among the Japanese Canadians of Toronto in 1961. The Toronto sample comprised 450 families selected from an estimated 1,000 households in metropolitan Toronto. The observations from which we will draw were derived from analysis of 255 'acculturated' and 'unacculturated' families, from which 381 children (12-14 years of age) and their mothers were selected for interviews. It is helpful to begin by acknowledging some of the salient features of the traditional Japanese family in the Maiji era. The family was patriarchal, patrilineal, and patrilocal. In general, a wife was subordinate to her husband, although they played complementary roles. A household comprised many members related through kinship. Ideally, each person subordinated his or her personal ambitions and desires to the survival of the extended family of which he or she was part.

It is interesting to note, parenthetically, that Japan has emerged as a highly industrialized and modernized nation despite such a nonindividualistic family pattern. We noted a comparable situation among the Jews, so that it seems that 'individualism' is *not* a necessary condition for modernization and industrialization.

About 9,000 Japanese Canadians lived in households dispersed throughout Toronto by 1961. Maykovich found no school with any significant concentration of their children, underscoring the fact that the Japanese Canadians are not confined to residential enclaves, at least in Toronto. One may be tempted to the further inference, that under conditions of dispersal, they do not constitute a 'community'. It is true that residential clustering is likely to encourage the formation of community ties, and that the dispersal of households is likely to discourage them. However, the telephone and the automobile may to some degree overcome communication problems and so encourage community-formation if independent grounds for such a formation exist. We frankly do not know what the facts are in this matter. A significant implication of our ignorance is that we cannot yet determine the extent to which the Japanese-Canadian families are subsumed within wider groups on a community-basis and/or a kinship-basis.

Most of the Toronto households studied by Maykovich were made up of parents and their unmarried children. In some cases, she found a sprinkling of other relatives. We may entertain two kinds of interpretations. Her data may indicate

(1) that the Japanese-Canadian family is predominantly nuclear now, due to the Canadianization or 'breakdown' of the traditional extended family; or

(2) that the presence of 'other relatives' in some cases testifies to the tenacity of the traditional patterns.

We are tempted to respond to both alternatives in the negative.

The traditional Meiji-period Japanese family no longer exists, even in Japan, and has been a rarity in all areas of that country since 1920. Contraction of the household unit has been going on in Japan for some decades. The extra-nuclear family relatives who are occasionally found in the Toronto households are apparently involved in the process of migration, according to Maykovich. The imagery of the Japanese-Canadian family, then, is not one of 'breakdown' or of 'continuation' of something traditional. The image is one of adjustment to, and mastery of, local circumstances together with the new use of old bonds.

The traditional, large, kin-based household grouping was based on a variety of factors, chief of which was traditional practices of land tenure. The relevant factors now occur neither in most parts of urban Japan nor in metropolitan Toronto. In both settings, therefore, the residential unit is pushed to one of the two possible minima:

(1) the nuclear family; or

(2) the matri-focal family.

The Japanese urbanites and the Japanese Canadians face choices which, under the circumstances, produce the nuclear family and not the matri-focal family. The crux of our argument is that the fact of the 'nuclearization' of the family as household units in Toronto must not be glibly interpreted as a consequence of the mystique of increasing 'Canadianization'. It is primarily a matter of housing space, both in Canada and in some of the Tokyo wards. Moreover, the first generation Japanese immigrants, whatever may have been their ideas about ideal households, arrived not in units of extended families, but as individuals. In other words, the raw material from which to build extended families was simply not available. Later, the housing situation and the absence of an ecological base for large household groupings of kinsmen, prevented the implementation in Canada of the ideal-structure of the Japanese family, an ideal which the first generation Japanese may have brought with them. In such a situation and as time passed, we suspect that even the ideal became, at best, a distant memory.

Finally, Maykovich found that the subordination of the individual to the family has diminished in a variety of ways. The traditional practice of 'arranged marriage', for instance, has virtually disappeared. The vast majority of the mothers interviewed (usually in their forties) apparently selected their own mates, independent of their parents. Most mothers believed that their children should select their own mates, too.

Concluding Remarks

We are fully aware of the limitations of our attempt to illustrate how actual familial forms and functions are generated as forces of variability and uniformity interact. We have ignored, due to limitations of space and lack of valid data, a whole range of problems, processes, and patterns that arise from interrelations between the family in the narrow sense and various social formations based on kinship and non-kinship principles.

A thorough study must describe and analyse the family in its total setting. The setting includes a great range of specialized agencies which in Canada determine the ways families actually operate. We have said nothing about so-called problem families, their problems of poverty, mental health, education, and actual obstacles to social mobility in a society nominally based on egalitarian ideals.

Our objective was limited. We wished only to illustrate that there is a *prima facie* case for a searching examination of the concept of the Western urban family as applied to the Canadian scene. We consider that such an examination is basic to systematic research on the family, in the sense that the stereotype of the 'Western, urban family' used to characterize Canada has hampered the formulation of important research.

As the rural segments of Canada's ecological structure are environmentally, technologically, ethnically, and organizationally more complex than the segments of the outpost, so the urban segments are more complex than the rural ones. Population aggregates in urban areas depend directly on a varying but wide range of non-agricultural activities for their sustenance and survival. These processes make for interesting variations and uniformities in family structure and therefore require complex documentation.

The census report documents the near-universality of the nuclear family in Canada. It is generally believed, as we noted at the outset, that the nuclear family is the typical Western urban family of today and that Canada is no exception. We believe that the significance of wider kin-groups is being slowly rediscovered by some family sociologists interested in Canada. After Porter's synthetic study, enough is now known about class variations in Canada to encourage at least preliminary formulations of research issues specifically focused on familial forms and functions. The relevance of ethnicity is vaguely sensed by family sociologists. What is needed, however, are intensive family studies among some of our ethnic peoples, inquiries conducted within the orientation that empirical forms are the product of complex interactions among forces of variability and uniformity.

It may well be that research will show that there is little variation, or that pressures towards uniformity are continuously eroding the variations that immigrants introduce. Our own assessment strongly favours the view that careful research is bound to reveal that situational pressures not only generate but also maintain variations, quite often in reaction to the very pressures of uniformity which work to erode variations.

NOTES AND BIBLIOGRAPHY
The author is indebted to Mr. P. G. Ganguly whose suggestions and criticisms have been immensely helpful in the preparation of this paper. The empirical material represented in this paper is based largely on a number of studies published in K. Ishwaran (ed.), *The Canadian Family*, Holt, Rinehart and Winston, Toronto, 1971. I am especially indebted to the contributing authors to that volume.

Ausubel, N. *The Pictorial History of the Jewish People.* N.Y.: Crown Publishing, 1969.

Bennett, J. W. *Hutterian Brethren: The Agricultural Economy and Social Organization of a Communal People.* Stanford: Stanford University Press, 1967.

————— *Northern Plainsmen: Adaptive Strategy and 'Agrarian Life.*

Chicago: Aldine Publishing Co., 1969.

———— and Kohl, S. "Succession to Family enterprises and the Migration of Young People in a Canadian Agricultural Community," in *The Canadian Family*, K. Ishwaran, ed. Toronto: Holt, Rinehart and Winston, 1971.

Cohen, R. "Modernization and the Hinterland: The Canadian Example," in W. E. Mann, ed., *Social and Cultural Changes in Canada.* Vol. 2. Toronto: Copp Clark, 1970.

Cruickshank, J. "The Matri-Focal Families in the Canadian North," in K. Ishwaran, ed., *The Canadian Family.* Toronto: Holt, Rinehart and Winston, 1971

Damas, D. "The Problem of the Eskimo Family," in K. Ishwaran, ed., *The Canadian Family*. Toronto: Holt, Rinehart and Winston, 1971.

Dunning, R. W. "Changes in Marriage and the Family Among the Northern Ojibway," in K. Ishwaran, ed., *The Canadian Family*. Toronto: Holt, Rinehart and Winston, 1971.

Elkin, F. *Families in Canada.* Ottawa: Vanier Institute of the Family, 1968.

Ferguson, J. "Social Change in the Western Arctic," in W. E. Mann, ed., *Social and Cultural Change in Canada.* Vol. 2. Toronto: Copp Clark, 1970.

Fortin, G. "Woman's Role in the Evolution of Agriculture in Quebec," in W. E. Mann, ed., *Social and Cultural Change in Canada.* Vol. 1. Toronto: Copp, Clark, 1970.

Goode, W. J. *World Revolution and Family Patterns.* Glencoe, Ill.: Free Press, 1963.

Jacobson, H. "The Family in Canada: Some Problems and Questions," in K. Ishwaran, ed., *The Canadian Family*. Toronto: Holt, Rinehart and Winston, 1971.

Jones, F. E. "Some Social Consequences of Immigration for Canada," in Bernard R. Blishen, Frank A. Jones, Kasper D. Naegele and John Porter, eds., *Canadian Society – Sociological Perspectives.* Toronto: Macmillan, 1968.

Latowsky, E. "Family Life Styles and Jewish Culture," in K. Ishwaran, ed., *The Canadian Family.* Toronto: Holt, Rinehart and Winston, 1971.

Litwak, E. "Geographic Mobility and Extended Family Cohesion." *American Sociological Review*, 25 (1960), 386-394.

———— "Extended Kin Relations in an Industrial Democratic Society," in E. Shanas and G. F. Streibe, eds., *Social Structure and the Family: Generational Relations.* Englewood Cliffs, N.J.: Prentice-Hall, 1965.

Maykovich, M. K. "The Japanese Family in Tradition and Change," in K. Ishwaran, ed., *The Canadian Family.* Toronto: Holt, Rinehart and Winston, 1971.

Moreux. "The French-Canadian Family," in K. Ishwaran, ed., *The Canadian Family.* Toronto: Holt, Rinehart and Winston, 1971.

Peter, K. A. "The Hutterite Family," in K. Ishwaran, ed., *The Canadian Family.* Toronto: Holt, Rinehart and Winston, 1971.

Porter, J. "Rural Decline and New Urban Strata," in W. E. Mann, ed., *Social and Cultural Change in Canada.* Vol. 1. Toronto: Copp Clark, 1970.

Shamas, E. and Streib, G. E., eds., *Social Structure and the Family: Generational Relations.* Englewood Cliffs, N.J.: Prentice-Hall, 1965.

Simmons, J. and Simmons, R. *Urban Canada.* Toronto: Copp Clark, 1969.

Vallee, F. G. "Kinship, the Family and Marriage in the Central Keewatin," in K. Ishwaran, ed., *The Canadian Family.* Toronto: Holt, Rinehart and Winston, 1971.

5. Civil Rights and Political Space **

Frank R. Scott/*McGill University*

The legal order is a basic condition of civil society. Yet it is paradoxical: since by its very nature it must treat unique persons, situations and events in categorical terms it can be used to serve the cause of injustice while maintaining formal legality. This next selection by one of Canada's foremost authorities on civil rights draws to our attention the anomalies inherent in the law. It is confronted with the difficult task of defining boundaries between the public and private spheres, while reconciling the tenuous relation between the law intended to serve the cause of individual justice and the law used as an instrument of social control.

The case of the deportation of the Canadian Japanese during World War II is a classic example of the law being used to effect the deprivation of a categorical group's social and private space. This same law, as Scott hints, was used in October 1970 to take away the political rights of all of us.

Another extreme example of the total annihilation of private space is the action, cited by Scott, of one Quebec municipality at the time when the law was being used in that province as an instrument of social control against a particular religious sect,

prohibiting the distribution of literature (any kind) inside (any) private house. As lawyer Scott so trenchantly observes, when individuals or groups of individuals are defined by the law as having no civil rights (and hence no private space) they are thereby disenfranchised in all respects. Being 'outside the law' they are deprived the protection of the law. This insight applies to others in our society whose private and political space is so constricted – inmates of mental hospitals and prisons, social and political deviants of all kinds.

Law, as the ultimate definer of political and social space, must be amenable to continuous reinterpretation and reformulation as social conditions change to make it responsive to the needs of the people it serves.

** Eds. This is a portion of the second lecture which Professor Scott gave at the University of Toronto in 1959 in the Alan B. Plaunt Memorial series. The Bill of Rights to which he refers was introduced by John G. Diefenbaker when he was Prime Minister, and was approved by Parliament in 1960. The second portion of the lecture, not reprinted here, dealt specifically with that Bill.

Reprinted from *Civil Liberties and Canadian Federalism*, by F. R. Scott, by permission of University of Toronto Press. © Canada, 1959, by University of Toronto Press.

I was speaking in my first lecture of the growth of our constitution since 1867 in its various aspects, and of our awakening concern over civil liberties and fundamental freedoms. I concluded with an analysis of the role of the judges in the protection of our basic rights against legislative or bureaucratic infringement. This judicial function is so important that I intend to open this lecture with an examination of some typical cases that have arisen in the past, in order to show just what attitude the courts have taken in the face of concrete situations. We shall be in a far better position to judge of the necessity and nature of a Bill of Rights if we have some knowledge of these facts of our constitutional history. We need particularly to know about the leading civil liberties cases that have come before the Supreme Court of Canada in the past decade. In no other period of our history have so many important questions of this kind arisen. I shall not confine myself, however, to recent history, but shall include a selection of older cases that illustrate both the nature of our constitution and the kinds of behaviour of Canadians in different provinces which gives rise to court battles over civil liberties.

Before explaining these cases I must be a little more specific as to what I mean by civil liberties and human rights. It seems to me that in Canada we must think of human rights and fundamental freedoms as comprising at least four main types of rights. I think we must include our minority rights among them. The United Nations Declaration does not contain minority or group rights, but in our history they have been of the first importance, and I would say without question that they rank ahead of nearly all other rights in the minds of most people in Quebec. I think that if the English were an equally surrounded minority they would feel the same way. At any rate the notion of minority rights guaranteed in the constitution is so fundamental to us and so closely related to the idea of a Bill of Rights that we should include them in our thinking on human rights. This does not mean, however, that they must be rewritten in the new Bill of Rights, if it is adopted; their place in the present constitution is fully entrenched and need not be changed.

A second group of rights are more usually called civil liberties or fundamental freedoms. They include freedom of religion, of the press, of speech and association. With these I would put freedom of the person – the right to move about unmolested, to be free from arbitrary arrest or unlawful detention, and the right to live where one chooses. Here too I would put the right to participate in one's government: the right to vote and to stand as candidate for legislative bodies. And I think academic freedom belongs among the civil liberties, as one aspect of freedom of speech and of conscience. A third kind of right is concerned with protecting the equality of status of citizens against discrimination due to race or religion: I would include here the types of statute we call Fair Employment Practices Acts and Fair Accommodation Practices Acts, and the Equal Pay for Equal Work Acts. These categories of rights I mention can never be exact; somewhere in this second or third group we should have to place not only the right to a fair trial in criminal cases but also a right to a fair hearing and to be treated in accordance with the principles of natural justice before all administrative boards and tribunals. Fourthly there is a vaguely defined group of economic and cultural rights. The right to own property and not to be deprived of it without compensation is well recognized, but we must think today of many other and even more basic rights such as the right to work and to protection against unemployment, the right to health and education and social security, and so on. These are spelled out more fully in articles 22-27 of the Universal Declaration of Human Rights. While these rights may not lend themselves so readily to legal protection in constitutions, they are as vital a part of a free society today as the older civil liberties. We have learned from bitter experience that the satisfaction of basic human needs is essential for the survival of any form of orderly government, and in a highly industrialized society the state cannot leave this task to unregulated private enterprise.

Taking this wide area of law and rights as our field of enquiry, let us look then at some of the judicial decisions that have illuminated this part of the law of our constitution. I must be highly selective, but I shall choose some examples from the earlier days before coming to the important cases that have crowded upon us in the last few years. The interpretation of the minority rights clauses in the BNA Act was the first problem to be judicially resolved in the field of human rights after Confederation. In 1871 the Privy Council held that, whatever separate

schools may have existed in practice at the Union in New Brunswick, none existed by law, and therefore the Common Schools Act adopted by the province in 1871 was constitutional. At the creation of Manitoba, the rights to separate schools existing either by law or by practice were guaranteed, and in consequence our Supreme Court held ultra vires the 1890 legislation which destroyed the separate school system set up in 1871; by a unanimous judgment our judges felt that rights enjoyed in practice at the Union were prejudicially affected. The Privy Council overruled, and added fuel to the great fire that died down, but was not extinguished, by the election of Laurier in 1896. Provincial autonomy had won over minority rights.

The same autonomy prevailed in the Ontario language dispute occasioned by Regulation 17 of the year 1913: it was found that the class of persons whose rights were protected under section 93 of the BNA Act was a class formed by religion and not by language and hence the province was not prevented by the constitution from requiring instruction to be carried on in the schools in the language of its regulations. We can see the Privy Council in these cases showing the same favourable view of provincial legislative authority as their lordships disclosed in other questions involving provincial jurisdiction. The right to appeal to the federal government for remedial legislation was upheld, and Ontario was checked in certain measures taken to enforce Regulation 17, but I think we can say that the result of judicial interpretation was to confine the school rights of the BNA Act within sharply defined limits. Other separate school cases since then have turned more on the interpretation of provincial laws than the BNA Act itself, and so do not directly concern our topic of tonight, but I would refer again to the very interesting judgment of the Quebec Court of Appeal in the Chabot case in 1957 where the right of the parent to choose the kind of religious instruction to be given to the children was firmly upheld. This is a right spelled out in article 26 of the United Nations Declaration.

Turning to the language provisions of the BNA Act, and dealing only with the legal questions that have arisen, I have already noted how it was held that the right to use a particular language in the schools was not protected in the constitution. Strangely enough the validity of Manitoba's statute of 1890 abolishing French as an official language in that province was never tested in the courts; had it been, I personally do not see how it could be upheld. It has always seemed to me that Manitoba was placed on the same footing as Quebec, and that if the Manitoba law of 1890 establishing English as the sole official language was valid, then there is no security for the English language in my province. The abolition of the use of French in the Territories was on a different footing since it occurred before the creation of provincial governments in Saskatchewan and Alberta.

An interesting language question arose on the interpretation of a federal statue in 1935 when it was found that there was a difference between the English and French texts of the law; our Supreme Court held that since both texts were equally authoritative that version was to be preferred which best expressed the intention of the legislature, which in that instance was clearest in the French. It was held, partly because of the French text, that a government car on a road could not be a 'public work'. I like to point out to English-speaking practitioners in provinces other than Quebec that in order to practise law with the utmost skill they must always compare the two texts of the federal statutes if they want to make sure that they are giving their clients the full protection of the law. Appropriately enough, the cause of action in this case arose in a locality called Britannia. It was on the same principle of equal authority of the two languages that Mr. Duplessis was induced to repeal a statute that the legislature of Quebec had passed in 1937 which purported to make the French text of the Civil Code prevail over the English in all cases of conflict.

Questions of racial discrimination, both in employment and in exercising the right to vote, gave rise to a number of cases from the turn of the century onward, particularly in the province of British Columbia. The power of disallowance was also used to set aside several of the provincial statutes aimed at the Asians on the ground that they affected Imperial relations with Japan. Among these cases I would single out *Cunningham v. Tomey Homma in 1903* as having established a very important principle. It held that a British Columbia law barring Chinese, Japanese and Indians, whether naturalized or not, from the provincial franchise was a valid exercise of the province's power to amend its own constitution. British Columbia has of course removed these discriminations since then, but the case remains as a reminder that the possession of Canadian citizenship is no guarantee of the equal protection of the right to vote. Once again provincial autonomy stands as a potential threat to equal status before the law. This case did much to overrule the earlier case of *Union Colliery v. Bryden* which had held that a British Columbia statute which prohibited Chinamen from working underground in coal mines was an invasion of the federal power over 'naturalization and aliens'. There are still some aspects of the law of citizenship which have not been fully worked out, and it may be that the status of Canadian citizen may come to mean more than it seems to now, but we have to take the cases as we find them and racial discrimination in electoral laws seems clearly within provincial powers. No purely federal Bill of Rights could change this fact. With regard to employment, we have a Supreme Court of Canada decision of 1914 holding that a Saskatchewan law prohibiting white girls from working in Chinese restaurants and places of business was valid. Fair Employment Practices Acts are now taking care of this situation; we now have a federal statute and six provincial statutes of this type. Something else we can see looming on the judicial horizon is the question of the validity of the Alberta legislation limiting the right of the Hutterites to purchase land near the existing brotherhoods. Are we to make forms of Christian communism a legal offence? Is the right to own property to be restricted to those who use it in a capitalistic manner?

Two other examples of discrimination will illustrate the wide area of provincial law covering this aspect of human rights. The problem of the restrictive covenant in leases and sales has received attention in the well-known cases of *In re Drummond Wren*, and *Noble v. Wolf*. The question is whether a vendor or landlord can attach a condition to the premises excluding their purchase or lease by persons of a particular race or religion. Here we see the right of private contract, and the right of a man to do what he likes with his own property, coming in conflict with the notion that no person should be discriminated against on grounds of race, religion or colour. Mr. Justice Mackay's courageous judgment in the *Drummond Wren* case invoking the Universal Declaration of Human Rights as evidence that such a condition was contrary to public policy will be perhaps more remembered outside than inside the law courts, for the decision in the *Noble v. Wolf* case went on less humane grounds. I may quote part of what his Lordship said:

> In my opinion, nothing could be more calculated to create or deepen divisions between existing religious and ethnic groups in this province, or in this country, than the sanction of a method of land transfer which would permit the segregation and confinement of particular groups to particular business or residential areas....

Ontario and Canada, too, may well be termed a province, and a country, of minorities in regard to the religious and ethnic groups which live therein. It appears to me to be a moral duty, at least, to lend aid to all forces of cohesion, and

similarly to repel all fissiparous tendencies which would imperil national unity. The common law courts have, by their actions over the years, obviated the need for rigid constitutional guarantees in our policy by their wide use of the doctrine of public policy as an active agent in the promotion of the public weal.

...If the common law of treason encompasses the stirring up of hatred between different classes of His Majesty's subjects, the common law of public policy is surely adequate to void the restrictive covenant which is here attacked.

As Mr. Smout said in commenting on these cases in the *Canadian Bar Review*:

> The courts did not wait for education to convince the gamblers of the moral impropriety of gambling, but meanwhile held the gambling contract unenforceable. There would seem to be no reason why the courts should wait for the intolerant to become tolerant before holding the discrimination covenant to be also unenforceable.

Unfortunately we have not arrived at that point either, it seems, in the law of Quebec or in the common law provinces. The courts have it in their power to come to the aid of racial equality, but unless the proposed Bill of Rights be taken by future judges as having clearly defined Canadian public policy more surely than has the Universal Declaration it will not affect provincial law.

Besides restrictive covenants, we have had cases of racial discrimination in the refusal of restaurant keepers and others to serve customers on grounds of race and colour. The Fair Accommodation Practices Acts are designed to make this an offence. It is indeed encouraging that Ontario and Saskatchewan have adopted such Bills and that one is being contemplated in Nova Scotia. In Quebec the law seems to be fixed by the *Christie* case which went to the Supreme Court of Canada in 1941; there damages were denied to a negro who had been refused a glass of beer because of his colour, in the York Tavern, though tavernkeepers can only operate under provincial licence and might reasonably be considered as acting under public authority. Freedom of commerce prevailed over racial equality, the tavern not being held to be a restaurant or hotel which by Quebec law are obliged to serve all comers. In choosing the particular result in this case, the majority of the judges exercised a discretion that could as well have gone the other way; once again we see the important role the judges must play in selecting which of two alternative views they will adopt.

I do not propose to go into the special problem of civil liberties in wartime, or to recount the various forms of censorship imposed under the Defence of Canada Regulations. It was said by Mr. Justice Stuart in a sedition case in 1916: "There have been more prosecutions for seditious words in Alberta in the past two years than in all the history of England for over 100 years, and England has had numerous and critical wars in that time." We can hardly expect normal rules to apply in times of such stress, yet we must I think be as vigilant in wartime as we should be in peacetime to see that the bounds of reasonable limitation are not exceeded. Because the freedoms may have to be less does not mean that they should cease to exist. In particular we are left with a legacy from World War II that I think should be discarded. The Privy Council, going a little further than our Supreme Court, upheld in full the Orders-in-Council of 1945 providing for deportation of the Canadian Japanese. Surely this interpretation of our constitution is as frightening as the policy of deportation was reprehensible. For it means that even Canadian-born citizens can be deported by Order-in-Council under the War Measures Act – assuming of course that a country can be found willing to receive them. I fail to see on what conceivable ground such a power can be felt to be necessary in the hands of our federal government. As citizens have we not the right to pay whatever penalty the law may require of us for breach of the law, and then to return to our own community after release from prison? In the case of the Japanese, of course, they had committed no crime whatsoever. I notice that the proposed Bill of Rights does not save us from this power in any future emergency. I suggest that the War Measures Act should be amended at least to prevent the federal executive from possessing this authority.** To take it away from Parliament itself would seem to require an amendment to the BNA Act.

Now I wish to look at the cases which have recently come before our Supreme Court and which have so sharply focussed our attention upon questions of fundamental freedoms. The first I wish to mention is that of *Boucher v. The King*, decided in 1951. This was a charge of seditious libel taken against Boucher, a Witness of Jehovah, for having distributed the pamphlet known as "Quebec's Burning Hate" to several persons in the district of Beauce, Quebec. The pamphlet was written in protest against the numerous arrests of members of the sect which had been going on in Quebec for some years, and against what was alleged to be the mob violence used on various occasions. It undoubtedly contained strong language directed to the conduct of officials in church and state; the question was, was it seditious? This involved the court in defining closely the Canadian law of sedition, particularly in the light of certain recent amendments to the Criminal Code. The lower courts agreed that the pamphlet was seditious, but the Supreme Court by a majority found otherwise. The decision is of the greatest importance to the law on freedom of speech, in my view, since it removed a rather vague idea that merely saying or writing something that might stir up feelings of ill-will between different classes of subjects constituted sedition in itself, whether or not there was an intention to incite to violence. Such an intention to promote violence of resistance or defiance for the purpose of disturbing constituted authority is now essential to the crime. As Mr. Justice Rand observed:

> There is no modern authority which holds that mere effect of tending to create discontent or disaffection among His Majesty's subjects or ill-will or hostility between groups of them, but not tending to issue in illegal conduct, constitutes the crime, and this for obvious reasons. Freedom in thought and speech and disagreement in ideas and beliefs, on every conceivable subject, are of the essence of our life. The clash of critical discussion on political, social and religious subjects has too deeply become the stuff of daily experience to suggest that mere ill-will as a product of controversy can strike down the latter with illegality. A superficial examination of the word shows its insufficiency: what is the degree necessary to criminality? Can it ever, as mere subjective condition, be so? Controversial fury is aroused constantly by differences in abstract conceptions; heresy in some fields is again a mortal sin; there can be fanatical puritanism in ideas as well as in morals; but our compact of free society accepts and absorbs these differences and they are exercised at large within the framework of freedom and order on broader and deeper uniformities as bases of social stability. Similarly in discontent, affection and hostility: as subjective incidents of controversy, they and the ideas which arouse them are part of our living which ultimately serve us in stimulation, in the clarification of thought and, as we believe, in the search for the constitution and truth of things generally.

** Eds. Professor Scott gave this lecture in 1959, long before the October 1970 events confirmed that the danger he foresaw was not just an academic one.

This case provides an excellent example of how in the definition of terms the area of freedom can be broadened or restricted. But I would point out that this was simply an interpretation of the present criminal law; if Parliament chose to tighten the law it could do so by amending the code, and no Bill of Rights short of an amendment to the BNA Act would save us.

I take next the case of the *Alliance des Professeurs catholiques*, decided in 1953. The Alliance was an association of Catholic school teachers which had been certified as a bargaining agent for the Catholic schools of Montreal by the Quebec Labour Relations Board. The Alliance was never popular with the School Commission, to say the least, and a request for decertification was made to the Board. The request came from Montreal, but it was accorded on the same day by the Board sitting in Quebec and the Alliance was notified by telegram immediately without having been summoned for a hearing and before even the written document containing the request had reached the Board. As Chief Justice Rinfret aptly remarked, "Voilà une justice expéditive." The decertification was held invalid on the ground that one of the principles of natural justice, *audi alteram partem*, had not been followed. The case fully supports this great principle of administrative law; unfortunately in the outcome the Alliance lost its suit because by the time it reached the Privy Council the Quebec legislature had amended the Labour Relations Act retroactively. Provincial autonomy won over the power of judicial interpretation, and this will ever be the case in all matters falling within provincial jurisdiction if we do not have a true Bill of Rights in the constitution.

In the same year as the *Alliance* case came a somewhat similar trade union case from Nova Scotia, and again our Supreme Court, this time upholding the courts below, took a liberal view of the law. The Nova Scotia Labour Relations Board had refused to certify a union because it found that its secretary-treasurer was a communist. No justification for this refusal was found in the law. Again quoting Mr. Justice Rand:

> There is no law in this country against holding such [i.e. communist] views. This man is eligible for election or appointment to the highest political offices in the province: on what ground can it be said that the legislature of which he might be a member has empowered the Board, in effect, to exclude him from a labour union?

Here the court drew the distinction, so necessary for us to maintain in times of strong controversy, between unpopularity and illegality. How much more fair and reasonable this approach is than that of the British Columbia Court of Appeal which upheld the Bar of the province in refusing permission to practice law to a law graduate believed to be a communist. It is not difficult to make out an argument that no man with a loyalty outside Canada should hold public office, but in that case why bar only communists? Why not Catholics and others who may conscientiously place religious obligation above their duty to the state?

I pass now to a case that is not easy to analyse because of the variety of judicial opinion it contains, but which raises a question of the utmost importance to civil liberties – the *Saumur* case. Saumur was a Witness of Jehovah in Quebec who attacked the validity of a city by-law forbidding the distribution in the streets of the city of any book, pamphlet, circular or tract whatever without permission of the chief of Police. Let us pause a moment to reflect upon the thoroughly menacing nature of this type of by-law, which any Quebec municipalities may adopt under a special statute enacted in 1947 by the legislature. It means that freedom of the press is placed under the censorship of the police. In Montreal at one time even federal election literature could not be distributed from door to door without the approval of the city executive, so that the operation of the federal election act was subject to municipal control. A man walking down the street would commit an offence if he pulled a pamphlet out of his pocket and gave it to his friend beside him. One zealous Quebec municipality went so far as to prohibit the distribution of literature inside private houses. This form of violation of civil liberties is not peculiar to Quebec; similar by-laws have been enacted in the United States and have been held unconstitutional by the American Supreme Court, though I know of no other province of Canada which has adopted them. Aimed at the Witnesses, communists and, very probably, trade unions, such by-laws take away the rights of all of us.

Now the holding in the *Saumur* case was satisfactory in that the Quebec City by-law was found not to prohibit the Witnesses from distributing in the streets, principally because of the Quebec Freedom of Worship Act. But the by-law itself was not held invalid, and it would seem that a majority of the Supreme Court at that time considered that a city might properly exercise such control over literature distributed in the streets. If this decision stands, a more damaging blow at our traditional electoral practices and at freedom of the press and of speech and of association can hardly be imagined. For a circular announcing a public meeting would require police approval, so that the ability of the citizens to meet together and to hear public speakers discuss the issues of the day is struck at by the simple process of controlling this means of communication. While there are other ways of announcing meetings, for those who can afford to pay for them, these too are liable to be under other forms of censorship and control from private persons. There was a time when the Montreal Star would not take a paid advertisement calling a CCF meeting. The City of Montreal by-law dealing with distribution of literature has been held unconstitutional by the Superior Court, but we are left in a somewhat uncertain state as to the general right of municipalities to affect fundamental freedoms under their authority to regulate what goes on in the streets.

I shall refer now to two cases which illustrate the danger to civil liberties from illegal police behaviour. These are the *Chaput* and the *Lamb* cases, decided in the Supreme Court in 1955 and 1959. Both involved Jehovah's Witnesses; in both the police were condemned to pay personal damages to the persons whose rights were violated. In the *Chaput* case the police, on orders from a superior officer, broke up an admittedly orderly religious meeting being conducted in a private house. Religious books and pamphlets were seized, and the officiating minister was forced to leave the premises. No charge of any kind was laid against anybody. In a unanimous judgment, overruling the Quebec courts, Chaput was awarded damages. The case brings out several important rules of our constitutional and administrative law. On the constitutional side, Mr. Justice Taschereau enunciated with great clarity the doctrine that in Canada there is complete equality among the various religious beliefs. He said:

> Dans notre pays, il n'existe pas de religion d'Etat. Personne n'est tenu d'adhérer à une croyance quelconque. Toutes les religions sont sur un pied d'égalité, et tous les catholiques comme d'ailleurs tous les protestants, les juifs, ou les autres adhérents des diverses dénominations religieuses, ont la plus entière liberté de penser comme ils le désirent. La conscience de chacun est une affaire personnelle, et l'affaire de nul autre. Il serait désolant de penser qu'une majorité puisse imposer ses vues religieuses à une minorité. Ce serait une erreur fâcheuse de croire qu'on sert son pays ou sa religion, en refusant dans une province, à une minorité, les mêmes droits que l'on revendique soi-même avec raison, dans une autre province.

On the administrative law side, the case illustrates the well-known rule that orders from a superior officer are no defence. The lesser official in the governmental hierarchy is not protected in wrong-doing because the superior officer tells him to do something; the illegal order merely makes the superior officer liable too. This rule is essential to the preservation of the rule of law as we have inherited it; it makes each and every public officer personally responsible for right behaviour, and unable to hide behind some cloak of authority. In this case the police were actually committing a crime, that of disturbing a religious ceremony. How can orders to commit a crime make the crime lawful? This is the expression in our domestic law of the rule we wish to write firmly into international law, so that those who commit crimes against humanity may be brought to book, as at Nuremberg, without being able to plead superior orders.

Another aspect of this, as of some similar cases, deserves comment. Sociologists may explain how it is that even in our supposedly civilized societies we seem capable of developing the concept of the outlaw. The outlaw is – outside the law; he has no rights of any kind, and therefore no one can do wrong in attacking, defaming, arresting or assaulting him, or even in destroying his property. It seems that the Witnesses of Jehovah were placed in that category in some parts of Quebec. Because one of their pamphlets was once held to be seditious, it was assumed by some officials that not only were all their other pamphlets seditious but that every member of the sect belonged to a seditious conspiracy though no court had ever held this and no such charge was ever laid. Roncarelli, for instance, was accused of fomenting sedition and had his private business deliberately destroyed when all he had ever done, besides being a member of the Witnesses, was give lawful bail in a lawful court with the lawful approval of the presiding judge. So too it seemed at one time as though every person called a communist was immediately outlawed. The outlawry of certain trade unions in Newfoundland has been attempted by more formal means, but the intention is the same. There is no more dangerous concept than this to the cause of civil liberties. Civil liberties are always needed most by unpopular people. Even the worst criminals after conviction have rights, and of course before conviction they are presumed innocent. It is the function of the law, and of the independent judges who apply it as well as of the independent barristers who practise it on behalf of all clients who need their help, to uphold the notion of legality against the pressures of angry opinion. Should the lawyers be afraid to take unpopular clients, and judges afraid to give unpopular decisions, all the principles of the law would be worthless.

The *Lamb* case is merely another example of police illegality, but it is part of the dismal picture that has too often been exposed in Quebec in recent years. Miss Lamb, another Jehovah's Witness, was illegally arrested, held over the weekend in the cells without any charge being laid against her, not allowed to telephone a lawyer, and then offered her freedom on condition she signed a document releasing the police from all responsibility for the way they had treated her. When reading such a story one wonders how many other innocent victims have been similarly treated by the police but have not had the courage and the backing to pursue the matter through to final victory – in this instance twelve and a half years after the arrest had taken place. We should be grateful that we have in this country some victims of state oppression who stand up for their rights. Their victory is the victory of all of us.

It will be noted that both these police cases from Quebec involve a defence of civil liberties by the normal process of the action in damages against the officials who have violated them. We see here the civil law of Quebec being brought into operation exactly as is the common law in similar cases. The rule of law of Dicey, whether based on civil law or common law, operates in very much the same way. It is probable however that the protection afforded by the civil law is somewhat wider than that given by the common law, for the reason that the civil law of delict is more fully evolved than the common law of tort. There is a universal principle of delict and quasi-delict, whereas there are only specific torts. Hence it is easier to bring a new situation under the law of delictual responsibility than it is to bring it under the ancient torts. This is theory, however; all will depend upon judicial willingness in interpretation, and unfortunately in almost every case coming from Quebec recently the provincial courts have not seen their way to protect civil liberties whereas the Supreme Court of Canada has. Technicalities seem to loom more largely in the minds of the Quebec Judges, whereas the Supreme Court appears to find more ways of securing that substantial justice shall be done.

Let me refer now to two cases which involved interpretations of the BNA Act, namely the *Birks* case and the Padlock Act case. In the *Birks* case a Montreal by-law, passed in virtue of a provincial statute, required that storekeepers should close their stores on the six Catholic holy days. Question: is this a law providing more holidays for employees, or is it a law for compulsory observance of the religious practices of one religion upon all people whether belonging to that religion or not? By a unanimous judgment the Supreme Court, overruling the Quebec Court of Appeal, found that religious observance was the pith and substance of the law, since, among other reasons, no additional holiday was provided for the employees of the stores if one of these holy days happened to fall on a Sunday. But in so holding the wider rule was laid down that laws affecting religious observance belonged within the field of criminal law and hence were exclusively within federal jurisdiction. This is therefore a leading case on the meaning of the BNA Act, and will have future consequences much more important than those decisions which, like the *Chaput* and *Lamb* cases, turned primarily upon provincial law which the legislature could amend if it wished.

The same results follow from the Padlock Act case. This was a statute which purported to make illegal the preaching of communism or bolshevism in houses in Quebec, and the printing and distribution of literature propagating or tending to propagate these ideologies anywhere in the province. The Attorney-General of Quebec, upon any evidence that seemed to himself adequate, could order the padlocking of houses where the offence was committed, and the seizure of all such literature, without trial or conviction of any sort. Outside of the Defence of Canada Regulations in wartime, I know of no other equivalent attempt at thought control in the history of Canada. The Act had been upheld in earlier judgments in the Quebec courts, the late Chief Justice Greenshields having once remarked from the bench: "I fail to find in the statute any interference with freedom of speech." Fortunately this judicial blindness did not affect the Supreme Court, which held that the subject matter of the Act fell under the criminal law power. Had the opposite view prevailed, we would have had the extraordinary situation in Canada that while the federal Elections Act would decide who could be a candidate for Parliament, a province might have barred the use of any public hall or building to members of any particular party. We would have been left with what I call the 'open-field' theory of democracy; freedom of speech would have existed only in the open air. As Mr. Justice Rand said:

> Parliamentary government postulates a capacity in men, acting freely and under self-restraints, to govern themselves; and that advance is best served in the degree achieved of individual liberation from subjective as well as objective shackles. Under that government, the freedom of discussion in Canada, as a subject-matter of legislation, has a unity of interest and significance extending equally to every part of the Dominion.

And he added: " . . . Legislatures and Parliament are permanent features of our constitutional structure, and the body of discussion is indivisible . . . ."

I come now to the last of the recent cases I wish to refer to – that of *Roncarelli v. Duplessis*. This case has many angles and lends itself to a variety of interpretations, but I think can be reduced to a very simple and reasonable proposition. When a public officer exceeds his authority, and thereby causes damage, he must pay for it personally. This is a basic rule of English constitutional and administrative law which Quebec inherited along with all other Canadian provinces. It is really what we mean when we say, as we can say with pride, that in our polity the state is under the law. For the state is nothing but the people who compose it, arranged in various groupings called legislatures and courts and senates and crowns-in-council. Constitutional law prescribes the groupings and their functions; administrative law tells us what authority each official possesses and how he may exercise it. No public officer has any power beyond what the law confers upon him, and the courts say what the law is. Thus the law puts a definite boundary around each official beyond which he acts at his peril. I say this, in Ottawa, with all the emphasis at my command. Any citizen – and this is a crucial corollary to which there are few exceptions – – can sue any official in the ordinary courts if that official has damaged him in a manner not permitted by law. No one is immune, not even a Prime Minister.

Now I am happy to note that no judge in any court in the *Roncarelli* case disagreed with this fundamental proposition. Where the disagreement came was on the facts of the case (for instance, did the Prime Minister actually cause the licence to be cancelled, or did he merely give advice that it could be cancelled?) or on the legal question as to whether the powers of an Attorney-General included that of ordering a cancellation under the circumstances of the case, or whether or not notice of action should have been given. No judge said a Prime Minister could not be sued. None said that he was free to exceed his powers.

I do not think there is any new law in this holding; it is really the same rule as was applied to the policemen in *Chaput* and *Lamb*. But it is always a triumph for the law to show that it is applied equally to all without fear of favour. This is what we mean when we say that all are equal before the law. The statement is by no means as true as it should be; Anatole France's quip that the law is the same for the rich, as for the poor, since both are allowed to sleep under bridges, has its counterpart in the statement that it is the same for both rich and poor since both are allowed to pay what it costs to carry their case to the Supreme Court of Canada. Yet the truth in the statement is, I suggest, even more important than the element of untruth, and woe betide any nation that loses sight of it.

Another reflection is appropriate upon the *Roncarelli* case. Our administrative services in Canada are carried on in the main by two methods; either through a government department, headed by a Cabinet minister, or through some public board or commission like the Canadian Broadcasting Corporation or the Quebec Liquor Commission. Some of these boards must be under close supervision of a Minister or even of the Cabinet, but some should be and are intended to be independent. Where they are independent, no politician has a right to interfere or to tell them how to behave. If he does, he exceeds his powers. This rule is essential for our protection against a too powerful state machine. When we distribute our powers, we want them to stay distributed, and here the courts can help as they did in *Roncarelli's* case. Politicians must learn that political power is not the same as legal authority.

Finally, the case is important in upholding the citizen's right to give bail. Bail is a great protection for civil liberties; it prevents the innocent from being held in prison pending trial, and every case starts with a presumption of innocence. To punish a man for giving bail is like punishing jurors for their verdicts or witnesses for their testimony. It is, or should be, in my view, a crime and not just an excess of authority. For it is interfering with a judicial process.

These are some of the civil liberties cases that have come into the courts.**

* * * *

** Eds. The rest of this lecture, which has been deleted here, dealt with reservations Professor Scott had concerning the Bill of Rights Legislation which Prime Minister Diefenbaker was proposing at that time (1959). The Bill was, in fact, passed in 1960.

6. Toward a Constitutional Bill of Rights

Pierre Elliott Trudeau

This is an excerpt from a speech given to the Canadian Bar Association on September 4th, 1967 by Mr. Trudeau when he was Minister of Justice in the Pearson government. Agreement on a Constitutional Bill of Rights, which Mr. Trudeau is talking about here, has continued to flounder on the shoals of subsequent Dominion-Provincial Conferences, including the latest at Victoria in June, 1971.

Much work has already been usefully done in the field of civil rights in Canada, particularly in connection with the enactment of the Canadian Bill of Rights in 1960. We are now aiming at a new Bill which will be broader and entrenched constitutionally. The Canadian Bill of Rights sets out the legal rights of the citizen in respect of life, liberty and the security of the person, and such basic political rights as freedom of speech and the press, freedom of religion, and freedom of assembly. There are also various provincial measures against discrimination and invasion of human rights. All of these measures are, however, statutory and do not preclude future encroachments of rights by Parliament or the Legislatures. They may be amended in the same way as any other statute. Moreover, they do not cover certain rights which are special to a country like Canada, founded on two distinct linguistic groups.

Accordingly, we envision a Bill of Rights that will be broader than the existing legislation. We all agree on the familiar basic rights – freedom of belief and expression, freedom of association, the right to a fair trial and to fair legal procedures generally. We would also expect a guarantee against discrimination on the basis of race, religion, sex, ethnic or national origin. These are the rights commonly protected by bills of rights. They are basic for a society of free men.

But there are rights of special importance to Canada arising from the fact, as I have said, that it is founded on two distinct linguistic groups. While language is the basic instrument for preserving and developing the cultural identity of a people, the language provisions of the British North America Act are very limited. I believe that we require a broader definition and more extensive guarantees in the matter of recognition of the official languages. The right to learn and to use either of the two official languages should be recognized. Without this we cannot assure every Canadian an equal opportunity to participate in the political, cultural, economic and social life of this country. I venture to say that, if we are able to reach agreement on this, we will have found a solution to a basic issue facing Canada today. A constitutional change recognizing broader rights with respect to the two official languages would add a new meaning to Confederation.

It is true that if we agree on the general content of a Consti-

tutional Bill of Rights, a number of further questions will arise, important for everyone but, from a technical point of view, of special concern to all of those who, like ourselves, are trained in the Law. Should the rights be declared generally, or defined precisely with exceptions clearly specified? For example, if we guarantee freedom of speech without qualification, will this invalidate some of our laws with respect to obscenity, sedition, defamation, or film censorship? Is freedom of religion compatible with compulsory Sunday closing legislation? What of a constitutional guarantee of 'due process of law'? In the United States this phrase has in the past created many problems because of its vagueness. At times the courts have construed it so broadly as to invalidate a variety of social legislation which we would now accept as essential. Should we avoid the possibility of such an application of 'due process' in Canada, by using a more precise term to guarantee the rule of law? What of the right to counsel? Should this 'right' impose a duty on the government to provide counsel for those who cannot afford it? If we recognize the right of every person to use and to be educated in either of the official languages, should we limit the exercise of this right to places where there is a concentration of one or the other language group?

These are some of the questions which will arise as we try to develop a Constitutional Bill of Rights. I mention them here not because I expect immediate answers, but to illustrate the complexities involved in any basic constitutional reform. I hope that the Canadian Bar Association will study some of these problems and in due course give us the benefit of its advice in the light of its long-standing interest and research in the protection of human rights.

I have said that I envision a Bill of Rights which will not only be broader in its content than the existing legislation but will also be entrenched constitutionally. The Canadian Bill of Rights of 1960 is a statute binding only at the federal level of government. And even at that level, the Courts have shown some reluctance to give it an over-riding effect. Also, it obviously does not apply to the exercise of provincial powers. And moreover, the effect of most existing human rights legislation in Canada is rendered uncertain by the present division of legislative powers. It is not clear to what extent Parliament or the Legislature can validly act in the protection of human rights. We will face this problem as long as we try to protect human rights by ordinary legislation. It is for these reasons that I believe the time has come to place the necessary safeguard in the constitution.

I am thinking of a Bill of Rights that will be so designed as to limit the exercise of all governmental power, federal and provincial. It will not involve any gain by one jurisdiction at the expense of the other; there would be no transfer of powers from the Federal Parliament to the Provincial Legislatures, or from the Provincial Legislatures to the Federal Parliament. Instead, the power of both the federal government and the provincial governments would be restrained in favour of the Canadian citizen, who will be better protected in the exercise of his fundamental rights and freedoms.

I have already said that agreement on entrenching a Bill of Rights will raise other basic constitutional issues. First, what procedure is to be followed in amending the Constitution? How is the Bill to be entrenched? Shall we ask the Parliament at Westminster to enact the necessary change in the British North America Act? Or will we finally agree on a formula for amending our constitution in Canada? It is inevitable that discussion of an entrenched Bill of Rights will lead to a renewed attempt to agree upon an amending formula – something we have as yet failed to achieve after years of effort. I can think of no better occasion than when we reach agreement on constitutional protection of the basic rights of the citizen to find a solution to the problem of developing a Canadian constitution in Canada – of finally 'patriating' our constitution.

We shall also face other constitutional issues. A constitutional Bill of Rights would modify even further the concept of parliamentary sovereignty in Canada. Once fundamental rights are guaranteed, they will be beyond the reach of government at all levels. This will confer new and very important responsibilities on the courts because it will be for the courts to interpret the Bill of Rights, to decide how much scope should be given to the protected rights and to what extent the power of government should be curtailed. This will inevitably bring us to consideration of the system of final adjudication in the constitutional field by the Supreme Court of Canada as presently constituted.

A Bill of Rights entrenched by an amending formula which 'brings home' the constitution, and applied throughout Canada by our supreme constitutional tribunal, will open the door to further constitutional reform. For example, will not the powers of reservation and disallowance of provincial legislation lose their meaning once a Bill of Rights has been entrenched in the Constitution? Are there not other antiquated features of the British North America Act which might well at that time be reconsidered?

And so, you see why I said at the outset that the adoption of a constitutional Bill of Rights opens the door wide to necessary constitutional change. I believe that, once we have agreed on a Bill of Rights, an amending formula, and a system of final adjudication, little would stand in the way of a general constitutional conference to discuss such other particular changes as may be necessary to adapt our constitution to the requirements of our day. We look forward to such discussions. Our policy is not opposed to any reasonable initiative or proposal. It should be apparent from the foregoing, Mr. Chairman, that the government's policy in regard to the constitution has been consistent and progressive throughout. It has been and remains a policy of *controlled development*, which does not fear change, indeed which even fosters it as I have shown today, provided that it maintains the integrity of Canada. Our aim is the maintenance of a strong Federal Government and strong Provincial Governments. That is what Federalism means.

---

7. Class, Mobility and Migration

John Porter /*Carleton University*

Social positions, ranked as higher, lower or simply equivalent, constitute the rank structure of society, a crucial dimension of social space. Where we are placed in the rank structure defines our range of movement, our world view, our life chances. In his book The Vertical Mosaic, *from which the next selection is taken, Professor Porter draws to our attention the intricate and complex way in which Canadian immigration patterns have affected, directly, mobility in this rank structure and, indirectly, the whole basis of Canadian political life.*

Firstly, there is considerable evidence that immigration into Canada has been carefully controlled to maintain Anglo-Saxon dominance numerically as well as politically. There are some indications that this historic pattern has been reversed over this past decade, although it is still too early to be sure. Nonetheless (as Kelner's essay later in this volume makes clear) non-Anglo-Saxons have not had as much room for movement in the social and political structure as have Anglo-Saxons.

Secondly, our reliance on immigration from abroad to fill our topmost positions whether in the universities, in the professions or in business, has meant that those already living here have found their opportunities to enter these occupations more restricted than would otherwise be the case. Present policy continues to be avowedly biased in favour of highly skilled, highly educated immigrants. Thus, although the figures Porter uses to support it are now outdated, his argument remains valid.

Thirdly, in many ways Canada has been a way-station – "a reception centre" Porter calls it – for the United States. Persons have passed through Canada rather than putting down root here. This has had very real consequences for national identity and national unity which have always been precarious. The major political focus has had to be on problems ensuing from this. Because ethnic consciousness has superceded class consciousness in Canadian political life, what sporadic attempts have been made to develop a class-based politics have not been very successful, says Porter.

For all these reasons ethnicity plus class position have been more important than class position alone in determining an individual's rank, and hence his social space, in this country.

People are the basic element of all social structure. Human beings create a society and its traditions. If a population is increasing, if it is always moving about, if it has a large proportion of immigrants, if it has to push out large numbers who cannot find work, if it is made up of a variety of cultural groups, it will clearly be a different kind of society than it would be if these conditions did not prevail. This is not to suggest that the prime mover of social structure is the population factor. Demographic changes do not take place independently of social values. As we know family size is not determined by reproductive capacity. We know, too, that community values can be strong enough to prevent the moving of a free labour force out of depressed areas. To account for social structure and change in solely demographic terms is almost to reduce sociology to biology. The more acceptable view is that the relationship between demographic structure and social structure is reciprocal rather than one way. We are here interested in Canadian demographic structure for any clues it might provide to the structure of Canadian social class.

Uncertain Growth

The most striking features of Canada's population are its uneven rate of growth and its geographical mobility. The two components of population growth are natural increase (the excess of births over deaths) and net migration (the excess of immigrants over emigrants), both of which have been important in the 110-year period between 1851 and 1961 when the Canadian population increased from 2.5 million to 18 million.[1] Natural increase, however, has always been much more important than net migration. Throughout its history Canada has experienced high birth rates and low death rates, the latter probably because large-scale urbanization with its public health hazards took place later in Canada than in Europe. Nathan Keyfitz, who has attempted to reconstruct the relative importance of these two components for each 10 year period between 1851 and 1950, estimated that 7.1 million arrived in Canada from other countries while 6.6 million left for other countries, mainly the United States. Natural increase during this period added about 10.5 million people to the population.

These large migrations have not been at a constant rate. Rather short periods of high immigration have been followed by longer periods of "gradual dissipation of the gains."[2] Large migrations are of course a response to economic conditions, one factor of production, labour, moving with another, capital. Economic factors can be either a 'push' or a 'pull'. The push comes when economic or political conditions in a country are so bad that they lead to desperation migration as when Scottish crofters were "combed off the hills like lice," or when, after the Irish potato famine, the Irish navvies came to work on projects such as the Rideau Canal system where they were reported to have "worked like horses" and "died like flies."[3] The pull of migration is the prospect of upward social mobility, of being better off by moving elsewhere than by staying put. The push and pull factors are not wholly separate, and often they work together.

It is impossible to separate the pull of Canada from the pull of North America as a whole. The period of massive immigration into Canada was between the turn of the century and World War I, the period when the western provinces were being opened up by the vigorous immigration policies of Sir Clifford Sifton. As long as the United States maintained its *laissez-passer* system of immigration, large numbers who came from Europe to Canada undoubtedly stayed only for a short time and then moved on to the United States.[4] The extent to which Canada played this role of a reception centre is indicated by the fact that 3,356,000 immigrants entered Canada between 1901 and 1921, but during that time the number of foreign-born in the Canadian population increased by only 1,256,000.[5] To be precise we would have to know the foreign-born mortality during the period, but there is no doubt that a large number of immigrants did later become emigrants.

Because grossly inadequate records were kept during these great population shifts, estimates of population movements vary, but between 2 to 3 million people came into Canada between 1901 and 1915, the only period when net migration augmented the population as much as natural increase.[6] During the same period well over a million left. The decade after World War I also saw large population movements through Canada with roughly a million people coming in and a million going out.

From 1931 to 1944, the depression and early war years, more people left the country than came in, but the actual number migrating during this period was much smaller. After World War II rapid economic growth led to a resurgence of immigration (although it was not as great as in the decade following the turn of the century) as well as a decline in emigration, making net migration positive. One estimate for 1946 to 1956 (and immigration statistics for this period are much more reliable) put immigration at 1.3 million and emigration to the United States alone at 300,000.[7] One 1960 estimate put immigration at over 1.5 million and emigration at 600,000 for the period 1950 to 1959.[8] As economic activity falls, or levels off, immigration is reduced partly as a result of government policy, and emigration increases creating the possibility of an over-all loss through migration. Although it is unlikely that net migration was negative there is little doubt that in the early 1960's it was close to becoming so.

The 1961 census provides the most reliable check on demographic movements during the boom decade since the 1951 census. There were 4,229,000 more people in Canada in 1961 than in 1951. This growth was made up of a natural increase of 3,148,000 (that is 4,468,000 births less 1,320,000 deaths) and net migration of 1,081,000 (that is, 1,543,000 immigrants less 462,000 emigrants). The emigrants here are those 'missing' after births, deaths, and immigrants have been accounted for, although the movement of an estimated 175,000 Canadian-born who emigrated and returned within the ten years would not be included in the tabulations. The actual movement out was then around 637,000. From one-fifth to one-quarter of all immigrants to Canada between 1951 and 1961 had left by 1961.[9]

The United States has been the main recipient of emigrants from Canada. With the imposition of quota restrictions after World War I only the Canadian-born could move freely into the United States from Canada. During the depression years they too were restricted. In the 1920's the number going south was roughly 925,000, and for the 10 years after World War II it was 300,000, more than three-quarters of whom were native-born Canadians.[10]

Although we have been dealing with the population of the whole of Canada, it is worth separating briefly the French-Canadian part of the population. French Canada has been traditionally a society of high fertility.[11] Most of its population growth, from about 65,000 at the time of the conquest in 1763 to 5.5 million in 1961 came from natural increase. Statements by two demographers put in startling terms the importance of this factor: "During the last two centuries, world population has been multiplied by three, European population by four, and French-Canadian population by eighty",[12] and, "If the population of France had multiplied in the same proportion [as that of French Canada] it would today be much larger than that of the entire world."[13] In comparison, immigration has had a negligible effect on the French-Canadian population. One demographer has placed total immigration to Canada from France during the 150 years of the French regime at no more than 10,000 people. After 1763, because of an ideological separation between New France and its former homeland following the French Revolution and because of the lack of population pressure in France, Frenchmen were not disposed to emigrate. Even a regulation placing natives of France on an equal footing with Commonwealth (white) and United States citizens did not result in any appreciable French immigration. French-Canadian population growth has thus had little help from the outside. There has, however, been a considerable French-Canadian emigration to the United States. This net loss has been estimated at 800,000, most of it beginning around 1830 and coinciding with the first shortage of land in Quebec and continuing until 1930. Industrialization of the United States became a lure to the *habitant* denied access to land.

It is clear that natural increase and immigration have been different for the French and non-French groups, and that the fertility of French Canada has made a considerable contribution to the natural increase of the Canadian population as a whole. In 1950 the French-Canadian birth rate was 32 per 1,000 compared to 24.5 per 1,000 for the non-French.[14] Before this date the ratio of the two groups was considerably greater. By 1961, although among those 65 and over there were 2.7 times as many British as French, among children under 15 years there were only 1.2 times as many. Thus after 200 years a military victory is on the way to being reversed through population growth.

Varying rates of growth have added to Canadian population instability. The rapid growth between 1951 and 1961, from roughly 14 to 18 million, about a 28-per-cent increase, was a reversal of falling rates of growth per decade that had prevailed since the heavy immigration of the first ten years of the century. The low point was the decade 1931 to 1941 when growth was only 11 per cent compared to 34 per cent in the first 10 years of the century. The rapid growth after World War II is attributed to positive net migration and high birth rates, the latter caused by more marriages, earlier marriages, and earlier family formation during a period of economic prosperity rather than by changed values about the size of families.

Social Psychology of Population Instability

Canada is not the only society which has been created by large numbers of human beings moving into vacant areas, but it is unlikely that any other society has resembled a huge demographic railway station as much as has the non-French part of Canada. As well as a society receiving immigrants it has been one producing emigrants, either naturally or by harbouring the 'birds of passage' who have stopped over in Canada while making the move from Europe to the United States. What is likely to be the effect on social institutions, and in particular on class structure, of such a kinetic population?

Emile Durkheim argued that what keeps a society together, what provides its solidarity and its sense of identity, is some kind of a collective conscience or set of values and ideas created in the process of living together and carried around in the minds of the members of the group.[15] He called these ideas – embodying both values and instrumental knowledge – collective representations. People behave in accordance with these collective representations or, what he sometimes called, currents of opinion. Social change and accompanying change in ideas he attributed to changes in population densities which affected the circulation of collective representations. He was of course seeking to refute the liberal notion of a society of atom-like individuals bound together only by the contracts they made. Although he did not give a satisfactory account of cohesion in the large industrial society, perhaps because he did not pay adequate attention to the importance of power, he did make the point that social life is given its structure by collective sentiments and ideas which in turn are affected by population densities and mobility. A later writer, David Riesman, has looked for national character in the processes of population growth.[16]

Collective efforts to create a Canadian society have been marked by periods of population stagnation and social despair or rapid population growth and the promise of greatness. Throughout their history, Canadians have had to find their identity in the shade of a giant neighbour whose pace of development has always been greater and whose way of life has been an eldorado to large sections of Canada's own population as well as to the people of Europe. "There is scarcely a farm house in the older provinces," wrote the *Toronto Mail* in 1887, "where there is not an empty chair for the boy in the States."[17] The construction of the first transcontinental railroad was an undertaking of heroic proportions. Before its construction, people in large numbers could not cross the barren rock to the great plains of the north, and the surplus population found its outlet southwards to the American mid-west. The completion of the Canadian Pacific in the middle of the world-wide depression from 1873 to 1896 did not bring the promised rewards. Homesteads in the new west were being abandoned by the thousands. As Sir Richard Cartwright put it, "The Dominion which began in Lamentations seemed to be ending in Exodus."[18]

Then a series of events brought a vitality of such strength that it seemed inevitable that the twentieth century would indeed "belong to Canada." Economic conditions throughout the world improved; the arable land of the west was occupied and the consequent surplus production of wheat made Canada a participant in a new international division of labour. Population grew by one-third, an increase which was not to be matched again until the new vitality which followed World War II. In the inter-war years, after brief prosperity, there came increasing discontent, reflected in the rise of new political parties and eventually the national trauma of drought and depression.

Two periods of great vitality and two longer periods of faltering stagnation summarize the social development of Canada as a nation. Canadian society has a brief history, and the traditions and loyalties of its people as Canadians are obscure, or at least lack a sufficient clarity and tenacity to produce a cohesiveness which will withstand the gravitational pull of the United States. Traditions and social values are carried in the minds of a society's population, but the ebb and flow of migrations make a kind of flotsam of those sentiments which should accumulatively produce a consensus about what Canada is. For example, the events of the pre-Confederation period and the evolution of self-government have little meaning for the European immigrant. Nor can they enter much into the consciousness of the native as he prepares to leave.

The French and non-French parts of the population provide a striking contrast. The high degree of cohesion of French Canada has been possible because its population growth has come from natural increase rather than immigration, and the proportion of French who have emigrated is less than the respective proportion in the non-French group. Some loosening of bonds may come as French Canadians become dispersed within Canada. Non-French Canadians, at least at the level of political rhetoric, and sometimes intellectual inquiry, search for what is essentially Canadian in the fact of biculturalism and a binational state. Something new supposedly is generated by the two major groups, but in effect the cultural division is so great that neither group breaks through the barriers of its own culture. The French struggle to retain their identity, while the non-French are looking for one.

A further aspect of Durkheim's social psychology of cohesion is the strain which collective values undergo in periods of economic prosperity. He was struck in his study of suicide[19] with the increase in the suicide rate which accompanied the boom periods of economic activity, and he was led to conclude that periods of rapidly increasing prosperity are also periods of instability in the collective conscience and moral ideas which regulate behaviour. Prosperity brings a great increase in means without a corresponding articulation of ends. The collective goals of prosperity are uncertain. Canada has experienced two periods of rapid economic expansion, of 'onwards and up-wards,' without much knowledge of the goals that lay ahead or above. It is unlikely that a society can define itself during short bursts of economic development.

If large-scale population movements have inhibited the development of a Canadian consensus they may also have inhibited the emergence of class cultures and class polarization with strong class identifications. The conditions which Marx saw as producing solidarity of the proletariat obviously would have to include the proletariat's sense of being captured in an industrial environment from which it could not escape. Had it not been possible for large numbers of the deprived English and European populations to move to North America class revolutions of the kind that Marx predicted might well have taken place. These immigrants probably carried with them sufficient hope of improvement to ameliorate the frustrations which were met in the new world and which could help to create class solidarity. In Canada there has always been the additional ameliorative condition that the way out was relatively easy and cost little. The choice of leaving or staying was open to all until the 1920's and for the Canadian-born most of the time. The significant examples of violent class conflict in Canada after World War I were centred in Winnipeg and Vancouver, both areas with a high proportion of foreign-born. This was also a period of heavy emigration from Canada to the United States. Had this outlet been closed the possibilities for increased class polarization would no doubt have been much greater. As it was, the outlet soon became closed to those born outside Canada. The large proportion of foreign-born adults who were residing in the prairie provinces and in British Columbia and who were therefore 'captured' in the system in which they found themselves may be one factor, in addition to many others, including economic ones, to account for the radicalism of the west. At the time of the 1921 census the proportion of the native-born in the population became progressively smaller from east to west. In the Maritimes it was 93 per cent, in Quebec 92, in Ontario 78, in both Manitoba and Saskatchewan 63, in Alberta 53, and in British Columbia 50. In almost all the large western cities the population came close to being half immigrant.[20]

Class traditions and sentiments, like those which bind the whole society together, develop over time and are carried around in the minds of people who see themselves as members of the same class. Some class consciousness is also necessary for non-violent forms of class-based political behaviour. Only rarely has this type of politics existed in Canada. The migratory character of the Canadian population may help to explain this fact, for large migrations into, out of, and across the country are not likely to be the conditions which give rise to class sentiments. Moreover, this migratory population has been ethnically heterogeneous, thus making it possible for class hostility to be deflected into ethnic hostility. After World War I, when immigration went increasingly to urban areas, large segments of Canada's immigrant proletariat spoke different languages, and they met hostility from English-speaking workers. The labour movement, the usual vehicle for political expression of the 'working classes', was becoming split by western labour radicalism and eastern conservative craft unionism. It is important to keep in mind that the United States has been accessible to two opposite types of people who are important to political movements: those with strong mobility aspirations who feel their opportunities restricted, and those who feel their status threatened by the prospect of downward mobility.[21]

Nationalism with its intense identifications is in the twentieth century frequently seen as an expression of the far right of the political spectrum. But it is also an important ingredient of the leftist expression. An underprivileged class comes to feel that it has claims on the productive resources of the homeland, and seeks to change the conditions which it sees as oppressive. National institutions are the machinery through which change can be brought about. However, national sentiments, the sense of a shared and common homeland against which claims can be made, are unlikely to develop when the population of a country has been built up and dissipated as Canada's has been. A further consequence of the 'safety valve' of migration to the United States is that the range of social welfare legislation necessary for class abatement can always be delayed.

Migration and Occupational Levels

The need and desire to migrate is not the same for all people. The migratory population is selective, usually made up of younger adults and those who are seeking work or who hope to improve their status. In 1960 one-fifth of all immigrants were between the ages of twenty and twenty-four, and slightly more than one-quarter were between the ages of twenty-five and thirty-four. Three-quarters of all immigrants were under the age of thirty-five.[23] Emigrants, it would seem, also come more from the young adult ages, and as we shall see later on the same holds for the large migrations within Canada. Because migrations continue during varying economic conditions they are not made up entirely of a jobless class at the bottom of the economic system. Rather they are made up of people who feel they can do better by coming into the country or getting out of it. Immigrants include, for example, skilled and professional people from Great Britain who come to particular jobs or who intend to practise, and they include *contadini* from the Abruzzi mountains who will work on the construction of deep sewers in Toronto. All three groups will settle in Canada at different levels in the class system, but all no doubt move because of the prospects of improving themselves. Similarly the Canadian-born who leave the country, whatever their class level, see better opportunities for themselves in the United States.

Upward mobility strivings and the prospects of doing better can exist at any level of the class system although they may not be equally strong at all levels. Many Canadians have achieved high status in American academic, professional and business life. In the years 1950 to 1959 almost 37,000 Canadian professional workers emigrated to the United States, the largest groups being graduate nurses and engineers.[24] (There was a reverse flow of United States professional workers to Canada although the number was much smaller – about 11,000 during the same period.) For high levels of technical competence based on a scientific and professional knowledge there is an international labour market. Although we do not know the educational standards of the Canadians who emigrate, impressionistically it might be said that there is a considerable loss of highly educated and skilled. One estimate places the number of skilled workers leaving for the United States between 1951 and 1955 at 13,500.[25] But there is a replacement of these professional and skilled groups through immigration; in fact, since 1945 there has been a considerable net gain.

The mass of migration, however, has not been of professional or skilled classes, but rather of lower class levels who have been motivated by the desire to find work or more money in the countries of emigration. Indeed, the educated and the skilled, although increasing in proportion, have never made up a majority of the migrating forces. David Corbett in his study of post-war Canadian immigration has shown that, between 1946 and 1951, 7 per cent of 'labour force' immigrants were professionals, but almost half the workers who came during this period went into agriculture, logging, mining and quarrying, construction, service occupations, and labouring occupations.[26] One-quarter of them were in the last two categories.

Manufacturing and mechanical occupations took in almost another quarter of the immigrant workers. Corbett has also pointed out that during the same period immigrants were represented in these lower occupations in greater proportion than was the labour force which they were to enter. For example, 25 per cent of immigrant workers as opposed to about 16 per cent of the labour force were engaged in the service and labouring occupations. There was a similar difference of representation in the manufacturing and mechanical occupations. However, at the level of professional workers the proportion of immigrants for this period was about the same as that of the total labour force, and in the middle level, white collar occupations – managerial, clerical, and commercial – immigrants were a smaller proportion, about 15 per cent immigrants compared to 25 per cent of the labour force.

Although it may be true, as Corbett has suggested, that this comparison of the occupational distribution of immigrant workers and the total Canadian labour force showed "no very great differences between the two groups," these gross figures and wide occupational categories tend to cover up the process of class formation that was taking place as a result of changes in the Canadian occupational structure. During the 1950's the primary and goods producing industries continued to decline in terms of the proportion of the total labour force they employed, and, correspondingly, the white collar occupations continued to increase. As well, skill levels within the manual occupations increased greatly. Both old and new Canadians were involved in the status shuffle that went with these changes. Immigration has always been an important source of recruits for unskilled lower status jobs, but it has also been an important source of recruits for skilled and professional occupations. In general it may be said that the immigrant labour force has been a polarized one. At the lower level are those who come in to do work which Canadians seem to dislike, and at the higher levels are those who come to do work for which not enough Canadians are trained.

In considering some of the reasons why immigrants were so readily absorbed into the Canadian economy Corbett notes that "some, but by no means all, of the immigrants have been recruited to industries where Canadian labour has been hard to get – in the rural areas, the northern and more remote regions, and in the manual and unskilled occupations in the cities. . . . It is equally possible that Canadians have eagerly moved to more enjoyable urban jobs, gladly leaving the frontier and the rough work to newcomers."[27] Certainly, in absolute numbers more immigrants were going into lower level than higher level occupations, but the skilled and professional component of the immigrant labour force has always been of such a size as to demonstrate the deficiency of the native labour force in the range of skills required by a growing industrial society. This inadequacy of Canadian education became more evident during the 1950's when continued industrial growth was accompanied by an increase in the proportions of professionals in the immigrant labour force. By 1959 and 1960 the proportion was 13.4 per cent,[28] almost double what it had been in the earlier years of the decade. In 1959, 14 per cent of those entering professional occupations in the scientific and technical fields were either recent immigrants or were recruited outside Canada.[29] From 1950 to 1958 almost a third of the increase in the supply of engineers came from net migration.[30] Therefore Canadians have not been moving from rural to more enjoyable urban jobs quite as easily as Corbett has suggested, because many have lacked the urban skills and have found themselves without work, however eagerly they may have turned citywards.

Agricultural occupations also illustrate the relationship between immigration and the existing stratification system. Although these occupations had in 1951 about 16 per cent of the total labour force and 11 per cent of the immigrant labour force, the immigrants were more likely to become farm labourers rather than proprietors or tenants. It has been calculated that between 1950 and 1958 no more than 3,900 immigrants had purchased farms and only 850 had become farm tenants.[31] No doubt some were missed in this count by the federal Department of Labour, but it is clear that immigrants of that period entered the stratum of farm owners in insignificant proportions. Canada has always looked upon farmers as preferred immigrants. As settlers – that curious word which has persisted in the language of immigration officials – they opened up the west. By 1950, however, immigrants were wanted as farm labourers to replace the young generation of farmers' sons who despite their lack of urban skills saw the urban work world as more attractive. It is not surprising, of course, that only a very small number of immigrants became farm owners. Throughout the 1950's great changes were taking place in farming as an occupation, changes which were to bring about a great reduction in the number of farms and the size of the farm labour force. Farms were larger and required larger investments of capital as well as new skills in the operating of modern farm equipment. The post-war immigrant did not fit these requirements.[32]

Some indication of the size of the migrating work force can be seen from the fact that between 1950 and 1959, 850,000 immigrants came into the labour force, and roughly 250,000 labour force members emigrated, making a net gain of 600,000 out of a total migration of 1.1 million workers.[33] The total civilian labour force in 1950 was 5.2 million, in 1955 5.7 million, and in 1960 6.4 million. Thus within this 10-year period approximately one-fifth to one-sixth of Canadian workers were involved in this occupational redistribution through immigration and emigration. Close to one-half of the increase in all the Canadian labour force during these 10 years came from net migration.[34]

Immigration and emigration take place within a structure of class which here we are regarding in terms of occupational levels. In turn, migrations affect the patterns of upward mobility within this structure, and at the same time the opportunities for upward mobility have their effect on migrations. Upward social mobility has been a characteristic of all industrial societies in that industrialization brings with it a great proliferation of occupations requiring great variations of skill and specialization. There appears a great new range of middle and professional occupations which must be filled from the previously unskilled classes. Because families at the middle occupational levels are too small to supply all the recruits for these constantly increasing middle level occupations, industrialization has meant, as well as a continual upgrading of the labour force, a general historical trend of upward social mobility. These historical facts stand in sharp contradiction to the Marxian prediction that industrialization would lead to a polarization of the labour force with increasing misery for the proletariat and increasing wealth and comfort for the bourgeoisie.

In societies with large scale immigration and emigration this process of upgrading may take a different form. If the lower level manual occupations are over-represented in the immigrant labour force relative to the existing labour force, and as long as middle level occupations are increasing as a proportion of total occupations, the immigrants act as a force to replace the existing working population as the latter move into the higher status skilled and professional jobs. This proposition assumes of course that the labour force in the receiving country has the facilities, such as formal educational institutions and various kinds of training within industry, to upgrade itself. On the other hand, if the newly emerged middle level occupations become over-represented in the immigrant labour force compared to the native labour force, immigration then has an adverse effect on, and in some respects is actually the result of, the mobility opportunities of the native-born. If the native labour force has not been upgraded to meet the new industrial growth, the natives may not be adequately motivated towards upward mobility, perhaps owing to the generally low evaluation of the latter in the society's culture. The evidence to be presented later gives some indication that Canada is not a mobility oriented society and has had to rely heavily on skilled and professional immigration to upgrade its labour force in periods of industrial growth.

Emigration is also an important variable in this upgrading process. If those who leave are from middle and higher level occupations they increase the opportunities for those who stay behind. When emigration of middle and higher level occupational groups is considerable it can strain the educational resources of the society which is losing its trained people. Underdeveloped countries are placed in this position when advanced societies accept from them only skilled immigrants. If the lower level occupations are over-represented among working emigrants the latter may be leaving because new opportunities are not appearing for them or their families. They may be drawn from a society which is not mobility oriented to one which is. If a society relies heavily on external recruitment for upgrading its labour force instead of bringing about changes in its educational system it can expect to lose those who have mobility aspirations. The perceptions of a society's minority groups may also affect the assessment of mobility opportunities. Members of some of these groups may feel that they have fewer opportunities than does the majority group, and may leave for other countries where they think opportunities are better. When minority groups from Canada establish communities in the United States, they provide an additional attraction, apart from economic considerations, for those in Canada of the same ethnic origin or religion.

There is then a set of interrelated variables operating on class structure during periods of industrial expansion – immigration, emigration, and mobility patterns in both the receiving and the losing societies. We shall now look at some occupational data to see how Canada has relied on external sources to upgrade its labour force. One illustration of this reliance has been the way in which Canada has recruited its medical profession during the 1950's. Writing in 1962, Dr. J. S. Thompson, Dean of the Medical Faculty at the University of Alberta, said that 35 per cent of doctors registering to practise in Canada at that time were graduates of foreign medical schools. "We thus have an anomalous situation wherein a rich country like Canada must today depend for one-third of her practitioners upon foreign countries. Tomorrow her needs will be greater, and we have as yet no plans to meet these prospective needs from Canadian sources alone."[35] The provision of adequate educational facilities is crucial for the process of social mobility and upgrading. Without them a society will never realize its potential for industrial growth.

Professions and Skills

Upgrading of the labour force with industrialization can be measured by the increase in the number of jobs requiring skills and specialized training. If we take a given list of professional and skilled occupations at two points in time and determine the increased numbers in these occupations in the intervening period, we shall have some indication of how the labour force has been upgraded. If there were no immigration or emigration the increment to skilled and professional occupations between the two periods would represent the upward mobility of the native labour force. Our task is to try to estimate the extent to which the increment to professional and skilled occupations which

came with the industrialization of the 1950's provided upward mobility for the native labour force. In addition, we shall try to discover the extent to which the increase was supplied by external recruitment.

A point of departure is the study of specialized manpower made by the federal Department of Labour for the Royal Commission on Canada's Economic Prospects.[36] The occupational categories of professional and skilled used in this study were more refined than the general industrial categories used in Corbett's study which was mentioned earlier. For example, the skilled occupations in the Department of Labour study included the more technical manual occupations as well as the inspectional and supervisory occupations within all industries. This study estimated that in 1956 there were 357,000 professional and 940,000 skilled workers in Canada, 6.2 per cent and 16.3 per cent respectively, or, when taken together, 22.5 per cent of the Canadian labour force.[37] In the period 1951 to 1955, 30.3 per cent of immigrant workers were in these specialized occupations,[38] a fact which indicates that the immigrant labour force was richer in skills than was apparent by consideration of such broad categories as 'mechanical and manufacturing', and that these specialized occupations were over-represented in the immigrant labour force. Viewed in another way, about one-tenth of all those working in professional and skilled occupations in 1956 were immigrants who had entered during the previous 5 years.

The number of professional immigrants during the period 1950 to 1960 was about 85,000, and from 1946 to 1960 it was almost 92,000.[39] The latter number amounted to about one-quarter of the number of all professional workers in the Canadian labour force in 1956. These highly qualified immigrants made a sizable contribution to the increment of professional workers required for the industrial growth of the 1950's. From the census it can be estimated that between 1951 and 1961 the increment of professional workers was 243,000. If we assigned all 85,000 professional immigrants to this increment they would have supplied about 35 per cent of it.[40] For the selected group of professional occupations used in the Department of Labour study referred to above the increment between 1951 and 1961 was 185,000. If all 85,000 professional immigrants were assigned to this increment of selected professional occupations they would account for a little under one-half of it (46 per cent). This latter estimate is probably too high because the category of professional occupations of immigrants may be wider than that used by the Department of Labour. Moreover, some proportion of the 85,000 professional immigrants between 1951 and 1961 left the country before 1961. If as many as 20 per cent of them left[41] the contribution of immigration to the increment of professional workers would have been 32 or 36 per cent rather than 35 or 46 per cent as estimated above.

Apart from immigration the main sources of supply for professional workers are the various training facilities, particularly universities. Not only must they supply replacements for withdrawals from the labour force because of deaths, retirements, and emigration, but also, if they are properly geared to industrial growth, they must supply the increment. The estimated number of graduates from Canadian universities during the 1950's was 166,000.[42] Many of these university graduates were women who would eventually withdraw from the labour force to get married; some emigrated without entering the labour force; and many did not enter professional jobs. To offset these losses in supply there are those who take professional training outside the universities (nurses and public school teachers, for example). Unfortunately we do not know the numbers involved to establish accurately the total supply of professionals available for the labour force, but we can take the number of university graduates as a rough total for the supply from Canadian sources. (During the 1950's the total number of immigrant professionals was equal to about one-half of the total supply from Canadian universities.) We know that around 40,000 professionals, many of whom would be from the supply of university graduates, emigrated to the United States during the decade. In a mobility oriented society, with fully available education, withdrawals of professional workers through emigration would leave more room at the top for those who remained behind.

It is doubtful, however, that the post-war economic and social development in Canada provided as much mobility opportunity for the native-born as it might have done because the institutions of higher learning were not sufficiently democratized, nor did they have the physical capacity to train the number of specialized workers required. There is probably, too, the cultural factor of a relatively low evaluation of education. Canadians have not made demands through the political system for extensive educational reform, or if they have the demands have not been effective. Nor have Canadians made adequate use of the facilities which already exist. A society in which trained people are produced at a sufficient rate only to replace those who die or retire is static. A dynamic society, on the other hand, anticipating industrial growth will invest heavily in its training facilities and make them open to all in a general search for talent.

More than one-half (53 per cent) of the immigrant professionals who came between the end of the war and 1960 were from Great Britain,[43] and many of these no doubt had been trained subsequent to the educational reforms of 1944 which made university training less of a class privilege than it has been in Canada. Perhaps one of the reasons that these professionals moved to Canada is because in Britain they found that, even though they were highly trained, they experienced difficulty in being accepted socially at the class level appropriate to their new professional status. They may have emigrated to Canada, where their social origins may not be so apparent, to achieve more upward mobility. The United States was the second largest supplier (15.5 per cent) of professional workers.

Complaints are often heard in Canada that trained people are lost to the United States, but these complaints overlook the fact that Canada too through its immigration policy raids other countries for trained people. In fact the international raiding for talent would suggest that industrial and scientific development throughout the world has proceeded at such a pace that the shortage of professionals is world-wide. Unlike the United States and the United Kingdom, Canada had not by the 1960's moved towards the creation of fully democratized education, either in its formal educational systems or through upgrading schemes in industry. Hence, Canadians did not have the same opportunities for upward mobility, either at home or elsewhere, as did the populations of these other countries.

Canadian emigrant professionals no doubt see the United States as providing greater opportunities for later periods in their professional careers. Why they should come to this conclusion can probably be explained by an analysis of selection and promotion procedures within industry and government, the bureaucracies of which constitute the major labour markets for the highly trained. Many are exposed to American career systems while doing advanced training. For most years of the 1950's there were 5,000 to 6,000 Canadians taking advanced training in the United States,[44] a further indication of Canada's reliance on other countries. Other important factors include the role of the United States subsidiary corporation in the Canadian economy, and the greater ease of geographical mobility between Canada and the United States than between some parts of Canada. As some studies of migration and job opportunities show, the opportunity at the shorter distance will be the one taken up. For many Canadians this proposition would seem to apply even when a change of citizenship is involved.

What has been said of Canada's reliance on immigrant pro-

fessionals applies also to her reliance on immigrants with trade skills. The number of new workers in the labour force between 1951 and 1960 in the group of skilled occupations selected by the Department of Labour for their Royal Commission study can be estimated at 340,000 – that is the estimated number in 1960 less the known number in 1951. Of this class 201,000 entered Canada between 1950 and 1960.[45] Thus, by a conservative estimate, about 50 to 60 per cent of the new skilled jobs that came with the industrial development of the decade were filled by immigrants, and less than 50 per cent were taken by members of the existing labour force through training schemes in industry, upgrading of workers after experience on the job, or through apprenticeship or vocational training. We have not, of course, included the skilled jobs vacated by deaths, retirements, and emigration because they would not have been included in the increment of skilled jobs during the decade, although they would certainly have to be replaced from the overall supply.

Skilled workers have been emigrating at a much lower rate than professional workers. In the selected group of skilled occupations, 15,000 workers emigrated to the United States between 1950 and 1955.[46] If the same number left in the second half of the decade a crude estimate for the 10 year period would be 30,000. On this basis we might say that skilled workers formed a smaller part of the emigrant work force than did professional workers. Over the decade between 2 and 3 per cent of this class of worker emigrated.

The process which we are here seeking to analyze is the expansion of the more highly skilled occupations that comes with increasing industrialization and that affords opportunities for upward mobility. If there were no migration the 'native' labour force would be over all a more skilled one through upgrading and technical training, a process which has characterized all societies which have become industrialized. When the number in the age group entering the labour force from school exceeds the number in the age group retiring from work there is no shortage of persons to meet retirements and deaths as well as the increment of skilled jobs, providing the entering group has been properly trained or those already in the labour force are upgraded. In Canada in 1956 the school leaving age group 15 to 19 years exceeded the retiring age group 65 to 69 by almost 700,000.[47] The way in which these new entrants fit into the labour force depends on their skills. They may enter at lower levels of unskilled or semi-skilled and push up the more experienced in the skill hierarchy, or if they are already skilled they can fill the vacancies left by retirements and deaths and provide for the increment that comes with industrial expansion.

* * * *

NOTES
1. This brief account of Canadian population history relies mainly on four papers: Nathan Keyfitz, "The Growth of the Canadian Population," *Population Studies*, IV (June 1950); N. B. Ryder, "Components of Canadian Population Growth," *Population Index*, April 1954; A. H. LeNeveu and Y. Kasahara, "Demographic Trends in Canada, 1941-56," *C.J.E.P.S.*, XXIV, no. 1 (Feb. 1958); and Duncan M. McDougall, "Immigration into Canada 1851-1920,' *ibid.*, XXXVII, no. 2 (May 1961).
2. Ryder, "Canadian Population Growth," 73.
3. See H. C. Pentland, "The Development of a Capitalistic Labour Market in Canada," *C.J.E.P.S.*, XXV, no. 4 (Nov. 1959).
4. Cf. H. B. Brebner, *The North Atlantic Triangle* (New Haven, 1945), 221ff.
5. *Census of Canada, 1951*, vol. X, 17ff.
6. See McDougall, "Immigration into Canada," Table III; and Keyfitz, "The Growth of the Canadian Population."
7. LeNeveu and Kasahara, "Demographic Trends."
8. Canada, Senate, Special Committee on Manpower and Employment, *Proceedings* (Ottawa, 1961), no. 1, p. 10.
9. The data for this review of intercensal changes were supplied by

the Dept. of Citizenship and Immigration, Ottawa.

10. LeNeveu and Kasahara, "Demographic Trends."

11. This account of French-Canadian population is based mainly on J. Henripin, "From Acceptance of Nature to Control," *C.J.E.P.S.*, XIII, no. 1 (Feb. 1957).

12. *Ibid*, p. 15.

13. A statement attributed to the French demographer Sauvy in William Peterson, *Planned Migration: The Social Determinants of the Dutch-Canadian Movement* (Berkeley, 1955), 121. It is a slight overstatement. The true figure appears to be closer to two-thirds of the world population in 1950.

14. Ryder, "Canadian Population Growth."

15. E. Durkheim, *The Division of Labour in Society*, trans. G. Simpson (Glencoe, Ill., 1951).

16. D. Riesman, *The Lonely Crowd* (New Haven, 1950)

17. Quoted in D. G. Creighton, *Dominion of the North* (New York, 1944), 354.

18. Quoted in A.R.M. Lower, *Colony to Nation* (Toronto, 1957), 390.

19. E. Durkheim, *Suicide*, trans. J. A. Spaulding and G. Simpson (Glencoe, Ill., 1950).

20. *Canada Year Book, 1925* (D.B.S., Ottawa 1926), 108. The term foreign-born here means born outside Canada. For many Canadians those born in Great Britain are not 'foreigners.'

21. See S. M. Lipset and H. L. Zetterberg, "A Theory of Social Mobility," in International Sociological Association, *Transactions of the Third World Congress of Sociology*, vol. III (London, 1956), for a discussion of social mobility and political behaviour.

22. Canada, Dept. of Citizenship and Immigration, *Immigration, 1962* (Ottawa, 1963), Table 1A. See also "Immigration at Lowest since 1947," *Globe and Mail*, Jan. 26, 1962.

23. Canada, Dept. of Citizenship and Immigration, *Quarterly Immigration Bulletin, Dec. 1960.*

24. Committee on Manpower and Employment, *Proceedings*, no. 2, p. 56, and no. 4, pp. 204-5. Estimates will vary depending on which occupations are classed as professional. According to one Dept. of Labour estimate that takes a fairly wide definition of professional, during the eleven years 1950-60 inclusive the loss of professional workers was 42,000. See Canada, Dept. of Labour, *The Migration of Professional Workers into and out of Canada 1946-1960* (Ottawa, 1962).

25. Canada, Dept. of Labour, for Royal Commission on Canada's Economic Prospects, *Skilled and Professional Manpower in Canada, 1945-1965* (Ottawa, 1957), Table 21.

26. David C. Corbett, *Canada's Immigration Policy* (Toronto, 1957), 171.

27. *Ibid.*, 170-71.

28. *Quarterly Immigration Bulletin*, Dec. 1960, 2.

29. Canada, Dept. of Labour, *Employment Outlook for Professional Personnel in Scientific and Technical Fields, 1960-62*, bull. no. 8 (Ottawa, 1960), 16.

30. Canada, Dept. of Labour, *Engineering and Scientific Manpower Resources in Canada*, bull. no. 9 (Ottawa, 1961), 47.

31. See the brief of the Canadian Federation of Agriculture to the Committee on Manpower and Employment, *Proceedings*, no. 9; and Canada, Dept. of Labour, *Trends in the Agricultural Labour Force in Canada* (Ottawa, 1960).

32. Brief of the Canadian Federation of Agriculture.

33. Committee on Manpower and Employment, *Proceedings*, no. 1, p. 10.

34. *Ibid.*, p. 11

35. Quoted in David Spurgeon, "The Supply of Doctors," *Globe and Mail*, April 9, 1962.

36. *Skilled and Professional Manpower*, Table 7.

38. Computed from *ibid.*, Tables 20 and 21.

39. *The Migration of Professional Workers*, Table 1.

40. *Census of Canada, 1951*, vol. V, and *Census of Canada, 1961*, vol. 3. 1-3, Table 6. The figure of 85,000 professional immigrants was modified slightly so that it would conform to the census period. Four thousand were added for the first half of 1961 and 2,000 subtracted for the first half of 1951 because the census was taken in June in both years.

41. Twenty per cent seems a reasonable estimate for professional occupations. Approximately 383,000 immigrants of the decade 1951 to 1961 were 'lost' by 1961. Assuming 26,000 of them died then roughly 25 per cent of the 1,543,000 immigrants later became emigrants.

42. *The Migration of Professional Workers*, Table 18.

43. *Ibid.*, Table 3.

44. *Ibid.*, p. 26.

45. *Skilled and Professional Manpower*, Table 21. The increment of skilled workers between 1951 and 1960 was calculated by assuming the skilled occupations to be 17.6 per cent of a labour force of 6.4 million in 1960. Because of many changes in the titles of occupations it was not possible to check these estimates with the 1961 census. The number of skilled immigrants for the years 1956 to 1960 was taken from expected occupations of immigrants in *Immigration*, 1956, 1957, 1958, 1959, and 1960.

46. *Skilled and Professional Manpower*, Table 29. Fifteen hundred added for 1950.

47. *Census of Canada*, 1956, "Age Composition of the Population."

Section Two

Definitions of Public and Private Spheres

THE IGLOO

*The familiar
Western notion of enclosed
space is foreign to the Aivilik. Both
winter snow igloos and summer sealskin
tents are dome-shaped. Both lack vertical walls
and horizontal ceilings; no planes parallel each other
and none intersect at 90 degrees. There are no straight
lines, at least none of any length. Generally each igloo has
several rooms. To enter Amaslak's, an Iglulik one, you went
first through a vestibule, next past a storage room for dead
seals, and then through a 'hallway' off of which opened three
'rooms', each with a snow sleeping platform and a stone lamp burning seal
oil. Amaslak, his wife, two children and I had one room; to the left lived
his parents and their favourite grandchild; to the right, his sister, her husband and child. Visually and acoustically the igloo is 'open', a labyrinth
alive with the movements of crowded people. No flat static walls arrest the
ear or eye, but voices and laughter come from several directions and the
eye can glance through here, past there, catching glimpses of the activities
of nearly everyone. The same is true of the sealskin tent. Every sound outside can be heard within, and the women inside always seem to be turning
and stretching so they can peer out through holes in the tent.*

Reprinted from *Eskimo*, by Edmund S. Carpenter, Frederick Varley,
and Robert Flaherty, by permission of University of Toronto Press.

Definitions of Public and Private Spheres

This section introduces the central theme of this book; the distinction between public and private space, which is fundamentally a political distinction. As the preceding section made clear, social space is bounded by normative constraints, laws, modes of interaction, as well as by physical space and time factors. Central to the whole discussion are the dual concepts of access *and* control. *Access involves the principle of inclusion-exclusion and that implies boundaries. Control involves the principle of regulation and that implies limitations on freedom. The questions to be asked, then, are: ''Who has access and under what conditions?'' and, ''Where is the locus of control?'' The separation of the public from the private is not as clear as we sometimes like to think it is; there is a good deal of ambiguity. There are private spatial aspects to those areas of social life commonly thought of as public, and public aspects to those areas commonly thought of as private.*

When we describe public space, we refer to those areas of political interaction to which all members of a society have access. The prerequisite of public space is that people are free to move into it, not necessarily that they are free to do what they like when they are there. The fundamental political question relating to public space, therefore, is whether the rules governing activity within the public space area are such that people choose to accept limitations on some areas of freedom in order to use the facilities offered in the public area. Anybody may join a political party, but what he can do inside it is determined by rules governing interaction. Thus one of the important questions affecting public space is how freedom of access is used to ensure conformity when inside the space area. Although a territory is notionally 'free', individuals within the territory, much like a dog marking out his own area, may have created their own rules which restrict this freedom. Public parks, for example, may be open to anyone, but what people do inside is determined by codes governing the scatter of litter, physical indecency, keeping dogs on leads and so on. These rules may be the result of external control (the local authority prescribing that people should not undress in a park) or they may be the result of the attitudes of people who have marked out their own territorial rights within the park (the park attendant may have decided that certain types of activity are too inconvenient to tolerate).

Politically, one of the effects of this distinction is that what is formally public may in fact be 'private': or what Lyman and Scott, in the selection below, refer to as 'home territory'. Anybody may join a political party, but in practice those who are in it may so formulate the rules that no one outside would, barring a mental breakdown, want to get in anyway. The important political question is whether the rules are framed inside the public area or from outside it: if they are framed inside, then the central issue is under what conditions do people use a public space to create private territory. If the rules are externally produced, then the problem is whether a private group is dominating a public space or whether – in a sense akin to Rousseau's 'Public Will' – the rules were framed in order to prevent a private group taking over. Even under this last condition it is possible for the 'Guardians of the Public Will' to constitute a closed group who progressively impose a definition on the society (contemporary Russia is a good case of this).

The general political problem regarding territoriality, however, is that the distinction between 'public' and 'private' space may largely be in terms of formal codes but much less in terms of actual practice. From the point of view of those outside a private or public space, the distinction may be important (if a space is formally public then those outside may, from time to time, want to make use of it). From the point of view of those who regularly use a public or private area, the difference may be less important; to all intents and purposes the territory is theirs whatever others

may think of it.

In their analysis below, Lyman and Scott also refer to interactional territories and body territories. Interactional territories are much more loosely structured than public or private areas. They may be described either as aspects of structure (people interact because structures determine that they should), or as situational (people interact because they happen to be in the same place at the same time, whatever the structural factors). Obviously neither of those definitions can be entirely correct. Structures are not possible independent of physical constraints. The importance of situational factors in political analysis is that certain kinds of political behaviour – whatever the 'structural' inputs – could only take place because of the physical proximity of the people involved. This physical proximity does not have to be accidental (though it may frequently appear to be). People may come together for a specific purpose or may have been called together by other people for a particular event; the importance of interactional territories lies not so much in the formal purpose of the meeting but in what people do once they are there. Interactional territories are important because we all have regular and systematic forms of interaction and we also use casual interactional situations both as points of reference (it is useful to know that MPs have consulting days to use if the need arises) and as forms of instantaneous catharsis or even action. Politically, interactional territories are the most commonly used by the great majority of any country's population, in that few people have their own private political territories and only a few more use the public territories except as vehicles for ad-hoc interaction (such as voting, drawing welfare benefits or contacting their elected representatives).

Finally, body territories concern relations between people as physical presences; essentially, these refer to the visible characteristics that individuals bring with them into any interactional situation. While in wider sociological issues these must include many physical features, including various forms of stigma, politically the two most important issues are sex and race. Significantly the crucial problem is whether physical characteristics affect other forms of interaction and, if so, whether physiology and pigmentation act as the basis for creation of private territories or the narrowing down of the rights of some groups in public ones. If discrimination on the basis of sex and race is widespread we would expect the creation of private political territories by aggrieved groups which may not only cater to these groups but also be closed to members of the dominant groups.

None of these territories, as will be clear from the above outline, is clearly bounded: a public territory may be taken over by a private one in such a way as to make it difficult for the public to use it; body territories may define rights in a public territory and act as the basis for private territory; interactional territories may exist in public, private or body territories, and so on. In all cases, however, the problem of boundaries has two definitions: that of the people who inhabit a territory and that of those who are outside. If a territory is inhabited by people who appear to be a threat to outsiders, or who are holding territory coveted by others, then conflict over territorial rights would seem to be inevitable. This conflict may manifest itself in three ways: people who disapprove of the rules and codes governing a territory may deliberately break the rules in order to bring the rulemakers into disrepute; groups from outside may invade a territory in order to break it up or take it over; a territory may be designated as contaminated by other groups in an attempt to discredit it. Political examples of these courses of action are infinite. The recent veterans' demonstration in Washington, DC, (May 1971), which was designed to bring the administration to a halt, is an example both of rule-breaking and invasion; the banning of the IRA in Northern Ireland, the FLQ in Quebec, and the Black Power groups in Trinidad, are all attempts at discrediting private territories that were considered dangerous by using military and legal powers to define the areas as contaminated. Frequently, if territory is 'invaded', it is then declared contaminated – witness most socialist parties' difficulties with their youth groups. The conceptions of purity and pollution are of great use in itemizing the ways that groups respond to territorial encroachment. In the NDP, for example, conflicting views of pollution affect the definitions of policy debates and leadership contests: the left wing defines reformism as polluting because it seems to work against the purity and purpose of the party; the right wing sees the left as polluted by foreign and alien ideologies. In this case, accommodation is possible as long as one group is prepared to accept the dominance of the other while retaining its own freedom of action. But in many cases the polluters are resisted by various devices – by creating fresh social barriers against invaders (e.g. the Rhodesian escalation to Apartheid); by subtle use of in-group language (e.g. the terminology used by some Marxist groups); and by physical defense (e.g. the use of strong arm gangs to eject unwanted hecklers from political rallies).

One of the consequences of these strategies is that certain groups are always excluded from political public space. If the definition of 'politics' is such that public territory does not allow various groups to operate freely, and if private territorial activities are branded as contaminated, then groups who fail to get into a political arena may somehow have to carve out areas for themselves, knowing that whatever they do they may be branded as contaminated. These alternatives may involve glorification of their pariah state (the activities of the Rastafari sects in Jamaica and the Doukhobors in British Columbia are suggestive examples); modification of the symbols of exclusion so that they appear to conform while in fact not doing so (a characteristic of so-called 'front' organizations); or an abandonment of all political activity in favour of quietistic, personal 'salvation' (suggested by the organization and activities of some youth communes). Whether contaminated groups are allowed even these alternatives depends in large measure on the extent to which other groups in society see them as threats or as occupying valuable space.

---

1. Territoriality: A Neglected Sociological Dimension

Stanford M. Lyman/*University of Nevada*
Marvin B. Scott/*Sonoma State College*

In this perceptive essay, Lyman and Scott, two American sociologists, make use of the insights and concepts developed in ethology and social ecology to examine various modes of managing space as a fundamental human activity. Territory affords, to those whose claims to it are recognized, opportunities for the expression of their desired identities. When these claims are challenged, certain defensive responses ensue which may or may not be successful. The maintenance of territorial boundaries, then, is always problematical. There are, however, some persons or categories of persons whose claims to territory are never recognized; such spatially deprived persons respond in typically privatized ways.

The four types of territory distinguished here are not readily reducible to the public-private dichotomy. Rather, they are types of claim and modes of response that might be made in either sphere.

All living organisms observe some sense of territoriality,[1] that is, some sense – whether learned or instinctive to their species – in which control over space is deemed central for survival.[2] Although man's domination over space is potentially unlimited, in contemporary society it appears that men acknowledge increasingly fewer *free* territories for themselves.[3]

Free territory is carved out of space and affords opportunities for idiosyncracy and identity. Central to the manifestation of these opportunities are boundary creation and enclosure. This is so because activities that run counter to expected norms need seclusion or invisibility to permit unsanctioned performance, and because peculiar identities are sometimes impossible to realize in the absence of an appropriate setting.[4] Thus the opportunities for freedom of action – with respect to normatively discre-

Reprinted from *A Sociology of the Absurd*, by Stanford M. Lyman and Marvin B. Scott, by permission of Appleton-Century-Crofts, Educational Division, Meredith Corporation. ©Meredith Corporation 1970.

pant behavior and maintenance of specific identities – are intimately connected with the ability to attach boundaries to space and command access to or exclusion from territories.

In American society where territorial encroachment affects nearly all members of society, certain segments of the population are particularly deprived, namely, Negroes, women, youth, and inmates of various kinds. With these categories in mind, this paper re-introduces a neglected dimension of social analysis important to understanding deprived groups.

Our strategy is twofold: first, to bring together under a new set of organizing concepts the notions of types of territory, types of territorial encroachment and types of responses to encroachment; and second, to specify the reactions of spatially deprived groups.

The Types of Territories

We can distinguish four kinds of territories, namely, *public territories, home territories, interactional territories* and *body territories.*

Public territories

Public territories are those areas where the individual has freedom of access, but not necessarily of action, by virtue of his claim to citizenship.[5] These territories are officially open to all, but certain images and expectations of appropriate behavior and of the categories of individuals who are normally perceived as using these territories modify freedom. First, it is commonly expected that illegal activities and impermissible behavior will not take place in public places. Since public territories are vulnerable to violation in both respects, however, policemen are charged with the task of removing lawbreakers from the scene of their activities and restricting behavior in public places.[6]

Second, certain categories of persons are accorded only limited access to and restricted activity in public places. It is expected, for instance, that children will not be playing in public playgrounds after midnight; that lower class citizens will not live — although they might work – in areas of middle class residence; and that Negroes will not be found leisurely strolling on the sidewalks, though they might be found laying the sewer pipe under the streets of white neighborhoods.

Since the rights of such discrepant groups to use these territories as citizens sometimes contradicts the privileges accorded them as persons, such territories are not infrequently the testing grounds of challenges to authority. The wave of sit-ins, wade-ins, and demonstrations in racially segregated restaurants, public beaches, and schools constitute an outstanding recent example. Informal restrictions on access to public territories often violate unenforced or as yet untested rights of citizens. Since the informal delineation of some of these territories implies the absence of certain persons, their presence stands out. Policemen frequently become allies of locals in restricting citizenship rights when they remove unseemly persons from territories which they do not regularly habituate, or when they restrict certain categories of persons to specific areas.[7]

Public territories are thus ambiguous with respect to accorded freedoms. First, the official rights of access may be regularly violated by local custom. Second, status discrepancy may modify activity and entrance rights. For example, the ambiguity in the distinction between minors and adults is a source of confusion and concern in the regulation of temporal and access rights to those whose status is unclear. Finally, activities once forbidden in public may be declared permissible, thus enlarging the freedom of the territory; or activities once licit may be proscribed thus restricting it. Hence display of female breasts is now permitted in San Francisco night-clubs, but not on the streets or before children. Nude swimming enjoys police protection at certain designated beaches, but watching nude swimmers at these same beaches is forbidden to those who are attired.

Home territories

Home territories are areas where the regular participants have a relative freedom of behavior and a sense of intimacy and control over the area. Examples include makeshift club houses of children, hobo jungles, and homosexual bars. Home and public territories may be easily confused. In fact "the areas of public places and the areas of home territories are not always clearly differentiated in the social world and what may be defined and used as a public place by some may be defined and used as a home territory by others."[8] Thus, a home territory that also may be used as a public one is defined by its regular use by specific persons or categories of persons and by the particular 'territorial stakes' or 'identity pegs' that are found in such places. The style of dress and language among the patrons at a bar may immediately communicate to a homosexual that he has arrived in home territory, while a heterosexual passerby who pauses for a drink may be astonished or outraged when he is accosted for sexual favors from the stranger seated next to him. Large-scale clandestine brotherhoods indoctrinate their members in secret codes of dress and demeanor so that regardless of their later travels they can unobtrusively communicate their fraternal identity and ask for assistance from one another in otherwise public places. Home territories sometimes enjoy a proactive status, beyond the presence of their inhabitants, in the form of reserved chairs, drinking mugs, signs or memorabilia that serve to indicate special and reserved distinctions.

Home territories may be established by 'sponsorship' or 'colonization.' An example of the former is found in the merchant emigrants from China who established caravansaries in certain quarters of Occidental cities which served as public trading establishments but also as living quarters, employment agencies, meeting places, and courts for their *Landsmänner*.[9]

Colonization occurs when a person or group lays claim to a formally free territory by virtue of discovery, regular usage, or peculiar relationship. Thus certain restaurants become home territories to those who are impressed with their first meal there; to those who eat there on specific occasions, such as luncheons, birthdays, or after sporting events; and to those who are intimate with the waitress.

Loss of home status may be occasioned by the death or resignation of a sponsor, by violation of the previously established usages, by rejection, or by conquest. Erstwhile 'regulars' at a bar may discover they are no longer warmly greeted nor eligible for a free drink when the proprietor dies or when their patronage becomes irregular. Homosexuals may desert a 'queer bar' when it becomes a place which heterosexuals frequent to observe deviant behavior.

It is precisely because of their officially open condition that public areas are vulnerable to conversion into home territories. The rules of openness are sufficiently broad and ambiguous so that restrictions on time, place, and manner are difficult to promulgate and nearly impossible to enforce. Armed with a piece of chalk children can change the public sidewalk into a gameboard blocking pedestrian traffic. Despite building codes and parental admonitions youngsters convert abandoned buildings or newly begun sites into forts, clubs, and hideaways.[10]

But children are not the only colonizers on the public lands. Beggars and hawkers will stake out a 'territory' on the sidewalks or among the blocks and occupy it sometimes to the exclusion of all others similarly employed. The idle and unemployed will loiter on certain streetcorners, monopolizing the space, and frightening off certain respectable types with their loud, boisterous, or obscene language, cruel jests, and suggestive leers. Members of racial and ethnic groups colonize a portion of the city and adorn it with their peculiar institutions, language, and rules of conduct.[11] Ethnic enclaves, like certain notorious homosexual bars and prisons on open-house day, are often 'on display' to non-ethnics who thus grant legitimacy to the colony's claim for territorial identity.

Among the most interesting examples of colonizing on the public lands are those attempts by youths to stake out streets as home territories open only to members of their own clique and defended against invasion by rival groups. Subject always to official harassment by police and interference by other adults who claim the streets as public territories, youths resolve the dilemma by redefining adults as non-persons whose seemingly violative presence on the youth's 'turf' does not challenge the latter's proprietorship. Streets are most vulnerable to colonizing in this manner and indeed, as the early studies of the Chicago sociologists illustrated so well, streets and knots of juxtaposed streets become unofficial home areas to all those groups who require relatively secluded yet open space in which to pursue their interests or maintain their identities.[12]

Interactional territories

Interactional territories refer to any area where a social gathering may occur. Surrounding any interaction is an invisible boundary, a kind of social membrane.[13] A party is an interactional territory, as are the several knots of people who form clusters at parties. Every interactional territory implicitly makes a claim of boundary maintenance for the duration of the interaction. Thus access and egress are governed by rules understood, though not officially promulgated, by the members.

Interactional territories are characteristically mobile and fragile. Participants in a conversation may remain in one place, stroll along, or move periodically or erratically. They may interrupt the interaction only to resume it at a later time without permanently breaking the boundary or disintegrating the group. Even where 'settings' are required for the interaction, mobility need not be dysfunctional if the items appropriate to the setting are movable. Thus chemists may not be able to complete a discussion without the assistance of a laboratory, but chess players may assemble or disassemble the game quite readily and in the most cramped quarters. Similarly, so long as Negroes were chattel slaves, slaveholders might move them anywhere where their services or appearance were needed.

The fragility of interactional territories is constantly being tested by parvenus and newcomers. The latter, even when they possess credentials entitling them to entrance into the interactional circle, break down ongoing interaction and threaten it by requiring all to start over again, end it instead and begin a new subject of common interest, or disintegrate.[14] Parvenus are a greater threat since their presence breaks the boundaries of the interaction and challenges the exclusiveness of the group. They may be repulsed, or accepted fully, though the latter is less likely than the granting of a 'temporary visa,' i.e., rights to interact for the instant occasion with no promise of equal rights in the future.

Body territories

Finally, there are body territories, which include the space encompassed by the human body and the anatomical space of the body. The latter is, at least theoretically, the most private and inviolate of territories belonging to an individual. The rights to view and touch the body are of a sacred nature, subject to a great restriction. For instance, a person's rights to his own body space are restricted where norms govern masturbation, or the appearance and decoration of skin. Moreover, rights of others to touch one's body are everywhere regulated, though perhaps modern societies impose greater restrictions than others.[15]

Body territory is also convertible into home territory. The most common method is marriage in a monogamous society in which sexual access to the female is deemed the exclusive right of the husband so long as he exercises propriety with respect to his status. Ownership, however, is not necessarily or always coterminous with possession, so that sexual rivalry might continue illegitimately after a marital choice has been made and erupt in trespass on to the husband's sexual property.[16] Under situations where women are scarce, such as nineteenth-century overseas Chinese communities in the United States, sexual property was institutionalized through organized prostitution, and the few Chinese wives among the homeless men were carefully secluded.[17]

Body space is, however, subject to creative innovation, idiosyncrasy, and destruction. First, the body may be marked or marred by scars, cuts, burns, and tattoos. In addition, certain of its parts may be inhibited or removed without its complete loss of function. These markings have a meaning beyond the purely anatomical. They are among the indicators of status or stigma. They can be signs of bravado as was the dueling scar among German students, or of criminality as is a similar scar on Italians and Negroes in America. Loss of an eye may prevent one's entrance into dental school, but at least one clothing manufacturer regards one-eyed men as status symbols for starched shirts. Tattoos may memorialize one's mother or sweetheart as well as indicate one's seafaring occupation.

The human organism exercises extraterritorial rights over both internal and external space. In the latter instance the space immediately surrounding a person is also inviolate.[18] Thus conversations among friends are ecologically distinguishable from those between acquaintances or strangers. A person who persists in violating the extraterritorial space of another of the same sex may be accused of tactlessness and suspected of homosexuality, while uninvited intersex invasion may indicate unwarranted familiarity.[19] Moreover, eye contact and visual persistence can be a measure of external space. Thus two strangers may look one another over at the proper distance but as they

near one another propriety requires that they treat one another as non-persons unless a direct contact is going to be made.[20]

Control over 'inner space' is the quintessence of individuality and freedom. Violations of 'inner space' are carried out by domination, ranging in intensity from perception of more than is voluntarily revealed to persuasion and ultimately hypnosis.[21] Demonstration of idiosyncrasy with respect to 'inner space' is exemplified by the modifications possible in the presentation of self through the uses of the several stimulants and depressants.

Territorial Encroachment

We can distinguish three forms of territorial encroachment: violation, invasion, and contamination.

Violation of a territory is unwarranted use of it. Violators are those who have repulsed or circumvented those who would deny them access. Violators are also by virtue of their acts claimants in some sense to the territory they have violated. Their claim, however, may vary in scope, intensity, and objective. Children may violate the graves of the dead by digging 'for treasure' in the cemetery, but unlike ghouls, they are not seeking to remove the bodies for illicit purposes. Some territories may be violated, however, merely by unwarranted entrance into them. Among these are all those territories commonly restricted to categorical groups such as toilets, harems, nunneries, and public baths – areas commonly restricted according to sex. Other territories may not be necessarily violated by presence but only by innovative or prohibited use. Thus some parents regard family-wide nudity as permissible but hold that sexual interest or intercourse among any but the married pair is forbidden. Interactional territories are violated when one or more of the legitimate interactants behaves out of character.[22]

Invasion of a territory occurs when those not entitled to entrance or use nevertheless cross the boundaries and interrupt, halt, take over, or change the social meaning of the territory. Such invasions, then, may be temporary or enduring.

Contamination of a territory requires that it be rendered impure with respect to its definition and usage. Cholera may require that a portion of the city be quarantined. In a racial caste society the sidewalks may be contaminated by low caste persons walking upon them. Home territories may be contaminated by pollution or destruction of the 'home symbols'. Orthodox Jews may destroy their dinnerware when an unwary maid has accidentally mixed the milk and meat dishes. Heterosexuals who regularly congregate at a bar sometimes discontinue their patronage when known homosexuals begin frequenting the bar. (This example illustrates a continuum in the process of territorial encroachment from invasion to contamination.) Interactional territories may be contaminated by sudden odors, especially if they emanate from one of the interactants, or by indiscreet language, e.g., obscenity, among those for whom identification with such language constitutes a loss of face or a reduction in status.[23]

Contamination of bodily territories occurs whenever the immediate space of or around the body is polluted. The removal by bathing of material involuntarily attached to the skin constitutes a ritualized purification rite of considerable importance in industrial societies.[24] However, body space may be contaminated in many ways, by smell, look, touch, and by proximity to contaminated persons or things. The sensitivity with respect to touch illustrates the complex nature of this contamination and also its peculiarly social character. The rules regarding touch are highly developed in American society and are clear indicators of social distance between individuals and groups.[25] Typically older people can touch younger ones, but suspicions of sexual immorality modify such contacts. Women who are friends or relatives may greet one another with a light kiss (commonly called a 'peck') on the cheek, but not on the lips. Men who are long absent may be greeted by male friends and relatives with a hearty embrace and touching of the cheeks, but the embrace must not be overlong or tender. Indeed, 'rough-housing,' mock-fighting, and pseudo-hostility are commonly employed in masculine affective relationships. Touch which would otherwise be contaminating is exempt from such designation when it takes place in situations of intense social action, e.g., on a dance floor, or in situations when the actors are not privileged to interact, e.g., crowded buses. At other times bodies contaminated by impermissible contacts are restored to their pure state by apologies.

Body space may be 'contaminated' by a kind of negative charismatic contact whereby objects which, though neutral in themselves, carry contaminating effect when transferred directly to the body. Thus a comb or toothbrush may not be lent or borrowed in certain circles since to use someone else's tools of personal hygiene is to contaminate oneself. Typically when clothing, especially clothing that will directly touch the skin, is lent, it is proper for the lender to assure the borrower that the apparel is clean, and that it has not been worn by anyone since its last cleaning.[26] A more striking example involves the rule of some shops forbidding Negroes from trying on clothes – their skin being regarded as a source of pollution. Similarly, drinking from the same glass as another is discouraged as a matter of hygiene among the middle class and as a source of pollution if it occurs among persons of different races or castes.

Reaction to Encroachment

We have already suggested that something of a reciprocal relation exists between the territorial types. For example, a public swimming pool – while officially open to all persons – might be conceived by certain regular users as an exclusive area. Strangers seeking access by virtue of their diffuse civic rights might be challenged by those whose sense of peculiar propriety is thus violated. Such a confrontation (sometimes called 'when push meets shove') could result in retreat on the part of the party seeking admittance, flight on the part of the contending parties to expand the area of legitimate access on the one hand, and withhold entirely or restrict the meaning of entry on the other.

Of course, the occupants of a territory may extend its use to others whose presence is not regarded as a threat. The most common situation is that in which common usage will not destroy or alter the value of the territory.[27] When public territories have been colonized by users who do not fully monopolize the space, who embroider it by their presence or whose occupancy still allows for other public and colonizing usages, the colonists will not be seriously opposed. Delinquent gangs who often define the streets of a neighborhood as a home territory do not usually regard the presence of local adults and children as an encroachment on their own occupancy. Unwarranted intrusion on interactional territories may be countenanced if the unwelcome guest indicates his willingness to be present on this occasion alone with no future rights of re-entry, or to listen only and not to interrupt the proceedings. Bodies usually invulnerable to feel and probe by strangers may be violated if the act is defined as physically safe, socially irrelevant, or emotionally neutral. Thus female nurses may massage their male patients with mutual impunity, and striptease dancers may perform unclothed upon a raised stage out of reach of the audience.[28] However, all such contacts will tend to be defined as territorial encroachment when the claimants threaten obliteration, monopoly, or fundamental alteration of a territory. Under these conditions, the holders of territory are likely to react to unwelcomed claimants in terms of *turf defense, insulation,* or *linguistic collusion.*

Turf defense

Turf defense is a response necessitated when the intruder cannot be tolerated. The animal world provides a multitude of examples which are instructive with respect to the human situation.[29] Here we may be content, however, to confine ourselves to the human scene. When Chinese merchants sought 'colonizing' rights among the urban merchants of San Francisco, they were welcomed and honored. A few years later, however, the appearance of Chinese miners in the white Americans' cherished gold fields called forth violent altercations and forced removals.[30] In contemporary American cities delinquent gangs arm themselves with rocks, knives, tire irons, and zip guns to repel invaders from other streets.[31] Among the 'primitive' Kagoro the choice of weapons is escalated in accordance with the social distance of the combatants; poison spears and stratagems are employed exclusively against hostile strangers and invaders.[32]

Turf defense is an ultimate response, however. Other more subtle repulsions or restrictions are available to proprietors wishing to maintain territorial control.

Insulation

Insulation is the placement of some sort of barrier between the occupants of a territory and potential invaders. The narrow streets, steep staircases, and regularized use of Cantonese dialects in Chinatowns serve notice on tourists that they may look over the external trappings of Chinese life in the Occidental city but not easily penetrate its inner workings. Distinct uniforms distinguishing status, rights, and prerogatives serve to protect military officers from the importunities of enlisted men, professors from students, and doctors from patients.[33] Bodily insulation characteristically takes the form of civil inattention and may be occasioned by a subordinate's inability to repel invasion directly. Another common form of insulation involves use of body and facial idiom to indicate impenetrability. It may be affected by the use of sunglasses,[34] or attained accidentally, by dint of culturally distinct perceptions of facial gestures, as, for example, often happens to orientals in Western settings.[35] It can also be attained by conscious efforts in the management and control of the mouth, nostrils, and especially the eyes.[36]

Linguistic collusion

Linguistic collusion involves a complex set of processes by which the territorial integrity of the group is reaffirmed and the intruder is labeled as an outsider. For example, the defending interactants may engage one another in conversation and gestures designed to so confuse the invader that he responds in a manner automatically labeling him eligible for either exclusion from the group or shameful status diminution. In one typical strategy the defending interactants will speak to one another in a language unfamiliar to the invader. Ethnic enclaves provide numerous examples. Jewish and Chinese storekeepers will speak Yiddish and Cantonese respectively to their clerks when discussing prices, bargaining rights, and product quality in the presence of alien customers. Negroes may engage one another in a game of 'the dozens' in the presence of intruding whites, causing the latter considerable consternation and mystification.[37] And teenagers develop a peer group argot (frequently borrowed from Negro and jazz musician usages) which sets them apart from both children and adults, and which, incidentally, is most frequently cited as proof for the claim that a distinctive youth culture does exist in the United States.

In another recognizable strategy, the participants continue to engage in the same behavior but in a more exaggerated and 'staged' manner. Mood and tone of the voice are sometimes regulated to achieve this effect. Thus persons engaged in conversation may intensify their tone and include more intra-group gestures when an outsider enters the area. Professors may escalate the use of jargon and 'academese' in conversations in the presence of uninvited students or other 'inferiors'. Homosexuals engaged in flirtations in a 'gay' bar may exaggerate their femininity when heterosexuals enter the establishment. Such staged displays call attention to the exclusive culture of the interactants and suggest to the outsider that he is bereft of the cards of identity necessary to participate.

Reaction to the Absence of Free Space

There are some segments of society that are systematically denied free territories. One outstanding example is that of lower-class urban Negro youth. Their homes are small, cramped, and cluttered and also serve as specialized areas of action for adults; their meeting places are constantly under surveillance by the agents of law enforcement and social workers; and, when in clusters on the street they are often stopped for questioning and booked 'on suspicion' by the seemingly ever-present police.[38]

What is the condition of Negro youth in particular appears to be an exaggerated instance of the trend with respect to denial of freedom among youth in general. Thus it has been suggested that youth are adrift somewhere between humanism and fatalism, i.e., between situations in which they feel they have control over their destinies and those in which such control is in the hands of forces outside youth's individual direction and influence.[39] In such a situation one response is to seek to maximize the area of freedom, the situations in which one can exercise liberty and license, the times one can be cause rather than effect. Among lower-class youth the carving of home territories out of the space provided as public ones is common and has already been noted. Note also, however, the frequency with which youth-created home territories are subject to invasion, violation, and contamination and the relative vulnerability of youth home territories to such encroachments.

Exercising freedom over body territory provides a more fruitful approach to those for whom public territories are denied and home territories difficult or impossible to maintain. The body and its attendant inner and external space have an aura of ownership and control about them that is impressed upon the incumbent. The hypothesis we wish to suggest here is that as other forms of free territory are perceived to be foreclosed by certain segments of the society, these segments, or at least those elements of the segments not constrained by other compelling forces, will utilize more frequently and intensively the area of body space as a free territory. Three forms of such utilization are prominent: *manipulation, adornment,* and *penetration.*

Manipulation rests upon the fact that the body is adjustable in a greater number of ways than are positively sanctioned and that by modifying the appearance of the self one can establish identity, and flaunt convention with both ease and relative impunity. Thus children, separated from one another for being naughty and enjoined from conversation, may sit and 'make faces' at one another, conforming to the letter of their punishment but violating its principle. Teenagers, denied approval for the very sexual activity for which they are biologically prepared and also enclosed more and more from private usage of public territories for such purposes, have developed dance forms which involve little or no body contact but are nevertheless suggestive of the most intimate and forbidden forms of erotic interaction. Further, male youth – enjoined from verbal scatalogical forms by customs and by rules of propriety – have developed a gesture language by which they can communicate the desired obscenity without uttering it.

Adornment of the body is another response.[40] By covering, uncovering, marking, and disfiguring the body individuals can at least partly overcome whatever loss of freedom they suffer from other encroachments. Both the French 'bohemians' of the nineteenth century and the disaffected American Negro youths of the twentieth have exhibited themselves as 'dandies,'[41] while the ascetic Doukhobors of British Columbia disrobe entirely and in public when challenged by authority.[42] Body space may also be attended by filling in the apertures in nose, mouth and ears by rings, bones, and other emblematic artifacts; by marking upon the skin with inks and tattoos; and by disfigurements, scars, and severance of non-vital members. An alternative mode of adornment, that appears to be directed definitely against elements of the core culture, is the refusal to use instruments of personal hygiene. We have already noted how these intruments acquire a peculiar aspect of the personal charisma of the user so that people do not customarily borrow the comb, toothbrush, and razor of another unless the contamination that occurs thereby is neutralized. Here, however, adornment occurs by simply *not* washing, combing, shaving, cutting the hair, etc. Like public nudity this form of assertiveness and reaction to oppression has the advantage of inhibiting a like response among those who are offended by the appearance created thereby, but, unlike stripping in public, the added advantage of being legal.

Penetration refers to the exploitation and modification of inner space in the search for free territory. One might hypothesize that the greater the sense of unfreedom, the greater the exercise of body liberty so that penetration is an escalated aspect of manipulation and adornment. There is, as it were, a series of increasing gradations of body space. The ultimate effort is to gain freedom by changing one's internal environment. The simplest form of this is cultivating a vicarious sense of being away, of transporting the self out of its existential environment by musing, daydreaming, or relapsing into a reverie.[43] However, voluntary reorganization of the inner environment can be assisted by alcohol and drugs. Contemporary college youth sometimes partake of hallucinogenic and psychedelic drugs in order to make an inner migration (or 'take a trip' as the popular idiom has it).

Conclusion

The concept of territoriality offers a fruitful approach for the analysis of freedom and situated action. Although the early school of ecology in American sociology provided a possible avenue for this kind of exploration, its practitioners appear to have eschewed the interactionist and phenomenological aspects of the subject in favor of the economic and the biotic. Nevertheless, much of their work needs to be examined afresh for the clues it provides for understanding the nature and function of space and the organization of territories. Similarly the work done by the students of non-human animal association provides clues to concept formation and suggestions for research. Here we may mention several potentially fruitful areas. The first involves cross-cultural studies of territoriality. Such studies would attempt to describe in greater specificity the constituent features of types of territoriality, the ways in which they vary, and their interrelationships. Using a cross-cultural perspective would also serve to specify generic forms of reactions to territorial encroachment and to establish how certain contexts predispose one type of response rather than another. A second area of research would focus on a variety of deviant behaviors (e.g., crime, juvenile delinquency, drug addiction, with the purpose of understanding the part the territorial variable plays in the etiology of such behaviors. Finally, we may suggest that micro-sociological studies of territoriality – which are perhaps more amendable to rigorous research design – may be extrapolated to an analysis of macro-sociological inquiries, especially in the realm of international affairs.

NOTES

1. The concept of territoriality was introduced into sociological analysis in the twenties under the label of 'the ecological school.' For an early statement see Robert E. Park, Ernest W. Burgess and R. D. McKenzie, *The City*, Chicago: University of Chicago Press, 1925. For a summary and bibliography of the school see Milla Aissa Alihan, *Social Ecology*, N.Y.: Columbia University Press, 1938. An updated version of this school is found in James A. Quinn, *Human Ecology*, N.Y.: Prentice-Hall, 1950, and Amos H. Hawley, *Human Ecology, A Theory of Community Structures*, N.Y.: The Ronald Press, 1950.

Originating in animal studies, 'territoriality' still looms large as an organizing concept in ethology. For a summary statement see C. R. Carpenter, "Territoriality: A Review of Concepts and Problems," in A. Roe and G. Simpson, editors, *Behaviour and Evolution*, New Haven: Yale University Press, 1958, pp. 224-50.

For a challenging argument that sociological investigation can fruitfully employ the techniques of comparative ethology – especially to such subjects as territoriality – see Lionel Tiger and Robin Fox, "The Zoological Perspective in Social Science," *Man*, I, i, (March, 1966), esp. p. 80.

Only very recently have sociologists revived ecological thinking to include a truly *interactional* dimension. The outstanding contributor is, of course, Edward T. Hall. See his *The Silent Language*, Garden City, N.Y.: Doubleday and Co., 1959, and *The Hidden Dimension*, Garden City, N.Y.: Doubleday and Co., 1966. For a masterful application of the concept of territoriality in interactional terms see Erving Goffman, *Asylums*, Garden City, N.Y.: Doubleday and Co., Anchor Books, 1961, pp. 227-248. In a slightly different vein see the interesting efforts of Robert Sommer, "Studies in Personal Space," *Sociometry*, 22 (September, 1959), pp. 247-60, and the writings of Roger Barker, especially his "Roles, Ecological Niches, and the Psychology of the Absent Organism," paper presented to the conference on the Propositional Structure of Role Theory, University of Missouri, 1962.

2. For the argument that human territoriality is a natural rather than a cultural phenomenon see Robert Ardrey, *The Territorial Imperative*, New York: Athenum, 1966, pp. 3-41.

3. The idea of 'free territory' is derived from Goffman, *loc. cit.*

4. See Erving Goffman, *The Presentation of Self in Everyday Life*, Garden City, N.Y.: Doubleday Anchor Books, 1959, p. 22.

5. The term 'citizenship' is used in a sense similar to that employed by T. H. Marshall in *Class, Citizenship and Social Development*, Garden City, N.Y.: Doubleday Anchor Books, 1965, esp. pp. 71-134.

6. See Harvey Sacks, "Methods in Use for the Production of a Social Order: A Method for Warrantably Informing Moral Character," Center for the Study of Law and Society, University of California, Berkeley, 1962; and Aaron Cicourel, *The Social Organization of Juvenile Justice*, New York: John Wiley, 1968.

7. See Jerome Skolnick, *Justice Without Trial*, New York: John Wiley, 1966, pp. 96-111 *et passim*; and Sacks, *op. cit.*

8. Sherri Cavan, "Interaction in Home Territories," *Berkeley Journal of Sociology*, 8 (1963) p. 18.

9. See Stanford M. Lyman, *The Structure of Chinese Society in Nineteenth Century America*, unpublished, Ph.D. dissertation, Berkeley: University of California, 1961.

10. Indeed, children are among the most regular and innovative creators of home territories from the space and material available to the public in general. Speaking of their peculiar tendency to violate the rules governing trespass, William Prosser has aptly observed, "Children, as is well known to anyone who has ever been a child, are by nature unreliable and irresponsible people, who are quite likely to do almost anything. In particular, they have a deplorable tendency to stray upon land which does not belong to them, and to meddle with what they find there." "Trespassing Children," *California Law Review* (August, 1959), p. 427.

11. Ethnic Groups in the process of assimilation sometimes discover to their astonishment that the isolated slum wherein they have traditionally and unwillingly dwelt is in fact a home territory possessed of cherished values and irreplaceable sentiments. A militant Negro thus writes: "For as my son, Chuck, wrote me after exposure to the Negro community of Washington: 'I suddenly realized that the Negro ghetto is not a ghetto. It is home.'" John Oliver Killens, *Black Man's Burden*, New York: Trident Press, 1965, p. 94.

12. Harvey W. Zorbaugh, *The Gold Coast and the Slum*, Chicago: University of Chicago Press, 1929. See also Jane Jacobs, *The Death and Life of Great American Cities*, N.Y.: Vintage Books, 1961, pp. 29-142.

13. See Erving Goffman, *Behavior in Public Places*, N.Y.: The Free Press of Glencoe, 1963, pp. 151-165 *et passim*.

14. An excellent illustration of the several facets of this process and attendant issues in social gatherings is found in David Riesman, *et al.*, "The Vanishing Host," *Human Organization* (Spring, 1960), pp. 17-27.

15. Talcott Parsons notes that "the very fact that affectionate bodily contact is almost completely taboo among men in American Society is probably indicative of [the limited nature of intra-sex friendship] since it strongly limits affective attachment." *The Social System*, Glencoe: Free Press, 1951, p. 189. For an empirical study and analysis of touching relations see Erving Goffman, "The Nature of Deference and Demeanor," *American Anthropologist*, 58 (June, 1956), pp. 473-502.

16. See Kingsley Davis, *Human Society*, New York: Macmillan, 1948, pp. 189-193.

17. Lyman, *op cit.*, pp. 97-111.

18. The perceptions of Simmel on this subject surpass all others and we are indebted to his work. Thus Simmel has noted: "In regard to the 'significant' [i.e., 'great'] man, there is an inner compulsion which tells one to keep at a distance and which does not disappear even in intimate relations with him. The only type for whom such distance does not exist is the individual who has no organ for perceiving distance.... The individual who fails to keep his distance from a great person does not esteem him highly, much less too highly (as might superficially appear to be the case); but, on the contrary, his importune behavior reveals lack of proper respect.... The same sort of circle which surrounds man – although it is value-accentuated in a very different sense – is filled out by his affairs and by his characteristics. To penetrate this circle by taking notice, constitutes a violation of personality. Just as material property is, so to speak, an extension of the ego, there is also an intellectual private property, whose violation effects a lesion of the ego in its very center." Georg Simmel, "Secrecy and Group Communication," reprinted in T. Parsons, *et al., Theories of Society*, New York: The Free Press of Glencoe, 1961, p. 320. For an updated statement of Simmel's point see Goffman, *Behavior in Public Places, op. cit.*

19. An interesting dilemma in this respect arises for the deaf and myopic. In attempting to appear as 'normals' they may overstep another's territorial space and thus call attention to the very stigma they wish to conceal. On the problems of those who are stigmatized see Goffman, *Stigma*, Englewood Cliffs, New Jersey: Prentice-Hall, 1963.

20. Goffman refers to this as 'civil inattention.' See *Behavior in Public Places, op. cit.*

21. Compare the remarks by Simmel, *op. cit.*, p. 321. "In the interest of interaction and social cohesion, the individual *must* know certain things about the other person. Nor does the other have the right to oppose this knowledge from a moral standpoint, by demanding the discretion of the first: he cannot claim the entirely undisturbed possession of his own being and consciousness, since this discretion might harm the interests of his society.... But even in subtler and less unambiguous forms, in fragmentary beginnings and unexpressed notions, all of human intercourse rests on the fact that everybody knows somewhat more about the other than the other voluntarily reveals to him; and those things he knows are frequently matters whose knowledge the other person (were he aware of it) would find undesirable." See also Goffman, *The Presentation Of Self in Everyday Life, op. cit.*, pp. 1-16.

22. The structural properties and parameters of interactional territories in unserious gatherings have been admirably presented by George Simmel. See his "The Sociology of Sociability," *American Journal of Sociology*, (November, 1949), pp. 254-261. Reprinted in

Parsons, *et al., Theories of Society, op. cit.,* pp. 157-163.

23. Here perhaps it is worth noting that language has a 'tactile' dimension, in the sense that to be 'touched' audially by certain terms is to be elevated or reduced in status. For Southern Negroes to be publicly addressed as 'Mr.,' 'Miss,' and 'Mrs.,' and by last names is considered so relevant for removal of caste barriers that legal action to require these usages has been undertaken. We may also note that genteel persons are polluted by audial contact with slang, obscenity, and on occasion, idiomatic expression.

24. See Horace Miner, "Body Ritual Among the Nacirema," *American Anthropologist,* 55, No. 3, (1956).

25. Note such phrases as 'I wouldn't touch him with a ten-foot pole'; 'she's under my skin'; 'he's a pain in the neck,' and 'Look, but don't touch'. For the rules regarding touch see Erving Goffman, "The Nature of Deference and Demeanor," *op. cit.*

26. Robin Williams has shown that one test of social distance among the races in America is their unwillingness to try on clothing at an apparel shop when they have witnessed that clothing tried on and rejected by members of another – and supposedly inferior – race. Robin Williams, *Strangers Next Door,* Englewood Cliffs: Prentice-Hall, 1964, pp. 125-130.

27. Our usage is similar to that employed in describing the relationships in plant-communities. "The majority of individuals of a plant-community are linked by bonds other than those mentioned – bonds that are best described as *commensal.* The term commensalism is due to Van Beneden, who wrote 'Le commensal est simplement un compagnon de table'; but we employ it in a somewhat different sense to denote the relationship subsisting between species which share with one another the supply of food-material contained in soil and air, and thus feed at the same table." Robert E. Park and Ernest W. Burgess, *Introduction to the Science of Sociology,* Chicago: University of Chicago Press, 1921, p. 175. (Adapted from Eugenius Warming, *Oecology of Plants,* London: Oxford University Press, 1909, pp. 12-13, 91-95.)

28. Ann Terry D'Andre, "An Occupational Study of the Strip-Dancer Career," paper delivered at the annual meetings of the Pacific Sociological Association, Salt Lake City, Utah, 1965.

29. See Ardrey, *op. cit.,* p. 210, who writes: "Biology as a whole asks but one question of a territory: is it defended? Defense defines it. Variability becomes the final description." See also Konrad Lorenz, *On Aggression,* New York: Harcourt, Brace and World, 1966, pp. 33-38 *et passim.*

30. See Mary Coolidge, *Chinese Immigration,* New York: Henry

Holt, 1909, pp. 15-26, 255-56.

31. See Lewis Yablonsky, *The Violent Gang,* New York: MacMillan, 1962, pp. 29-100 for a good ethnography of urban gangs. For an analytical treatment see Frederic M. Thrasher, *The Gang,* Chicago: University of Chicago Press, 1927, pp. 97-100, 116-129.

32. See M. G. Smith, "Kagoro Political Development," *Human Organization* (Fall, 1960), pp. 137-149.

33. It is now a commonplace of sociological irony that persons thus insulated are vulnerable once the insulating material is removed or ubiquitously available. Thus non-coms will insult officers in clubs when both are out of uniform, psychiatrists will be mistaken for patients at dances held in the recreation room of an insane asylum, and students will adopt an inappropriate familiarity with professors not wearing a coat and tie.

34. See Goffman, *Behavior in Public Places, op. cit.,* p. 85 for a succinct account of the elements of this process as a form of civil inattention.

35. Kathleen Tamagawa, *Holy Prayers in a Horse's Ear,* New York: Long, Smith Inc., 1932, pp. 144-151 *et passim.* Andre M. Tao-Kim-Hai, "Orientals are Stoic," in F. C. Macgregor, *Social Science in Nursing,* New York: Russell Sage, 1960, pp. 313-326.

36. See Georg Simmel, "The Aesthetic Significance of the Face," in Kurt H. Wolff, editor, *Georg Simmel 1858-1918,* Columbus: Ohio State University Press, 1959, pp. 280-281.

37. The usual situation is quite the reverse, however. The 'dozens' and other verbal contest forms are most frequently used by Negroes within the ethnic enclave out of earshot and view of whites. See Roger D. Abrahams, *Deep Down in the Jungle,* Hatboro, Penn.: Folklore Associates, 1964, esp. pp. 41-64.

38. See Carl Werthman, *Delinquency and Authority,* M. A. Thesis, University of California, Berkeley, 1964.

39. David Matza, *Delinquency and Drift,* New York: John Wiley, 1964.

40. Many suggestive essays on this subject can be found in *Dress, Adornment, and the Social Order,* ed. by M. E. Roach and J. B. Eicher, N.Y.: John Wiley, 1965.

41. See Cesar Grana, *Bohemian vs. Bourgeois,* New York: Basic Books, 1964, and Harold Finestone, "Cats, Kicks, and Color," *Social Problems,* V. 5, 1 (1957), pp. 3-13.

42. See Harry B. Hawthorn, editor, *The Doukhobors of British Columbia,* Vancouver, B.C.: The University of British Columbia and Dent & Sons, 1955.

43. Goffman, *Behavior in Public Places, op. cit.,* pp. 69-75.

---

2. Distances in Man

Edward T. Hall/*Northwestern University*

Territoriality, as this concept was used in the preceding essay, refers to behavior by which individuals lay claim to an area and defend it from encroachment. Personal space – or personal distance – has to do with what the author of this next selection calls 'that invisible bubble' or 'spatial envelope' which surrounds a person, separating him from his fellows. As this chapter from Professor Hall's book The Hidden Dimension *makes clear, it is a physical distancing that has social and psychological origins. Ethologists go further in suggesting it has biological and physiological origins as well. Personal distance protects the individual's 'persona' from the undesired intrusion of others. The extent of this distance – or the size of the 'bubble' if you will – is culturally determined and is a function of the social situation.*

Edward T. Hall, whose major interest is non-verbal

communication, is Professor of Anthropology at Northwestern University. As well as The Hidden Dimension *from which this selection is taken, he is the author of* The Silent Language.

Reprinted from *The Hidden Dimension,* by Edward T. Hall, by permission of Doubleday and Company Inc. © Edward T. Hall 1966.

> Some thirty inches from my nose
> The frontier of my Person goes,
> And all the untilled air between
> Is private *pagus* or demesne.
> Stranger, unless with bedroom eyes
> I beckon you to fraternize,
> Beware of rudely crossing it:
> I have no gun, but I can spit.
>
>   W. H. AUDEN
>   "Prologue:
>   The Birth of Architecture"

Birds and mammals not only have territories which they occupy and defend against their own kind but they have a series of uniform distances which they maintain from each other. Hediger has classified these as flight distance, critical distance, and personal and social distance. Man, too, has a uniform way of handling distance from the fellows. With very few exceptions, flight distance and critical distance have been eliminated from human reactions. Personal distance and social distance, however, are obviously still present.

How many distances do human beings have and how do we distinguish them? What is it that differentiates one distance from the other? The answer to this question was not obvious at first when I began my investigation of distances in man. Gradually, however, evidence began to accumulate indicating that the regularity of distances observed for humans is the consequence of sensory shifts.

One common source of information about the distance separating two people is the loudness of the voice. Working with the linguistic scientist George Trager, I began by observing shifts in the voice associated with changes in distance. Since the whisper is used when people are very close, and the shout is used to span great distances, the question Trager and I posed was, How many vocal shifts are sandwiched between these two extremes? Our procedure for discovering these patterns was for Trager to stand still while I talked to him at different distances. If both of us agreed that a vocal shift had occurred, we would then measure the distance and note down a general description. The result was the eight distances described at the end of Chapter Ten in *The Silent Language*.

Further observation of human beings in social situations convinced me that these eight distances were overly complex. Four were sufficient; these I have termed intimate, personal, social, and public (each with its close and far phase). My choice of terms to describe various distances was deliberate. Not only was it influenced by Hediger's work with animals indicating the continuity between *infra*culture and culture but also by a desire to provide a clue as to the types of activities and relationships associated with each distance, thereby linking them in peoples' minds with specific inventories of relationships and activities. It should be noted at this point that *how people are feeling toward each other* at the time is a decisive factor in the distance used. Thus people who are very angry or emphatic about the point they are making will move in close, they 'turn up the volume', as it were, by shouting. Similarly – as any woman knows – one of the first signs that a man is beginning to feel amorous is his move closer to her. If the woman does not feel similarly disposed she signals this by moving back.

The Dynamism of Space

Man's sense of space and distance is not static, and it has very little to do with the single-viewpoint linear perspective developed by the Renaissance artists and still taught in most schools of art and architecture. Instead, man senses distance as other animals do. His perception of space is dynamic because it is related to action – what can be done in a given space – rather than what is seen by passive viewing.

The general failure to grasp the significance of the many elements that contribute to man's sense of space may be due to two mistaken notions:

(1) that for every effect there is a single and identifiable cause; and

(2) that man's boundary begins and ends with his skin.

If we can rid ourselves of the need for a single explanation, and if we can think of man as surrounded by a series of expanding and contracting fields which provide information of many kinds, we shall begin to see him in an entirely different light. We can then begin to learn about human behavior, in-

cluding personality types. Not only are there introverts and extroverts, authoritarian and egalitarian, Apollonian and Dionysian types and all the other shades and grades of personality, but each one of us has a number of learned *situational* personalities. The simplest form of the situational personality is that associated with responses to intimate, personal, social, and public transactions. Some individuals never develop the public phase of their personalities and, therefore, cannot fill public spaces; they make very poor speakers or moderators. As many psychiatrists know, other people have trouble with the intimate and personal zones and cannot endure closeness to others.

Concepts such as these are not always easy to grasp, because most of the distance-sensing process occurs outside awareness. We sense other people as close or distant, but we cannot always put our finger on what it is that enables us to characterize them as such. So many different things are happening at once it is difficult to sort out the sources of information on which we base our reactions. Is it tone of voice or stance or distance? This sorting process can be accomplished only by careful observation over a long period of time in a wide variety of situations, making a note of each small shift in information received. For example, the presence or absence of the sensation of warmth from the body of another person marks the line between intimate and non-intimate space. The smell of freshly washed hair and the blurring of another person's features seen close up combine with the sensation of warmth to create intimacy. By using one's self as a control and recording changing patterns of sensory input it is possible to identify structure points in the distance-sensing system. In effect, one identifies, one by one, the isolates making up the sets that constitute the intimate, personal, social, and public zones.

The following descriptions of the four distance zones have been compiled from observations and interviews with non-contact, middle-class, healthy adults, mainly natives of the northeastern seaboard of the United States. A high percentage of the subjects were men and women from business and the professions; many could be classified as intellectuals. The interviews were affectively neutral; that is, the subjects were not noticeably excited, depressed, or angry. There were no unusual environmental factors, such as extremes of temperature or noise. These descriptions represent only a first approximation. They will doubtless seem crude when more is known about proxemic observation and how people distinguish one distance from another. It should be emphasized that these generalizations are not representative of human behavior in general – or even of American behavior in general – but only of the group included in the sample. Negroes and Spanish Americans as well as persons who come from southern European cultures have very different proxemic patterns.

Each of the four distance zones described below has a near and a far phase, which will be discussed after short introductory remarks. It should be noted that the measured distances vary somewhat with differences in personality and environmental factors. For example, a high noise level or low illumination will ordinarily bring people closer together.

Intimate Distance

At intimate distance, the presence of the other person is unmistakable and may at times be overwhelming because of the greatly stepped-up sensory inputs. Sight (often distorted), olfaction, heat from the other person's body, sound, smell, and feel of the breath all combine to signal unmistakable involvement with another body.

Intimate Distance – Close Phase

This is the distance of love-making and wrestling, comforting and protecting. Physical contact or the high possibility of physical involvement is uppermost in the awareness of both persons. The use of their distance receptors is greatly reduced except for olfaction and sensation of radiant heat, both of which are stepped up. In the maximum contact phase, the muscles and skin communicate. Pelvis, thighs, and head can be brought into play; arms can encircle. Except at the outer limits, sharp vision is blurred. When close vision is possible within the intimate range – as with children – the image is greatly enlarged and stimulates much, if not all, of the retina. The detail that can be seen at this distance is extraordinary. This detail plus the cross-eyed pull of the eye muscles provide a visual experience that cannot be confused with any other distance. Vocalization at intimate distance plays a very minor part in the communication process, which is carried mainly by other channels. A whisper has the effect of expanding the distance. The vocalizations that do occur are largely involuntary.

Intimate Distance – Far Phase
(Distance: six to eighteen inches)

Heads, thighs, and pelvis are not easily brought into contact, but hands can reach and grasp extremities. The head is seen as enlarged in size, and its features are distorted. Ability to focus the eye easily is an important feature of this distance for Americans. The iris of the other person's eye seen at about six to nine inches is enlarged to more than life-size. Small blood vessels in the sclera are clearly perceived, pores are enlarged. Clear vision (15 degrees) includes the upper or lower portion of the face, which is perceived as enlarged. The nose is seen as overlarge and may look distorted, as will other features such as lips, teeth, and tongue. Peripheral vision (30 to 180 degrees) includes the outline of head and shoulders and very often the hands.

Much of the physical discomfort that Americans experience when foreigners are inappropriately inside the intimate sphere is expressed as a distortion of the visual system. One subject said, "These people get so close, you're cross-eyed. It really makes me nervous. They put their face so close it feels like they're *inside you*." At the point where sharp focus is lost, one feels the uncomfortable muscular sensation of being cross-eyed from looking at something too close. The expressions 'Get your face *out* of mine' and 'He shook his fist *in* my face' apparently express how many Americans perceive their body boundaries.

At six to eighteen inches the voice is used but is normally held at a very low level or even a whisper. As Martin Joos, the linguist, describes it, "An intimate utterance pointedly avoids giving the addressee information from outside of the speaker's skin. The point . . . is simply to remind (hardly 'inform') the addressee of some feeling . . . inside the speaker's skin." The heat and odor of the other person's breath may be detected, even though it is directed away from subject's face. Heat loss or gain from other person's body begins to be noticed by some subjects.

The use of intimate distance in public is not considered proper by adult, middle-class Americans even though their young may be observed intimately involved with each other in automobiles and on beaches. Crowded subways and buses may bring strangers into what would ordinarily be classed as intimate spatial relations, but subway riders have defensive devices which take the real intimacy out of intimate space in public conveyances. The basic tactic is to be as immobile as possible and, when part of the trunk or extremities touches another person, withdraw if possible. If this is not possible, the muscles in the affected areas are kept tense. For members of the non-contact group, it is taboo to relax and enjoy bodily contact with strangers! In crowded elevators the hands are kept at the side or used to steady the body by grasping a railing. The eyes are fixed on infinity and are not brought to bear on anyone for more than a passing glance.

It should be noted once more that American proxemic patterns for intimate distance are by no means universal. Even the rules governing such intimacies as touching others cannot be counted on to remain constant. Americans who have had an opportunity for considerable social interaction with Russians report that many of the features characteristic of American intimate distance are present in Russian social distance. As we shall see in the following chapter, Middle Eastern subjects in public places do not express the outraged reaction to being touched by strangers which one encounters in American subjects.

Personal Distance

'Personal distance' is the term originally used by Hediger to designate the distance consistently separating the members of non-contact species. It might be thought of as a small protective sphere or bubble that an organism maintains between itself and others.

Personal Distance – Close Phase
(Distance: one and a half to two and a half feet)

The kinesthetic sense of closeness derives in part from the possibilities present in regard to what each participant can do to the other with his extremities. At this distance, one can hold or grasp the other person. Visual distortion of the other's features is no longer apparent. However, there is noticeable feedback from the muscles that control the eyes. The reader can experience this himself if he will look at an object eighteen inches to three feet away, paying particular attention to the muscles around his eyeballs. He can feel the pull of these muscles as they hold the two eyes on a single point so that the image of each eye stays in register. Pushing gently with the tip of the finger on the surface of the lower eyelid so that the eyeball is displaced will illustrate clearly the work these muscles perform in maintaining a single coherent image. A visual angle of fifteen degrees takes in another person's upper or lower face, which is seen with exceptional clarity. The planes and roundness of the face are accentuated; the nose projects and the ears recede; fine hair of the face, eyelashes, and pores is clearly visible. The three-dimensional quality of objects is particularly pronounced. Objects have roundness, substance, and form unlike that perceived at any other distance. Surface textures are also very prominent and are clearly differentiated from each other. Where people stand in relation to each other signals their relationship, or how they feel toward each other, or both. A wife can stay inside the circle of her husband's close personal zone with impunity. For another woman to do so is an entirely different story.

Personal Distance – Far Phase
(Distance: two and a half to four feet)

Keeping someone at 'arm's length' is one way of expressing the far phase of personal distance. It extends from a point that is just outside easy touching distance by one person to a point where two people can touch fingers if they extend both arms. This is the limit of physical domination in the very real sense. Beyond it, a person cannot easily 'get his hands on' someone else. Subjects of personal interest and involvement can be discussed at this distance. Head size is perceived as normal and details of the other person's features are clearly visible. Also easily seen are fine details of skin, gray hair, 'sleep' in the eye, stains on teeth, spots, small wrinkles, or dirt on clothing. Foveal vision covers only an area the size of the tip of the nose or one eye, so that the gaze must wander around the face (*where the eye is directed* is strictly a matter of cultural conditioning). Fifteen-degree clear vision covers the upper *or* lower face, while

180-degree peripheral vision takes in the hands and the whole body of a seated person. Movement of the hands is detected, but fingers can't be counted. The voice level is moderate. No body heat is perceptible. While olfaction is not normally present for Americans, it is for a great many other people who use colognes to create an olfactory bubble. Breath odor can sometimes be detected at this distance, but Americans are generally trained to direct the breath away from others.

Social Distance

The boundary line between the far phase of personal distance and the close phase of social distance marks, in the words of one subject, the 'limit of domination'. Intimate visual detail in the face is not perceived, and nobody touches or expects to touch another person unless there is some special effort. Voice level is normal for Americans. There is little change between the far and close phases, and conversations can be overheard at a distance of up to twenty feet. I have observed that in overall loudness, the American voice at these distances is below that of the Arab, the Spaniard, the South Asian Indian, and the Russian, and somewhat above that of the English upper class, the Southeast Asian, and the Japanese.

Social Distance – Close Phase
(Distance: four to seven feet)
Head size is perceived as normal; as one moves away from the subject, the foveal area of the eye can take in an ever-increasing amount of the person. At four feet, a one-degree visual angle covers an area of a little more than one eye. At seven feet the area of sharp focus extends to the nose and parts of both eyes; or the whole mouth, one eye, and the nose are sharply seen. Many Americans shift their gaze back and forth from eye to eye or from eyes to mouth. Details of skin texture and hair are clearly perceived. At a sixty degree visual angle, the head, shoulders, and upper trunk are seen at a distance of four feet; while the same sweep includes the whole figure at seven feet.

Impersonal business occurs at this distance, and in the close phase there is more involvement than in the distant phase. People who work together tend to use close social distance. It is also a very common distance for people who are attending a casual social gathering. To stand and look down at a person at this distance has a domineering effect, as when a man talks to his secretary or receptionist.

Social Distance – Far Phase
(Distance: seven to twelve feet)
This is the distance to which people move when someone says, "Stand away so I can look at you." Business and social discourse conducted at the far end of social distance has a more formal character than if it occurs inside the close phase. Desks in the offices of important people are large enough to hold visitors at the far phase of social distance. Even in an office with standard-size desks, the chair opposite is eight or nine feet away from the man behind the desk. At the far phase of social distance, the finest details of the face, such as the capillaries in the eyes, are lost. Otherwise, skin texture, hair, condition of teeth, and condition of clothes are all readily visible. None of my subjects mentioned heat or odor from another person's body as detectable at this distance. The full figure – with a good deal of space around it – is encompassed in a sixty degree glance. Also, at around twelve feet, feedback from the eye muscles used to hold the eyes inward on a single spot falls off rapidly. The eyes and the mouth of the other person are seen in the area of sharpest vision. Hence, it is not necessary to shift the eyes to take in the whole face. During conversations of any significant length it is more important to maintain visual contact at this distance than it is at closer distance.

Proxemic behavior of this sort is culturally conditioned and entirely arbitrary. It is also binding on all concerned. To fail to hold the other person's eye is to shut him out and bring conversation to a halt, which is why people who are conversing at this distance can be observed craning their necks and leaning from side to side to avoid intervening obstacles. Similarly, when one person is seated and the other is standing, prolonged visual contact at less than ten or twelve feet tires the neck muscles and is generally avoided by subordinates who are sensitive to their employer's comfort. If, however, the status of the two parties is reversed so that the subordinate is seated, the other party may often come closer.

At this distant phase, the voice level is noticeably louder than for the close phase, and it can usually be heard easily in an adjoining room if the door is open. Raising the voice or shouting can have the effect of reducing social distance to personal distance.

A proxemic feature of social distance (far phase) is that it can be used to insulate or screen people from each other. This distance makes it possible for them to continue to work in the presence of another person without appearing to be rude. Receptionists in offices are particularly vulnerable as most employers expect double duty: answering questions, being polite to callers, as well as typing. If the receptionist is less than ten feet from another person, even a stranger, she will be sufficiently involved to be virtually compelled to converse. If she has more space, however, she can work quite freely without having to talk. Likewise, husbands returning from work often find themselves sitting and relaxing, reading the paper at ten or more feet from their wives, for at this distance a couple can engage each other briefly and disengage at will. Some men discover that their wives have arranged the furniture back-to-back – a favorite sociofugal device of the cartoonist Chick Young, creator of 'Blondie'. The back-to-back seating arrangement is an appropriate solution to minimum space because it is possible for two people to stay uninvolved if that is their desire.

Public Distance

Several important sensory shifts occur in the transition from the personal and social distances to public distance, which is well outside the circle of involvement.

Public Distance – Close Phase
(Distance: twelve to twenty-five feet)
At twelve feet an alert subject can take evasive or defensive action if threatened. The distance may even cue a vestigial but subliminal form of flight reaction. The voice is loud but not full-volume. Linguists have observed that a careful choice of words and phrasing of sentences as well as grammatical or syntactic shifts occur at this distance. Martin Joos' choice of the term 'formal style' is appropriately descriptive: "Formal texts . . . demand advance planning . . . the speaker is correctly said to think on his feet." The angle of sharpest vision (one degree) covers the whole face. Fine details of the skin and eyes are no longer visible. At sixteen feet, the body begins to lose its roundness and to look flat. The color of the eyes begins to be imperceivable; only the white of the eye is visible. Head size is perceived as considerably under life-size. The fifteen degree lozenge-shaped area of clear vision covers the faces of two people at twelve feet, while sixty degree scanning includes the whole body with a little space around it. Other persons present can be seen peripherally.

Public Distance – Far Phase
(Distance: twenty-five feet or more)

Thirty feet is the distance that is automatically set around important public figures. An excellent example occurs in Theodore H. White's *The Making of the President 1960* when John F. Kennedy's nomination became a certainty. White is describing the group at the 'hideaway cottage' as Kennedy entered:

Kennedy loped into the cottage with his light, dancing step, as young and lithe as springtime, and called a greeting to those who stood in his way. Then he seemed to slip from them as he descended the steps of the split-level cottage to a corner where his brother Bobby and brother-in-law Sargent Shriver were chatting, waiting for him. The others in the room surged forward on impulse to join him. Then they halted. A distance of perhaps thirty feet separated them from him, but it was impassable. They stood apart, these older men of long-established power, and watched him. He turned after a few minutes, saw them watching him, and whispered to his brother-in-law. Shriver now crossed the separating space to invite them over. First Averell Harriman; then Dick Daley; then Mike DiSalle, then, one by one, let them all congratulate him. Yet no one could pass the little open distance between him and them uninvited, because there was this thin separation about him and the knowledge they were there not as his patrons but as his clients. They could come by invitation only, for this might be a President of the United States.

The usual public distance is not restricted to public figures but can be used by anyone on public occasions. There are certain adjustments that must be made, however. Most actors know that at thirty or more feet the subtle shades of meaning conveyed by the normal voice are lost as are the details of facial expression and movement. Not only the voice but everything else must be exaggerated or amplified. Much of the non-verbal part of the communication shifts to gestures and body stance. In addition, the tempo of the voice drops, words are enunciated more clearly, and there are stylistic changes as well. Martin Joos' *frozen style* is characteristic: "Frozen style is for people who are to remain strangers." The whole man may be seen as quite small and he is perceived in a setting. Foveal vision takes in more and more of the man until he is entirely within the small circle of sharpest vision. At which point – when people look like ants – contact with them as human beings fades rapidly. The sixty degree cone of vision takes in the setting while peripheral vision has as its principal function the altering of the individual to movement at the side.

Why 'Four' Distances?

In concluding this description of distance zones common to our sample group of Americans a final word about classification is in order. It may well be asked: Why are there four zones, not six or eight? Why set up any zones at all? How do we know that this classification is appropriate? How were the categories chosen?

The scientist has a basic need for a classification system, one that is as consistent as possible with the phenomena under observation and one which will hold up long enough to be useful. Behind every classification system lies a theory or hypothesis about the nature of the data and their basic patterns of organization. The hypothesis behind the proxemic classification system is this: it is in the nature of animals, including man, to exhibit behavior which we call territoriality. In so doing, they use the senses to distinguish between one space or distance and another. The specific distance chosen depends on the transaction; the relationship of the interacting individuals, how they feel, and what they are doing. The four-part classification system used here is based on observations of both animals and men. Birds and apes exhibit intimate, personal, and social distances just as man does.

Western man has combined consultative and social activities and relationships into one distance set and has added the public figure and the public relationship. 'Public' relations and 'public' manners as the Europeans and Americans practice them are different from those in other parts of the world. There are implicit obligations to treat total strangers in certain prescribed ways. Hence, we find four principal categories of relationships (intimate, personal, social, and public) and the activities and spaces associated with them. In other parts of the world, relationships tend to fall into other patterns, such as the family/non-family pattern common in Spain and Portugal and their former colonies or the caste and outcast system of India. Both the Arabs and the Jews also make sharp distinctions between people to whom they are related and those to whom they are not. My work with Arabs leads me to believe that they employ a system for the organization of informal space which is very different from what I observed in the United States. The relationship of the Arab peasant or fellah to his sheik or to God is not a public relationship. It is close and personal without intermediaries.

Until recently man's space requirements were thought of in terms of the actual amount of air displaced by his body. The fact that man has around him as extensions of his personality the zones described earlier has generally been overlooked. Differences in the zones – in fact their very existence – became apparent only when Americans began interacting with foreigners who organize their senses differently so that what was intimate in one culture might be personal or even public in another. Thus for the first time the American became aware of his own spatial envelopes, which he had previously taken for granted.

The ability to recognize these various zones of involvement and the activities, relationships, and emotions associated with each has now become extremely important. The world's populations are crowding into cities, and builders and speculators are packing people into vertical filing boxes – both offices and dwellings. If one looks at human beings in the way that the early slave traders did, conceiving of their space requirements simply in terms of the limits of the body, one pays very little attention to the effects of crowding. If, however, one sees man surrounded by a series of invisible bubbles which have measurable dimensions, architecture can be seen in a new light. It is then possible to conceive that people can be cramped by the spaces in which they have to live and work. They may even find themselves forced into behavior, relationships, or emotional outlets that are overly stressful. Like gravity, the influence of two bodies on each other is inversely proportional not only to the square of the distance but possibly even the cube of the distance between them. When stress increases, sensitivity to crowding rises – people get more on edge – so that more and more space is required as less and less is available.

3. Household Space and Family Organization

Dorothy Smith/*University of British Columbia*

Using the familiar but unmapped territory of the household, Professor Smith provides in this essay a sensitive analysis of the relationships between physical and social space. You will want to compare it with the first selection in this section by Lyman and Scott. Although Smith does not explicitly use their territorial categories, examples of each can be found in her discussion. Note the emphasis the author accords to conditions of access and types of control as key variables for the analysis of spatial relations.

The household is an organization which is defined by its occupancy of a specific physical location. Its members daily travel through and about it in the course of their various activities. Their paths, whether individual or communal, must intersect and diverge within the bounds of the spatial arrangements peculiar to the dwelling. These arrangements are made up partly of physical boundaries of one sort or another (walls, doors, and the like), partly of rules about the treatment of boundaries (e.g., whether doors are left open, burst open, or knocked on), and partly also of the allocation of the space available as zones to different functions and persons.

The visible concrete features of the house are rather readily accessible even to the casual visitor in a way that the inner life of the family is not. It is relatively easy for respondents to describe their daily patterns of spatial usage and traffic. Questions about the territorial arrangements can be made concrete and distinct and are not ordinarily threatening. The systematic study of patterns of spatial usage characteristic of the family can give us information about its inner life which cannot be gained in any other way – firstly, because its participants are often not aware of this aspect until their attention is directed to it; secondly, because they cannot be reproduced directly in any other situation.

Let me emphasize first of all that I am concerned with the spatial arrangements that are made in a household and not solely with the raw features of floor area and rooms. Some of the arrangements are part of the fixed equipment or design of the premises. The rooms and doors and windows constitute the physical limits within which individual family arrangements are made. The kitchen plumbing and bathroom, and so forth, are normally stable aspects of the physical plant which can be modified to suit particular family needs only with major expenditures. A number of studies indicate how important to relations with neighbours is the placing of the major entry and exit to the household (for example, Kuper, 1953; Festinger et al. 1950).

Within a given arrangement of rooms, doors, and windows which constitute the gross physical conditions of the household, there are indefinite possibilities of individual household adaptation. In a general way, these possibilities are culturally limited, but individual variations even within a standard form of housing may be considerable. The aspects of spatial arrangement, such as the placing of furniture, which can be adjusted to the preferred patterns, normally become fixed by custom. When they are changed, their changes will represent or precipitate changes in patterns of contact among household members – though these changes may be quite minor. At any one time, however, the chosen arrangement of movable or modifiable spatial arrangements will have its current effect and changes in

Reprinted from *Pacific Sociological Review*, 14:1 (January 1971), by permission of the author and Sage Publications Inc.

long-established usages will cause a noticeable disruption of habitual patterns.

Once we make the simple observation that all social action is anchored in space, then the studies we have of how the spatial properties of relations between houses and apartments affect neighbourly interaction, interesting as they are, seem hardly to scratch the surface. The purpose of this paper is to explore the spatial arrangements in the home and between households and their implications for patterns of interaction and relationships. The treatment is discursive and I have made an eclectic use of instances, some drawn from observation, others from informal reports, some from the architectural literature and others from ethnographic accounts. The topics discussed are governed by a single perspective. This is that spatial arrangements structure the ways in which people become directly accessible to one another.

Accessibility

The concept of accessibility is derived from Goffman's (1963) formulation of 'public' situations.[1] People are considered accessible to one another when the actions or appearance of one becomes directly (through the ordinary sensory equipment of the human organism) available to another as potential information or cues relevant to each other's behaviour. Under such circumstances the individual has direct access to those features of the other's situation of action which are realized in the behaviour setting common to both. In each other's presence they reciprocally influence one another's behaviour, even when there is no current interchange or conscious surveillance. Four main sources of mutual influence can be placed under this heading:

(1) Proximity increases the probability of interaction between persons who are copresent. Interaction may then be readily initiated without going through special procedures to arrange for a meeting. Indeed a special demeanor may be needed to avoid entering into interaction. Interaction may, therefore, be started and dropped on much slighter grounds and in connection with more casual foci of interest than when it must be prearranged.[2] Spatial arrangements may thus affect the 'weight' or formality of interpersonal relations.

(2) The activities of individuals who are copresent, which are not directed towards eliciting a response from another, may necessitate adaptive behaviour as a by-product – as for example to avoid interfering with another's task. Two people passing in a hallway must normally engage in mutually adaptive behaviour even if only to a minor degree. Spatial arrangements may thus constrain concerted activities, even when these are of avoidance rather than of engagement.

(3) Since the behaviour of others is immediately visible or audible, or both, it is also immediately available for judgment and evaluation and hence for correction when appropriate.

(4) There is a generalized influence upon behaviour which derives from what those present attribute to others as expectations of their own behaviour. Others present constitute reference individuals regardless of whether their expectations or evaluations are known or made known.

These direct ways in which spatial arrangements may modify the interactional possibilities fall into two main classes: one, the likelihood of individuals making contact with one another, and second, the likelihood of individuals observing others and being themselves observed. Without pushing this too far, these focus attention on two different features of the spatial arrangements of the household (or indeed of any other set of premises).

(a) It is the siting of domestic activities in a territory which patterns encounters between members of a household or between households in a neighbourhood. The meetings and separations of members are spatial events. The siting of different household functions (cooking, cleaning, and so on) create, inhibit, or preclude opportunities for encounters. The spatial location of events brings people together or keeps them apart, both at the time of the event and in transition from one thing to the next. Here then we are concerned with the spatial arrangements which allocate activities to a territory.

(b) When we focus on the second effect, then we are concerned with barriers, with the walls, doors, and windows, and with how and to whom they disclose or conceal the activities of participants. When situations of action are regularly exposed to the overview of nonparticipants, then the norms governing behaviour of those situations will not only take into account the attitudes of participants but also those attributed to the others who merely observe (or are in a position to be supposed to be doing so). The physical barriers which restrict this effect are thus boundaries to the scope or jurisdiction of norms identified with others than those present. Thus private regions – i.e., regions which are secluded from the overview of all but participants – create normative enclaves in an encompassing normative order. They are territorially defined and encapsulated zones of autonomy. There is a direct relation here between the provision of physical barriers and these processes of social control.[3]

Thus the patterning of mutual access realized by the spatial usage of a particular household states the effective boundaries and articulations of social control within the family. The autonomy of members of a household with respect to local norms or of subgroups of individuals within the family with respect to the jurisdiction of collective family norms arises from the spatial structuring of accessibility within the home. Variations in spatial arrangements and the rules of usage that particular families develop constitute the basic structure of mutual accessibility of family members to one another and of the family to its neighbours.

The Social Structure of the Outer Boundary

The household stands in a fixed relationship to other household units, whether these are close, whether they share certain facilities in common (as elevators and stairways in apartment buildings), or whether they are largely self-contained units proximate to but otherwise unconnected with their neighbours, or whether they are miles distant, as in some rural areas. Distance establishes a preliminary determination of possible interrelations. But I shall neglect that fact and discuss only those situations where the household units are close enough to make accidental contacts possible.

The physical barriers created by the exterior walls of the house are not necessarily tight social barriers. The boundaries between household and neighbourhood may be more or less permeable and further articulated by the structure of garden or yard areas. One factor of importance here is how far household boundaries are inclusive of domestic activities. Certain basic activities are very generally, perhaps universally, characteristic of households – sleeping, sex, some aspects of personal care, for example. Other activities (leisure, business, craft, study, and the like) may be incorporated into the household according to cli-

matic variations and institutional differences. In some technologically primitive and climatically suitable areas, the dwelling is little more than shelter used for sleeping, sex, and some storage of personal belongings – cooking, food preparation, personal toilet are all done outside, very much as on a campsite among vacationing Americans.

There must be systematic variations in the internal structure of the household according to the structure of its exterior boundaries, if for no other reason than that zones defined as private must necessarily be subtracted from what is potentially accessible to a wider and more comprehensive collectivity. At one extreme is the household boundary which seals off the domestic life of householders from the external world. In Frank Lloyd Wright's (1963: 98-99) work, for example, a major theme is the turning away of the nuclear family from local neighbourhood ties. In his design for a housing project in Massachusetts, he arranges entrances and windows so that neighbours could not overlook one another. This is complemented in his design by an open interior plan which exposes everyone to everyone else situationally and all to visitors (with the exception of bedrooms and bathrooms).

Hoggart (1957: 33), in his description of an English working-class neighbourhood, also makes a connection between the interior closeness of family living and insulation from neighbours. The house defines the boundaries between 'family living' and the neighbourhood. Family is a wider kinship unit than just members of the one household. Its members have generous access to the warmth, food, and close family relations of the living room. The drawn shades or little lace curtains exclude the neighbours. This emphasis on privacy is an emphasis on the reservation of the family domain from the penetration of *local norms*. Physical seclusion means that the norms governing how the family members interact among themselves need neither be reflected upon in light of imputed neighbourly views nor be sustained and shaped by knowledge of how others do it or that others are aware of deviations.

Chermayeff and Alexander (1963: 129) adopt a similar strategy in their discussion of the principles of domestic design. Their dwelling is totally inclusive of all domestic needs. It is designed, indeed, like a fortress against an intrusive world. Since traffic through the zones between households is designed for car transportation, the opportunities for 'accidental', i.e., unprogrammed, contacts between neighbours is minimal. Their plan maximizes the isolation of the individual household. Moreover, the existence of an external world is architecturally obliterated. Their scheme provides no 'fenestrations' which allow the housewife to overlook the passerby or the businesses, activities, and lives of her neighbours. Unlike the Hoggart example, however, seclusion from the locality is not a means of securing to an extended family linkage the special privileges of warmth and generosity identified with the living room/kitchen.[4] Their internal layout perpetuates the theme of privacy. From each possible other member of the family who might constitute a source of constraint and expectation, there is a further place of withdrawal. Their principle of design provides a means of securing the ultimate autonomy of the individual.

The mutual screening of neighbour from neighbour may be a means of keeping the family available for external relationships of other kinds. We might expect, for example, that insulation from local expectations would be important to people whose orientations were more 'cosmopolitan' than 'local' (Merton, 1957). Concealment of the inner life of the family and its furnishings and equipment would become important when visitors to the dwelling represent other standards and reference groups than the local. Insulation of the dwelling in liberating individual families from the permeation of local standards permits conformity to nonlocal reference groups. The insulation provided by walls, curtained windows, and screened entryways serves to keep separate sets of relationships whose different membership norms might create embarrassment if they were mutually exposed.

At the other extreme are households with highly permeable boundaries. Under climatically suitable conditions, shortage of space within the dwelling means that territory between dwellings, instead of being neutral ground, becomes a resource among other resources which are shared among a number of households. This may be associated with the sharing of domestic resources to which a middle-class American family expects exclusive access – water supply, for example – or as in the *vecindad* described by Oscar Lewis (1959), bathing facilities.

The spilling over of family life into interstitial areas appears to be the basis of the relations of proximity described by Michel (1960) in her study of a group of French working-class families. These were families who resided more or less permanently in furnished hotels because other accommodation was not available. Relations among neighbours in hotels took on many of the functions normally performed by members of the kin group. Michel suggests that one important factor in the emergence of this pattern was the shortage of space and facilities in the individual apartments. As a result, the hallways and courtyards were shared for many purposes, and, in particular, the hotel courtyard came to be shared as a playground for the children. Relationships among adults developed around their common interest in the children. Babysitting services were exchanged, godparents for the newborn were chosen from among apartment dwellers, children might sleep at a neighbour's, or sometimes live entirely with a neighbour. Children starting school were accompanied, guided, and protected by a child from the same hotel rather than a sibling or cousin, as would otherwise be the case. Shortage of space made the interstitial territory a zone in which surrounding households had common rights and interests. The courtyard and the children became the common responsibility and concern of the inhabitants of the hotel.

Under such conditions the zones between households become the basis for informal contacts between members of different households. The multiplicity of informal contacts leads to the emergence of norms regulating interaction on interstitial territories. The normative boundaries between household and neighbourhood are blurred. The social life of the neighbourhood and the social life of the family are not discontinuous. Accordingly, the normative autonomy of the household is markedly reduced compared with the previous types. Michel comments on the amount of 'busybodying' among tenants of the hotel she studied. In some instances, for example, the *favela* of Rio as Caroline de Jesus (1962) describes it, local standards of disorder and informality may be as binding as standards of respectability are elsewhere. Since spatial arrangements do not provide for the maintenance of a front which can be kept separate from backstage regions, household members have little opportunity to manage and hence control their image. Those who choose to be different must hazard the hostility of their neighbours.[5]

The converse effect of the permeability of household boundaries is their members' sense of rightful concern in neighbourhood affairs. Fried and Gleicher (1961) have suggested that a sense of common ownership of interstitial areas between dwellings is especially characteristic of 'slum' neighbourhoods. In the slum neighbourhood, walls, doors, and windows do not constitute barriers. The social life of the neighbourhood flows around and in and through them. In a middle-class neighbourhood the boundaries are characteristically less permeable. The dwelling itself (and its yard, if any) may be sharply marked off from the surrounding areas between dwellings which are defined as public. They suggest that people living under these two types of conditions have a different relationship to the surrounding territory. The slum dweller inhabits and has a sense of ownership of a territory which includes the unit in which he resides. To the middle-class individual the surrounding territory is primarily a zone in which people travel between dwellings or other types of individualized units. It belongs to no one.[6]

Variations

The structure of household boundaries is not a simple continuum from totally inclusive to open. There are a variety of modifications to the simple picture. In many midwestern communities, for example, where domestic activities are territorially restricted to the household and garden area, there is no fencing around the household territory either in front or in back. Backyard boundaries are demarcated by token shrubs or a line of flowering plants. There is nothing to inhibit the free track of children. Neighbours working in their gardens or hanging out the wash are directly accessible to one another.

According to the account of one informant,[7] this lack of physical barrier between household territories is associated with a lack of normative autonomy. The neighbours are not only interested in one another's family life, they also feel a sense of rightful concern in the conduct of others' domestic affairs, insofar as these are accessible to them. In such communities, privately owned areas adjacent to the actual dwelling appear to come within the scope of communal norms. All the comings and goings and business which are visible to neighbours – even down to the contents of the garbage (with its empty bottles) – are their legitimate concern.

The quasi-public character of visible aspects of domestic life may be combined with areas of seclusion sufficient to create a life of private deviance from public standards of proper domestic behaviour. For example, an informant[8] reported that on a university housing estate where the children played in a common court surrounded by private apartments, communal norms prohibited using physical punishment. This area, and therefore the behaviour of adults to children in this area, was highly visible. The interior of the apartments, on the other hand, was secluded. My informant reported that he and his wife resolved the problem of discipline this rule created for them by bringing the child inside the apartment before smacking him. The peculiarity of this only came home to him when he discovered accidentally one of his neighbours doing the same. The ecology of hypocrisy appears to be that of an abrupt disjunction between areas of domestic use highly accessible to the mutual overview of neighbours and the private boundaries of the dwelling itself.[9]

So far we have considered only the relationship of the household as a whole to the locale. An additional source of variation lies in the fact that the relationships of individual members of the household to the neighbourhood may differ from its relationship as a whole. Housewives may meet and converse on the street or may talk over the backyard fence without engaging their respective families in intimacy. Informal colleague group relations among housewives on a local basis are, in fact, rather common.[10] The evening return of the husband to the home is often associated with a turning away from the neighbourhood and in upon the family itself.

Children's activities are a particularly important source of variation in this connection. Some house designs, such as Frank Lloyd Wright's housing project in Massachusetts (Wright, 1963: 98-99), involve a total enucleation of the nuclear family. Indoor and outdoor play areas for children are included in this individual household unit. But in many neighbourhoods, play areas for children are communal. This is particularly likely when space in the home is markedly limited. In the *vecindad* (Lewis 1959, 1961), the children played in the interstices between dwellings. Kerr (1958: 64-65), in her study of an English slum, describes how children were kept outside the house as much as possible during the day. If they were not on the street, they were sent to the cinema (see also Spinley, 1953). If the boundaries of the household largely circumscribe the local lives of its adult members, while the children occupy the territory between, then there is a lack of coincidence between adults' and children's worlds and the latter may develop a pronounced autonomy. Thus the household may stand in a different relation to the locale, depending upon which status category is concerned.

The Orientation of The Dwelling

The accessibility structure within the home itself is articulated with a more encompassing structure which orients the strictly domestic territories to those outside. The progression from these areas nearest the outside – and most accessible to neighbours, the public, or visitors – to those innermost areas reserved exclusively for family use can be assigned to persons and activities in a variety of ways. In our society, we tend to take for granted a distribution from public to private according to differences in function. Those activities which take place 'backstage' are allocated the innermost parts of the dwelling – sleeping, dressing, sex, bathing, toilet, and the like. The frontstage-backstage dichotomy is a basic assumption of our housing practice.

In other societies and times, however, the orientation can be quite different. One pattern arranges innermost and outermost by status rather than by function. Commonly, the basis of differentiation is sexual – the area assigned to the men being closest to the public domain while the women's area is secluded at the rear or center. The Greek house of classical period was of this type (Rider, 1916: 217-218). It was ordered around two courts. The men's court (the *andronitis*) was closest to the street and the women's court (the *gunaikonitis*) was placed to the rear of the building and was accessible only through the men's court. When household zones are assigned by status rather than function, a range of functions is performed in each zone. The men in their zone near the public ways eat, sleep, dress, and so on. The women's area is also functionally autonomous and generally incorporated, or is adjacent to, the zone allocated to food preparation and storage.

In our own society, the main differentiation is between adults and children, and household arrangements locate these status categories differently with respect to the outside. In some homes, the visitor is immediately engaged, or potentially engaged, with any member of the family who may be present. In others, a distinct area for adult encounters is demarcated. In most instances I have observed neither extreme is present, but there is a pronounced tendency to reserve certain areas in the less public part of the house for children.

The differentiation between outermost and innermost partly depends upon the extent or the way in which the dwelling is accessible to people from the outside. For example, in the Algerian enclosed courtyard dwelling (Chombart de Lauwe, 1959), the dwelling is shut off from the outside by the windowless walls, and the whole life of the dwelling is oriented toward an inner courtyard. The main public life of the township takes place outside the home, and there is very limited access – apart from relatives – to the inside. The boundaries between public and private are abrupt. The public areas do not intersect with the private at all, and hence there is no special internal provision for public encounters, such as we find in the Greek village household (Friedl, 1962), or in the parlor of the rural nineteenth-century American homes (Lynes, 1963: 138-154).

The principles of design put forward by Chermayeff and Alexander (1963) also establish a coincidence of exterior wall and the socially structured boundary between public and private. There is a major jump at the transition. The entryway is designed so that the inhabitants cannot be taken by surprise and can see their prospective visitor before he can see them. Their conception of the relationship of individual to dwelling to locality to community is of nested series of domains ranging from the most private to the most generally public, but there is a major transition between public and private at the perimeter wall of the dwelling.

The internal orientation will also represent the relations with the public sector. Households to which are admitted only persons who are on terms of intimacy with the family, other family members, or close friends may be arranged without a specific area set aside for ceremonial usage. In this society, this pattern is more characteristic of the working class, whereas in upper-class urban or suburban practice, extensive areas of the dwelling, including work areas, may be more accessible to visitors other than intimate friends or family. This openness and ceremonial informality of the interior has influenced styles of decor so that the work areas and the like have been made decorative, and in some cases designed specifically for display (Kennedy, 1953). These areas of ceremonial informality may, however, be sharply separated from areas of further privacy, such as the master bedroom.

Inside the Household

Activities and Contacts

Household space is a scarce resource for which there are competing uses. The people who share this space have to adjust their behaviour to one another within the amount of space available. The allocation of space in the household to activities and to individuals provides a basic ordering of contacts among family members. Some contacts may arise in the course of cooperative activity and others accidentally out of a coincidence of individual activities in a single area. The arrangement of zones and relationships between them shape the accidental as well as the planned contacts.

Here too the amount of space available is important in determining whether choice can be exercised in the allocation of activites to a given space. Where space is limited, and even when climatic conditions do not prevent the extension of domestic activities into areas outside the home, the coincidence of basic domestic activities in a small space brings family members into close proximity. Sleeping, at least, and sex, and often eating and cooking must all share the same area, and family members are necessarily in each other's presence. The privacy of sex relations between husband and wife are protected only by darkness. The nightmares and snores and itchings of neighbouring sleepers are inescapable. Under such conditions, the likelihood of mutual interference in the course of ordinary daily activities is great. If this is to be avoided, the activities of individual participants must be adjusted and arranged so as to accord with the activities of others. This constitutes a special problem of order. If an institutionalized irritability (Plant, 1960) does not result, the autonomy of the individual must be sharply reduced, and the range of individual behaviour occurring within the domain must be integrated as part of a coordinated structure.[11] Descriptions of shipboard life such as Dana's *Two Years Before the Mast* (1948) show the nicety to which individual habits are adjusted in the course of long-term close-quarters living. But the successful integration of personal habits is not always reached. For example, in *The Children of Sanchez* (Lewis, 1961), we find the problem of order solved (and perhaps perpetuated as a problem) by the personal dominance of Sanchez himself, who directly and arbitrarily controlled the entries, exits, and bedtimes of household members.

Where there is more space to play with, the location of different activities and phases of the day becomes of importance in influencing the placing of participants engaged in those activities, and the accidental contacts among family members which arise as a by-product of travel between situated activities. For example, one kind of floor plan opens up all the differentiated functions – kitchen, living room, bedrooms, bathroom, and so on – to one central hall, so that the probability of accidental contacts in making transitions between activities is rather high. Some architects believe in building this feature into the living room as the central room or 'hub' of the house, because the amount of casual traffic enhances the informal relationships among family members. Others believe in placing the living room as a secluded *cul-de-sac*, so that a special journey must be made to reach it (for example, Chombart de Lauwe, 1959: 179).

Ordinarily, in contemporary Western society, there are fixed locations for certain functions. Some of these are defined primarily by the location of fixed equipment, in the kitchen and bathroom, for example. Others are defined by differentiation of furnishings – the bedrooms versus the living room or the dining room. These differentiated locations are not universal, of course, and many societies have a much more flexible ordering of things. In traditional Japan, for example, the sleeping arrangements are provided for by a bedroll which can be taken up and put down at need, so that the need for a special sleeping area is done away with by the lack of provision of special heavy equipment for sleeping. 'Room' boundaries may also be changed at will through the use of portable screens or dividers. In our society, however, the major transitions of the day are ordered spatially, as well as in time. However, we may note that families, arrangements, and houses differ greatly in the extent to which other than basic functions are specially provided for by zoning. This is particularly the case with unplanned interplay, informal exchanges, play, chatting, gossip, and so on.

In some families and houses, these unprescribed activities are assigned specific areas. Generally the living room (which may double as a ceremonial reception room) is the scene of these residual forms of action. Lynes (1963: 116) describes the kitchen in the nineteenth-century home as the locus of informal interaction among family members. Children's play may be confined to their rooms or the yard. In some families, the kitchen is an important conventionalized locus for random interplays and chatting. In other families, however, interactional clusters may arise in almost any part of the house and may shift rapidly with the movement of participants or shifts in cluster participation, or of the center of interest. Interaction arises where people are, rather than where it is arranged for. This may be contrasted with the ceremony which attends upon a high degree of spatial fixing of functions of all kinds which we associate with nineteenth-century styles of architecture.

In the most ceremonially elaborated houses characteristic of the later nineteenth century, each major phase of the daily order and each major activity was given a separate room with furnishings, accoutrements, appropriate to its function. There is an elaboration of furnishings by setting and function so that the same article will have a special design and character according to the room in which it is placed. Dining room chairs differ from morning room, living room, or library chairs. Each room thus also provides a decor and a setting and is associated with situational norms which regulate the forms of behaviour proper to it. The formalized situation constitutes a supplementary means of control of behaviour, for once the situational norms are learned, entry to the zone provides the cues to initiate the appropriate sequences of behaviour.

The extent to which family members are likely to be in, or to come into, each other's presence without having meetings programmed or arranged is, I believe, an important determinant of what might be called the 'texture' of family relationships. When there is plenty of space to play with, household routines and the inventory of domestic occasions may be mapped into a permanently differentiated set of behaviour settings. Routines and occasions thus are given specific physical embodiment, and the order of the home is fully realized in its spatial arrangements. The location of settings in relation to one another will usually be planned to facilitate routine transitions between them, so that opportunities for accidental contact and casual interchange are reduced. By contrast, restricted space makes the assignment of definite activities to definite locations difficult. Something can be managed by ordering changes of scene in the same location through time, but the ceremonial differentiation of occasions is much more difficult to achieve unless the props it requires are extremely simple. Under such circumstances, relationships are likely to be less exclusively realized in the formal terms provided by the structure of definite occasions. A variety of information about the persons of participants which is not part of a controlled 'performance' becomes available. Participants are seen or heard in other contexts and situations of action than when they are immediately engaged in interaction with one another. Then, too, the climate of the situation is affected because the level of background and extraneous noise and the variegation of movement and visible differentiation are increased.

The Articulation of Accessibility

Various dwelling plans and arrangements of the household group participants in different ways at different times. Territorial arrangements act as supplementary means of control by bringing certain members together for certain functions while segregating them from others. This is the dual effect of any alignment. The household pattern of alignments will appear in its territorial arrangements. Thus an open arrangement emphasizes the communality of relations among family members. It increases the area of communal exposure and reduces zones of individual or subgroup differentiation. Frank Lloyd Wright (1963), for example, in his designs, opened up the living areas of the house and separated only the sleeping quarters (and a study for the man of the house). A major innovation was the planning of the kitchen as a distinct zone spatially continuous with the living area of the house. He associated the undivided plan with an extension of the warm, farmhouse atmosphere to the whole communal living area. His conception eliminated the physical segregation of the cooking housewife and made the communal living room life more accessible to the cook and the cook more accessible to those using the communal living room.

The general acceptance of this type of kitchen plan seems to be associated with a special view of the housewife's role which gives less importance to the craft aspects of cooking and homemaking and more prominence to the expressive aspects of the role. There is some feeling here of the family as a kind of ongoing social gathering from which the housewife should not be excluded (see Kennedy, 1953: 232). This view can be contrasted with a more traditional view which emphasizes the role of cook and housekeeper as a work role. The kitchen tends then to be treated as a work area in which the cook is entitled to be protected from interference. In such contexts the kitchen constitutes a domain distinct from communal living areas and to which access of other family members is generally restricted (Chombart de Lauwe, 1959: 178).

The communal versus differentiated zones of the family living can be variously provided for. The open plan provides for communal accessibility in all daily activities of family members, but differentiates nightly in bedroom areas between parents and children. Generally also in our culture, children are segregated by sex. An alternative plan provides for the planned or programmed use of a communal living room, rather than treating it as a place where family members happen to be together because they are engaged in their own pursuits in a common territory. Segregation of adults and children otherwise may primarily dovetail with their different sleeping schedules. Or separate areas may be assigned for a much greater range of activities. Chermayeff and Alexander (1963) provide elaborate arrangements for the separation of zones assigned to children and adults. Their designs create circumstances in which child and adult lives may be lived largely separately with intersections at meals and at planned meetings in a communal living room. They emphasize the provision even of separate entrances so that the comings and goings of children are autonomous. These arrangements are in the tradition of English upper-class planning for children which assigned them quarters distinct from those in which the ceremonial upper-class life was lived. It is a principle of design that not only assumes the separation of children from the adult world (note that Chermayeff and Alexander [1963: 204-209] are not only concerned with the protection of adults from interference by children but also with protecting children from the intrusive supervision of adults), but helps to reinforce it. Arrangements which separate parents and children during an extensive range of daily activities reduce the frequency of casual and unregulated contact between parents and child. They reduce the information each has about the other. They create the conditions under which adult and child may inhabit separate normative worlds.

If a group of siblings are separated from the rest of the family, we may expect the development of a more or less autonomous group culture, just as children extruded to the street will tend to develop a group culture largely independent of adult norms and ideas. We have only to look at some of the autobiographical literature which describes the world of children in English upper-class homes at the turn of the century to find extreme disjunctions between the adult and the child worlds (Grahame, 1964). An additional effect must be noted in the character of supervision. If children play and live in the area where parental life is pursued, supervision of their activities can be provided as a by-product of whatever else the parent is doing. The visual or acoustical openness of a house creates these conditions. The housewife in the kitchen can hear what is going on in the rest of the house, and can pick up sounds indicating potential trouble – e.g., the click of scissors from the living room when only the baby is there, or the incipient fight in the bedroom. Under such acoustical circumstances, the whole house is under her surveillance. But when areas are markedly segregated, the supervision (if it is to be provided at all) must be provided for by more formal checking procedures, by visits of inspection (however casual), informal interrogations, and the like, and such methods of control are quite different in character from processes of supervision which may not in fact be visible as such either to parent or child.

Many of these features would normally be discussed under the heading of privacy. But this term only identifies that set of rules which establish for the occupant or occupants of a territory an exclusive access to what goes on within it. Therefore it identifies only simple dichotomies. A closer examination reveals more delicate articulations of spatial practice. Take, for example, the bathroom. Family practices vary widely with respect to who may do what in whose presence in the bathroom. In some the user has absolute privacy. In others, washing, shaving, and so forth, do not command that privilege. In yet others, probably rare, there are no reserves. Moreover, privacy practices in the bathroom vary with the age and sex of the occupant and the relationship of occupant and 'intruder'. Yet another problem arises from the performance of the cleaning functions in the home. If the housewife and mother does it all, which is common in our culture, she then has access to any room and any storage place, and, in consequence, also to the 'traces' of activities otherwise not displayed – diaries, letters, the

condoms in her growing son's coat pocket, and so on.

Analysis of spatial arrangements and the movements of household members through that space add a new dimension to the conception of a family structure of control. A household set in a neighbourhood so as to make it virtually an island may have interior arrangements which provide for extensive maternal surveillance of the children's activities. When this is combined with a very permissive style of control, the effect may be described as 'benevolent totalitarianism'. By contrast the authoritarian structure and 'tight' discipline of another family may operate within a much more restricted scope, in a household which provides for substantial regional autonomy. The implications of structures of control must vary with variations in the internal structuring of front and back regions – the rules about who has access to whom in what 'phase' of self.

Conclusion

The purpose of this paper was to see where an analysis of spatial arrangements in the home and outside might take us. If one begins with a phenomenon defined empirically rather than theoretically, then there are a number of different directions in which analysis of its relation to social structures might proceed. A preliminary exploration is thus necessarily open-ended and serves rather to delimit and define than to specify a determinate course arriving at determinate conclusions. Rather than summarize, rather than attempting a final but necessarily deceptive synthesis, I list below a set of implications or suggestions that this analysis has raised.

(a) Most studies of household-neighbourhood relations work with a conceptual model of the household as a discrete social unit. The neighbourhood begins outside the front door. We tend to take for granted that the normative boundaries of the dwelling coincide with its physical boundaries. The instances presented in the section of the paper on the social structure of boundaries suggest that this model represents only one type of household-neighbourhood relations. The social structure of boundaries provides sometimes for an interpenetration of household and neighbourhood normative structures. Clearly for there to be anything that can be called a household at all, there must be some practices which preserve its character as a discrete territory. But what these are and how they work in different kinds of locations is an empirical question.

(b) The same kind of thinking treats the family as if it had a 'floating' relation to the wider social structure, linked to wider institutional structures through the multiple participation of its members. The perspective outlined here begins with the empirical observation that families are located in definite spatial relations to other families. The effective detachment of the family from local relations is then treated as problematic. One would ask, how is it done? What type of relations between household and neighbourhood establish the household as an island? What are the alternatives?

(c) Examining cultural and subcultural differences in the orientation of the dwelling suggests that the differentiation of front and back regions is not an invariant feature of housing practice. Sometimes front and back regions are separated and sometimes not. Insofar as the work of impression management depends upon this provision, spatial arrangements here create sets of different possibilities. Moreover, there are clearly cultural differences in the allocation of persons and activities to front and backstage regions, suggesting that cultural differences in housing practice may have something to contribute to an understanding of the character and ideal content of the social order, which is realized in the presentation of selves.

(d) Largely through the work of Erving Goffman we have come to recognize settings as normative structures which cue in behaviour appropriate to the occasions with which they have come to be associated. This is as much so in the home as in any other social organization. Of particular interest, then, is the extent to which settings are or may be differentiated and specific to a type of occasion. This, I have suggested, may be an important factor in the degree of formality or ceremony which characterizes particular family relationships.

(e) Studies of the family which focus on its role structure recover for the sociologist a model which is the family as respondents see it, using a frame of reference provided by the sociologist's interview schedule. The relation of this model to actual patterns of interaction and to other features of interpersonal process is necessarily indeterminate. There are two ways, I think, in which an analysis of spatial arrangements is relevant here:

(1) Perhaps rather obviously, the investigation of patterns of movement in the home and outside may show up alignments and isolations among family members which they may not themselves recognize or conceptualize.

(2) Similar types of control structures may have quite different implications depending upon the structure of accessibility in the home and in the locality. This seems to be of particular importance with reference to socialization of the child. Perhaps we do not pay enough attention to the kinds of childhood experiences which, according to children's literature or the literature of childhood, often seem crucial. The differences between the childhood experiences recounted in, say, *Huckleberry Finn* (Twain, 1948), Mary McCarthy's (1957) *Memoirs of a Catholic Girlhood*, or Kenneth Grahame's (1964) *The Golden Age* indicate that this aspect of household and local structures of accessibility is of very great significance in the child's experience of the world and his relations with adults.

NOTES AND BIBLIOGRAPHY

1. See Goffman's specification of face-to-face relations as it appears in Chapter 2 of *Behavior in Public Places* (Goffman, 1963). He discriminates the elements of such relationships more finely and elegantly than I can. Those who are familiar with Goffman's work will notice a good deal of overlap in the concepts used. I should emphasize here that I have adapted aspects of his theoretical approach to different analytical purposes, and I should like to take this opportunity of acknowledging my dependence upon his work without implicating him in any way with the uses I have made of it. He uses the term 'accessible' in much the same sense as I have, but in a more restricted context (Goffman, 1963: 154).

Other sociologists have dealt with the same general theme that I have identified here as accessibility, notably Merton (1957: 336-353) and Stinchcombe (1968).

2. Dobriner (1963: 10) quotes a suburban dweller's remark as follows: "On Saturday, when the weather is nice, I spend quite a bit of time outdoors – you know, just knocking around, doing a bit here and there. *When you see someone else out, cutting the grass or something,. it's easy to strike up a conversation"* (italics added).

3. Of course, this does not preclude reference group process of other kinds. Nor does it apply in a simple way to action which *will have* sensibly present results for others. So it is stated as one type of boundary only. The problem of how the jurisdiction of different normative sets is established is an important and neglected area of study. Organizational theory and practice, as well as ordinary observation, suggest that the presence or imminent presence of another who represents a given set of norms to the actor brings those norms into the actor's presence with him.

4. We should not take this form of seclusion for granted. It is not a universal practice. For example, in some cities in the Netherlands, the uncurtained windows of the family living room give directly on to the street so that the family may gaze upon and be gazed upon by passers-by.

5. This observation suggests that the front-backstage phenomenon described by Goffman (1960) is not an invariable feature of social interaction. The required separation of regions is beyond the spatial re-

sources of the favela.

6. Hoggart's (1957: 51-56) description of slum living contradicts Fried and Gleicher's (1961) here. The latter ignore the possible significance of climatic differences. In areas where there is marked seasonal variation, household organization in crowded neighbourhoods may move from an open and permeable structure in summer and hot weather to a closing up and focusing upon intrafamilial relations when cold weather comes.

7. Personal communication.

8. Personal communication.

9. Warriner (1958) writes of a communitywide ecology of hypocrisy. He describes the dual standards of communal and private virtue in a midwestern community. Its special character may be associated with a formal jurisdiction of communal norms over domestic behaviour coupled with the effective inaccessibility of the household to a neighbourhood surveillance.

10. Berger (1960: 96) describes patterns of backyard chatting and kaffee klatching among housewives which do not implicate other members of their families. In the Greek village described by Friedl (1962), the housewives' circuit and that of the family unit may involve the same persons, but the situations of housewives' meetings and interfamilial meetings are ceremonially segregated.

11. In descriptions of crowded slum living, parents are often characterized as arbitrary in their disciplining of children. An action permitted at one time is punished at another. This may arise from the problem of scheduling changes in activities and hence situational norms through the same location. Children thus may have to be disciplined to discourage current interference in a particular situation rather than to discourage behaviour which is in breach of a general rule of conduct.

Bell, N. and E. P. Vogel (eds.) 1960 *A Modern Introduction to the Family*. Glencoe, Ill.: Free Press.

Berger, Bennett M. 1960 *Working Class Suburb: A Study of Auto Workers in Suburbia*. Berkeley: Univ. of California Press.

Chermayeff, S. and C. Alexander 1963 *Community and Privacy: Toward a New Architecture of Humanism* New York: Doubleday.

Chombart de Lauwe, Paul Henry 1959 *Famille et Habitation,* a volume in *Sciences Humaines et Conceptions de l'Habitation.* Paris: Centre National de Recherche Scientifique, Groupe d'Ethnologie Sociale.

Dana, Richard Henry 1948 *Two Years Before the Mast.* New York: Dodd, Mead.

Dobriner, W. M. 1963 *Class in Suburbia.* Englewood Cliffs: Prentice-Hall.

Festinger, Leon, S. Schachter, and K. Back 1950 *Social Pressures in Informal Groups.* New York: Harper.

Fried, M. and P. Gleicher 1961 "Some sources of residential satisfaction in an urban slum." *J. of the Amer, Institute of Planners* 27 (November): 4.

Friedl, E. 1962 *Vasilika, A Village in Modern Greece.* New York: Holt, Rinehart & Winston.

Goffman, E. 1960 *The Presentation of Self in Everyday Life.* New York: Doubleday Anchor.
1963 *Behavior in Public Places.* Glencoe, Ill.: Free Press.

Grahame, K. 1964 *The Golden Age and Dream Days.* New York: Signet.

Hoggart, R. 1957 *The Uses of Literacy.* London: Chatto & Windus.

de Jesus, Caroline Maria 1962 *Child of the Dark.* New York: Signet.

Kennedy, Robert Woods 1953 *The House and the Arts of its Design.* New York: Reinhold.

Kerr, Madeleine 1958 *The People of Ship Street.* London: Routledge & Kegan Paul.

Kuper, L. (ed.) 1953 *Living in Towns.* London: Cresset.

Lewis, Oscar 1959 *Five Families, Mexican Case Studies in the Culture of Poverty* New York: Basic Books.
1961 *The Children of Sanchez: Autobiography of a Mexican Family.* New York: Random House.

Lynes, Russell 1963 *The Domesticated Americans.* New York: Harper & Row.

McCarthy, Mary Therese 1957 *Memories of a Catholic Girlhood.* New York: Harcourt, Brace & World.

Merton, R. K. 1957 *Social Theory and Social Structure.* Glencoe, Ill.: Free Press.

Michel, A. V. 1960 "Kinship relations and relationships of proximity in French working-class households." In N. Bell and E. F. Vogel (eds.)

A Modern Introduction to the Family. Glencoe, Ill.: Free Press.

Plant, J. 1960 "Family living space and personality development." In N. Bell and E. F. Vogel (eds.) *A Modern Introduction to the Family.* Glencoe. Ill.: Free Press.

Rider, B.C. 1916 *The Greek House*, Cambridge, U.K.: Cambridge Univ. Press.

Spinley, Betty L. 1953 *The Deprived and the Privileged.* London: Routledge & Kegan Paul.

Stinchcombe, A. K. 1968 *Constructing Social Theories*, New York: Harcourt, Brace & World.

Twain, Mark (Samuel L. Clemens) 1948 *The Adventures of Huckleberry Finn.* New York: Grosset & Dunlap.

Warriner, Charles K. 1958 "The nature and functions of official morality." *Amer. J. of Sociology* 64 (September): 165-168.

Wright, Frank Lloyd 1963 *The Natural House.* New York: Mentor.

4. Social Network as a Subjective Construct: A New Application for an Old Idea

Robert Stebbins/*Memorial University of Newfoundland*

Network analysis is a relatively new tool, first developed by anthropologists to take into account the loose web of affiliation that links together individuals variably placed in one or possibly several different societies. As yet there is no widespread agreement on a definition of network. Some use the concept to include all forms of social relations; others use it as a residual category to include those relationships that are outside the readily recognizable social institutions, groups or categories of structural analysis. To this extent networks lack clearly defined boundaries. Networks affect the range of options available to individuals in deciding any given course of action in as much as individual variability and choice-making are functions of communication circuits and an individual's perception of his placement in the network. Contemporary youth movements, for example, might be viewed as a world-wide network of age-status peers which, in some respects, enlarges and, in other respects, constricts behavioral patterns.

If we accept Stebbins' thesis, so cogently developed in this essay, that "a social network is also a psychological disposition to respond," then the importance of networks to social spatial analysis is clear. The degree to which one's space, or room to manoeuvre, is restricted by these predispositions and interpersonal relations is exemplified in several selections in this volume. Consider, for example, Archibald's essay on women, or Nagler's on Indians in the next section, or Desbarats on the Quebec 'family' in Section Six. As Stebbins observes, "the social network is very much a reality to the individual because of the pressures which originate within it."

The ever-growing body of literature incorporating the notion of 'social network' into its analysis is strong evidence for the fertility of an idea formally introduced into social science by J. A. Barnes (1954). The numerous studies which have appeared since that time have related social network to an extensive array of subjects. A majority of these have employed this idea as an explanatory factor, explaining or helping to explain such diverse phenomena as social change, efficiency of communities as melting pots, links between the various groups in a society, social class, maintenance of rural ties, and nature of contacts outside the family (Epstein, 1961; Gutkind, 1965; P. Mayer, 1962; Mitchell, 1966; Srinivas and Beteille, 1964; Bott, 1957;

Reprinted from the *Canadian Review of Sociology and Anthropology*, 6: 1 (1969), by permission of the author and the publisher.

Nelson, 1966; Young and Wilmott, 1957; Barnes, 1954). A somewhat smaller proportion of studies or summaries has treated social networks as objects of explanation while investigating influences of rural to urban migration on networks, formation of interpersonal relationships as they affect networks, types of networks, gossip and networks, and how networks originate (Frankenberg, 1965; Katz, 1966; Adams, 1967; Bott, 1957; Barnes, 1954; Hannerz, 1968).

For the purposes of this introductory discussion we can accept Bott's definition of social network as a "set of social relationships for which there is no common boundary" (Bott, 1957: 59). In the strict sense of the word a network is not a structure, since it has no shared boundaries (boundaries recognized by everyone in the social network) and no commonly recognized hierarchy or central co-ordinating agency. Nevertheless, there are interconnections between others in the network in that some of its members are directly in touch with each other while others are not. Thus, it is also a characteristic of networks that their mesh may be 'closely-knit' (many members having direct contact) or 'loosely-knit' (few members having direct contact) (Barnes, 1954; Bott, 1957: 59). Many of the studies mentioned above provide evidence for Bott's definition of social networks as comprised of social relationships.

A certain amount of confusion has sprung up among those who have endeavoured to consider the idea of network on a theoretical plane. This confusion is almost entirely centred in the question of whether a network should be approached from the point of view of a particular person (ego-centred perspective) or from a more totalistic stance in which the component relationships are seen as a sum total of every person's network (holistic perspective). The ego-centred perspective is like the standpoint used in kinship analysis, whereas the holistic perspective focuses less on any particular point in the network than on the total structure of relationships.

What has happened, as Adrian Mayer (1966) recently observed, is that Bott used network in an ego-centred sense, a usage which Barnes originally reserved for the term 'set' which he never developed to any definitive degree.[1] Most subsequent writers have continued to follow Bott, and we shall do the same here. This definition has become established in the parlance of anthropologists and sociologists.

Outside of these few attempts at conceptual clarification, there has been a regrettable paucity of theoretical discussion about the concept of social network. In order to strengthen the explanatory power of this idea, we shall examine its logical connection with the concept of interpersonal or social relationship (IR) and the implications which this link has for the network as an explanation. The set of statements below will serve as a sort of itinerary for the theoretical excursion which follows:

1. Interpersonal relationships as mutual orientations between persons are basically psychological predispositions to respond which guide behaviour in the social situation.

2. Interpersonal relationships are the component parts of social networks.

3. If one or more of a person's IRS influence his actions as they are being carried out with reference to still another IR, then we can say that part or all of that person's social network directly guides his situated behaviour.

4. Therefore, we can say that a social network is also a psychological predisposition to respond.

5. The observation that the network is a predisposition which can directly explain behaviour, although perhaps not wholly new, has received little or no systematic empirical or theoretical attention in the past.

Interpersonal Relationships

Max Weber (1947: 118) can be given credit for setting the basic theoretical foundation of the contemporary approach to social or interpersonal relationships: "The term 'social relationship' will be used to denote the behaviour of a plurality of actors in so far as, in its meaningful content, the action of each takes account of that of the others and is oriented in these terms. The social relationship thus *consists* entirely and exclusively in the existence of a *probability* that there will be, in some meaningfully understandable sense, a course of social action."[2] It is clear from this quote and Weber's subsequent discussion that 'mutual orientation' is the essence of IR . In order to have a more concise definition at hand, which emphasizes this subjective quality, we shall redefine the interpersonal relationship as *ego's sustained orientation toward a particular alter which is perceived by ego to be reciprocated by that alter*.[3]

Certain basic characteristics of IRS must first be discussed as a prerequisite to our later consideration of IRS as predispositions. Accordingly, we shall briefly review the intimate nature of IRS, their changeability, some of the reasons for their continuation, the relationship of sentiments to IRS, and the private culture of IRS.

Interpersonal relationships are born in the prolonged interaction of two people, and it is not unusual to find that more than one has sprung up between them (Znaniecki, 1965: 89).[4] Related to this observation is the fact that there is a "strain toward totality" whereby "as time goes on, the flow of external events calls forth more and more of the total set of identities of the individuals involved" (McCall and Simmons, 1966: 186).

Each of the parties in an IR recognizes the other as a distinct individual about whom he has some degree of prior knowledge (McCall and Simmons, 1966: 169). This knowledge is not only historical knowledge about one's partner but intimate knowledge as well, a facet of IRS which probably characterizes all but the marginal cases (Simmel, 1950: 126-127).[5]

It is probably acknowledged by most participants in IRS that they are by no means totally static conditions even though some exhibit a greater constancy than others. Strauss notes that "involvements are evolvements – in the course of which parties and their relationships become transformed (Strauss, 1959: 37). Thus, there are unevenly spaced high points in the career of any IR after which one is a different person to the other and the other is different to oneself. Such experiences along with less dramatic ones may actually effect the development of additional IRS, as when the boss invites his subordinate to accompa-

ny him on a fishing trip thereby initiating a sequence of interaction which may lead to a friendship relationship.

It is also important for our purposes to recognize that while IRS quite frequently terminate, there are forces which may prevent this from happening. 'Reward dependability' is a characteristic feature of many IRS and a major reason for their existence and continuation.[6] Ascription, both desired and undesired, is a second compelling reason for maintaining a certain relationship, as well as for initiating it. Men may also be more or less forced to remain in an IR for reasons other than ascription. 'Commitment', as this process is sometimes referred to, is manifested by means of a variety of arrangements, such as the existence of pension funds and seniority rights which make it costly for a person to quit his job simply because he does not get along with his boss (Becker, 1960). Of course, the person may also become positively 'attached' or involved in an IR.[7] Furthermore, one's investment in terms of time and other resources may operate to sustain a relationship. The effectiveness of these forces apparently depends somewhat upon the IR under consideration; for instance, kin relationships, at least for some segments of the population, are harder to break than others (Bott, 1957: 93; McCall and Simmons, 1966: 179).

Sentiments and Interpersonal Relationships

Essential to any discussion of IRS is the idea of sentiment, or the basic unit of organization of affect (Pear, 1964: 634-635).[8] A sentiment is the generalized feeling which one person has for the other in an IR, and it is to be identified through a pattern of response, rather than through any particular act (Shibutani, 1961: 333). Thus, a man in love with a woman expresses different emotions according to the situation in which he finds himself; he expresses joy in her presence, sorrow in her prolonged absence, fear when her life is in danger, and so forth. Sentiment organizes the appropriate emotions in the ongoing situation and it must be stressed that neither this underlying sentiment nor its emotional manifestations need always be positive in a relationship. One can have a negative IR with a neighbour or work superior, for instance, based upon the sentiment of hate, and it seems that this is especially likely to happen where he is committed to that IR. Although there is considerable empirical and theoretical work on specific negative relationships, general discussions of the nature of IRS tend to overlook this characteristic by limiting their focus to relationships built on positive bonds only.[9]

Of course, the intensity of the sentiment in an IR varies from situation to situation for each person, as well as varying over the career of the relationship. Variation in the intensity of sentiments alerts us to the fact that sentiment is only part, albeit a very important part, of the meaning which an enduring IR may have for a person. An IR may also have rational, evaluative, and traditional meanings for those involved in them, and these forms of meaning may also vary from situation to situation and over the career of the relationship. If there were not several kinds of meaning contained in an IR, many relationships would probably disintegrate or come dangerously close to disintegration with each dip of the intensity of the supporting sentiment. We are assuming, of course, that no one will maintain an IR which does not hold some meaning for him.

The Private Culture

Because IRS are basically subjective constructs, it should be apparent that they develop from 'virtual social identities' or the categories to which the parties of the relationship judge the other to belong (Goffman, 1963: 2).[10] These are to be distinguished from 'actual social identities' or those categories to which one can be proved, by objective analysis, to belong and those attributes which one can be proved to possess.

In the broad sense of the term, identities have roles attached to them; roles shall be defined here as sets of expectations of behaviour. This set of expectations can always be subdivided into a publicly-recognized component and a private component, the latter having been generated exclusively in the interaction of the two participants. The public expectations are generally acknowledged by members of the community to apply to those persons claiming to have or imputed to possess certain attributes and to those claiming to be or said to be members of certain categories. While there are always some community-wide or public expectations associated with them, for certain kinds of IRs (e.g., enemy, friend, and lover) the private aspect, nevertheless, is said to be by far the largest (Nadel, 1957:42).

This private aspect of role is part of the larger 'private culture' associated with the IR, which may include a rudimentary common language, common goals, memories of common experiences, and so forth. The recognition of a private culture associated with an IR contributes to the perception of the relationship as being unique among other relationships.

Interpersonal Relationships as Predispositions

By treating interpersonal relationships as predispositions, we give them a more explicit psychological foundation, a foundation implied in the words 'reciprocal' or 'mutual' orientation found within the definitions presented earlier. Furthermore, as we shall see later, the proposition that IRs are predispositional is an essential part of the causal nexus linking this concept and that of social network to situated behaviour. Social relationships have traditionally been seen in this latter role of guiding behaviour, a view which can be traced back to Weber's statement on this subject. However, their conceptualization as predispositions and, hence, as subjective constructs has never been clearly formulated.

The usage of the term 'predisposition' follows that of Campbell (1963: 97-112). He limits his statement to acquired states, stressing the importance of the fact that predispositions (or as he calls them, 'acquired behavioural dispositions') are enduring and that they remain dormant until 'activated' by situational stimuli. When activated, these products of past experience impinge upon our awareness, equip us with a specific view of the world, and guide behaviour in the immediate present. Values, attitudes, bits of knowledge, memory, habits, and meanings all have predispositional qualities about them.

The use of the term 'orientation' in definitions of the IR is itself a clue to the latter's status as a predisposition. Webster's Third International Dictionary defines an orientation in one sense of the word as the "choice or adjustment of associations, connections, or dispositions." It is of interest that Campbell includes 'adjustment, 'orientation' and 'disposition' in his extensive list of acquired behavioural dispositions. In harmony with the definition of orientation as an adjustment of predispositions, there are several subsidiary predispositions to be found in any IR. Knowledge about the other person, whether intimate or simply historical, may be considered as one such predisposition. The same is also true of the knowledge ego holds about alter's expectations of him and other aspects of the private culture. Commitment or attachment to a particular IR is a predisposition and so are the sentiments and other meanings which are part of any relationship.

Interpersonal relationships are also special views of the world; views which develop from their component subsidiary predispositions. It is perhaps this facet of IRs which explains best Nadel's observation (1957: 9) that there is a consistency about the many diverse acts which take place within them. Within wide limits "we may still say of persons in a given relationship that they act towards each other always in the same manner."

To the people in them IRs when activated have a very poig-

nant reality which is manifested in at least three ways. First of all, the continuous interaction between the two parties works to emphasize the existence of the relationship. Secondly, the high points in the career of the IR also make the participants conscious of it. Finally, the basic sentiment and its various emotional expressions make the person aware of the relationship.

The Social Network

As we have already observed, Bott's definition of social network (1957: 59) indicates the importance of interpersonal relationships as the basic elements of this construction. She viewed a social network as a "set of social relationships for which there is no common boundary." However, we have also noted that the traditional approach to IRs is essentially predispositional which means that upon activation these mental states help guide behaviour in the immediate setting. Now, since most people have several relationships at any one period in their lives, there is a strong possibility that one or more of them will be activated during interaction with members of the community. Where the ongoing interchange is with one of ego's relationship partners and his behaviour is at least partially guided by his reflection about one or more other IRs activated because they are relevant to the business at hand, we can say that all or a portion of his social network is influencing his actions. Because clusters of IRs, and perhaps not infrequently even the total set of IRs, can influence a person's action in the situation, we are forced to conclude that the social network also has subjective or predispositional qualities.[11]

Awareness of the Social Network

Like an IR, a social network as an activated predisposition must also be subjectively real to the individual whose network it is; that is, we are aware of activated predispositions. There is a considerable amount of theoretical discourse and empirical evidence in various social science fields which support this assertion. We shall briefly review some of them here.

One of the ways subjective awareness is manifested is through the direct and indirect effects which IRs in a network have upon each other. Direct contact between others in the various IRs is especially likely where the social network is closely-knit. Under these circumstances what transpires between two people in one relationship may affect another relationship through transactions in the social network of the second person. In this way a chain reaction can be set up, becoming, for example, a form of social control (Epstein, 1961; Hannerz, 1968). This direct influence is also seen where a third party, an IR significant in the network of both individuals, intercedes or threatens to intercede in the affairs of their IR.[12] For instance, Kemper (1968) found that wives and parents influence ego's response to alter in IRs established in a work organization.

Another possibility of direct influence is seen in Newcomb's A-B-X theory of the symmetry of orientation (1961, chap. 2). Where A is the central actor in an IR, B is his partner, and X is another person (for our purposes one with whom both have IRs), the following postulate may be advanced: "The stronger the forces toward A's co-orientation in respect to B and X, (a) the greater A's strain toward symmetry with B in respect to X; and (b) the greater the likelihood of increased symmetry as a consequence of one or more communicative acts."[13] The influencing force here is the desire on the part of the central actor to maintain some sort of cognitive equilibrium with respect to the elements of his social network through communication about this matter to his partner, B. The intensity of co-orientation determines which X's will require symmetry. The possibilities of disequilibrium, and hence awareness of the network, are considerable when we remember that A may see himself in a positive or negative relationship to B as well as to X.

The various IRS also may have indirect effects through the person whose network it is. Much, if not all, of this can be fitted into one of the various balance theories, which are in many ways like Newcomb's A-B-X model but do not involve communication with the actor's partner. In general, a state of balance exists for the actor when the elements in the social network have non-contradictory relationships for him. The basic proposition in balance theory is that where there is imbalance a person strives to restore the state of balance. Unlike the A-B-X model the elements themselves are not, as a rule, in contact. Thus, when in one man's social network his clergyman demands attitudes of racial equality whereas close friends in his neighbourhood demand attitudes of discrimination, a state of imbalance prevails. Balance theory hypothesizes that the individual in question will strive for balance, which may be achieved in various ways. Unfortunately, it is beyond the scope of this paper to examine these at the present time; our objective is simply to point out that the social network is very much a reality to the individual because of the pressures which originate within it.[14]

In addition to the pervasive influence of the component IRS on each other, the problems of trying to intermesh the daily and weekly routines associated with each relationship create an awareness of the over-all network. One comes to realize which IRS mean the most to him as he distributes his time to each. As McCall and Simmons (1966: 246) put it, it is a concern of "agenda-construction," and one's agenda "is not altogether a personal matter but must be *interactively* determined."

Because of the problems of agenda-construction connected with maintaining several IRS, the addition or loss of an IR also calls for a certain amount of planning, an activity which in itself makes one conscious of his network. Moreover, gaining new IRS or losing old ones may upset network balance or symmetry. It may be hypothesized that these problems are especially acute in what Bott (1957: 95) has called the 'transitional network': where one is changing from a tightly-knit to a loosely-knit network, or vice versa. Finally, Moreno's discussion (1960:64) about death in the social atom (see footnote 15) can be interpreted as illustrating these points: "If we happen to survive the ones we love or hate, we die a bit with them as we feel the shadow of death marching from one person in our social atom to another."

Size is also an important factor for agenda-construction; only so many IRS can be properly maintained in any given period of time. Thus, we can say that size makes the network subjectively real by curtailing the addition of new relationships and by pushing the claims on one's time resources to the limit. After assessing a variety of IRS, Jennings (1950: 309) discovered that the typical maximum number was twelve. Nelson (1966) has provided some evidence from his study of families that tightly-knit networks are more demanding of time than the loosely-knit ones. Another important observation on the factor of size is supplied by Goodenough (1965: 7) to the effect that the number of IRS depends upon how many are available, and this may vary from one culture to another. Finally, we may note that even if further expansion is possible from the point of view of the agenda, the psychological necessities of maintaining balance and symmetry set or strongly favour network growth in particular directions, directions which are compatible with the existing IRS. It would seem, in light of this last statement, that people also become at least partially committed to networks, as well as to certain IRS.

Social Networks as Predispositions

If social networks are to be accepted as predispositions, then we must be able to demonstrate this characteristic of them in a way independent of the dispositional nature of their component

IRS. Just because each individual IR in the network is a tendency to respond is not reason enough to assert that the network as a whole or any subpart of it also has this quality when activated. What features of a social network and its various segments give it the alleged predispositional character?

We can answer this question by pointing out that, like an IR, a social network is an orientation or an adjustment of subsidiary dispositions. The knowledge which a person has about the direct influence which IRS in his network have upon each other may be taken as one of these dispositions. Imbalance stemming from the presence of contradictory elements is definitely a state of mind which also predisposes a person to respond. Conflict of the daily and weekly routines associated with each IR not only creates awareness of the over-all social network but activates an adjustment disposition which is manifested in agenda construction. The same sort of conflict emerges when one attempts to increase the size of his set of IRS. Adjustment, in this case, may be simply to refuse to interact with the person in question, thereby preventing the development of a relationship.

Bott's earlier definition of social network while noting the role of IRS does not adequately convey this subjective characteristic which we have been discussing. It has been pointed out that she generally takes an ego-centred approach. A social network from our perspective is not ego-centred, in that the individual is merely the point from which analysis may begin, but person-centred: it is seen from the subjective standpoint of the individual whose network it is. Thus, we can now redefine social network as *the orientation which develops from considering all or a portion of one's interpersonal relations.* Formulated in this way this notion differs from several related ones which have appeared in the sociological and social psychological literature.[15]

Social Network in Explanations of Behaviour

The principal use to which networks have been put in the past is that of helping to account for the pattern of distribution of values, attitudes, or some sort of information. The kind of content conveyed may be gossip, rural values in the city, news about kin, or any number of other interests which can be spread by human contact. Recognizing and treating the social network as a predisposition does not in any way supplant this approach, but rather the predispositional point of view complements the communications network stance by opening up a new avenue of application: the direct explanation of behaviour in the social situation. Just how 'new' this use of social network actually is could be a matter of conjecture. Observations like the following from Elizabeth Bott's study (1957:94) have, no doubt, appeared from time to time in the network literature: "But although external people may help the elementary family, close-knit networks may also interfere with conjugal solidarity. A wife's loyalty to her mother may interfere with her relationship with her husband. Similarly her relationship with her husband may interfere with her relationship with her mother. A man's loyalty to his friends may interfere with his obligations to his wife and vice versa."

The point which should be stressed is that there has been no explicit formulation of a predispositional or subjective approach to networks. And, such an approach has utility as an explanation for certain kinds of human action as it is played out in social settings.

We can begin by asking when is this predispositional point of view of social networks and IRS called for in explanations? Or, perhaps, why is it needed at all? Is not the ordinary objective stance adequate? In answering these questions we may note that first of all, the predispositional point of view is required when the object of explanation is human social action of some kind: e.g., migration to an urban centre or the channels of gossip, to name two recent foci of network studies. More specifically, and this is the second point, it is needed when structural or cultural explanations or both fail to do their job adequately – when there is variation in social action which these frameworks cannot account for. When this happens we may be sure that personal interpretation has entered the picture. This personal interpretation has been referred to as the definition of the situation (see Stebbins, 1967b); the combination of internalized (and therefore previously interpreted) elements of culture and social structure, of personality, and of the situation which when reflected upon and defined in the ongoing setting can lead to behaviour that is to some degree different from what is categorically expected. The significance of the process of interpretation for the social sciences has been clearly stated by Herbert Blumer in his critique of variable analysis: "In my judgment, the crucial limit to the successful application of variable analysis to human group life is set by the process of interpretation or definition that goes on in human groups. This process, which I believe to be the core of human action, gives a character to human group life that seems at variance with the logical premises of variable analysis.... Any scheme designed to analyze human group life in its general character has to fit this process of interpretation" (1956:686).

The definition of the situation is basically an interrelation and interpretation of other predispositions which have been activated by certain situational factors. It is our contention that among the person's predispositions will be found specific IRs and all or a portion of his social network, where activated. Thus, the strength of this predispositional view lies in the fact that it enables us to study people's social networks at the situational level where it is hypothesized that on some occasions these networks modify culturally expected behaviour.

Research utilizing these concepts in this way should not be difficult. Interpersonal relationships can be inferred in a variety of ways; such as, by length of time in which ego has known alter, by amount of contact between the pair, by ability to predict the other's behaviour, as well as by the chances of re-establishing the relationship as suggested by Schutz and cited earlier in this article. Whether or not any particular IR was influencing behaviour in a given situation could easily be discovered by in-depth interviewing with regard to alter's salience at that time. Social networks could be determined by getting the respondent to report all interpersonal relationships of sufficient length, intimacy, and frequency of contact in various spheres of life: occupational, familial, recreational, neighbourly, religious, political, educational, commercial, and governmental. The activation of one's social network in any specific situation could be uncovered by a question like "were there certain things you wouldn't do with or say to certain other persons present because you were afraid it would get back to a mutual acquaintance?" Information about the respondent's awareness of the incompatibility of expectations stemming from various IRs as they affect his behaviour indicates influence of the network as does awareness of a conflict of routine.

Summary and Conclusions

Our main purpose has been to examine the logical connection between the concept of interpersonal or social relationship (IR) and that of social network, and to determine the implications of this link for network as an explanation. On the basis of the observation that since Weber's time IRs have been regarded as reciprocated orientations between two people, we presented a definition which more adequately conveyed this subjective or predispositional nature of the relationship. It follows that because of their status as predispositions IRs influence actual behaviour in the social situation. Bott's definition of social network as a set of relationships was assessed from this point of view. If one or more of a person's IRs influence his actions as they are being carried out with reference to one or more other IRs, then it is possible to conclude that part or all of that person's social network directly guides his situated behaviour. Therefore, we can say that a social network is also a psychological predisposition. This observation that the network is fundamentally a subjective construct which can be used as a direct explanation of behaviour, although perhaps not wholly new, has received little or no systematic empirical or theoretical attention in the past. Yet, such an application of network could be very fruitful in helping to account for why men define situations as they do and hence, why they act as they do. Moreover, as Boissevain (1968:546-9) has pointed out, non-group phenomena like networks help to free social anthropology from the grip of functionalism, thus opening new vistas for research and explanation.

NOTES AND BIBLIOGRAPHY

I would like to express my gratitude to D. Ralph Matthews and Robert Paine for their valuable comments on a draft of this paper.

1. For a critique of the term 'social network' and the closely related notion of 'field' (also used by Barnes), which is somewhat contradictory to Mayer, see Jay (1964).

2. Cooley (1922: 114-120) also approached IRs from a subjective point of view by treating them as clusters of sentiments attached to a symbol or image of another person.

3. Because IRs develop through sustained contact, it is probably safe to say that, in fact, they are reciprocated. There appears to be little likelihood that a normal person would see an IR between himself and another individual while the latter did not see one between them. Of course, the intensity of the sentiments involved may vary, as we shall see shortly. Evidence that IRs, in fact, are reciprocated can be found in Newcomb (1961). Schutz (1964: 111) presents what is basically an operational definition of an interpersonal relationship: "each of them [the partners in the IR] has the chance to reestablish the we-relation, if interrupted, and to continue it as if no intermittency had occurred."

4. A common example of two IRs between the same parties is that of the father-son and employer-employee relationships.

5. Schutz (1964: 113) has also defined intimacy in an operational manner: "the degree of reliable knowledge we have of another person."

6. Most of these forces are presented by McCall and Simmons (1966: 179).

7. For a further discussion of the distinction between attachment and commitment, see Stebbins (1969).

8. Some of the basic works on sentiment are those of Shand (1920), McDougall (1908), and Shibutani (1961).

9. See, for example, Simmel (1950: 118-142) and McCall and Simmons (1966, chap. 7).

10. 'Identity' is preferred over closely related ideas like 'status,' 'position,' and 'rank' because of its apparently broader scope. For example, one can have the identity of neighbour, but we would not ordinarily call this a position or a status.

11. Statements by Blumer (1956), Cicourel (1964: 119), and Fenton (1968) all support the belief that if structural variables can be said to influence ongoing behaviour, then they are mediated by the personal interpretation of the actor; and if personal interpretation has not been demonstrated, then any putative causal link between structure and behaviour may actually be no more than a chance correlation.

12. Nadel (1957: 86-87) refers to this situation as the 'triadization of roles.' See also Blau (1964: 31-32).

13. The term 'co-orientation' or 'simultaneous orientation' is equivalent to 'attitude' in the more inclusive sense of referring to both cathectic and cognitive tendencies. 'Symmetry' refers to the similarities of A's and B's orientations to X.

14. For a further discussion and bibliography of some of the various balance models, see Brown (1965, chap. 11).

15. The formulation which comes closest to being synonymous with our version of social network is Moreno's 'social atom' (1960: 52-54). However, the following two features of social atoms disqualify them as social networks from our point of view. (1) Moreno states that actors can be related to others even when those others do not know it.

However, the best evidence to date suggests that IRS as we have been discussing them in this paper, are reciprocated (Newcomb, 1961). (2) Moreno includes wished-for relationships in his social atom, while the idea of social network as developed in this paper is comprised only of ongoing IRS. Other similar formulations like Merton's 'status-set' and 'role-set' (1957: 368-384) or Znaniecki's 'social circle' (1965: 203-209) focus on one role or identity of the individual actor, while a social network encompasses all of the actor's identities and roles as long as there are established IRS involved. Finally Kemper's 'reference-set' (1966) should be mentioned since it includes the total aggregation of others from whom one derives central notions about oneself. Certainly any social network would include many of these, but it would, at the same time, exclude certain reference others with whom there are no IRS established (e.g., the prominent baseball star for the ten-year-old boy) and it would include certain non-reference others (e.g., the hated superior or the hostile neighbour).

Adams, B. N. 1967 "Interaction theory and the social network." *Sociometry* 30:64-78.

Barnes, J. A. 1954 "Class and committees in a Norwegian island parish." *Human Relations* 7:39-58.

Becker, H. S. 1960 "Notes on the concept of commitment." *American Journal of Sociology* 66:32-40.

Blau, P. M. 1964 *Power and Exchange in Social Life*. New York: John Wiley & Sons.

Blumer, H. 1956 "Sociological analysis and the variable." *American Sociological Review* 21:683-690.

Boissevain, J. 1968 "The place of nongroups in the social sciences." *Man* 3:542-556.

Bott, E. 1957 *Family and Social Network*. London: Tavistock Publications.

Brown, R. 1965 *Social Psychology*. New York: The Free Press.

Campbell, D. T. 1963 "Social attitudes and other acquired behavioral dispositions," pp. 94-172 in Sigmund Koch (ed.), *Psychology: A Study of a Science*. Vol. 6. New York: McGraw-Hill Co.

Cicourel, A. V. 1964 *Method and Measurement in Sociology*. New York: The Free Press.

Cooley, C. H. 1922 *Human Nature and the Social Order*. New York: Schocken Books.

Epstein, A. L. 1961 "The network and urban social organization." *Rhodes-Livingstone Journal* 29:29-62.

Fenton, C. S. 1968 "The myth of subjectivism as a special method of sociology." *The Sociological Review* 16:333-349.

Frankenberg, R. 1965 *Communities in Britain*. Harmondsworth Middlesex: Penguin Books.

Goffman, E. 1963 *Stigma*. Englewood Cliffs, N. J.: Prentice-Hall.

Goodenough, W. H. 1965 "Rethinking status and role," pp. 1-24 in Association of Social Anthropologists, *The Relevance of Models for Social Anthropology*, vol. 1. London: Tavistock Publications.

Gutkind, P. W. 1965 "African urbanism, mobility, and the social network." *International Journal of Comparative Sociology* 6: 48-60.

Hannerz, U. 1968 "Gossip, networks, and culture in a black American ghetto." *Ethnos* 32:35-60.

Jay, E. J. 1964 "The concept of field and network in anthropological research." *Man* 64: 137-138.

Jennings, H. H. 1950 *Leadership and Isolation*, 2nd ed. New York: Longmans, Green & Co.

Katz, F. E. 1966 "Social participation and social structure." *Social Forces* 45: 199-210.

Kemper, T. D. 1966 "Self-conceptions and the expectations of significant others." *Sociological Quarterly* 7:323-344.

1968 "Third party penetration of local social systems." *Sociometry* 31:1-29.

Mayer, A. C. 1966 "The significance of quasi-groups in the study of complex societies," pp. 97-122 in Association of Social Anthropologists, *The Social Anthropology of Complex Societies*, vol. 4. London: Tavistock Publications.

Mayer, P. 1962 "Labour migrancy and the social network," pp. 21-34 in J. F. Holleman, et al. (eds.), *Problems of Transition: Proceedings of the Social Science Research Conference held in University of Natal*, Durban. Pietermaritzburg: Natal University Press.

McCall, G. J., and J. L. Simmons 1966 *Identities and Interactions*. New York: The Free Press.

McDougall, W. 1908 *An Introduction to Social Psychology*. London: Methuen & Co.

Merton, R. K. 1957 *Social Theory and Social Structure*, rev. ed. New York: The Free Press.

Mitchell, C. J. 1966 "Theoretical orientations in African urban studies," pp. 37-68 in Association of Social Anthropologists, *The Social Anthropology of Complex Societies*, vol. 4. London: Tavistock Publications.

Moreno, J. L., et al. 1960 *The Sociometry Reader*. New York: The Free Press.

Nadel, S. F. 1957 *The Theory of Social Structure*. New York: The Free Press.

Nelson, J. I. 1966 "Clique contacts and family orientations." *American Sociological Review* 31:663-672.

Newcomb, T. M. 1961 *The Acquaintance Process*. New York: Holt, Rinehart & Winston.

Pear, T. H. 1964 "Sentiment," pp. 634-635 in Julius Gould and W. L. Kolb (eds.), *A Dictionary of the Social Sciences* New York: The Free Press.

Schutz, A. 1964 *Collected Papers II: Studies in Social Theory*. The Hague: Martinus Nijhoff.

Shand, A. F. 1920 *The Foundations of Character*. London: Macmillan.

Shibutani, T. 1961 *Society and Personality*. Englewood Cliffs, N. J.: Prentice-Hall.

Simmel, G. 1950 *The Sociology of Georg Simmel*, trans. K. Wolff. New York: The Free Press.

Srinivas. N. M., and A. Beteille 1964 "Networks in Indian social structure." *Man* 64:165-8.

Stebbins, R. A. 1967 "A theory of the definition of the situation." *Canadian Review of Sociology and Anthropology* 4:148-164.

——. 1969 *Commitment to Deviance: the Non-professional Criminal in the Community*. New York: Greenwood Publishing Corp.

Strauss, A. L. 1959 *Mirrors and Masks*. New York: The Free Press.

Young, M., and P. Wilmott 1957 *Family and Kinship in East London*. New York: The Free Press.

Znaniecki, F. 1965 *Social Relations and Social Roles*. San Francisco: Chandler Publishing Co.

5. Public and Private Space

John O'Neill/*York University*

Without real neighbourliness, you are no longer responsible for anything nor for anyone. But without the feeling of responsibility of each toward others, there is no possible civic freedom; dictatorship becomes inevitable in every society whose maxim is 'each for himself and God for all,' which is the maxim of those who do not believe in God. . . . The sense of one's neighbour, responsibility and liberty are things intimately linked, they engender one another mutually and can not long subsist without one another. And order is born of their alliance.**

** Denis de Rougement, *The Devil's Share* (New York: Pantheon, 1944) pp. 205-6

This seminal reflection expresses succinctly the thesis developed in this next essay: through the aegis of the corporate economy the boundaries between the public and private domains have become blurred, or even erased; the public has been subordinated to the private; the privatization of individual sensibilities renders them impervious to the arousal of a genuine public consciousness. It is instructive in this regard to examine the political philosophy that has been dominant in Canada throughout her history. The statements from McKenzie King and Lester Pearson which are quoted in Herman's essay in the next section are particularly telling.

Elsewhere, others have exposed the contradictions inherent in the institution of property and a moral code informed by the ethical precepts of justice and equality. As long as property is seen as a sacred and hence inalienable right, the state exists to ensure private privilege even at the expense of collective well-being. The recent controversies surrounding government intervention to block the sales of certain private firms in Canada to American corporations as being 'against the public interest' suggest the extent to which the sacredness of private property is embedded in the institutional structure of Canadian society. Or, consider the controversy that raged around the Spadina Expressway proposal in Toronto. Though the sales were blocked and the expressway stopped, the appeal that achieved this was at least as much to expediency as to principle.

Social space refers to claims. Inasmuch as the institution of property legitimates private claims, public space becomes a residual category, that space which is left over after private claims have been recognized.

Political imagination is shackled by the corporate organization of modern society. The traditional antitheses of individual and state, state and society, public and private rights, conflict and order, no longer serve to orient men's private lives toward their political contexts. Modern society is increasingly consensual and apolitical; it generates a comfortable reality which tempts us to identify the rationality of its industrial metabolism with the whole of rationality and thus to disengage ourselves from the critical tasks of reason. The tendency to identify technological rationality with social rationality is the major threat to the survival of the political imagination.[1] It underlies the liberal abdication of politics in favour of the market economy. By contrast, the subordination of technological rationality to social rationality is the program of a genuine Marxian political economy.

Political economy remains nerveless so long as it rests upon a concept of government which does not question the social distribution of resources between the public and private sectors of the economy. No modern government can retain power which fails to control industrial technology and the power of large corporations to shape the national ecology and psychic economy of individuals. The corporate economy stands between the state and the individual. Its power to determine the life-style of modern society must be recognized as the principal subject of political economy. The critique of the forces working to produce what Herbert Marcuse has called one-dimensional society must avoid the elitist fiction that mass society is the cause of our political troubles as well as the liberal illusion that pluralistic countervailing power is the only viable formula for political conduct.[2] At the same time, the basic organizational form of modern industrial society is so closely tied to such a small number of corporate and bureaucratic structures that the ideas of pluralism can hardly be said to exercise a qualitative effect upon the system.

Reprinted from *Agenda 1970: proposals for a creative politics*, edited by Trevor Lloyd and Jack McLeod, by permission of University of Toronto Press. © University of Toronto Press 1968.

"In a specific sense advanced industrial culture is *more* ideological than its predecessor, inasmuch as today the ideology is in the process of production itself. In a provocative form, this proposition reveals the political aspects of the prevailing technological rationality. The productive apparatus and the goods and services which it produces 'sell' or impose the social system as a whole. . . . The products indoctrinate and manipulate; they promote a false consciousness which is immune against its falsehood. And as these beneficial products become available to more and more individuals in more social classes, the indoctrination they carry ceases to be publicity; it becomes a way of life. It is a good way of life – much better than before – and as a good way of life, it militates against qualitative change. Thus emerges a pattern of *one-dimensional thought and behavior* in which ideas, aspirations, and objectives that, by their content, transcend the established universe of discourse and action are either repelled or reduced to terms of this universe. They are redefined by the rationality of the given system and of its quantitative extension."[3]

One-dimensional society is characterized by a systematic linkage between the subordination of public space to private space through the agency of the corporate economy and an ideological privatization of individual sensibilities which reinforces corporate control over the allocation of social resources and energies. One-dimensional society has its roots in the liberal concept of society as a field in which the private pursuit of economic interests produces public benefits without political intervention. The emergence of a 'social universe', which is, strictly speaking, neither public nor private, is a modern phenomenon that arises from the public significance accorded to the business of making a living and that has no counterpart in the ancient world. It is a phenomenon which has forced upon us the hybrid term 'political economy' and with it the challenge to rethink the relation between the public and private domains in modern industrial society.

Public and Private Space

In the Graeco-Roman world the boundary between the public and private realms was clear and men were conscious of the threshold between public and private life. Although the ancient city-state grew at the expense of the family household and kinship group, the boundary between the public and private realms was never erased. Indeed, the definition of the public realm as an area of freedom and equality presupposed the recognition of 'necessity' in the household economy.[4] The needs of maintenance and reproduction defined the social nature of man and the family, and the sexual and social division of labour between man and woman, master and slave.

In the modern period this ancient boundary between public and private realms was dissolved with the emergence of 'society' and the liberal concept of mini-government. A whole new world – the social universe – emerged between public and private life. The public significance of the social universe has its roots in the subjectivization of private property and the subordination of government to a minimal agenda in the social equilibration of individual and public interests. The seventeenth century reduced the political domain to the narrow limits of 'government' in order to exploit the boundless domain of possessive individualism, which Professor C. B. Macpherson has described as the central impediment of modern liberal-democratic ideology. "Its possessive quality is found in its conception of the individual as essentially the proprietor of his own person or capacities, owing nothing to society for them. The individual was seen neither as a moral whole, nor as part of a larger social whole, but as an owner of himself. The relation of ownership, having become for more and more men the critically important relation determining their actual freedom and actual prospect of realizing full potentialities, was read back into the nature of the individual.... Society becomes a lot of free individuals related to each other as proprietors of their own capacities and of what they have acquired by their exercise. Society consists of relations of exchange between proprietors. Political society becomes a calculated device for the protection of this property and for the maintenance of an orderly relation of exchange."[5]

The liberal practicality shied away from any utopian conception of the public domain and was content with an order that seemed to emerge through non-intervention in the natural processes, or rather in the metabolism, of society. As Hannah Arendt has argued, this extraordinary identification of society with its economy may be traced in part to the liberal devaluation of politics. "What concerns us in this context is the extraordinary difficulty with which we, because of this development, understand the decisive division between the public and private realms, between the sphere of the polis and the sphere of household and family, and, finally, between activities related to a common world and those related to the maintenance of life, a division upon which all ancient political thought rested as self-evident and axiomatic."[6]

All the spaces of the modern world are absorbed into a single economy whose rhythms are linear and mechanical. The architecture of public and commercial institutions, the furnishings of the home, and even the styles in which we clothe our bodies threaten to destroy the dialectic between the things that are to be shown and the things that are to be hidden. The results vary from the inhuman naked space of the typing-pool to the democratic open spaces of Toronto's new City Hall where the shocking exposure of secretarial knees produced demands for privacy in the design of working areas. Even more desperate is the loss of the values of privacy in the very sanctuary of the home. Le Corbusier has called the modern house 'a machine to live in', a machine that mechanizes living in a mechanical world. In a strange, disordered repetition of ancient symbolism, the modern household is hooked into the centre of the universe through its television navel and suspended by an aerial (*universalis columna quasi sustinens omnia*) between heaven and hell. "The Kwakiutl believe that a copper pole passes through the three cosmic levels (underworld, earth, sky); the point at which it enters the sky is the 'door to the world above.' The visible image of this cosmic pillar in the sky is the Milky Way."[7] Through the picture-frame windows of the modern house the metabolism of family life is projected into the public realm and from there it completes its circuit back into the home through a magical aether populated by waxes, deodorants, soap-suds, and tissues.

In one-dimensional society desire born of necessity is no longer domesticated. Now the whole of society is organized to satisfy domestic passions. And this is an arrangement eminently suited to the ethic of individualistic-familism and the socialization of the members of society into their 'calling' as consumers whose needs are the self-imposed agency of social control. It is this continuity of psychic and socio-economic space which grounds the coherent fantasy of consumer sovereignty at the same time that it fills the air with the noise and filth that are the by-products of the commercial narcosis.[8]

Metabolism and Political Economy

In the period between the decline of the feudal family order and the rise of modern nation-states geared to a fully industrialized economy there emerged a microcosmic version, in the Court circle and the salon of high society, of the tragic alienation of the individual in a universe hidden from God and abandoned to the play of social forces.[9] Whether it is through the identification of the individual with his title at Court in the *ancien régime* or with his occupational status in the modern corporation, the modern individual encounters a bureaucratization of private sensibilities, a wasteland between the boundaries of the heart and the public presentation of the self.[10] The rise of modern society is the history of the decline of feudal community, the growth of the nation state, industrial technology, and political democracy. But it is also the paradox of the affinity of individualism for conformism through the erosion of the communal bases of the family, the guild, the village, and the Church.[11] The emergence of the 'total community' has its origins in the growth of rationalism in economics, politics, and religion. In each of these areas modern individualism receives its impulse from the subjectivization of the bases of the feudal community and a simultaneous assimilation of the individual into the abstract community of market society. "Thus, from the viewpoint of this enlightened political economy which has discovered the *subjective* essence of wealth within the framework of private property, the partisans of the monetary system and the mercantilist system, who consider private property as a *purely objective* being for man, are *fetishists* and *Catholics*. Engels is right, therefore, in calling Adam Smith the *Luther of political economy*. Just as Luther recognized religion and *faith* as the essence of the real *world* and for that reason took up a position against Catholic paganism; just as he annulled *external* religiosity while making religiosity the *inner* essence of man; just as he negated the distinction between priest and layman because he transferred the priest into the heart of the layman; so wealth external to man and independent of him (and thus only to be acquired and conserved from outside) is annulled. That is to say, its *external* and *mindless objectivity* is annulled by the fact that private property is incorporated in man himself, and man himself is recognized as its essence. But as a result, man himself is brought into the sphere of private property, just as, with Luther, he is brought into the sphere of religion. Under the guise of recognizing man, political economy, whose principle is labour, carries to its logical conclusion, the denial of man. Man himself is no longer in a condition of external tension with the external substance of private property. What was previously a phenomenon of *being external to oneself*, a real external manifestation of man, has now become the act of objectification, of alienation. This political economy seems at first, therefore, to recognize man with his independence, his personal activity, etc. It incorporates private property in the very essence of man, and it is no longer, therefore, conditioned by the local or national *characteristics of private property* regarded as existing outside itself. It manifests a cosmopolitan, universal activity which is destructive of every limit and every bond, and substitutes itself as the *only* policy, the *only* universality, the *only* limit and the *only* bond."[12]

The identification of the metabolism of the household with the national economy, which results in the hybrid concern of 'political economy' is the outcome of the alienation of private property and labour from their anchorages in use-values. In their endlessly reproducible forms, as the exchange-values of capital and labour power, private property and labour enter the public realm and subordinate the public realm to the needs of market society. The emancipation of labour is the precondition of the substitution of exchange-values for use-values which leads to the subordination of all fixed forms of life and property to the accumulation and expansion of wealth. In the remarkable passage from the *Economic and Philosophical Manuscripts* quoted above, Marx explains how private property becomes the subjective impulse of industrial activity through its definition as *labour-power*. The Physiocrats identified all wealth with land and cultivation, leaving feudal property to the later attacks on ground rent. The objective nature of wealth was also in part shifted to its subjective basis in labour, inasmuch as agriculture was regarded as the source of the productivity of land. Finally, industrial labour emerged as the most general principle of productivity, the factors of production, land, labour, and capital, being nothing else than moments in the dialectic of labour's self-alienation.

Private Opulence and Public Squalor

Marx's expectation remains unfulfilled that capitalism would collapse because of the conflict between the technological rationalization of its economy and the irrationality of its social and political structure. The question is whether the Marxian diagnosis is as irrelevant as the phenomena of welfare and affluent capitalism[13] are taken to suggest. Certainly, the metabolism of the corporate economy absorbs more than ever the public and private energies of modern society. Under the banner of a neo-feudal ideology of corporate responsibility,[14] a new psychic serfdom to brand-loyalties and occupational status immunizes monopoly capitalism from the processes of social and political criticism. It is increasingly difficult to discuss the nature of the good society where everyone is mesmerized by the *goods* society.

In the North American context, there are historical and environmental factors which contribute to the equation of politics and abundance. "The politics of our democracy was a politics of abundance rather than a politics of individualism, a politics of increasing our wealth quickly rather than dividing it precisely, a politics which smiled both on those who valued abundance as a means to safeguard freedom and on those who valued freedom as an aid in securing abundance."[15] The ideological roots of the affluent society have been traced by John Kenneth Galbraith to the hold upon the liberal mind of certain imperatives which flow from the 'conventional wisdom.' Adam Smith, Ricardo, and Malthus were clear enough that the mass of men were powerless against the class of property owners. But in view of the factors of scarcity, against which any proposal for social redistribution could only mean a relapse into barbarism, it seemed that the mutual interests of the rich and the poor lay in the expansion of industrial activity. However, in the conventional wisdom the imperative of production remains just as imperious as it ever was, despite intervening changes in the modern economic environment which have made abundance a technological possibility, if not a sociological certainty. "These – productivity, inequality and insecurity – were the ancient preoccupations of economies. They were never more its preoccupations than in the nineteen thirties as the subject stood in a great valley facing, all unknowingly, a mountainous rise. In a very large measure the older preoccupations remain."[16] The paradox of the affluent society is that it has exhausted the liberal imagination in a 'solution' of the problems of inequality and insecurity through a mindless expansion of production.

The instrument of this paradoxical situation is the corporate organization of the economy whose success in controlling its economic environment[17] has won for it political acceptance from its employees and the stabilizing support of state-administered anti-depressants for those moments on which the soulfulness of the corporation threatens to reach a low-point. The power of the corporation to control its environment assumes a variety of forms, ranging from its ability to control price-cost relationships, levels and composition of investment, the nature of research and innovation, the location of industry with its effects upon local communities and, of course, its power to influence governmental intervention, and, last but not least, the power to shape the physical and socio-psychological environment of the consumer public. In each case, these powers of the corporation are of enormous social and political consequence.[18]

In the face of the reality of corporate power, Galbraith's theory of countervailing power is hardly more than a figleaf for corporate respectability and liberal prudishness. It is in any case a desperate gesture in view of Galbraith's own understanding of the corporate practice of integrating its production and sales efforts through the generation of wants. By engineering consumer response, the corporation is able to get an *ex post facto* ratification of its commitment of social resources as determined by corporate agenda. While paying lip-service to consumer sovereignty in the final allocation of social resources, the corporation can in fact assume the conventional distribution of social resources between the public and private sectors of the economy. This presumption is a political reality inasmuch as the demand for public services presently arises out of the needs of low-income groups who are powerless to compete away social resources from the private uses of higher-income groups. It is only in the context of the unequal distribution of income, which remains as much as ever a defining characteristic of affluent capitalism, that one can properly understand the imperative of production or, rather, of *relative overproduction for the private sector*, which in turn promotes the secondary imperatives of consumption and other-direction. Despite the heralds of the age of high mass consumption, the fact is that monopoly capitalism is a production system continually faced with the problem of deficient consumption structurally related to the class distribution of income.[19] Because of this conventional restraint upon the economic space of the capitalist system, it is necessary to invade the psychic space of workers and consumers through raising levels of expectation or through deepening levels of credit.

There are, of course, attempts to expand the economic space of the capitalist system through extensions of the public sector, overseas operations, and the conquest of outer space. But in no case do these extensions result in a significant alteration of the flow of social resources between the public and private sectors. The commanding position of the corporation in the face of governmental efforts to redistribute social income is evident from the relative stability of corporate profits after taxes as a share of national income during the last forty years.[20] In effect, the government merely uses the corporation to collect its taxes and is therefore dependent upon the corporate economy's agenda having been substantially realized before it can undertake its own program. Indeed, it must be recognized that the determination of the balance between the public and the private sectors of capitalist society depends increasingly on the identification of welfare and warfare. The American war psychosis is an obvious manifestation of the increasingly militarized production imperatives of the corporate economy. The significance of the social unbalance created by military spending is lost when considered simply as a proportion of total gross national product. From this perspective, the one-tenth of GNP absorbed in military expenditure seems negligible and easily enough absorbed in alternative expenditures. However, once it is realized that military expenditures represent half of total federal government expenditures,[21] it is clear that the issue is neither negligible nor easily corrigible. It is not negligible because it represents the impoverished conception of the public domain in capitalist society. Nor is it easily corrigible, since to find alternative paths of governmental spending involves a reconsideration of the balance between the public and private sectors which would expose the poverty of the liberal ideology.

The institution of advertising can now be understood as the essential means of expanding the economic space of capitalism in a manner compatible with the liberal ideology. What Galbraith calls the 'dependence effect' is in reality a political option which, if unrelated to the class structure of capitalist society and its effects upon the distribution of social resources between public and private uses, appears as the myth of an evil genius. "Were it so that a man on arising each morning was assailed by demons which instilled in him a passion sometimes for silk shirts, sometimes for kitchenware, sometimes for chamber pots, and sometimes for orange squash, there would be every reason to applaud the effort to find the goods, however odd, that quenched the flame. But should it be that his passion was the result of his first having cultivated the demons, and should it also be that his effort to allay it stirred the demons to even greater and greater effort, there would be question as to how rational was his solution. Unless restrained by conventional attitudes, he might wonder if the solution lay with more goods or fewer demons.

"So it is that if production creates the wants it seeks to satisfy, or if the wants emerge *pari passu* with the production, then the urgency of the wants can no longer be used to defend the urgency of the production. Production only fills a void that it has itself created."[22]

It is not the dependence effect as such which is responsible for the irrationality of consumer behaviour. For in every society wants are largely cultural acquisitions. The real problem is the nature of the social order which determines the content and pattern of wants. A society which fails to maintain the necessary complementarities between private and public goods and services drives itself even deeper into the accumulation of private amenities in order to compensate for the public squalor which this very process leaves in its wake.

The automobile becomes the true symbol of the North American flight into privacy.[23] It has hollowed the cities and drained the countryside, melting each into the atomized living-space of suburbia; it is the instrument of urban congestion and rural uglification. At the same time, the automobile is perfectly geared to the values of technical rationality, private ownership, individual mobility, sex equality, and social rivalry – pre-eminently the values of the liberal ideology and the stock-in-trade of the corporate economy. The automobile is eminently the equilibrator of the tensions in corporate culture: it is a family headache and a family joy, an air-pollutant indispensable for trips into the fresh-air of the countryside, an escape mechanism from all the problems with which it is structurally integrated.

The role of the automobile in modern society makes it evident that we can no longer consider machines from the purely technological standpoint of the mastery of nature. We must take into account the interaction between machinery and the social relations between men not only in the context of machine production but in the wider context in which machinery patterns our style and ecology of life. Short of such an understanding, we find ourselves hallucinating the conquest of distance while all the time the road which opens up before us is the distance between a humane living-space and the little boxes which house our automobile.

But any criticism of the automobile is likely to be dismissed as quixoticism. For the power to respond to such criticism has been sapped through the cultivation of psychic identification with the automobile as an extension of individual personality. Even where slightly less elongated extensions have been preferred by four-wheeled man, the apparent rationality of that choice actually only deepens the commitment to private as opposed to public transportation alternatives. The result is a chain-process in the privatization of other social resources integrated with the automobile culture at a time when more than ever we need to break that circuit.

The difficulty of intervention on behalf of the public domain is nowhere better seen than in the light of the potential hue and cry against interference with the individual's freedom to buy, own, and drive, wherever and whenever, that capsule which seals him off from physical and social reality while making him completely dependent upon them. Likewise, the course of public intervention in regard to the automobile is indicative of the impoverished conception of government in liberal society. The result so far is the confusion of the growth of public space with the extension of public highways which breeds more automobiles and accelerates the dislocation of urban spaces in favour of suburban locations. Commuting by means of private transportation becomes the only link between living spaces and working spaces. Finally, the rationale of this living arrangement is given a coherent projection through television advertisements in which the enjoyment of suburban values can be 'seen' in the happy use of the automobile to take children to school, mother to the stores, father to work, and the dog to the veterinarian, without anyone even wondering how everything got so far away.

Alienation and the Sublimation of Politics

There is a trend in industrial society toward the interpretation of freedom and equality in terms of consumer behaviour rather than of political action about the nature and conditions of production and consumption. "Equality for the working-classes, like freedom for the middle-classes, is a worrisome, partially rejected, by-product of the demand for more specific measures."[24] In the context of corporate capitalism, the rhetoric of freedom and equality no longer swells into a coherent political ideology as it once did as a strategy of bourgeois and proletarian emancipation. Just as the terrible freedom of market society has not always been tolerable to the middle class without escapes, so the working class response to market society has varied from class struggle to the becalmed acceptance of inequality softened by improvements to the social basement. This ambivalence in the response to the symbolism of freedom, equality, and reason must be understood in terms of the changing social contexts from which these notions derive their meaning and significance. Robert A. Nisbet has commented upon the changing contexts of individuality.[25] He observes that when we speak of 'the individual' we are dealing with an ideal type or moral abstraction whose symbolic currency depends upon the existence of an institutional context which is favourable to its assimilation in everyday life. The liberal image of man, its possessive individualism, is the result of the imputation of the properties of market society to the interior life of the individual. The liberal theory of society and the individual was plausible just so long as the historical situation which liberalism presupposed effectively linked its vocabulary of motives with typical contexts of action.[26] However, once the evolution of market society moves in the direction of corporate society, the vocabulary of liberalism merely evokes lost contexts, arousing a nostalgia haunted by the loss of meaning.

The loss of a meaningful, social or public context for the ideals of individualism, freedom, and equality is reflected in the alienated and confused symbolism of David Riesman's *Lonely Crowd* or Paul Goodman's *Growing Up Absurd*. Each of these works confronts us with the paradox that society may be free without individuals being free. The liberal identity of individual and social interests, or, rather, the liberal perception of the challenge and opportunity offered to the individual by society, has withered away into a conviction of the absurdity of society and the idiocy of privatization which is its consequence. For want of a genuine public domain, in which the political and social activities of individuals can achieve a focus and historical perspective, men abandon politics for the civic affairs of suburbia or the 'bread and butter' questions of unionism. By shifting awareness toward improvements in consumption styles, these tactics deflect attention from the social imbalance which results from the pursuit of intra-class benefits that leave whole sectors of the population outside of their calculus. This tactic is further strengthened by the ideological acceptance of social improvement through the escalation effect of an expanding economy upon all classes rather than through any radical redistribution of class income or the extension of chances of individual mobility between classes.

As individual awareness is increasingly shifted toward a concern with consumption, economic knowledge is reduced to a concern with prices in abstraction from the corporate agenda which determines prices. The result is a loss of any coherent ideological awareness of the political and economic contexts of individual action. However, this does not represent an end of ideology. It is simply the nature of the dominant ideology of individualism shaped by the context of corporate capitalism. In order to break the tendency to monetize all individual experience, and in order to shift individual time perspectives away from short-term consumer expectations, it is necessary to institutionalize more universal goals of collective and long-term value. Such a requirement falls outside the pattern of instant satisfactions projected by the consumer orientation. The latter substitutes the thin continuity of progress for the solid accumulation of social history. The result is the paradox upon which Robert E. Lane has commented. "Is it curious," he asks, "that a nation that has so emphasized progress should have no sense of the future? I do not think so," he replies, for "progress is a rather thin and emotionally unsatisfactory continuity. It is the continuity of differences, the regularity of a rate of change, almost a rate of estrangement."[27] Any concern with social balance, institutional poverty, and waste, or the interaction between politics, economics, and culture presupposes a collective and historical framework; but this is foreign to the liberal ideology of individual agency and its moralistic acceptance of inequality and failure within a natural order of social competition and private success.

In a society where individual interests are so privatized that people prefer private swimming pools to public swimming pools, common effort is likely to be viewed only as a substitute for private effort. Moreover, any comparison between public and private enterprise will be moralized in favour of the fruits of individual effort owing to the very real struggle involved in the acquisition of private pools, homes, and education. The loss of community functions resulting from the privatization of social resources makes individual accumulation appear all the more 'rational'. In reality, the individual is driven toward this pattern of privatization not from genuine choice but because he is deprived of alternatives whose systematic provision would require a public sector powerful enough to compete with the private economy. The provision of alternatives to the patterns of production and consumption in the corporate economy never gets beyond the platitudes of 'variety' and consumer sovereignty which are virtually meaningless once attention is diverted from increasing the size of the goods basket to questions about the quality of a single item in it, such as bread.[28] The 'efficiency' of private enterprise must be discounted by the loss of social energy involved in trying to choose a reasonable (unmagical, unwrapped, uncut) loaf of bread, and reaches an absurdly low point once the individual retreats to 'home-baking', or, indeed, any kind of hobby which is a *substitute* for satisfaction in the private economy. The rise of para-social, political, and economic activities is an indication of individual withdrawal from 'society'. It is the expression of an abstracted individualism that is the ideological alternative to political action on behalf of a world that men can have in common. This loss of a common world separates society into a corporate hierarchy and a multitude of individuals who are turned in upon themselves in the competition to maintain occupational status and at the same time other-directed in their attempt to rationalize their loss of community in the pursuit of the good life – family-style. Where there is no common world between working life and private life the individual's public life is reduced to shopping expeditions, church attendance, and movie-going, all homogenized to suit family-tastes, which are, of course, presensitized to the appeal of the 'goods life'.

It is in keeping with the liberal ideology of individualistic familism that tensions are personalized and at best call for individual therapy. Any attempt to relate private troubles to institutional contexts, which would suggest public or political action, is regarded as projection, the evasion of difficulties best tackled within the four walls of the home, if not in one particular room. The result is that men lack bridges between their private lives and the indifference of the publics that surround them. "Nowadays men often feel that their private lives are a series of traps. They sense that within their everyday worlds, they cannot overcome their troubles, and in this feeling they are often quite correct. What ordinary men are directly aware of and what they try to do are bounded by the private orbits in which they live; their visions and their powers are limited to the closeup scenes of job, family, neighbourhood; in other milieux, they move vicariously and remain spectators. And the more aware they become, however vaguely, of ambitions and of threats which transcend their immediate locales, the more trapped they seem to feel."[29]

It is the task of the political and sociological imagination to conceive men's private troubles in the contexts of public concern and to furnish bridging concepts which will enable individuals to translate their private uneasiness into public speech and political action. It must undertake to shift the contexts of freedom, equality, and reason away from the private sector and out of the household into a public domain which will constitute a genuine common world. And this is a task which must be articulated in a conception of government which is bold enough to seek understanding and responsible control over the human and social values generated but largely dissipated in the corporate economy which enforces the privatization of men's lives. Such a positive conception of government would help to create a public domain in which men share common assumptions about their moral and physical environment and exercise them in a concern for truth of speech and beauty of form in public places – places cleared of their present monuments to financial cunning and fear of the future that wastes private lives.

NOTES

1. Herbert Marcuse, *One-Dimensional Man*, Studies in the Ideology of Advanced Industrial Society (Boston, 1964). For the distinction between technical or 'functional' rationality and 'substantial' rationality see Karl Mannheim, *Man and Society in an Age of Reconstruction* (London, 1940), pp. 51-60.
2. "*To be socially integrated in America is to accept propaganda, advertising and speedy obsolescence in consumption.* The fact is that those who fit the image of pluralist man in pluralist society also fit the image of mass man in mass society. Any accurate picture of the shape of modern society must accommodate these ambiguities." Harold L. Wilensky, "Mass Society and Mass Culture: Interdependence of Dependence?" *American Sociological Review*, vol. 29, no. 2 (April 1964), p. 196.
3. Herbert Marcuse, *One-Dimensional Man*, pp. 10-11. For an empirical confirmation of the ideological content of the consumer orientation, see Sanford M. Dornbusch and Lauren C. Hickman, "Other-Directedness in Consumer-Goods Advertising: A Test of Riesman's Historical Typology," *Social Forces*, vol. 38, no. 2, pp. 99-102.
4. Aristotle, *Politics*, 1252 a.2.
5. C. B. Macpherson, *The Political Theory of Possessive Individualism: Hobbes to Locke* (Oxford, 1962), p. 3. The liberal concept of 'society' provoked the counterconcept of 'organic society' in Conservative and

Marxian thought which have more in common than either has with liberalism. Karl Mannheim, *Essays on Sociology and Social Psychology* (New York, 1953), chap. II, "Conservative Thought."

6. *The Human Condition* (Chicago, 1958), p. 28.

7. Mircea Eliade, *The Sacred and the Profane (New York, 1959), p. 35.*

8. "To behold, use or perceive any extension of ourselves in technological form is necessarily to embrace it. To listen to radio or to read the printed page is to accept these extensions of ourselves into our personal system and to undergo the 'closure' or displacement of perception that follows automatically. It is this continuous embrace of our own technology in daily use that puts us in the Narcissus role of subliminal awareness and numbness in relation to these images of ourselves. By continuously embracing technologies, we relate ourselves to them as servomechanisms. That is why we must, to use them at all, serve these objects, these extensions of ourselves, as gods or minor religions. An Indian is the servomechanism of his canoe, as the cowboy of his horse, or the executive of his clock." Marshall McLuhan, *Understanding Media: The Extensions of Man* (New York, 1965), p. 46.

9. Lucien Goldmann, *Le dieu caché: Etude sur la vision tragique dans les pensées et dans le théâtre de Racine* (Paris, 1955).

10. Locke shows no awareness of the alienation of man in society, unlike Hobbes, who, nevertheless, has no solution for it. It is Rousseau who first attempts to link the experience of alienation with social criticism.

11. Robert A. Nisbet, *Community and Power* (New York, 1962). Cf. Karl Marx, *Communist Manifesto* (New York, Gateway Editions, 1954), p. 12. Marx's sketch of the breakdown of feudalism is brilliantly developed in Karl Polanyi, *The Great Transformation* (Boston, 1957).

12. *Karl Marx: Early Writings*, T. B. Bottomore, trans. and ed. (London, 1963), pp. 147-8.

13. For a careful appraisal of the relations between welfare capitalism and the affluent society, see T. H. Marshall, *Sociology at the Crossroads*, (London, 1963), Part Three, "Social Welfare," and Richard M. Titmuss, *Essays on the "Welfare State"*, with a new chapter on "The Irresponsible Society" (London, 1963).

14. It has been argued that the corporate exercise of political power is in principle continuous with the natural-law tradition of the separation of sacred and profane power and its institutionalization in the countervailing powers of feudal nobility. St. Augustine's 'City of God', understood as the theory that in every age there is a moral and philosophical framework which constrains power, has been claimed as the model of corporate politics. Adolf A. Berle, *The Twentieth Century Capitalist Revolution* (London, 1955).

15. David M. Potter, *People of Plenty: Economic Abundance and the American Character* (Chicago, 1954), p. 126.

16. J. K. Galbraith, *The Affluent Society* (Boston), p.77.

17. "By and large, corporations have been able to exert sufficient pressure on governments, and on social institutions generally, to stabilize the field in their favour. *This stabilizing of the environment is the politics of industry.*" John Porter, *The Vertical Mosaic; An Analysis of Social Class and Power in Canada* (Toronto, 1965), p. 269 (my italics). The weakness of government planning in America has been attributed to the competitive nature of its political institutions which weaken it relative to the more monolithic structure of business. Andrew Shonfield, *Modern Capitalism: The Changing Balance of Public and Private Power* (New York, 1965), p. 353.

18. Carl Kaysen, "The Corporation: How Much Power? What Scope?," and Norton Long, "The Corporation, Its Satellites and the Local Community," in Edward S. Mason, ed., *The Corporation in Modern Society* (Cambridge, Mass., 1961), pp. 85-105, 202-17.

19. Gabriel Kolko, "The American 'Income Revolution'," in Philip Olson, ed., *America as a Mass Society* (New York, 1963), pp. 103-16; Porter, *The Vertical Mosaic*, pp. 125-32 for an evaluation of the validity of the middle-class and middle-majority image in Canada.

20. Irving B. Kravis, "Relative Shares in Fact and Theory," *American Economic Review*, Dec. 1959, p. 931, quoted in Paul A. Baran and Paul M. Sweezy, *Monopoly Capital: An Essay on the American Economic and Social Order* (New York, 1966), p. 148. There is consistent empirical evidence of long-run tax-shifting by corporations. Two recent studies emphasize the long-run maintenance of a stable after-tax rate of return on investment despite substantial increases in corporation income tax, E. M. Lerner and E. S. Hendrikson, "Federal Taxes on Corporate Income and the Rate of Return in Manufacturing 1927-1952," *National Tax Journal*, vol. IX (Sept. 1965), pp. 193-202; R. E. Slitor, "The Enigma of Corporate Tax Incidence," *Public Finance*, vol. XVIII (1963), pp. 328-52.

21. In a record US budget of $135 billion for the fiscal year 1967 $72.3 billion were allocated to military expenditures, a sum exceeded only by the figure of $81.3 billion spent in 1945. *Globe and Mail*, Toronto, Jan. 25, 1967, p. 1.

22. Galbraith, *The Affluent Society*, p. 153.

23. Housing would illustrate the problems of over-privatization and the impoverishment of the public sector just as well as the automobile to which it must be related. The housing situation is especially illustrative of the tendency to privatize even explicitly public functions. "Public money totalling hundreds of millions of dollars has been advanced as National Housing Act loans for middle- and upper-middle-income families, to help them buy houses. But few lower-middle-income families and no poor families can get these loans . . . many persons in Europe look on the Canadian system as socialism for the rich, private enterprise for the poor. The North American welfare approach to public housing singles out low-income tenants as conspicuous recipients of public bounty. It hives them off in ghettos for the poor. The European approach, on the other hand, treats housing as a public utility. It contains a big public sector, in which non-profit housing is provided to persons in a broad income range – not merely the poor. It also contains a large area in which private enterprise operates freely and profitably." G. E. Mortimer, "Canada's Leaky Housing Program," *Globe and Mail*, Toronto, Jan. 5, 1967, Women's Section, p. 1.

24. Robert E. Lane, *Political Ideology: Why the American Common Man Believes What He Does* (New York, 1962), p. 60.

25. *Community and Power*, chap. 10, "The Contexts of Individuality." Compare C. B. Macpherson's discussion of 'social assumptions', *The Political Theory of Possessive Individualism*, chap. I, II, III, VI.

26. C. Wright Mills, "Situated Actions and Vocabularies of Motive," in *Power, Politics and People: The Collected Essays of C. Wright Mills*, I. L. Horowitz, ed. (New York, 1963), pp. 439-52.

27. *Political Ideology*, p. 290.

28. "I say we make the foulest bread in all the world. We pass it off like fake diamonds. We advertise it and sterilize it and protect if from the germs of life. We make a manure which we eat before we have had time to eliminate it. We not only have failed God, tricked Nature, debased Man, but we have cheated the birds of the air with our corrupt staff of life." Henry Miller, "The Staff of Life," in *The Intimate Henry Miller*, with an introduction by Lawrence Clark Powell (New York, 1959), pp. 73-4.

29. C. Wright Mills, *The Sociological Imagination* (New York, 1961), p. 3.

6. On the Classification and Framing of Educational Knowledge

Basil Bernstein/*University of London Institute of Education*

Most of our conceptions of education are based on the restrictions on how people are selected for places in schools, colleges and universities (see the analysis by R. Pike in the next section which deals with social class as a determinant in higher education, and the essay by M. and J. Maxwell in Section Four which isolates an enclave of 'privilege' in the school system). But once we have accepted that educational systems are inegalitarian, further – and perhaps more crucial – problems arise: if educational institutions are concerned with transmitting knowledge, what is that knowledge, who decides its content and how do different kinds of educational structures determine the boundaries of 'knowledge'? Or, in other words, why, if at all, is sociology at the Université de Montréal 'different' from sociology at the University of Toronto? Who makes the decisions? And to what extent is the societal context important in determining what goes on in the institutions and in the relationships between the so-called 'disciplines'?

Some of these questions were raised at the end of the nineteenth century by Emile Durkheim (in e.g. Moral Education: *New York, Free Press of Glencoe, 1961) and more recently by Pierre Bourdieu and Jean-Claude Passeron* (La Réproduction, *Paris: Editions de Minuit, 1969). A Brazilian educationalist, Paulo Freyre in* The Pedagogy of the Oppressed *(New York: Harder and Harder, 1970) has raised similar questions in the context of Third World Education. This difficult essay by Basil Bernstein is, however, probably the first attempt by an English-speaking sociologist to tackle the important theme of knowledge boundaries in educational institutions. By using a comparative framework he illustrates how we may study the ways that our conceptions of knowledge are bounded by social structural, physical, temporal and cultural definitions of space.*

Introduction

How a society selects, classifies, distributes, transmits and evaluates the educational knowledge it considers to be public, reflects both the distribution of power and the principles of social control. From this point of view, differences within and change in the organisation, transmission and evaluation of educational knowledge should be a major area of sociological interest. (Bernstein, B. 1966, 1967, Davies, D. I. 1970, 1971; Musgrove, 1968; Hoyle, 1969; Young, M. 1970.) Indeed, such a study is a part of the larger question of the structure and changes in the structure of cultural transmission. For various reasons, sociologists have fought shy of this question. As a result, the sociology of education has been reduced to a series of input-output problems; the school has been transformed into a complex organisation or people-processing institution; the study of socialization has been trivialized.

Educational knowledge is a major regulator of the structure of experience. From this point of view, one can ask "How are forms of experience, identity and relation evoked, maintained and changed by the formal transmission of educational knowledge and sensitivities?" Formal educational knowledge can be

Reprinted from *Class, Codes and Control*, Routledge and Kegan Paul, 1971, by permission of the author.

considered to be realized through three message systems: curriculum, pedagogy and evaluation. Curriculum defines what counts as valid knowledge, pedagogy defines what counts as a valid transmission of knowledge, and evaluation defines what counts as a valid realization of this knowledge on the part of the taught. The term, educational knowledge code, which will be introduced later, refers to the underlying principles which shape curriculum, pedagogy and evaluation. It will be argued that the form this code takes depends upon social principles which regulate the classification and framing of knowledge made public in educational institutions. Both Durkheim and Marx have shown us that the structure of society's classifications and frames reveals both the distribution of power and the principles of social control. I hope to show, *theoretically*, that educational codes provide excellent opportunities for the study of classification and frames through which experience is given a distinctive form. The paper is organized as follows:

1. I shall first distinguish between two types of curricula: collection and integrated.

2. I shall build upon the basis of this distinction in order to establish a more general set of concepts: classification and frame.

3. A typology of educational codes will then be derived.

4. Sociological aspects of two very different educational codes will then be explored.

5. This will lead on to a discussion of educational codes and problems of social control.

6. Finally there will be a brief discussion of the reasons for a weakening of one code and a strengthening of the movement of the other.

1. Two Types of Curricula

Initially, I am going to talk about the curriculum in a very general way. In all educational institutions there is a formal punctuation of time into periods. These may vary from ten minutes to three hours or more. I am going to call each such formal period of time a 'unit'. I shall use the word 'content' to describe how the period of time is used. I shall define a curriculum initially in terms of the principle by which units of time and their contents are brought into a special relationship with each other. I now want to look more closely at the phrase 'special relationship'.

Firstly, we can examine relationships between contents in terms of the amount of time accorded to a given content. Immediately, we can see that more time is devoted to some contents rather than others. Secondly, some of the contents may, from the point of view of the pupils, be compulsory or optional. We can now take a very crude measure of the relative status of a content in terms of the number of units given over to it, and whether it is compulsory or optional. This raises immediately the question of the relative status of a given content and its significance in a given educational career.

We can, however, consider the relationship between contents from another, perhaps more important, perspective. We can ask about any given content whether the boundary between it and another content is clear cut or blurred. To what extent are the various contents well insulated from each other. If the various contents are well insulated from each other, I shall say that the contents stand in a *closed* relation to each other. If there is reduced insulation between contents, I shall say that the contents stand in an *open* relationship to each other. So far then, I am suggesting that we can go into any educational institution and examine the organization of time in terms of the relative status of contents, and whether the contents stand in an open closed relationship to each other. I am deliberately using this very abstract language in order to emphasize that there is nothing instrinsic to the relative status of various contents, there is nothing intrinsic to the relationships between contents. Irrespective of the question of the intrinsic logic of the various forms of public thought, the *forms* of their transmission, that is, their classification and framing, are social facts. There are a number of alternative means of access to the public forms of thought, and so to the various realities which they make possible. I am therefore emphasizing the social nature of the system of alternatives from which emerges a constellation called a curriculum. From this point of view, any curriculum entails a principle or principles whereby of all the possible contents of time, some contents are accorded differential status and enter into open or closed relation to each other.

I shall now distinguish between two broad types of curriculum. If contents stand in a closed relation to each other, that is, if the contents are clearly bounded and insulated from each other, I shall call such a curriculum a *collection* type. Here, the learner has to collect a group of favoured contents in order to satisfy some criteria of evaluation. There may of course be some underlying concept to a collection: the gentleman, the educated man, the skilled man, the non-vocational man.

Now I want to juxtapose against the collection type, a curriculum where the various contents do not go their own separate ways, but where the contents stand in an open relation to each other. I shall call such a curriculum an integrated type. Now we can have various types of collection, and various degrees and types of integration.

2. Classification and Frame

I shall now introduce the concepts, classification and frame, which will be used to analyse the underlying structure of the three message systems, curriculum, pedagogy and evaluation, which are realizations of the educational knowledge code. The basic idea is embodied in the principle used to distinguish the two types of curricula: collection and integrated. Strong insulation between contents pointed to a collection type, whereas reduced insulation pointed to an integrated type. The principle here is the strength of the *boundary* between contents. This notion of boundary strength underlies the concepts of classification and frame.

Classification and Frame

Classification, here, does not refer to *what* is classified, but to the *relationships* between contents. Classification refers to the nature of the differentiation between contents. Where classification is strong, contents are well insulated from each other by strong boundaries. Where classification is weak, there is reduced insulation between contents for the boundaries between contents are weak or blurred. *Classification thus refers to the degree of boundary maintenance between contents*. Classification focuses our attention upon boundary strength as the critical distinguishing feature of the division of labour of educational knowledge. It gives us, as I hope to show, the basic structure of the message system, curriculum.

The concept, frame, is used to determine the structure of the message system, pedagogy. Frame refers to the form of the

context in which knowledge is transmitted and received. Frame refers to the specific pedagogical relationship of teacher and taught. In the same way as classification does not refer to contents, so frame does not refer to the contents of the pedagogy. Frame refers to the strength of the boundary between what may be transmitted and what may not be transmitted, in the pedagogical relationship. Where framing is strong, there is a sharp boundary, where framing is weak, a blurred boundary, between what may and may not be transmitted. Frame refers us to the range of options available to teacher and taught in the *control* of what is transmitted and received in the context of the pedagogical relationship. Strong framing entails reduced options; weak framing entails a range of options. *This frame refers to the degree of control teacher and pupil possess over the selection, organization, and pacing of the knowledge transmitted and received in the pedagogical relationship.*[1]

There is another aspect of the boundary relationship between what may be taught and what may not be taught and consequently, another aspect to framing. We can consider the relationship between the non-school everyday community knowledge of the teacher or taught, *and* the educational knowledge transmitted in the pedagogical relationship. We can raise the question of the strength of the boundary, the degree of insulation, between the everyday community knowledge of teacher and taught and educational knowledge. Thus, we can consider variations in the strength of frames as these refer to the strength of the boundary between educational knowledge and everyday community knowledge of teacher and taught.

From the perspective of this analysis, the basic structure of the message system curriculum is given by variations in the strength of classification and the basic structure of the message system pedagogy is given by variations in the strength of frames. It will be shown later that the structure of the message system evaluation is a function of the strength of classification and frames. It is important to realize that the strength of classification and the strength of frames can vary independently of each other. For example, it is possible to have weak classification and exceptionally strong framing. Consider programmed learning. Here the boundary between educational contents may be blurred (weak classification) but there is little control by the pupil (except for pacing) over *what* is learned (strong framing). This example also shows that frames may be examined at a number of levels and the strength can vary as between the levels of selection, organization, pacing and timing of the knowledge transmitted in the pedagogical relationship.

I should also like to bring out (this will be developed more fully later in the analysis) the power component of this analysis and what can be called the 'identity' component. Where classification is strong, the boundaries between the different contents are sharply drawn. If this is the case then it pre-supposes strong boundary maintainers. Strong classification also creates a strong sense of membership in a particular class and so a specific identity. Strong frames reduce the power of the pupil over what, when and how he receives knowledge and increases the teacher's power in the pedagogical relationship. However, strong *classification* reduces the power of the *teacher* over what he transmits as he may not over-step the boundary between contents *and* strong classification reduces the power of the teacher vis-à-vis the boundary maintainers.

It is now possible to make explicit the concept of educational knowledge codes. The code is fully given *at the most general level* by the relationship between classification and frame.

3. A Typology of Educational Knowledge Codes[2]

In the light of the conceptual framework we have developed, I shall use the distinction between collection and integrated curricula in order to realize a typology which includes types and sub-types of educational codes. The *formal* basis of the typology is the strength of classification and frames. However, the sub-types will be distinguished, initially, in terms of substantive differences.

Any organization of educational knowledge which involves strong classification gives rise to what is here called a collection code. Any organization of educational knowledge which in-volves a marked attempt to reduce the strength of classification is here called an integrated code. Collection codes may give rise to a series of sub-types, each varying in the relative strength of their classification and frames. Integrated codes can also vary in terms of the strength of frames, as these refer to the *teacher/pupil/student* control over the knowledge that is transmitted.

The diagram sets out general features of the typology.

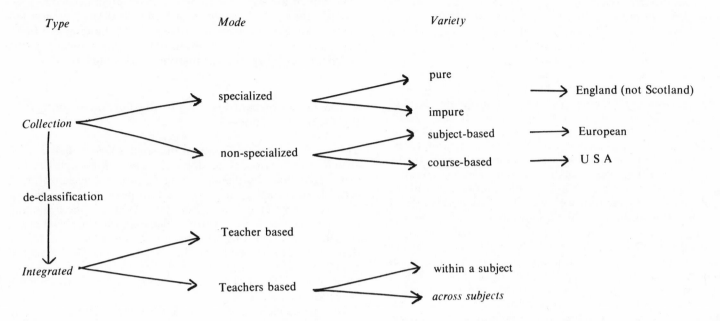

Collection Codes

The first major distinction *within* collection codes is between specialized and non-specialized types. The extent of specialization can be measured in terms of the number of closed contents publicly examined at the end of the secondary educational stage. Thus in England, *although there is no formal limit*, the student usually sits for three 'A' level subjects, compared with the much greater range of subjects which make up the Abitur in Germany, the Baccalaureate in France, or the Studente Exam in Sweden.

Within the English specialized type, we can distinguish two varieties: a pure and an impure variety. The pure variety exists where A level subjects are drawn from a common universe of knowledge, e.g. Chemistry, Physics, Mathematics. The impure variety exists where A level subjects are drawn from different universes of knowledge, e.g. Religion, Physics, Economics. The latter combination, although formally possible, very rarely sub-stantively exists, for pupils are not encouraged to offer – neither does timetabling usually permit – such a combination. It is a matter of interest that until very recently the pure variety at the University level received the higher status of an honours de-gree, whereas the impure variety tended to lead to the lower status of the general degree.[3] One can detect the beginnings of a shift in England from the pure to the impure variety, which appears to be trying to work towards the non-specialized type of collection.

Within the non-specialized collection code, we can distin-guish two varieties, according to whether a subject or course is the basic knowledge unit. Thus the standard European form of the collection code is non-specialized, *subject* based. The USA form of the collection is non-specialized, course based.

I have so far described sub-types and varieties of the collec-tion code in simple descriptive terms, as a consequence it is not easy to see how their distinctive features can be translated into sociological concepts in order to realize a specific sociological problem. Clearly, the conceptual language here developed has built into it a specific perspective; that of power and social control. In the process of translating the descriptive features into the language of classification and frames, the question must arise as to whether the hypotheses about their relative strength fit a particular case.

Here are the hypotheses, given for purposes of illustration:

1. I suggest that the European, non-specialized, subject based form of collection involves strong classification but *exceptionally* strong framing. That is, at levels *below* higher education, there are relatively few options available to teacher, and espe-cially taught, over the transmission of knowledge. Curricula and syllabus are very explicit.

2. The English version, I suggest, involves *exceptionally* strong classification, but relatively weaker framing than the European type. The fact that it is specialized determines what contents (subjects) may be put together. There is very strong insulation between the 'pure' and the 'applied' knowledge. Cur-ricula are graded for particular ability groups. There can be high insulation between a subject and a class of pupils. 'D' stream secondary pupils will not have access to certain subjects, and 'A' stream students will also not have access to certain subjects. However, I suggest that framing, relative to Europe, is weaker. This can be seen particularly at the primary level. There is also, *relative* to Europe less *central* control over what is transmitted, although, clearly, the various requirements of the University level exert a strong control over the secondary level.[4] I suggest that, although again this is *relative*, there is a weaker frame in England between educational knowledge and the everyday community knowledge for certain classes of stu-dents: the so-called less able. Finally, relative to Europe, I sug-gest that there are more options available to the pupil within the pedagogical relationships. The frame as it refers to pupils is weaker. Thus I suggest that framing as it relates to teachers and pupils is relatively weaker, but that classification is relatively much stronger in the English than the European system. Scot-land is nearer to the European version of the collection.

3. The course-based, non-specialised USA form of the collection, I suggest, has the weakest classification *and* framing (especially over pacing) of the collection code, especially at the secondary and university level. A far greater range of subjects can be taken at the secondary and university level, and are capable of combination; this indicates weak classification. The insulation between educational knowledge and everyday community knowledge is weaker, as can be evidenced by community control over school; this indicates weak frames. The range of options available to pupils within the pedagogical relationship is, I suggest, greater. I would guess then, that classification and framing in the USA is the weakest of the collection code.

Integrated Codes

It is important to be clear about the term 'integrated'. Because one subject uses the theories of another subject, this type of intellectual inter-relationship does not constitute integration. Such intellectual inter-relation may well be part of a collection code at some point in the history of the development of knowledge. Integration, as it is used here, refers minimally to the *subordination* of previously insulated subjects *or* courses to some *relational* idea, which blurs the boundaries between the subjects. We can distinguish two types. The first type is *teacher* based. Here the teacher as in the infant school has an extended block of time with often the same group of children. The teacher may operate with a collection code and keep the various subjects distinct and insulated, or he can blur the boundaries between the different subjects. This type of integrated code is easier to introduce than the second type, which is *teachers* based. Here, integration involves relationships with other teachers. In this way, we can have degrees of integration in terms of the number of teachers involved.

We can further distinguish two varieties according to whether the integration refers to a group of teachers *within* a common subject, or the *extent* to which integration involves teachers of different subjects. Whilst integrated codes, by definition, have the weakest classification, they may vary as to framing. During the initiating period, the frames the teachers enter will be weak, but other factors will effect the final frame strength. It is also possible that the frames the *pupils* enter can vary in strength.

Thus integrated codes may be confined to one subject or they can cross subjects. We can talk of code strength in terms of the range of different subjects co-ordinated by the code, or if this criterion cannot be applied, code strength can be measured in terms of the *number* of teachers co-ordinated through the code. Integrated codes can also vary as to frame strength as this is applied to teachers or pupils, or both.

Differences within, and between, educational knowledge codes from the perspective developed here, lie in variations in the strength and nature of the boundary maintaining procedures, as these are given by the classification and framing of the knowledge. It can be seen that the nature of classification and framing affects the authority/power structure which controls the dissemination of educational knowledge, and the *form* of the knowledge transmitted. In this way, principles of power and social control are realized through educational knowledge codes and through the codes enter into, and shape, consciousness. Thus variations within and change of knowledge codes should be of critical concern to sociologists. The following problems arise out of this analysis.

1. What are the antecedents of variations in the strength of classification and frames?[5]

2. How does a given classification and framing structure perpetuate itself? What are the conditions of, and resistance to, change?

3. What are the different socializing experiences realized through variations in the strength of classifications and frames?

I shall limit the application of this analysis to the consideration of aspects of the last two questions. I feel I ought to apologize to the reader for this rather long and perhaps tedious conceptual journey, before he has been given any notion of the view to which it leads.

I shall examine the patterns of social relationship and their socializing consequences which are realized through the European, particularly English, version of the collection code and those which are *expected* to arise out of integrated codes, *particularly those which develop weak framing*. I shall suggest that there is some movement towards forms of the integrated code and I shall examine the nature of the resistance towards such a change. I shall suggest some reasons for this movement.

4. Classification and Framing of the European form of the Collection Code

There will be some difficulty in this analysis, as I shall at times switch from secondary to university level. Although the English system has the distinguishing feature of specialization, it does share certain features of the European system. This may lead to some blurring in the analysis. As this is the beginnings of a limited sociological theory which explores the social organization and structuring of educational knowledge, it follows that all statements, including those which have the character of descriptive statements, are hypothetical. The descriptive statements have been selectively patterned according to their significance for the theory.

One of the major differences between the European and English versions of the collection code is that, with the specialized English type, a membership category is established early in an educational career, in terms of an early choice between the pure and the applied, between the sciences and the arts, between having and not having a specific educational identity. A particular status in a given collection is made clear by streaming and/or a delicate system of grading. One nearly always knows the social significance of where one is and in particular, *who* one is with each advance in the educational career. (Initially, I am doing science, or arts, pure or applied; or I am not doing anything; later I am becoming a physicist, economist, chemist, etc.) *Subject loyalty* is then systematically developed in pupils and finally students, with each increase in the educational life and then transmitted by them as teachers and lecturers. The system is self-perpetuating through this form of socialization. With the specialized form of the collection it is banal to say as you get older you learn more and more about less and less. Another, more sociological, way of putting this is to say as you get older, you become increasingly *different* from others. Clearly, this will happen at some point in any educational career, but with specialization, this happens much earlier. Therefore, specialization very soon reveals *difference from* rather than communality with. It creates relatively quickly an educational identity which is clear-cut and bounded. The educational category or identity is *pure*. Specialized versions of the collection code tend to abhor mixed categories and blurred identities, for they represent a potential openness, an ambiguity, which makes the consequences of previous socialization problematic. Mixed categories such as bio-physicist, psycho-linguist, are only permitted to develop after long socialization into a subject loyalty. Indeed, in order to change an identity, a previous one has to be weakened and a new one created. For example, in England, if a student has a first degree in psychology and he wishes to read for a higher degree in sociology, either he is not permitted to make the switch or he is expected to take a number of papers at first degree level in sociology. In the process of taking the papers, he usually enters into social relationships with accredited sociologists and students through whom he acquires the cognitive and social style particular to the sociological identity. Change of an educational identity is accomplished through a process of re-socialization into a *new* subject loyalty. A sense of the sacred, the 'otherness' of educational knowledge, I submit does not arise so much out of an ethic of knowledge for its own sake, but is more a function of socialization into subject loyalty: for it is the subject which becomes the linchpin of the identity. Any attempt to weaken or *change* classification strength, or even form strength, may be felt as a threat to one's identity and may be experienced as a pollution endangering the sacred. Here we have one source of the resistance to change of educational code.

The specialized version of the collection code will develop careful screening procedures to see who belongs and who does not belong, and once such screening has taken place, it is very difficult to change an educational identity. The various classes of knowledge are well insulated from each other. Selection and differentiation are early features of this particular code. Thus, the deep structure of the specialized type of collection code is *strong boundary maintenance creating control from within through the formation of specific identities.* An interesting aspect of the protestant spirit.

Strong boundary maintenance can be illustrated with reference to attempts to institutionalize new forms or attempts to change the strength of, classification, within either the European or English type of collection. Because of the exceptional strength of classification in England, such difficulties may be greater here. Changes in classification strength and the institutionalizing of new forms of knowledge may become a matter of importance when there are changes in the structure of knowledge at the higher levels and/or changes in the economy. Critical problems arise with the question of new forms, as to their legitimacy, at what point they belong, when, where and by whom the form should be taught. I have referred to the 'sacred' in terms of an educational identity, but clearly there is the 'profane' aspect to knowledge. We can consider as the 'profane' the property aspect of knowledge. Any new form or weakening of classification clearly derives from past classifications. Such new forms or weakened classifications can be regarded as attempts to break or weaken existing monopolies. Knowledge under collection is private property with its own power structure and market situation. This affects the whole ambiance surrounding the development and marketing of new knowledge. Children and pupils are early socialized into this concept of knowledge as private property. They are encouraged to work as isolated individuals with their arms around their work. This phenomena, until recently, could be observed in any grammar school. It can be most clearly observed in examination halls. Pupils and students, particularly in the arts, appear from this point of view, to be a type of entrepreneur.

There are, then, strong inbuilt controls on the institutionalizing of new knowledge forms, on the changing of strength of classification, on the production of new knowledge which derive from both 'sacred' and 'profane' sources.

So far, I have been considering the relationship between strong classification of knowledge, the concept of property and the creation of specific identities with particular reference to the specialized form of the collection code. I shall now move away from the classification of knowledge to its *framing* in the process of transmission.

Any collection code involves an hierarchical organization of knowledge, such that the ultimate mystery of the subject is revealed very late in the educational life. By the ultimate mystery of the subject, I mean its potential for creating new realities. It is also the case, and this is important, that the ultimate mystery of the subject is not coherence, but incoherence; not order, but disorder; not the known but the unknown. As this mystery, under collection codes, is revealed very late in the educational life – and then only to a select few who have shown the signs of successful socialization – then only the few *experience* in their bones the notion that knowledge is permeable, that its orderings are provisional, that the dialectic of knowledge is closure and openness. For the many, socialization into knowledge is socialization into order, the existing order, into the experience that the world's educational knowledge is impermeable. Do we have here another version of alienation?

Now clearly any history of any form of educational knowledge shows precisely the power of such knowledge to create endlessly new realities. However, socialization into the specific framing of knowledge in its transmission may make such a history experientially meaningless. The key concept of the European collection code is discipline. This means learning to work *within* a received frame. It means, in particular, *learning* what questions can be put at any particular time. Because of the hierarchical ordering of the knowledge in *time*, certain questions raised may not enter into a particular frame.

This is soon learned by both teachers and pupils. Discipline then means accepting a given selection, organization, pacing and timing of knowledge realized in the pedagogical frame. With increases in the educational life, there is a progressive weakening of the frame for both teacher and taught. Only the few who have shown the signs of successful socialization have access to these relaxed frames. For the mass of the population the framing is tight. In a sense, the European form of the collection code makes knowledge safe through the process of socialization into its frames. There is a tendency, which varies with the strength of specific frames, for the young to be socialized into assigned principles and routine operations and derivations. The evaluative system places an emphasis upon attaining *states* of knowledge rather than *ways* of knowing. A study of the examination questions and format, the symbolic structure of assessment, would be, from this point of view, a rewarding empirical study. Knowledge thus tends to be transmitted, particularly to elite pupils at the secondary level, through strong frames which control the selection, organization and pacing[6] of the knowledge. The receipt of the knowledge is not so much a right as something to be won or earned. The stronger the classification and the framing, the more the educational relationship tends to be hierarchical and ritualized, the educand seen as ignorant, with little status and few rights. These are things which one earns, rather like spurs, and are used for the purpose of encouraging and sustaining the motivation of pupils. Depending upon the strength of frames, knowledge is transmitted in a context where the teacher has maximal control or surveillance, as in hierarchical secondary school relationships.

We can look at the question of the framing of knowledge in the pedagogical relationship from another point of view. In a sense, educational knowledge is uncommonsense knowledge. It is knowledge freed from the particular, the local, through the various languages of the sciences or forms of reflexiveness of the arts which make possible either the creation or the discovery of new realities. Now this immediately raises the question of the relationship between the uncommonsense knowledge of the school and the *commonsense* knowledge, every day community knowledge, of the pupil, his family and his peer group. This formulation invites us to ask how strong are the frames of educational knowledge in relation to experiential, community based non-school knowledge? I suggest that the frames of the collection code, very early in the child's life, socialize him into knowledge frames which discourage connections with everyday realities, or that there is a highly selective screening of the connection. Through such socialization, the pupil soon learns what of the outside may be brought into the pedagogical frame.

Such framing also makes of educational knowledge something not ordinary or mundane, but something esoteric which gives a special significance to those who possess it. I suggest that when this frame is relaxed to include everyday realities, it is often and sometimes validly, not simply for the transmission of educational knowledge, but for purposes of social control of forms of deviancy. The weakening of this frame occurs usually with the less 'able' children whom we have given up educating.

In general then, and depending upon the specific strength of classification and frames, the European form of the collection code is rigid, differentiating and hierarchical in character; highly resistant to change particularly at the secondary level. With the English version, this resistance to change is assisted by the discretion which is available to headmasters and principals. In England, within the constraints of the public examination system, the heads of schools and colleges have a relatively wide range of discretion over the organization and transmission of knowledge. Central control over the educational code is relatively weak in England, although clearly the schools are subject to inspection from both central and local government levels. However, the relationship between the inspectorate and the schools in England is very ambiguous. To produce widespread change in England would require the co-operation of hundreds of individual schools. Thus, rigidity in educational knowledge codes may arise out of highly centralized *or* weak central control over the knowledge codes. Weak central control does permit a series of changes which have, initially, limited consequences for the system as a whole. On the other hand, there is much stronger central control over the organizational style of the school. This can lead to a situation where there can be a change in the organizational style *without* there being *any* marked change in the educational knowledge code, particularly where the educational code, itself, creates specific identities. This raises the question, which cannot be developed here, of the relationships between organizational change and change of educational knowledge code, i.e. change in the strength of classification and framing.

In general, then the European and English form of the collection code may provide for those who go beyond the novitiate stage, order, identity and commitment. For those who do not pass beyond this stage, it can sometimes be wounding and seen as meaningless. What Bourdieu calls 'la violence symbolique'.

Integrated and Collection Codes

I shall now examine a form of the integrated code which is realized through very weak classification and frames. I shall, during this analysis, bring out further aspects of collection codes.

There are a number of attempts to institutionalize forms of the integrated code at different strengths, above the level of the infant school child. Nuffield Science is an attempt to do this with the Physical Sciences, and the Chelsea Centre for Science Education, Chelsea College of Technology University of London, is concerned almost wholly in training students in this approach. Mrs. Charity James, at Goldsmiths College, University of London, is also producing training courses for forms of the integrated code. A number of comprehensive schools are experimenting with this approach at the middle school level. The SDS in Germany, and various radical student groups, are exploring this type of code in order to use the means of the university against the meaning. However, it is probably true to say that the code at the moment exists at the level of ideology and theory, with only a relatively small number of schools and educational agencies attempting to institutionalize it with any seriousness.

Now, as we said in the beginning of the paper, with the integrated code we have a shift from content closure to content openness, from strong to markedly reduced classification. Immediately, we can see that this disturbance in classification of knowledge will lead to a disturbance of existing authority structures, existing specific educational identities and concepts of property.

Where we have integration, the various contents are subordinate to some idea which reduces their isolation from each other. Thus integration reduces the authority of the separate contents, and this has implications for existing authority structures. Where we have collection, it does permit, in principle, considerable differences in pedagogy and evaluation because of the high insulation between the different contents. However, the autonomy of the content is the other side of an authority structure which exerts jealous and zealous supervision. I suggest that the integrated code will not permit the variations in pedagogy and evaluation which are possible within collection codes. On the contrary, I suggest there will be a pronounced movement towards a common pedagogy and tendency towards a common system of evaluation. In other words, integrated codes will, at the level of the teachers, probably create homogeneity in teaching practice. Thus, collection codes increase the discretion of teachers (within, always, the limits of the existing classification and frames) whilst integrated codes will reduce the discretion of the teacher in direct relation to the strength of the integrated code (number of teachers co-ordinated by the code). On the other hand, it is argued that the increased discretion of the teachers within collection codes is paralleled by *reduced* discretion of the pupils and that the reduced discretion of the teachers within integrated codes is paralleled by *increased* discretion of the pupils. In other words, there is a shift in the balance of power, in the pedagogical relationship between teacher and taught.

These points will now be developed. In order to accomplish any form of integration (as distinct from different subjects focussing upon a common problem, which gives rise to what could be called a *focused* curriculum) there must be some relational idea, a supra-content concept, which focuses upon general principles at a high level of abstraction. For example, if the relationships between sociology and biology are to be opened, then the relational idea (amongst many) might be the issue of problems of order and change examined through the concepts of genetic and cultural codes. Whatever the relational concepts are, they will act selectively upon the knowledge within each subject which is to be transmitted. The particulars of each subject are likely to have reduced significance. This will focus attention upon the *deep* structure of each subject, rather than upon its surface structure. I suggest this will lead to an emphasis upon, and the exploration of, *general* principles and the concepts through which these principles are obtained. In turn, this is likely to affect the orientation of the pedagogy, which will be less concerned to emphasize the need to acquire *states* of knowledge, but will be more concerned to emphasize *how* knowledge is created. In other words, the pedagogy of integrated codes is likely to emphasise various *ways* of knowing in the pedagogical relationships. With the collection code, the pedagogy tends to proceed from the surface structure of the knowledge to the deep structure; as we have seen, only the elite have access to the deep structure and therefore access to the realizing of new realities or access to the experiential knowledge that new realities are possible. With integrated codes, the pedagogy is likely to proceed from the deep structure to the surface structure. We can see this already at work in the new primary school mathematics. Thus, I suggest that integrated codes will make available from the beginning of the pupils' educational career, clearly in a way appropriate to a given age level, the deep structure of the knowledge, i.e. the principles for the generating of new knowledge. Such emphasis upon various *ways* of knowing, rather than upon the attaining of *states* of knowledge, is likely to affect, not only the emphasis of the pedagogy, but the underlying theory of learning. The underlying theory of learning of collection is likely to be didactic whilst the underlying theory of learning of integrated codes may well be more group or self-regulated. This arises out of a different concept of what counts as having knowledge, which in turn leads to a different concept of how the knowledge is to be acquired. These changes in emphasis and orientation of the pedagogy are initially responsible for the relaxed frames, which teacher and taught enter. Relaxed frames not only change the nature of the authority relationships by increasing the rights of the taught, they can also weaken or blur the boundary between what may or may not be taught, and so *more* of the teacher and taught is likely to enter this pedagogical frame. The inherent logic of the integrated code is likely to create a change in the structure of teaching groups, which are likely to exhibit considerable flexibility. The concept of relatively weak boundary maintenance, which is the core principle of integrated codes, is realized both in the structuring of educational knowledge *and* in the organization of the social relationships.

I shall now introduce some organizational consequences of collection and integrated codes which will make explicit the difference in the distribution of power and the principles of control which inhere in these educational codes.

Where knowledge is regulated through a collection code, the knowledge is organized and distributed through a series of well-insulated subject hierarchies. Such a structure points to oligarchic control of the institution, through formal and informal meetings of heads of departments with the head or principal of the institution. Thus, senior staff will have strong horizontal work relationships (that is, with their peers in other subject hierarchies) and strong vertical work relationships within their own department. However, junior staff are likely to have only vertical (within the subject hierarchy) allegiances and work relationships.

The allegiances of junior staff are vertical rather than horizontal for the following reasons. Firstly, staff have been socialized into strong subject loyalty and through this into specific identities. These specific identities are continuously strengthened through social interactions *within* the department *and* through the insulation between departments. Secondly, the departments are often in a competitive relationship for strategic teaching resources. Thirdly, preferment within the subject hierarchy often rests with its expansion. Horizontal relationships of junior staff (particularly where there is no *effective* participatory administrative structure) is likely to be limited to *non-task based* contacts. There may well be discussion of control problems ("X of 3b is a _____ how do you deal with him?" or "I can't get X to write a paper"). Thus the collection code within the framework of oligarchic control creates for *senior* staff strong horizontal and vertical based relationships, whereas the work relationships of junior staff are likely to be vertical and

Ideal Typical Organizational Structures

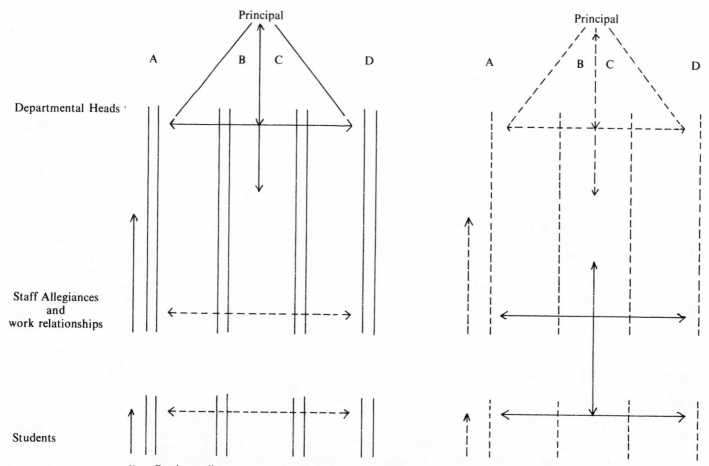

Key: Continuous lines represent strong boundaries. Continuous arrows represent direction of strong relationships.
Dotted lines represent weak boundaries. Dotted line arrows represent direction of weak relationships.
Collection Code Type = Strong Classification: Strong Frames.
Integrated Code Type = Weak Classification: Weak Frames.

the horizontal relationships limited to non-work based contacts. This is a type of organizational system which encourages gossip, intrigue and a conspiracy theory of the workings of the organization for *both* the *administration* and the *acts of teaching* are *invisible* to the majority of staff.

Now the integrated code will require teachers of different subjects to enter into social relationships with each other which will arise not simply out of non-task areas, but out of a shared, co-operative educational task. The centre of gravity of the relationships among teachers will undergo a radical shift. Thus, instead of teachers and lecturers being divided and insulated by allegiances to subject hierarchies, the conditions for their unification exists through a common work situation. I suggest that this changed basis of the relationships, among teachers or among lecturers, may tend to weaken the separate hierarchies of collection. These new work-based horizontal relationships may alter both the structure and distribution of power regulated by the collection code. Further, the administration and specific acts of teaching are likely to shift from relative invisibility to *visibility*.

We might expect similar developments at the level of students and even senior pupils. For pupils and students with each increase in their educational life are equally sub-divided and educationally insulated from one another. They are equally bound to subject hierarchies and, for similar reasons, to staff; their identities and their future are shaped by the department. Their vertical allegiances and work-based relationships are strong, whilst their horizontal relationships will tend to be limited to non-task areas (student/pupil societies and sport) or peripheral non-task based administration. Here again, we can see another example of the strength of boundary maintenance of collection codes; this time between task and non-task areas. Integrated codes may well provide the conditions for strong horizontal relationships and allegiances in students and pupils based upon a common work task (the receiving and offering of knowledge).[7] In this situation, we might expect a weakening of the boundary between staff, especially junior staff, and students/pupils.

Thus, a move from collection to integrated codes may well bring about a disturbance in the structure and distribution of power, in property relationships and in existing educational identities. This change of educational code involves a fundamental change in the nature and strength of boundaries. It involves a change in what counts as having knowledge, in what counts as a valid transmission of knowledge, in what counts as a valid realization of knowledge, *and* a change in the organizational context. At the cultural level, it involves a shift from the keeping of categories pure to the mixing of categories; whilst, at the level of socialization, the outcomes of integrated codes *could* be less predictable than the outcomes of collection codes. This change of code involves fundamental changes in the classification and framing of knowledge and therefore changes in the structure and distribution of power and in the principles of control. It is no wonder that deep felt resistances are called out by the issue of change in educational codes.

5. Collection, Integrated Codes and Problems of Order

I shall now turn to aspects of the problem of order. Where knowledge is regulated by collection codes, social order arises out of the hierarchical nature of the authority relationships, out of the systematic ordering of the differentiated knowledge in time and space, out of an explicit, usually predictable, examining procedure. Order internal to the individual is created through the formation of specific identities. The institutional expression of strong classification and framing creates predicta-

bility in time and space. Because of strong classification, collection does allow a range of variations between subjects in the organization, transmission and evaluation of knowledge. Because of strong classification, this code does permit, *in principle*, staff to hold (within limits) a range of ideologies because conflicts can be contained *within* its various insulated hierarchies. At levels below that of the university, the strong frames between educational knowledge and non-educational/relevant knowledge, *in principle*, may facilitate diversity in ideology held by staff because it cannot be explicitly offered. At the same time, strong framing makes such intrusion highly visible. The range of personal freedoms at the *university* level is symbolized in the ethical system of some collection codes and so forms the basis for the cohesion of the differentiated whole.

Whilst it is usually the case that collection codes, relative to integrated codes, create strong frames between the uncommonsense knowledge of the school and the everyday community-based knowledge of teacher and taught, it is also the case that such insulation creates areas of privacy. For, in as much as community-based experience is irrelevant to the pedagogical frame, these aspects of the self, informed by such experiences, are also irrelevant. These areas of privacy reduce the penetration of the socializing process, for it is possible to distance oneself from it. This still means, however, that the socialization can be deeply wounding either for those who wish for, but do not achieve, an identity or for the majority for whom the pursuit of an identity is early made irrelevant.

Order created by integrated codes may well be problematic. I suggest that if four conditions are not satisfied, then the openness of learning under integration may produce a culture in which neither staff nor pupils have a sense of time, place or purpose. I shall comment briefly on these four conditions as I give them.

1. There must be consensus about the integrating idea and it must be very explicit. (It is ironic that the movement towards integration is going on in those countries where there is a low level of moral consensus). It may be that integrated codes will only work[8] when there is a *high* level of ideological consensus among the staff. We have already seen that, in comparison with collection, integrated codes call for greater homogeneity in pedagogy and evaluation and therefore reduce differences among teachers in the form of the transmission and assessment of knowledge. Whereas the teaching process under collection is likely to be invisible to other teachers, unless special conditions prevail, it is likely that the teaching process regulated through integrated codes may well become visible as a result of developments in the pedagogy in the direction of flexibility in the structure of teaching groups. It is also the case that the weak classification and relaxed frames of integrated codes permit greater expressions of differences among teachers, and possibly among pupils, in the selection of what is taught. The moral basis of educational choices are then likely to be explicit at the initial planning stage. Integrated codes also weaken specific identities. For the above reasons, integrated codes may require a high level of ideological consensus and this may affect the recruitment of staff. Integrated codes at the surface level create weak or blurred boundaries but at bottom they may rest upon closed explicit ideologies. Where such ideologies are not shared, the consequences will become visible and threaten the whole at every point.

2. The nature of the linkage between the integrating idea and the knowledge to be co-ordinated must also be coherently spelled out. It is this linkage which will be the basic element in bringing teachers *and* pupils into their working relationship. *The development of such a co-ordinating framework will be the process of socialization of teachers into the code. During this process, the teachers will internalize, as in all processes of sociali-*

zation, the interpretative procedures of the code so that these become implicit guides which regulate and co-ordinate the behaviour of the individual teachers in the relaxed frames and weakened classification. This brings us to a major distinction between collection and integrated codes. With a collection code, the period of socialization is facilitated by strong boundary maintenance both at the level of *role* and at the level of knowledge. Such socialization is likely to be continuous, with the teacher's own educational socialization. With integrated codes, both the role and the form of the knowledge have to be *achieved* in relation to a range of different others and this may involve re-socialization if the teacher's previous educational experience has been formed by the collection code. The collection code is capable of working when staffed by mediocre teachers, whereas integrated codes call for much greater powers of synthesis, analogy and for more ability to both tolerate and enjoy ambiguity at the level of knowledge *and* social relationships.

3. A committee system of staff may have to be set up to create a sensitive feed-back system which will also provide a further agency of socialization into the code. It is likely that evaluative criteria are likely to be relatively weak, in the sense that the criteria are less likely to be as explicit and as measurable as in the case of collection. As a result, it may be necessary to develop committees for both teachers, students, and where appropriate, pupils which will perform monitoring functions.

4. One of the major difficulties which inhere in integrated codes arises over what is to be assessed, the form of assessment, and the place of specific competencies in such assessment. It is likely that integrated codes will give rise to multiple criteria of assessment compared with collection codes. In the case of collection codes, because the knowledge moves from the surface to the deep structure, this progression creates ordered principles of evaluation in time. The form of temporal cohesion of the knowledge regulated through the integrated code has yet to be determined and made explicit. Without clear criteria of evaluation, neither teacher nor taught have any means to consider the significance of what is learned, or any means to judge the pedagogy. In the case of collection codes, evaluation at the secondary level often consists of the fit between a narrow range of specific competencies and states of knowledge, and previously established criteria (varying in explicitness) of what constitutes a right or appropriate or convincing answer. The previously established criteria together with the specific social context of assessment create a relatively objective procedure. I do not want to suggest that this necessarily gives rise to a form of assessment which entirely disregards distinctive and original features of the pupil's performance. In the case of the integrated code under discussion (weak frames for teacher and taught) then this form of assessment may well be inappropriate. The weak frames enable a greater range of the student's behaviour to be made public and they make possible considerable diversity (at least in principle) among students. It is possible that this might lead to a situation where assessment takes more into account 'inner' attributes of the student. Thus if he has the 'right' attitudes then this will result later in the attainment of various specific competencies. The 'right' attitude may be assessed in terms of the fit between the pupil's attitudes and the current ideology. It is possible, then, that the evaluative criteria of integrated codes with weak frames may be weak when these refer to specific cognitive attributes but strong when they refer to dispositional attributes. If this is so, then a new range of pupil attributes become candidates for labels. It is also likely that the weakened classification and framing will encourage more of the pupil/student to be made public; more of his thoughts, feelings and values. In this way, more of the pupil is available for control. As a result the socialization could be more intensive and perhaps more penetrating. In the same way

that pupils/students defend themselves against the wounds of collection or distance themselves from its overt code, so they may produce new defences against the potential intrusiveness of the integrated code and its open learning contexts.

We can summarize this question of the problem of order as follows. Collection codes have explicit and strong boundary maintaining features and they rest upon a tacit ideological basis. Integrated codes have implicit and weak boundary maintaining features and they rest upon an explicit and closed ideological basis. The ideological basis of the collection code is a condensed symbolic system communicated through its explicit boundary maintaining features. Its covert structure is that of mechanical solidarity. The ideological basis of integrated codes is *not* a condensed symbolic system; it is verbally elaborated and explicit. It is an *overt* realization of organic solidarity and made substantive through weak forms of boundary maintenance (low insulations). Yet the covert structure of mechanical solidarity of collection codes creates through its specialized outputs *organic* solidarity. On the other hand, the overt structure of organic solidarity of integrated codes creates through its *less* specialized outputs *mechanical* solidarity. And it will do this to the extent to which its ideology is explicit, elaborated and closed *and* effectively and *implicitly* transmitted through its low insulations. In as much as integrated codes do not accomplish this, then order is highly problematic at the level of social organization and at the level of the person. In as much as integrated codes do accomplish such socialization, then we have the covert deep closure of mechanical solidarity. This is the fundamental paradox which has to be faced and explored.[9]

6. Change of Educational Code

I have tried to make explicit the relationships between educational codes and the structure of power and principles of social control. Attempts to change or modify educational codes will meet with resistance at a number of different levels irrespective of the intrinsic educational merit of a particular code. I shall now briefly discuss some reasons for a movement towards the institutionalizing of integrated codes *of the weak classification and weak framing (teacher and taught) type*, (see note 1), above the level of the primary school (see note 2).

1. The growing differentiation of knowledge at the higher levels of thought, together with the integration of previously discreet areas, may set up requirements for a form of socialization appropriate to these changes in the structure of knowledge.

2. Changes in the division of labour are creating a different concept of skill. The in-built obsolescence of whole varieties of skills reduces the significance of context-tied operations and increases the significance of general principles from which a range of diverse operations may be derived. In crude terms, it could be said that the nineteenth century required submissive and inflexible man, whereas the twentieth century requires conforming but flexible man.

3. The less rigid social structure of the integrated code makes it a potential code for egalitarian education.

4. In advanced industrial societies which permit, within limits, a range of legitimizing beliefs and ideologies, there is a major problem of control. There is the problem of making sense of the differentiated, weakly co-ordinated and changing symbolic systems and the problem of inner regulation of the person. Integrated codes, with their stress on the underlying unity of knowledge, through their emphasis upon analogy and synthesis, could be seen as a response to the first problem of 'making sense'. The *inter-personal* rather than *inter-positional* control of the integrated code may set up a penetrating, intrusive

form of socialization under conditions of ambiguity in the system of beliefs and the moral order.

If these reasons operate, we could consider the movement towards integrated codes as stemming from a technological source. However, it is possible that there is another and deeper source of the movement away from collection. I suggest that the movement away from collection to integrated codes symbolizes that there is a crisis in society's basic classifications and frames, and therefore a crisis in its structures of power and principles of control.[10] The movement from this point of view represents an attempt to de-classify and so alter power structures and principles of control and in so doing, to unfreeze the structuring of knowledge and to change the boundaries of consciousness. From this point of view, integrated codes are symptoms of a moral crisis rather than the terminal state of an educational system.

Conclusion

In this paper, I have tried to explore the concept of boundary in such a way that it is possible to see *both* the power and control components. The analysis focuses directly upon the structuring of transmitted educational knowledge.

Although the concept, 'classification' appears to operate on a single dimension, i.e. differences in degrees of insulation between contents (subjects/courses etc.) it explicitly points to power and control components. In the same way, the concept, 'frame' appears to operate in a single dimension; what may or may not be taught in the pedagogical relationship. Yet the exploration of the concept again points to power and control components. Through defining educational codes in terms of the relationship between classification and framing, these two components are built into the analysis at all levels. It then becomes possible in one framework to derive a typology of educational codes, to show the inter-relationships between organizational and knowledge properties, to move from macro- to micro-levels of analysis, to relate the patterns internal to educational institutions to the external social antecedents of such patterns, and to consider questions of maintenance and change. At the same time, it is hoped that the analysis makes explicit tacit assumptions underlying various educational codes. It attempts to show at a *theoretical* level, the relationships between a particular symbolic order and the structuring of experience. I believe that it offers an approach which is well capable of exploration by diverse methods at the empirical level.

It should be quite clear that the specific application of the concept requires at every point empirical evidence. I have not attempted to bolster the argument with references because, in many cases, the evidence which is required does not exist in a *form* which bears directly upon the chain of inferences and therefore would offer perhaps spurious support. We have, for example, little *first* hand knowledge which bears upon aspects of framing as this concept is used in the paper. We also have next to no *first* hand knowledge of the day by day encounters realized by various types of integrated codes.

I hope that the kinds of questions raised by this approach will encourage sociologists of education to explore, both theoretically and empirically, the structure of educational knowledge which I take to be the distinctive feature of this field.

NOTES

I am most grateful to Professor Wolfgang Klafki and particularly to Mr. Hubertus Huppauf of the University of Marburg for many valuable suggestions and constructive criticism. I should also like to acknowledge many hours of discussion with my colleague Mr. Michael Young. I have also learned much from Mr. David Adelstein, graduate student in the Department of the Sociology of Education, University of London Institute of Education. I am particularly grateful to Mr. W. Brandis, research officer in the Department's Research Unit. I have also benefited from the stringent criticisms of Professor R. Peters, and Mr. Lionel Elvin, of the University of London Institute of Education. My greatest debt is to Professor Mary Douglas, University College, London.

I should like to thank the Director of the Chaucer Publishing Company, Mr. L. G. Grossman, for a small but vital grant.

Note 1.

In the paper, I suggested that integrated codes rest upon a closed explicit ideology. It should then follow that this code would stand a better chance of successful institutionalization in societies where (a) there were strong and effective constraints upon the development of a range of ideologies and (b) where the educational system was a major agency of political socialization. Further, the weak boundary maintaining procedures of the integrated code would (a) increase the penetration of the socialization as more of the self of the taught is made public through the relaxed frames and (b) deviancy would be more visible. On the other hand, integrated codes carry a potential for change in power structures and principles of control. I would therefore guess that in such societies, integrated codes would possess weak classification but the frames for teacher and taught would be strong.

Note 2.

It is a matter of interest that, in England, it is only in the infant school that there is relatively wide-spread introduction of this form of integrated code. This raises the general question of how this level of the educational system was open to such change. Historically, the primary school developed distinct concepts of infant and junior stages and distinct heads for these two stages. Given the relative autonomy over the transmission of knowledge which characterises the British system of education, it was in principle possible to have change. Although only a ceiling may separate infant from junior departments, two quite distinct and often incompatible educational codes can develop. We can regard this as a necessary, but not sufficient, condition for the emergence of integrated codes at the infant school level. It was also the case, until very recently, that the selection function started in the Junior department, because that department was the gateway to the grammar school. This left the infant school relatively free from control by levels higher than itself. The form of integration in the infant school, again until recently, was *teacher* based, and therefore did not set up the problems which arise out of *teachers* based integration. Finally, infant school teachers are not socialized into strong educational identities. Thus the English educational system, until recently, has two potential points of openness – the period between the ages of five to seven years, before selection began, and the period post eighteen years of age, when selection is virtually completed. The major control on the structuring of knowledge at the secondary level is the structuring of knowledge at the tertiary level, specifically the university. Only if there is a major change in the structuring of knowledge at this level can there be effective code change at lower levels, although it is still probable that in any one secondary school in England we will find a variety of codes.

NOTES AND BIBLIOGRAPHY

1. It follows that frame strength for teacher and taught can be assessed at the different levels of selection, organization, and pacing of the knowledge.

2. Elaborated codes are formally developed in educational institutions. Different educational codes represent different forms of the institutionalizing of elaborated codes. Thus educational knowledge codes are public regulators of the form and contents of elaborated codes.

3. Consider the recent acrimonious debate over the attempt to obtain permission at Oxford to develop a degree in Anthropology, Sociology, Psychology & Biology – a relatively 'pure' combination.

4. The content of public examinations between the secondary and the tertiary level is controlled by the tertiary level directly or indirectly, through the control over the various syllabi. Thus, if there is to be any major shift in secondary schools' syllabi and curricula, then this will require changes in the tertiary level's policy, as this affects the acceptance of students. Such a change in policy would involve changes in the selection, organisation, pacing and timing of knowledge at the tertiary

level. Thus, the conditions for a major shift in the knowledge code at the secondary level is a major shift in the knowledge code at the tertiary level. Changes in the knowledge code at the secondary level are likely to be of a somewhat limited nature without similar changes at the tertiary level. There clearly are other interest groups (industry) which may affect a given curriculum and syllabus.

5. Variation in the strength of classification and frame are in principle traceable to variation in the developments of class structures.

6. What is often over-looked is that the pacing of the knowledge (i.e. the rate of expected learning) is implicitly based upon the middle-class socialization of the child. Middle-class family socialization of the child is a hidden subsidy, in the sense that it provides both a physical and psychological environment which immensely facilitates, in diverse ways, school learning. The middle-class child is oriented to learning almost anything. Because of this hidden subsidy, there has been little incentive to change curriculum and pedagogy; for the middle-class child is geared to learn; he may not like, or indeed approve of, what he learns, but he learns. Where the school system is not subsidised by the home, the pupil often fails. In this way, even the *pacing* of educational knowledge is class based. It may well be that frame strength, as this refers to pacing, is a critical variable in the study of educability. It is possible that the weak frame strength (as this refers to *pacing*) of integrated codes indicates that integrated codes pre-suppose a longer average educational life. Middle-class children may have been potential pupils for progressive schools because of their longer educational life.

7. It is possible that the weak boundary maintaining procedures of integrated codes at the level of the organizational structure, knowledge structure and identity structure may increase the pupils/students informal age group affiliations as a source of identity, relation and organization.

8. In the sense of creating order.

9. If educational codes can be considered as a repeater system we can ask, what is the *social basis* of a repeater system which produces the unlikely.

10. I am suggesting that the internal organization and focusing of meanings with individuals are initially structured and focused by the distribution of power and the principles of control.

Bernstein, B., Peters, R. and Elvin, I. "Ritual in Education." *Philosophical Transactions of the Royal Society of London*, Series B, 251:1, 1966.

Bernstein, B. "Open Schools, Open Society?" *New Society*, September 14th, 1967.

Davies, D.I. "The Management of Knowledge: A Critique of the Use of Typologies in Educational Sociology," Sociology 4 No. 1.; reprinted in *Knowledge and Control*,(ed.)M. Young, London: Collier-Macmillan, 1971.

Davies, D. I. "Knowledge, Education and Power." Paper presented to the British Sociological Association Annual Conference, Durham. Published in R. Brown (ed.) *Education, Culture and Sociology*, London: Tavistock, 1971.

Douglas, M. *Purity and Danger*, Routledge & Kegan Paul, 1966.

Douglas, M. *Natural Symbols*, Barrie & Rockliff, The Cresset Press, 1970.

Durkheim, E. *On the Division of Labour in Society*, The Free Press, Glencoe, Illinois, 1947.

Durkheim, E. *Moral Education*, The Free Press, Glencoe, Illinois, 1961.

Durkheim, E. & Mauss, M. *Primitive Classification* (Translated by Needham, R.) Cohen & West, 1963.

Keddie, N. G. "The Social Basis of Classroom Knowledge," M. A. Dissertation, University of London Institute of Education, 1970.

Hoyle, E. "How Does The Curriculum Change? (1) A Proposal for Enquiries (2) Systems and strategies," *Journal of Curriculum Studies*, 1:243, 1969.

Jeffrey, G. B. *The Unity of Knowledge: Reflections on the Universities of Cambridge and London*. Cambridge University Press, 1950.

Musgrove. F. "The contribution of sociology to the study of the curriculum"; in *Changing the Curriculum* (ed.) Kerr, J. F., University of London Press, 1968.

Young, M. "Curricula as Socially Organised Knowledge," in *Knowledge and Control* (ed.) Young, M., Collier-Macmillan, 1971.

Restrictions on Public Space

Restrictions on Public Space

Public space encompasses those social institutions that are formally open to all members of the society by virtue of their claim to citizenship (actual or anticipated) who meet commonly agreed upon, universal criteria. However, as the selections in this section indicate, it is very difficult to separate universal criteria from particularistic ones. Consequently some persons, groups or social categories are effectively excluded from ostensibly public areas because they do not meet the informal, privately defined standards for admission, or because once in they do not conform to the 'private' rules. Universities tend to become gentlemen's clubs, the civil service and certain occupations a male preserve, the city a racial filter.

Here the central question is: does not the very structure of imequality that generated the excluded and underprivileged groups operate so as to keep them from acquiring the power, the skills and the self-recognition of their own worth that they would need to have their claims recognized? Part of the answer, at least, lies in the very complexity of social life. Exclusion is never total, nor control ever absolute. There is a continuing though tenuous reciprocal relation between universalistic and particularistic principles that makes for continuous adjustment and for the possibility, at least, of major structural change.

---

1. Social Class as a Factor in Selection for Higher Education

Robert Pike/*Queen's University*

Access to the full rights of citizenship in an industrial society, at least until now, has been primarily through education. In Canada all able-minded children are required to go to school for about eight years from the age of six on (there are variations from province to province) and ostensibly, at any rate, they are free to continue thereafter for as long as their ambitions and their abilities permit them. Access may be equal but, as this excerpt from a much longer examination of accessibility to higher education so forcefully documents, opportunities once inside are not. The net result is a progressive shoring-up of privilege of the favoured classes and ethnic groups at the expense of the less advantaged. This stubborn paradox, which others have noted elsewhere as well, might be raised almost to the level of a social law: every attempt to remove inequities that operate to the disadvantage of certain categories and groups invariably reward the most favoured in proportion to the distribution of power and occupational success.

The Definition of Social Class

A sociologist who writes about 'the class structure of Canadian society' is liable to meet a hostile reaction from the general reader. 'Class' is a nasty word, which suggests a desire to make invidious distinctions between 'upper' and 'lower', 'better' and 'worse' or between the 'haves' and 'have nots' – in short, it suggests an unsubtle snobbery or a conscious acceptance of Karl Marx's belief in the inevitability of class warfare. As I have often been told by returning Canadian tourists, Britain contains social classes, whereas Canada does not. In Britain, so the tourists say, people dress according to their class, speak with the accents of their class, and go to schools which reinforce their class position and class consciousness. In Canada, these Old World social distinctions are popularly presumed to have been dissipated by a healthy injection of New World equalitarianism. It is hard to explain, therefore, that when we talk about social class in Canada, we are not claiming that the

Reprinted from *Who Doesn't Get to University – and Why*: A Study on Accessibility to Higher Education in Canada, by Robert M. Pike, by permission of the author and The Association of Universities and Colleges of Canada, Ottawa. © 1970.

average Canadian (like an old-fashioned but rapidly disappearing race of Englishmen) labels a man as 'lower class', and then damns him, because he drops his 'h's', or eats peas with his knife. Very often 'social class' is simply used as a convenient short-hand device which enables a sociologist to classify differences in behaviour and attitudes between individuals and groups of individuals.

The various definitions of 'social class' have been thoroughly explored by John Porter in his outstanding Canadian study, *The Vertical Mosaic*.[1] I use the term, as does Porter much of the time, to refer to artificially constructed statistical groups in which individuals are placed on the basis of occupation, level of income or education. To quote Porter, "When people within a particular income range, or at a particular skill or educational level, are grouped together it will be found that they behave in ways different from people grouped together in another income range or at another skill or educational level. The farther removed one class is from another the greater will be differences in behaviour".[2] Since the behaviour of an individual, and the attitudes and opinions which he holds, are greatly influenced by his immediate social environment (i.e. where he lives, whom he meets, how much money he has to spend) and since his immediate social environment is to a considerable extent determined by his occupation, income or level of education, it is not surprising to find that people classified in one occupational category or income-group tend to behave differently from people classified in another. We would hardly expect men engaged in labouring work, characterized by low incomes, poor education, and the threat of seasonal unemployment, to behave, and think, in just the same way as those engaged in highly-qualified professional occupations.

From the point of view of the sociologist, the most widely used measure of the social class of school children is father's occupation. The occupation of a school pupil's father sums up a series of socio-economic factors which at a very early stage begin to influence the child's educational progress and expectations, and for this reason it is a good predictor of whether or not the child will complete high school and enter university. Other objective measures which the sociologist might use as indicators of a child's social class background, and which also are significantly correlated with his educational progress and chances of university admission, include family income and the educational attainment of his parents. Sometimes, the sociologist will use a combination of such measures as indicative of a child's social class background. Alternatively, however, he may use just one of them – say, the father's occupation as ranked on a widely used occupational prestige scale – and assume that this measure is inter-related and interlinked with the other measures which he might have used. Thus, to take an example of the second approach, if the sociologist classifies a group of school children as being 'upper-middle-class' because their fathers are engaged in high status professional occupations, he might expect his reader to take for granted that the great majority of these children also come from homes where family income is relatively high, and where the parents (or, at least, the father) have received an advanced education. Furthermore, as a result of this expectation, he is likely to use such terms as 'upper-middle-class children', 'children from the high income groups', 'children of professionals and executives' (or alternatively, 'lower-working-class children', 'children from low income families', 'children of unskilled manual workers') very much as if they refer to the same group of people. To be strictly accurate they do not, since it is possible to think of many cases where a child would be classified in one social category on the basis of his father's occupation and in quite another on the basis of disposable family income. For example, the child of a clergyman will usually be classified as 'professional' in origins, but nevertheless the income received by many clergymen is lower than that received by many skilled manual workers. However, the rationale behind the approach is that in an advanced industrial society, the economic, occupational and educational hierarchies tend to be interrelated and reinforce each other. Thus terms such as 'middle-class' or 'working-class' should simply be regarded as broadly indicative of groups with certain social characteristics. They are not intended to be exhaustive social categories.

Social Class Differentials in University Attendance

Most of our existing information on Canadian class differentials in educational opportunity has to be gleaned from pieces of research which were carried out during the 1950's, or during the first couple of years of this decade. However, because the 1960's have witnessed a revolution in Canadian secondary and post-secondary education – for example, an increasing proportion of school children completing high school, a very large increase in university and college enrolments, the establishment of new types of post-secondary institutions, and the development and expansion of student financial aid programs – we are in no postion to assume that the class factors which influenced selection for higher education during the 1950's still retain their erstwhile significance. The lack of contemporary research on the changes which may have occurred in class differentials in educational opportunity as a result of this revolution is quite deplorable. But, in such circumstances, all we can do is to describe the situation as it existed ten or so years ago, and then to point out the main areas in which further research is required.

a) Social Class and University Attendance During the 1950's
During the 1950's, children whose fathers were employed in relatively highly paid professional and white-collar occupations were very greatly over-represented amongst Canadian university students relative to their total numbers in the Canadian population. On the other hand, children whose fathers were engaged in poorly paid, semi-skilled or unskilled manual occupations were very greatly under-represented, and had a very poor chance indeed of reaching university. We know these facts largely as a result of John Porter's analysis of the social class origin of some 8,000 university students, drawn from all provinces in Canada, who were attending the universities in 1956-57.[3] Porter classified the occupations of the students' fathers in accordance with the Blishen occupational scale – a scale of classes in which occupations are classified on the basis of the average annual income, and average years of schooling, of members of the occupation.[4] He then compared the proportion of students falling within a particular occupational class with the proportion of all children in the Canadian population (all those at home with fathers in the work force) who fell within that class. Details are given in Table I. The 'ratios of representation' in the final column of the table are obtained by dividing column II (percentage of all children at home with fathers in the work force) into column I (percentage of university students).

Table I: Social class origins of 7,947 Canadian university students 1956-57 (Blishen Occupational Scale)

| Fathers' Occupational Class | I % of Students | % of Labour Force | | % of Children at Home with Fathers in Labour Force | | IV Ratio of Representation[2] |
		Total	Male Heads of Family with Children[1]	II All Children[1]	III Children Aged 14-25 Years[1]	
Class 1	11.0	.9	1.4	1.1	1.0	10.00
Class 2	34.9	10.7	14.7	10.4	13.5	3.36
Class 3	4.8	6.3	4.0	3.5	3.1	1.37
Class 4	7.1	7.0	5.0	4.9	4.7	1.45
Class 5	19.7	23.9	24.8	22.6	18.4	.87
Class 6	5.8	19.6	15.1	16.1	15.5	.36
Class 7	5.3	21.3	13.8	14.9	14.5	.36
Farmers[3]	11.4	10.3	16.8	20.7	26.0	.55
Unclassifiable[4]			4.4	5.7	3.3	

[1]Computed from Census of Canada, 1951, Vol. III, Table 141.
[2]Obtained by dividing column I (% of students) by column II (% of all children at home with fathers in labour force).
[3]Census occupation class of 'farmers and stock raisers.'
[4]'Others' and 'not stated' in Census.
Source: John Porter, *The Vertical Mosaic*, Table XXIII, p. 186.

They indicate the extent to which children from each occupational class were over-represented or under-represented amongst the university sample in terms of the numbers of all children at home.[5]

A glance at the table shows that children with fathers in the professional occupations (class I of the Blishen Scale) constituted 11.0 per cent of the total sample of university students , but only 1.4 per cent of all Canadian children at home in families with the male head in the work force. At the other end of the class spectrum, children whose fathers were engaged in relatively poorly paid, semi-skilled or unskilled occupations (classes 6 and 7) constituted 11.1 per cent of the university sample, although no less than 31.0 per cent of all children at home had fathers who were engaged in class 6 or 7 occupations. Between these extremes, children in classes 2, 3 and 4 (father engaged in white-collar and high blue-collar occupations) were over-represented amongst university students, although to a considerably smaller extent than children from the highly-paid professional group. And finally, children whose fathers were engaged in skilled trades (class 5) were slightly under-represented, but certainly not to the extent of children from semi-skilled and unskilled groups. The category of 'farmers' does not constitute a homogeneous economic group for it included children whose fathers were engaged in all kinds of farming – everyone from the prosperous cattle rancher to the dirt farmer eking out a poor living on a few acres of land. Even so, the children of farmers contributed only about one-half of the numbers of university students that this group would have contributed if children from all socio-economic categories had had 'equality of representation' at the university level. In 1957, Professor W. G. Fleming described Canadian university education as being "to a considerable extent the privilege of a numerically small occupational class"[6] He was hardly overstating the situation which existed at that time, for over one-half of the students attending Canadian universities (those in classes 1-4) were drawn from a social segment of the population which, in total, contained only about one-fifth of the country's children.

It is not difficult to describe the patterns of social selection which led to these class inequalities in university participation. Throughout the 1950's (and it is undoubtedly still the case today) Canadian children from working-class homes were more likely to leave school before reaching the 'university eligibility grade' than children whose fathers were engaged in professional and white-collar occupations. This meant that the group of pupils still at school in the university eligibility grade was not only generally superior in terms of intellectual capacity and scholastic performance but contained disproportionately large numbers of school children from financially well-off, middle-class families. It follows naturally from this that those students who entered university also tended to be drawn in disproportionately large numbers from financially well off, middle-class families. Indeed, as the decision to enter university involved a series of practical calculations on the part of students and their parents – most notably, whether the costs of university attendance could, or could not, be met – we find that the university students were, in general, a more 'class-biased group' than the matriculant population from which they were drawn.[7] This generalization, however, needs to be qualified by the observation that the extent of the 'class bias' varied considerably from university faculty to university faculty, and probably also from university to university. As shown in a nationwide study of university student expenditure income carried out by the Dominion Bureau of Statistics in 1961-62, some faculties, notably education, had a relatively strong appeal for children from clerical, manual working-class and farming backgrounds. Others, notably the professional faculties of law and medicine, drew the majority of their students from the professional and managerial middle-classes.[8]

As the dimensions of class differential in educational opportunity during the 1950's have been well documented,[9] there is not a great deal of point in continuing this brief outline. It is sufficient to note that, whether the measure of social class then used was the composite Blishen Scale (composite in the sense of classifying occupations in terms of the average annual income and education of members of the occupation) or the less sophisticated device of classifying university students simply on the basis of parental income or parental education, university students were found to come in disproportionately large numbers from the higher occupational classes, the higher income groups, and from homes where the level of education of the parents was relatively high. Of course, this does not mean that all university students were the children of wealthy, well-educated parents any more than it means that all the children of wealthy, well-educated parents attended university. Indeed, in view of the limited amount of money then available in the form of student financial aid, it is rather surprising that, in the Dominion Bureau of Statistics' student expenditure and income survey, between 10 per cent and 22 per cent of the undergraduate respondents (the percentages depending on the university faculty in which they were enrolled) reported gross parental incomes of less than $3,000 a year.[10]

b) Social Class and University Attendance During the 1960's
In 1965-66, the Canadian Union of Students undertook a sample survey of Canadian undergraduate students which supported the conclusions of earlier studies insofar as it found that Canadian university students are "...by and large not representative of the Canadian class structure but rather bear the characteristics of the middle and upper classes of Canadian society".[11] There is thus some indication that, whatever changes may have taken place in the social composition of the university population since the mid-1950's, we are still very far removed from an idealistic, and probably unobtainable, state of 'perfect educational mobility'; a state in which young people all find their 'natural' educational levels in accordance with variations in their 'natural' inherent abilities, uninfluenced by family background, school or neighbourhood. The educational developments which have taken place during the past fifteen years have been very substantial. Nevertheless, young people from middle-class homes and from families in the higher income categories are still over-represented amongst university students in terms of their total numbers in the Canadian population.

Even if we accept that there is still a 'class bias' in selection for Canadian higher education, we might hope, nevertheless, that the class differentials which characterized participation in university education in the mid-1950's – most notably the massive under-representation of children from unskilled working class homes – have since been somewhat reduced. On this score, however, recent studies carried out in England and the United States give us few grounds for optimism. In their study of class differentials in educational opportunity in England and Wales, Allan Little and John Westergaard have shown that the expansion of the English universities in recent years has, if anything, benefited children of middle-class people and skilled workers more than those from semi-skilled and unskilled workers' homes.[12] Similarly, Christopher Jencks and David Riesman in their recent monumental analysis of higher education in the United States, suggest that the expansion of the two-year and four-year colleges in that country has benefited upper middle-class children as much as, or more than, it has benefited those from the lower-middle and working classes.[13] In both countries, children of predominantly middle-class parents appear to have maintained their privileged educational position. In both countries, the 'university attendance chances' of young people from very low-income, unskilled backgrounds do not seem to have increased relative to those of young people in the middle and upper strata. Class differentials in chances of access to the universities would appear, therefore, to be more remarkable for their dogged persistence than for their diminution over time – and this despite increased university enrolments, better secondary school provisions, and financial aid to university students.

Since the socio-economic classification of 'father's occupation' which was used in the survey carried out by the Canadian Union of Students is not directly comparable with the Blishen Scale used by John Porter, we are not in a position to assess the relevance of these English and American studies to the Canadian scene. In such circumstances, all we can do is to review the developments and changes in educational behaviour, and educational policy, which have taken place since the mid-1950's, and then to speculate on the possible social consequences of each of these developments and changes. I would list the major relevant ones as follows:

1. A large increase in the numbers, and proportions, of young people matriculating from high school.

2. A doubling, since the mid-1950's, in the proportion of the 18-24 age group enrolled in full-time university courses.

3. The establishment of new types of post-secondary institutions which are designed to offer young people increasing opportunities for post-high school education outside the aegis of the universities.

4. A growing public concern with problems of educational inequality. In practical terms, this concern has shown itself not only in measures designed to combat cultural deprivation, and to improve school facilities, but also through a massive increase in government expenditures on student financial aid. Canadian government expenditures on repayable and non-repayable aid to full-time undergraduate students rose about thirty-fold between 1957-58 and 1967-68, with the bulk of the increase being designed to provide assistance to those students in need of financial help.[14] I will begin my speculations with an examination of the possible social consequences of the growth in senior high school and university enrolments.

I) THE GROWTH IN SENIOR HIGH SCHOOL AND UNIVERSITY ENROLMENTS

It should be obvious that a growth in Canadian senior high-school and university enrolments does not by itself ensure a reduction of social inequalities in educational opportunities; it does so only if the expanded facilities in high schools and universities are made proportionately more accessible to those previously least able to take advantage of them. To put this proposition in another way: unless the growth in the numbers, and proportions, of young Canadians finishing high school and entering university has been primarily a consequence of increased working-class access to and interest in higher education, class differentials in chances of university attendance may have remained the same despite the growth in enrolments. A theoretical example may help to clarify this statement. Just suppose that as a result of the expansion in the number of university places over a 10 year period, an intelligent working-class child's overall chances of attending university increases from, say, 10 in 100, to 15 in 100 (an increase of 50 per cent). However, over the same period, an intelligent middle-class child's chances of attending university increases from 40 in 100 to 60 in 100 (also an increase of 50 per cent). In this case, the expansion in the number of university places has increased the overall chance of university attendance both for the middle-class and working-class child. Nevertheless, the social inequalities in chances of university attendance are as sharp as ever, since the middle-class child is still 4 times as likely as the working-class child to enter university.

Some practical implications of this theoretical discussion are

Table 2: Children living at Home and in School aged 14-24, 1951 and aged 15-21, 1961 (Blishen Occupational Scale)

Occupational Class	I No. of Children Living at Home 1951	II Percentage at School 1951[1]	III No. of Children Living at Home 1961	VI Percentage at School 1961[1]	V Absolute Percentage Increase Over 1951	VI Relative Percentage Increase Over 1951[2]
Class 1	13,502	71.0	20,641	83.3	12.3	17.3
Class 2	173,937	55.2	229,496	69.2	14.2	25.7
Class 3	40,130	50.6	33,727	67.0	16.4	32.4
Class 4	60,739	45.6	110,364	58.6	13.0	28.5
Class 5						
(With Farmers)	573,095	38.9	412,969	52.5	13.6	34.9
(Without Farmers)	(237,925)	(45.6)	(205,071)	(56.5)	(10.9)	(23.9)
Class 6	200,517	38.2	249,295	44.4	6.2	16.2
Class 7	186,862	34.8	150,124	43.2	8.4	24.1
Occupations Unstated in Census or Unclassifiable	41,316		162,922			
TOTAL	1,290,098		1,369,538			

[1] All figures shown in the table cover only those children living at home at the time of the 1951 and 1961 Censuses. Children not living at home are excluded. It will be noted that the table compares children in the 14-24 age group in 1951 with children in the 15-24 age group in 1961. The comparison is reasonable since in most provinces the legal minimum age of school leaving was raised from 14 to 15 years during the interim period.

[2] For comment on the nature of 'relative percentage increase over 1951', see footnote 18 of this chapter.

Sources: i) *Census of Canada 1951*, Vol. III, table 141.

    ii) *Census of Canada 1961*, Vol. II, table 82.

    iii) John Porter, *The Vertical Mosaic*, table XIX, p. 180.

illustrated in Table 2. The first two columns of the table, which are based on John Porter's analysis of relevant data on 'father's occupation' contained in the report of the 1951 Census of Canada, show the magnitude of class differentials in the proportions of young people in the 14-24 age group who were attending school or university (i.e. had not entered the work force) at the time of the 1951 Census.[15] The third and fourth columns of the table provide an estimate of class differentials in the proportions of 15-24 year olds who were attending school or university at the time of the 1961 Census, and represent my attempt to replicate Porter's investigation using corresponding occupational data contained in the 1961 Census report. The Blishen Occupational Scale, which was referred to earlier in this chapter, has been used throughout as the basis of socio-economic classification.[16] However, for various technical reasons, the application of this scale to the occupational data contained in the 1961 Census turned out to be a hazardous operation. The reader is, therefore, advised to consult footnote 17 to this chapter in order that he may be aware of the nature of the technical problems involved.[17] He is further advised (for reasons made apparent in the footnote) that changes, between the two Census dates, in the proportions of young people from each socio-economic category described in Table 2 as being 'at school' constitute only a very rough guide to trends in educational participation amongst Canadian children from different social class backgrounds.

Granted that Table 2 should be treated as 'a very rough guide' to certain trends in educational participation, what are its major features? The first, and most obvious, is the significant increase between 1951 and 1961 in the numbers and proportions of young Canadians remaining at school beyond the minimum school leaving age (up to 14 years of age in most provinces in 1951 and up to 15 years of age in most provinces in 1961); an increase which was not limited to any particular social class, or classes, in Canadian society but which reflected an absolute increase in levels of educational attainment amongst young people from all social classes in the population. Thus, no social class was entirely isolated from the trend to late school leaving. If valid, this conclusion indicates that there has been an overall increase in the 'holding power' of Canadian school systems.

So far so good. Yet – and here is the catch – it will be noted that at the time of the 1951 Census, the proportions of young people in the 14-24 age group who were then attending school or university varied from 71.0 per cent of those whose fathers were engaged in highly skilled professional work (class 1) down to 34.8 per cent of those whose fathers were engaged in unskilled manual occupations (class 7). Ten years later, at the time of the 1961 Census, the proportions of young people in the 15-24 age group who were attending school or university varied from 83.3 per cent of the children of professionals down to 43.2 per cent of the children of unskilled manual workers – percentages which show the maintenance of very wide class differentials in school retention rates despite the absolute increase in these rates. Thus, it is quite possible (although the evidence is by no means irrefutable) that the trend towards later school leaving between 1951 and 1961 raised the general level of educational attainment without effectively disturbing existing class differentials in educational opportunity, at least not at the extremes of the class spectrum. Certainly, there may have been a narrowing of 'the educational opportunity gap' between children of certain occupational classes – notably between the children of highly-paid professional workers and the children of executive-white-collar and skilled workers (classes 2-5) – but the children of semi-skilled and unskilled manual workers (classes 6 and 7) remained the group least likely, by far, to continue their schooling beyond the minimum leaving age.[19]

From the point of view of access to the universities, it is obvious that an analysis of this kind (based as it is on very broad age groupings) is a poor substitute for a long-term study of changes in the likelihood that. a young person of given social origins will actually enter university. Furthermore, it is possible that the rapid growth in senior high school and university enrolments since 1961 has subsequently led to some significant changes in these class differentials in school and university participation. However, the only point that I am emphasizing here is that we cannot be sure that increased school and university participation has been accompanied by a significant decrease, at the extremes of the class ladder, in social inequalities in educational opportunity. Indeed, the reverse is possible – that the new technology of automation, with its emphasis on the acquisition of skills and learning, may have begun to cleave Canadian society, particularly its younger members, into two clearly distinguishable classes; two classes with relatively little social movement between them. Timothy Reid made this suggestion in a thought-provoking article published in *The Labour Gazette* in 1965.[20] According to his definition, one of the two classes – the 'favoured' class – is made up of people who have, at the very minimum, 4 years of secondary school education, and most of whom, because they have sufficient formal education, are continuously employed and because they are continuously employed, have incomes of at least $5,000 per annum. In stark contrast, however, the second – the 'disadvantaged' class – is made up of the under-educated most of whom, because they are under-educated, are chronically unemployed or work only sporadically, and who, because they are unemployed, live in relative deprivation and poverty. The children of the 'favoured' class are able to participate fully in the growing educational employment opportunities offered by the society. Children from the 'disadvantaged' class tend, like their parents, to be under-educated and under-employed; to face with inadequate skills a world in which advancing technology is reducing the number of unskilled jobs for which they may apply. Reid's suggestion, as noted above, is lent some support by the findings of a recent Canadian study which examines the association, over a number of generations, between the educational attainments of parents and the educational attainments of their children.[21] The study, undertaken by Michel D. Lagacé, on the basis of questions appended to the Dominion Bureau of Statistics Labour Force Survey of June 1966, suggests that those children whose parents have received only an elementary education are perhaps becoming isolated from the increasing opportunities for educational advancement enjoyed by other groups in the educational structure. The data on which this suggestion is based is too detailed to discuss here, but it shows a consistent, and long-term, high degree of self-recruitment, whereby 90 per cent of the under-educated of one generation are the children of the under-educated of the preceding generation.[22] In other words, lack of education, with its corresponding ills of unemployment and poverty, tends to perpetuate itself.

In the light of the foregoing discussion, I would hazard a guess that if we were in a position to compare the 'university attendance chances' of children of different social class backgrounds who were enrolled in the high schools in the mid-1950's with the 'university attendance chances' of children of different social class backgrounds who are attending high school today, we might reach two conclusions: first that, in absolute terms, children of all social classes are more likely to attend university now than was the case fifteen years ago – this would be a natural concomitant of the rapid growth in university enrolments – and, secondly, that in terms of class differentials in chances of access to the universities, there might have been a narrowing of the 'accessibility gap' between the children of highly-paid professional workers on the one hand, and the children of relatively well-off white-collar workers and skilled manual workers on the other – a narrowing born of rising levels of real income and rising educational expectations. I should note, however, that (subject to the two sets of qualifications made in the final paragraphs below) it is highly questionable whether, in relative terms, there has been any narrowing of the accessibility gap between children in these social strata and the children of semi-skilled and unskilled manual workers (amongst whom would be included most of the children belonging to Reid's disadvantaged class) in fact the gap may actually have widened. The two sets of qualifications are as follows:

First of all, in instances where provinces have recently subjected their educational systems to a series of far reaching reforms – Quebec would be a good example – the claim that there has been no narrowing of the accessibility gap for lower-working-class children (i.e. those from semi-skilled and unskilled manual backgrounds) needs to be subjected to critical evaluation. It would certainly be suprising to learn that Quebec's 'quiet educational·revolution', with its emphasis on measures designed to promote greater equality of educational opportunity amongst the children of the province, had not led to a relative improvement in the university attendance chances of lower-working-class children vis-à-vis children from other social class backgrounds.

Secondly, some consideration must be given to changes over time in the numbers and proportions of young Canadians with a given level of educational opportunities, as well as to changes in differentials in educational opportunity between existing social classes. For example, since the proportions of the Canadian labour force engaged in professional, white-collar and service occupations have been increasing steadily over the past few decades, with a concomitant decrease in the proportions engaged in unskilled manual work and in farming, it is probable that changes over time in the size and composition of the various social classes, resulting from changes in the occupational composition of the labour force, have led to a proportionate increase in the numbers of young Canadians whose chances of university attendance are relatively high: i.e. the growing numbers of those whose fathers are employed in professional and white-collar occupations.[23] Thus, from a national viewpoint, we might well argue that there has been an overall increase in young people's chances of university attendance simply as a result of changes in the Canadian occupational class structure.

With these thoughts in mind, I turn now to the second of the major developments of the past fifteen years: the development and expansion of government programs designed to provide financial aid to university students.

II) THE ROLE OF STUDENT FINANCIAL AID[24]

Insofar as class differentials in chances of access to the universities persist, they do so in the face of a very great increase in Canadian government expenditures on student financial aid. During the past four or five years alone, the proportions of Canadian university and college students receiving financial aid through the Canada Student Loans Plan, and similar aid programs, has risen substantially. This increase is taken by many student-aid administrators as evidence, first of all, that young people from the lower-income groups are becoming more equitably represented amongst university and college students, and secondly, that the growing availability of student financial aid is one of the major reasons for the increased participation in higher education of young people from these groups. In other words, many aid administrators see student financial aid as playing an increasingly important role in the 'democratization'

of university and college studies.

It should be abundantly clear that we are not in a position either to support, or refute, a claim that student financial aid is playing an increasingly important role in the 'democratization' of higher education. In order to support such a claim, we would have to be able to show there had been over the past few years, a substantial proportionate increase in the numbers of young people from low-income homes remaining at school to matriculation level, and/or a substantial proportionate increase in the numbers of qualified matriculants from low-income homes going on to university or college. In addition, we would have to be reasonably sure that the growing availability of student financial aid (rather than changing motivational patterns or better educational facilities) was the prime reason for these increases. The lack of information on the social effects of aid-giving in Canada and other countries can be summed up very neatly by quoting the authors of an international study of student financial aid programs which was published in 1963. The authors noted as follows:

> Few countries are in a position to evaluate the effects of aid programmes and their success in achieving the objectives for which they were set up. This situation undoubtedly springs mainly from the lack of statistical information available. It seems that until we approached them many countries had little information on how these figures were growing both in total and in relation to the student body. Hardly any countries have any statistical basis on which to assess the effects of aid programmes on the total size and the composition of the student body, nor is there any clear idea – though many theories are propounded – on the influence of aid on academic standards . . . So, sizable sums of money are being spent yet no one knows to what effect.[25]

It is accordingly not at all evident that the increased coverage of student-aid programs has been accompanied by an influx of young people from low-income homes into the universities. However, I do a little to remedy our basic lack of statistical information in the second half of this report.

The comments I make above should not in any sense be taken as a denial that existing student financial aid programs perform an important 'enabling function' – i.e. that they make university or college attendance possible for many students who would otherwise be unable, for financial reasc.s, to continue their studies – but rather that we do not know very much about their long-term effects on the social composition of the student body. In my mind, there is little doubt that, at any one point in time, such programs do indeed provide essential financial support to university and college students coming from families in the lower and middle-income ranges. To take an example drawn from one province, the data in Table 3 show the numbers of dependent students with parents in given income categories who were receiving aid through the Canada Student Loans Plan and the province of Nova Scotia's provincial aid program during the 1967-68 academic year. About two-thirds of the Nova Scotian students receiving public financial aid came from families where combined parental income before taxes was $6,000 a year or less, and 11 per cent actually came from families where combined parental income before taxes was $2,000 a year or less.[26] We have no indication of the proportions of all Nova Scotian university and college students with parents in given income ranges who actually received financial aid through government programs, but one would have a hard time arguing that those students whose parents earned a combined income of, say, $4,000 a year or less would have been able to attend a post-secondary institution if it had not been for the ready availability of student financial

Table 3: Nova Scotia. Numbers of Dependent Full-Time Students with Parents in Given Income Categories Receiving Aid through the Canada Student Loans Plan and the Nova Scotia Government Bursary Program, 1967-68[1]

Combined Parental Income Before Taxes	Numbers of Students	Percentage	Cumulative Percentage
$0 - $2,000	433	10.8	10.8
$2,001 - $4,000	961	24.0	34.8
$4,001 - $6,000	1,300	32.2	67.0
$6,001 - $8,000	759	18.9	85.9
$8,001 - $10,000	367	9.1	95.0
$10,001 - $12,000	135	3.4	98.4
$12,001 - $14,000	46	1.1	99.5
$14,001 - $16,000	19	.5	100.0
TOTAL	4,020	100.0	

[1] Aid-receivers attending universities and other post-secondary institutions both inside, and outside, the Province of Nova Scotia are included in the table. Aid-receivers not considered to be dependent upon their parents are excluded.
Source: Unpublished data received from Student Aid Section, Department of Education, Province of Nova Scotia.

aid.

If we accept that existing student-aid programs enable many qualified matriculants from low-income homes to continue their studies then we also have to accept that, by definition, such programs cannot provide direct assistance to those young people from low-income homes who leave school from the lower grades. This is the most obvious limitation placed on the 'equalizing' role of a student-aid program, and it may help to explain why a large increase in expenditures on student financial aid is not inevitably accompanied by a large proportionate increase in the numbers of young people from very low-income families entering the universities. I noted that the great majority of those young people who matriculate from high school probably continue their education at a university or some other type of post-secondary institution.[27] However, I also noted that only a small (although growing) proportion of young Canadians do, in fact, matriculate from high school, whilst many drop out after receiving only an elementary, or limited secondary education.[28] In view of these facts, I would not hesitate to argue that any loss of 'college potential' which may occur through the failure of high-school matriculants from low-income homes to continue on to university or college, is overshadowed by the loss which undoubtedly occurs during the course of elementary and secondary schooling. Let us not forget the conclusion reached by the Economic Council of Canada that in 1961, some 27 per cent of the total non-farm population of Canada, including 1.7 million children under 16 years of age, were living in a state of 'total poverty'.[29] We have to face up to the likelihood that very few children from this large segment of the Canadian population are represented amongst high-school matriculants. A shortage of money alone does not necessarily account for their premature withdrawal from school, but shortage of money is associated with many other social and cultural factors which are inimical to continued school attendance.

Given these circumstances, it is fairly obvious that student financial aid at the university or college level cannot by itself ensure 'equality of access' to higher education, unless we interpret 'access' simply in terms of the processes of social selection which occur between high-school completion and university or college admission. Student financial aid can perhaps ensure that no academically qualified student from a low-income fami-

ly is deprived of the chance of going on to university or college. And it may encourage young people from low-income homes to remain at school in the knowledge that they will be able thereafter to continue their education. But there its influence ends, and we are still confronted by the distasteful fact that there are many, many intelligent children from the 'disadvantaged' classes in Canadian society for whom the availability or non-availability of student financial aid is of little practical importance. The principal of Glendon College, York University, recently observed that " . . . one million dollars spent on kindergartens for 4 and 5 year old children of the poor will be more effective in moving towards our objective of equality of educational opportunity than $10 million spent on bursaries for students at universities, provided that the 4 and 5 year olds who are given a head-start by going on to first-rate kindergartens, go on to first-rate primary schools".[30] He could have added that if the children of the poor who are given this head-start then proceed on through secondary school to university, we might, in some future year, have to spend $20 million to keep them there. The role of student financial aid as a dynamic 'equalizing' agent, therefore, largely depends on how many children from low-income homes we can keep in school to matriculation level. Financial aid is one weapon – but inevitably a weapon of limited range – to be used in our attack on the broad problems of educational inequality.

I have two further comments to make. First of all, it should be obvious that increased Canadian expenditures on student financial aid are not being entirely devoted to making it *possible* for qualified matriculants, who would otherwise have been unable to attend university or college, to continue with their studies. Some of the money at least is being expended in order to make it *easier*, and certainly much more pleasant, for numbers of our young people to attend university or college, even though many of these young people might, in fact, still have attended if no financial aid had been available. There is certainly no obvious conflict between this 'easing function' of a student-aid program and its 'enabling' function,[31] although they might oblige an aid-giving body to establish an order or priorities. Thus, for example, it is the argument of the New Brunswick Higher Education Commission that no matter how desirable it might be to make it easier for New Brunswick students to attend university, the first object of the provincial government's student aid program should be " . . . to knock down those financial barriers which keep out those who are capable, qualified and interested in university and college studies".[32] In view of the limited public funds available for student financial support in many of Canada's less prosperous provinces such a definition of priorities may be inevitable.

Finally, it is, of course, possible that high-school students may be led to aspire to a university or college education by the knowledge that financial aid will be available to them; in other words, the availability of financial aid may be taken into consideration by high-school students when they formulate their educational plans for the future. This possibility may be described as the 'retention function' of an aid program; the program may well change social attitudes by creating a general feeling amongst potential university students and their parents that 'the money is there if I need it'.[33] Whether student-aid programs in Canada do perform such a function it is quite impossible to say. Nevertheless, I think we have to work on the assumption that the availability of student financial aid may lead some young people to aspire to a university or college education, and that it may encourage some young people from low-income homes to remain in school in order to complete their studies. On the basis of this assumption it is imperative that vocational guidance counsellors in high schools and student-aid officers in universities, colleges and provincial departments of education, cooperate in order to ensure that high-school students are made fully aware that financial aid is available for university and college studies. For, to adapt a well known expression, 'what high school students don't know won't help them'.[34]

III) THE DEVELOPMENT OF POST–SECONDARY ALTERNATIVES
TO UNIVERSITY STUDIES

Throughout this discussion, 'accessibility to higher education' has primarily been defined as 'accessibility to the universities'. This being so, I have not paid much attention to the social role played by non-university post-secondary institutions (hereafter generally referred to as 'post-secondary colleges') within the class structure of Canadian society.[35] Yet we have to concede that the development and expansion of these institutions over the past decade may have begun to widen the educational opportunities of certain segments of the Canadian population. In most provinces, a Canadian who completes high school is not now faced (as he once might have been) with the choice between either entering a university or entering the work force. He can also, where adequate college provision is made, choose between entering a university on the one hand, or entering a College of Applied Arts and Technology or a Collège d'Enseignment Général et Professionnel on the other. Thus, education at a CAAT, CEGEP or some such similar institution, becomes an alternative of choice to education at a university. It is doubtful, of course, whether the former alternative is regarded by all students and their parents as being equally desirable to the latter. The prestige value of a university education with its increasingly outdated implications of social and intellectual elitism, is a formidable barrier to the creation of 'equality of esteem' between universities and post-secondary colleges.[36]

Canadian post-secondary colleges, although by no means all of a kind, differ from Canadian universities in certain essential respects. First of all, the type of education they provide, although certainly not exclusively vocational, tends to lean towards the applied arts and sciences. Secondly, their admission requirements are frequently more flexible, and in the case of admission to some programs, lower than the admission requirements of the universities. Thirdly, the duration of some of the

certification courses that they offer is relatively short, although others may extend to three years or more. Fourthly, and highly significant, many post-secondary colleges are tuition-free or charge only low tuition fees. We would reasonably expect, therefore, in view of these differences, that the group of students which aspires, and has access, to the kind of education offered by the post-secondary colleges does not have just the same social class characteristics as the group which aspires, and has access, to a university education. For example, if relatively high university tuition and residence fees should impose a financial barrier which children from low-income families find hard to surmount, then a locally-situated tuition-free post-secondary college may offer them a viable alternative.

Despite a growing concern on the part of Canadian governments with the development and organization of post-secondary colleges, research into the social characteristics of the college population is remarkable only for its paucity. However, there is some evidence from the province of Quebec that, compared with the university student body, a relatively large proportion of post-secondary college students are drawn from the lower-income groups in Canadian society. In 1966, the Quebec government with the co-operation of the Centre de Recherches sur l'Opinion Publique (CROP) undertook a questionnaire survey of the entire Quebec post-secondary population, with the primary task of ascertaining, for student financial aid purposes, existing levels of income and expenditure amongst Quebec university and college students.[37]

At the time of writing, the results of this survey have not been made widely available, but nevertheless, I have had the opportunity to analyse some preliminary statistical returns. Thus, those statistics shown in Table 4, taken from the preliminary report of the Quebec government's study, compare the distribution of the unmarried student population of Quebec universities on the one hand, and Quebec post-secondary colleges on the other, by father's income before taxes. It will be seen that over one-half (51.4 per cent) of the college students who responded to the questionnaire came from families where the father earned a gross income of $4,999 a year or less, compared with just 32.7 per cent of the university students. At the higher income levels, only 10.7 per cent of the college students responding to the questionnaire, compared

Table 4: Quebec: Distribution of Unmarried Full-Time Students Attending Universities and Post-Secondary Colleges by Father's Income before Taxes 1966-67[1]

Father's Gross Income	Technical Colleges No.	%	Classical Colleges[2] No.	%	Other Post-Secondary[3] Colleges No.	%	Total Post-Secondary Colleges No.	%	Universities No.	%
$3,000 and Less	474	21.0	528	12.4	1,041	28.5	2,043	20.1	1,103	9.5
3,001 - 4,999	795	35.2	1,142	26.8	1,242	34.0	3,179	31.3	2,678	23.2
5,000 - 6,999	689	30.5	1,236	29.0	890	24.4	2,815	27.7	3,121	27.0
7,000 - 8,999	184	8.1	566	13.3	295	8.1	1,045	10.3	1,500	13.0
9,000 - 10,999	68	3.0	278	6.5	104	2.9	450	4.4	976	8.4
11,000 and More	48	2.1	510	12.0	78	2.1	636	6.3	2,179	18.9
TOTAL	2,258	100.0	4,260	100.0	3,650	100.0	10,168	100.0	11,557	100.0
Others[4]	552		1,472		1,521		3,545		2,931	

[1]Based on response from 49 per cent of full-time university students, and on returns received from post-secondary colleges where the total response from the students was 60% or higher.
[2]Classical college students in the grades "Belle-Lettres" to "Philosophie II" only, and students in "centres d'études universitaires".
[3]Teachers' colleges, nursing schools, fine arts and music.
[4]Fathers deceased, unemployed or income unknown.
Source: Robert Ayotte, *Etude du Budget des Etudiants au Niveau Collégial et Universitaire Pour L'Année 1966-67.* table 21, p. 40 and table 22, p. 42.

with 27.3 per cent of the university respondents, came from families where the father earned a gross income of $9,000 a year or more. Furthermore, in view of the popular belief that post-secondary education in Canada is the *de facto* prerogative of high-income families, it is interesting to note that 20.1 per cent of the Quebec college students, and 9.5 per cent of the university students, came from families where the father's income was $3,000 a year or less. However, it should also be noted that over one-half of the 98,146 Quebec university and college students to whom questionnaires were sent, failed to return them. A subsequent check by the Quebec investigators amongst 289 college students who failed to respond, suggests that the college non-respondents came from slightly higher income families than the college respondents.[38] Hence, there may have been a bias in response amongst the college students toward the lower levels of the income distribution.

As the Canadian provinces continue to develop and expand their post-secondary college facilities, the need for research into the social implications of post-secondary expansion becomes more and more pressing. Are the highest enrolment rates in Canadian post-secondary colleges (as some sociologists would claim to be the case in recruitment to American junior colleges) found amongst those less able children from affluent families who cannot gain admission to university?[39] Or are these colleges, as the Quebec survey would seem to hint, beginning to open up the vistas of post-high-school education to a growing number of intelligent children from the less well-off classes in Canadian society? Furthermore, if the latter alternative is the correct one – that these colleges are beginning to provide new educational opportunities for children from the lower-income classes – then why should this be so? Do the vocationally oriented courses they offer perhaps have a particular attraction to the practically-minded children of working-class parents? Or does a low level, or absence, of tuition fees hold peculiar charms? Finally, does the placing of these institutions (some being placed in rural areas far away from the nearest university) cater to an immediate clientele, i.e. the children of low-income rural families? This final question is of vital importance. In planning the establishment of junior colleges as 'feeders' to the universities, or post-secondary colleges designed primarily to provide vocationally oriented programs, a government may hit on the strategy of locating these institutions in areas where post-secondary facilities are limited, or non-existent. By so doing, it helps to overcome what may well be one of the greatest barriers to equality of access at the post-secondary level (whether access to the universities or to post-secondary colleges) – the lack of locally available post-secondary facilities in thinly populated parts of the country.

Some Concluding Remarks

Although I have devoted a good deal of space to a discussion of the relationship between social class and university attendance, there are many other aspects of this relationship, equally worthy of investigation, which I have not even touched upon. For example, studies undertaken in a number of European countries have found that the effects of social inequalities in educational opportunities are felt more by girls than by boys. In these countries (as in Canada) a smaller number of boys and girls enter the universities, but a larger proportion of those girls than of those boys, who do enter the universities are drawn from the professional classes and a smaller proportion come from the homes of manual workers.[40] It has indeed been suggested that the image of the woman as a 'homemaker' who does not require a very high level of education, is more widespread amongst members of poorer families. Hence, where such traditional attitudes prevail, relatively few girls from working-class homes will be encouraged by their parents to continue their education beyond high school.

There are other areas of concern too. If the effects of social inequalities in educational opportunity may be felt more by girls than by boys, then, within the Canadian context, the cumulative effects of social inequalities on educational behaviour are likely to be more apparent in some provinces and regions than in others. It is obvious, for example, that the proportion of children falling within that class which we have described as the 'disadvantaged class' in Canadian society is not uniform from province to province, or from region to region. Provincial variations in school retention rates, and possibly in university participation rates, therefore, bear the markings of differences in the class composition of provincial populations. Such are the regional implications of social class inequalities.

As this chapter is probably more remarkable for the questions it asks than for the questions it answers, I can only request the reader to treat the questions which have been asked (but not answered) as recommendations for further research in the field. At present we are in the country of the blind – rushing ahead with university expansion, spending more money on student financial aid, and developing new kinds of post-secondary institutions, yet all this without having any clear idea of the social consequences of our actions (although we hope that these actions, and their consequences, are the right ones).

N O T E S
1. John Porter, *The Vertical Mosaic: An Analysis of Social Class and Power in Canada,* Toronto: University of Toronto Press, 1965, Chapter 1, *passim.*
2. *Ibid.,* p. 10.
3. *The Vertical Mosaic,* pp. 183-188. Porter obtained the information on the occupations of the students' fathers from a nation-wide survey of student income and expenditure carried out by the Dominion Bureau of Statistics in 1956 – See, Dominion Bureau of Statistics, *University Student Expenditure and Income in Canada, 1956-57,* Ottawa: Queen's Printer, 1959.
4. Bernard R. Blishen, 'The Construction and Use of An Occupational Class Scale', *Canadian Journal of Economics and Political Science,* Vol. XXIV, no. 4, Nov. 1958, p. 523. In Blishen's occupational scale, *Class 1* covers the higher professions requiring high levels of education and having a high income-earning power; *Classes 2 and 3* are primarily white-collar occupations with some higher blue-collar occupations included; *Class 4* contains some high level blue-collar jobs as well as lower level white-collar ones; *Class 5* is the class of skilled trades, and *Classes 6 and 7* consist mainly of semi-skilled and unskilled occupations requiring a limited education and having a relatively low earning power. Because they are based on average income and years of schooling these occupational classes, with the exception of 'farmers', constitute relatively homogeneous socio-economic groups.
5. In table 1, a ratio of representation of one would be equal representation; a ratio greater than one, over-representation, and a ratio of less than one, under-representation. Thus, children in class 1 have a ratio of representation of 10 which means that they contributed about 10 times as many students to the university sample as they would have done if representation from all classes had been equal. However, as Porter has pointed out, the ratios for classes 5-7 might actually over-estimate the representation of children from working-class homes amongst the university population. The reason for this is that columns 2 and 3 of the table refer 'to children at home' and, at the time of the study, the higher classes had a greater proportion of the 14-24 age group at home and in school than the lower classes. See, *The Vertical Mosaic,* p. 186.
6. W.G. Fleming, "Background and Personality Factors Associated With Educational and Occupational Plans and Careers of Ontario Grade XIII Students," *Atkinson Study of Utilization of Student Resources, Report* no. 1, p. 8.
7. John Porter, *The Vertical Mosaic,* Chapter VI, p. 183.
8. See, Dominion Bureau of Statistics, *University Student Expenditure and Income in Canada, 1961-62,* Part II, Ottawa: Queen's Printer, 1963,

table 16. In this study, it was found that approximately 53 per cent of undergraduate law students, 52 per cent of medical students, 47 per cent of arts and science undergraduates and just 29 per cent of undergraduates pursuing education programs, came from families where the father was engaged in professional, managerial or executive work. On the other hand, however, 48 per cent of the education students compared with 30 per cent of the law students, and 32 per cent of the medical students, came from families where the father was engaged in manual work or in farming. To account for these class variations between students enrolled in different faculties, we would have to take into consideration the costs, and duration, of the various academic programs, and also the probability of a significant element of 'self-recruitment' (i.e. the son entering the occupation of the father) in certain occupational fields, notably medicine.

9. For three main sources of documentation, see Porter, *The Vertical Mosaic,* Chapter VI, *passim;* C. T. Bissell (ed.), *Canada's Crisis in Higher Education,* National Conference of Canadian Universities, Toronto: University of Toronto Press, 1957, section 3; Frank E. Jones, *The Social Bases of Education,* Toronto: Canadian Conference on Children 1965, Chapter II, *passim.*

10. Dominion Bureau of Statistics, *University Student Expenditure and Income in Canada 1961-62,* Part II, table. 18.

11. Robert Rabinovitch, *An Analysis of the Canadian Post-Secondary Student Population, Part 1: A Report on Canadian Undergraduate Students,* Ottawa: CUS, Feb. 1966, p. 41. For example, the CUS study (p.45) concluded that only 35 per cent of Canadian undergraduate students were from 'blue-collar' or working-class families compared with 64.1 per cent of employed Canadians who held jobs that were so classified.

12. Allan Little and John Westergaard, "The Trend of Class Differentials in Educational Opportunity in England and Wales", *British Journal of Sociology,* 15: 4, Dec. 1964, pp. 301-316.

13. Jenks and Riesman, *The Academic Revolution,* Chapter III, *passim.*

14. See Chapter XIV of R. Pike, *Who Doesn't Get to University – And Why,* Ottawa: A.U.C.C., 1970.

15. John Porter, *The Vertical Mosaic,* table XIX, p, 180.

16. For details of the Blishen Occupational Class Scale see footnote 4 to this chapter.

17. John Porter's analysis of class differentials in educational participation in 1951 was based on an examination of the occupations of fathers of children who were in and out of school at the time of the 1951 Census. The appropriate table contained in the report of the 1951 Census lists approximately 340 specific occupations of fathers with children in and out of school, and hence the task of classifying these children in accordance with the Blishen Occupational Class Scale was relatively simple. By way of contrast, however, the corresponding table contained in the report of the 1961 Census lists less than 100 specific occupations (or groups of closely related occupations) of fathers with children in and out of school on the Census date, with the rest subsumed into broad occupational categories. In such circumstances, it was frequently necessary for me to make an arbitrary decision on the classification of children in a particular socio-economic category (for example, the Blishen Scale places specific professional engineering occupations in classes 1 and 2 whereas I was obliged to place all children of 'professional engineers' in class 1 since this was the only category used in the Census table), so that a margin of classification error undoubtedly occurred. Furthermore, the residual number of 162,922 'unclassifiables' shown in column III of table 2 includes 17,-947 children whose fathers' occupations were not stated in the Census, and 144,975 children whose fathers' occupations were not stated specifically enough to permit reasonably accurate classification on the basis of the Blishen Scale. The large number of children in the latter category gives further grounds for caution in interpreting the nature of social class changes in educational participation over the ten year period.

18. See Chapter III, section entitled "Trends in High School and University Enrolment" in Pike, *op. cit.*

19. Column V of table 2 shows the *absolute* percentage increase in retention rates between 1951 and 1961 for children of each occupational class. On the basis of this absolute percentage increase, the children of semi-skilled and unskilled manual workers (classes 6 and 7) ran a poor second to children with fathers in the other occupational classes. By way of comparison, column VI of the table shows the

relative percentage increase in retention rates for children in each class (i.e. the absolute percentage increases in class retention rates between 1951 and 1961 as proportions of the percentages of children from each class at school in 1951), and this column probably provides a somewhat better indication of the charges in class differentials in school and university participation over the 10 year period. This comparatively high relative percentage increase in retention rates amongst children in classes 2-5 suggests that the educational gap between these children and the children of highly skilled professional workers (class 1) may have narrowed somewhat between the two Census years. Similarly, the children of unskilled manual workers (class 7) may have improved their position relative to the children of semi-skilled manual workers, (class 6), but both groups nevertheless, remained firmly entrenched at the bottom of the educational ladder.

20. Timothy E. Reid," Education: The Key to Freedom in Automated Society", *The Labour Gazette,* Department of Labour, Canada, Vol. LXV, no. 10, Oct. 29, 1965, pp. 887-896.

21. Michel D. Lagacé, *Educational Attainment in Canada: Some Regional and Social Aspects,* Dominion Bureau of Statistics, Special Labour Force Studies, no. 7, Ottawa: Queen's Printer, Oct. 1968.

22. See Lagacé, esp. pp. 16-28.

23. For an examination of occupational trends in Canada between 1931 and 1961, see Noah M. Metz, *Changes in the Occupational Composition of the Canadian Labour Force, 1931-1961.* Economics and Research Branch, Department of Labour, Ottawa: Queen's Printer, March 1965.

24. In the discussion which follows, I am concerned solely with an analysis of the functions of 'needs-based' student aid programs – i.e. loans and non-repayable aid provided on the basis of a means test to university and college students who can prove a need for financial assistance.

25. The Economist Intelligence Unit Ltd.,"Financial Aid to Students" in Frank Bowles, *Access to Higher Education,* Vol. 1, Liège: UNESCO and International Association of Universities, 1963, appendix C, pp. 179-198.

26. Table 3 does, however, also show that 'needs-based' aid is by no means provided only to students coming from families in the lower and middle-income categories. Since the decision to give financial aid depends not only on an assessment of parental income, but also takes into consideration the number of other dependents in the family, exceptional expenses incurred by the family and so on, it is quite possible that a student coming from a large family will receive aid even if combined parental income before taxes is $10,000 a year or more.

27. Chapter IV, section entitled"High School Matriculation and Admission to University",in R. Pike, *op. cit.*

28. Chapter IV, section entitles "Retention to Matriculation Year", *ibid.*

29. Economic Council of Canada, Fifth Annual Review, *The Challenge of Growth and Change,* Ottawa: Queen's Printer, Sept. 1968, p. 109.

30. Escott Reid, *The Universities in the Seventies,* Opening Address to the Annual Conference of District 32 of the Ontario English Catholic Teachers Association, Feb. 14th, 1969, p. 18 (mimeographed document).

31. I suppose that a conflict could arise between the 'enabling' and 'easing' functions of a student-aid program if an argument that student financial aid simply 'eases the way' for some university students is transformed into an argument that all those students receiving aid would still have attended a university or college even if no aid had been made available to them. In its more reasonable form, the latter argument may rest on a belief that once a student has reached high school matriculation level, he is not likely to be discouraged from continuing his studies by a shortage of money. The student has proved his intellectual capacity to deal with post-secondary studies, and presumably he has planned for a number of years to attend a university or college, so he will undoubtedly find some way of supporting himself through university even in the absence of student financial aid. However, in its crasser form, such an argument can also rest on the belief that university students (although not necessarily those students attending post-secondary institutions other than universities) are all 'rich kids from rich homes' and that student financial aid is simply a form of regressive taxation which takes from the poor in order to give to the wealthy. Whilst it is certainly true that a disproportionately large number of university students are indeed drawn from the middle and

upper-income groups in Canadian society, this belief is easily refuted by the kind of statistical data presented in table 3. Are we to presume that all those Nova Scotian university students whose parents earn a combined income of $4,000 a year or less are in some mysterious way 'rich kids'? Both lines of argument can be used to support a 'laissez-faire' approach to student financing.

32. New Brunswick Higher Education Commission, *Investing in the Future: A Program For Government Assistance to Universities, Technical Schools and Their Students*, Fredericton: Government Printer, Jan. 1969, p.63.

33. Quotation from New Brunswick Higher Education Commission *Investing in the Future*, p. 63.

34. Some universities and provincial departments of education do arrange meetings with high-school vocational guidance counsellors and high school students in order to explain the nature, and scope, of existing financial aid programs. I suspect, however, that, in general, more could be done to provide easily understandable publicity material on student financial aid and that more could be done to ensure that this material is made available to young people in the junior grades of the high schools. During the course of writing this report, I received approximately 30 briefs from high school guidance counsellors, many of which contained criticisms of existing student-aid publicity schemes. One of the major criticisms was that publicity material is only made available to those high school students who are about to matriculate (although whether this is the fault of the guidance counsellors themselves, or of the universities and provincial departments of education, I would hesitate to say). Another was that the information on student aid which is currently provided in most university calendars is often too abstruse, and vague, for many students to understand. Finally, some counsellors (and also some student-aid administrators in provincial government departments) deplored the fact that they were unable to obtain information on government student-aid programs established in provinces other than their own. This put them at a considerable disadvantage when advising those high-school students who wished to attend university or college outside their province of residence.

35. Throughout the discussion which follows, I define 'post-secondary colleges' as institutions offering an alternative pattern of post-secondary studies to that offered by the universities. I am aware, however, that some post-secondary colleges – notably the Quebec CEGEPs – will eventually offer the only route beyond the secondary school, with all students intending to enter university going through the general or vocational college program first. Furthermore, some post-secondary colleges offer transfer programs which permit students to transfer to university after one or two years of college studies. The distinction between a 'post-secondary college education' and a 'university education' may, therefore, be rather blurred.

36. I do not think that this is unfair comment. Some of the 'status'

problems of the Ontario community colleges were, for example, brought to light in the acrimonious discussion surrounding the possibility of student transfer between community colleges and universities, which erupted in the columns of the Toronto *Globe and Mail* early in 1968. Much of this discussion revolved around the statement of a university administrator that the lack of adequate transfer facilities might lead the community colleges to become known as "places for dull clods who cannot obtain entrance to university", a statement which aroused considerable ill-feeling amongst community college teachers. See the editorial article entitled"Opportunity Narrowed" which was published in the *Globe and Mail* on January 16th, 1968, and also the subsequent discussion which arose in the letter columns of that newspaper.

37. See Robert Ayotte, *Etude du Budget des Etudiants au Niveau Collégial et Universitaire Pour L'Année 1966-67*, Québec: Ministère d'Education, rapport préliminaire 1969.

38. Robert Ayotte, *Etude du Budget des Etudiants au Niveau Collégial et Universitaire*, pp. 5-8. Also personal correspondence with M. Ayotte. It will be noted that as a result of the low response from some post-secondary colleges in Quebec, the post-secondary college student data contained in table 4 is based only on those institutions from which the total response was 60 per cent or higher. These institutions were representative of all categories of post-secondary colleges and all regions of the province.

39. See particularly, Christopher Jencks,"Social Stratification and Higher Education"in *Harvard Educational Review*, 38: 2, Spring 1968, pp. 277-316. One of Jencks' main themes in this article is that for various reasons – most notably class differences in educational motivation – the US junior colleges have not dramatically improved the competitive position of children from poorer homes vis-à-vis those from the affluent middle classes.

40. A survey of a number of European studies dealing with the influence of social class factors on the educational opportunities of boys and girls can be found in the report of the 1967 Conference of Ministers of Education of European Member States of UNESCO entitled *Access to Higher Education in Europe*, Paris: UNESCO, 1968, pp. 67-73. It is also quite possible that a relatively large proportion of girls attending university in Canada are drawn from the upper social strata. Thus, the first report of the Atkinson Study of Utilization of Student Resources shows that 57 per cent of those girls who matriculated from Ontario Grade XIII in 1956 and entered university in the following fall came from families where the father was employed in 'professional, managerial and executive' work, and 23 per cent came from the homes of manual workers. The corresponding percentage amongst Ontario male matriculants entering the universities in 1956 were 45 per cent and 31 per cent; W. G. Fleming, *Background and Personality Factors Associated With Educational and Occupational Plans and Careers of Ontario Grade XIII Students*, appendix table II.8.a.

---

2. Sex and the Public Service: Differences in Opportunity and Treatment

Kathleen Archibald

Throughout the history of Western civilization and stemming to a large extent from the Judaeo-Christian tradition, women have been accorded a status subordinate to men. The handful of women who, in each age, have had the tenacity, the courage, the ability and the opportunity to break through the sex barrier have been held up by both men and women as token symbols that exclusion

Reprinted from *Sex and the Public Service*: A Report made to the Public Service Commission of Canada (1970), by Kathleen Archibald, by permission of Information Canada.

from the full rights of citizenship – even, some would say, exclusion from the fully 'human' race – on the basis of sex does not exist. Yet the evidence everywhere is abundantly to the contrary.

In this next selection, which is an excerpt from an extensive report made for the Public Service Commission of Canada by Dr. Archibald, herself a Canadian woman of no mean accomplishment, we are presented with irrefutable evidence of the subtle yet potent ways in which women are effectively barred from higher level positions in the Public Service.

"When she behaves as a human being," Simone de Beauvoir

has said in speaking of woman in the The Second Sex, *"she is said to imitate the male."* *That such an attitude is deeply ingrained in Canadian society is supported by the evidence presented here. Other evidence, collected by the recently concluded Royal Commission on the Status of Women, strengthens this claim. Gradually, and largely through the efforts of the now world-wide Women's Liberation movement, women are being raised to a new level of consciousness both with regard to the extent of their exclusion from full participation in society and to the myths and pseudo-scientific theories that reinforce and seek to justify it.*

Each member for which this Convention is in force undertakes to declare and pursue a national policy designed to promote, by methods appropriate to national conditions and practice, equality of opportunity and treatment in respect of employment and occupation, with a view to eliminating any discrimination in respect thereof.

> Article 2, Convention III of the International Labour Organization, ratified by the Government of Canada in 1964.

Are opportunities for occupational satisfaction and advancement in the Canadian public service more limited for women than for men? Must a woman be better qualified than a man to achieve the same degree of success? In other words, is discrimination one factor that explains the differential success of women in the public service?

The weight of evidence presented in this report points to an unequivocal 'yes'. Preceding chapters have shown that differences in capability, experience, and work interests do not fully explain the lower levels and salaries of women. This suggests the remaining difference in occupational success is a result of restricted opportunities for women within the public service.

This conclusion is supported by results of the interview study. Three-quarters of the senior women and one-half of the men said they were aware of prejudice or discrimination against women in the public service; approximately half the women and 10 per cent of the men said it existed within their own departments. Twelve per cent of the women and 30 per cent of the men said discrimination was the most important reason why so few women reached senior levels in the public service.

And many of these men and women were defining both prejudice and discrimination narrowly. Using standard definitions of these terms, an examination of the interviewee's perceptions shows fully 90 per cent of both men and women saw some prejudice, and 86 per cent of the women and 60 per cent of the men saw some current discrimination, even though not all were willing to so label what they perceived. In addition, 14 per cent of the women reported, without being asked, that they had been told explicitly at some point in their public service careers that they could not get a certain position because they were women.

That discrimination against women exists within the public service should surprise no one. Discrimination against women in the work world has a long history and is widespread; there was no particular reason to expect the Canadian public service in 1969 to be free of it.

The exact extent of discrimination within the public service is impossible to estimate. Some data in this report could be used as indices, for instance, differences in salary when education and experience are controlled or in the probability of a man besting a woman with identical qualifications in an experiment. But all such indices have serious draw-backs as general measures of discrimination. Suffice it to say that discrimination is not limited to a few isolated cases – there is a fair amount of it – and any future attempt to measure improvement should look at several indices.

While the degree of discrimination cannot be measured, one can ask where and how it occurs. What barriers within the public service inhibit occupational advancement for women? Which of these barriers can be considered discriminatory?

Differences in opportunities for and treatment of men and women will be considered under three headings: beliefs and attitudes, the structure of work, and personnel practices.

Beliefs and Attitudes

Apparently, those who practise much of the discrimination which occurs in the public service do not see it as discrimination at all. This failure to understand the nature of discrimination is the most serious problem under the category 'beliefs and attitudes.' There is no point in prohibiting discrimination unless those making personnel decisions know what discrimination is.

Stereotypical beliefs about, and negative attitudes toward, women in the work world are also a problem, although less can be done about them. Prejudice is a matter of belief, discrimination a matter of action. Nondiscrimination can be enforced to some extent, nonprejudice can not – although prejudice can perhaps be reduced. Negative beliefs and attitudes are of concern since they are likely to influence personnel decision, especially when there are misunderstandings about what kinds of actions are discriminatory.

Misunderstandings About the Meaning of Discrimination
Discrimination may be defined in a number of ways, but it always refers to impairing the opportunity of individuals solely on the basis of their membership in a particular group. The 1958 Discrimination (Employment and Occupation) Convention of the International Labour Organization (ILO) defines discrimination thus:

> ...any distinction, exclusion or preference made on the basis of race, colour, sex, religion, political opinion, national extraction or social origin, which has the effect of nullifying or impairing equality of opportunity or treatment in employment or occupation.[1]

and goes on to point out that:

> Any distinction, exclusion or preference in respect of a particular job based on the inherent requirements thereof shall not be deemed to be discrimination.[2]

Misunderstanding about discrimination in the public service is not trivial: its essential meaning is often misunderstood. For instance, it is quite widely considered fair to base decisions about individuals on probabilities derived from the behaviour of a group. Fully 40 per cent of the the senior women interviewed, 55 per cent of the men, and 60 per cent of Public Service Commission (PSC) Staffing Program Directors believe "it is not discriminatory to limit the number of women employed in areas where job tenure is important if females have a higher turnover rate in that area."

It is also generally believed that many jobs are 'male only' or 'female only' and that excluding the opposite sex from competitions for these jobs is all right. In fact, very few jobs require a 'male' or 'female' inherently because of the large overlap between men and women on most variables. Yet, it was found that departments think of about half of all jobs under PSC Staffing Programs as being 'male', or 'female'.

Until 1969, the staff request form, going to the Public Service Commission when a department had a position open, permitted departments to specify sex – a specification ignored by most Staffing Programs, at least since the 1967 Act prohibited discrimination on the basis of sex. Requests for staff to the PSC between October 23 and November 7, 1968, were monitored, however, to see to what extent departments still thought of jobs as either 'male' or 'female'. Of 90 requests during that period, 41 specified 'either'; 28 were marked 'male' and 21 'female'.

Sex is not mentioned on the new form. If a position genuinely requires exclusively a man or a woman, the department may state this with supporting reasons under 'remarks'.

When one is certain that no member of a particular group could conceivably meet the requirements of a particular job, then it is reasonable to exclude all members of that group. But if even a small percentage of that group might be able to handle the job, it is not fair to exclude them. It is difficult to think of a government job which inherently requires a person of one particular sex. In a few cases, however, moral conventions strongly suggest limiting a particular job to members of one sex, for instance, where sleeping quarters must be shared and in certain institutional or custodial positions.

In addition to misunderstandings about the meaning of discrimination, interpretation of the nondiscriminatory clause in the Public Service Employment Act has presented some problems. The Act mentions selection standards only, and there has been a tendency to construe this narrowly, despite Canadian ratification of the ILO Convention which should help interpret the spirit of the Act.

Misunderstanding about discrimination, combined with the tendency to interpret the Act narrowly, suggested one recommendation to the PSC during this study: preparation of a general statement on principles underlying the concept of equal employment opportunity, and of specific statements on particular problems in each area of discrimination, for instance, on race, on religion, on sex, etc. It was also recommended that the PSC circulate a preliminary statement on "equal career opportunities without regard to sex" near the beginning of 1969 to tie in with removal of the specification 'male', 'female' or 'either' from the 'staff request form'. This preliminary statement was circulated to Deputy Heads and Personnel Directors for comment. Both this statement and the idea of preparing a more general statement, met with generally favourable response.

Beliefs about the Relative Productivity of Women

Beliefs that women have a short work-life expectancy, a very high absenteeism rate, lack of involvement in work, are unable to travel, lack supervisory competence, etc., seem quite prevalent within the public service. They are used often to explain the differential success of women, and, sometimes quite openly, to justify differences in the kinds of jobs offered to men and women. While there is some factual kernel to most of these beliefs, the difference between men and women on these variables is too small to explain their differential success. Nor does it justify differential treatment on grounds of economic efficiency – even if the Public Service Employment Act did not prohibit discriminatory treatment on the basis of sex.

Two things about beliefs concerning the relative productivity of women deserve mention, aside from the fact that most are quarter-truths at best. One, a number of these beliefs can turn into self-fulfilling prophecies. If, for instance, a manager assumes short work-life expectancy, he is less likely to give a woman on-the-job training and responsible assignments. Thus the woman seeking challenge and a future in her work is likely to fulfill the manager's original prediction and quit.

Second, all the most prevalent beliefs have negative consequences for working women; all imply women should expect fewer of the rewards of work. If beliefs were chosen randomly, or based on the strongest available evidence about job-relevant differences between men and women, one would not expect this to happen. For instance, the female turnover rate is about double the male rate, and many think this should influence employment practices. The male crime rate is 600 to 700 times the

female crime rate,[3] yet how often does anyone argue that women, rather than men, should be hired in jobs requiring moral probity, for instance handling money?

Prejudicial Attitudes

Traditional norms consign women to a position socially inferior to men. These sex-grading norms spill over into the work world, which explains some of the differential success of men and women. But only a portion of this spillover involves prejudice and discrimination: if women themselves adhere to these norms, they will not aspire to supervisory posts, nor perhaps even to responsible staff positions where they will have to interact with men on equal footing. That is their choice. But the evidence shows that those women who are interested in responsible posts are more restricted than their male counterparts. This is discrimination.

There is no justification for perpetuating a set of norms and attitudes with no intrinsic relevance in the work world when they put one group at a distinct disadvantage. This kind of discrimination is understandable; indeed it often seems quite natural. For this very reason it requires particular attention if it is to be effectively countered.

Paternalistic attitudes, derived from traditional notions of women as the weaker sex, present the final problem. If anyone thinks 'protective' attitudes toward women are long since outmoded, or that women should not mind them, the following excerpt from a recent memo prepared by a junior personnel officer for his Assistant Deputy Minister should prove instructive:

> Yet another major factor which must be considered with regard to isolated posts is that of segregation and privacy. Other than in exceptionally large communities in direct contact with the outside world, it would not be feasible to guarantee the virtue of any female in an isolated area – for obvious reasons. Accepting that the occasional individual female may consider herself capable of safeguarding herself, or even not particularly desirous of protecting herself, the resultant problem of moral and/or pregnancy [sic] would be, at least undesirable.

Exclusions based on 'protective' attitudes, however kindly their intent, are no less discriminatory than other exclusions. Job applicants, male and female, should be warned about unpleasant or risky aspects of the work in question, but from there on they must be considered as capable of deciding on their own needs for protection.

The Structure of Work

Opportunities for women in the public service are most severely restricted by structural features of the service: occupational segregation, foreshortened career ladders in 'female' fields, and an overall organization of work around the concept of the continuing, full-time employee. The implications of each of these structural features for women, and the extent to which they can be deemed discriminatory, will be considered in turn.

Occupational Segregation by Sex

There is a high degree of occupational segregation by sex in the public service. One consequence is that wages in predominantly female fields tend to be depressed and opportunities restricted.[4] Women in 'male' or mixed fields tend to fare considerably better than those in 'female' fields.

Insofar as segregation is a consequence of the preferences and capabilities of men and women, it is not morally repugnant, although its consequences may still give cause for concern. Insofar as segregation is imposed on men and women, it is clearly discriminatory.

What of segregation within the public service? Is any of it imposed or is it all the product of differing preferences and capabilities of men and women?

A small amount is, currently, definitely imposed – for instance, women are often excluded from field work in isolated or difficult areas. Another instance is an agreement with the Council of Graphic Arts covering non-supervisory employees in the Printing Operations Group. At first, this agreement seemed to be an example of unequal pay for equal work, since 'journeymen' were paid more than 'journeywomen'. On further exploration, this proved to be exclusion instead. Journeywomen received lower pay because they are 'bindery girls' and are not trained as long, nor for the same jobs, as journeymen. A woman cannot become a journeyman, nor, presumably, a man a journeywoman. This is imposed segregation and it is discriminatory, unless it can be demonstrated that 'femaleness' is a *bona fide* qualification for the one apprenticeship program and all jobs it leads to, and 'maleness' for the other.

A small degree of the existing sex segregation, then, is directly imposed. But how much of the rest can be considered the result of differing preferences and capabilities, and how much the result of discrimination against women in earlier years? Do most working women really want to be typists, secretaries, lower-level clerks, nurses, social workers, librarians, and elementary school teachers? Or is it because these were the fields which welcomed women for many years and, in fact, remain the only fields in which women are sure of a welcome? Surely, the concentration of women – almost 83 per cent of all those in the service – in the Administrative Support Category has something to do with the fact that, in the early 1900's, non-professional women were barred from all but dead-end office support jobs, and even professional women had difficulty being classified as anything but clerks. This situation improved but little until World War II, and did not improve significantly until the mid-1950's. It is extremely doubtful that the occupational distribution of women would look as it does today if opportunities had been equal over the past sixty years.

So long as the current degree of occupational segregation continues, women will have only limited opportunities to demonstrate they can be as productive as men on many jobs, and salaries in 'female' fields are likely to remain depressed.

Foreshortened Career Ladders in 'Female' Fields

We have noted (a) 'female' professional fields in public service tend to top out at lower salaries than 'male' ones, and (b) the seemingly unjustifiable separation of Social Workers and Welfare Program Administrators into two occupational groups – the former as a female 'professional' field requiring more education and paying less than the second, a male 'administrative' field. But career ladders in female professional fields are a joy to behold compared to those in the secretarial, stenographic and typing (ST) group.

The ST group really consists of four sub-groups, so its levels do not actually represent a career ladder. Levels 1 and 2 are typist positions; 3 and 4, stenographers; 5 to 8, secretaries; and Level 9, court reporters. A normal line of career progression exists between stenographic and secretarial positions, but not between Levels 8 and 9 (although those training to be court reporters, usually men, are paid at ST 6-8 rates) nor, necessarily, between ST 2 and 3, since the latter requires shorthand and the former does not.

For typists, in fact, one can scarcely even refer to a career 'ladder': only two steps appear under the new classification system. Previously, a typist could aspire to be a senior typist; now, if she is ever to earn even $4000, she must either acquire shorthand (an unpopular choice and for good reason, as shown

below) or transfer into the clerical (CR) class. While such transfer seems quite common, those whose only experience has been in a typing pool are liable to be at a disadvantage in competing for a CR 2 position against a Level 1 clerk with more varied experience.

In other words, good transcribing and typing skills bring very little reward in the public service, unless they are combined with shorthand skills. This is a somewhat peculiar requirement considering:

(1) only about 20 per cent of all government correspondence is dictated to a stenographer [5]

(2) machine dictation is cheaper than stenography [6]

(3) taking dictation is not an important part of many ST 3–8 jobs and – considering the preference of many officers for hand drafting or machine dictation – does not even enter into many stenographic and secretarial jobs

(4) the perennial shortage of stenographers and secretaries.

What rhyme or reason is there to a classification scheme that is costly to the government and which so curtails careers for typists that any rational girl would opt for a CR 1 or 2 position[7] in preference to ST 1 or 2? The Administrative Support Staffing Program has argued against making shorthand a prerequisite for entry into stenographic and secretarial positions, but such arguments have so far fallen on deaf ears in the Treasury Board's Bureau of Classification Revision.

The structural features which make ambition unrealistic in the ST group can be seen most clearly by comparing it with the clerical group. Figure 1 illustrates the hierarchical structure of the two.[8]

Top salary in the clerical group is higher than in the ST group, and the chances of getting anywhere near top pay are far higher: no more than 6 per cent of all ST's make over $5000 a year (and no more than 9 per cent of those in ST 3-8) yet 45 per cent of all clerks make over $5000[9] – 5 to 7 times the chance for 'success'.

Further, some clerks, although certainly a minority, do move laterally to occupational classes with greater advancement opportunities. The chances for an ST to do this are smaller. She can move into the clerical group and hope to move out and up from there, but even this process becomes difficult or costly above ST 3.[10] Clerical training is acquired primarily on the job, so an ST 4 or 5 is unlikely to have the skills needed to move into a CR 3 post – yet if she transfers to a lower level CR position, she must take a cut in pay. A further obstacle is the quite reasonable tendency of supervisors to promote their own clerks to any open higher level positions rather than bringing in an occupational outsider.

The woman who does not transfer may move rapidly to an ST 4 position but things get sticky at this point, and at Level 5 she is liable to get stuck. The chances of moving from ST 5 to another occupational class have been low, at least until recently,[11] and the chances of moving to a higher ST level are severely limited: 'rug-ranking' takes over above ST4. This means a secretary's status and salary is determined by the status of her boss, not by the demands of her job. One becomes an ST 5 by working for an Assistant Director, an ST 6 for a Director, ST 7 for an Assistant Deputy Minister and an ST 8 by working for a Deputy Minister. Opportunities narrow severely above ST 5; since very few men get to be Directors of Branches, very few secretaries get to make over $5000.

The career structure of STs (Figure I) looks more like a steeple than a pyramid. This is attributable to rug-ranking, which not only curtails opportunities for STs, but also means that lower level officers whose work requires a very good secretary either cannot get one or, should they have an exceptional stenographer, cannot treat her fairly nor increase the chances of her staying, by rewarding her adequately. This formal linking of the fate of secretaries to the fate of their bosses has

Figure 1 – Career Ladders in the Administrative Support Category, July, 1967

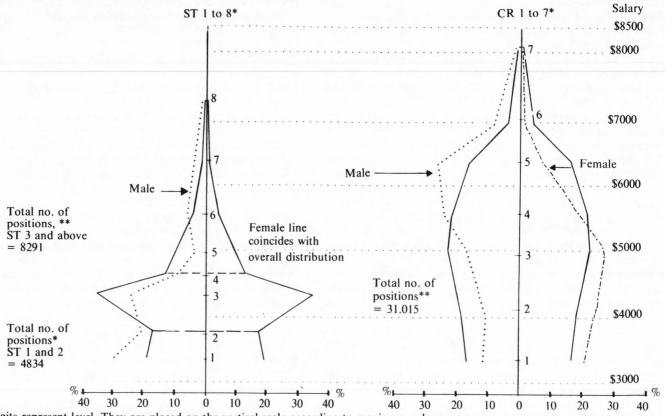

* Single digits represent level. They are placed on the vertical scale according to maximum salary.
** Numbers actually represent the no. of incumbents, so are an underestimate of the no. of positions.
Source: Prepared from data obtained from Pay Research Bureau

another interesting hooker in it: a woman at ST 6 level or higher may well find herself in a state of suspended animation if her boss leaves the public service, since the incoming boss will be inclined to promote his own secretary.

Rug-ranking is a good example of the inappropriate intrusion of male and female social roles into the work world.

It does not reflect the concept of a working team but relates rather to family roles. The secretary (woman) of the office (household) plays a supportive role, and her status in the department (community) is only peripherally related to her own achievement, instead it depends largely on the status of her boss (husband). This association is understandable and may be quite sensible in many individual relationships given the tenacity of sex-grading norms among both men and women. Age-grading norms often produce an equivalent situation: a father and son tone commonly enters the interaction between senior and junior men in an office. But rug-ranking is inappropriate and anachronistic in that the husband-wife model does not merely evolve in individual situations, it is imposed by the formal classification system.

It is all too often assumed that most STs are content with routine and unwilling to exert themselves, that their principal interests are coffee breaks and pay cheques. An examination of the structural features of their occupational group demands caution about such assumptions. If you limit opportunities severely and see to it much of the work is dull, you make ambition and work involvement unrealistic as motivating forces. A study of office secretarial services, recently completed for the Treasury Board, identified a number of other factors that tend to make the work of ST 1-4s in typing and transcribing pools not only unrewarding, but often very frustrating.[12] The fact that separation rates are considerably higher in the ST class than in the clerical class also suggests job dissatisfaction.

How does all this concern the employer? In two ways. Firstly, in terms of economic efficiency and effectiveness, it is reasonable to assume that greater opportunities for work satisfaction and advancement will improve the performance of those supplying secretarial services – which, in turn, should increase the productivity of officers using those services. The study for the Treasury Board, based on interviews with STs in typing and transcribing units and with the officers who depend on them, argues strongly for reorganization of office support services on grounds of operational effectiveness.

Secondly, the career structure within the ST group should concern the government on grounds of equity and freedom of choice. Opening lines to better career ladders for STs will make opportunities for women more equal to those for men and increase their freedom of choice. While this may not be a compelling argument in itself, it gains considerable weight when considered in historical perspective: ST jobs are dead-end jobs now because they were deliberately made dead-end jobs sixty years ago to limit the advancement of women.

Problems related to employees who are not 'continuing, full-time'
Employment structures are generally designed to conform to the work patterns and needs of continuing, full-time employees. Yet a number of capable workers either cannot or do not wish to work continually and full-time for one employer. Our main concern in this report is married women, who often need or wish to work part-day, part-week, or part-year so they can deal with family responsibilities.[13] But other kinds of workers have similar needs or desires: students, the elderly, persons with health problems, people trying to establish themselves in the creative arts, etc.

Employers have difficulty handling these kinds of employees

and often do not wish to be bothered with them. As Ginzberg has pointed out:

> With respect to utilization, employers give unequivocal evidence that they prefer stupid men to smart women. They are usually unwilling to make even modest adjustments in hours, vacations, and other scheduling to attract able women. Admittedly it is easier to run a large organization according to a single set of rules. But women are not men and one set of rules is seldom adequate for all men and never for both men and women[14].

The public service has gone further than many Canadian employers in attempting to organize a part-time, part-year program for 'highly qualified' married women with school-age children. This program, begun in August, 1967, was developed by the Treasury Board and Public Service Commission and operated by the PSC's Socio-Economic Staffing Program.

In its first year, the program was limited to mothers of school-age children with university degrees in one of three areas with a shortage of full-time employees: economists, statisticians and librarians. The program authorized hiring a maximum of 30 women in Ottawa/Hull to work 20 to 30 hours a week during the elementary school year (i.e., with summers off).

The project was well-publicized and attracted considerable interest. There were 230 initial inquiries which, when screened, produced 78 serious applicants. Of these, 54 were rejected on the basis of their written applications. Of the 24 interviewed, 7 were considered qualified for professional positions and 10 for technical ones. Though only 17 were qualified when 30 had been planned for, placement proved difficult. Several departments, which had expressed early interest in the program, were reluctant to tie up continuing positions with part-time employees in view of 'establishment' cuts imposed in October, 1967, a reluctance increased by the employment 'freeze' announced in March, 1968. Departments also said they had been hoping for more highly-qualified women, yet 7 did qualify for professional positions and only 4 could be placed – one of these only as a technical officer because no economist positions were available. Only 4 of the 10 who qualified for technical positions could be placed.

Seven of these eight accepted jobs, and six were still working in late spring of 1968. Their supervisors, when interviewed, all expressed satisfaction and all wanted to retain the part-time employees on their staff. Several mentioned, however, they would prefer a full-time employee if one were available.

A new Treasury Board authorization has extended the program to March, 1970 and expanded it to include more women – a maximum of 50 – with university degrees in more varied fields, covering shortages in Scientific and Professional, Administrative and Foreign Service, and Technical categories. The program has more or less lain dormant under this authorization. There has been discussion about it, but no active recruiting nor any attempt to identify or develop interest within departments.

The reasons for this slowdown are several. The program took a great deal of time – at least five man-months of officer time – in its first year, with rather meagre results. While the first-year program hired only in occupational groups under the Socio-Economic Staffing Program, the current one cuts across several staffing programs so no one section has clear responsibility for implementing it. The employment freeze suggested it might be more useful to worry about 'redundancies' than about part-time people and made departments reluctant to employ part-time people. On top of this, departments have demonstrated a general reluctance to use part-time people, or at least part-

time married women. The part-time program tends to be seen at best as a frill or a side-issue and at worst as a terrible nuisance. Contributing to its nuisance value is the fact that the benefits and conditions of employment for part-time people are confusing. And for 'seasonal', part-timers – which is what the women under this special program are – they are so confusing that special authorization was obtained to hire these women even though special authorization was not, theoretically, required.[15]

All the problems faced by the part-time employment program for 'highly qualified' married women sum up to this: systems of manpower utilization in the public service are designed for the continuing, full-time employee. Any other type of employee is seen as a special case, a nuisance and, often, as a second class citizen.

We have focused on this part-time program because it has attracted so much attention. The essential problem is wider: how does the employment system respond to those who wish to work other than on a continuing, full-time basis? How should it respond? Since women tend to be part-time, or casual, or 'discontinuous' employees more often than men, this issue is important in any discussion of women's opportunities and treatment in the work world.

The various policy instruments – Acts, regulations, directives, etc. – which shape the government's employment system have been formulated with the idea of the continuing, full-time employee in mind. Sections on other types of employees have usually been tacked on as afterthoughts.

This means that aspects of the employment system pertaining to such employees are often inconsistent, unclear, incomplete or counter-productive (i.e., they encourage inefficient use of manpower resources). Some confusion exists about how most employees other than continuing, full-time ones should be handled.

The introduction of collective bargaining confuses the matter even further. Only those working more than one-third time are subject to a collective agreement, so the old rules presumably apply to those working one-third time or less. Some collective agreements do not refer specifically to part-time people. Are their terms, then, pro-rated for those working over one-third time, or do the old rules apply? Since unions are not exactly famous for their love of part-time employees,[16] who protects their interests?

The Manpower Allocation and Control System[17] in effect since April, 1969, promises to facilitate the flexible and efficient use of part-time and casual employees. But it adds its own set of problems and confusions which may dilute this promise. Under this new system, the Treasury Board sets ceilings on departmental utilization of manpower on two bases; total man-years in a fiscal year and number of 'continuing, full-time employees' on strength at year end. The 'man-year' ceiling is generally the higher of the two because it includes all employees who are part-time, casual, seasonal, etc. The general concept is excellent, but details of the system as it now stands, raise several problems.

(1) The Treasury Board circular suggests the simplest way to measure 'man-year utilization' is with paylist counts. For instance, "where employees are paid twice a month, there are two regular paylists each month, and each entry on one of those paylists will be taken as representing one-twenty-fourth of a man-year". If this is done, a part-time person will use as large a fraction of a 'man-year' as a full-time person. Departments will certainly remain reluctant to use part-time people as long as two half-time employees working for one year adds up to two 'man-years' in the eyes of the Treasury Board.

(2) The very notion of a *continuing*, part-time employee has no place in this new system. This implies either that the govern-

ment has no continuing 'commitment' to any non-full-time employee or that 'year-end strength' will underestimate the number of employees to whom the government does have a continuing 'commitment'. 'Commitment' is in quotes because the government is not actually committed to any employee, but certainly the need to report and control 'year-end strength' in addition to 'man-year utilization' indicates the belief that those so counted are likely to be around for awhile. Continuing or regular part-timers form a special category of employees and it is important to distinguish them from casual or intermittent employees. (Regular part-time employment is a permanent and increasingly significant feature of the labour market. But, because it does not fall within our traditional ways of thinking about manpower obligation, it has been referred to as "one of the major problems in the world of tomorrow".)[18]

(3) When a casual employee works more than six months, he or she comes under the pertinent collective agreement, and must also be certified by the Public Service Commission. These two facts alone may suggest to departments that any 'casual' needed for more than six months should be fired and re-hired every six months. The incentive to do this is even stronger if any full-time union member certified by the PSC is considered as 'continuing, full-time' under the new allocation and control system. It is not clear whether this is or is not the case as the Treasury Board circular explaining the new system does not define 'continuing, full-time'. But, since the practice of firing and re-hiring casuals is already well established, a department in doubt is likely to continue this practice.

An employment structure favouring continuing, full-time employees means (1) other types of employees do not receive equal treatment; (2) built-in complications and confusions discourage use of other types of employees, even when this would be of advantage to the government; and (3) employment opportunities for women with family responsibilities are more limited than need be. These three problems will be considered in turn, using continuing, part-time employment as an example.

The total package of pay and benefits per hour worked is less for continuing, part-time employees than for continuing, full-time ones. (For instance, part-timers receive no increments unless specifically called for in a collective agreement.) Lower pay and benefits are commonly justified on the grounds that overhead costs are higher per hour worked by part-time employees. But this is not necessarily true. Consider two half-time typists or librarians. If one works in the morning and the other in the afternoon, accommodation costs are the same as for full-time employees. Employee output per hour tends to be higher the shorter the working day.[19] Part-time employees' absenteeism rate tends to be lower and turnover rates may be lower as well.[20] Given all these considerations, overhead costs could well be less for part-time employees, in some cases, than for full-time employees.

Current regulations on dismissal procedure do not distinguish continuing part-time employees from casual ones. Thus the continuing, part-time employee has far less job security than his continuing, full-time co-worker.

These problems connected with continuing, part-time employees are common throughout Europe and North America; sufficiently so that the authors of two recent OECD studies both recommend the position of part-time workers be regularized or 'decasualized' and that measures be taken to ensure equitable rights and benefits for such employees.[21] Both studies argue that part-time workers should be given, "where appropriate, the same rights and benefits as full-time workers, prorata to their weekly hours of work".[22]

Part-time employment fills a need for certain sectors of the population in particular for women with family responsibilities. It enables them to handle dual responsibilities and, more important for the employer, allows those with special qualifications to retain their skills until they are again able to work full time. A system which tends to discourage use of part-time employees and offers them less than equitable rights and benefits, needlessly restricts employment opportunities for women with family responsibilities.

As one of the OECD studies states:

> A fundamental consideration is not how many people are affected by the system of part-time work, but to give each individual the possibility of choosing freely. Governments should make the necessary arrangements, employers the indispensable effort of adaptation, trade unions demand the essential safeguards for both full-time and part-time workers: all of them will be failing in their obligations if they reject out of hand a system which might offer the optimum solution for various sections of the population.[23]

If it were most efficient for the government to hire only continuing, full-time employees, the issues raised here would not deserve so much attention. But that is not the case. It is often advantageous for the government to hire other types of employees.

For instance, a continuing, part-time employee is a better investment than a continuing, full-time one when the work will not keep a full-time employee busy, when available part-time workers are more skilled or competent than available full-time ones (this may sometimes be true in the Administrative Support category), and in particular fields where full-time employees are in short supply.

Summary

Restrictions on employment opportunities for women are built right into the current system of manpower utilization. It appears, in fact, that this structural discrimination accounts for more of the earnings gap between men and women than any other set of variables. That the very structure of federal employment is discriminatory is in large part a function of earlier policies which openly and explicitly used sex and marital status as reasons to offer unequal opportunities and inequitable treatment.

Without structural changes – changes in the classification system designed to reduce occupational segregation; changes in classification, selection standards, and work organization that will improve career ladders for Administrative Support employees; 'decasualization' of continuing, part-time employees; and clarification of the benefits and terms of employment for all employees who are other than 'continuing, full-time' – there will be little improvement in the relative position of women in the public service. For no matter how fairly the current system of manpower utilization is administered, it will continue to be discriminatory in its consequences simply because it was developed as a system of manpower utilization not womanpower utilization.

A number of changes could be effected at no cost – excepting set-up costs – to the government, or at a net benefit.

Personnel Practices

This section examines some specific personnel procedures and practices as they relate to women.

Recruiting

With very few exceptions, posters and notices of open competitions for jobs within the public service have not specified 'male' or 'female' for the last several years. All illustrated recruiting materials picture women as well as men, and a few show women working in areas not usually deemed 'female'. No special brochures are designed for a female audience.

The one active recruiting campaign specifically directed to women is conducted in Ottawa Valley high schools by the Ottawa Regional Office of the PSC to interest girls in ST jobs. Such active recruiting is a response to the perennial shortage of competent STs in the service. Other responses, like making the jobs less dead-end and the work less frustrating, have seldom been considered. The Treasury Board's insistence on putting lower level STs in typing and transcribing pools and in using 'line-count' to measure productivity seems to have been based on notions of how to get good work out of efficient machines not on notions of how to get better work out of ordinary human beings. And certainly the idea of getting and holding better STs in the service did not enter into it.

The University Recruitment Program, at least before 1968, probably gave preferential treatment to male candidates, but since this is related to departmental preferences, it is discussed in a later section.

In general, the recruiting activities of the PSC have tended to reflect and thus help preserve the current occupational distribution of men and women.

Selection Procedures

Selection in the public service is based on the 'merit principle'. All candidates supposedly have an equal chance, and the job is offered the best candidate. For entry level jobs in the Administrative Support category, candidates are placed on an eligibility list in order of their score on the competitive written examination. For other positions, a selection board (usually three people) evaluates candidates in terms of education, experience, and personal suitability. Both methods – written examination and selection boards – present problems if one is concerned about equal opportunities.

A selection board produces a list of percentage scores, ordering all candidates on a scale of presumed merit, but the quantitative neatness of this list implies an objectivity it does not in fact possess. Evaluation of experience and, particularly, of personal suitability involves considerable subjective judgement. Thus prejudices may affect the scoring of candidates. An experiment suggests this: subjects were far more likely to give top ranking to a fictional candidate when they thought the candidate was a man than when they thought the candidate was a woman. Subjects in the experiment worked alone; discriminatory tendencies might have been reduced in groups of three. Anti-feminine prejudices are so common, however, that it would be overly optimistic to assume that merely having three judges on a selection board would solve the problem.

In fact, no procedure for selecting candidates for higher level jobs would completely eliminate the possible influence of prejudice. Matching people to jobs which require complex skills involves, *per force*, a strong subjective component. The objection to current procedure concerns not their subjectivity, but their facade of objectivity. On grounds of statistical reliability alone, current eligibility lists do not really order all candidates; at most they cluster them into groups of rough equality. It might be fairer to let the supervisor choose from three to four top candidates; at least all concerned would know that the final decision on who is hired is really a subjective, and sometimes rather personal, choice.

While the current system assumes the PSC staffing officer on the selection board will prevent prejudice from affecting decisions, several staffing officers said quite frankly it was very difficult to insist on giving a female candidate a job if her future supervisor did not want a woman. They also pointed out that placing a woman in such a situation might not be doing her any favour. Thus the line manager often does, in fact, choose between top candidates. Bringing this into the open should not make things any worse, and *might* make things better if it gives the slightly-prejudiced manager more of a chance, through a personal interview rather than the formality of the selection board, to decide "this particular woman is an exception." This is not posed as a solution; but the problem is posed as one needing some serious consideration.

The problem with eligibility lists derived from written examinations arises clearly in the clerical group. All applicants take the same tests, but the jobs within this group vary considerably – for instance, some involve working outside, handling heavy objects, climbing ladders, etc. Since these sound like male jobs, males were always sent to fill them until very recently. In fact, until 1969 staff request forms included a box which allowed departments to specify 'male', 'female', or 'either' thus leading at least the Ottawa Regional Office to develop a convenient rule of thumb for placing clerks: men were always sent when requested and women when the card was marked 'female' or 'either' as more females were typically on the eligibility list than males. Given the situation, this procedure was efficient. Most women would not have been interested in the jobs reserved for men. But the procedure – since stopped – was also discriminatory and other methods are available which are as efficient, or more so, and would not be discriminatory in effect. As simple a procedure as having clerical candidates indicate what kinds of jobs they would not accept when taking the written examination would solve much of the problem.

Departmental variations

The longer women remain in the service, the worse off they are in salary compared to men with similar experience and education. Some of the general barriers, particularly structural features of the employment system, which help account for this have been discussed.

While these structural barriers are the same in all departments, beliefs and attitudes are not. Thus in-service opportunities for women to advance vary within different departments.

Table V–1 ** provides a succinct, but not terribly satisfactory, comparison of departments in terms of opportunities for women. The table supports the good reputation of several departments (Dominion Bureau of Statistics, Public Archives and National Library, Public Service Commission and Secretary of State) but it neither confirms nor disproves bad reputations unless it is supplemented with information about occupational mix within the department. The nature of Post Office work is well enough known, however, to point out that Table V–1 confirms its reputation as one of the departments most inhospitable to women.

There seems to be a tendency for those departments with a significant proportion of women in upper salary groups to also pay attention to opportunities for work satisfaction and career advancement for women at lower levels. Public Archives and National Library, for example, has a well-developed plan for upgrading promising girls who start as typists, by transferring them first into clerical, then other classes. The Dominion Bureau of Statistics also has put some thought and effort into the particular problems connected with ST and CR groups.

Another indication of differences lies in the departments' attitude toward female Administrative Trainees. This program was scrutinized closely in this study because of the special problems faced by women moving into administrative posi-

** Eds. In the interests of space, this table has not been reproduced here. Interested readers are referred to the original report.

tions. Apparently, at least until 1968, the number of women recruited into this program was partially determined by the number that could be placed in departments. Most departments prefer more male trainees, and some prefer no women at all.

In 1967, 36 per cent of the June graduates who were qualified to enter the service as Administrative Trainees or Foreign Service Officers were women, but only 20 per cent of those offered jobs were women. In 1968, the proportion of women among those qualified (21 per cent) and among those offered jobs (20 per cent) did not drop off. It would be pleasant to think this represented an improvement, but note the percentage of women among those offered jobs in the two years did not change. It was the percentage of women among those qualified that dropped. If more women had been qualified in 1968, would more have been offered jobs?

Discriminatory practices within departments pose a serious problem for the Public Service Commission. While the PSC has legislative responsibility for ensuring equal opportunity, the problem of monitoring the many personnel actions taken within departments is extremely difficult, and will be more so as staffing authority is increasingly decentralized.

Training

The departments themselves handle a great deal of training, and no central records are kept of these activities. The PSC and the Treasury Board are jointly responsible for training programs that cut across all departments and are administered by the PSC's Bureau of Staff Development and Training (BSDT).

The proportion of women in courses administered by BSDT seems to be about the same as the proportion of women in the occupational groups and levels from which the trainees are drawn, but this was *not* checked closely because it could only have provided a partial picture of training activities in the government. There are few women in management courses, except the course for 'Senior Supervisors' which draws trainees from the clerical group, because there are few women in the occupational groups, such as Program Administration, from which these trainees are drawn. In the top-level Career Assignment Program, three women were admitted in the first year (one dropped out) out of a total of 70 – actually an over-representation of women given the proportion of women at the levels from which CAP candidates are drawn.

The government does not now provide in-service training for STs, although it used to. A re-organization of office support services, as recommended by the Treasury Board study previously mentioned, would require a training program – for officers using the services as well as for those providing them. The study points out that there are now fairly serious problems of coordination between officers and STs in the typing pools; neither knows what the other needs to improve performance.[24]

Training is important but only as an adjunct to other, broader programs. An attempt to increase the number of women in management training, for instance, would have to be combined with efforts to give women more opportunity to move into management else it would have little effect.

Maternity Leave and Child-care

Maternity leave in the public service is without pay; when it ends, a woman is reinstated in her old job or given another position of an appropriate nature and level. The normal pre-natal leave is eight weeks, but may be increased; post-natal may last up to twenty-four weeks. During maternity leave, a woman must pay the full premium on health and superannuation plans.

No central records are kept on number of women taking maternity leave nor on the average length of such leave, so information from those departments with readily available records was requested. The mean proportion of women taking maternity leave in one year was 2.6 per cent, and the range 0.1 to 7.6 per cent with those in Agriculture, appropriately enough, being most fertile. Average length of leave (pre- and post-natal) was 3.7 months, with a range of 2.3 to 6 months.

Government policy on maternity leave resembles that of Ontario employers surveyed by the Ontario Women's Bureau,[25] but is somewhat below the minimum standards of maternity protection laid down in ILO Conventions (which Canada has not ratified) and Recommendations.[26]

An interesting anomaly has recently been introduced in this area. Most collective agreements signed thus far give a married man one day of paid 'paternity leave' every time his wife bears a child. The negotiating teams included no women, so the question of an equitable response to the family responsibilities of working women was, presumably, not raised. *Equal* treatment, called for by the ILO Convention on Discrimination suggests one day of paid maternity leave. *Equitable* treatment is more complex but ILO standards and recommendations related to maternity protection deserve, at least, serious consideration.

Granting paid paternity leave, even for only one day, without granting paid maternity leave, and the example of different pay and different jobs in the printing trades mentioned earlier, raise a serious issue. What government agency is responsible for ensuring that negotiated agreements do not violate the non-discriminatory policy of the Canadian government? The Public Service Staff Relations Act states that no union which discriminates on the basis of sex, race, religion, etc., can be recognized as a bargaining agent, but it makes no mention of any checks or safeguards on potential discriminatory consequences of a collective agreement.

Child-care facilities near the place of employment or near the home, are particularly helpful to mothers of pre-school children with low family incomes. Approximately 10 per cent of female public servants in the capital have pre-school children. Without even counting casual employees, this means that about 1,600 women in the Ottawa/Hull area alone are faced with the problem of arranging adequate care for young children. Many more have to worry about the care of school-age children. Should the Canadian government help these working mothers by providing child-care facilities (as the American government is now doing on a pilot basis) or by encouraging other agencies to do so?

The more general question is: when should a certain class of employees receive special assistance? (The relevant class here, it should be noted, includes wifeless working fathers as well as working mothers.) This is discussed in the next section. First, however, let us pose a question which places employer-subsidized child care within a perspective that suggests it merits serious consideration. Which is more reasonable in a just society, and for a socially responsible employer: to provide free parking facilities for high-status employees or to subsidize child-care facilities for low-status employees? The cost per child should be about the same as the cost per car.

Towards Equal Employment Opportunity

Special treatment that attempts to expand opportunities or improve conditions for persons who would otherwise be at a disadvantage is not considered discriminatory.[27] But what is special treatment? Is it anything that is difficult to do under the current system? Or should something other than administrative ease determine what is special treatment and what is not? If administrative ease is the criterion, *then any change* becomes special treatment.

It is suggested here that special treatment might best be defined as anything which decreases efficiency or productivity (i.e., is costly to the employer) in the medium run – say for two to five years. It may or may not be costly over the long run.

An equal employment opportunity policy may be implemented in any of three ways: through a passive approach, an active approach, or an aggressive approach.

What is here called a *passive approach* is one that merely attempts to ensure that the existing structure is administered fairly. It does not concern itself with inequities built into the structure, but concentrates on educational campaigns to change attitudes, individual cases of discrimination brought to light through formal or informal complaints, and 'token' appointments, that is, active attempts to get minority group members into a few particularly visible positions.

An *active approach* is one which attempts to adjust the structure itself in those areas where it imposes unfairly on particular groups and where such adjustments, while sometimes disruptive and costly in man-hours in the short-run, are expected at least not to increase costs or decrease productivity in the medium-run. In other words, an active approach, as here defined, involves no special treatment.

An *aggressive approach* is one that includes the elements of the passive and active approach and special treatment in addition. In other words, it initiates changes that are expected to be costly, in dollars or decreased productivity, in both the short- and medium-run, although not necessarily in the long-run. Current public service efforts designed to provide more equal employment opportunities for French-speaking Canadians provide an excellent example of an aggressive approach. Language training for English-speaking Canadians, for instance, will be very costly for a number of years but the benefits to be derived from this in the long-run are expected to more than compensate for the medium-term costs.

The Canadian government has in the last few years adopted a passive approach with respect to equal employment opportunities for women. For several years before that, there was no approach. And before that, the approach was on the negative side of passive – it was one of promoting unequal opportunities for women.

NOTES
1. Convention III, Article 1, sec. 1 (a).
2. *Ibid.*, Sec. 2.
3. Bernard Berelson and Gary A. Steiner, *Human Behavior: An Inventory of Scientific Findings*, New York: Harcourt, Brace, 1964, pp. 626-627
4. Occupational distribution accounts for a fairly large portion of the income difference between men and women. See Sylvia Ostry, *The Female Worker in Canada*, Ottawa: Dominion Bureau of Statistics, 1968, pp.40-43 and Henry Sanborn, "Pay Differences between Men and Women", *Industrial and Labor Relations Review*, 17 (1964), pp. 534-541.
5. Glassco Commission report, Vol. 1, p. 520: "The Royal Commission on Government Organization," Ottawa, Queen's Printer, 1962-3.
6. Estimates in the early 1960's were $1.50 compared to $1.75 (Glassco Commission, *ibid.*). The cost of both would be higher now.
7. Given that the CR 1 position offers good experience. There is great variation on this among the CR positions.
8. ST 9, Court Reporter, has been omitted from Figure V – 1 since

there is such disparity between it and the rest of the ST series. The other three sub-groups – typists, stenographers, and secretaries – are shown by the broken lines, the less broken one between ST 2 and 3 indicating greater discontinuity here than between ST 4 and 5.
9. There was a four per cent raise for all levels in both classes in the fall of 1967, but this does not change this distribution.
10. There is little agreement as to whether such transfers have become easier or more difficult under the new classification system and selection standards, see Chapter VI, K. Archibald, *Sex and the Public Service*, Ottawa, Queen's Printer, 1970.
11. Hence, transfers to other occupational classes decrease as level increases. See Planning and Special Projects Division, "Unilingual Secretaries' Career Opportunities", Ottawa: Public Service Commission, March, 1969, p.4.
The recommendations of this study are excellent: that more opportunities be opened up for STs to transfer into clerical or administrative service positions. While the recommendations are made with respect to unlingual secretaries, they will benefit bilingual secretaries as well. This is as it should be. While the study points out that an increasing number of ST 6-8 positions are available only to bilingual secretaries and this decreases opportunities for unilingual secretaries, it does not point out that the opportunities are severely limited even for bilingual secretaries. In terms of numbers of positions available, the unilingual secretary has only a 7 per cent chance of making it into an ST 6-8 position, but the bilingual secretary does not do much better. She has only a 9 per cent chance.
12. "A Study of Office Secretarial Services in the Federal Government", Treasury Board Project 21/67, Ottawa, Canada, August, 1968.
13. One-fifth of all women in the Canadian labour force work part-time and many more would like to. See Patricia Cockburn, *Women University Graduates in Continuing Education and Employment*, Canadian Federation of University Women, 1966.
14. Eli Ginsberg, "Paycheck and Apron – Revolution in Womanpower", *Industrial and Labour Relations Review*, 7 (1968), p. 202.
15. Except to allow accumulated sick and special leave to be carried forward if a woman terminated employment and then was re-hired within six months. For other 'annually-rated' part-time employees, it is three months.
16. Not all unions are against part-time employment, but many are – for a variety of reasons, some legitimate and some not. See Jean Hallaire, *Part-time Employment: Its Extent and its Problems*, Paris: Organizations for Economic Co-operation and Development, 1968, esp. pp. 58-68 and Viola Klein, *Women Workers: Working Hours and Services*, Paris: OECD, 1965, p. 86.
17. Treasury Board Circular No. 1968-39.
18. Hallaire, *op. cit.*, pp. 13-16.
19. *Ibid.*, p. 45.
20. *Ibid.*, p. 46.
21. *Ibid.*, pp. 100-101 and Klein, *op. cit.*, p. 88.
22. Hallaire, *op. cit.*, p. 101.
23. *Ibid.*, p. 100.
24. "A Study of Office Secretarial Services . . .," *op. cit.*
25. Sixteen southern Ontario companies were selected that had at least *some* provision for maternity leave. ("Maternity Leave Practices in Ontario", brochure prepared by the Women's Bureau of the Ontario Department of Labour, Toronto, June, 1968.) Most of these firms guaranteed reinstatement; over one-half required the woman to pay the full premium on most fringe benefits, as the government does on health and superannuation plans, but almost one-third continued to contribute the employer's share. Neither the government, nor most other Ontario employers surveyed, permit employees to use accumulated sick leave to cover maternity leave. The government does not provide any income maintenance during maternity leave, nor do most companies – although some, particularly manufacturers, do.
26. These include cash benefits and breaks during working hours to allow nursing mothers to breast-feed their children. ILO Maternity Protection Conventions (1919 and 1952) and Recommendations (1921 and 1952) and the Social Security (Minimum Standards) Convention of 1952.

3. A Québécoise View of the Parameters

Léandre Bergeron/*Sir George Williams University*

A decade ago an editorial in Canada's leading English-language newspaper asked, "What does Quebec want?" That question revealed how very wide was the gulf that separated the 'two solitudes' at that time. Since then, many Québécois have endeavoured to articulate, for themselves, the answer. Here, a historian and fervent nationalist, draws his own vivid picture of the social structure of Quebec society. While some may say it is overdrawn, informed more by passion than by scientific rigour, it offers an emphatic statement of the extent to which the Québécois has perceived and continues to perceive himself excluded from full membership in his own society.

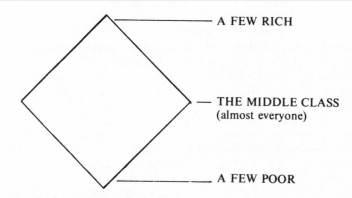

Apparent Political Structure

The people elect the Members of Parliament.

The MP's of the majority party form the government. The leader of the majority party becomes Prime Minister and finds among his colleagues the various cabinet ministers he needs to govern the country.

The MP's of the minority party form the opposition. Their work consists of criticizing the government so that it will pass better laws for the people.

Real Political Structure

The people elect Members of Parliament, who are attached to parties. The parties 'win' their elections with electoral campaigns financed by big business.

The party in power first of all must pass laws to favour the companies, then other laws to appease the people (such as family allowance, labour laws, welfare, etc.)

The government is in the service of the companies. It is a caretaker government.

This kind of democracy is called bourgeois democracy.

This bourgeois democracy is really a dictatorship by the possessor class.

Apparent Social Structure
(what they want us to accept)

They tell us that:
- The rich are richer than the others because they have worked harder. So that they deserve the grand life they lead.
- Everybody can become rich like them.
- The middle class means everybody, or almost; it includes the labourer, the judge, the doctor, the janitor, the Prime Minister, the farmer, you and me. If we worked a little harder and saved a little more we could become very rich, but we stay where we are because we do not have the *will*, the *courage* or the *ability*. However we really shouldn't complain because there are those who are poorer than we are
- The poor are stupid and don't have the courage to work. Look at them: when you give them money they waste it in the tavern. They deserve their fate.

The Real Structure of Quebec Society

There are two main groups involved—the workers and the

Reprinted from *The History of Quebec: A Patriot's Handbook*, by Léandre Bergeron, (originally published as *Petit Manuel d'Histoire du Québec*, Editions Québécoises, 1971), by permission of New Canada Publications, a division of NC Press Ltd.

bourgeoisie. The worker is the producer par excellence. He converts material into a product which is used for the subsistence and development of society.

The bourgeois owns the means of production. He has under his control:
- the materials
- the equipment

Then he buys the labour-power of the worker and appropriates all of his production in return for a wage.

The materials can be natural wealth (forests, mines, etc.) or semi-finished products which undergo a transformation. The equipment includes the buildings, machines, tools, everything needed to convert the materials. Labour-power is the energy the worker uses to convert the material with the aid of equipment.

The bourgeois controls the entire productive process but he does no productive work himself.

The Bourgeois

The bourgeois wants to make profits.

To do this:
- he looks for real or imagined human needs to satisfy
- he looks for raw materials to process to satisfy these needs and the equipment to manufacture them
- he accumulates money, capital, either from his own business or from other bourgeois through a financial institution
- he buys the labour-power needed to produce his commodity

The wheels of industry can now be set in motion. The bourgeois sells his commodity at a price that allows him to pay for his materials and equipment, to repay the capital he has borrowed, and to pay his workers' wages. At the same time, he keeps enough to satisfy his own needs and to expand his industry.

The Worker

His only property is his labour-power and a few personal belongings. In a society of exploitation like ours, his labour-power is considered a commodity—and to survive he must sell it to the bourgeois, his employer. In return he receives a wage, just enough to keep him and his family alive to continue their lives as slaves.

He tries in vain to work harder to escape; it is almost always impossible. His wages will disappear in the purchase of necessities and some indispensable entertainment to escape momentarily from the conditions of his life.

The bourgeois takes *all* of the goods that the worker produces in his working day. Now, the special quality of the commodity 'labour-power' is that it can produce more than it costs the capitalist. A worker may produce enough commodities in the first two or three hours to cover the wage he is paid for the whole day. The rest of the day he works for the bourgeois for free.

In taking everything the worker produces, the capitalist is taking a surplus value,[1] some of which goes to pay back his loans and taxes, and the rest he keeps for personal consumption and for re-investment. Also out of this surplus value comes the money to pay a large number of working persons whom we will call non-productive workers.

PRODUCTIVE AND NON-PRODUCTIVE WORKERS
A *productive worker* produces a commodity[2] which will realize surplus value for the bourgeois. The class of productive workers is known as the proletariat. It is because the whole capitalist system is based on the fact that workers produce the surplus value which is the source of capital, that the proletariat – along with the bourgeoisie which appropriates that capital – is the most important class in that social system.

Productive workers include:
1. Those who extract raw materials: *lumberjacks, miners, wage-earning fishermen, wage-earning agricultural workers*
2. Those who convert raw materials into goods for sale (commodities): *manual workers and technicians in the factories, construction workers*
3. Those who bring the commodities to market: *stevedores, truck drivers, warehouse workers, railway workers.*

A *non-productive worker* is one whom the bourgeois, or the state apparatus, hires as his servant, either personally or professionally and who is paid by him out of the suplus value created by the worker; for example, a textile worker works in the mill for twelve long hours and the factory owner uses part of her unpaid labour (surplus value) to hire her sister as a maid, her brother as a teacher and her cousin as a policeman or soldier.

This does not mean that only productive workers are dominated by the bourgeoisie. All those who work for wages or salaries, without ownership of means of production and without power of decision, are oppressed like the workers. This includes the secretary, the civil servant, the school teacher, the professor, the artist, the writer.

One might object by saying that the announcer at the CBC sees nothing in common between himself and the doorman who opens the door for him. Here we must distinguish between subjective outlook and objective reality.

The announcer subjectively sees himself in a white shirt, admires himself on the television screen, receives admiration from many viewers because of his deep voice and charm. The doorman sees himself in the doorman's uniform opening the door to these important ladies and gentlemen.

These two subjective outlooks are radically different and correspond to two different objective realities. But these different objective realities (talking on TV and opening a door) are determined by one common fundamental reality. Both men own no means of production and have no real power of decision. Both submit to a system of oppression that makes them sell their ability to work and prevents them from participating in the decisions that affect every aspect of their lives.

Blue collar or white collar workers, the difference in their standard of living may not be too great. Blue collar workers work mostly with their hands whereas white collar workers work more with their head and fingers. The point is, they are all oppressed, all without the power of decision. The bourgeoisie uses the difference in the colour of their shirts to keep working people divided, to prevent them from uniting and becoming a force that could threaten their privileged position.

The semi-proletariat
The *semi-proletariat* consists of those non-productive workers who both in the kind of work they do and in their standard of living are very close to the productive workers. They are often paid less than productive workers, they may work harder under worse conditions, but *they do not produce surplus value.*

The semi-poletariat includes;
1. those who do the maintenance work of society: *garbagemen, janitors, dry-cleaning workers*
2. those who tend to the personal needs of the bourgeoisie: *domestic servants, gardeners*
3. those whose functions exist only in a money economy: *store clerks, certain clerical workers.*

SOCIALLY USEFUL AND SOCIALLY USELESS WORK
Another distinction that must be made is that between socially useful work and socially useless work. Socially useful work is work that contributes to the well-being of society as a whole. Socially useless work is that which is detrimental to society.

Policemen in our society do socially useful work when they direct traffic or look for lost persons. But when they beat up workers on strike or students demonstrating against the bourgeois regime, they are nothing but instruments in the hands of the class which is trying to prevent the oppressed from bettering their conditions.

Office workers, salesmen and retail clerks are socially useful but non-productive workers. They do not produce commodities; rather, they carry out certain functions which are absolutely essential to the capitalist system, to a system which distributes goods not according to need but according to ability to pay. In society which is not divided into exploiting and exploited classes, a society where no one needs to steal to eat or to prove his self-worth through his possessions, it is not necessary to have a huge army of people who produce nothing, but simply guard merchandise, bookkeep it, sell it, and collect bills.

A few people are necessary in any system to allocate and dispatch goods. But, we don't really need to put all this effort into selling the goods of the bourgeoisie and keeping track of their money.

The Petit-Bourgeoisie
The petit-bourgeoisie consists of three categories:
1. The small capitalist who must work himself in his own enterprise in order to live; that is, part of his income is gained from the labour of others and part from his own labor: *shop keepers, small manufacturers, family farmers*
2. those whose specific function is to maintain the system of exploitation by ideological means: *teachers, artists, clergy, members of parliament, judges, civil servants, lawyers, military and police brass, salesmen, office workers*
3. professionals who market their expertise (as distinguished from workers who sell their ability to produce commodities): *doctors, dentists, architects, engineers, scientists, computer programmers.*

SMALL CAPITALISTS
Small manufacturers own small means of production incidental to the main functioning of the economy and they hire few workers. While they exploit their workers by appropriating the surplus value they create, most often they are personally involved in the productive process. Such small businessmen are the first to go out of business when times get tough and are continually being taken over by the middle and big bourgeoisie.

Businessmen, shop keepers and salesmen derive their income from selling goods. Their power of decision is exercised in selecting and sticking price tags on merchandise and selling it.

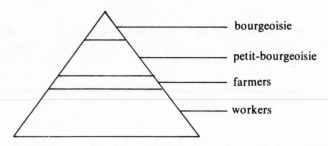

To the extent that they make goods available to the population, they do useful work. But their work is harmful when they buy up all the goods and sell them at a price few can afford. By such profiteering they work, not for the sake of improving the conditions of humanity, but to accumulate money for selfish use.

FARMERS

Quebec farmers, owners of a few acres of land, produce goods like the worker. But can they be considered workers, strictly speaking?

They are not wage-workers.

They are owners of small means of production – their farms.

They have some power of decision.

These are characteristics of the petit-bourgeoisie. Unlike the bourgeois, their holdings are small and they generally employ few if any workers.

However, it must be noted that agriculture in Quebec today is feeling the effects of industrial society and now accounts for only 6 per cent of the working population. Because of this, the small farmer has to change his life.

He might leave the farm to become a worker in the city, or he might manage to buy some land, hire some employees and set himself up as a real country bourgeois farmer. Or, as a third alternative, he might get together with other farmers to form co-operative farms. In the first case he becomes a worker. In the second case he becomes a bourgeois. In both of these cases he is either exploited or exploiter. But, in the third case, he directs himself toward a society where neither exploited nor exploiter exists.

IDEOLOGICAL WORKERS

The ideological sector employs workers to convey the ideology– the attitudes and way of thinking which enables the dominating class to stay in power and keep the working class and other oppressed classes down.

Teachers perform two functions. They convey knowledge necessary to train workers: auto mechanics, chemistry, typing, mathematics. But their main function is to convey to students the ideology of the dominating class and the values that will make them useful members of the society: neatness, narrowness of vision, unquestioning obedience,etc. At great risk, teachers can choose to make their students conscious that the system we live in is a system of exploiters and exploited.

Commercial artists most often participate in the sale of consumer goods which promotes individualism without contributing to a generalized betterment. They can help the people when they use their skills to depict and encourage the struggle of the people against their exploiters.

Parish priests spread bourgeois ideology to the extent that they defend the interests of the bourgeois class by preaching submission to and respect for authority. However, they help the people if they break their ties with the bourgeoisie and integrate into the working class and struggle with it against the exploiters.

Artists journalists, authors and radio and TV producers are in the same position as teachers. They transmit messages: they have the same responsibility. Those who choose the side of the

people will play an important role.

THE PROFESSIONALS

There are those who work at trades considered as 'professions': doctors, dentists, lawyers, notaries, architects, consulting engineers. They do not work for a salary or a wage and because of their specialized knowledge they can demand high fees for their services. They can charge what they like—up to a point. The instruments of exploitation are in their hands. This establishes a distinction between themselves and the workers and so they tend to identify with the exploiters. In their respective fields they have the power to make some decisions but they employ few. The 'means of production' which they own are generally their own skills. Their work cannot be considered 'labour' in the strict sense because, unlike the productive workers, they are not hired to *produce commodities.*

THE FUNCTIONARIES OF THE STATE APPARATUS

This stratum of the petit-bourgeoisie—members of parliament, judges, policemen, soldiers, civil servants—are employed by the bourgeoisie to run their state in their own interests. They work indirectly for the owners of the means of production and have little, if any, power of decision.

The Member of Parliament in Canada or Quebec today may think he has nothing in common with a kindergarten teacher. He may think he is superior to teachers, that he has decision-making powers and a salary that places him in the bourgeois class. But, in fact, he owns no means of production: he is salaried and for his fat salary he has sold his power of decision. He accepts the decisions dictated to him by the party. And, in Canada, political parties, whatever their class base, accept decisions dictated to them by the big bourgeoisie that is dominated by the bourgeoisie of another country, the United States. There are no parties in Canada or Quebec today which represent the working class.

As for the judge, he too may think himself a big bourgeois with a huge salary and sweeping powers of decision. He can send men to the scaffold. In fact, he receives a salary to make decisions already made for him in the law books by the exploiter class. The lawyer is handsomely paid as well, for helping the judge.

PHYSICAL ARM OF THE REPRESSIVE APPARATUS

Those whose function is to maintain the system of exploitation (or extend it) by directly repressive means: *policemen, jail guards, soldiers.*

SPECIAL CASES

The unemployed are workers. They are paid to do nothing until they are needed. These reserve workers are part of the labour bank of the capitalist system. As such they have no power of decision.

What distinguishes the unemployed from other workers is that they do not do any productive work. They are workers who are not workers.

They are forced to live with this contradiction.

WELFARE RECIPIENTS

This large group of people is rejected by bourgeois society. They are considered unable to produce in a capitalist system because of physical, emotional or intellectual handicaps or because of police records. Nevertheless, society supports them, by dishing out a mere pittance, in order to keep its conscience clear by being 'generous to the disinherited'.

Although welfare recipients are at the mercy of others and have no power of decision over anything at all, they are not workers. They do no productive work and their allowance cannot be considered to be a salary. It is, rather, a pension for the demobilized.

Students form a complex group. To begin with, as students they are neither bourgeois nor workers. They have neither ownership of means of production nor a wage or salary. They have no power of decision. As for productive work, this depends on the future career they choose. The training of a student can make him into a bourgeois or a petit-bourgeois or a specialized worker.

Since students do not participate in production, either as exploited or exploiter, they are really marginal to society. They can be sympathetic or offer moral support to either the exploited or the exploiter, but as long as they are students and not involved in the relations of production as definite bourgeoisie, petit-bourgeoisie, or workers, they are demobilized just like welfare recipients. They are kept outside of the exploiter exploited relationship at the level of production because they are financially supported outside of the relations of production. Therefore they have no real involvement in the struggle between the exploited and the exploiters.

The student revolt is predominantly the result of this demobilization, of this state of waiting on the margin of the relations of production, of this state of privileged welfare recipients being prepared for a specific role in the system of exploitation.

The Bourgeoisie

The bourgeois in the real sense of the word owns the means of production.

His income comes not from wages but from profits derived from the unpaid labour of his workers at the point of production.

He buys the workers' labour-power at a price well below the value of the product of this same worker's work. The difference between the two is surplus value and from it comes the bourgeois' profit.

The bourgeois has the power to make decisions not only concerning his own life but his workers' lives as well. He spends his time giving orders to those who do the productive work. The money he has accumulated gives him control of production but he produces nothing at all. He is the perfect parasite.

The bourgeois system of production is the world upside down. The real producers, those who produce goods, have no power of decision over their lives and end up with only enough to survive. The non-producers enjoy the power of decision and goods produced by others.

UPPER AND MIDDLE BOURGEOISIE

The bourgeoisie per se consists of two groups, the upper and the middle. What is the difference between the two groups?

Both exploit their workers on a large scale; both have significant powers of decision over our daily lives. However the 'big' bourgeoisie is in all respects bigger and this difference in degree leads to a difference in kind.

The upper bourgeoisie is made up of capitalists whose investments and economic power of decision dominates wide sectors of the country and in a good many cases extends to other countries. It is the ruling class both in its home country and in the countries it dominates.

The middle bourgeoisie is made up of capitalists whose investments and economic power of decision are more modest. It is greatly dependent on decisions made by the upper bourgeoisie and in most cases limits itself to national territory.

The owners of American companies, who exploit not only in the United States but also in other countries in Latin America and Europe and Canada and Quebec, are members of the upper bourgeoisie, and constitute the ruling class in these countries. However, the owners of a company like Vachon Biscuits, in Quebec, are part of the Quebec middle bourgeoisie and have no such power.

This difference between the members of the bourgeois class causes conflicts between them. The upper bourgeoisie tends to become increasingly powerful because it has more capital and so it is always on the look-out to absorb the enterprises of the middle bourgeoisie. There are numerous examples of this phenomenon of absorption of small companies by large ones. Canadair, a middle bourgeois enterprise, was bought out by General Dynamics, a huge company belonging to some upper bourgeois Americans.

The middle bourgeoisie which is often called the national bourgeoisie, identifies with its national territory and may try to rally other classes to help it rid the country of these foreigners so that it may rule in their place. It is, however, quite incapable of this task at this stage of capitalist development.

Members of the upper echelons of the underworld are part of the middle bourgeoisie to the extent that they own means of production and exchange. Until recently most of the bosses of organized crime were local criminals. But, just like other businessmen, they have been brought under the control of New York.

It is known that in some places the underworld controls the distribution of cigarettes, just as it controls prostitution, the drug market, fraudulent bankruptcies and part of show business as well as many 'legitimate' businesses. By so dominating the market for the exploitation of human passions, the underworld is an integral part of bourgeois society where exploitation is the rule.

This is why in private clubs (where important decisions are made) we find members of parliament and leaders of the underworld rubbing shoulders. Everyone remembers the visit of Cotroni, boss of the Montreal under world, during the Union Nationale leadership convention in June 1969 in Quebec City. M. Cotroni came to 'softly pressure' for *his* candidate for leadership of the Union Nationale in exactly the same way as industrialists concerned about government contracts.

The capitalist owners of Dupont of Canada or Canada Packers are more exploitative, more base, more grasping than the underworld bigshots, but they can pass as do-gooders because their kind of exploitation is accepted by official ethics. Members of the underworld are considered bad guys because their kind of oppression is forbidden (in theory only) by the same ethics.

Respectable capitalists and notorious underworld characters are merely two sides of the same coin: exploitation of man by man in every possible way.

Nationalities and Social Classes in Quebec

The Bourgeoisie

Both strata of the bourgeoisie which exploit our manpower and resources in Quebec are for the most part foreign.

The upper bourgeoisie are foreigners. The big companies and financial institutions which exploit and govern Quebec belong to Americans and English-Canadians. The companies that extract our natural resources (lumber and minerals) are in the hands of American capitalists. American or English-Canadian capital dominates the secondary sector—conversion of raw materials, pulp and paper mills, textiles etc.

The Québécois upper bourgeoisie is practically non-existent.

The middle bourgeoisie is dominated by English-Canadians. Those who own small factories, loan companies, small transport or construction companies, stores, radio or TV stations and newspapers are predominantly English-Canadian, many of whom are Jewish[3] and a few are Québécois.

SOME EXAMPLES

Noranda Mines	American and English-Canadian
Iron Ore Co.	American and English-Canadian
General Motors	American
Canadair	American
General Electric	American
Canadian International Paper	American
Dupont of Canada	American
Canada Packers	English-Canadian
Domtar	American and English-Canadian
Seagram's	Jewish-Canadian and American*
Dominion Textile	American and English-Canadian
C.P.R.	American and English-Canadian
Bell Telephone	American and English-Canadian
Alcan	American and English-Canadian

* Its head office is in New York

Jewish Canadian capitalists have important holdings in food stores, footwear, fur and clothing businesses. French-Canadian capitalists and religious orders are trying to catch up with the English in banking, transport, construction (buildings, houses, roads) in mass media (radio, newspapers, TV) and in food stores. And there are now new immigrants from Italy, Germany, and France who have managed to get a foothold in some sectors of the economy.

Every Québécois can rhyme off the list: Eaton's, Simpson's, Ogilvy's are English-Canadian; Steinberg's is Jewish-Canadian; Dupuis, Sicotte Construction, Poupart are French-Canadian. But a systematic examination of Quebec business is yet to be done.

francophones   Red Man   anglophones

The Petit-Bourgeoisie
Virtually absent from the upper bourgeoisie and in the minority in the middle bourgeoisie, the Québécois make up the majority in the other classes: petit-bourgeoisie, workers and farmers, students, unemployed and welfare recipients.

They represent a bare majority in the upper ranks of the petit bourgeoisie. English-Canadians and especially Jewish-Canadi-

ans are well established in the liberal professions and small businesses.

The Workers
Most Québécois are workers. Again, among white collar workers we find English-Canadians and recent immigrants. With the Québécois majority, we find Italian and Portuguese immigrants and some English-Canadian blue collar workers.

WELFARE RECIPIENTS
Most of the welfare recipients are Québécois. There is also a large proportion of Red men on welfare, kept on 'reserves'. If we place the whole of the Quebec population in a pyramid we find that the Québécois, who make up 82 per cent of the population, are at the bottom of the ladder. Of the other 18 per cent, two-thirds are of British origin, the rest of Jewish or German or other national origin.

Recent Events

The Fifties and Sixties
Boosted by the Second World War, American capitalism resumed its expansionism throughout the world, constantly increasing its hold on the Canadian economy and, consequently on the Quebec economy. Industrialization in Quebec continued to displace traditional Québécois society. The rate of migration from the country to the city continued to grow, along with the rate of integration of farmers into the working class. Soon the majority of Québécois became cheap labour in industrial centres for American, English-Canadian, French-Canadian and Jewish capitalists.

The habitants brought a rural mentality with them from the farms, but this had to go. A worker does not think like a habitant who owns thirty acres of land. The Québécois in the back country and little industrial centres had been kept in ignorance by Duplessis and the Clergy, so that they could be properly exploited by American and English-Canadian capitalists. However the new 'city guys' could not be kept from asking questions and wanting to change the old ways of behavior and thought.

At the same time the Québécois small and middle bourgeoisie, who had benefitted from the post-war economic boom, began to feel strong enough to establish themselves as a national bourgeoisie—a new elite with the power to dominate Québécois society. American capitalists and the English-Canadian bourgeoisie were willing to collaborate with this Québécois bourgeoisie because they recognized in them an ally that would 'modernize' Quebec and train the Québécois masses to qualify as workers for their factories, and buy their products obsessively, just like the American masses.

The role played by the former Negro-Kings, Duplessis and the Clergy, was not useful enough to our colonizers, American and English-Canadian capitalists, in the modern system of exploitation. The requirement was no longer a Negro-King preaching hard work and an austere existence, but a Negro-King who could make the Québécois people believe that they had to work hard and live extravagantly. That is, that they had to consume, and consume. Therefore, a new elite was needed, a liberal lay elite who would adopt and preach the *American way of life,* gradually Anglicizing the Québécois to make them into 'real' Canadians—in other words, second-rate Americans who are submissive producers and servile consumers for American imperialism.

So our colonizers supported our small and middle bourgeoisie morally and financially, concentrating on the provincial

Liberals. The Party came to power in 1960, led by Jean Lesage's crack team that proceeded to launch the 'Quiet Revolution'.

Our colonizers were happy. The Negro-King, Lesage, was going to modernize the education system as we have seen by creating a Ministry of Education and by applying the Parent report. Every Québécois would have a minimum American education, An American professional and technical education to become good American producers and consumers. This would integrate the entire population into modern capitalism.

The Negro-King, Lesage, was going to nationalize electricity to permit the planned distribution of this source of energy to industry and all important centres. Nothing very revolutionary about this: Ontario had done the same thing at the beginning of the century. Electricity is another service the state offers to industry, just like the roads it builds.

Negro-King Lesage was going to create Soquem (*Société Québécoise d'Exploration Minière*), which would help capitalists find our minerals in the Quebec subsoil.

Negro-King Lesage would create a pension fund, offer hospital insurance, increase aid to the under-privileged, and modernize the Labour Code; all the so-called social measures to appease popular discontent, and to help the Québécois population cope with the capitalist system of exploitation. Each person could find his own secure pigeon-hole – workers at work, welfare people at home, bourgeois in their beautiful clean districts, students at their studies – and everybody would be consuming way over their means with a well-oiled credit system, the golden chain of modern slavery.

As Lesage began to play his new role of Negro-King, a belief was growing among certain elements of the petit-bourgeoisie and certain white collar workers that the Québécois bourgeoisie would have to go further than the Negro-King role and become the national bourgeoisie of an independent country. So, the struggle for Quebec's independence was launched in 1960 with the formation of the RIN (*Rassemblement pour l'Indépendence Nationale*). It believed that the Québécois had to fight against domination by the English-Canadian bourgeoisie whose political centre of control is in Ottawa, and that the Québécois bourgeoisie was to assume its role as a ruling class in a nation independent of any other bourgeoisie.

But these new Patriotes were not at first mindful of the fact that the English-Canadian bourgeoisie, along with our middle bourgeoisie, are just the means by which we are dominated by the American capitalists.

Soon, a group of young people formed who were enthusiastic about the changes taking place in Quebec and wanted to see them happen faster. The FLQ-63 planted some bombs. These young men thought that the Québécois people would spontaneously rise up as a single man to the noise of the bombs and quickly make Quebec independent. Since the national reflex of the colonized is fear of change, the Quebec people were scared. "The Québécois violent? Impossible." But underneath this fear, complicity and some deep hope lay hidden.

Bombs are a formal protest – they challenged the whole system. The obedient Lesage responded according to his role and quickly jailed the young people who were upsetting the 'Quiet Revolution,' the evolution toward a comfortable consumer society.

When the Queen of England came to see her subjects on the road to Americanization in 1964, Lesage unleashed Minister Claude Wagner, who in turn unleashed the Quebec municipal police on the students who were mournfully chanting "We are joyful, we are overflowing with joy." Wagner's qualities as a defender of law and order were exposed by this 'Saturday of the bludgeons'.

The same year, the radical monthly *Parti Pris*, which had been publishing concrete analyses of Québécois society since October 1963, rallied together some young people who wanted to change things. In 1965 they created the MLP (*Mouvement de Libération Populaire*), whose manifesto proclaimed the necessity to politicize the workers, demonstrate in the streets, and arouse the masses to overthrow the bourgeois system of exploitation.

In 1966, Pierre Vallières and Charles Gagnon left the MLP to join the FLQ-66, while the other members of the MLP joined the PSQ (*Parti Socialiste du Québec*) where some senior members like Michel Chartrand were trying to rally unionized workers with a programme similar to that of the NDP (New Democratic Party). During the summer of 1966, the FLQ planted a bomb at La Granade Shoe Company.

Vallières and Gagnon went to the United Nations to plead the cause of the Quebec liberation struggle. They were arrested, brought back to Quebec, and accused of murder, robbery, conspiracy and in fact everything that would keep them behind bars for an indefinite time.

Meanwhile, more adherents were being won to the *Québec Libre* cause. In the elections of June, 1966, surprise! – Lesage's Liberals were defeated. The Union Nationale came back to power with Daniel Johnson as leader. The RIN led by Pierre Bourgault won 10 percent of the votes but did not get any seats. The Union Nationale, however, got more seats than the Liberals with fewer votes.

The number of seats obtained is no real indication of support because the electoral map is unbalanced. The Union Nationale took almost all the county-side, where the counties are over-represented in the Assembly, whereas the Liberals kept the large urban centres where the population per county is larger and consequently under-represented in the Assembly.

What is significant in this election is that during its six years in power the Liberal Party was not able to make the rural population believe that the Liberals represented their interests. The habitants identified Lesage with the Americanization of Quebec, and refused to go along. At this point the Union Nationale could exploit the situation by promising a return to a former 'security'.

The colonizer was not too happy about the Union Nationale's return to power, but soon got over it when Daniel Johnson showed that he was ready to take his turn as Negro-King. With the nationalists he spoke of independence; with American financiers, of internal stability good for investment; with farmers, of better agriculture; with the Clergy, of modernization of rites and rituals; with English-Canadians, of a new federalism; with the city dwellers, of a revival of the 'Quiet Revolution'. Subtle and calculating, Daniel Johnson knew how to give the impression of governing without ever doing so.

Meanwhile in the RIN there was tension between the left and right wings. The left wanted to relate to the workers, support strikes, and institute a radical programme; the right preferred to look for favours from the petit-bourgeoisie.

One member of Lesage's crack team of Liberals, which represented the new lay elite at the service of American and English-Canadian interests, was René Lévesque. Lévesque was becoming ill at ease. He was aware that the crack team was playing the role of Negro-King, and he did not like it. Having some respect for himself as an individual and as a Québécois, he could no longer see himself as a puppet like his Liberal or Union Nationale colleagues. As a Québécois he felt he had to fight for the Québécois. Within the framework of a capitalist economy, this meant fighting for the rise of a Québécois national bourgeoisie which would take charge of the future of the whole Québécois people. Having conceived this kind of alternative, he was now thinking along the same line as the RIN Patriotes.

René Lévesque did not consider getting rid of capitalism and American imperialism in Quebec. His kind of independence means severing the ties of Confederation in order to keep revenues, that are now handed over to the federal government, in Quebec so that the Québécois can benefit from them in a more equitable system of social security. It means 'civilizing' foreign capitalists by asking them to re-invest their profits in Quebec and give more consideration to the population they exploit. It means that the state will aid Québécois enterprises (the bourgeoisie) with credit so that they can be dominant in Quebec and no longer at the mercy of Americans and English-Canadians.

We have seen that our Patriotes of 1837 wanted the same thing: to establish the bourgeoisie as the leadership of the Québécois people; in other words, a national bourgeois revolution.

So, René Lévesque quit the Liberal Party to form the MSA (*Mouvement Souveraineté-Association*) in November, 1967. In the spring of 1968, the left in the RIN quit, and a few months later, those who remained dissolved the RIN with the promise to join Lévesque's MSA. In October 1968, the MSA became the *Parti Québécois*. After 130 years of repression, the movement was reborn.

These new Patriotes wanted to make a national bourgeois revolution in Quebec. They wanted the Québécois middle bourgeoisie to replace the English-Canadian bourgeoisie, to a certain extent, and to negotiate new relations of exploitation with the American capitalists. In order to reach its goal, this Québécois bourgeoisie must take control of the state by way of elections, declare Quebec independence, and negotiate diplomatic, financial and commercial agreements with Ottawa and use all of the state's powers to finance a Québécois capitalist economy.

René Lévesque had rallied a good part of the petit-bourgeoisie and a number of white collar workers to his side. He was now trying to convince the class he was serving, the Québécois middle bourgeoisie, to support him and join his party. Lévesque invited workers of all types to join, but on certain conditions. They could not demand large social changes; they had to accept the capitalist system of exploitation and the leadership of the Québécois bourgeoisie as well as its growing power over the fate of the Québécois people.

While the PQ was slowly but surely consolidating its base and preparing for the electoral contest, other movements were channeling the widespread popular discontent. The Québécois people were beginning to realize how they were being exploited as producers and consumers, and how they have been manipulated by the American capitalists, the English-Canadian bourgeoisie, and by their own elite who play the role of Negro-King. Every day, Québécois were becoming more conscious of their right to sovereignty as a nation and of their dignity as productive workers.

Students were rebelling, striking, and occupying schools and universities. They do not want to be brainwashed into being good, obedient workers or professionals in a system of exploitation which considers them mere instruments of production.

The citizens of the so-called disadvantaged areas were getting together to form committees and engage in a direct struggle against municipal power. Such committees develop workers' solidarity, the consciousness of being exploited and struggling against all those who keep them in that situation. The LIS (*Ligue pour l'Intégration Scolaire*), led by Raymond Lemieux, entered the struggle for unilingualism, starting at St Léonard. The LIS wanted to extend the fight for the Québécois language into every area where it was threatened.

The CSN (Confederation of National Trade Unions or CNTU) was moving farther away from the trade-union mentality, that is the striving for little salary hikes. It was becoming

radical and spoke of a 'second front,' a workers' political struggle against the exploiters. Michel Chartrand, elected president of the Montreal Central Council of the CSN, was increasing his attacks against the capitalist system and all those who support it in Quebec – the Americans, English-Canadians and our sellout elite.

The Left was organizing demonstrations to 'awaken the population.' The St-Jean-Baptiste parade of 1968 turned into bitter fight between demonstrators and the Montreal police in front of the honoured guests in the reviewing stand at Parc Lafontaine. Following this, the municipal authorities created an anti-riot squad – in other words, a little army specialized in repressing demonstrations.

In February, *Opération McGill français* brought out 15,000 demonstrators in front of McGill. The purpose of this demonstration was to expose this university as one the fortresses of English-Canadian and American capitalism, which is keeping the Québécois in a state of economic, political and cultural servitude. Several bombs exploded in Montreal – a few at Eaton's, another at the Montreal Stock Exchange. Three hundred special police hunted for members of the new FLQ-69. Pierre-Paul Geoffroy was arrested, judged and condemned to life imprisonment.

The FLP (*Front de Libération Populaire*) organized a demonstration following the St-Jean-Baptiste '69 parade. There were a few scuffles and the float carrying St-Jean-Baptiste was knocked over. The symbol of the Quebec people's servitude lay on the ground. Québécois youth had knocked down the traditional image that the elite had imposed on the people after the defeat of the Rebellion.

In June, 1969, *Opération Anti-Congrès* brought thousands of workers to the gates of the Quebec Coliseum to ridicule the Union Nationale leadership convention which was actually a circus. The police attacked from helicopters with tear gas.

On October 7th, the day of the Montreal policemen's strike, the MLT (*Mouvement de Libération du Taxi*) and sympathizers attacked the Murray-Hill garage. Murray-Hill is the company which enjoys the monopoly for passenger service between the airport and downtown. The demonstrators burned several buses. The son of the owner, Hershorn, ordered his employees to guard the garage and fire into the crowd if necessary. The employees, guarding from the roof and the windows, did exactly that. Several demonstrators were wounded and one was killed. The fatality turned out to be a certain Dumas of the Provincial Police, an *agent provocateur* disguised as a demonstrator. The inquest into his death concluded that it was impossible to determine who had killed him. This protection of Hershorn and his hired killers is a striking example of justice – Mr. Hershorn belongs to the class that makes the laws, and makes them for its members. 'Justice' accepts the fact that a bourgeois defends his property by shooting people. Bourgeois property has priority over human life. Hershorn's property was more sacred than a man's life.

In that same month of October, the Bertrand government was trying to pass a bill (Bill 63) that would give parents the right to choose the language of instruction in school. This meant that all anglophones and immigrants who chose English would have the right of English schools. The French language, already badly battered, was now to see its inferiority couched in articles of law.

Bill 63 was the legal confirmation of the domination of the colonizer's language. Bertrand, the Negro-King, was forced by the colonizer to run this bill through parliament 'full steam ahead', even though every Québécois was against it. The colonizer wanted his privileges written into the law, in order to have a legal weapon against any movement favouring French unilingualism. All he had to do was play around with the Union Nationale's campaign funds to get caretaker Bertrand to make the necessary arrangements.

The opposition of the Québécois people was clear. For two weeks they demonstrated on the streets all over Quebec, and there were teach-ins and general walk-outs in the universities, Cégeps (community colleges), and secondary schools. One of these demonstrations in Montreal numbered 45,000 people. In front of the Quebec Parliament a gathering of 30,000 people declared their opposition. Officially, this fight against Bill 63 was led by the FQF (*Front du Québec Français*) which included hundreds of organizations of all kinds, among others, the St-Jean-Baptiste Society, the CSN, the CEQ (*Corporation des Enseignants du Québec*), *l'Alliance des Professeurs de Montréal*, and the LIS. But, for most of the demonstrations, the population was mobilized by the *Front Commun Contre le Bill 63*, which rallied more radical groups together, such as the FLP, MSP (*Mouvement Syndical Politique*), LSO (*Ligue Socialiste Ouvrière*), and workers committees.

Bill 63 passed with the support of the Liberals, despite opposition from René Lévesque and a few recalcitrant Union Nationale MPs.

On November 7th, the *Comité de Défense de Vallières et Gagnon* organized a demonstration of several thousand people in front of the Montreal Law Courts. Following the demonstration, some demonstrators broke windows at banks and financial institutions on St. James Street to show the population that the capitalists are the ones who oppress the Québécois people.

There was a climate of insecurity in the bourgeois districts in the province. Anglophones were leaving for Ontario. Some companies were moving to Toronto. American imperialists were keeping a close watch on the evolution of the province. The Québécois people felt the need for great changes.

The Québécois people were once subjected to the old kind of colonialism that kept them in the mines, forests and factories as cheap-labour. Now they are subjected to a new colonialism that still exploits them but, in addition, asks them to disown themselves and become average American robot-consumers, narrow limited individualists. Like rats in a cage, the Québécois are to be conditioned in work, family life and recreation to think only of little possessions, of gadgets to be accumulated, of the security which is like that of a worm in its cocoon.

The Québécois people, those who were the undesirables, who were driven back into the wilderness and then drawn to the cities to be made slaves of the capitalist production system, those who were brutally crushed every time they tried to revolt, are making their entrance into history.

1970 Before October

The Bertrand government had come to the end of its term of office, and to the end of its rope. The American and English-Canadian colonialists, who had never really been confident in the Union Nationale although they had tolerated its return in 1966, were more than ever anxious to see the Liberals in power.

The sloppy caretaker Bertrand called elections for April 29th. The Parti Québécois entered the campaign actively in the country-side with a programme of political reform (Quebec independence) and of social reform (better distribution of wealth within the capitalist system).

The Liberal Party with its new puppet leader, Robert Bourassa, tried to regain power by playing on the Québécois' ingrained fears. He spoke of the flight of capital, the collapse of the Quebec economy and the possibility of a bloody revolution if the PQ ever came to power.

The Union Nationale, following its tactic of trying to please everybody at once, displeased more and more people.

The Social Credit, which is the reactionary federalist party regrouping the rural petit-bourgeoisie and Quebec farmers who are afraid of the great capitalist monopolies, joined the province's contest against the PQ and its 'dirty bearded commie revolutionaries'.

But the enthusiasm for the PQ began to shake Westmount. "Are the people going to elect those dirty separatists who want to eat us all up?" the Anglo-Saxophones asked themselves.

The fear of a Parti Québécois landslide was felt throughout the entire province. Some English had already packed their bags.

But there was nothing to fear. Order was restored, thanks to an electoral system rigged to favor the bourgeois, who are already in power, and block the petit-nationalist bourgeois who try to replace them. The Liberals, along with 'Bourassa-the ideal-caretaker,' came back to power with 44% of the vote and the disproportionate number of 72 seats.

The PQ obtained 24% of the votes but only 7 seats.

The Union Nationale obtained only 20% of the votes, but nevertheless won 17 seats to become the official opposition.

The Créditistes got 11% of the votes and 12 seats.

The disillusionment was great. The Québécois were slowly learning that bourgeois democracy is bourgeois dictatorship; and that any contest for power that follows the rules of those who will not relinquish it is as predictable as a stacked deck of cards.

The Québécois were also learning that those ridings which elect PQ members are the workers' ridings in Montreal. In other words, the Québécois workers are the ones who vote for what seems to be a change, whereas the bourgeois ridings and the francophone petit-bourgeois areas of the metropolis hide behind their dearly-bought Liberal security. The PQ thus found itself in the dilemma of working for the cause of the small and middle bourgeoisie while being supported by the working class. This contradiction, and many others, shook the party.

Proud of their overwhelming majority, fraudulent as it was, the Liberals made a grand gesture. They freed Vallières on bail, Gagnon having been released several months earlier by the Bertrand government.

Some young Québécois, angered by the outcome of the elections, resumed bombing. No week could pass without a few downtown businesses and some private homes in Westmount shaking with an explosion. It became part of the 'normal' way of life in Montreal.

Despite the noise of the intermittent bombings, a heavy silence permeated Québécois society. We were in the trough of a huge wave preparing to crash.

October 1970

On Monday, October 5, James Richard Cross, British Trade Commissioner in Montreal, receives an unscheduled visit in his comfortable mansion on the slopes of Mount Royal. The armed visitors identify themselves as members of the FLQ and ask him to follow them.

Mrs. Cross phones the police. The news spreads like wildfire. An earthquake could not have caused a greater shock.

An FLQ cell called *Libération* tries to get communiqués to certain journalists, but the police intercept them. At a press conference, Minister of Maintenance of Quebec, Jérôme Choquette, spells out the FLQ demands for the release of Mr. Cross:

1. an immediate stop to the police hunt.
2. broadcast of the FLQ Manifesto.
3. liberation of certain political prisoners.
4. their free passage to Cuba or Algeria.
5. the rehiring of the Lapalme drivers.
6. $500,000 in gold ingots.
7. identification of the informer on the last FLQ cell.

Through this action, the FLQ-70 seeks to polarize the social forces at play: on the one hand, the bourgeois class and the state apparatus it has at its disposal; on the other, the working class, the exploited class of Quebec. The FLQ-70 believes that in directly attacking the state apparatus by kidnapping a foreign diplomat, it can help the working class become conscious of its exploitation as well as the strength it can develop through unity to overthrow the bourgeois state.

But since this action does not spring from the very concrete struggle of the workers, since this action seems to be done more *for* the workers than *with* them, it awakens some support but can hardly lead to mobilization of any kind.

Yet this action shakes up the structure of Québécois and Canadian society. The existing social order is threatened. The caretakers have some work cut out for them. In this case, the Great Caretaker himself will take over. The federal government is to take all the decisions in this affair, and the sub-caretaker government of Bourassa simply has the job of carrying them out.

Arrests are made.

Ottawa indicates it is willing to negotiate through a mediator. The *Libération* cell replies that it rejects all mediation.

Ottawa, then, broadcasts the FLQ-70 Manifesto. Following this, the *Libération* cell reduces its demands to two, an immediate stop to the police hunt and the liberation of the political prisoners.

On Friday, October 10, Jérôme Choquette whose Montreal office is in constant contact with Ottawa offers the kidnappers safe conduct to a foreign country in exchange for Cross' release.

Jérôme Choquette has barely finished speaking when Pierre Laporte, Minister of Labour and Immigration in the Bourassa cabinet is kidnapped in front of his St. Lambert home. The Chénier cell that claims to be the author of this second kidnapping re-issues the seven original demands for Laporte's release.

These kidnappings relegate to the background the negotiations under way between the provincial government and the specialists on medicare, as well as the municipal election campaign in Montreal where mayor Jean Drapeau is facing the rise of a real opposition in FRAP (*Front d'action politique*), a coalition of citizens' committees of Montreal.

The government talks of possible negotiations to kill time and give the police a chance to discover the kidnappers' hideouts, but on Thursday, October 15, it rejects the FLQ demands. That same evening, 3,000 people rally in Paul-Sauvé arena to show their support for the FLQ.

Students are starting to move. Classes are boycotted in high schools, *Cégeps* (community colleges) and universities. The FLQ manifesto is discussed everywhere, and everybody is following the match between the government and the FLQ with the greatest interest. Support for the FLQ is mounting in the masses of Quebec. Thousands of Québécois support the goals of the FLQ although they may not endorse the means taken to achieve them. FRAP and the Central Council of the CNTU of Montreal come out with statements to this effect.

In the face of this mounting support, the government panics and imposes the War Measures Act on Quebec. On Friday, October 16, Quebec again witnesses the military occupation of its territory. The *habeas corpus* is again suspended and the police have the right to arrest and search without warrant as well as to detain 'suspects' for three weeks without charging them. More than 12,000 police and soldiers are at work. Over 340 Québécois will be thrown in jail in the coming days. The forces of repression behave like Hitler's SS troops. In the middle of the night, they knock doors down, wake up 'suspects' with machine guns in the ribs, brutalize them, cart them off like criminals and leave behind them terrified women and terrorized children.

Among those arrested are Michel Chartrand, chairman of the Central Council of the CNTU of Montreal, Robert Lemieux, counsel for many political prisoners, Pierre Vallières,

Charles Gagnon, Doctor Serge Mongeau, chairman of the Movement for the Defense of Political Prisoners of Quebec (MDPPQ), poet Gaston Miron, singer Pauline Julien, and journalist Gérald Godin.

The state is hitting back in anger. All FLQ sympathizers or supporters not in jail shut up and duck. The bourgeois state is taking its revenge for the scare it got. The bourgeois have to be reassured.

On Saturday October 17, an anonymous telephone call gives the place where the body of Pierre Laporte can be found. Near the St Hubert air-base the police find the body in the trunk of a car. Searches, arrests, dragnets, questionings continue.

Marcel Pépin, chairman of the CNTU, Louis Laberge, head of the FTQ (Quebec Federation of Labour), Yvon Charbonneau, chairman of the CEQ (Quebec Teachers Association), Claude Ryan, editor-in-chief of *Le Devoir*, René Lévesque, leader of the Parti Québécois, all beg the government to negotiate the release of Mr. Cross.

In spite of all that's going on, the municipal elections of Montreal take place on Sunday, October 25. The Civic Party of the Boss of Montreal, Jean Drapeau, exploits the situation to the full. Drapeau accuses FRAP of being a front for the FLQ. The trick works. His Civic Party takes all the seats while FRAP gets 15 percent of the votes, despite the imprisonment of a number of its candidates and Drapeau's terrorist campaign.

On November 6, Bernard Lortie, alleged member of the Chénier cell, is arrested.

On November 9, Maintenance Minister Jérôme Choquette holds a press conference to tell the underworld it should not fear that the special powers granted the government by the War Measures Act will be used against it. The underworld is reassured.

On November 11, Father Charles Banville, curé of Saint-Paul-de-Matane (Gaspésie), states, "The great majority of the population and the priests of Matane and Matapédia ridings agree with the FLQ manifesto"!

A few days later, the member of the National Assembly for Matane (Gaspésie) advocates the restoration of capital punishment, a compulsory ID card, a very strict control of demonstrations, censorship of the press, TV, movies, the cleaning-up of colleges and universities, a strict ideological training for all teachers and professors and compulsory military service.

The police stick up posters of Marc Carbonneau, Jacques Lanctôt, Paul Rose and Francis Simard with a reward of $150,000 for anyone giving information leading to the arrest of these individuals.

On November 25, at the coroner's inquest into the death of Pierre Laporte, Paul Rose's sister, Lise, refuses to testify and cries out how the police stripped and beat her in her cell. The judge condemns her to six months' imprisonment for contempt of court.

The Provincial Police threaten to go on strike over the criticism of their conduct by some of the politicans.

On December 3, an apartment in number 10,945 on rue des Récollets in Montréal-Nord is surrounded. The *Libération* cell holding Mr. Cross there negotiates his release and its own safe conduct to Cuba. Jacques Lanctôt, his wife and child, Jacques Cossette-Trudel and his wife, Marc Carbonneau and Yves Langlois leave for Cuba on an RCAF plane and Mr. Cross is set free.

On December 28, Paul Rose, Jacques Rose and Francis Simard are arrested in a farmhouse near St. Jean and accused of the murder of Pierre Laporte.

The state apparatus considers it has the guilty ones behind bars and can now start easing the hold of repression while at the same time trying to plaster over the cracks of its public image.

A few hundred 'suspects' are gradually released while the

better-known ones are accused of membership in an illegal organization and seditious conspiracy.

It is now the turn of the judicial arm of the state apparatus to fight those who question its order. The accused accuse the judges and Crown attorneys. The judges fight back with contempt of court charges, expulsions, in-camera sessions and adjournments.

With its image tarnished, the judicial apparatus finds a way to free Chartrand and Lemieux on bail, though Paul Rose is prevented from even attending his own trial.

The reigning order is defending itself while the Québécois are thinking things over.

History is in progress.

Time-Table of History

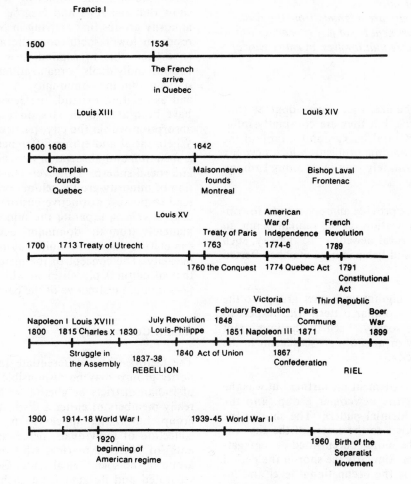

Note: above the line are important reigns and noteworthy events in the metropolis and, below the line, noteworthy events in Quebec.

NOTES
1. Workers produce *value*. Some of this value they get back in their wages. The rest is surplus value that is appropriated by the capitalist.
2. A *commodity* is a product used as exchange value.
2. Persons of Jewish origin form the third largest national group in Montreal. Almost all have become English-speaking rather than French-speaking and now comprise nearly 25 per cent of the English population of Montreal. Thus they must be considered by-and-large part of the English-Canadian nation rather than part of the Québécois.

4. Patterns of Social Adjustment of Indians in the City

Mark Nagler/*Canadian Research Centre for Anthropology, St. Paul University*

This selection, taken from a more extensive analysis of the problems encountered by Indians in the city, nicely illustrates several points made earlier in this volume concerning the interrelatedness of physical, cultural and social space. It tells us something, as well, about the difficulties that attend even the most responsible attempts to render any social space fully public. The claims which, in this case, Indians make are misunderstood because cues are misread owing to the wide cultural differences that exist between them and the varied others with whom they share the city. As Edward Hall warns in his book The Hidden Dimension, *the difference between them and the dominant culture are "basic and have to do with such core values as the use and structuring of space, time, and materials, all of which are learned early in life."*

Moreover, as some of Nagler's informants make so plain, the social distance that exists is not solely because of ethnic differences. Indians new to the city are migrants from the rural environment as well. Their adjustment is not just economic: it is a matter of physical and social scale that involves an entire way of life.

When Indians attempt to urbanize, they must adopt at least some urban behaviour patterns, but they are constantly influenced by their traditional and rural background. Many of the severe physical, social, and economic problems which new city dwellers face are disproportionately manifest among Indians, the most recent urban arrivals:

> ...immigrant populations provide an opportunity for observing the impact of urbanization on the human being. In the accommodation of the rural newcomer to the city, such transformation in thought and behaviour as may be effected may be traced.[1]

The majority of the earlier migrant newcomer groups to the city have followed essentially a similar pattern with respect to place in the economy and in society. Each of the immigrant strains found its port of entry or area of first settlement in the older blighted sections of the city.

> The longer the period of settlement the farther out was the medium location point of the newcomer group, and the more dispersed was its residential pattern. The shorter the period of settlement, the closer to the centre of the city was its medium location, and the more concentrated or segregated was its residential pattern. Similarly the shorter the period of settlement, the lower was the occupational level and income of the newcomers. The longer the period of settlement, the higher the educational and occupational level and income. Finally, with respect to social status, a common pattern was also visible. Each of the newcomer groups was in turn greeted with hostility, suspicion, distrust, prejudice, and discriminatory practices. With the passage of time each of the newcomer groups climbed the economic ladder to achieve access to the broader social and cultural life of the community and increased general acceptability.

The patterns by which immigrant groups became 'Canadianized' indicate in general the process by which the newest newcomers – the Canadian Indian – will make the transition from traditional behaviour in their rural areas of origin to urbanism as a way of life. The process of acculturation will be similar in many respects to the process by which immigrants before them settled in Canadian cities. This is not to say that there will not also be differences arising from greater visibility and differences in cultural background.[2]

In this study, the term urban adjustment is used to define myriad patterns of association and accommodation to the urban complex. Such adjustment entails association with institutions and organizations, both formal and informal, which embrace the economic, social, political, religious, and perhaps

Reprinted from *Indians in the City*, by Mark Nagler, by permission of the author and The Canadian Research Centre for Anthropology, St. Paul University, Ottawa. © 1970.

even psychological spheres.

'Successful adjustment' not only includes participation in and association with these aspects of the community, but also the development of precise relationships to such institutions as the law and to members of the community at large.

For example, the studies by Wirth[3] and Drake and Cayton[4] show that the Jews and Negroes respectively, like most other minority groups first arriving in North American cities, tend to reside in lower socio-economic areas. The Jews in particular have been able to expand their patterns of association with various individuals, organizations, and institutions of higher status within the community. As their levels of communication and association expand, the Jews, like most minority groups, have been able to embark on a slow but persistent pattern of absorption within the city, particularly in the economic sphere. Where racial and ethnic differences are not readily observable, association and absorption may also take place in the religious and social spheres. However, complete integration and absorption of minority groups seldom occurs because minority groups tend to possess distinctive customs which, in addition to racial distinctiveness, separate the minority group more or less permanently from the dominant society. However, North American culture does not require cultural, social, and religious homogeneity. The concept of the melting-pot has been replaced by that of cultural pluralism in which pride is taken in the practices that are distinctive of the participating minority groups.

Indian Community

The factors which differentiate Indians from other urban minority groups may be responsible for the lack of development of Indian districts or ghettos within Toronto. Indians are not really members of either a distinctive cultural, racial, or ethnic group, but rather appear to be members of an amorphous collection of individuals, descendants of the 'original inhabitants' of North America, who may gradually evolve into a group in the sociological sense. Geographically they have been separated and isolated from each other, and several different patterns of culture have evolved.

This lack of commonality is illustrated by the following incident at a tavern in the Jarvis-Dundas area of Toronto. A lone Indian, seated in the corner, was encountered by the author who from previous visits to this bar had developed an acquaintance with five Indians at another table. This lone Indian had just arrived in Toronto. After a brief conversation the author remarked, "At least two of those fellows across from us came from the same area as you [Six Nations]. Why don't you ask them to help you find what you are looking for?"

"Don't be silly. Would you ask a Japanese or a nigger for help?"

"But they are Indians."

"So what. They can understand me like a nigger understands you. My friends are from my own place and I don't know them."

Indians do not possess any of the common attributes which those of distinctive ethnic and minority groups usually have. Racial distinctiveness is not usually an attribute which is applied to Indians in the ethnological or anthropological sense. Indians may possess racial characteristics that are very similar to those of Caucasians, while others demonstrate racial characteristics that are more 'oriental'. North American Indians have sometimes been designated as 'members of the Red Race'. Racial categorization is not universally accepted as there is so much diversity in the physical characteristics of these people.

But they are all labelled 'Indian' and their subsequent treatment is influenced by this identification. This outside group definition is an important factor in their group development.

The failure to acknowledge commonality prevents the creation of Indian communities within the urban place. To have racial or ethnic 'neighbourhoods', there must be an acknowledgement by those who would form the 'community' of some common background. The factors which might act as communal ties are non-existent among the diversified Indian population in North America. Only in the case of specific areas and specific projects, such as the Denver Navaho Relocation program,[5] is it possible to transpose a group of Indians from a reserve area into a relatively specific urban neighbourhood. Indians come to the city from a variety of locations, and most of them do not possess the common bonds which would bring them together.

Also preventing the emergence of Indian 'neighbourhoods' is the fact that most reserves are located near urban areas, or in areas that may be easily reached.

Most immigrants, when relocating in North American urban areas, have been exposed to the cultural and social shock of being almost completely separated from their places of origin. It is difficult, if not impossible, for most foreign immigrants to return to their homelands; because immigrants cannot easily maintain personal relationships with their homeland, in North America they tend to create their own 'ghettos'. Indians, on the other hand, do not suffer as complete a social and cultural shock as do most immigrants, for they can easily return to their reserve with a minimum of effort and expense.

The reserve, therefore, continues to act as a social and cultural centre for many Indians who may reside in Toronto or other cities. Indians in the blue collar and transitional categories usually maintain strong ties with their home reserves. Likewise, most white collar Indians tend to maintain a relationship with their reserve friends. It appears that the white collar workers and skilled blue collar workers maintain their reserve relationships even more than other Indians, as in addition to visiting their former homes they also remain in contact through written correspondence.

The majority of Indians in Toronto are located in an area bounded by the Don Valley expressway on the east, Bloor Street on the north, Church Street on the west, and King Street on the south. This concentration of Indians has not, however, had the effect of creating any Indian organizational structure which could even be vaguely construed as the beginnings of an Indian 'urban reserve'. In this Toronto district one finds large concentrations of individuals of lower socio-economic status. There are cheap accommodations, restaurants, bars, and hostels. It is low socio-economic status which draws many Indians

into this area, but lower socio-economic status does not in itself create the conditions necessary to spawn 'Indian urban neighbourhoods'.

Table 1 presents some of the factors which serve to differentiate the urban process of urban assimilation and absorption from those of other immigrant and migrant groups.

Broom and Kitsuse[6] have said:

Many Indians are attempting to validate their acculturation by moving into the larger stream of American life. Many of them are not sufficiently acculturated to behave within the larger system; or, on the other hand, the acculturative experience of some has been defective, or has had a corrosive effect upon them. At best, Indian enclave communities and parallel ethnic institutions are only at an incipient stage of development in most communities.

Perhaps these Indian enclaves will not emerge, and Indians may become directly assimilated into urban areas.

Social Assistance

The majority of the white and blue collar Indian workers are permanently adjusted to urban life and many of them are becoming integrated members of the urban milieu. On the other hand, members of the 'transitional Indian group'* demonstrate unstable patterns of adjustment. Similarly, some of those Indians who use the city for short-term purposes, such as the seasonal workers and those who journey to Toronto to secure supplies and entertainment, exemplify under-developed patterns of urban association and adjustment.

Of the Indian population in Canada, thirty-eight percent are on some type of welfare[7] while only eight percent of the total Canadian population receives such aid. The number of Indians receiving welfare benefits in urban areas cannot readily be determined.

Many Indians who are not permanent city residents have become relatively skilled in utilizing the social welfare facilities available in the city. These Indians are adept in soliciting the aid of various social agencies that are able to provide free meals, accomodation, and employment. In Toronto the Scott Mission and the Salvation Army hostel, the Harbour Light, together with such organization as the Good Shepherd, provide these services. In addition, civic and private welfare agencies provide funds which are usually sufficient to meet minimal living expenses.

White collar, established blue collar, and seasonal workers seldom appear on the welfare rolls. Of the transitional Indian group, those who are students and of Indian status may obtain assistance in the form of student support. This permits them to acquire training, and is provided mainly by the Indian Affairs Branch.

Indians receive federal government aid on their reserves. It has been hypothesized that in many instances this aid has had the effect of retarding their desire for achievement, and of preventing many of them from seeking independence either on the reserve or within the urban setting. However, the limited scope of this study did not reveal sufficient evidence to validate this hypothesis.

One type of social welfare aid which Indians receive in the urban setting is provided by civic or private authorities. This

Table I: Characteristics of Migrants Groups to Urban Areas

Acknowledged Characteristics	Rural Migrant	Foreign Immigrant	Indian Migrant
1. Common ethnicity	No	Yes	No
2. Proximity to home	Yes	No	Yes
3. Common culture	No	Yes	No
4. Strong family ties	No	Yes	Usually yes
5. 'Ghetto' urban formation	No	Yes	No
6. Language problems	No	Yes	Yes
7. Cultural traits			
A. Saving and security	Yes	Yes	No
B. Established organization	Yes	Yes	No
C. Common language	Yes	Yes	No

*The transitional Indian group are those Indians who desire to become urban in all aspects, but who have not as yet maintained permanent residence in the city.

assistance permits its recipients to maintain themselves, at least to a minimal extent, in the urban area. Its Indian recipients may find living conditions superior to those which they experienced in their reserve environments. Twenty-one of the Indians encountered in the course of the study had been on welfare for long periods of time. These individuals expressed little or no desire to change their life pattern.

Indians brought into the city under the auspices of Program 5 and similar programs receive funds from civic, provincial, and municipal authorities in order that they may participate in specific educational endeavours. Upon completion of their programs, the majority of these Indians are supposed to become self-supporting individuals. Those interviewed who had received this type of assistance remained in Toronto or some other urban area, as the skill or trade which they had acquired was not usually in demand within the reserve setting.

Thirty-five of the Indians in the present study received social assistance from municipal and private authorities. Nine respondents received assistance to qualify for educational programs. It is impossible to ascertain how many received assistance on the reserve, as many of them would receive it indirectly and not be aware of its existence. The attitude of the Indian toward receiving assistance is difficult to assess. Those enrolled in government training programs expressed tempered gratitude as they desired to obtain the educational benefits which the assistance permitted, but they resented being subject to or controlled by outside authority. An example of this situation was expressed by a twenty-three-year-old Indian enrolled in Program 5.

> I arrived here last fall. Every so often I have to go to the Indian Affairs Branch. Usually I get money orders. Have you ever walked into a store with a money certificate for $3.18 to buy a shirt? They look at you. You are different. Of course we are different, but why do you do this? I would pay them back but that type of control by my supervisor is not right. Why can't they give us cheques?

This situation occurred only among those individuals enrolled in programs under the supervision of the Indian Affairs Branch. Seven individuals who had completed their program training, and who subsequently obtained permanent work in Toronto, maintained that at the time of their assistance they felt alienated because of the way in which it was dispensed. Social assistance can be a stigma to those who receive it, when it tends to distinguish them from others. Some Indians felt that government supervision was probably necessary. In retrospect, they felt that during their training periods, which took place during the course of their initial exposure to the city, they were in no position to manage funds efficiently as "we may have gotten boozed up."

Nine of the Indians interviewed who had recently arrived in the city were not aware of the existence of social welfare. An Indian woman from the Hudson Bay area commented, "You mean I can get money and not work? Where – what do you have to do for them?"

Organizational Participation

There are two organizations in Toronto which have as their main interest the welfare of Indians. These two organizations are the Indian Friendship Centre and the Indian-Eskimo Association. The former organization is primarily a grouping of Indians, while the latter is organized and operated primarily by whites for the benefit of Indians.

The Indian Friendship Centre is becoming a focal point for many Indians visiting, relocating, or residing in the city. Centres like it have been developing in many of the major metropolitan areas of Canada since 1957, including Vancouver, Calgary, Edmonton, Regina, Winnipeg, Kenora, and Toronto. Although each Friendship Centre is organized differently, they all strive to act as counselling, referral, courtwork, and social service agencies. They usually receive grants from various levels of government, and in some instances they are sponsored by a church-centred group. The organizations function primarily through the voluntary services of Indians and non-Indians. In some cases other organizations help to extend the Centres' programs.

The main purpose of the Friendship Centre is to aid the Indians' adjustment to the urban world. It is aware of the problems which are faced, not only by Indian arrivals but also by long-term city residents. Its main concerns are to institute programs such as educational services, and to act as a coordinating body to direct Indians to agencies that are able to deal with the problems they encounter in Toronto.

On occasion, the Friendship Centre institutes programs in conjunction with such other organizations as the YMCA and Alcoholics Anonymous. Other programs, such as those of employment agencies and, to a lesser extent, social welfare agencies, are channelled through the Centre in order to make its members and associates aware of facilities available in the urban community and how to take advantage of them.

The Centre experiences difficulties in solving all the needs of Indians. To meet these requirements, substantial financial resources and organizational expansion would be required. The Friendship Centre cannot contact all of the Indians who are in the city, or who enter the city, but only those who choose to take advantage of its facilities. It makes a concerted effort to publicize the existence of its facilities in the reserve areas around Toronto. In spite of this publicity many Indians within Toronto never visit the Centre, either because they cannot find it or because they have no idea of its existence.

> One of the major failures of the Centre is its restricted ability to be in contact with all Indians within the Community. If the Centre, because of its structure cannot do it, then it ought to erect para-centre structures that could successfully reach the at present unreachable.[8]

Another of the major functions which the Centre may accomplish is to co-ordinate welfare and social services available within the community. Indians in most metropolitan areas experience difficulty in obtaining employment, social welfare, and other benefits which are available only through specific agencies. Those in charge of employment services, social welfare agencies, and other similar facilities may not be aware of the agencies which Indians must contact in regard to specific situations. Many Indians, especially those not versed in the ways of the city, may be sent from one welfare agency to another, and in the process become discouraged.

The Friendship Centre is endeavouring to eliminate situations of this type. The organization strives with other concerned bodies, to organize a scheme or system so that Indians arriving in the city can embark on a definitive program to secure their maintenance. It has encountered only limited success, as many welfare agencies and people in authority are apparently not interested in the adjustment problems faced by Indians. Efforts of co-ordination within Toronto have sometimes led to confusion and antagonism between the Centre and other welfare organizations.

The Centre endeavours to proceed through group work programs rather than individual services, as it is difficult, given their present resources, to formulate specific programs for each newcomer. Some services for migrant Indians must be organized on an individual basis in order to solve such problems as employment and housing, but the Centre's functions also go beyond solving the immediate concerns of new arrivals. The established urban Indian is also served by the Friendship Centre through services of a different nature, represented more in terms of group activity. Many Centres, such as the one in Toronto, have consciously developed a social program organized to create national pride in Indian identification.

In view of the fact that there is no uniform Indian culture, many Indians who visit the Centre feel they cannot easily establish social contact with other Indians there. The Centre attempts to create a congenial atmosphere so that its users can communicate in an environment free from tension. One tension-relieving device is the Centre's program of employing as large an Indian staff as possible. However, problems occur because there are only a few Indians qualified to administer the programs and functions of the Centre. In some cases, Indians would rather communicate with non-Indians than acknowledge their inadequacies and difficulties to members of their own group. While some Indians refuse to talk about their problems with Indians, others refuse to converse with whites concerning similar problems. To overcome this situation, group programs are undertaken, as Indians are in many instances able to communicate their problems and arrive at solutions more readily within a group atmosphere.

The larger centres, such as the one in Toronto, organize programs for teens, home-makers, and other segments of the Indian population, not only through their own programming, but also in co-operation with outside organizations.

Programming is thus the major function of the Centre's work:

Whether adjustment will be successful depends greatly on the opportunity for the Indian to learn a little about his environment through as tension free programs as possible. It is imperative that the program director be knowledgeable about 'Indian culture' as well as white culture if he wants to secure stability and consistency of process in the urbanization of the Indian. Such a process is likely to produce better results if, after a certain period of programming within the city, the program moves out to some community facilities where the Indian can be offered the opportunity of crosscultural experiences with non-Indian persons interested in the same activities. Even activities restricted entirely to Indians would have some benefits if they took place in premises other than the Centres.

The program director must strive for a well balanced program which should encompass activities being held within and without the Centre as well as activities for all age groups of both sexes, varied according to the degree of acculturation of each specific group. In addition, program activities must meet the following basic emotional needs which are inherent in most individuals: companionship, opportunities to create, enjoyment (or freedom from tension), sense of achievement, social recognition, sense of well-being and relaxation from tensions caused by job or other difficulties of adjustment.[8]

The Indian Friendship Centre appears to be the most influential organization within the city endeavouring to promote successful urban adjustment among the Indians. However, reaction toward the Centre varies. A white collar Indian who participates actively in the Centre commented:

Since the Centre moved to Beverley (Street) I have been making an effort to come to the Centre, or to have my wife come to the Centre, twice a week. We can both help these

people to get located in the city and to obtain employment. However, we don't want to become socially too involved with the Centre as we would have our bedrooms filled every night. I was able to obtain an education and I really desire to make things easier for as many Indians as possible. Unfortunately, as in all organizations, there is probably only a few of us who care, and who are doing the work. I think the Centre is a great institution but I will not do all the work. I think more resources should be contracted to the Centre as unfortunately a great deal of, especially, government funds are given to the Indian-Eskimo Association who employ people who give stupid talks and who organize expensive conventions for themselves to go to. If you ever want to see professional conference makers and conference goers, you should see the Indian-Eskimo Association, conferences here, conferences there – a big conference in Winnipeg that cost the Federal Government probably thousands, and what do they do – they draw up a few memorandums, and at times they give the Centre some help. As far as I am concerned it is a completely useless organization, and it is not even an Indian organization anyway.

Another Indian white collar worker said:

The Indian Friendship Centre is for Indians just coming into the city who need help. We have no time to help these people as we have our own responsibilities, and we are not members because they do not need us. You only join a group when you need them and they need you.

An Indian in the transitional category made the following observation:

I came here (to the Centre) with a friend of mine who has been living in the city for some time. They sent me to the Indian Affairs Organization [probably the Indian Affairs Branch]. Through them I was able to be accommodated and go to school. I come to the Centre now for fun. You meet a lot of people here and usually one is lonely in the city.

For some Indians the organization is only a social centre, but for others it has served as an employment agency and a planning organization. As the functions of the Centre are recognized it may be able to obtain more government aid.

It is impossible to assess the success of the Indian Friendship Centre in any concrete terms such as services offered, adjustment opportunities, or the number of Indians who may directly or indirectly benefit through the Centre's direction. But by the very nature of its program this organization is the prime association which provides the directives, resources, and facilities necessary to promote the urban adjustment of Indians.

The Indian-Eskimo Association, like the Indian Friendship Centre, has counterparts in many larger communities. Its goals are to "insure that Indians, Métis, and Eskimos have opportunities to progress and fulfillment equal to other Canadians." To achieve this goal the Indian Eskimo Association aims to:

(1) assist them in breaking the cycle of poverty among native peoples

(2) shift the emphasis from relief to employment, restoring dignity and self-respect

(3) help native people who leave the reserve adjust to modern urban life

(4) help Indians and Eskimos get the education they require for today's industrial society.

The organization "studies the problems and opportunities for Indians and Eskimos, provides a sounding board for all organizations concerned with improving the lot of native citizens, encourages the native people to develop their own programs, promotes better understanding between the native peoples and the Canadian public, and seeks to improve existing services through consultation with government."*

The Indian-Eskimo Association may do all these things as claimed. The goals are general and it is difficult to pinpoint the specific efforts and programs which are supposed to work toward accomplishing these goals. The Association sponsors conventions which are intended to bring interested and informed individuals together to discuss various facets of the so-called Indian problem. Some of these conventions appeared loosely organized and relatively ineffective. An example is the Winnipeg Convention in October, 1966, to discuss urban problems of Canadian Indians. With the exception of the keynote speaker, most participants, and particularly some of the important resource people, seemed to have little acquaintance with the problems at hand. Many of the Indian participants were utilized as 'show pieces' rather than participants. During the final evening of the convention an entertainment program was held during which Indians from across the country gave a display of 'Indian dancing'. This display had all the appearances of a freak show. A reporter for the *Winnipeg Free Press*, who wished to remain unnamed, stated:

To use Indians in a display of this nature is not only childish and disrespectful to the Indians, but it has in fact defeated the whole purpose for which this convention was called. By performing thus these Indians create the impression that they are nothing more than the common stereotype of the Tom Clappers of Indians resident on backward reserves. A social performance of this sort should give an audience a true picture of a segment of Indian culture, but in view of the fact that Indian culture is apparently an amorphous term referring to a multitude of Indian practices, such display can hardly be held to be a meaningful example of Indian culture.

The conventions may act as sounding boards for preparation of briefs to the Indian Affairs Branch, and they may increase public awareness of the Indian 'problem'.

One Friendship Centre official expressed the view that the "Indian-Eskimo Association support of our activities is not what it should be." He maintained:

Unfortunately the Indian-Eskimo Association appears to be an organization of individuals who are professional conference creators and conference goers. As far as I am concerned the data in their reports is frequently in error, or of such elementary scope that it could not be of much use to anybody. A good example was that urban conference last fall where there was only one useful speech given by 'a successful Indian' and this speech was subsequently mimeographed and given to all participants. Why did they not just send a copy of the speech to everybody who attended the convention and forget it? In the first place, surely they must realize that the problem which Indians face in Canada is to a great extent regionally determined, as such a national conference can do little more than act as a sounding board for gross generalities. To debate urban difficulties of Canadian Indians one should hold regional conferences in areas that possess the same social, economic and psychological environment. A National conference on such issues is like having a National conference on the weather – so what.

Although the Indian-Eskimo Association is making efforts to publicize 'the Indian problem', their efforts appear to be duplicated by the activities of the Indian Affairs Branch and the

*Membership application form.

Indian Friendship Centre. Some Indians in the white collar category prefer to use this organization for their own advancement and publicity. In essence, this organization may be using 'the Indian problem' as an excuse for its own existence. It has been able to solicit financial support and personnel to carry on its own program, but it may not really perform a worthwhile function in terms of the movement to aid the Indian.

There are other organizations in which Indians participate within the city. Members of the white collar category in particular participate in such organizations as service clubs, political parties, and, to a lesser extent, religious and social organizations. The blue collar workers participate in such organizations, and the other categories defined seldom, if ever, participate in formal or voluntary organizations.

Unlike members of other minority groups, Indians in the city have not created their own permanent organizations which function in social, economic, political, or religious areas. Many social clubs have emerged within the city at one time or another, but they inevitably disband. There are reasons which explain why these 'Indian organizations' fail to become permanent. As previously discussed, Indians do not possess a common ethnic or cultural background. Except for the Iroquois, Indians seldom acknowledge their tribal identity. In essence, Indians in Toronto and most other Canadian communities lack ties of commonality which could act as bonds to bring them together.

When a small number of urban Indians desire to create formal or informal groups, they often meet with hostility and lack of cooperation from other Indians in the community. Large numbers of Indians within the urban setting are sceptical because Indian organizations frequently claim to speak for all Indians. In view of the fact that Indians have not developed any *esprit de corps*, they resent and tend to work against any Indian sub-group which may pretend to represent them within the urban matrix. Occasionally, social organizations like the Thunderbird Club emerge on a short-term basis, but support for them diminishes and they subsequently falter. These organizations have become "wild social clubs which organize wild free-for-alls." Thus when such organizations are formed, they are seen by many Indians as a threat to Indian self-interest. Hence pressure is applied to hinder Indian organizational development.

One Indian merchant noted:

I don't like Indian groups. We have enough trouble as Indians in the city. In Toronto the Thunderbird Club proved very wild. We Indians have enough trouble without creating more, besides no organization knows all the Indians. I want to speak for myself and I don't want anyone to speak for me.

This undermining of potential Indian organizations hinders the development of leadership. Indians in Toronto and other centres do not have acknowledged leaders who may represent them on a community level. The Indian-Eskimo Association or Friendship Centre spokesmen may act as 'Indian leaders' but they are seldom widely acknowledged by Indians as legitimate spokesmen. Indians generally acknowledge in the broadest sense only the fact that 'they are Indians'. Indians have not yet developed a set of objectives and goals for which they strive as a group. When and if these objectives are agreed upon, Indian power groups may be formed to accomplish these objectives.* But it is difficult, if not impossible, to establish such power groups among a population that refrains from acknowledging

*In 1968-69 a National Indian Brotherhood was formed in Canada. At the time of writing, it is impossible to tell what direction this group will take and how effective it will be.

itself as an existent group in the sociological sense.

In many instances the problems which Indians face are derived from the fact that they are relatively unorganized. They have no established means of communicating or relating their inhibitions and frustrations. Alcohol becomes a social agent which not only permits them to resolve at least temporarily their frustrations, but also serves as a source of recreation.

Alcohol Consumption

To Indians who are not members of the white collar category, the consumption of alcohol has become one of the main sources of recreation. Among the lower categories of Indians it also provides a strong motivating force for economic activity, for without financial resources it is impossible to purchase liquor. In the lower-class bars of the Jarvis-Church area of Toronto, one frequently finds Indians drinking. In general for these Indians there are no negative consequences in becoming 'drunks'. Some drink for the sole purpose of getting drunk because there are few, if any, accepted cultural inhibitions against the use of alcohol. In white society there is usually guilt and stigma attached to inebriation.

Alcoholism among Indians appears to be negligible because it is impossible to drink unless one can obtain financial resources. According to Dailey[9] the alcoholic problem for the Indian is:

> ... not one that involves a threat to health – but rather an economic problem in that a greater proportion of cash income may be spent on drink rather than on the essentials of modern living.... The modern day Indian is not facing the problem of food shortage.... Nowadays the Indian has a number of welfare agencies from which to derive the necessities of life if he cannot afford to secure them for himself. Certainly the Indian has a sense of security insofar as relief is readily available, but from the point of view of most whites, this is not a desirable situation.

In spite of the fact that Indians in the blue collar, transitional, and urban user categories may drink excessively, the author did not find any Indians who could be considered alcoholics. According to studies by Dailey[10] and Littman[11] very few Indians turn up in hospitals or clinics with the organic complications of alcoholism. If anything, the excessive drinker in the Indian population is more likely to develop tuberculosis and other diseases which may strike when resistance has been lowered through over-indulgence and concomitant dietary deficiencies.

Because the economic resources of most drinking Indians are generally low, alcoholic beverages must be secured in quantities large enough to share, and therefore they tend to confine themselves to the consumption of the cheapest alcohol, which is usually beer, sherry, and apple cider. At no time in Toronto did the author encounter Indians resorting to drinking alcohol substitutes such as vitalis or rubbing alcohol. In Vancouver some Indians in the skid row area, especially the prostitutes, are addicted to narcotics, but in Toronto, drinking and 'social thrills' were limited to consuming legal alcoholic beverages.

The type of drinking and the social attitudes toward drinking are undergoing change. In Toronto, as in most places in Canada, Indians may consume liquor legally. Therefore the Indian 'gulping habit' and 'alley drinking' are beginning to disappear. There still remain some Indians who do not know that the interdiction concerning alcohol has been removed, and they are still secretive about their drinking and show considerable apprehension when questioned on such behaviour. Bootlegging has declined as a result of the removal of interdiction, but Dailey[12] finds in his study that it is still as prevalent on weekends and after hours among Indians as it is among non-Indians.

The major difference between Indian and white drinking patterns seems to lie not so much on what is consumed, but rather in attitudes towards its use. Many Indians drink to get drunk although the reasons may be different. None the less, drinking, and drinking to get intoxicated remain a desired end. Little, if any, prestige falls on an Indian who can hold his liquor, nor do Indians compete with one another in drinking bouts to determine capacity.

It appears that Indian drinking is a social pastime which serves as recreation and a response to frustration and boredom. One seldom sees an Indian drinking alone, as much of his satisfaction is derived from the social environment in which the drinking takes place.

Criminal Offences

Although official statistics are not available, the number of Indians arrested for alcoholic offences is probably much higher than for any other group. In Toronto, in the lower class bars of the Dundas-Jarvis area, one notices many intoxicated or semi-intoxicated Indians. A sergeant of detectives maintained that there exists an unofficial dictum to arrest only those Indians who are the cause of major public disturbances. He said:

> On practically any day of the week we could load up the paddy wagon, but such procedure would only cause increased public expense, inefficiency, and book work. There is not too much point in having these Indians become public wards on our account, because we have more important matters to be concerned with.

The Indian's relationship with alcohol is not the only cause of his frequent difficulties with the law. In addition to alcohol, the two most common offences for which Indians are arrested are vagrancy and prostitution.

Sometimes those who are arrested for vagrancy may not understand the offense. Those who arrive in the city from distant areas do not realize they are committing an offense by being without funds, as they are in the habit of walking around without money. As in the case of alcohol offenses, arresting officers sometimes choose to ignore these 'potential vagrants'.

Indian prostitution is in evidence in the city. The five Indian prostitutes who were interviewed were 'self-employed'. All of the girls had been arrested and convicted at least three times. They apparently became prostitutes as a reaction to their economic situation, as they were unskilled and could obtain only very low-paying jobs in domestic service and other similar pursuits. They claimed that they had to resort to prostitution to pay for rent, clothing, and entertainment. For them prostitution has not always meant an easy way to make a living. Three of the girls had been beaten up severely, and sometimes they were unable to "collect for their efforts". Although the girls interviewed claimed that they were not working for an agent, they maintained that there are advantages in such an arrangement, as "you can always keep part of what you earn." One of the girls had previously worked for an agent and she related that "it may be just as difficult to work for pimps because sometimes they don't pay you enough, and if you collect and hold back, you will be beaten up and wish you were dead."

The prostitutes solicited the lower-class hotels and bars in the Jarvis, Church, Dundas area. None of them had ever worked at the upper-class hotels and bars, as people there were interested in "high class professionals, and those types of hooks are not interested in Indian girls." Prostitution may not pay for some of these girls. Three claimed to have friends who had been 'hookers,' but who had subsequently gone straight. "At least at $10 a day you can always receive your money." "A good hooker can earn as much as $100 a day," but these girls seldom earned more than $30 to $35 a day.

Two of the prostitutes interviewed were only temporary residents of the city. They claimed that they resorted to prostitution in order to pay their bills and return to their reserves.

Patterns of offences amongst Indians are typical 'lower class patterns of legal violations.' As Indians gradually integrate or assimilate within urban communities, their criminal patterns will probably become more evenly distributed throughout all 'levels' of crime.

Attitudes of Urban Indians to their Ancestry

Many of those Indians interviewed illustrated stable patterns of urban adjustment. Most of these adjusted Indians are white collar and blue collar workers. They are scattered throughout Metropolitan Toronto and do not demonstrate any signs of uniting into a community-type organization or neighbourhood.

These Indians can be analysed according to their attitude toward their ancestry. That is, some Indians readily identify and are proud of their ancestry, and they usually participate in both Indian and non-Indian activities and organizations. A white collar Indian who has been teaching in the region for twenty years commented:

I do very well in Toronto. The reasons I have been fortunate to be where I am are in no doubt due to my parents and the priest who were responsible for me staying in school, and finally becoming a teacher. Indians need others, preferably Indians, to act as 'influences' to guide them along so that they may acquire the necessary tools for participation and self-sustaining activity in city life. This is probably the main difficulty. These individuals need the guidance of those qualified to give them advice. By my own experience I have learned the ropes, so to speak. I spend a lot of my free time at the Friendship Centre helping Indians who are in similar positions to what I was when I was young.

But, I also, and by I, I mean myself and my family, belong to and participate in activities and organizations which are not Indian. When you live in a mixed society it is important for you to mix with some elements of the society. You can't mix with all of them because you just don't have the time, and you have to select appropriately. My children have never had any difficulty mixing. My family is proud of all our ties and we try to do our share insofar as keeping the obligations are concerned.

Another Indian who planned on entering university commented:

Yes, some day I will be a successful Indian. I have been told that it is difficult to be successful and to be Indian because, unfortunately, those of your Indian friends who cannot make it by themselves begin to rely on you and expect all sorts of things from you. I think successful Indians in many cases are more or less forced to give up their Indian associations. I hope I don't have to because I don't know.

There are other Indians in the white and blue collar categories who believe that their Indian ancestry only serves to inhibit their general participation and advancement in the various respects of urban life. One Indian athlete chased the author from his premises when he discovered the intent of the interview. He was under the impression that the author had intended doing a magazine article. His comments were: "Get the hell out of here. People like you are always trying to stir up trouble. Just leave us alone. Don't bother me again."

An Indian civil servant commented:

I don't like to let people know I am an Indian. Right away you are different. They treat you differently. In the government anyway they like to show off their successful Indians. It is also difficult for my children. They don't admit they are Indian. That just causes problems. We spend most of our time by ourselves, although we do belong to the church and the Y. At the Y my boy participates in everything, and my oldest son who is fourteen is just beginning to go out with girls. I don't think my children have any Indian friends. We are not Indians, we are Canadians. I do not have to help other Indians. I had enough of being an Indian when I was young.

However, I go home to see my family in North Bay. There we have some friends who are all Indian, but being an Indian just does not work in Toronto. I myself can't do anything for them. I want to do the best for my family. If I do my best I am not Indian.

Some Indians, like the two described, seldom acknowledge their Indian background. When these Indians must maintain affiliations with their families and other Indians, they tend to compartmentalise their relationships. They do not want their non-Indian associates to be aware of their Indian ties. These people feel that Indian identification serves to inhibit their functioning economically, politically, and particularly socially, within the urban environment.

In addition to the preceding two groups there are some Indians in the white and blue collar categories who are ambivalent concerning their Indian status. One of these observed:

I don't care what you call me. Whether you think I am Indian or not, I don't care. I work with people who are not Indian, and I live beside them, but most of my friends are Indian. They are at the Friendship Centre and sometimes we play sports together. But I just live. When you are doing television repairs in Toronto it doesn't matter whether you are Indian or not. When I go out on call for the company the people I visit just want their appliances fixed. They don't care whether I'm Indian or not. It doesn't make any difference. This is why I live in Toronto. In Toronto it doesn't make any difference, but if I was living in a small town, even St. Catharines, I don't think I could get a job because I am Indian, at least the type of job I have here in Toronto. I made $6,400 last year. I did not make all that in repair work as I made money at night on a gardening crew, but no Indian makes that kind of money in small towns. There you have to be an Indian. Here it does not make any difference. My children know a few Indians here in the city but they have friends who are both Indian and not. I want them to grow up here in Toronto because if they know how to get along with these people, it will be better for them.

For some Indians, personal perceptions dictate priorities of importance which may influence them to disguise their Indian background. There are also a few Indians, particularly in the white collar group, who may obtain 'mileage' out of the fact that they have Indian ancestry. These individuals may be involved in 'Indian associated organizations'. Usually these Indians believe in the goals toward which they are working, but some of them become involved in these activities for personal glory and are only marginally interested in the goals of the organization.

Those who appear to be ambivalent about their Indian status usually are satisfied with city life, and not at all concerned with problems of discriminatory practices. One Indian of this type commented:

It really does not matter whether you are an Indian or not. There are those who cry because they are Indian, and not getting anywhere. They are not getting anywhere because they are lazy or because they just don't know how. Then there are other guys like that – on the stage. He really enjoys being an Indian, and he really thinks he is god's gift. The ones you call adjusted I guess are like me. I don't care. I do my work. I am what I am, that's what everybody should be.

NOTES

1. Hauser, Philip M. "Urbanization: An Overview," *The Study of Urbanization*, Philip M. Hauser and Leo F. Schnore eds., New York, Wiley, 1965.
2. *Ibid*, p. 22
3. Wirth, L. *The Ghetto*, University of Chicago Press, 1928
4. Drake, St. Clair and Horace Cayton *Black Metropolis: A Study of Negro Life in a Northern City*, Toronto, McLeod, 1945.
5. Graves, T. D. "Navaho Relocation Research: Perceived Opportunities, Expectation and the Decision to Remain on Location," mimeographed. University of Colorado, 1965.
6. Broom, L. and J. I. Kitsuse "The Validation of Acculturation: A Condition to Ethnic Assimilation," *American Anthropologist* 47: 44-45, 1955.
7. Currie, Walter "The Indian in the City," Address to the Indian-Eskimo Association Convention, Winnipeg, 1966.
8. Lagasse, Jean H. "A working paper on Friendship centres," Department of Citizenship and Immigration, 1965, pp. 10; 20-21.
9. Dailey, R. "Alcohol and the Indians of Ontario past and present," unpublished ms. p. 31, n.d.
10. *Ibid*.
11. Littman, Gerald "Some observations on drinking among Indians in Chicago," Paper presented at the 27th International Congress on Alcohol and Alcoholism, Frankfurt, Germany, September 7th, 1964.
12. Dailey, R. *Op. cit*.

5. The Emerging Welfare State: Changing Perspectives in Canadian Welfare Policies and Programs, 1867-1960

Kathleen Herman/*Queen's University*

Canada, like other modern states founded upon liberal utilitarian principles, has had to confront throughout her history the delicate and difficult task of deciding what to do with her economically and socially 'useless'. In the absence of any constitutional guarantee of basic human rights as the corollary of citizenship, what claim has been made by or on behalf of the 'useless' has had to be based on an appeal to their utility to the society in the past (as in the case of veterans or the aged) or in the future (as in the case of children, the ill and disabled, the unemployed). The difficulty is, of course, that with each new attempt to reduce the gaps created by inequity, new ones arise. Inevitably, the boundaries between the public and the private become even more attenuated and ambiguous. Another anomaly of the Welfare State, which is not brought out in this selection but which is made forcibly clear in the selection on social planning that appears in Section Six, is that in making public space more accessible to them, the private space of those so helped is, paradoxically, restricted.

Although the term 'welfare state' is of relatively recent origin,[1] and its meaning vague and imprecise, it conceptualizes a trend that is common to all industrialized nations in the twentieth century: the drive towards equality in social rights that T.H. Marshall suggests is "the latest phase of an evolution of citizenship which has been in continuous progress for some 250 years".[2] Social equality implies, he says, "an invasion of con-

Published for the first time in this collection.

tract by status, the subordination of market price to social justice, the replacement of the free bargain by the declaration of rights".[3] Embodied in the notion of the 'welfare state' is a dimension of governmental intervention which aims to control, either by persuasion or edict or both, the free play of market forces in such a way as to cushion, if not eliminate, the extreme social and economic inequalities that are likely to be manifest in a ruthlessly competitive system.[4]

All definitions of the 'welfare state' incorporate this dimension of state intervention, but there is little agreement as to the nature or the extent of that intervention. A well-known American economist speaks of the welfare state "which *promotes* the general welfare of all its inhabitants, within a democratic framework".[5] A British historian defines the welfare state as one "in which organized power is deliberately used ... in an effort to *modify* the play of market forces in at least three directions: 1) to guarantee individuals and families a minimum income, 2) to enable them to meet certain 'social contingencies' (for example, sickness, old age, and unemployment) and 3) to ensure all citizens access to a certain agreed range of social services without regard to status or class".[6] A German authority, on the other hand, would restrict the use of the term to those mechanisms of government which *supersede* the free play of market forces.[7] The definition used in this paper offers a synthesis of these notions:

The Welfare State is one in which deliberate measures are adopted by government either to influence, to interfere with, or to supersede the free play of market forces in the interests of the well-being of all its citizens.[8]

One restriction of our definition must be noted. It includes only those governmental measures that are explicitly and consciously directed at the realization of equity with respect to the social rights of citizenship. It does not include for example, the whole field of taxation policy even though implicit within it there may be a self-conscious principle of social equity.[9]

The theoretical framework for this paper is derived from Bendix's discussion of modernization and the nation-state. Using Marshall's delineation of the evolution of citizenship, Bendix asserts,

> A core element of nation-building is the codification of the rights and duties of all adults who are classified as citizens. *The question is how exclusively or inclusively citizenship is defined* . . . (C)itizenship at first excludes all socially and economically dependent persons . . . (T)his massive restriction is gradually reduced until eventually all adults are classified as citizens.[10]

Bendix discerns two principles that have informed the evolution of citizenship rights in the modern nation-state. The 'functional principle' is at work when special privileges are accorded to or withheld from special groups in the society by virtue of their status and function. That is, a citizen is accorded rights and assumes duties by virtue of his membership in some particular categorical group such as 'all persons whose income is under $1,000', or 'all members of academia' and so on. Bendix juxtaposes this essentially feudal principle with the 'plebiscitarian principle' according to which "all citizens as individuals possess equal rights before the sovereign national authority."[11] The one is a principle of exclusion, the other a principle of inclusion. To this extent they are conflicting principles. Usually, as Bendix notes, there is some measure of plebiscitarianism and functionalism in any society and the relations between them are frequently paradoxical and tenuous. Each society must work out its own accommodation within its own unique economic and political development.

One way to trace a society's evolution into a modern welfare state and the way in which it has worked out its particular accommodation to these two conflicting principles is to examine its legislative debates on these issues. This paper presents a content analysis of Hansard from 1875 to 1960 on the subjects of health, welfare and social security.[12] Firstly, I shall present a sketch of Canadian society at the turn of the century paying particular attention to the political structure which has had special implication for Canadian social welfare policies. Then, I shall trace the historical development of these policies and the changing attitudes underlying them as they are reflected in the parliamentary debates from 1900 to 1960. Finally, I shall look briefly at Canadian society today in order to assess the extent and direction of change.

Canadian Society, 1867 - 1900

Canadian Confederation, in 1867, was a compromise, born of fear and need and not from any strong bond of common identity or loyalties. Great Britain's disenchantment with empire had led to the reversal of imperial preferences with dire consequences for the economy of her North American colonies, already strained as a result of the changes being wrought by the Industrial Revolution. Coupled with this, the territorial aggrandizement of the United States impelled a defensive union of the British colonies to the north.[13]

The Constitution, perhaps deliberately in the light of the spirit of compromise out of which it was fashioned, is vague and imprecise and does not spell out in any detail the intent of the founding fathers. Trade and commerce and national defence, the chief reasons for union, were the principal functions assigned to the federal government, while to the provincial governments were left all functions 'of purely local concern'. Unlike the United States, the residue of powers not expressly given to the provinces was reserved to the Dominion (federal government); to the Dominion, too, was given unlimited powers of taxation. This has led to continuing judicial and legislative disputes, with the issues decided almost unanimously in favour of the provinces. In the field of health and social welfare legislation, which is the central interest of this paper, the consensus over the years and until the early 1940's has been that these are matters for provincial and even municipal jurisdiction, and that the federal government had neither responsibility for nor control over the welfare of Canadians generally.

At the time of Confederation, about 3,500,000 people lived in the British North American colonies. Four-fifths of the population was rural; most people were engaged in agriculture, lumbering or fishing. Montreal, much the largest city, had about 100,000 population; Quebec and Toronto were the only other towns boasting more than 30,000 population. Barely 12 per cent of the total population lived in towns exceeding 5,000. Almost two-thirds of the population was under 29 years of age, and a mere 5 per cent was 60 years or over (See table 1). The family was a self-sufficient economic and social unit, accepting responsibility for its own members when they were sick, aged or unable to work, or economically deprived.

The doctrine of *laissez-faire*, accentuated by the frontier spirit of rugged individualism with its strong tradition of reliance on individual enterprise and initiative, was at the peak of its authority. However, at no time in Canada was this force of frontier individualism allowed to go unchecked to the extent that it was in the United States. Because her large southern neighbour was exhibiting good evidence of aggressive designs, and because of her lack of any revolutionary tradition, Canada's history has been one not only of political protection, but of more favourably disposed attitudes towards economic and social protection as well.[14] The more ruthless manifestations of the frontier mentality of freedom and independence were held in check, first by the presence of British troops and then, later, by a strong national police force, both evidence of a powerful central authority. Contemporary observers have noted that, in contrast to those in the United States, cultural values and social patterns in Canada seem much more muted. The same values are valued, it is argued, but with more hesitancy. There is less emphasis on equality and a more ready acceptance of hierarchical patterns. There seems to be less optimism, less faith in the future, less willingness to take risks.[15]

From the beginning, as is evidenced in the early parliamentary debates, Canadians not only accepted but expected government intervention and assistance in the development of the country and in the creation of a social climate in which the weaker and less competitive members would be assured of survival. The issue was not one of private initiative versus government authority, but rather *which* government had the greater authority. "A kind of grandfatherly paternalism," notes J.A. Corry, "which distributes sweetmeats and is sparing of restraint has been a striking feature of Canadian government since Confederation."[16] Furthermore, "the state has lacked the awe and mystery with which age and ceremonial surrounded it in older countries, and it never had the record of bad behavior which made men fear it in England." Although there was neither fear of or resistance to government authority, no government on any level assumed much responsibility for the health and welfare of its citizens during the first thirty years of Canada's

Table 1: Canadian Population, Percentage Distribution by Age Groups
1871 - 1961

Age Group	1871	1881	1891	1901	1911	1921	1931	1941	1951	1961
	%	%	%	%	%	%	%	%	%	%
0-19 years	52.8	49.9	47.2	44.9	42.6	43.6	41.7	37.5	37.9	41.8
20-39 years	28.3	29.3	30.4	30.6	33.3	30.6	29.8	31.3	29.5	27.1
40-49 years	13.5	14.4	15.3	16.8	17.0	18.3	20.1	21.0	20.4	20.3
60 yrs. & over	5.5	6.4	7.1	7.7	7.1	7.5	8.4	10.2	10.2	10.8
Total pop. (in thousands)	3,578	4,268	4,833	5,371	7,207	8,788	10,377	11,507	14,009	18,238

(Adapted from Dominion Census Reports, 1931, 1941, 1951, 1961)

history. The self-sufficiency of the rural population combined with the constant renewal of fresh economic opportunities in a new country retarded the demand for state intervention in the development of social services.

At the federal level, the main concern of the government as far as the health of its citizens was concerned had to do with quarantine regulations covering ships bringing immigrants to the new land, (as well as to protect Canadians from the cholera and small-pox epidemics that were sporadically breaking out in the United States), and with standards to regulate against the adulteration of food, drink, and drugs.[17] The Quarantine and Health Act was passed in the first year of Confederation and was administered by the Department of Agriculture. When health matters were discussed in Parliament, which they were infrequently, it was either with a righteous moral indignation that it was the duty of legislators to control by edict the baser instincts of the common people, or with a concern for the heavy economic consequences of the high mortality and morbidity rates. When Prime Minister Alexander McKenzie in 1876 entered the debate for the establishment of a Bureau of Sanitary Statistics, he declared that the principal causes of disease were the "want of proper ventilation and light, hastily and ill-constructed houses, and the excessive use of stimulating liquors" (1876, p. 734). In the same debate, in which there was generous and laudatory reference to the remarkable success being achieved by other countries in the reduction of death and disease through the introduction of state-regulated sanitary measures, the emphasis was on the economic saving that would thereby accrue. "Twelve million dollars annually could be saved," it was claimed, "if proper sanitary precautions were taken" (1876, p. 733). Throughout this period, from 1875 to 1900, there is no reference in any of the debates to such concepts as 'social justice' or health as a 'social right'. "It was the duty of the statesman and philanthropist to initiate sanitary measures" (1876, p. 733) but this was because it was the duty of the statesman to encourage the economic development of the nation more than from any sense of responsibility for the health and social well-being of individual citizens. Charles Tupper, one of the Fathers of Confederation, felt "it was a matter of regret that the subject of public health had not been under the purview of the federal powers" for "pragmatic economic reasons" and because stricter sanitary control could "make the country more attractive to immigrants" (1876, p. 736). However, the efforts at the federal level to establish such a bureau of sanitary statistics, the function of which would be to provide "a central point, where they might receive all information relating to diseases peculiar to our climate and soil, and everything in this regard concerning the children on the streets, the artisans in their workshops, the thieves in their prisons, the insane in

their asylums, etc." was successfully resisted by the provinces until after the turn of the century. The first chink in this armour of provincial resistance was made in 1899 when a Director General of Public Health was appointed, still responsible to the Minister of Agriculture, whose chief function was to be the administration of the Public Works (Health) Act, passed in that year, which required contractors on such public works as the national railroad to "provide necessary hospital accommodation in cases of communicable disease" among their workers, as well as "suitable housing." Thus by 1900 what little responsibility the federal government had assumed with regard to health matters was in the nature of a policing function and no more.

The provincial governments, however, had begun to take an increasing responsibility for the public health that had hitherto been left to the local municipalities. Ontario passed its Public Health Act in 1884 which provided for a permanent Provincial Board of Health and for the compulsory organization of local boards of health. The efficacy of strong central power was demonstrated in the small-pox epidemic of 1885. In Quebec, where there was no such provincial legislation, there were 7,000 deaths; in Ontario, there were only 18. After this demonstration, Quebec enacted its public health legislation in 1866, and the other provinces quickly followed.[18] However, governmental responsibility, at any level, was more or less confined to such public health measures as sanitation and the control of communicable disease. Except for a few municipally operated insane asylums, provision of facilities for the care of the sick was left largely to private charity and especially to the church. Although by the turn of the century it was becoming apparent that it had been no more than a pious hope, yet the attitude expressed at the time of Confederation that, "hopefully a time would come when private charity would relieve the governments of their existing commitments for public welfare,"[19] had not yet been entirely dispelled.

The Transition Period: 1900-1940

By 1900, Canada was beginning to feel the impact of the Industrial Revolution. Owing to improvements in transportation and growing industrial development, Canada was losing its predominately rural character. The urban population rose from 20 per cent of the total to 38 per cent, although the overall growth in population had been disappointingly slow (from 3.6 million in 1871 to 5.4 million in 1901, an increase of less than fifty per cent). The age distribution of the population was changing too (See table 1). Where, in 1871, only 19 per cent of the population was over forty years of age, by 1901 that proportion had risen to 24.5 per cent, with a corresponding percentage drop among the younger age groups. For twenty-five years Canada had languished in economic stagnation and the enthusiasm for nation-building, that had accompanied Confederation, had all but vanished. Discouraged and frustrated by repeated setbacks, the federal government was only too willing to leave to the provinces the authority that they claimed was rightfully theirs. Now, by the turn of the century, the rapid industrial development in Western Europe and the United States had given to Canada a new economic importance as she was called upon to provide more of the foodstuffs and raw materials for these other nations. New lands opened up, settlers flowed in, cities grew, new employment opportunities, particularly in the service occupations, mounted rapidly. An expanding national economy united the provinces, as they had not been united before, in a common material interest and with it a growing national consciousness and confidence. Caught up in the enthusiasm, and encouraged by the examples of industry, commerce and finance that were rapidly centralizing control in a few of the larger eastern cities, the federal government was ready to assume a new and larger role of aggressive leadership and action.

By 1913, over 45 per cent of the population was classed as urban, and the self-sufficiency of the farm household and village community, which had marked Canadian life through the nineteenth century, had largely passed. The open frontier had almost disappeared. With the coming of a highly specialized interdependence, the capacity of individuals to overcome economic reverses and mischances by their own efforts were greatly impaired and the material conditions which force governments into costly expenditures for social security were begun. With intensive industrial development came the shift from the country to the cities, bringing in its train a greater demand and a greater need for collective provision of various services.

On the health front, the deadly ravages of tuberculosis dominated the concern of the federal legislators. Over the whole period from 1875 to 1900, a scant .16 per cent of the parliamentary debates had been given to health matters; in the two years, 1905 and 1910, the amount of 'health talk' had increased fivefold to .8 per cent, with almost all of it devoted to a discussion of the federal government's responsibility in helping to combat this dread disease. In 1905, it was estimated, 40,000 persons were afflicted with tuberculosis and there were 8,000 deaths. Yet only one province (Nova Scotia) operated a sanitorium with 18 beds; while six, with 234 beds, were operated by private charity. One legislator spoke the obvious when he said, "Private charity has not yet been able to cope with this difficulty to any extent" (1905, p. 1354). Thus, "an obligation devolves upon this House to provide some means of lessening this great evil. If we wait for municipalities and private charities to come to the rescue of these unfortunate people, many of them will die ... Besides being so fatal, this disease costs the people of this Dominion millions of dollars every year" (1905, p. 1355). But, while the economic cost to the nation remained the principal argument for federal assistance, the tone of the debates was changing. In some of the speeches one can detect a faint acknowledgement of collective responsibility for the human side of the equation.

> This is not a political question. ... It is non-partisan question (that can) be dealt with simply in the interest of the population at large. If it is true that we can save the lives of at least 4,000 of our people annually ... what a triumph that will be! ... Economic authorities place the value of a human life to the state at from $1,000 to $1,500. It is easy to see the financial gains that will come to the Dominion if we can effect this saving of life ... But I appeal to this House from the standpoint of sympathy, from the humanitarian stand-

point. ... (1905, p. 1364).

Large sums of money, it was argued, were being spent on bringing immigrants to Canada yet "it must be better statesmanship to save the lives of our own citizens, for I maintain that one good Canadian whose life has been saved is better than a score of Doukhobors" (1905, p. 1361). To counter the argument that health was a matter for provincial and municipal jurisdiction and not Dominion, one impatient legislator noted:

> Half a million dollars was spent last year ... in preserving the lives of domestic animals. ... If the government feels the responsibility of protecting and preserving the lives of ... animals, surely the government must feel their responsibility in preserving the lives of the people. (1910, p. 1398).

In the end, the Dominion government did little more than increase its annual grant to the voluntary National Tuberculosis Association for an extension of its public education work, but the debate clearly revealed a growing sense of national responsibility for the health of all citizens. A way had to be found to circumvent the constitutional obstacles that stood in the way. A disease such as tuberculosis, aetiologically correlated with poverty and expensive to treat because of the long period of time required, could not be combated successfully as long as government responsibility for health remained at the municipal level. It was the poorest municipalities, in which the rate was the highest, who were the least able to provide the services and facilities that were needed. Central governments, at first the provincial and then later at the federal levels, had to become involved in order to provide to all citizens at least a minimum of equality so far as the right to health was concerned. Although the pace at which this was done in Canada was uneven and often hesitant, the direction of change was unmistakable. By 1930 all provinces were involved in cost-sharing arrangements with municipalities for the treatment and control of tuberculosis, with control definitely in the hands of the provincial governments; by 1940, 3 provinces (Alberta, Saskatchewan, and Ontario) had assumed full financial responsibility; by 1950, the federal government, through its health grants program, was assuming fifty per cent of the cost.

With the close of the first World War, alarmed by the lack of physical fitness revealed by recruiting statistics (over fifty per cent of the young men called to military service had been rejected as medically unfit), and by their high rates of morbidity and mortality, especially infant mortality, as compared with other nations in the Empire and in Europe, Canadians began to be more insistent that the national government could no longer sit back and leave to the provinces such an important matter as the health of its citizens. During that decade, interest groups, particularly women's organizations and organized labour, started making representations to the federal government that it must assume a larger role in both the treatment and the prevention of disease. In 1918, the Canadian Manufacturers' Association and the Trades and Labour Congress joined forces to present a brief urging the federal government to establish a Bureau of Public Welfare "to deal with such matters as health, sanitation, town planning, housing plans, accident prevention, and every other matter pertaining to the physical efficiency of the nation." In response to this popular demand, and despite the vigorous resistance of some of the provinces, especially the two larger ones, on the grounds that it was unconstitutional, a national Department of Public Health was established in 1919. In addition to the health functions already the responsibility of the federal government, this new Department was to provide leadership to the provinces and coordinate their activities with respect to child welfare, venereal disease control, public hospitals and sanitoria. Its functions, however, were confined to purely health matters; the federal government was not yet ready to acknowledge its responsibility for the much broader spectrum of social welfare, although there were some in parliament who saw this need.

With regard to the creation of the proposed Department of Public Health, I would rather that the wider appellation had been used of 'public welfare', because it would express more fully, I think, what is in the minds of the people. I hope that . . . this wider meaning will be kept in mind, and that all matters pertaining to the welfare of the people will be taken care of.   (1919, p. 456.)

However, despite the limitations of its formal functions, the legislators saw a great role for the newly established department:

This (Public Health Department) is in line with what I believe this Government, as all governments in Canada, will have to do in the next few years – give greater attention to social problems. After all, the importance of our country is determined by our people, and unless we have a vigorous, virile, healthful people we cannot have a country of the first importance. Universal health conservation is . . . the duty of the nation.   (1919, p. 97).

It was still with a strongly paternalistic attitude, however, that many legislators viewed this new and expanded role of government:

To protect our people from the conditions which I have been describing (poverty, disease, unemployment – which could only lead to crime and destitution) is to perform work of the highest and most patriotic character, work worthy of the attention of any Government.   (1919, p. 99).

There were others, though, and they were among the country's greatest leaders, who were coming to talk in terms of 'social justice'. Gradually, during the decade of the 20's, this attitude began to reveal itself alongside that of the benevolent paternalism which still remained strong. Mackenzie King, who a few years later was to become Canada's Prime Minister and who was to remain in that office for more than twenty-five years, published a book on labour problems in 1917 in which he wrote:

Social insurance, which in reality is health insurance, in one form or another, is a means employed in most industrial countries to bring about a wider measure of *social justice*, without on the one hand, disturbing the institution of private property and its advantages to the community, or on the other, imperilling the thrift and industry of individuals. Social insurance looks upon industry as in the nature of social service. . . . Insurance against unemployment recognizes that an isolated human being . . . must be cared for when idle. It recognizes also that nothing is so dangerous to the standard of life or so destructive of *minimum conditions* of healthy existence, as widespread or continued unemployment. When idleness is the fault of the social order . . . it places *the onus on the state* to safeguard its own assets, not more in the interests of the individual than in the interests of social well-being . . . Much invalidity and penury . . . is evidence of want of effective social control. What society fails effectively to prevent, society is in some measure under obligation to meet.[20]

This philosophy was incorporated into the platform of the Liberal Party at the 1919 Convention at which time Mackenzie King was elected leader. Since this party has held power almost continuously since 1920, a programme of extended social security in a free enterprise economy has been the avowed government objective since that time. But the Liberals are just as dedicated to the principle of a truly federal state and have tried to find ways and means of inaugurating the welfare state while preserving, nominally at least, the principle of provincial autonomy. The two other principal parties, the Conservatives and the CCF[21] have been much firmer advocates of a strong central government, ready to assume what they consider its rightful residue of wider powers in the health and social welfare field. Nor were all Liberals enthusiastic supporters of the welfare state principle. One cannot escape the feeling, when reading the House of Commons debates, that the constitutional issue has been at times a convenient escape for a government that was, in reality, hesitant to initiate such sweeping social change.

During the second half of this 'interim' period, from 1920 to 1940, there is no doubt that there was widespread public agitation for government action in this direction. Many of the smaller and less economically favoured provinces were also urging the federal government to assume a large share of the responsibility for health and welfare expenditures. Nor were the vested interests, in particular the medical profession and the financial community, as strongly organized in opposition to the welfare state as they came to be later. In fact, during the late 1920's and 1930's the most eloquent spokesmen in the House of Commons for state medicine were members who were medical doctors.

It was during this period that two formal amendments to the British North America Act were made, both of them to authorize the federal government to assume complete responsibility for major welfare programs: old age pensions and unemployment insurance. Old age pensions were first mentioned in the House of Commons in 1907 when a resolution was introduced "that in the opinion of this House the subject of improving the conditions of the aged, deserving poor is worthy of and should receive the early and careful attention of this Government." No action was taken on this resolution at that time but in 1912 and again in 1913 committees of the House were appointed to study the system in other countries. It was not, however, until 1927 that legislation was finally passed. By the terms of this legislation the federal government offered to reimburse 50 per cent of the cost to any province willing to inaugurate an old age pension scheme of its own. The responsibility for the initiation of a scheme and its administration remained with the provinces. The scheme itself was in the nature of poor relief in that a stringent means test was involved and the amount of the pension ($20 per month) was intended to cover minimal needs only. There was no notion of pensions as a *social right* though the concept of *social justice* inspired some of the debates. In 1926, denying that old age pensions were 'socialistic', the Prime Minister said:

There is need for society to assist in the protection of its members against a condition which simultaneously places burdens upon the worker whose day's work is done, and the worker whose day's work is just beginning. If the young are to be given a fair start in life the care of the aged should not be their first responsibility.

It was a good indication of how far Canadian society had moved from the time, a half-century earlier, when the family was a self-sufficient social and economic unit.

Since 1926 there has not been a session of the federal parliament when the subject of old age pensions has not been discussed. At first the debate centred around the geographic inequities of the 1927 Act. As long as old age pensions were left to provincial initiative and as long as some provinces could not afford the heavy expenditures that their 50 per cent share would entail, it meant that all Canadians were paying through federal taxes for assistance to destitute aged in only a few provinces. By 1931, the 5 western provinces and the Northwest Territories had entered into agreements. In 1931 the federal share was raised from 50 to 75 per cent and this encouraged the then remaining 4 eastern provinces to enter the plan. Although some legislators spoke feelingly for increasing the amount paid and for reducing the age limit, there was not, during this period, any argument that old age pensions should be extended to all aged citizens as a matter of right. They were still seen as a form of poor relief.

In 1930 a resolution before the House proposed that Old Age Pensions should be paid to destitute blind persons at 40 years of age and legislation to this effect was introduced in 1935.

The Depression, that hit Canada with full force in the mid-1930's, revealed how great the disparities between the different regions of Canada really were, and on what an insecure foundation the prosperity of the 1920's had been based. The wheat-growing provinces, in particular Saskatchewan, confronted first with an almost total loss of market for their only product, and then later, by the loss of the product itself through prolonged and devastating drought, were overwhelmed and absolutely unable to meet the economic burden of depression relief. The Maritimes, too, felt the economic pinch keenly but they had never shared in the economic prosperity to the same degree as had the rest of Canada and so the burden was somewhat more tolerable. But, for the West, the previously cherished constitutional rights had to be set aside in favour of grim economic reality. The federal government had to assume the biggest part of the cost, and the provincial governments were eager for the central government to assume the administrative responsibility as well.

Canada had never experienced an unemployment problem of such magnitude. During previous periods of economic depression, the problems of unemployment and destitution had usually found their resolution in the self-sufficiency of the household, in the solidarity of the family, in the establishment of new homes on the agricultural frontier, in the decline of immigration, and in the increase of emigration to the United States. By 1930 such opportunities for self-reliance and mechanisms of adjustment had all but disappeared. The livelihood of hundreds of thousands of citizens was entirely dependent upon government relief. While the constitutional responsibility of the provinces was still adhered to in form, in fact the Dominion government assumed more than 40 per cent of the total cost. In 1930 relief and other public welfare had absorbed 11 per cent of government income at all levels; by 1937 the proportion had risen to 25 per cent (Table 3).

Although there had been some agitation earlier for a sound government-sponsored system of unemployment insurance, the problem had not been so urgent and it had been easy to forestall federal responsibility by recourse to the now-familiar constitutional argument. In 1926, organized labor had asked both major political parties to declare their stand on unemployment insurance and the reply had been that the federal government would be "willing in case of serious emergency . . . to cooperate with the provinces" (1930, p. 1122). In 1929, a parliamentary committee, appointed to study the matter, reported that while "social insurance had a federal aspect, nevertheless legislative jurisdiction is vested entirely in the provinces" (1930, p. 2359). To this the Prime Minister added, "In my opinion a system of unemployment insurance would be a constructive way to deal with the unemployment problem . . . If the provinces make a move in this matter . . . the federal government will be pleased to take the matter under consideration" (1929, p. 107).

Now, five years later, the extreme emergency had arisen and the provinces had made the move. By 1935 the Conservative government presented to the House an Unemployment Insurance Bill the intent of which, if not the manifest provisions, was to lay the foundation for a much broader program of social security.

In introducing the Bill to the House, the Prime Minister stated:

> It is expedient to introduce a bill to establish an employment and social insurance commission, to provide for a national employment service, for insurance against unemployment, for aid to unemployed persons, and for other forms of social insurance and security. . . . (1935, p. 277)

The Unemployment Insurance Bill would be a first step in an eventual nation-wide health insurance program in that it would provide a clearing-house of information "useful to the provinces should they decide to set up health insurance schemes" (1935, p. 1066). The people of Canada were promised "not only insurance against unemployment but also health insurance, invalidity insurance, and insurance against old age" (1935, p. 1066).

The Bill was passed but it was later declared *ultra vires* by the Privy Council for going beyond rightful federal power. However, in 1940, the newly-elected Liberal government was able to get the British Parliament to agree to an amendment to the BNA Act which cleared the way for a new National Unemployment Insurance Act. Under the terms of this Act employees (with certain important exceptions) were required to contribute monthly premiums, collected in the form of payroll deductions; the federal government contributed an equal share (though not the employer) and the worker was thereby entitled, by right of contract, to the payment of benefits in the event of unemployment. What is of interest to us here, is that first the benefits of this Act were not extended to all Canadians. In particular, self-employed persons such as farmers and fishermen, as well as persons above a moderate income level, were not covered. Although the Act was revised from time to time to widen the participant categories, to increase both premiums and benefits, and to raise the income ceiling, it still retained its 'functional' character.[22] Secondly, and perhaps of even greater interest for this study, it is to be noted that the introduction of this Act and the parliamentary debates that preceded it, mark the first time that the 'insurance principle' was introduced into notions of social welfare. Prior to this time, nineteenth century attitudes of poor relief had dominated government welfare policy; persons who were receiving government aid, at whatever level, were a class separated from the rest of the community by the proven demonstration of their indigency and, by implication, their own inadequacy. The insurance principle operates as a form of contract: benefits are paid as a matter of right and the recipient is not set apart from the rest of the community. However, while removing one form of inequality, the principle of insurance introduces a new inequity: the payment of insurance 'premiums' falls most heavily upon those in the lower income groups since it is usually calculated as a percentage of daily wages. The higher wage earner pays the same percentage premium as the lower wage earner. In the evolution of the welfare state, and Canada has been no exception in this regard, the continuing dilemma with which legislators must wrestle is the minimization of new inequalities that arise as old inequalities are removed.

Over this transition period, 1900 to 1940, the Canadian population structure had shifted considerably. In 1901, 45 per cent of the population was under 20 years of age; by 1941 that percentage had dropped to 38 per cent. The percentage of persons over 60 years of age increased from 8 per cent to 10 per cent. Much of this change was a depression phenomenon which has not continued into the modern period (See Table 1). In 1900, 6 per cent of government expenditures at all levels (municipal, provincial, federal) were given to health and welfare services. During the depression years, the proportion rose sharply until, by 1940, it amounted to 25 per cent at which level it has more or less remained to the present. This increase in government activity led to a corresponding increase in the size of the government bureaucracy. The principle of selection by merit was introduced in 1908 with the passage of the Civil Service Amendment Act. At that time there were fewer than 10,000 persons in the employ of the federal government. War, followed by expanded government activities in the boom years of the 20's and the depression years of the 30's, resulted, by 1940, in a federal Civil Service of some 50,000 persons of whom 12 per cent were in the departments engaged in health and welfare activities. The federal government had moved a long way, despite the Constitution, in assuming active responsibility for the health and welfare of all Canadians.

The Modern Period, 1940 - 1960

During these two decades the shape and nature of the Canadian Welfare State began to emerge in bolder outline. The first major piece of social legislation that involved a redistribution of national income, with benefits payable to all, irrespective of income or status, was the Family Allowances Act passed in 1944. Utilizing the 'plebiscitarian principle,' this was a form of social legislation which elicited little discussion either before or after its passage. The idea of a baby bonus to be given to parents of large families was first mooted in parliament in 1920, when France was presented as a model in this regard by one of the French-Canadian members of parliament (who admitted to having twenty-eight children himself!) (1920, pp. 3297). The proposal was rejected without much discussion, one of the reasons given for not considering it further being that it would benefit only French-Canadians. One legislator considered such a bonus to be in the nature of avoiding one's duty to the State:

> It fails to distinguish between a man's parental duties and his duties to the State. A man's parental duties are primary duties which he ought to be pleased to discharge. . . . But a man's duties to the State are entirely different and to say that he ought to be helped in his parental duties by being exempted from his State duties is a proposition to which I could not give my consent (1920, p. 3301).

In 1929, the Standing Committee on Industrial and Internal Relations had brought in a report to parliament suggesting that the question of jurisdiction between Dominion and provinces on the granting of family allowances be considered and, by 1935, questions were beginning to be asked in the House as to the government's intentions in this regard. (1935, p. 1007). When the legislation was introduced in 1944, which was approved unanimously, it was described in these terms in the Speech from the Throne:

> The family and the home are the foundation of national life. . . . To aid in ensuring a *minimum* of well being to the children of the nation and to help gain for them a closer approach to *equality* of opportunity in the battle of life . . . (1944, p. 32. Emphasis mine)

Though the allowances aimed only at a minimum of well being, the aims of the legislators were lofty:

As the years go by, family allowances can help to reduce sickness, disease, crime, illiteracy, inefficiency, and other social ills that have their roots in child upbringing. Since they are given to people who will spend the money, they will create a continuous demand for necessities which will result in increased production and employment (1949, p. 900).

Though they have not been effective in the elimination of such social 'problems' from Canadian society, family allowances have had the very important consequence of redistributing national income between provinces which has been of greater import than the redistribution among families. While the amount per family is relatively negligible, they have been a way of providing current circulating income to those provinces commonly labelled the 'have-not' provinces of Canada (Quebec, the Maritimes, and Newfoundland). Thus, one of the more inequitous forms of stratification of Canadian society – the geographic – has been somewhat muted.

Until the start of this decade (1970), the institution of family allowances was viewed as an inviolable social right accepted by all classes and all income groups. Only occasionally and somewhat half-heartedly would an NDP (CCF) member nudge the government for its 'callous attitude' in failing to increase the amount to keep pace with rising costs. However, because they were a heavy drain on the federal treasury, any increase was neither economically feasible nor politically desirable. Now (1971) with new legislation pending, the 'plebiscitarian' principle of universality appears to have been abandoned in a return to the now primordial 'functional' approach.

This modern period has seen, too, a change in philosophy with respect to old age pensions. Initiated as poor relief and maintaining the principle of provincial responsibility, such a philosophy had become untenable to both labor and industry by 1950. During the war, when wages were frozen, industry bargained for scarce labor by offering a variety of fringe benefits including retirement pensions. As long as government pensions continued to be based on the principle of a means test, they would be denied those persons entitled to industrial pensions. By 1950 there was considerable public agitation that this inequity be removed and that state pensions should be paid to older citizens as a matter of right rather than because of need. Discussion in parliament at this time did not question this principle as much as how universal pensions might be financed. Contributory schemes (based on the insurance principle) were urged because they "encouraged self-respect" (1950, p. 674). On the other hand, the inequity of contributory schemes was also argued in that a fixed contribution would impose hardships upon the lower income groups whose members would be most in need of pensions in their retirement years.

It is within the power of the dominion to finance its share of the combined cost of health insurance and of old age pensions out of the consolidated revenue fund with such modification of taxation as would be justified . . . by the universal benefits of health insurance and old age pensions. . . .

> There are however . . . advantages in terms of administrative efficiency, compliance, and popular understanding of the plans in introducing features more specifically contributory in nature and tied up more closely with the provisions (of insurance principles) . . . (1950, p. 471).

This viewpoint had to be balanced with the other argument:

> The old age pension should be given as a right of citizenship when a person reaches the age of 65. . . . It should not be contributory; the income tax is in effect a contributory system. . . . What we need in this country is not social security but *social justice* . . . (1950, pp. 476, 582).

In the end, a compromise was worked out. The Old Age Security Act of 1951 provided for the payment of a pension to all residents at age 70, who had resided in Canada for twenty years (citizenship is not a requirement), to be financed by a special Social Security Tax payable on a graduated income tax basis up to a maximum of $60 (later increased to $90) and by special sales tax and corporation tax levies. With the agreement of all provinces, the federal government assumed full responsibility for these pensions; such unanimous agreement made a constitutional amendment unnecessary. The amount of pension has been increased at regular intervals, always as an election plum or to fulfill an election promise, until by 1971 it was $80 a month. The age limit has remained at 70, though the residence requirement has been considerably reduced.

Government pensions are seen as a minimum allowance, a supplement to industrial pensions which have been a matter of negotiation between employer and employees. Supplementary Old Age Assistance is provided for by the Old Age Assistance Act which was passed in 1951 and which allows for additional monthly benefits for persons 65 and over subject to a means test. These benefits are paid out of taxation, shared equally by the provinces and the federal government, and are in effect a vestige of the earlier form of poor relief. Thus, old age pensions are a peculiar amalgam of 'plebiscitarian' and 'functional' principles.

Like old age pensions, unemployment insurance, and other welfare measures, health insurance has long been an issue before the House of Commons. It was one of the plans in the Liberal party platform in 1925; by 1944 a Health Insurance act had been drafted but it was never presented to the House, presumably because of objections from the provinces that had been called together in a special conference to discuss it. During the 1930's, the house debated each year a resolution concerning health insurance and/or state medicine. There were several medical doctors in the House and they were its most ardent proponents. In 1931, for example, when Dr. Howden introduced his resolution "that a measure of federal state medicine would be in the best interest of the Canadian people" (1931, p. 1574), thirteen members took part in the debate, all but two of them speaking in favour of the resolution. By 1939, one of the non-medical members of the House, debating a similar resolution, could say:

The people of this country are more and more taking an interest in public health.... In former days ... when a resolution of this nature came up there was usually a doctors' field day.... Now the members of this House are becoming more health conscious ... We have placed behind us the view that sickness, disability and illness were each man's own concern ... and we have reached a stage where ... sooner or later we must see to it that every citizen of the state obtains at least the *minimum* of medical care and attention. (1939, p. 1580 ff.)

As early as 1932 a Committee of the House had been appointed to study the matter of state medicine. Between then and 1960 when a Royal Commission was appointed to explore a full-scale program of health insurance and state medicine in all its many ramifications, there had been no fewer than nine such parliamentary committees appointed, all of them urging government action in this regard. But, as in the 1935 report, caution was counselled: "While realizing the desirability of some form of state medicine ... the matter has to be approached very gradually because the medical profession have (sic) to go along with it" (1935, p. 1137). Some legislators, while in favour of a system of health insurance for the poor, argued against a universal plan:

Health insurance is most applicable to low wage earners and persons in the middle income group – it should not be all inclusive of the higher income group. If it applied to everyone in the state, it would be an invitation to state medicine, which I believe would be entirely undesirable and unacceptable in Canada. (1945, p. 2839).

The draft Health Insurance Act was presented to the provinces at a special Dominion-Provincial Conference in 1945. While the Act itself was rejected as being precipitous, one constructive consequence of that Conference was agreement on a plan of National Health Grants. Under this plan, which was inaugurated in 1948 with all provinces but Quebec participating, the federal government agreed to pay to the provinces stated sums of money for health purposes, and in particular for the construction of hospitals, on the proviso that the provinces would provide an equal amount of money. These grants, while greatly facilitating the extension of government health services, still had the effect of favouring the wealthier provinces since many of the poorer provinces could not afford to accept the total grant allotted them because it was based on the matching grant principle. As long as the principle of provincial autonomy in health matters was insisted upon, no other plan appeared feasible.

The goal of a national health insurance plan was not abdicated by the federal parliamentarians. Entering the debate on the subject in 1950, the Minister of Health declared:

We should give the highest priority in the next few years (to) a national health plan to make available to our people, as freely as our primary schools now are to our children, all the health services that the people of Canada require. I hope that such a plan can be developed in cooperation with the medical and nursing professions and all others interested, so that we shall not have a conflict of interests preventing or delaying the coming into effect of a great national health plan. (1950, p. 3870).

"One of the greatest drawbacks to a national health scheme," it was stated in 1955, "is the fact that we are under a federal system" (1955, p. 6242). In urging the government to take positive aggressive action one of the most eloquent spokesmen, a Socialist, (Knowles) argued:

No one now suggests that health insurance should be bureaucratically administered at the centre.... Everyone accepts the idea, laid down in 1945 ... that it should be provincially administered.... The responsibility of the federal government is to take those financial and other steps that will put the provincial governments in a position to carry through a programme of health insurance ... (1955, p. 3402).

This action was taken by the government when, in 1957, it passed its Hospital Insurance and Diagnostic Services Act. The year before, under insistent pressure both from within the House and from the general public which had no vested interest in provincial autonomy and was becoming increasingly impatient with the constitutional argument, the federal government announced its willingness to enter into health insurance agreements provided that a majority of the provinces were ready to participate. By 1967 all provinces were participating in the hospital insurance program,[23] although the plans vary from province to province. Following the report of the Royal Commission on Health Services in 1963, this same insurance principle has been extended to include medical care.

By 1960 the welfare state was accepted by all major political parties, although it was recognized that, in practice, the Canadian legislation had been piece-meal and incomplete. Social justice, said Prime Minister Diefenbaker:

> means dedication on a continued and practical basis to the concept of fairness to each and fairness to all. . . . It is the duty of government to reconcile (opposing views of social justice) . . . and to take action to achieve for all Canadians the highest measure of social justice within the resources of the nation. (1960, pp. 503-504).

To this, the Leader of the Opposition, Lester Pearson, added:

> The state has the responsibility of providing by social security legislation a cushion between the citizen and catastrophe, to help him in circumstances where he cannot help himself or support himself. That is why we have pensions, unemployment benefits and such things. They are a recognition of the social responsibility of the state to *all* its members. (1960, p. 7231).

Concluding Remarks

Through an analysis of the debates in the House of Commons, I have endeavoured to trace the evolution of the welfare state in Canada from the time of Confederation to the present. Though complicated and delayed because of the peculiar nature of Canada's federal structure and the uneven rate of industrialization and population growth, Canada has changed from a nation in which the principles of *laissez-faire*, supported by the individualism of the open frontier, prevailed, to one in which the idea of the welfare state, if not its actual realization, is supported by all political parties and by all governments. However, as long as Canada continues to adhere to the federal principle of provincial autonomy with respect to health and social welfare measures, there will always be inequities between provinces with widely disparate economic and human resources. Without formal constitutional changes, peculiar Canadian compromises have been worked out that preserve the federal form, while greatly altering its substance.

In the early years of Canada's history the dilemma confronting the legislators had been to achieve equality of opportunity for all Canadians while maintaining the principle of the federal division of powers. The new dilemma that now confronts them is how to preserve the rights of individual citizens in the face of increasing government powers that are concomitants of the welfare state. This was most eloquently expressed by the then Prime Minister, L.B. Pearson, in the 1960 Debate on the Human Rights Bill:

> In recent years the asserted claims of the individual on the State have been matched by his protests against the State's interference in his activities and in his private life, an interference which his own demands have made easier and in some cases inevitable. The state cannot provide services and support for the citizen without acquiring the power and authority which is necessary and desirable for that purpose. . . . More social security, desirable and even necessary that it is, may often be the means to greater State powers, and the latter persistently press against the freedom and rights of citizens who are to benefit from these powers.
> Now, that pressure is often embodied in masses of legislation and regulations . . . (that) only with difficulty can be reconciled to the equal necessity of defining and protecting the rights of an individual against the state from which he demands these services and protection. This is the great dilemma of a democracy in the changing circumstances of today. (1960, VII, 5666).

Just as industrialization can occur only once, with other nations being able to follow the example of their predecessors, so it seems the fully socialized welfare state with its implied threat to the rights of its individual citizens can only occur once. Canada, through the unique conjunction of her geography and history was evolving, by the late 1960's, a form of Welfare State that tried to preserve the citizenship rights of freedom and initiative of enterprise while guaranteeing at least a minimum of social rights for all. The functional principle that singled out special groups for government relief was giving way to the plebiscitarian principle of benefits to all as a matter of social right. Now, in the decade of the 70's, confronted with a host of new problems – economic and political – Canadians are having to rethink and refashion much of their welfare legislation. Economic considerations have led to an attenuation of the plebiscitarian principle; political tensions have exacerbated and made even more visible the vast social disparities that continue to exist within the country. New social and political movements are challenging the basic premises upon which the welfare state has been constructed. The dilemma sounded in Mr. Pearson's warning has taken on added urgency in the wake of recent political events. The resolution of this dilemma presents a challenge to Canadians.

Table 2: Canadian Population – Rural – Urban Distribution, 1891 - 1961

	1891	1901	1911	1921	1931	1941	1951	1961
	%	%	%	%	%	%	%	%
Rural:	68.2	62.5	54.6	50.5	46.3	45.7	43.3	30.4
Urban:	31.8	37.5	45.4	49.5	53.7	54.3	54.7	69.6

(From Dominion Census Reports, 1931, 1941, 1951, 1961)

Table 3: Expenditures on Public Health and Welfare Canadian Governments, All Levels, 1866 - 1957

% of Total Government Expenditure:	1866	1874	1896	1913	1921	1930	1937	1945	1955
	%	%	%	%	%	%	%	%	%
	4.2	3.4	7.0	6.1	5.6	10.4	25.2	26.1	27.3

(From Rowell-Sirois Commission Report, 1940; and Canada Year Book, 1962)

Table 4: Cost of Social Security, Expressed as a Percentage of National Income
Certain Specified Countries, 1954

Australia	8.1%	New Zealand	12.5%
Austria	17.0%	United Kingdom	10.0%
Canada	9.1%	United States	5.2%
France	18.5%	Sweden	11.2%
German Fed. Republic	19.2%		

The Cost of Social Security, 1949-1957. International Labour
Office: Geneva, 1961.

Table 5: Proportion* of Parliamentary Debates, House of Commons, Ottawa Devoted to Health, Welfare, and Social Security; Selected Years, 1900-1960

Year	Health (Genl.)	Welfare: Old Age & Disability Pensions	Family Allowances & Child Welfare	Unempl. Insurance	Health Insurance	Total Percentage	Total # Pages Hansard All Debates
	%	%	%	%	%	%	
1900	.2	—	—	—	—	.2	(5,250)
1905	.8	—	—	—	—	.8	(4,911)
1910	.8	—	—	—	—	.8	(4,431)
1915	.1	—	—	—	—	.1	(2,629)
1920	.1	—	.1	—	—	.2	(2,495)
1925	.2	.1	—	—	—	.3	(2,533)
1930	1.9	—	—	7.7	—	9.6	(2,948)
1935	.1	.5	—	7.0	1.0	8.6	(4,314)
1940	2.7	—	—	7.0	.1	9.8	(2,611)
1945	1.0	3.0	2.1	4.0	.3	10.3	(2,511)
1950	1.0	3.0	—	2.0	.7	6.7	(4,465)
1955	1.0	.4	.4	2.0	.6	4.4	(6,965)
1960	1.0	1.0	—	1.2	.6	3.8	(7,905)

*Estimated on the basis of a content analysis of Hansard for each year cited.

NOTES AND BIBLIOGRAPHY
I am grateful to Mr. Reinhard Bendix, University of California (Berkeley) for his helpful comments during the preparation of this paper, and for his critical reading of it.

1. Evidently, it was first used in Britain by Archbishop Temple in a book entitled *Citizen and Churchman* (1941) in which he spoke of the 'welfare state' as the opposite of the 'power state' of the dictators. See Margaret S. Gordon, "US Welfare Policies in Perspective", *Industrial Relations*, 2 (Feb. 1963), p. 33 for information on this point.
2. T. H. Marshall, *Class, Citizenship, and Social Development*, (Garden City, New York: Doubleday & Co., Inc., 1964) p. 71.
3. *Ibid*, p. 111.
4. The 'welfare state' has always been under fire from the Right. It is only recently that it has been bitterly castigated by the far Left as well. See particularly Alvin Gouldner's devastating indictment in his *The Coming Crisis of Western Sociology*, New York: Basic Books, 1970. Gouldner exposes the Utilitarian ethic that informs welfare statism which he argues is pernicious in its separation of the 'useless' from the 'useful'. (pp. 73 ff)
5. Kenneth E. Boulding, *Principles of Economic Policy* (Englewood Cliffs, N.J.: Prentice-Hall, 1958), p. 11. Quoted by Margaret Gordon in *op. cit.* p. 33.
6. Asa Briggs, writing in *The European Journal of Sociology*, 2:2 (1961), quoted by T. H. Marshall, *op. cit.*, p. 281. Also by Margaret Gordon in *op. cit.*, p. 33.
7. The authority referred to, by T. H. Marshall in *op. cit.*, p. 281, is Professor Boettcher, writing in the *European Journal of Sociology*, 2:2 (1961).
8. This is an adaptation of the definition suggested by T. H. Mar-

shall in *op. cit.*, p. 281.
9. Richard Titmuss argues that discussion of taxation policy is central to any analysis of the welfare state. The problem, he says, is one "of reconciling ... the imperious demands of preferential social policies with a general equitable principle of fairness.... The more that the uniqueness of individual needs and dependencies is recognized and relieved in any occupational society based on rewards, the more may principles of individual equity fall into disrepute". I agree; see Richard M. Titmuss, *Essays on the Welfare State*, London: Geo. Allen and Unwin Ltd., 1958, p. 49.
10. Reinhard Bendix, *Nation-Building and Citizenship*, New York: John Wiley & Sons, 1964. Page references are to the 1969 Doubleday Anchor Books edition, p. 90, underlining mine.
11. *Ibid*, p. 91.
12. Hansard is the *Official Record of the Debates of the House of Commons, Canada*. References are cited in the body of the text of this paper in the following manner: (Year, page number). For the purposes of this content analysis, all Hansards from 1875-1900 were examined. Thereafter, volumes were selected at 5 yr. intervals, (1900, 1905, 1910, etc.). A count was made of all references to anything referring to health, health insurance, medical insurance, old age pensions, disability pensions, unemployment insurance, family allowances, and other such welfare measures. The proportion of space given to these topics is tabulated in table 5.
13. Texas was annexed in 1845; Oregon in 1846; and Alaska purchased in 1867. Minnesota, which lay just to the south of the tiny Red River settlement, was admitted to the Union in 1858. This quick advance across the continent was accompanied by hymns to 'manifest destiny' and by repeated, though largely irresponsible demands for the annexation of the British colonies to the north.

14. This argument has been forcefully presented by S. D. Clark, *The Developing Canadian Community* (Toronto, University of Toronto Press, 1962), and in his numerous articles on the effects of the frontier on Canadian political, social, and religious development.

15. See, for example, Kaspar Naegele, "Canadian Society: Some Reflections," in *Canadian Society* (Toronto: Macmillan Co., 1961) 1st edition, esp. pp. 21ff; Seymour M. Lipset, "The Value Patterns of Democracy: A Case Study in Comparative Analysis", *American Sociological Review*, 28 (Aug. 1963), pp. 515-531; also S. D. Clark *op. cit.* There is mounting evidence that centennial celebrations triggered a new self-consciousness in Canadians. Their 'passivity', whether myth or no, is giving away to a more active, self-confident stance. Some of these claims concerning the 'Canadian character' made a decade ago and cited above are, without question, losing their credibility in the more politically active 1970's.

16. J. A. Corry, *The Growth of Government Activities since Confederation* (Ottawa, 1939), p. 5.

17. Even as early as 1876 there must have been a powerful dairy lobby in Canada for in that year the 'Adulterated Food Bill' was passed to prohibit the sale of oleomargarine which, it was contended, was a "fraud upon the consumers.... It was necessary ... to guard and protect not only the consumers, but also the producers of butter". (Debates of the House of Commons, 1878, p. 2033).

18. J. A. Corry, *op. cit.*, p. 96.

19. *Speech on the Proposed Union*, John A. Macdonald, 1864. Quoted on p. 43, Book 1, *Report of the Royal Commission on Dominion-Provincial Relations*, Ottawa, 1940.

20. Quoted by Mackenzie King in the Debate in the House of Commons on unemployment insurance (1930, pp. 1231-32).

21. CCF – The Cooperative Commonwealth Federation, a Socialist political party. Originally a strongly agrarian party it merged with labor in the 1950's to become the NDP (New Democratic Party).

22. Legislation now before the House (1971) goes a long way towards making unemployment insurance more plebiscitarian in Bendix's terms.

23. Quebec was the last province to come in. It resisted for many reasons. It is interesting to note that one argument advanced in Parliament by some members from Quebec, was that the care of the sick was the traditional and proper function of the Church, and should not be 'usurped' by Government.

Official Documents:

Debates of the House of Commons, Government of Canada, 1875-1960 inclusive

The Canada Year Book, Dominion Bureau of Statistics, Ottawa, 1930-1960 incl.

Report of the Royal Commission on Dominion-Provincial Relations (Rowell-Sirois Commission), Government of Canada, Ottawa, 1940.

The Canadian Sickness Survey, Queen's Printer, Ottawa, 1950-51.

Corry, J. A., *The Growth of Government Activities since Confederation*, Queen's Printer, Ottawa, 1939. (Report prepared for Rowell-Sirois Commission).

Grauer, A. E., *Public Health in Canada*. Queen's Printer, Ottawa, 1939. (A Study Prepared for Royal Commission on Domn.-Provl. Relations)

————, *Public Assistance and Social Insurance*. Queen's Printer, Ottawa, 1939. (A Study Prepared for Royal Commission on Domn.-Provl. Relations).

Clark, Robert M., *Economic Security for the Aged in the United States and Canada*, 2 Vols. Queen's Printer, Ottawa, 1960.

Other:

Bendix, Reinhard, *Nation Building and Citizenship*, New York, John Wiley and Sons, 1964.

Blishen, Bernard R., et. al. *Canadian Society*, Toronto: Macmillan Co., of Canada Ltd., 1961.

Clark, S. D., *The Developing Canadian Community*. Toronto: University of Toronto Press, 1962.

Gordon, Margaret S., "US Welfare Policies in Perspective", *Industrial Relations*, Vol. 2 (February, 1963), pp. 33-61. (Reprint).

Gouldner, Alvin, *The Coming Crisis of Western Sociology*, New York: Basic Books, 1970.

Lipset, Seymour, M. "Value Patterns of Democracy: A Case Study in Comparative Analysis", *American Sociological Review*, Vol. 28 (August, 1963), pp. 515-531.

Marshall, T. S., *Class, Citizenship, and Social Development*. Garden City, New York, Doubleday & Co., 1964.

Titmuss, Richard M., *Essays on the Welfare State*. London: Geo. Allen and Unwin Ltd., 1958.

---

6. Canadian Narcotics Legislation, 1908-1923: A Conflict Model Interpretation

Shirley J. Cook/*University of Toronto*

The three characteristics of social structure which the author of this selection pinpoints as at least partial explanation for Canada's drug control policy are those that we have already indicated are principal parameters of social space: economic stratification, ethnic hostility and cultural belief systems. In a different political and moral climate, she suggests, the law might not have been enforced so energetically.

The sociology of deviance has traditionally asked why people violate social norms, seeking to determine the properties of the culture or social structure which account for such forms of deviance as delinquency and drug addiction. More recently, however, attention has shifted to a related but different question: what properties of the culture or social structure account for the identification of certain kinds of behaviour as deviant?

This newer formulation partly stems from the realization that social-control policies sometimes create deviance. Cohen, for example, asserts "Deviance may be created or expunged by changes in rules. The study of the making and unmaking of rules is, therefore, an intrinsic part of the study of deviance" (1966:31).

Consistent with this approach, this article seeks to determine the properties of the Canadian social structure which account for the decision made in the 1920's, to label narcotic drug users as criminals, and to explain why a very punitive law was adopted to repress what was a relatively minor social problem.

The conceptual scheme adopted is a modified version of the 'conflict model' of society. We have incorporated the insights of Howard Becker (1963), Edwin Schur (1968), and I. L. Horowitz and M. Liebowitz (1968).

Reprinted from *The Canadian Review of Sociology and Anthropology*, 6:1 (1969), by permission of the author and the publisher.

A theoretical approach which stresses conflict and power customarily implies a criticism of the functionalist or equilibrium theories. The argument between these two schools of thought often centres around 'crucial' variables. Thus, Schur has criticized the functional approach by arguing that law is "crucially concerned with ... power-related aspects of social life." (Schur, 1968:87)

> Laws would not exist unless they served *some* functions, manifest or latent, for society at large or for important elements within the society. But what is positively functional for one unit may be dysfunctional for another. In the area of legal outcomes and policies, in which there are always 'winning' and 'losing' parties, or interests, such specification is absolutely essential. We can see this need most clearly, perhaps, when we consider the power and stratification aspects of the legal order ... (Schur, 1968:84-85)

The first anti-opium law was passed in 1908 as a result of Mr. Mackenzie King's private investigation and report on the use of opium in Vancouver. As deputy minister of labour, King was sent to supervise the compensations to be paid the Chinese and Japanese after the anti-Asiatic riots of 1907 in Vancouver.

Much to his surprise he received two claims from Chinese opium-manufacturing merchants whose stocks had been destroyed. King found that he could purchase opium over the counter in spite of a provincial ordinance forbidding such a practice. He submitted a report to the government and the Opium Act of 1908 was passed with little discussion.

In 1911 King, now a member of Laurier's cabinet, introduced a more stringent Opium and Drug Act. This second act apparently originated largely as the result of King's personal moral fervour. Having acquired the reputation of a specialist in opium, he was chosen to be one of the 5-man British delegation attending the Shanghai Opium Commission in 1909. By 1911 he had thus acquired additional stature as an opium specialist and appealed to the House to pass the proposed legislation to assist "a world wide movement which has for its object the suppression of this kind of evil in all countries" (House of Commons Debates, 1910-1911:2522).

King read many alarmist testimonials concerning drug abuse during the debate but it seems likely that these were not as 'unsolicited' as he claimed. A reference in the 1921 Hansard indicates that King requested letters on the subject from clergy, police officers, and welfare workers (House of Commons Debates, 1921:2901).

A year later, in 1912, the Hague Opium Conference was held. Ratification of this convention was mandatory for all those who signed the Versailles Peace Treaty in 1919. The Canadian government passed amendments to the 1911 legislation in 1920 to meet these international commitments.

The existence of narcotic drug legislation in itself, however, does not specify its punitive content nor the energy with which it will be enforced.

Even though Canada was already committed to strict prohibition, public agitation emerged from 1920-1923, calling for harsher penalties than those proposed by the Government. Maclean's magazine ran 5 sensationalist articles in 1920 in which vivid warnings of the dangers posed by opium, morphine, and cocaine were presented to the readers. The author was Mrs. Emily Murphy, a Juvenile Court judge in Edmonton. She later expanded her views in a book, *The Black Candle*, which sold 2,000 copies.

Alarmist speeches were made in the House of Commons in 1921 and 1922 by H. H. Stevens and L. J. Ladner, both of Vancouver. Their testimonials combined with enforcement difficulties resulted in severe penalties and unusually wide police enforcement privileges. The punishment for illegal possession came to be very severe, thus, in effect, making drug addiction a crime. Police enforcement of this law became very energetic. What characteristics of the social structure would account for the rise of these two characteristics of drug control policy in Canada?

The existing stratification order is the first relevant property of Canadian society. Howard Becker and others have argued that laws, as well as other normative rules, reflect differentials in power (Becker, 1963, chaps. 7 and 8).

A recent article which takes this point of view states that "A comprehensive analysis of deviance must include political factors by determining which decision-makers define deviance as a social problem, and indicate why they consider deviance a problem" (Horowitz & Liebowitz, 1968:281).

The authors suggest a 'conflict model of deviance'. Deviance is seen as a "conflict between at least two parties: superordinates who make and enforce rules, and subordinates whose behaviour violates those rules" (Horowitz & Liebowitz, 1968:282). This conflict model has not been used in the past "because for the most part, decision-making concerning deviance has been one-sided. The superordinate parties who regulate deviance have developed measures of control, while the subordinate parties, the deviants themselves, have not entered the political arena. The conflict, though existent, has remained hidden" (Horowitz & Liebowitz, 1968:282).

Thus, conflict can mean an open contest or an implicit set of incompatible interests. The history of narcotics legislation in Canada has disclosed both types of 'conflict'. The present public debate over marijuana exemplifies the open contest between decision-makers and deviants. The early years of 1908 to 1923 illustrate the hidden type of conflict. The opiate users did not enter the political arena, but this does not erase the superordinate-subordinate relationship implied in the Act and the incompatible interests of the two parties. Nor does the political passivity of those defined as deviant negate the fact that the law developed as a political process and reflected current power differentials.

There were several groups in the population which could have been designated offenders when the law was first proposed. The medical profession was probably responsible for as much opiate addiction as the Chinese opium pedlars when the issue was first discussed at length in Parliament in 1911. It could have been argued that in order to protect society, the legislators should attack the widespread indiscriminate use of medications containing opiates by ordinary citizens. Mothers frequently gave babies soothing syrups containing opiates, paregoric in particular. All the physicians in Parliament who spoke on this item were agreed that the practice was widespread but were not unanimous as to the degree of harm involved.

Furthermore, medical men commonly prescribed nostrums that contained opiates and allowed such prescriptions to be refilled many times. In 1911, Dr. Thomas Sproule told the House, "In the treatment of epilepsy or asthma, where spasms come regularly I give a prescription and instruct the patient to go to the druggist with a number and have it refilled when required" (House of Commons Debates, 1910-1911:2350).

Dr. Peter McGibbon who violently opposed the Opium and Narcotic Drug Act of 1920, described his medical practice as follows: "There is not a week when I am at home practising, that people do not telephone to me and complain of pains—symptoms of appendicitis, or colic, or something of the kind—and I ask them if they have any remedies in the house. They tell me probably that they have some laudanum or paregoric, and I have prescribed it over the 'phone hundreds of times. ..." (House of Commons Debates, 1920:1754).

Senator J. H. Wilson, also a physician, sounds as modern as sociologist Edwin M. Schur, when in 1911, he strongly objected to making addiction a crime. He was the only speaker to imply that a political decision was being made when the Chinese were singled out as the offenders rather than the medical profession.

The indiscriminate use of opium is a very deleterious habit, yet that is no justification for making the use of it a criminal offense. This habit is principally among the Chinese. Have we the right to make criminals of people, because they have learned the habit in their younger days and now desire to continue it? They give no offense except by injuring themselves. Much of the habit of using opiates, morphine or cocaine has been brought about by its indiscriminate use as authorized by physicians.... Why not punish the physician? (House of Commons Debates, 1910-1911:399).

Parliament did introduce the Patent and Proprietary Medicines Act in 1908 to deal with this indiscriminate use of harmful drugs. However, this law was much less drastic in its penalties than the Opium and Narcotic Drug Act and any medicine which had the formula printed on the label did not come under the restrictions of the Patent Medicines Act.

The fact that it was decided that the deviants were to be the Chinese opium users (and the unconventional people who associated with them), rather than the doctors, is emphasized for theoretical reasons. Returning to Schur's argument, it is clear that the 'losers' in this case were the low-status Chinese, not the high-status doctors. This law was dysfunctional for the former, however functional it might have been for other elements in society. The decision to label narcotic drug users as criminals reflected the prevailing stratification order.

The prevailing cultural attitudes and beliefs constitute the second property of Canadian social structure which influenced the history of narcotics legislation.

In the early decades of this century, moral reformers had the arena of social legislation-making to themselves. There were no countervailing views from social scientists. The evidence presented was very vague and highly moralistic. In his Report on the Need for the Suppression of Opium in Canada, Mackenzie King gave the following ominous statement regarding the extent of opium use amongst the white population: "... the amount consumed in Canada, if known, would probably appal the ordinary citizen who is inclined to believe that the habit is confined to the Chinese and by them indulged in only to a limited extent" (Government of Canada, Sessional Papers, 1908:36b).

In general, newspaper clippings were a prominent source of information about drug use. King told the House in 1911 that "One of the means whereby information is gathered by the Department of Labour in relation to matters affecting industrial and social conditions is the selection from newspapers of items which are classified and kept for reference. I have here a very large number of such clippings referring to this subject" (House of Commons Debates, 1910-1911:2525). He read or referred to four such items and the following from the *Montreal Witness*, 23 November 1910, is typical. Entitled *Cocaine a Social Plague*, it quoted the views of a Judge, Mr. R. Dupuis: 'This curse of cocaine has existed for a short time in the city. It is a real evil. It is a social plague and it goes on spreading so fearfully that it is time for society to take marked notice. Alcoholism and morphia are nothing to cocaine. It is the agent for the seduction of our daughters and the demoralization of our young men....' (House of Commons Debates, 1910-1911:2525).

The unchallenged right of the moral reformers to provide 'definitions of the situations' meant that there was an uncritical acceptance of the 'dope fiend' image of the drug user. The belief existed that the chemical action of drugs directly produced a totally changed personality: "The taking of drugs is

undoubtedly the cause of a great deal of crime because people under its influence have no more idea of responsibility of what is right or wrong than an animal" (Murphy, 1922:59). This quotation refers to 'noxious drugs' in general.

The following specifies the consequences of marijuana use.

Persons using this narcotic, smoke the dried leaves of the plant, which has the effect of driving them completely insane. The addict loses all sense of moral responsibility. Addicts to this drug, while under its influence, are immune to pain, and could be severely injured without having any realization of their condition. While in this condition, they become raving maniacs and are liable to kill or indulge in any form of violence to other persons, using the most savage methods of cruelty without, as said before, any sense of moral responsibility. (Murphy, 1922:333).

This same belief about the direct relationship between chemicals and personality was implicit in the fears expressed by prohibitionists in the House of Commons in 1908, during a private member's motion to outlaw tobacco. The following is typical of the alarmist views on the 'vice theory' of noxious chemicals. Speaking about the dangers of tobacco, Mr. Wm. Telford (Grey North) stated, "There is scarcely a town or city in Canada where you will not find boys, the sons of respectable parents, who have not dwarfed their bodies, ruined their intellect and damaged their moral perceptions to such an extent that they do not know the difference between right and wrong, and consequently many of them have had to be sent to reformatories" (House of Commons Debates, 1907-1908:5102).

If the chemical effect of tobacco was that it "produced cigarette fiends" (House of Commons Debates 1907-1908:5096), the chemical effect of opium could hardly be expected to do less.

The 'dope fiend' beliefs discussed above reflect a fundamental general supposition about the nature of man held by the Victorian middle class. The moral reformers of the time made an assumption about human nature which was the philosophical foundation for their views on tobacco, liquor, narcotics, and apparently any 'chemical comforts'. The assumption was the doctrine of the natural depravity of man. The premise of the prohibitionists' argument seems to have been as follows: "Poisonous chemicals can break down the defences erected by family and church against this natural depravity. Young persons are particularly vulnerable to these poisons because their defences are still developing and hence very frail."

This direct relationship between the chemical action of the substances and moral fibre of youth is implied in the following statement, one of numerous similar ones made in Parliament and elsewhere by those advocating total prohibition of various substances: "[Tobacco] unfits a man for proper physical or moral manhood and unfits him to be the parent of a generation with vigour and stamina" (House of Commons Debates, 1907-1908:1698).

In any case, it is clear that the moral reformers believed that the moral fibre of the citizens was constantly in need of protection. "The object of good government is to help people in every way and even to control people so that they may not do what injures themselves" (House of Commons Debates, 1907-1908:5117).

It is clear from the speeches and articles that the moral reformers believed that people needed to be controlled in order that they might not indulge in pre-marital sex. Frequently, in the narcotics debates, it was argued that severe measures were necessary to protect innocent young women and girls from moral ruin. It was probably believed that the use of opiates stimulated sexual drives. However, such a belief can only be inferred from the data. For example, in her book exposing the drug traffic, *The Black Candle*, Mrs. Emily Murphy shows a picture of a woman lying on a bed beside a Negro with opium-smoking equipment between them. The caption reads, "When she acquires the habit, she does not know what lies before her; later she does not care" (Murphy, 1922:30). In an article in *Maclean's* magazine, Mrs. Murphy declares that once a woman gets into the clutches of the Drug Ring, "she becomes a 'victim' in more ways than one" (1920).

Finally, those advocating punitive narcotic laws had very little valid pharmacological knowledge about the effects of the various 'narcotic' drugs. Numerous quotations in Mrs. Murphy's book, *The Black Candle*, show that there was no appreciation of the fact that cocaine is quite different from the opiates.* Cocaine is a stimulant, while all the opiates are true narcotics – drugs that slow down body response, soothe pain, and induce sleep. The following two quotations illustrate this confusion:

> When a man is criminally inclined, cocaine and heroin produce delusions which actually make him "insane and dangerous to be at large." These drugs also give him courage without reason; make his vision more acute, and steady his hand so that he may commit murder with ease. (Murphy, 1922:57)
> The most violent of the crimes were perpetrated by the users of heroin and cocaine... (Murphy, 1922:298).

The above elaboration of anxiety beliefs further illustrate the hidden nature of the conflict over drugs. The fact that these beliefs were not challenged in public, should not distract our attention from the fact that they were espoused by the superordinate group who made and enforced the rules. We can safely assume that the people defined as deviant would not have expressed the same views. In a different social structure the disagreement might have been expressed openly and been given publicity. Such was not the case in the 1920's in Canada.

Interracial conflict was the third and perhaps most important property of Canadian society to influence the history of narcotics drug legislation. Hostility toward immigrants from Asia predated any public concern over drug abuse. Many pages of Hansard during the years 1907-1908 are devoted to the subject of Oriental immigration, prompted by the proposed trade treaty with Japan which would allow Japanese immigration to Canada. The speeches were lengthy and antagonistic. The specific objections to the Chinese were that they were supposed to be very eager to come to Canada in overwhelming numbers and then to be unwilling to contribute anything positive to Canadian life. "[They] come in swarms, are single, do not marry, do not build up the country by constructing schools, churches, houses, etc., but crowd into large barn-like buildings" (House of Commons Debates, 1907-1908:750).

Mr. Duncan Ross of Vancouver, enumerated a long list of objections to the Asiatics. The last two items were that "They

make the country of no value as a home for the surplus population of Great Britain," and "We want to preserve the British type in our population" (House of Commons Debates, 1907-1908:743).

In the 1922 narcotics debates, the villain responsible for the moral ruin of innocent young people was identified as belonging to this foreign, inferior race. The moral indignation of the legislators increased accordingly and the penalties were increased. Reading the inflammatory speeches of L. S. Ladner (Vancouver South), leaves the impression that he hoped to eliminate two evils simultaneously – the distribution of opiates and the presence of a despised racial group.

Speaking of drug addiction he quoted with approval the following remarks of the Secretary of the Anti-Asiatic Exclusion League: "Here we have a disease, one of many directly traceable to the Asiatic. Do away with the Asiatic and you have more than saved the souls and bodies of thousands of young men and women who are yearly being sent to a living hell and to the grave through their presence in Canada" (House of Commons Debates, 1922:1530).

The editors of *Maclean's* magazine introduced the articles written by Judge Emily Murphy by saying that their purpose was to arouse public opinion and thus influence the government to pass more stringent measures to suppress the drug traffic. The visual impact of the first article was bound to arouse curiosity and indignation. Photographs of reclining opium smokers are surrounded with line drawings of the 'grim reaper' and Chinese goddesses. Each article contained a cartoon caricature of a Chinese opium smoker – swollen faced, slanted eyes closed, with puffs of smoke coming out of each ear.

The verbal images were equally exotic and coloured with sentiments of racial hostility toward the Chinese, as well as Negroes. In her book, *The Black Candle*, this antagonism toward the Chinese is even more explicit.

> It is claimed also, but with what truth we cannot say, that there is a well-defined propaganda among the aliens of color to bring about the degeneration of the white race.... It is hardly credible that the average Chinese pedlar has any definite idea in his mind of bringing about the downfall of the white race, his swaying motive being probably that of greed, but in the hands of his superiors he may become a powerful instrument to this very end... whatever their motive, the traffic always comes with the Oriental, and... one would, therefore, be justified in assuming that it was their desire to injure the bright-browed races of the world.... Some of the Negroes coming into Canada... have similar ideas, and one of their greatest writers has boasted how ultimately, they will control the white man. (Murphy, 1922:186-189)

Hansard records equally vivid accounts of the 'machinations' of the drug ring organized by Chinese. L. J. Ladner (Vancouver South) provided this type of colourful detail:

> What are known as 'snow parties' are held, Chinamen of great wealth, engaged in this odious practice, and living in expensive, luxurious quarters, give parties at which white women, whom they employ, act as hostesses. Young girls are invited from about the city to take part in these so-called social functions.... Interspersed among these young people are two or three addicts who are trained... to inveigle other people into the use of narcotics (House of Commons Debates, 1922:1529).

In support of the amendment which provided whipping as an additional penalty for giving drugs to minors, the same Mr.

---

* Dr. Harris Isbell has speculated about the consequences of this confusion between cocaine and heroin. "The abuse of cocaine... began in the under-world about the same time as the use of heroin, shortly after 1900. Like heroin, cocaine is a white powder and was taken as a snuff. Unlike heroin, which is a typical quieting, soothing opiate, cocaine is a stimulant drug, which in large repeated doses, causes extreme nervousness, bizarre behaviour, toxic psychoses and a paranoid state. Persons under the influence of cocaine are dangerous and may assault, or harm other persons. It seems natural that the public's idea about heroin, and hence about addicts, may have been confused by the association of heroin and cocaine. It is interesting to speculate that the term 'dope fiend' may have had its origin in this confusion" (1963:161).

Ladner elaborated further this stereotype: "The addict must be treated as a patient. The trafficker, generally an Oriental, a cool, calculating person, does not take the drug himself because he knows its terrible effects on those who become its slaves, but he ingeniously inveigles innocent people into the habit..." (House of Commons Debates, 1922:1529).

These two complementary stereotypes – the innocent addict victim and the cool, calculating Oriental trafficker, were presented to the House in 1922 in order to increase the penalties. At the suggestion of the Vancouver members, H. H. Stevens and L. J. Ladner, two amendments were incorporated into the law –

(1) whipping for giving drugs to minors and
(2) deportation of aliens convicted of drug trafficking.

A year earlier in 1921, Mr. Stevens told the House that drug traffickers actually distributed drugs to school children and that many "tragic cases" had been brought to light, "where these young people, especially girls, have been utterly ruined" (House of Commons Debates, 1921:1987). This speech was made in support of his amendments to increase the penalties for illicit trafficking. Indictment proceedings carrying a possible seven years' prison sentence, were added, and were mandatory for anyone accused of giving drugs to a minor. Mr. Stevens also wanted the latter offence to be penalized by whipping but this was rejected by the House in 1921. A year later, with the introduction of the negative racial stereotype the whipping clause was accepted.

Law-enforcement officials asked for two amendments which might not have passed the Senate unless the negative stereotype of the responsible agent had been available. The police wanted to obtain a 'drastic right of search.' That is to say, a police officer who had "reasonable cause to suspect that any drug was kept or concealed for illicit purposes in a store... or other place" (except a dwelling house), "could search by day or night" without first obtaining a warrant from a magistrate (Statutes of Canada 12-13). This proviso about the dwelling place was included at the insistence of Senator J. S. Daniel. He was satisfied that this would "conserve the liberty of ordinary law-abiding citizens" while agreeing that the police should have arbitrary powers as far as the 'Chinamen' were concerned. However, he argued, as the latter lived largely in their stores or in connection with their stores, his amendment would not thwart the activities of the police in this regard. Moreover, he said, "the words 'other place' would enable an officer to nab (a Chinaman) if he lived in a shack alongside this store" (Senate Debates 1922:480).

The 'drastic right of search' amendment was requested and secured in 1922. The same year the Department of Health asked that no appeals be allowed for convicted illicit traffickers. This was rejected by the Senate in 1922 but agreed to in 1923 when the government spokesman made it clear that this proviso would not apply to honest citizens but only to criminals who, as a rule, had no fixed residence or place of abode and thus simply vanished after serving notice of appeal. This ruling it was stated, would not apply to physicians, druggists, etc., "who have a place of business or interest in the community, and are not likely to disappear" (Senate Debates, 1923:407).

We can safely assume that most of the Senators were sure that it would be mainly Chinese drug pedlars who would suffer under the 'no appeals' clause and that this made the amendment more palatable.

Had the racial conflict between whites and Asiatics been absent, the moral indignation against drug use and the energetic enforcement of the law might have waned gradually as it has in the case of tobacco and liquor. The agents responsible for the manufacture of tobacco and alcohol were high-status citizens, many of British ancestry, whose industries contributed much revenue to the various governments in Canada. These people could not be vilified with the level of intensity directed against the Chinese. Furthermore, the latter continued to remain in a low-status level in Canadian society because of immigration restrictions, their occupational skills, and their high social 'visibility'. They thus remained a despised social category until after World War II.

In conclusion, the stratification order, the cultural beliefs, and interracial conflict influenced the content of Canadian narcotics legislation. The political process in a different culture and social structure might have produced a less coercive and repressive law. In a different political and moral climate the law might not have been enforced so energetically.

In Canada, as in the United States, stamping out addiction became not merely an enforcement chore but a moral crusade. The stereotype of the addict as an 'innocent victim' persisted for some time but in practice the addict was coming to be treated as a criminal. He too became the 'enemy' along with the trafficker.

The combined lack of tolerance for 'chemical comforts' and hostility toward the Asiatic immigrants produced a political climate which set in motion the feedback system outlined by Kitsuse and Dietrick (1959):

> Less tolerance
> leads to – more acts being defined as crimes
> leads to – more action against criminals
> leads to – more alienation of deviants
> leads to – more crime by deviant groups
> leads to – less tolerance of deviants by conforming groups.

This circular process continues today. A low tolerance on the part of public officials toward the use of marijuana and other psychedelic drugs combined with a distaste for the 'hippy' subculture has set the process in motion. (Marijuana was added to the schedule of the Narcotic Drug Act in 1923. Its addition provoked no comment in Parliament.) The most energetic enforcement of the law prohibiting marijuana occurs in places where the users are most visible and most defiant of traditional norms regarding dress, work, and sex.

The Narcotic Control Act provides law-enforcement officials with a weapon to suppress an undesirable subculture. The precedent for using narcotics legislation in this manner was established half a century ago.

BIBLIOGRAPHY

Becker, H. *Outsiders*. New York: Free Press, 1963.
Cohen, A. K. *Deviance and Control*. Englewood Cliffs, N.J.: Prentice-Hall, 1966.
Government of Canada Sessional Papers. Ottawa: Queen's Printer, 1908.
Kitsuse, J. I., and D. C. Dietrick "Delinquent boys: a critique." *American Sociological Review* 24, cited by L. T. Wilkins, p. 90, 1959.
Horowitz, I. L., and M. Liebowitz "Social deviance and political marginality: toward a redefinition of the relation between sociology and politics." *Social Problems* 15: 3, 1968.
House of Commons Debates 1907-1908, 1910-1911, 1920, 1921, 1922 Ottawa: Queen's Printer.
Isbell, H. "Historical development of attitudes towards opiate addiction in the United States," in *Conflict and Creativity*. New York: McGraw-Hill Book Co., 1963.
Murphy, E. F. "The Grave Drug Menace." *Maclean's* Magazine 33 (3):9, 1920; *The Black Candle*. Toronto: Thomas Allen, 1922.
Schur, Edwin *Law and Society*, New York. Random House, 1968.
Senate Debates Ottawa: Queen's Printer, 1922, 1923.
Statutes of Canada
  12-13 George v. Chap. 36, Sect. 3. Ottawa: Queen's Printer.
Wilkins, L. *Social Deviance*. London: Tavistock, 1964.

7. Aliens in Their Own Land

Leslie Armour/*Cleveland State University*

In their by now well-known book, Professors Mathews and Steele of Carleton University have stridently voiced their alarm over the extent to which non-Canadians, particularly Americans, are staffing our universities. That the process of constricting, for Canadians, their own academic space may be even more insidious than some might realize is suggested in this next selection. Mr. Armour, a native of British Columbia, was a professor of philosophy at the University of Waterloo at the time he wrote this article and is now Chairman-elect of the Department of Philosophy at Cleveland State University, Ohio. He is the author of The Rational and the Real, The Concept of Truth *and the forthcoming* Logic and Reality.

Being a foreigner in one's own country is a curious and unnerving experience. It is one that Canadians who teach in Canadian universities face with increasing frequency.

Some of the cruder facts are no longer much in dispute. In faculties of arts and science, Canadians comprised, by 1969, just about half the staff. The most reliable counts put the figure at 49 per cent. There are departments in which only one teacher in 10 is a Canadian.

The proportion of Canadians has probably fallen since then: 6 years ago, Canadians got more than 40 per cent of new appointments; 4 years ago the figure had dropped to 30 per cent. More recent figures are speculative, but the trend seems to have gone unchecked until about a year ago. By now, publicity may be having its effect; some sources suggest that in Ontario this year half the jobs will go to Canadians. But the basic position remains unchanged.

About half the non-Canadians who get jobs in Canadian universities are Americans. In 1968, for instance, 2,280 immigrants gave their occupation as 'professor'. They included 1,013 Americans, 545 Britishers and 672 others.

Arguments go on about the figures. Not all universities keep nationality counts and some universities won't reveal the counts they do keep. One way of counting is to notice where faculty members got their first degree. People usually take their first degrees at home. Most of the figures in circulation were collected by Profs. Robin Mathews and James Steele – two men from Carleton University whose names have become household words in Canada as the controversy has gathered wind – and no one has been able to provide any ground for believing that they are very far wrong.

The data about trends may be sneakier just because the phenomenon is a very old one and the movement of non-Canadians in and out of the universities may well have proceeded by fits and starts. When I was an undergraduate at the University of British Columbia – 20 years ago – just one of the 4 members of the Philosophy Department was a Canadian. A glance at the current university calendar suggests that the proportion hasn't changed much, though the department has grown four-fold. There are certainly many departments of the humanities and the social sciences at Canadian universities in which Canadians have never been in a majority. (One of Professor Steele's most startling findings was that in the History Department at the University of Toronto, one of the oldest and most Canadian universities in the country, Canadians are – or were a couple of years ago – in a minority: 46 per cent. Yet Canada not only has

Reprinted from *The Nation*, 212:26 (June 14, 1971), by permission of the publisher.

a history; it has also always been rich in historians. At Toronto now, the chairman of the Philosophy Department is also American-born.)

The most vulnerable areas have always been the social sciences and the humanities (law schools and medical schools tend to be staffed by Canadians, as do other disciplines that require 'licensing'), and the vast expansion in these fields during the last decade has made the issue more obvious and pressing.

Non-Canadians are not spread evenly throughout the various disciplines or across the fifty-nine universities and colleges in the country. I have taught for nine years in the Philosophy Department at the University of Waterloo. For most of that time, there have been two Canadians in a department which, recently, has had about twenty full-time members. When I leave for Cleveland in September (assuming that I am lucky enough to get a US immigrant visa), one Canadian will be left on the full-time regular staff. One of my graduate students, who got his PhD in May, has been hired for one year as a temporary assistant professor. About four others will be part-time instructors and other Canadians, pursuing their graduate studies as senior teaching fellows, will give introductory courses under supervision. But – barring the lucky arrival of a visiting professor – only one Canadian will be among the nineteen regular full-time teachers. I can think of a dozen other Philosophy Departments in which the situation is about the same and very few in English Canada differ significantly. Waterloo runs heavily to Americans – thirteen in the Philosophy Department. Other universities favor Englishmen or Scotsmen.

How did things get this way? Nobody really knows. The older universities in English Canada had their start at various times in the nineteenth century, England and Scotland most often providing the staffs for them. Young Canadians were sent abroad, at first often to the United Kingdom and then, increasingly, to the United States, for graduate studies. Frequently they couldn't find jobs at home when their studies were completed – the people doing the hiring preferred the domestic product. Some, of course, didn't want to come home.

It seems likely that during periods of surging national awareness (after each of the two World Wars for instance) more Canadians wanted to come home and more were welcome, but the pattern was never wholly broken. I went to the University of London and when, in 1956, I received my Ph D , there seemed to be no jobs in Canada. Some universities didn't even answer my letters. I went to Montana and on to California. Five years later I had become respectable enough to be invited home. My experience was by no means unique.

During the rapid expansion of the 1960's, Canadians either couldn't be found or just weren't found. The new universities, usually unable to attract staff from their established predecessors, looked to the United States. The vastness and complexity of the American academic scene make it inevitable that a considerable number of good people in bad places are willing to take a chance on new universities. Relatively high salaries, a short academic year (usually ending in April) and the push to establish and expand graduate studies also made Canada attractive to Americans.

This expansion was accompanied by the quite massive growth of graduate programs, and Canadians began not only to be available but visible – they were less often far away, being educated at Harvard or employed in South Dakota or North Carolina. Canadians who had come back also began to hear about more Canadians abroad who wanted to return home, and the new universities began to attract Canadians in the older universities.

Surprisingly, this doesn't seem to have led to the hiring of Canadians. In the last five years, my own department about doubled in size. Thirty-five qualified Canadians applied in those years, two or three of them being among the two dozen best-known philosophers in Canada. But not one was hired (or was offered a job). The pattern could be repeated any number of times.

It is at this point that people began to get by turns puzzled, worried and angry. Nowadays, hiring is done democratically in all decent universities. Candidates are rounded up, invited to read papers, argued over, and voted on. The majority wins. That is as it should be – other things being equal. The trouble is that, in this situation, things are often not equal.

Academics tend to rely heavily on the opinions of people they know and trust. If you're an Englishman or an American in Canada you've probably never heard of the Canadians who write letters on behalf of other Canadians, and Canadians phrase letters of recommendation a little differently from the American style. Traditionally, grading standards have differed: a 'B' used to be a very good grade at a Canadian university and a mediocre grade at most American universities. So the dice might be loaded against Canadian candidates. That problem is often compounded by differences of doctrine.

In philosophy, I suspect, it is a real problem. It is true that almost every philosophical position which a rational man could hold is held by someone, somewhere, in an American university. But at most times in this century there have been dominant fashions in doctrine.

Currently certain kinds of analytic philosophy – mostly given to deflating speculation, analyzing language and dissolving philosophical problems with a variety of real and pseudo-logical devices – are most popular in the United States. Certain existentialist and phenomenological theories also have large followings. Other views (including the native species of pragmatism) follow far behind. The Americans who staff Canadian universities mostly arrived during the full flower of the analytic movement.

The philosophical tradition in Canada has tended to be pluralistic, heavily influenced by some facets of Hegelianism and given to large-scale syntheses. Reason has figured rather as a device for illuminating possibilities and not, as if it were a substitute for force, a device for compelling assent. Many Canadian philosophers have become interested, of course, in the problems posed by the analytic philosophers, but they have usually taken a softer line about them.

Indeed, candidates interviewed by my department often seemed 'soft' and 'woolly' to my American colleagues. Cultural clash has turned out to be a reality. The business of justifying yourself (and your graduate students), when you think you're at home and working in your own tradition, becomes embittering, and those of us on the inside have suffered along with the candidates.

In the social sciences, I suspect, matters are even more complex. The modern social sciences – as they are practiced in the English-speaking world – are very much an American creation; they have grown out of the American experience and out of American aspirations. The distinction between economics and political science, for instance, surely has something to do with particularly American convictions. It has been brought to Canada as somehow an accepted fact – though the University of Toronto still has, in name at least, a Department of Political Economy. But is it so obvious in a country where no political party has ever accepted the distinction?

And what of the notion that one can study sociology apart from history? Or the distinction between sociology and anthropology? Both views imply a theory that one must hold before one begins research; perhaps they make less sense in Canada than in the United States.

At a much deeper level, the whole thrust of the so-called behavioral sciences, with their bias toward a behavioristic methodology, may well reflect things that Americans hoped were true. A society open to action and dependent on technology will tend, surely, to devalue the reflective inner life and, if the belief is strong enough, will contend that the inner life is mythical, or, at least, not part of what any scientist should investigate. Canadians, perhaps, have been more skeptical about these things.

For whatever reason, the social sciences, as they are now understood, developed rather slowly in Canada. The result was that when the demand came to staff the new Social Science Departments, the Americans and Englishmen imported to start them off claimed that there were no trained Canadians.

The theoreticians produced by our older schools of political economy, the psychologists who came out of our joint Departments of Philosophy and Psychology, the social theorists who fought the separation of history and sociology may no longer be numerous. Where they exist, they too often find themselves strangers in their own house, parties to an enterprise devoted to some other end.

Does it matter? The public issue is simple. If it is important to maintain options on the North American continent, if no government is so trustworthy that we can afford to turn over a whole continent to it, if human nature is too rich to be compressed into one mold, then, indeed it does matter.

The heroes of our minor revolutions – Riel, Mackenzie, Papineau – all found it necessary to flee to the United States at various times. Americans, from fugitive slaves to opponents of the war in Vietnam, have found the national differences worthwhile.

Squeezing Canadians out of their own universities – if that metaphor is not too active for what goes on – does endanger the alternatives. Canadian students complain bitterly that courses in sociology are based on American books and American problems, and leave their own lives untouched. Canadian students in political philosophy find that theories which might make their environment intelligible are not discussed and then rejected; they are not discussed at all.

What is it like to grow up feeling that your country has produced no thinkers and no one capable of teaching you? (A former chairman of my department wrote an official memorandum in which he said: "There *is* no Canadian philosophy as such." He went on to say that there was indeed an American philosophy.)

Nationalism is potentially dangerous – though not more dangerous than cultural imperialism. If it is to be defended, it must be on the ground that it is consistent with the legitimate interests of all men. The Canadian cultural tradition, though, has harmed no one and many Americans have been grateful for its existence.

Then there are practical and personal issues. Finding oneself cut off from one's roots, forced to defend one's every thought, can, all too easily, crack one's mind. (In my case, it has been even queerer: I have been massively overloaded with graduate students – about half of them Americans – who want at least to share my attitudes toward philosophy. Defending their right to do what they want has become a major occupation.)

Then, Americans can freely enter Canada, whereas Canadians wishing to move to the United States are now subject to a quota; the queue for a visa has averaged twelve to fourteen months, and it is hard to get a job that far in advance.

Other countries don't show the Canadian tolerance toward

aliens. The Institute of International Education quoted in 1969 that only 2.5 per cent of academics in the United States were non-Americans. Ninety-seven per cent of those who teach in British universities are British.

No one in Canada would suggest proportions like that. Demands for a quota have been growing, but the favorite demand is that two-thirds of the members of each department should be Canadian. Like many other Canadians who feel strongly about the issue, I remain suspicious of quotas. My interest is in seeing that some of the Canadian traditions are adequately maintained and I am disinclined to attach numbers or count birth certificates. Others think that people like me are unrealistic and perhaps we are.

I suspect that the real solution would be to make sure that, sometimes at least, Canadians decide who is to teach in Canada. In Ontario, with fourteen publicly supported universities inching their way reluctantly toward a University of Ontario, the solution would be simple: name a committee of Canadian scholars in each field and give them the power to make a significant proportion of the appointments in that field for the whole province (and power to make all appointments until an agreed upon proportion is reached and until it includes a reasonable share of the full professors). The committee would be charged with seeing that departments had a reasonable number of Canadians and, much more, that Canadian ideas were fostered and not stamped out. It could move its appointees from campus to campus as need arose.

Departments could still do what they liked with the rest of the appointments, but at least sometimes Canadians would decide who was to teach in Canadian universities and Canadian ideas would become a specific concern. That is a small and perhaps conservative dream.

Meanwhile, I am off to Cleveland in hope rather than despair. I have always enjoyed being a foreigner in someone else's country and, anyhow, Americans at home, freed from the need to feel defensive in the face of a vaguely strange culture, are rather different from Americans living in enclaves in other people's countries. As one lone Canadian, I shall not, I trust, be tempted to bring a cultural wall with me. (Being abroad in bands would be bad for Canadians, too, if they got a chance at it.)

I may not 'belong' in downtown Cleveland, but the American city is one of the places in which the future of civilization is apt to be decided. If we don't succeed there, none of us may belong anywhere. It is a good place to find out whether philosophers have anything to say to the young for whom the future too often has a desperate look. It is an honest place to stand, whatever one's nationality.

The Uses of Private Space

The Uses of Private Space

Not all of human group life takes place in the public realm. In fact, very little of it does. For the most part, most of us live out our lives in various social groupings that function to give us our identity by setting us apart from others. We preempt our own parcel of social space, as it were, and ward off intruders with a variety of signs all of which say, in effect: "Private property. No trespass allowed." We are not here speaking of personal space *in the psychological sense, which refers to the individual's management of his 'self' in the ways that Hall describes in his selection in Section Two. In contradistinction,* private space, *as we are using the term here, is a property of groups, social categories or associations. It is a sociological, not a psychological concept.*

We know who we are by knowing who – and what – we are not. George Orwell's trenchant observation in his probing inquiry into the nature of class distinctions in England that "the lower classes smell," expresses nicely, if somewhat pungently, the distancing techniques people use (in this case the distancers were Orwell's 'shabby-genteel families') in order to confirm for themselves their own separate and distinct identities.

Viewed in one way, society can be looked at as a congeries of competing claims. For the most part, these claims are not thought about very much. They are legitimated in the society's normative and institutional structure and are considered, if they are thought about at all, as the 'right' way of doing things. It is only when these claims come to intrude upon the claims of others that we become aware of them and of the extent of the ambiguity inherent in our shared 'understandings'.

Take the family, for instance. It is generally taken for granted that this is a private preserve, that parents are free to bring up their children in their own way and to decide how they will be sheltered, dressed, fed, educated, their health protected and maintained, and so forth. Instantly, of course, we recognize that there are many limitations to this freedom. In the first place there are legal constraints. Child neglect, child beating, sexual assault of minors – admittedly extreme examples – violate our most deeply-held moral sensibilities. Their prohibition by law we consider basic to any civilized society. Difficulties arise, however, when we attempt to define the outer limits of what we take to be

included under the rubric of such offences. Is it child neglect when parents refuse to allow a blood transfusion to be given to their child since this would violate their religious beliefs? Some say yes. And so we have the anomaly of a mother having to 'steal' her day-old baby (who is now no longer 'her' baby in the eye of the law!) from the hospital nursery and take it with her into hiding for several months as the only method by which she can protect it from what she considers to be pollution of the gravest degree.

Or consider the law which says parents must send their children to school for a given period of their lives. On the face of it this seems straight-forward enough, and for most people it presents no problem: they do not see it as an intrusion upon their private space. Most of us agree that education is a basic human right and so, in our society as in most others, the state uses public monies to provide children with schools and teachers. Problems arise, however, when parents – or the children themselves – decide they want a say in the kind of education the school provides (or even the mode of dress that will be worn!). School personnel may see this as an intrusion on their *private space. Other parents, wishing to set up their own school as an alternative to the state school will discover that the educational bureaucracy has staked prior claims; its officials have become the definers of what is or is not 'education' and who is qualified to dispense it.*

The examples are multitudinous. But as these homely ones indicate, the amount of freedom private space affords the individuals enclosed within it is a function of how 'private' the space is. This is a function of where the group is placed in the social power structure and/or how much the group threatens or intrudes upon others who are more powerful. The group that distances itself physically as well as socially, as for example the private school described by the Maxwells in their essay in this section, is usually more successful in maintaining control of its private space than one which does not have such physical boundaries. One of the reasons is that physical distance makes it easier to protect the members from pollution and so to sustain their purity and the purity of the group. The two essays in this section can be read, on one level, as analysis of purity-maintaining techniques and the consequences for identity affirmation should this purity be adulterated.

---

1. The Canadian Social Register

Frank R. Scott/*McGill University*

A Social Register for Canada was promoted in Montreal in 1947. On the advisory Committee were names like Rt. Hon. Louis St. Laurent, Sir Ellsworth Flavelle, Air-Marshal Bishop, Rear-Admiral Brodeur, Hon. J. Earl Lawson, Hartland Molson and others. A Secret Committee was to screen all applicants. All quotations in this poem are taken verbatim from the invitation sent out to prospective members.

Reader, we have the honour to invite you to become a
    "Member of the Social Register",
For the paltry fee of $125 per annum.
This "work of art, done in good taste", and listing annually the
    "Notables of the Dominion",

Will contain nothing but "Ladies and Gentlemen pre-eminent
    in the Higher Spheres",
A list, indeed, of "First Families",
Who are "the very fabric of our country".
Thus shall we "build up in the Nation's First Families
A consciousness of their rôle in the life of a civilized democra-
    cy".

Thus shall we bring "added dignity and profound significance
To our cultural way of life".
Through deplorable lack of vision, in times past,
Men who were "great Canadians, have everlastingly passed
    into oblivion",
Leaving no "footprints on the sands of time".
Somehow, despite their pre-eminence, they have disappeared.

Shall we, through "tragic shortsightedness", let the leaders of
   this era
"Disappear into the realm of eternal silence"?
"Shall there be no names, no achievements, to hearten and
   strengthen on-coming generations in time of stress"?
If they have failed to make history, shall they fail to make The
   Canadian Social Register?
No – not if they can pay $125 annually,
And pass our Secret Committee.
For there is a "Secret Committee of seven members",
Who will "determine the eligibility of those applying for mem-
   bership".
Thus will the Social Register be "accepted in the most fastidi-
   ous circles".
And to aid the Secret Committee you will send
The name of your father and the maiden name of your mother,
And the address of your "summer residence",
(For of course you have a summer residence).
You may also submit, with a glossy print of yourself,
"Short quotations from laudatory comments received on di-
   verse public occasions".
When printed, the Register will be sent,
Free, gratis, and not even asked for,
To (among many others) the "King of Sweden", the "President
   of Guatemala", and the "Turkish Public Library".

Reader, this will be a "perennial reminder"
Of the people (or such of them as pass the Secret Committee)
Who "fashioned this Canada of ours",
For "One does not live only for toil and gain",
Not, anyway, in First Families. It is comforting to believe
That while we "walk the earth", and pay $125,

And "after we have passed on", there will remain
"In the literature of the Universe", and particularly in the
   "Turkish Public Library",
This "de luxe edition", "these unique and dignified annals",
"These priceless and undying memories", with laudatory com-
   ments chosen by ourselves,
To which "succeeding First Families and historians alike will
   look",
For "knowledge, guidance and inspiration".
Lives rich in eligibility will be "written large",
(But within "a maximum of one thousand words")
"For all men to see and judge".
The "glorious dead", too,
These "selfless and noble defenders of Canada's honour",
Will be incorporated in the Social Register
"Without any financial remuneration",
Assuming, of course, that they are all
"Sons and daughters of its Members".

Reader, as you may guess, the Register
Was not "a spur of the moment idea".
It was "long and carefully nurtured",
And "counsel was sought in high and authoritative places",
So that it may "lay a basis upon which prominent Canadians
   will henceforth be appraised
As they go striding down the years",
Paying their $125,
And receiving a "world-wide, gratuitous distribution",
Even unto "the Turkish Public Library".

"Si monumentum requiris, circumspice!"
On this note, we both end.

---

2. Faith Healing

John Lee/*Scarborough College,
University of Toronto*

*There can be no more intensely private space than that created by
deeply-held religious beliefs. One gains access only through
conversion. The extent of the social distance that separates
believers from non-believers is conveyed in the words of one
informant quoted in this essay, "(We) call these people outside
the jailors." Or in the author's observation, "There was a strong
sense of unity in opposition to the cold, unfriendly world outside."*

*Private space, we have said, is not likely to be intruded upon
unless it threatens others. In this regard it is instructive to
examine the sequence of events surrounding the devil cult which is
described in this selection. The church authorities had known
about it for some time and had allowed it to continue even though
it espoused beliefs and engaged in practices that were contrary to
the official Anglican creed. It was not until the cult's activities
were exposed to full public view through the unfortunate death of
one of its members and the ensuing anger and indignation cast a
shadow upon the church's established and prestigious position,
that the diocesan authorities set up their own tribunal to rid the
church of the heresy.*

Reprinted from *Sectarian Healers and Hypnotherapy*: A Study for the
Committee on the Healing Arts (1970), by permission of the author
and The Queen's Printer of Ontario.

In popular usage the term 'faith healing' generally would be
understood to include most of the occult healing systems. Here
we are using the term in a more restricted sense, recognizing
that there are certain distinctions in metaphysical doctrine
which separate Christian Science, Unity, non-Christian spiritu-
alism and other forms of 'mind cure' from the faith healing
dealt with in this chapter.

History

The concept of intercession with divine powers for relief of
human distress is one of man's most ancient beliefs.

   Within the Judaic culture, incantation and intercession with
deities for evil purposes were forbidden, and this tradition continued in Christendom, where such practices were labelled
'witchcraft'. The Church took over and monopolized the positive tradition of intercession with the one God of Judaism and
of Jesus Christ. Jesus himself had set the example of personal
purity and godliness in his human life, and demonstrated the
power of a right relationship with God in his healing miracles.
However, He constantly emphasized that it was the sufferer's

own faith (right relationship with God), rather than any occult power under His control, which made the healing possible.

Although the Apostles and early Christians continued the healing work initiated by Jesus, the expansion of Christianity gradually reduced the proportion of extremely vital and devoted members, and increased the proportion of nominal adherents. At the same time, expansion necessitated organization. The care of the sick became a specialized duty. Hospitals were established. Inevitably a process of secularization shifted the emphasis from faith to medicine, from priest to doctor, from petitioner to patient.

In medieval times the tasks of healing were bifurcated between the Church, which specialized more and more in spiritual health, and the medical profession, which was carefully restricted to limited physical procedures. Religious opposition to dissection and other medical advances widened the gap. Mental illness was regarded as possession by evil spirits, rather than a province of medicine. Although charismatic figures arose from time to time, and brought both physical and mental healing to the ill, the worldly organization of the Church tended to discourage saintliness more and more. Monasteries cared for the sick, but with neither excellent medicine nor healing miracles.

The Protestant Reformation downgraded the role of saints and abolished monasteries. The rule of natural law was incorporated into Christian doctrine. Calvin concluded that "The grace of healing has disappeared, like all other miraculous powers." The physician must now heal the mortal man, while the Church cared for the immortal spirit. Though the Protestant churches established their own hospitals, in Catholic, Protestant and secular hospital alike healing had become the responsibility of the physician of materia medica.

The way was left open for new religious concerns for man's health and well-being, based on the early concept of the wholeness of man. The nineteenth century mind-cure movement was one response to this need, but it so distorted the traditional doctrines of Christianity that many 'orthodox' Christians found it profoundly dissatisfying.

Within 'orthodox' Christianity, only the Catholic Church has preserved an active concern for physical healing through faith, as for example at Lourdes and at St. Joseph's Oratory in Montreal. However, this healing has remained only a minor part of the Catholic Church's activity, and does not meet our criteria for selection of 'healing cults.' The same is true of the United Church's occasional support of Rev. Alex Holmes.

The Anglican Church of Canada has not made 'faith healing' a part of its activities, but the recent startling events at a Toronto Anglican church which *did* make healing a central activity bring this particular church within our criteria.

Among the 'fringe' or 'fundamentalist' Protestant groups, some persons have made healing their major activity and therefore are of concern to us. The most famous of these is Oral Roberts.

Oral Roberts

Oral Roberts, a member of the Pentecostal denomination, is probably the best-known living faith healer in North America. His 'crusades' visit many cities, and through television broadcasts of edited portions of these crusades, many millions more are reached each week. In two decades, Roberts has expanded from a small personal ministry to an incorporated structure employing hundreds of persons with a budget in the millions of dollars each year. A university is now part of that corporate structure.

Claims

Oral Roberts claims to be a divinely appointed channel for God's healing of all forms of human illness and distress. Numerous testimonials are published and broadcast to support this claim. Those seeking his intercession with God are urged to 'expect a miracle'.

Roberts does not rival medical practice in any way; on the contrary, he urges the use of physicians and recognizes their work as another equally valuable channel of God's healing power. Roberts also has been careful to avoid any conflict with other religious and occult healing groups.

Although he makes no personal claims for his own power, attributing all healing to God's action, Roberts does carry out his healing role in an extremely dramatic and personalized manner which inevitably attracts attention to his own actions rather than to the (unseen) actions of divine power.

Doctrine

Roberts shares the generally fundamentalist doctrines of the Pentecostal movement, concerning the nature of reality, the destiny of man, the nature of God. This includes a belief in Satanic power and the existence of demons as a cause of human illness and distress. Strangely enough, Roberts mentions his encounter with demons in his Brazilian crusade more frequently than any encounter with demons in North American society. He claims to have cast out demons.

Roberts argues that God is good and does not will disease, but may permit it as a test, or for purification, to demonstrate His own power for goodness. He urges the sufferer to trust in God's power and willingness to heal.

History

In 1947 Oral Roberts was pastor of the Pentecostal Holiness Church at Enid, Oklahoma. A decade earlier, he claims, he had been "miraculously healed of tuberculosis" at a revival meeting in Ada, Oklahoma. At that time, God promised him that he would take His healing power to the world. Roberts waited for a sign, and it came in 1947 in a series of dreams. He rented an auditorium, found that his "enthusiasm was contagious", and healed a woman whose hand had been crippled for thirty-eight years.[1]

Roberts resigned his post and moved to Tulsa, where he founded the "Healing Waters Revival Ministry" and began publication of a magazine. In 1948 he incorporated his ministry and began his crusades. During a meeting in Texas, a storm struck his huge tent, and half-ton steel poles slowly fell on the crowd of 7,000. No one was hurt, however – everyone was able to get out of the way of the poles – and the newspapers headlined a 'miracle'. Roberts rocketed to national fame.

From the beginning of his healing ministry, Roberts demonstrated his power to move a large crowd with effective preaching. He also showed great skill in the use of mass media. His radio ministry began in 1948, and in 1954 he began broadcasts of crusades by television.

Roberts' corporate affairs prospered enormously. His organization moved into its own modern office building in 1954, and in 1959 moved again into the 'Abundant Life' building, especially designed for his ministry, with equipment for production of radio, film, tape and television programs. He took crusades further afield, to India, Australia, South Africa and Europe.

Organization

Including staff at Oral Roberts University, the Roberts organization now numbers over 600 employees, with a budget of millions of dollars. Regional offices handle local affairs, but all are in close contact with Tulsa. In Canada, Oral Roberts' affairs are managed through a Toronto office by an Administrator and several full-time clerks. Replies to appeals for help and public response to the mass media outreach are handled through this office.

As well as dominating the healing crusades, Roberts remains in personal authority within the corporate structure. Most of the organization's literature is authored by him and he is the most frequent person featured in it (he is also shown in many photographs). The healing ministry remains very much the *Oral Roberts* ministry despite the development of a 'healing team'.

The organization of a crusade requires months of advance preparations. About one crusade a month is held somewhere in the world. In Canada, the Canadian Administrator assesses the proposed location about six months in advance to ascertain that a crusade will be successful.

A committee of local ministers willing to support the crusade's work is set up and takes the responsibility for local arrangements. If the location lacks a large enough hall, the Roberts tent will be used. Roberts always brings his own public address system, rather than depending on local equipment and risking failures.

Crusades cost between $15,000 and $25,000. Roberts' organization guarantees to cover any loss. On the other hand, if there is a surplus after all expenses are paid, it goes to the local sponsoring churches, as do all the names on the Prayer Cards.

No information is available on the exact budget of the Roberts' organization, his own salary, or similar matters. Nor are there any reliable data on the number of persons reached or 'healed'. The persons attracted to Roberts' crusades are likely to be in the working and middle-class range, but no statistics are available on typical age, income or education. Clearly the great majority would be favourably disposed to fundamentalist Protestant doctrine, and are therefore likely to be of less than university education, non-professional, and in the middle-to-older age range.

Therapy
Roberts does not ordinarily practise healing in a quiet private situation with the individual patient. He works in a crusade, a series of large daily meetings, carefully organized and stirred to enthusiasm (and even frenzy) by rousing hymn-singing and preaching.

Those wishing healing must register in advance and secure a Prayer Card. Individuals are called in alphabetical order, with all those not called prayed for en masse on the last day.

Following hymns and Roberts' dramatic sermon, the Prayer Line forms. Roberts usually sits on stage, on a high stool, with each petitioner coming before him in turn (and remaining standing). Roberts reads out the name and illness from the Prayer Card, and then exchanges a few personal words warmly with the sufferer.

Then with a forceful gesture, which may cause the sufferer to sway backward, Roberts firmly grasps him by the head or shoulders and cries out loudly, "In the name of Jesus Christ, be HEALED, be HEALED." The sufferer may shudder or shake, or even cry out.

Relaxing his hold, Roberts again converses with the sufferer, asking him, for example, "Did you feel that", or "How do you feel now?" or saying "I felt God's healing power that time". Usually the sufferer agrees that he or she felt something flow through from Roberts' hands, or that he or she is feeling better.

As the sufferer walks off stage, the limp may have disappeared, or the crippled arm may swing, or the back straighten. Whether or not the health of the individual is altered in a meaningful way, it is frequently possible to observe a marked difference in the posture, motion, general manner and facial expression of the petitioner.

Roberts often features return visits by persons he has healed at earlier crusades (especially in the same city). These individuals, now hale and hearty, testify to the healing they received from a previous crusade.

In many cases, no observable healing takes place. This is not frequent on the television coverage of crusades, since these programs are edited rather than presented 'live'. On stage, Roberts tends to emphasize, and devote more time to, those persons who seem to respond to his healing technique.

Training
The 'healing team' of assistants who aid Roberts in his crusades consists mainly of ministers who have developed abilities for faith healing in their own right, and who have joined the Roberts organization. The Oral Roberts University School of Evangelism is training its students in the doctrine and practice of Christian healing, among other things.

Other Faith Healers: Fundamentalist

Healing crusades regularly visit many smaller centres in Ontario where the Roberts organization would not find sufficient support to merit the large expense of a crusade. These smaller crusades usually feature a healer and several assistants. A tent, chairs, public address system, and other equipment are moved about by truck.

Contacts are made in advance with sympathetic local ministers to publicize the crusade. A week or so before the crusade arrives for the usual week-long series of meetings, advertising cards may be tacked on utility poles in the area. Advertising is placed in the local newspaper church page.

At a recent crusade of this type in southern Ontario, featuring a western Canadian faith healer, evening gatherings were held in a large tent raised on a department store parking lot. Several scores of persons sat scattered throughout the tent, which could have held at least 500. Rousing hymn-singing was followed by requests for all those who felt the power of God present in the tent to raise their arms . . . and then to stand up. A fiery sermon was then preached, in which the healer included his own story of miraculous recovery from a very terrible disease.

Those who desired healing were called to the stage. The healer grasped each in turn by the head, commanded the demons in possession to "loose this man" (or woman), and called on the healing power of Christ to make whole.

One woman, about thirty-five to forty years old, came up and disclosed her problem as 'oppressive fear and depression'. When the healer grasped her head and shouted to the demons to "Loose this woman", she swayed backward and fainted to the stage floor. The healer retained his grasp and the woman revived. He again exorcised the demons, and the woman broke into tears, babbling incomprehensibly. She shook and writhed on the stage.

Finally, after about five minutes, the healer left her on the stage floor and returned to the healing line. After a further five minutes the woman ceased shivering, got up, and returned to her seat. The gathering was punctuated with cries of 'Halleluja' and similar outbursts during all this time. The healer afterward assured the crowd that "God's healing power was truly with us tonight."

Other Faith Healers: Toronto Anglican 'Demon Cult'

A group practising the exorcism of demons was active for several years in St. Mathias Anglican Church in downtown Toronto, and came to sensational press and public attention in September 1967 following an inquest into the death of one of its members.

The spiritual leader of this group was well respected not only among his fellow churchmen, but also by ministers of other denominations who knew him well. Two Anglican priests who had served under him in the past described him as "almost a holy man, deeply religious, always concerned to help troubled persons, a man of peace."

The second Anglican priest in this group, the assistant at the church, was new to the ministry (having recently been ordained after serving as a teacher in a private school). He tended to be rather facile and dogmatic in his exposition of the group's doctrines.

The organizational leadership of the group was exercised by the estranged wife of a university professor. She was a woman of strongly held opinions, biting sarcasm, unyielding attitude, and almost 'hypnotic' persuasiveness.

The church in which the group operated is located in a downtown working-class area of Toronto. Most of the population are Italian or Polish immigrants, and Roman Catholic. The membership of the Anglican church is very small, and most apparently became involved in the demon-exorcising group.

"The ministry began as a group gathered for prayer for spiritual healing. Latterly it has become more and more concerned with the presence of evil in the lives of distressed people, . . . " reported the Anglican bishop at the time of the inquest.

The assistant priest freely conceded that the group believed in real, personal entities called demons, in the service of the Devil and Hell. Illness and distress were caused by the possession of an individual by demons, he claimed. An 'evil atmosphere' surrounded such a person. The demons could be exorcised by various prayers and rituals.

The woman in charge of organization, whose personality obviously dominated the group, acted as a 'house mother' to about sixteen persons living in the group's community house. The age of residents ranged from three years up. It included five theology students at the University of Toronto, and the assistant priest.

Most of these residents, especially the students, had come from emotionally troubled backgrounds. They clearly appreciated the strong emotional rapport possible with the leadership of the group. Anyone leaving the house first came into the living room and held hands briefly with the assistant priest and the woman while a protective prayer was said. Physical expressions of emotional attachment and dependence were frequent (holding hands, kissing and hugging).

Several of the resident students credited the group and its leadership with effecting great improvement in their health and emotional stability. Improvement in school performance also was mentioned. There was a strong sense of unity in opposition to the cold, unfriendly world outside.

The inquest found that the Anglican priest and his wife had been negligent in the death of an eighteen-year-old girl, a member of the occult group and a resident in the church rectory as the legal ward of the priest. She died in June 1967, from a brain abcess and meningitis.

The girl had been suffering an 'earache' for several weeks prior to her death, and had been treated on seven occasions by six different doctors at a Toronto hospital. The last treatment was nine days before her death, and at that time the examining doctor found her to be recovering well. He instructed her to return in two weeks.

During the twenty-four hour period prior to her death, she suffered great pain and was continually screaming. The priest and other members of the group believed her to be suffering from possession by the Devil. At the inquest, the priest admitted that his religious beliefs had 'clouded' his judgement, and

that he had believed his ward's troubles to be only emotional.

Instead of calling a doctor when the girl began screaming and showing great pain, the priest 'spanked' her ritually to force the devil out of her. Later two other members of the group came to exorcise the devil out of her, but found her dead.

When the girl's body was removed to the coroner's morgue, three members of the group went to the morgue and prayed over the body. They admitted that they fully expected that their prayers would bring the girl back to life, as Lazarus had been raised from the dead 2,000 years before.

At the inquest, concern was expressed at the lack of communication among the doctors at the hospital treating the girl, such that six different doctors should have become involved, a circumstance reflecting more cause for concern about hospital outpatient services than about faith healing. But the jury verdict attached no fault to the medical profession.

One of the most interesting rituals of this group, for our investigation, was paid little attention in the press. This was a ceremony for 'potting the devil'. When possessed of a demon, the individual suddenly fell asleep, as if in a trance; and, according to witnesses, the woman in the group leadership also went into a trance. Once she 'howled like a dog'. This ritual, and the extremely emphatic, persuasive manner of the woman in ordinary conversation suggest that phenomena resembling those of hypnosis were part of the group's ritual, whether the group was aware of this or not.

The group encouraged its adolescent members to break away from parents who were believed to be possessed by the devil and imprisoning the children in evil. "We call these people outside the jailors," explained a member of the group. The angry emotional divisions created (or exacerbated) in the families of some of the group members were frequently evident at the inquest.

Members of the group lived in daily fear of the devil, and were encouraged and assisted to remain always on guard. The devil was described by one witness:

> He was a live, active, dark mist surrounding things and penetrating them. If you cut a finger or drop a dish, that would be the devil's work. If I talked of my father and mother I would be picking up their bad atmosphere and that would have to be prayed away.[2]

The leadership and at least half a dozen of the members of this group had university-level education. The remainder were young persons of a working-class or white-collar background, most in their late teens or early twenties.

It should be emphasized that the events at St. Mathias in Toronto are in no way characteristic of the policy or practice of the Anglican Church of Canada on questions of healing.

Evaluation

Probably none of the larger denominations any longer propagates doctrines of demonology and demon exorcism, although doctrinal statements concerning belief in demons and Satan still remain part of most Christian Churches. It would be necessary to revise the New Testament substantially to eliminate such doctrines completely. However, most of the larger Churches not only discourage implementation of demonological concepts today; they are also moving in the direction of rejecting faith healing as a legitimate application of Christian belief.

The Church of England
In 1955 the Archbishop of Canterbury appointed a special

commission to study the role of the Church in healing. The practical investigations required were turned over to the British Medical Association (a fact which later served to cast doubt on the objectivity of the Report, but which on the other hand made its concessions to the power of occult healing all the more significant). Both the BMA and the Archbishop's Commission issued reports in 1956. ,

In its report, the Archbishop's Commission takes a general 'scientific' approach to healing. It rejects the doctrine that suffering is God's will but states that it can be a consequence of man's sin.

However, it denies that healing inevitably follows sufficient faith, or that God must heal, or that sickness is always caused by sin; and thus it undermines the doctrines of faith healing.

The Report considers that a scientifically inexplicable healing is no more important or wonderful than one brought about by medical means:

> Nor does the fact that an event is scientifically inexplicable constitute evidence of supernatural cause. Confronted with what is at present inexplicable, the scientist cannot resort to supernatural explanations without transgressing the limits of scientific thinking.[3]

The Report urges recognition of the *post hoc, ergo propter hoc* fallacy (the argument that because B followed A, A caused B) which frequently underlies testimonials of the efficacy of faith healing. It opposes use of the term 'faith healing' within the Church, on the grounds that it puts too much emphasis on faith and the faith healer as the operative aspects of healing. It also opposes *spiritual* and *divine* healing because these suggest that medical healing does not involve the spiritual or divine. The preferred term is 'the Church's ministry of healing'.

As might be expected, the Commission's Report deals largely with the theological aspects of the Church's ministry of healing; the BMA Report, undertaken at the Commission's request, deals with the specific experience of faith healing among British doctors.

British Medical Association Report

The Archbishop's Commission asked the BMA to investigate
  1) medical evidence of spontaneous cures or rapid recovery as a result of spiritual healing
  2) evidence of the value of healing services in the Church
  3) possible harmful effects, including delay in seeking medical advice.

Ten prominent doctors with an impressive array of qualifications constituted the BMA Committee. They held hearings, consulted individuals in the field, and distributed a questionnaire to all physicians.

> As far . . . as our observations and investigations have gone, we have seen no evidence that there is any special type of illness cured solely by spiritual healing which cannot be cured by medical means, which do not involve such claims.[4]

Actually, this conclusion is very carefully phrased. It does not say that spiritual healing cannot heal or has not healed any disease, but only that such healings could have been achieved by medical means. The Report does concede several major points, which occult healing practitioners have since cited as lending some support to their own claims.

First, the Report concedes that the patient may gain new courage from spiritual healing ministrations; his anxiety may be reduced, thus promoting healing, and his appetite may even be restored. But the Report goes further:

> The same drug given by two doctors may have a very

different effect according to the personality of the practitioner administering it, thus one may succeed where another fails; one patient may be cured because he has faith whereas the sceptical one is not; one method such as suggestion may cure where analysis failed, and vice versa.[5]

This statement tends to lend support to the doctrine taught in Christian Science, Concept-Therapy and other occult systems, that the efficacy of drugs depends (largely or entirely) on the doctor's suggestion.

The appendix of the Report contains a number of verified cases submitted by British doctors who themselves believed that some form of spiritual healing was at least partly responsible for the patient's recovery. Cases are reported where "recovery occurred usually in a very short time after healing services were held for patients with grave or hopeless prognosis":

> A case of disseminated sclerosis with widespread lesions; a lady in her forties with sinus for whom inhalations and antiseptics had provided no relief; an elderly lady of seventy-one who had been in bed for nine weeks following a stroke and had been told by her general practitioner that she would not walk again; a baby two and a half years old with tubercular intestinal peritonitis who had been given two weeks to live; a child of nine with diagnosis confirmed by biopsy, of cirrhosis of the liver; a woman in her forties who had ulcerative colitis with frequent haemhorrage from the rectum, a condition from which she had suffered a number of years . . .[6]

These *medical* testimonies attributing healing in whole or in part to spiritual treatment and prayer cover a very wide variety of disorders, both 'functional' and 'organic'. This probably accounts for the caution of the Committee in restricting its conclusion to the suggestion that the same cures might have been achieved by medical means, without denying the physicians' reports that they were in fact achieved without, or after the exhaustion of, medical means.

In the area of functional disorders, the Committee readily admits the efficacy of spiritual healing, suggestion and similar techniques:

> Disorders of psychological origin may be cured by many methods of treatment affecting the patient's mind and emotional state, including spiritual healing, laying on of hands, unction, forms of analytical treatment, suggestion (including hypnosis) . . . some of these methods direct themselves simply to the abolition of the symptoms, such as removal of pain or a hysterical paralysis; others, especially the analytical method, aim at discovering some of the causes and the meaning of the illness, and by allaying the anxiety, may cure the patient more radically and permanently.[7]

One possible explanation is suggested for the success of spiritual healing after exhaustion of ordinary medical means:

> All psychiatrists know of seemingly intractable physical illnesses or emotional disorders which did not respond to any form of treatment hitherto, but which under their care make a rapid and apparently complete recovery. It is this sort of case which responds to spiritual healing, and gives the false impression that the spiritual healing was the causal factor.[8]

Turning to the potential dangers of spiritual healing, the Committee warns that:

> . . . it is undesirable and even highly dangerous for anyone

to apply these methods of treatment without a knowledge of the nature of the disease from which the patient is suffering. To treat certain forms of depression by laying on of hands or to resort to the help of spirit media or suggestion when specific treatment is available is to do the patient the greatest disservice.[9]

The dangers of faith healing were believed by the Committee to be greatest among those who put the most hope in it and then were disappointed, since the resulting depression could reduce the efficacy of ameliorative medical treatment, even when a cure was not possible.

The majority of cases where physicians reported damage to the patient as a result of faith in an occult healing system were found to involve Christian Science.

Since 'incurable' patients who turn to occult practitioners and survive the physicians who predicted their early death are among the more frequent examples referred to by occult practitioners as proof of their success, the Committee takes pains to point out that such prognosis is made on a statistical basis. That is, the chances of survival may be only one in a hundred, but obviously it is that one who stays around to testify to his survival. Such survival need not involve any form of occult healing; it is simply a matter of statistical chance.

United Church of Canada

Perhaps the most critical assessment of faith healing by a Church is that recently issued by the United Church of Canada in its report, *Sickness and Health*.[10] This study was produced by a Committee of ministers and physicians, and it omits any objective survey of medical experience. It presents the following criticisms of faith healers (paraphrased below):

1) Most faith healers assume sickness is the work of Satan or a result of sin; this is not in accord with New Testament teaching.

2) Most faith healers wrongly assume a distinction between natural and supernatural healing.

3) Many faith healers make extravagant and unreliable claims, and use sensational testimonials given under emotional stress.

4) Many faith healers encourage suggestibility and credulity.

5) Some reliable studies have suggested that only in a very small proportion of cases is healing achieved. (The BMA and two other studies are cited.)

6) Much agony and heartbreak is suffered by many who are not healed.

7) Many faith healers disparage or discount the role of medicine.

8) The huge sums of money contributed to faith healers would be more productively used in medical research.

The Report concludes that "faith healers of the variety described above do not exercise a legitimate ministry of the Church and should be actively resisted in their practice."

'Scientific' Studies of Faith Healing

If by 'scientific' we mean objective, experimental, verifiable studies, then there are very few such in this field. Studies by survey of physicians do not qualify, since they are open to prejudice and emotion. The information gained from such surveys, carefully conducted, is certainly useful, but it cannot be regarded as definitive. The results of a survey of positive effects (the BMA study) and one of negative effects (our own survey of Toronto physicians) are reported elsewhere.

A study by A. C. Gabelein in 1925[11] found that of 350 persons who received healing from a faith healer in Vancouver, B.C., 301 showed no change, 39 died within 6 months, 5 became mentally ill, and 5 were cured. Of course, the cures were attributed to recovery from functional disorders, since physicians label any illness cured by a faith healer as (by definition) a functional disorder.

As the Anglican Archbishop's Commission pointed out, this is to be expected. Scientific medical practice cannot accept a supernatural explanation. Even if a faith healer caused an amputated limb to grow back on a patient, medicine would have to seek a natural explanation.

A study by Leslie D. Weatherhead[12] and his son, a psychiatrist, of miracle cures at Lourdes in France found that at least 98 per cent go home unhealed. He refers to Dr. George Day's study of the Lourdes miracles, which concluded that of the 68 million persons estimated to have visited the shrine since its opening, only 200 cures have been certified by the commission of physicians and priests responsible for such verification. Of course, these 200 cures have survived the most rigid investigation. Before recognition as a 'miracle', a cure must be verified with the patient's personal physician, with times and dates of treatment, and with opinions of specialists consulted; the patient is then examined by at least three doctors at Lourdes, and sent home for a year. At the end of a year he is again examined by three physicians. If in their opinion healing has taken place which can reasonably be attributed to the period of time of the visit to Lourdes, a commission is appointed, medical opinion is consulted, and finally, all being agreed, the cure is certified as a miracle.

Despite his grave doubts about the statistical efficacy of Lourdes, Weatherhead asserts that after examining several cases in detail, one involving a boy who was totally blind, "there cannot be any doubt that real cures of organic diseases have taken place."[13] However, he attributes the cures to factors other than supernatural intervention and the healing waters of the shrine:

> There is probably no stream in Britain which could not boast as high a proportion of cures as the stream at Lourdes if patients came in the same numbers and in the same psychological state of expectancy.[14]

In any event, the proportion is not very high: Day estimates it at .0003 per cent of those visiting Lourdes.[15]

Finally, we note a study conducted by a German physician[16] of three women: one with chronic inflammation of the gall bladder, with stones; one who was failing to recuperate from a major abdominal operation; and a third with widespread cancer. The physician first allowed a spiritual healer to pray for the patients without informing them. Nothing happened. He then informed them that he was requesting spiritual healing, and repeatedly emphasized this so that their expectations were increased over a period of several days. He named a specific time at which the spiritual healer would be praying, a time at which he was quite certain the healer would not be doing so. When the stated time arrived, all three patients improved 'quickly and dramatically'. The recuperating patient completely recovered; the cancer patient recovered enough to go home and do household duties until her death shortly thereafter; and the third went home well and did not relapse until several years later.

NOTES

1. Oral Roberts, *My Twenty Years of a Miracle Ministry*, Roberts Evangelical Mission, Tulsa, Oklahoma, 1967, p. 7.
2. *Globe and Mail*, September 29, 1967, p. 2.
3. *Archbishop's Commission Report*, 1956, p. 27.
4. British Medical Association, *Divine Healing and Co-operation between Doctors and Clergy*, 1956, p. 13.
5. *Ibid*, p. 11.

6. *Ibid*, p. 35.
7. *Ibid*., p. 11.
8. *Ibid*., p. 13.
9. *Ibid*., p. 11.
10. United Church of Canada, *Sickness and Health*, Board of Evangelism and Social Service, Toronto, 1967.
11. Cited by the United Church of Canada, *ibid*., p. 17.

12. Leslie D. Weatherhead, *Psychology, Religion and Healing*, Hodder and Stoughton, 1963, p. 157.
13. *Ibid*., p. 149.
14. *Ibid*., p. 158.
15. *Ibid*., p. 157.
16. H. Rehder, "Wunderheilungen". *Hippokrates*, Vol. 26, 1955, p. 577.

3. Boarding School: Social Control, Space and Identity

Mary Percival Maxwell/*Queen's University*
James D. Maxwell/*Queen's University*

The private school has had extensive influence in maintaining elite control of Canadian political institutions. In his book The Vertical Mosaic, *John Porter documented the extent to which students who had attended private schools, although they make up only four per cent of the school population, are disproportionately represented not only in the upper echelons of government but of business and other major institutions as well. It is the prototype of private space as we have defined it. Access is rigorously controlled, drawing from a pool of potential recruits that is confined to a very small segment of society. Control rests firmly within the institution. In their paper, the Maxwells provide us with compelling evidence that the social distance that separates private school members from the world outside is deliberately contrived and carefully managed; fear of pollution and taboos to protect purity are strong.*

On a second level, this paper is an excellent illustration of the sensitive application of the concept of territoriality as it is presented in Lyman's and Scott's essay in Section Two. Discerning examples of the four types of territory, the authors discuss the utility of each in the management of identity and social space.

This paper focuses on an elite Canadian private school for girls. It is particularly concerned with the organizational features and socialization practices which affect the 'moral career' of a 'new girl' in the boarding school, and the implications they have for the student's career after she graduates and leaves the School. A 'moral career' in this context is the series of stages, events, *rites de passage* which a girl goes through during her stay in the School. In addition, in Goffman's terms, this entails the sequence of changes in the person's image of self and felt identity, as well as in her social status (1961: 127-169). Institutions such as the School 'try to leave their mark', that is to say, they try to impose certain values, norms and identities on those who enter. We are describing a small segment of this process and its implications for those who enter the School and for their lives after they have left the School.

The School and the External World — Whence They Come

The School is of late nineteenth century Anglican origin and

Published for the first time in this collection. The research, upon which this paper is based, is from a larger study; Mary Percival Maxwell, "Social Structure, Socialization and Social Class in a Canadian Private School for Girls" (PhD dissertation, Cornell University, June 1970).

was founded in 1894 to unite "evangelical spiritual influences with a thorough intellectual culture." Historically, it has had close ties with the 'old Country' which implies that it has been closely tied to and has attempted to serve, in very large part, what Porter (1965) has called the British Charter Group. Only four per cent of the students enrolled in academic primary and secondary educational institutions in Canada are enrolled in private schools (Canada, Dominion Bureau of Statistics, 1963-64:30-31). Yet, as Porter has demonstrated, persons who have attended private schools exert considerably greater social power than their numbers would suggest. In Canadian society, private school attendance must be looked at as having a significant impact in the larger social sphere and the socialization practices in this school should be viewed as affecting the larger social system, even though this is a girls' school, and the corridors of power in Canadian society are not overcrowded by the female sex.

Life in any organization is affected by the type of person who is recruited as a potential member and the type of person who is eventually selected to become a member of the organization. By controlling transactions with the external environment, organizations can influence to at least some degree the 'society' which exists within them. Total institutions are those organizations where members are cut off from the world at large and where life is formally administered (Goffman, 1961:xiii). Members spend all their daily life there. The voluntary nature of the relationship is highly significant for such institutions which are obliged to 'put up with' their members around the clock and for those members who must fulfill their daily life in a 'public place'. They differ from such total institutions as prisons which must accept all those who come (and thus relationships may be involuntary) and public schools which are in a similar position (although they do not have their members with them around the clock). This School is in an advantageous position in terms of recruitment and selection; it does not accept any student who does not wish to come and it has no shortage of applicants.

Perhaps one of the best ways of looking at the homogeneity of the School is in terms of social class. The social class composition of virtually all independent schools in Canada is determined not only by the mutual selection of the upper classes and these schools but by the fee structures of the schools themselves. Except for a very small number of students on scholarships, the School recruits the daughters of the upper classes who can afford the $1000 a year day school fees and an additional $1000 or more for boarders. The homogeneity of social class is reflected in the fact that 97 per cent of the occupations of fathers of students fall into Class I or II of the Blishen Scale

(Blishen, 1958). In addition, 52 per cent of both the fathers and mothers of students in Grades IX-XIII had attended a private school and 14 per cent of the mothers had attended this same school. Not only does the School recruit from certain social classes, but it tends to select those whom it deems to have values appropriate to their class. Included among these in recent decades has been a high respect for academic ability and achievement; comparatively less emphasis has been placed on religious affiliation. The social orbit within the School into which a new student is placed is thus a restricted one. It is restricted in terms of those who can afford and have chosen to attend the School, and by the process by which the School selects its students. In many cases this sphere has been restricted in a like manner for several generations. The School thus relegates to the external environment a large portion of the socialization which might otherwise be required and students have undergone what we usually refer to as anticipatory socialization.

The School is located in one of Canada's largest cities on spacious grounds in what once were the 'suburbs'. Approximately 550 students attend the School at all levels from preschool to the end of high school. At the secondary level, the School offers only the four and five year academic courses in preparation for university indicating its strong orientation toward higher education. Students may attend the School either as 'day girls' or 'boarders' except in the early grades in which it accepts only day students. Most of the students come from within Canada but a variety of other countries are represented. Males attend the School – in the pre-school programme!

The spacious buildings and grounds and their relative seclusion permit the School to create and sustain a large number of activities which might not be as possible in more confined quarters. At the same time the easy access of the School to the facilities of the larger city permit it to enlarge, as it were, the social space of its members without undue inconvenience, but at the same time to control this enlargement. The success of the School is facilitated by this selective use of physical space, and the selective use of social mechanisms in conjunction with this physical space which allow for a rich but controlled institutional life. Other total institutions, at least in the past, have tended to suffer from a poverty of physical space and social activity. This, plus the involuntary nature of their recruitment, has resulted in deprivation for their members.

Delegated Authority and the Privilege System

The homogeneity of social class and value systems and the voluntarism of recruitment permit the School to utilize organizational features and modes of social control by which students themselves are co-opted as agents of socialization and control. Because of the prestige attached to private school attendance, especially to attendance at the most elite, the authorities are able to utilize the technique of appealing to the honour of the School to gain conformity by students. The School scotches much potential deviance, as well as reducing the likelihood of the recurrence of breaches of the official norms, by telling the students that they are, or would be 'letting the School down'. Behaviour within the School and in public places is thus controlled by this identification with the School to a much greater degree than is possible in other institutions. The School is able to assume an identity on the student's part while at the same time attempting to strengthen that identity. The assumption of a strong and increasing identification with the School underlies the privilege system[1] and operates as the principal mechanism of social control within the School. The School authorities recognize, of course, the role of developmental factors at work

during this period when increased privileges are granted.

The privilege system as it operates in the School seems to rest on two basic assumptions. The first is that the longer a girl spends at the School, the more she can be trusted; in effect, as we mentioned previously, her identity becomes stronger and she will not 'let the School down'. The second is that students will attempt to prevent their peers from letting the School down. Consequently, as the years pass, girls are allowed more and more privileges which would in the earlier years have been thought to involve too much risk. In addition, they are allowed to run for and be elected or appointed to a myriad of offices in houses,[2] sports and clubs which the School has created to sustain the process of identification.

The most significant among these systems of offices is the prefect system. The School, like other private schools, has a system by which the School co-opts senior student leaders in Grade XIII into prefect roles where they assist in the administration and discipline of the rest of the School body. Being a prefect, elected by a weighted system of voting among students and staff, is a privilege in itself but in addition, prefects are given special additional privileges which release them from rules and restrictions applying to others in return for the responsibility the first privilege entails.

Beyond the system of offices in the various sectors of the School is the grade structured privilege system which allows each succeeding academic grade new or extended privileges relative to the ones of the preceeding year. Privileges cover a wide range of practices, such as less staff supervision, a later 'lights out' hour and permission for boarders to leave the School grounds after classes on weekdays until five o'clock study. All share one aspect in common: that is, they all offer a carefully measured additional amount of personal autonomy to the members of the particular grades to which they apply and less staff supervision and control.

A third category of privileges are rewards for identification and behavioural conformity which are given regardless of one's age-grade status. These include less close staff supervision in general and, in particular, unsupervised study and greater access to free places. To the extent that they are attained, they allow less intrusion of the institution into the individual's private sphere. They have meaning of course only within the rules of the School in terms of their reward value.

The grade-stratified, hierarchical community structure tends to engender acceptance of authority from those in lower grades because one knows that in the future, one will 'get one's turn' in the authority structure. In contrast to these ascribed privileges, those given for good behavior and those offices for which achievement is open tend to encourage a more personal identification with the School. Students in the School are allowed greater range in terms of physical space (and the social activities which accompany these) and a greater range of social activities in leadership positions as they identify with the School more strongly. External social control and the way in which it impinges on the individual's private sphere is reduced as that individual identifies more closely with the collectivity.

Moral Career and Physical Space

In its organization, structure and patterns of authority, it is the Boarding School (the physical portion of the School where the boarders live *and* the boarders as a sub-system of the School) which most resembles Goffman's characteristics of a total institution mentioned previously. There is a relative lack of social and geographical separation of work and leisure roles; there is continuous supervision of 'inmates' by staff who have 'echelon' authority; there are systems of rewards and punishments which are institutionalized in the age-graded privilege system as well as 'house rules', 'privileges' and punishments applying to all. As we mentioned at the outset of the paper, we are discussing only the small segment of the process of identity conferral which relates to the use of space. Processes surrounding the moral career which are not directly related to space, particularly those which function at the level of expressive symbolism, will be alluded to rather than discussed in detail. In this section we shall examine how physical space is used in the Boarding School as a mechanism of social control in the process of conferring an identity on the new girl.

The Boarding School occupies the upper two floors of the School and the various age-grades are assigned rooms adjacent to each other so that a corridor or a section of a corridor contains the bedrooms of boarders of the same age-grade and the matron who oversees the age-grade. Grades X, XI, and XII share a floor and corridor with no physical barrier separating the grades. However, for much of the day interactional barriers can be observed, that is, students do not interact because of the institutional management of the students' activities and interests. Moreover, the matrons in charge of specific grades tend to try to reduce what interaction between grades might occur in order to maintain social control over their charges. These efforts are beyond those of institutional exigencies. Interactional territories,[3] that is territories where social gatherings might occur, are thus restricted in large part to grade groupings.

By comparison, Grades VI–IX and Grade XIII, the lowest and the highest status groups in boarding, have physical barriers separating them from each other and from the other grades. In addition, whereas all boarders are allowed, at certain times of the day, to frequent the corridor and even the rooms of boarders up to Grade XII, the Grade XIII corridor is reserved *exclusively* for its own members. This means that for the seniors, 'home territory', that is territory where "the participants have a relative freedom of behavior and intimacy and control over the area", (Lyman and Scott, 1967) extends to their corridor, whereas for the other grades, home territory is confined to the members' bedrooms and washrooms. The seniors also have their own common room whereas the other grades do not individually have similar 'home territory' specifically allocated for collective use.

The allocation of physical space just described might be regarded as part of the privilege system. These extra spheres of 'home territory' permit greater autonomy since they are less subject to staff supervision, and they allow seniors a place beyond the scrutiny of other students where they can drop the masks of authority which appear necessary for institution maintenance and identity conferral, and permit them to express the types of idosyncratic behavior which may be necessary for the personal adjustment[4] of 'public leaders' in the institutional system. This is particularly true for the Prefect of the Boarding School (the highest leadership office in the Boarding School). She has an additional 'site' for short periods of solitude, knowledge of which is passed on from one boarder prefect to her successor. This is not only Goffman's backstage in the figurative sense, but also literally; it is the backstage of the Assembly Hall where she can drop the facade of perpetual enthusiasm and cheerfulness which are the demands of her role and 'indulge in a good cry'.

Within the Boarding School, the self of the 'new girl' is systematically, if often unintentionally, mortified and the process[5] starts on the day on which the new boarders arrive at the School for initial orientation (the day before the 'returning' boarders arrive). The new boarder undergoes a form of admission procedure in which her height, weight and menstrual history are recorded by the nurses in the presence of several other students who are waiting their turn. The student is also told that she must come and sign a book in the infirmary at the commencement of each menstrual period. This 'health check' constitutes for the new boarder the first dramatic demand for the revelation of personal facts about herself which, up until then, she may have kept private. This procedure constitutes a violation of the student's 'informational preserve' (Goffman, 1961:23) regarding her 'self'. The new girl is also assigned to her room (shared with two or three others) on this day and must accommodate herself to a relative poverty of material furnishings and comforts, as well as a lack of privacy in bedroom and bathroom, in comparison to that to which she has been accustomed. Loss of this set of comforts reflects a certain loss of self-determination through invasion of the individual's private territory. However, unlike the inmates of custodial institutions, boarders may bring many of their private possessions, including clothes, with them. Physical 'props' in terms of the self are not entirely removed in this setting. However, during the Day School hours of academic instruction, the girls are required to wear the School uniform. The new girl, unaccustomed to seeing large numbers of people in uniform, tends to have initial difficulty in distinguishing individual students. The fact that, in addition to not being recognized, she is unable to use the 'physical props' or 'costumes for the self' which she has been used to is part of the mortification process. The fact that recognition of individuals proves difficult under the new circumstances symbolizes, in a material way, the predominance of the new collectivity and its 'absorption' of the individual as the process of identity conferral begins.

In spite of its mortification aspects, collective living is valued by virtually all boarders and few girls elect to have one of the half dozen single rooms. Many bedrooms for four share a common bathroom with connecting doors which, according to the informal norms, should be left open permitting free access of all eight boarders to the entire area. Thus eight people are 'john-mates' and the relationships fostered by this particular arrangement may continue throughout their lives. Great emphasis is placed on sociability both by the staff and by the students themselves and a high value is attached to being able to sustain constant interaction. At the same time, students feel a need to be alone from time to time and, in contrast to monastic orders, few formal opportunities are provided for solitude. Boarders utilize a number of 'secondary adjustments'[6] in order to obtain a few moments of solitude. Among these are the use of the toilet cubicles in the common bathroom 'to be alone', using the infirmary, going off the School grounds at permitted times but unaccompanied by a required companion, slipping off to sit alone on the landing of the unfrequented back stairway and other 'illegal mechanisms' of securing privacy. New girls, not yet adjusted to the intensity of collective life, frequently go to the infirmary claiming they are tired and want to rest for a while. The nurses, sensing their need to be alone, place them in one of the infirmary's single rooms. Boarders may request 'early bed', that is, to go to bed in the infirmary right after the evening meal and this too is used as means of gaining temporary control over space for private use.

New boarders also have to accustom themselves to morning uniform inspection and weekly 'bedroom inspection' by their matrons. A card with a boarder's marks on these bedroom inspections must be displayed at all times on her mirror, so that anyone entering her room has immediate access to this information. Personal belongings are open to the matron's perusal at any time and the matron confiscates any contraband items she may discover on her surprise inspections (which often take place in the girl's absence). The inspections are rationalized on the grounds that they help to instill tidiness and curtail the use of secondary adjustments. Nevertheless, they reinforce property dispossession and violate the territories of the self.

Access to the outside world is an additional dimension of physical space which must be examined in terms of social control and identity conferral. Access to the outside world is curtailed and programmed by several sets of rules. No boarder up to Grade XII may leave the School, even at permitted times, without signing herself out in a special book and she must state in writing where she is going and must be accompanied by one or more other boarders unless she has obtained written permission from the Principal to be accompanied by an adult host or hostess, who then acts *in loco parentis*. The names of such 'outsiders' must have been entered well in advance by the girl's parents on her 'visiting card'. Girls in Grades VI – IX are never allowed out unless chaperoned by a hostess or a member of the staff. Not only are the girl's exits and entrances carefully monitored but her external social relations are jointly controlled by parents and the School. In addition, the School term is divided into alternate 'In' and 'Out' Saturdays and only on the 'Out' Saturdays are the excursions described above allowed. Return times are determined by age-grade as are the distances which girls may go from the School. Only the students in Grades XII and XIII are permitted to go over a mile from the School without being accompanied by adults listed on the 'visiting card'. The privilege system, the element of greater trust with greater identification with the School, extends into the control of access to public space as opposed to the private space or home territory of the School as a whole. This appears to be a very finely regulated and controlled process of preventing contamination of a developing identity.

'In Saturdays' cannot be interpreted literally. Girls may leave the School but only with their fellow students, not with outsiders on the visiting card. Frequently, group activities are planned in the School on which occasions the girls are not expected to go out in groups. Group activities are also planned which take the girls out of the School to museums, art galleries and cultural events. On such occasions, the girls go with chaperones from the School (a group which often includes the Principal). On these occasions the School may be seen as attempting to enlarge its social space. Interestingly enough, on these occasions when the School does make of use of public space, it does not use public transportation. Although it may be for reasons of status, a bus is rented and the members of the School travel as a group and attend as a group, not as individual members of a group who assemble at a chosen destination. The result, regardless of the reasons for the choice of the type of space for transportation, is a greater degree of cohesion and morale in terms of the outing and a more effective appropriation of public space for the School's purposes. The 'In' Saturdays in this system (even though they involve excursions outside the School) must be looked upon as mechanisms for encouraging closer group identity and preventing the formulation of too highly regularized individual excursions into the outside world, which, even though controlled would undermine the process of identity conferral.

Moral Career and Personal Space

By 'personal space' we refer specifically to the aspects of moral career which have implications for a new boarder's status, feelings of self worth and sphere of social roles and role sets. Admission to the Boarding School, itself, seems to have two opposing kinds of effects on one's self-esteem. On the one hand, because admission is voluntary and membership in an elite private school carries considerable prestige in the eyes of the student, parents, and the community, the student's feelings of self-worth and potential social power are invariably increased. On the other hand, the physical confinement, curtailment of the self, and the rigidly disciplined activities and regimentation and constant supervision often produce in the new girl feelings of personal threat and lessened self-esteem through

the effects of the mortification practices. The latter lead to an initial reaction of alienation in the new boarder, typically expressed in describing the Boarding School as 'like a prison'. The student's feeling of isolation from her family and the outside world is reflected in the fact that perhaps most boarders view the period when telephone calls are permitted and when mail is delivered as the most important times of the day.

A number of significant factors affect the taking on of a new identity. Firstly, although a large number of new boarders describe the School as being like a prison, their decision to attend the School was a voluntary one, and the School, as we mentioned, attempted to ascertain the degree to which their decision to come was their personal wish. Secondly, the identities of the students are only partially formed. As opposed to institutions of resocialization, neither the School nor the students face the same problems of reshaping an identity which has been already forged. Thirdly, as mentioned previously, a balance of rewards over costs for students as a group and individually appears to exist in both the short and the long run. All these factors have implications for personal space. The fact that inroads can be viewed as yielding long run results, the fact that individuals in this age group as they are socialized are accustomed to experiencing some inroads into their personal space as well as the fact that in the School they experience them as a group (whereas in the home they are experienced individually), makes the experience more bearable and, after the initial trials of adjustment, enjoyable for the majority of girls.

In this regard the uniform of the School has significant moral significance. It proclaims one's student status in the organization as paramount and civilian status as not relevant within the School. It does this in a personal way since clothing is one significant way, in terms of the use of physical and material objects, of expressing one's identity. The uniform in the initial period thus emphasizes the regimentation of the School and its control over students. The wearing of the uniform can be seen to be an act and a symbol both of 'separation' from the outside world and of 'incorporation' into the student status of the School. By means of the uniform, role dispossession symbolically takes place. Further role dispossession occurs by virtue of the interaction barrier which the total institution places between the boarder and the wider world, and this marks perhaps the most dramatic curtailment of the self. The first weekend of the fall term is an 'In' weekend, so that the boarders do not visit away from the School for the first two weeks of term. For the new boarder this ensures "a deep initial break with past roles and an appreciation of role dispossession", (Goffman, 1961:14-15) which is characteristic of total institutions.

In the orientation talk given by a member of the staff on their second day at the School, new girls are told that they are extremely privileged to attend a School like this, and in oblique terms, the elite status the School confers on its members not only during their career at the School but for the rest of their lives is emphasized. The new girls also receive initial instruction in the rules of both the Boarding and Day School. Special emphasis is placed on both the need for rules and the specific rule that no day girl is allowed up into the Boarding School. This orientation talk not only strengthens the identity of the new boarder with the School and by extension the upper classes, but emphasizes that within the School itself her boarder status is paramount in her personal identity and supercedes at times, the more general status of 'student' which she also shares with day girls. New boarders are also given further instruction in the hierarchical authority structure, their age-grade status in it, and the deference patterns they are expected to display. The returning boarders arrive that day and greet each other with shrieks of excitement and hearty embraces. The new boarders look on with deeper realization of their isolation and lack of familiarity with the new life they have embarked on, but also with a realization that it must have its positive attributes in terms of personal relationships.

The period of initial 'separation'[7] in the *rite de passage* of the new boarders is essentially limited to their first day before the returning boarders have arrived. Apart from the process of mortification which is an aspect of separation, the School strives to incorporate the new girls and bring about her adjustment to Boarding School life within the first few weeks of the School year, or, at the latest, by Thanksgiving (the second Monday in October, six weeks after commencement of the School year for which the boarders have a long weekend vacation). To this end, returning boarders are encouraged to assist in the familiarization of the new boarder, inform her of the details of the privilege system and offer strong socio-emotional support particularly to those who exhibit marked signs of 'homesickness'. This goal of rapid socialization is further facilitated by a series of social gatherings, singing, games, small get-togethers, group visits to the apartment of the principal, and other events designed to bring everyone together. The relatively rapid socialization into boarding school life helps to strengthen the formal structure of authority.

As the process of instruction in the privilege system goes on, so does the new boarder's instruction in the informal norms binding boarders and roommates. She begins to learn the 'unwritten code' which controls boarders' behavior toward each other. In particular, she learns through instruction and during spontaneous interaction with other boarders, the dominant norm of peer-group solidarity. This very strong norm and the age-graded organization of the Boarding School both strengthens her identity with other boarders and fosters close friendships with her grade-mates. Frequently these friendships last for life.

The new girl is also socialized into the universalistic orientation of the privilege system and the need to turn to her roommates for more particularistic support and consideration. She is also socialized into the achievement oriented atmosphere of the School which is patterned most systematically through the house system and the inter-house competition. She begins to learn to pattern her personal space in relation to the School and the School's view of the 'outside world'.

The new girl goes through a series of initiation ceremonies, as when she is introduced to the members of her House and receives the House 'ribbon' and more subtly through the traditional ceremonies of the 'Old' and 'New Girls' Entertainment'. The 'Old Girls' Entertainment' is similar to 'the welcome' outlined by Goffman as a form of initiation in which the staff or inmates, or both "goes out of their way to give the recruit a clear notion of his plight" (1961:18). This entertainment is held in the Assembly Hall, usually on the third Saturday evening after term commences (an 'In' weekend). It is put on by the 'old' boarders and consists of songs and skits. Through mime and parody they teach the new boarders aspects of the 'underlife' of the Boarding School – the types of 'secondary adjustments' that are utilized, the peculiarities of different matrons, and effective strategies in dealing with them, that sex is a topic for informal discussion and that deprivation of heterosexual friendships is of concern to the boarders, etc. They also portray the formal status system and authority structure by caricaturing the matron's roles and the self-confidence and social power of the 'old' boarders. Two weeks later, the 'New Girls' Entertainment' is held in which the new boarders portray, in the same idioms, what they have 'learned' of the 'System' and its underlife, and that they are now capable of making out successfully in the life of the Boarding School.

During the first few weeks, the new boarder also hears and learns much of the esoteric language[8] of the Boarding School and the meaning of such terms as 'gating', 'Out' weekends, 'going up North', 'Orderly marks', 'Herbie' (the euphemism for the menstrual period), 'Prefects' and the nicknames for promi-

nent staff members, used in reference to these persons but never as terms of address or in the presence of other staff members. By learning the social structure of the School and the language of this social structure the new girl internalizes many of the expectations the School has of her. Although these may, in the beginning, only result in proper role performance, they obviously have some cumulative effect on the formation of the self and perceptions of personal space.

In general, as we have mentioned, although the boarders commonly experience a loss of considerable autonomy, there is a high degree of consensus that boarding-school life, with its bureaucratic structure and affectively neutral system of regulated interaction, facilitates the process of becoming more independent of the particularistic norms and emotional relations of the family in preparation for the more universalistic relations of adult life. Whereas the loss of autonomy is often lamented, the universalistic characteristics which prepare the student for adult life are generally seen by parents and students alike, as well as by the administrative personnel of the School, to more than compensate for the deprivation of particularism and autonomy which is endured. The invasions of personal space and the definitions of identity which the School holds are accepted as appropriate and desirable by those whose identity will be altered.

Moral Career and Social Space

The constraints and patterning of physical and personal space define, to a large extent, the boundaries and sphere of social relations, or social space. Attending the School has paradoxical effects on the boarder's social space. Becoming a boarder entails a serious curtailment of social space in terms of role dispossession, and role sets such as familial, neighbourhood, and to a large extent heterosexual are temporarily suspended. Attendance at the School also implies drastic curtailment in terms of the social class space the boarders occupy. Boarders are cut off from contacts with members of the lower classes which they previously had through physical presence and social membership in their neighbourhood, community and public schools (most boarders have transferred from the public school system). On the other hand, their social space is substantially enlarged *within* the social space of the upper classes. The enlarged intra-class space includes not only the substantial increase of friendships with fellow boarders but also expanded heterosexual friendships with class co-equals. At the same time a shrinking of the social space vis-à-vis boys of lower class status occurs.

Cross-sex relationships are strictly controlled by the School during the term when it is acting *in loco parentis*. No boarders in any grade up to and including grade X are permitted to have a date with any boy, except at the School-sponsored and supervised 'Grade Nine and Ten Dance' (boarders in these grades do not attend the 'Boarders' Dance' in the fall term) held at the School, for which dates are supplied exclusively from one or more of the elite private boys' schools which are in the School's orbit. This dance is held in the spring after new girls have been subjected to the School's socialization practices for most of an academic year and hence are likely to relate to their dates and the social setting in the appropriate ways. Since the boarders in these grades are usually chaperoned by a staff member during occasions when they are off the School property, there are few opportunities for *sub rosa* meetings with boys.[9]

All boarders in grades XI - XIII have the privilege of going out on two dates per term, which means, at most, six for the whole academic year; a definite curtailment in temporal terms of social space. In addition, a boarder must apply in writing to the principal and have a personal visit with her to obtain permission for a date. If the prospective date's name is not included on her visiting card, the girl is normally required to obtain in writing the consent of her parents to go out with the boy, before the School will grant permission. The principal may grant permission, if the boy is not on the visiting card, but this is rare and there is widespread belief among students that if the boy does not attend a private school, permission will not be granted. This practice of having to make formal application to the principal and the belief about private school membership of the prospective date have a profound effect on the student's requests for permission. Permission is also granted only if the principal feels the girl will be adequately chaperoned by adults, which usually means only formal events, such as a dance at one of the boys' private schools, a private formal dance given by a boy or girl who attends the School or another private school, a birthday dinner for self or friend or close relative or a special concert or other cultural event. These all involve social occasions with virtually exclusively members of the same social class. Moreover, the girl must be escorted to and from the School, preferably by private transportation, or taxi, and is required to be back at the School within half an hour after the event ends. The former rule is another example of how the School privatizes the public space and restrains personal space through its temporal limitation on the private space in which developing intimacy of the relationship is culturally patterned. Hence, it constrains the development of sexual intimacy, an indirect inroad on otherwise private space.

The School in a series of other subtle ways, moves the boarder's social activities and friendships into the private school orbit and away from groups to which the student may have belonged. Many of the shifts result from structural influences, although the latter have their attitudinal components. Foremost, is the influence of the new social system of the private school which exhibits marked differences from that experienced by students who attend the public schools. In the course of time the boarder's friendships with public school students wane because she begins to have less and less in common with them in terms of mutual friends, social climates and participation in the same social system. In both direct and subtle ways the School fosters and rewards the formation of friendships with boys and girls who attend private schools and at the same time reduces and devalues opportunities for friendship formation with those who do not attend private schools.

Several practices of the School foster friendship formation within the private school circuit. One way the School does this is by scheduling inter-scholastic competitions almost exclusively with other private schools, both boys' and girls'. The norm of reciprocity operates here: the other private schools invite its students to compete in athletic activities and attend social events, the School is expected to reciprocate. This also applies to the major social event of the year in most schools – the school dance; the major girls' schools always invite the school captains of the other schools to their annual formal dances. In addition, at one or more social occasions during the year, notably the 'Boarders' Dance' and the 'Grade IX – X Dance', the School officially invites boys from one or more of the boys' private schools to provide dates for the Boarders at the School. The prefect of the Boarding School coordinates the lists of the boys and girls and pairs them off on the basis of height and grade before the occasion and formally introduces the dates to each other when they arrive at the School. Apart from the norm of reciprocity, the School also feels greater assurance that the social background and behavior of boys from private schools will correspond to that considered appropriate by the School and that these boys will be adequately chaperoned by their own staff which reduces the problem of social control.

From time to time the School holds social events, other than dances, to which the boys' private schools, both boarding and day pupils, are invited. This further provides both boarders and day girls with opportunities to meet boys from private schools rather than public schools.

Many of the brothers of the students at the School are enrolled at private schools and to facilitate family reunions, the School makes a very careful attempt to schedule School holidays to coincide with those of the private boys' schools within their social orbit. This scheduling of holidays to coincide has another consequence, though formally unintended perhaps, which further acts to keep peer group friendships of the students within the private school social sphere. The private school holidays begin earlier and end later than those of public schools. The fact that they begin earlier is particularly relevant, for it means that when the students start a holiday, the only other students they can get together with for several days are those who are also at private schools. It seems reasonable to assume that this would produce the tendency to associate with these students throughout the holidays rather than associating with those at public schools. Thus, although physical space is enlarged geographically and temporally during holidays, this is unlikely to have a comparable effect on the enlargement of social space in terms of expanding social relations with a wider spectrum of the social classes.

It is more prestigious to attend events at the elite boys' private schools in the School's social orbit than at public schools, and also more prestigious to associate with private school than with public school boys, although when explicitly asked, staff and students both disavow that there is any difference. Nevertheless, in subtle ways the staff clearly communicated to new boarders that friendships with the former carried greater prestige. The overwhelming majority of the students also concur in this evaluation and consciously and unconsciously influence new boarders to accept this evaluation.

Moreover, the fact that these girls' brothers frequently attend private schools increases the girls' social contacts with other boys at these schools and the likelihood of the formation of friendships. The out-of-town boarder, cut-off from the home town boys, becomes dependent upon the School's semi-formal blind date system or on the informal system itself. Informally, day girls arrange blind dates for new girls, both day and boarder students, with classmates of their dates, who are generally at private schools. In this way, the new girl is further drawn into the same social sphere as her 'old-girl' friends.

But the School and the private-school peer group are not the only agents which influence a new student to identify with the private school ethos and seek friendships within it. New boarders often find they are regarded as snobs and snubbed by their former friends and cliques who continued to attend the public schools. This has the effect of making the new boarder even more dependent upon friendships formed within the School or with students at other private schools.

All the three types of curtailment and control of physical, personal and social space which are in Goffman's sense, both part of the 'stripping process' (1961:148) and the processes by which the self is reconstituted by the institution, can be seen as institutional invasions of private space. However, this invasion is done by the delegated authorities of the upper classes on their own juvenile members as a systematic socialization process which reinforces family and social class norms and behavioral styles to increase the solidarity of class identity in its young members. This is fostered by confining these three aspects of space primarily to spheres of interaction with class equals, provision of a shared distinctive culture and developmental experiences and the fostering of expanded intra-class primary group affiliations. Thus, in a sense, the spheres of social space become coextensive with social class membership. Boarders come to perceive space along social class lines and 'private space' is a replication of social class space and 'public' space tends to become 'extra-class' space.

The School and the External World — Return to Whence They Came

Private school education is perceived as helping to preserve elitist norms and behaviour patterns in the children of elites and thus aid in the inter-generational continuity of elitist status. It thus assists in the maintenance of the social space of a particular class. In the case of the School, it is possible for a student to have been in attendance for fifteen years and to have been in boarding for a period of eight years before she assumes the status of 'old girl' and returns to the elite world whence she came. Given the nature of the system we have described and the length of time a girl spends in it, it would be surprising if the School-sponsored and School-regulated life did not have an effect. We must be careful to point out, however, that the School is not effecting a 'Pygmalion'. By the nature of the recruitment processes, the School tends to maintain rather than create a style of life. Students do not come from the humble origins of Eliza Doolittle nor enter a world which is strange to them, even though, in the idiom the matrons use to describe social space, the School does have some 'pushed up paupers'.[10] On the contrary, the students enter a world which is entirely familiar to them, the only difference in their changed status is that they now have only the indirect sponsorship of the School rather than its direct support and assistance. Their social world, their friends, acquaintances, their pool of potential husbands have been carved out for them by the School. Unless they leave the country physically or forsake their identity, their life space has been provided for them, particularly if they remain in the city where the School is located.

To a very large extent, although times are changing, for an upper class woman, marriage is career. By virtue of marrying within her class, the upper class woman is expected, as part of her responsibility in the marriage to assume leadership positions within the community. The social skills and friendship patterns which the School has provided by the management of her social sphere operate in influencing marriage patterns and the marital career.

School sponsorship of sports days, and dances with boys' schools, tours of Europe arranged in conjunction with other boys' and girls' schools, School affiliation with summer camps, and the fact that many of the girls have brothers in the boys' private schools, perpetuates a courtship orbit, a mating pool. In other words, attendance at the School by the mechanisms we mentioned earlier, and those we mentioned here, is likely to result in a higher probability that a girl will marry within her class and that the social space of the elite will be preserved inter-generationally.

Once married, friendships continue within what once was the courtship pool. This is the social milieu of the 'younger set' in the upper classes. Although males may struggle and work hard at their career, they do not have to struggle up the social class ladder; they must work to *maintain* not to *attain* status while they advance their careers. In the advancement of the career of her husband, the upper class female may play an important role. The social contacts she brings to the marriage may result in 'sponsorship' of her husband in the work world. In addition her efforts in the world of culture and philanthropy may bring prestige and status to her husband as well as herself.

The alumnae association of the School plays an important role in fostering social contacts with charitable groups and organizations. Included in the alumnae association are members of the boards of the major cultural and philanthropic organizations upon which women sit in Canada. Through the 'old school tie' relationships these groups tend to be self-perpetuating, replacing their members with like situated individuals from younger age groups. Moreover, a number of branches of at least two charitable organizations have been formed by age-grade cliques at the School. These women thus have a source of independent status through their memberships, as well as assisting in the management of their husband's status. They also play a role in policy formation in various sectors of the society, not only indirectly through their husbands who are members of the elite, but also directly through their membership on boards. Their occupancy of this type of space in the national social structure has been in large part determined for them by the way in which the School and its alumnae operate. Although the way in which the School has been portrayed here may have led to an image of the School in which conformity is overemphasized, it must be remembered that in the myriad of offices and activities, the School prepares people to assume the responsibilities and innovativeness required in leadership roles. In addition to carving out the social space of the student, the School in its management of her personal space has given her the identity and skills to operate within this space. This management of space, as we have attempted to point out throughout the paper, is very carefully handled by the School. Although not all the consequences or the practices mentioned are planned, the School has a very high level of concern for its students both individually and collectively. It is because of this concern and because of the careful process of socialization which results from it that the School is able to arrange so successfully the social and personal space of its alumnae. However, we must stress in closing that it is the high degree of congruency in almost all aspects of social life between the School and its recruits and between the School and its alumnae which permits its goals to be realized.

As times have changed, private schools have been viewed as anachronistic. Although the clubwoman and the organizer of cultural and charitable activities is still required, other roles are becoming increasingly open to women of all classes. The School places a high value on academic achievement and, in contrast to the past when such schools were viewed as finishing schools, expects its students to go on to post-secondary education. Elites in society are those who occupy positions of power in the social structure. An elite which does not validate its status by its social activities is unlikely to maintain its social power in Canadian society in the long run. The School is very sensitive (possibly more than other private schools) to changing times and changing needs. It is more than likely that it will maintain, to some extent, its position and the position of its students in the social space of Canadian social structure, but it is also likely that it will bring about change in Canadian society which will result in a redefinition of its space within the social system.

NOTES AND BIBLIOGRAPHY

1. For a description of the role and consequences of 'privilege systems' in total institutions, see Goffman, (1961: 48-66).
2. 'Houses' at the School, of which there are six, are not residential units, but ascriptive, associational units containing members from all grades from VI-XIII and through which intramural competitions in sports and other activities, including the raising of money for charity, are organized.
3. Lyman and Scott define interactional territory as "any area where a social gathering may occur" and point out that the boundary of such a territory is essentially invisible, a kind of membrane (1967:236-248).
4. These types of idiosyncratic behavior are similar to Erving Goffman's 'secondary adjustments' though many are not prohibited.

5. For a description of the 'mortification process' see Erving Goffman (1961:14-74).

6. Goffman defines 'secondary adjustments' as "practices that do not directly challenge staff but allow inmates to obtain forbidden satisfactions or to obtain permitted ones by forbidden means" (1961:54).

7. Arnold Van Gennep, in his famous classic on initiation ceremonies, proposed that the initiation ceremony conveys three submeanings and phases – 'separation'. 'transition' and 'incorporation' which together may be summarized as a *rite de passage* or status transition (1960).

8. Goffman calls this the "institutional lingo" (1961:53).

9. When they have received permission to visit over a weekend and have been 'signed out' by their hostess who is then *in loco parentis* until the girl is signed in, they have a quasi-*sub-rosa* opportunity for seeing boys.

10. The phrase 'pushed up paupers' refers to daughters of the *nouveaux riches* and not to students from families of severely limited financial resources on scholarship. Thus 'paupers' indicates paucity of history of elite family status, traditions and way of life rather than financial poverty.

Blishen, Bernard R. "The Construction and Use of An Occupational Scale," *Canadian Journal of Economic and Political Science* 24 (November): 521-531, 1958.

Canada, Dominion Bureau of Statistics, Educational Division. *Preliminary Statistics of Education*, 1963-64. Ottawa: The Queen's Printer, 1965.

Goffman, Erving *Asylums: Essays on the Social Situation of Mental Patients and Other Inmates*. Garden City: Doubleday and Anchor Books, 1961.

Lyman, Stanford M., and Marvin B. Scott "Territoriality: A Neglected Sociological Dimension." *Social Problems* 15 (Fall): 236-248, 1967.

Porter, John *The Vertical Mosaic: An Analysis of Social Class and Power in Canada*. Toronto: University of Toronto Press, 1965.

Van Gennep, Arnold *The Rites of Passage*. (Tr. Monika B. Vizedom and Gabrielle L. Caffee). Chicago: University of Chicago Press, 1960.

Cultural Aspects of Relationships

Cultural Aspects of Relationships

In the introduction to this book it was stated that the Canadian tradition in Social Science was essentially interdisciplinary, and that one of the themes of this book was a dialogue between the political-economy tradition (best illustrated by Levitt in Section One) and the literary-sociological communications tradition, illustrated in this section by McLuhan. (Harold Innis might reasonably have claimed to be the father of both traditions). But traditions are useful only if they continue to act as the basis of a culture which is constantly being recreated and developed by the members of that culture. (Where this does not happen we have museums of dead cultures, such as contemporary Greece or Southern Spain.) But what is a culture and how can we tell if it is living or dead? In one sense even 'dead' cultures continue to live: the Greek colonels may care little for Pericles or Socrates (except to draw revenue from their monuments) but elsewhere elements of the Greek tradition enter into the culture of societies for whom democracy is more than a classical Greek word. But culture is other than mere borrowing or even a national tradition: centrally it is the way that a group of people make sense of their life-situation in terms of the language, technology, values and codes of behaviour that they inherit and recreate.

One of the essential parts of any study of culture is the analysis of Communication – such as language, vision, touch, as well as the various 'mass' media of communication. It was this latter task that provided the theme for the Explorations *school at the University of Toronto in the 1950's. (See introduction to the essay by McLuhan below.) But such an exercise is only part of the study of culture and only one of the ways that the analysis of culture might develop from the observations of Innis. An alternative route was to ground the study of culture firmly in the political-economy tradition. Danny Drache's essay does this by arguing that to understand the values and beliefs of the Canadian middle class we must begin by analyzing the part played by this same middle class in the American takeover of the Canadian economy. As such his essay is complementary to Kari Levitt's essay in Section One and Sandy Lockhart's in Section Eight. It also provides a beginning for a sophisticated Marxism of Class Consciousness in Canada.*

As Drache suggests, our perceptions are in a large part moulded by our socio-economic position. It may also be true, however, that whatever our class situation our interpretations of what happens to us may be framed by beliefs and traditions which seem to have nothing to do with class as such. Class may determine our life-style but religion may provide our 'commonsense' view of our relations with others and even our politics. In Section One S. D. Clark indicated the importance of religion in influencing Canadian political development. Here David Millett argues that the continuation of particular religions, institutions and practices has acted as a force to maintain ethnic divisions in Canada. It is important to compare this essay with that by Ossenberg in Section Eight, who suggests that the Catholic church in Quebec could only do this by collusion with the English economic elites.

Culture, then, is about 'making sense' of our social situations both in a cognitive and practical way. It is about how we account for the discrepancies in our daily lives, in the apparent inconsistencies between appearance and experience. It is also about how we make use of our natural resources to create a living environment and how, in turn, we are influenced in our symbolizations of reality by that environment. In the two final extracts in this section we find examples of such making sense. B. Y. Card's rather whimsical piece illustrates how even our private space is controlled from outside and how an individual tries to make sense of the fact; while Rémi Savard discusses the construction of a cosmology by Eskimos who have to take account of a vast but constricting environment.

The possibilities of expanding the analysis of aspects of Canadian culture are very great indeed. In doing so, and in creating a lively social science tradition concerned with culture, Canadian social scientists are seen here drawing not only on a vivid Canadian tradition but also foreign ones. Drache grafts Marx onto Innis, Savard develops from Claude Lévi-Strauss and Marcel Mauss in France, and B. Y. Card's writing is reminiscent of some California ethnomethodologists. The roots and prospects of developing a distinctive Canadian Sociological culture are perhaps most clearly seen in this section.

---

1. Five Sovereign Fingers Taxed the Breath

Marshall McLuhan/*University of Toronto*

Between 1953 and 1959 Explorations, *a journal on communications, was published at the University of Toronto. In 1960 an anthology of some of the articles that had appeared in that Journal was published under the title* Explorations in Communication, *edited by Edmund S. Carpenter and Marshall McLuhan. In their introduction to that anthology the editors stated,*

> Explorations *explored the grammars of such languages as print, the newspaper format and television. It argued that revolutions in the packaging and distribution of ideas and feelings modified not only human relations but also sensibilities. It further argued that we are largely ignorant of literacy's role in shaping Western man, and equally unaware of the role of elec-tronic media in shaping modern values. Literacy's vested interests were so deep that literacy itself was never examined. And the current electronic revolution is already so pervasive that we have difficulty in stepping outside of it and scrutinizing it objectively. But it can be done, and a fruitful approach is to examine one medium through another: print seen from the perspective of electronic media, or television analyzed through print.*

Since that time Marshall McLuhan, the author of this delightful next selection, has elaborated and extended these ideas in his many publications until now they have become familiar, if still somewhat bewildering.

The CITY no longer exists, except as a cultural ghost for tourists. Any highway eatery with its TV set, newspaper, and magazine is as cosmopolitan as New York or Paris.

The PEASANT was always a suburban parasite. The farmer no longer exists; today he is a 'city' man.

The METROPOLIS today is a classroom; the ads are its teachers. The classroom is an obsolete detention home, a feudal dungeon.

The metropolis is OBSOLETE. Ask the Army.

The INSTANTANEOUS global coverage of radio-tv makes the city form meaningless, functionless. Cities were once related to the realities of production and intercommunication. Not now.

Until WRITING was invented, we lived in acoustic space, where the Eskimo now lives: boundless, directionless, horizonless, the dark of the mind, the world of emotion, primordial intuition, terror. Speech is a social chart of this dark bog.

SPEECH structures the abyss of mental and acoustic space, shrouding the race; it is a cosmic, invisible architecture of the human dark. Speak that I may see you.

WRITING turned a spotlight on the high, dim Sierras of speech; writing was the visualization of acoustic space. It lit up the dark.

These five kings did a king to death.

A goose's quill put an end to talk, abolished mystery, gave architecture and towns, brought roads and armies, bureaucracies. It was the basic metaphor with which the cycle of CIVILIZATION began, the step from the dark into the light of the mind. The hand that filled a paper built a city.

The handwriting is on the celluloid walls of Hollywood; the Age of Writing has passed. We must invent a NEW METAPHOR, restructure our thoughts and feelings. The new media are not bridges between man and nature: they are nature.

The MECHANIZATION of writing mechanized the visual-acoustic metaphor on which all civilization rests; it created the classroom and mass education, the modern press and telegraph. It was the original assembly line.

Gutenberg made all history SIMULTANEOUS: the transportable book brought the world of the dead into the space of the gentleman's library; the telegraph brought the entire world of the living to the workman's breakfast table.

PHOTOGRAPHY was the mechanization of the perspective painting and of the arrested eye; it broke the barriers of the nationalist, vernacular space created by printing. Printing upset the balance of oral and written speech; photography upset the balance of ear and eye.

Telephone, gramophone, and RADIO are the mechanization of postliterate acoustic space. Radio returns us to the dark of the mind, to the invasions from Mars and Orson Welles; it mechanizes the well of loneliness that is acoustic space: the human heart-throb put on a PA system provides a well of loneliness in which anyone can drown.

Movies and TV complete the cycle of mechanization of the human sensorium. With the omnipresent ear and the moving eye, we have abolished writing, the specialized acoustic-visual metaphor that established the dynamics of Western civilization.

By surpassing writing, we have regained our WHOLENESS, not on a national or cultural, but cosmic, plane. We have evoked a super-civilized sub-primitive man.

NOBODY yet knows the language inherent in the new technological culture; we are all deaf-blind mutes in terms of the new situation. Our most impressive words and thoughts betray us by referring to the previously existent, not to the present.

We are back in acoustic space. We begin again to structure the primordial feelings and emotions from which 3000 years of literacy divorced us.

Hands have no tears to flow.

---

2. The Canadian Bourgeoisie and Its National Consciousness

Daniel Drache/*Atkinson College, York University*

In Section One we drew attention to the extent that Canada's geography, history and economic position in a colonial world have shaped Canadian political theories and institutions and how these, in turn, have made a deep imprint on the Canadian psyche and self-image. Canadians pride themselves on their capacity for accommodation and compromise. Disdaining what they see to be the political and economic aggressiveness of their southern neighbours, they retreat into what political scientist Drache calls a "sentimental nationalism" which, he argues, has blinded them to the economic realities of industrial capitalism. His argument, so forcibly presented is a cogent one – yet it is one many Canadians will reject. Perhaps the reasons for this rejection should provide the subject-matter of more detailed sociological investigation.

Ten years ago the dream of the Canadian bourgeoisie* had an air of reality. Its spokesmen made much of the fact that Canada's survival as a nation was assured, that national unity prevailed, that Canada was a land of prosperity. Now, the claims of the bourgeoisie are contradicted by the hard facts of Canadian life. National disunity, American imperialism, the collapse of federalism, labour unrest, student militancy, and Quebec separatism reveal a different truth about the policies and politics of Canada's ruling class. The disintegration of the country cannot be seen and studied in isolation from the historic man-

*The term normally refers to the owners of the means of production who form the governing class. The Canadian bourgeoisie own a fraction of the means of production and retain control of a minority of the country's resources. More correctly, they are part owners and more frequently the national managers and agents of the owners of the means of production. American capitalists have nationalized Canadian resources and industry. There can be no quarrel on this point. (See a special report in the *Toronto Daily Star* headlined, "Foreigners Buy 500 of Our Firms in 20 Months," October 17, 1969.) In speaking of the bourgeoisie I include also their representatives in the fields of

date of the bourgeoisie to rule Canada. With their unlimited self-assurance they have promoted the view that only one class of people can hold the country together, overcome regional and racial disunity, and build a national state with national policies. But the balkanization of Canada, north-south, east-west, is a fact that the most arrogant of the establishment cannot afford to ignore. Politically the result of this state of affairs is becoming clearer. The bourgeoisie are in the process of dismantling the Canadian state economically, socially, and culturally. By this process, Canadian history has come full circle – from a colony to a colonial dependency.

The Canadian plight between two imperialisms was documented in the 1930s and 1940s by a political economist, Harold Innis,[1] and by the conservative liberal historians, Donald Creighton[2] and A. R. M. Lower.[3] In more recent times its chief exponent has been George Grant. In his *Lament for a Nation*,[4] he has stated the Canadian dilemma in a single sentence: "Canada's disappearance as a nation is a matter of necessity." He argues that American imperialism has destroyed the basis of an independent Canada, and that the Canadian state has become an advanced colonial structure. He claims further that liberal capitalism has become the instrument for destroying the meagre foundations of Canadian independence. To say this is to argue that the policy of continental development adopted by the Liberal government as Canada's national policy is founded on an anti-national logic. That the Canadian economy has thus been placed at the disposal of American capital and in the hands of American capitalists substantiates the general truth of Grant's argument. The Watkins Report presents extensive evidence that the nationalization of Canadian resources by American imperialism has reached an all-time high.

The charge that Canada has become *de facto* a region of the United States is not new, and on one level it does not take Canadian liberals by surprise. For the bourgeoisie who have guided Canada into a deepened colonialism the wide spectrum of dependency is not a disgrace, nor is it regarded unfavourably. Near-prosperity, the illusion of prosperity, the spill-over from imperial prosperity have been reason enough to legitimize their policies in the political and economic spheres. Their success in living off the British and American empires has given the bourgeoisie enough political power to withstand the opposition from a long line of radical and radicalizing movements for social change. In the past, the politics sustained by regional disparity, class struggle, farmer militancy, and Quebec separatism never reached ascendancy. Hence, for good reason, the bourgeoisie were able to pursue policies which guaranteed them their place as managers and middlemen of a colonial economy.

If for the bourgeoisie of the ruling class the imperial presence does not present a crisis of confidence, it has created a crisis of power. They miscalculated the economic and political cost of remaining an advanced colony. While balkanization may suit the government's purposes, its increased economic helplessness in stopping the spread of inflation, regional depression, unemployment, and industrial stagnation does not meet with approval from three critical sections of the Canadian public – Quebec and the provinces, organized and unorganized workers, and students. Their collective reaction to the Americanization

education, culture, media, political life, labour, and military and state bureaucracies, who ally with and defend the interests and policies of resident and non-resident bourgeoisie. Marx describes the function of these people "as the active conceptualizing ideologists of the ruling class." A few of the leading spokesmen for the bourgeoisie in the nation include President Bissell of the University of Toronto; Dr. Solandt, Chancellor of the University of Toronto; Robert Fulford, literary critic; Patrick Watson, media propagandist; Bruce Hutchison, writer; the late Blair Fraser; a pyramid of civil servants lead by Bob Bryce; Ramsay Cook, historian; George Ignatieff and A.D.P. Heeney, diplomats; etc., etc.

of Canada in its many forms represents the beginning of a new era of politics in Canada.

The bourgeoisie are threatened by these political realities, and their paranoia dominates their politics. *Item:* They regard the struggle for a Free Quebec as a national crime. In simpler language, it is a felony to dismember part of the colony and seek national independence. *Item:* The Committee of Ontario Presidents does not lose any time in aping the imperial American universities and issues its liberal stand for law and order. Radical action in Ontario universities will henceforth be prosecuted. An Americanized faculty and Americanized universities will now be protected from Canadian students. *Item:* International construction unions in Toronto support a drive to crush an 'upstart' Canadian union. Canada's labour party, the NDP, gives no support to the Concrete Former's Union. *Item:* Inflation and more inflation. The government remedy is to create planned unemployment to cool off the economy. *Item:* Kierans announces reforms of the postal service. His intention is to make it pay its own way. Consequently, raising the postal rates is tantamount to a stamp tax; it is cheaper not to communicate; publish nationally and perish.

That the bourgeoisie view the political environment with hostility has an objective basis. Their once secure world has ceased to exist and their traditional methods of governorship, parliament, federalism, political parties, and compromise no longer function as national institutions. Their legitimacy is dying out; or, more simply, continental imperialism no longer needs the official channels of the bourgeoisie. But the bourgeoisie have no intention of discarding the pillars of their liberal faith. Such deviations from the norm as the class struggle or Quebec separatism are, in their eyes, unresolved difficulties of the present, not permanent features of a new social order – structural dependency. In blocking out the major social and economic forces of the present period of history, the bourgeoisie look upon such realities as class politics, imperialism, the colonialism of Canadian capitalism and nationalism as heresies in the minds of the left and not as the political condition of the real world. In part their refusal to recognize these realities, let alone understand them, reflects their historic role in Canadian history. On this point we shall have more to say presently. In another sense, the estrangement of the bourgeoisie is a self-willed act – the product of their provincialism and their insistence on Canadian exceptionalism. By their logic Canada stands in a unique relationship to history – history is a benign force which somehow has exempted Canada from the political economy of imperialism, class struggle, and racism. When this construct is broken apart by the national revolution in Quebec, by the nationalization of the Canadian economy by American capital, and by the demands of students to Canadianize Canadian universities, the eruption of the underground cannot be easily covered up. The very problems to which the bourgeoisie stringently denied an existence dominate the national politics of Canada.

The case against the bourgeoisie is not made on the grounds of style. Their general dullness, their abject defeatism on the national question, their contempt for democratic politics, their indifference to labour, play an important part in a managerial strategy of depoliticizing Canadian national life. Style is a convenience, the mark of authority. But style, however McLuhanesque and hence attractive in liberal eyes, is not the heart of the matter. The substantive strategic question is why the bourgeoisie support and welcome the American occupation of Canada. What is it that gives the bourgeoisie a vested interest in Canada as a dependency? Why are they powerless to stop the disintegration of the Canadian state? The answers can be found through study of the history of this class as it builds the national consciousness about nationalism and imperialism, and its use of liberalism as its political ideology. It is through an analysis of these questions that one begins to understand the tragedy of Canadian exceptionalism.

The Contradiction Within The Nationalism of Subordination

Nationalism joins together the linguistic, cultural, and political aspirations of the ruling class in support of the national economic unit, the nation-state. By virtue of political economy, capitalism is a force of the national interest and the ideology of national cohesiveness – that is, nationalism. Liberalism has made much out of appeals to nationalism, because of the obvious moral and political implications of this simple theory. But whatever the moral use-value of nationalism, its real power and authority stem from the material interest it advances. It is the latter part of this statement, "material interest it advances," which has been relevant to the Canadian experience.

One cannot fault the Canadian bourgeoisie with the charge that they have not identified with nationalist politics. Their espousal of national unity, national development, and national survival is evidence in their mind of their national interest. However, their methods of working towards these rhetorical goals denote a deep-seated ambivalence and a lack of will to build national economic structures, and hence a political and cultural nation. In the liberal view, Canada's problems grow out of the belief that Canada, if it is not a nation now, *can* be one in the future and that this idea of nationhood can be brought about by reasonable men working reasonably for its attainment. For liberal persuaders Canada can be a country, a nation unto itself, and can survive on the continent as an un-American, yet sovereign, state by virtue of the fact that the desire is a reasonable one, non-antagonistic to American interests, and because Canada's existence as a nation is recognized by law. Their perception of Canadian history resembles, then, a textbook of constitutional and legal pieties. For them the resilience of liberal optimism is that it acts as its own surrogate. It wishes away the unreasonable issues of Canada's situation. The Canadian liberal has never wanted to face the political economy of his situation. He believes that Canadian nationalism is essentially a nationalism of, and at one with, empire. This idea of nationhood was supposed to be a testament to the possibility of how the contradiction between national sovereignty and imperial control could be overcome. In the view of the national bourgeoisie, to join nation to empire was a sign of nationhood, coming of age within the empire; for the liberal tradition in Canada is founded on the historical experience that liberalism has grown out of empire and that colonies have grown into nations. As a colony it had experienced neither the best nor the worst of the imperial world; and although its place in the empire was ambivalent in certain respects, the Canadian ruling class had no serious misgivings about the necessity for empire and the importance of an imperial domain. But the bargain it attempted to strike first with the British and then with the United States empires failed to prevent Canada's integration economically and politically into the imperial fold.

As burghers of the industrial world in both the nineteenth and twentieth centuries, Canadian businessmen and industrialists have given priority, not to the search for worldwide markets and imperial monopoly after the Anglo-American pattern, but to a national goal of protection and preference, entry and accessibility into imperial markets.[5] This nationalism of empire, although not unlike the national philosophies of the British and American bourgeoisie, differed in a fundamental aspect. Whereas the latter 'big' bourgeoisie spoke from a developing if not a well-developed foothold of national capitalism, in Canada the bourgeoisie spoke from a much different position. Canada's economy was that of a colony, characterized by underdevelop-

ment of industry and overdevelopment of staples. The nationalism of Canadian capitalism contained the belief that it sought co-existence with 'mature' capitalism, not as an equal, never as a rival, but primarily as a subordinate and lately as a junior partner.* It was this economic outlook which Canadian governments drafted as their chief strategy with Britain before the end of the British Century in 1939. It solved the problem of getting a better deal for Canada in imperial affairs by adopting a rhetoric of Canadian absenteeism from imperial commitments. In reality, government policy amounted to a tactical ploy of hedging its bet in order to bargain for special concessions. It was this same strategy that the long reign of Liberal governments devised to establish Canada's colonial reliability with Washington. Reversing styles, the Pearson approach called for blanket endorsement of American Cold War politics – a free hand in a Free World for an American-continental market. In both instances the nationalism of subordination fit the material interests of the Canadian bourgeoisie.

If the task of nationalism on the economic level is to ensure the colonial relationship of the governing élite to the imperial establishment, politically nationalism is a dangerous instrument of class rule. This is no less true for the Canadian bourgeoisie than it is for any other colonial élite. By its very definition nationalism in the colony is an anti-imperialist doctrine. Too much talk of independence and economic development arouses the latently antagonistic national consciousness of the people. This is the explosive, socially progressive, politically formidable side of nationalism which the bourgeoisie seek to defuse. They know also that without national unity or a sufficient amount of national identity the economic state of the country suffers. Hence, the bourgeoisie do not relish nationalism. They look upon it as a tightrope which will bridge the distance between local growth and imperial concerns.†

No bourgeoisie, however, can afford to disown the rhetoric, nor the political task, of claiming to be nation-builders and supposedly the saviours of the country. Hence, in the colony or dependency, the bourgeoisie distort nationalism for their own ends. In their actions and in their programmes for national self-determination, they emphasize their support of independence and of continuing the relationship with the imperial metropolis. Their ingenuity in drawing up a nationalist programme deflects the independence movement from its immediate goal of overthrowing colonialism in all facets of life.

The Canadian bourgeoisie are no exception to the general rule – they have taken nationalism in hand and made it safe for domestic consumption. For them it was necessary to turn nationalism on its head by deploying it in support of imperial causes and in defence of their class rights. This concept of nationalism was directed, not to building a country, but to ruling it. On this basis alone, it suited the bourgeoisie to support national endeavours. As long as nationalism dissipated its energies in endless factional strife, they had nothing to fear from it. Thus they turned nationalism against itself; that is, in the past and in the present Canadian nationalism has been self-liquidating and therefore useful as a disabling device politically

*W. L. Morton, "British North America: A Continent in Dissolution," *History* (June 1962), argues that, for geo-political reasons connected with the American Civil War, the Canadian bourgeoisie would always be dominated and run by the needs of the American empire. The excellent analysis of this question by S. Ryerson in *Unequal Union* (Toronto, 1968), refines Morton's contention. He demonstrates that the petty bourgeois elements in Upper and Lower Canada were developing a national capitalist consciousness which was anti-imperialist. Historically the petty bourgeoisie have lacked political power to beat the imperial policies of Canada's big bourgeoisie. On this last point G. Myers, *History of Canadian Wealth*, is an invaluable source of information.

†The most successful colonial politicians, Macdonald and King, put

while losing little of its utility as a tonic economically. By draining nationalism of its progressive content, the bourgeoisie deployed it as a strategy of divide and rule. By turning nationalism into a force of division, they discovered their only basis, short of military dictatorship, for maintaining control of Canada's national affairs.

At all critical times in the nineteenth and twentieth centuries, the method of rule of the bourgeoisie followed the well-established pattern of the colonial era. The politics of a pre-Confederation Canada depended on equal amounts of authority and opportunism. This formula, which had served its purpose of bringing the bourgeoisie together so that a minimum transfer of power could occur, was not abandoned when the imperial authorities withdrew. Instead, it was adopted and used with the same advantage it had provided for pre-Confederation and Confederation politicians. But the birth of national politics so heavily committed to national-colonial or national-imperial principles did not have as its immediate objective a solution to the French-English question, any more than it was interested in developing strong inclusive national institutions. Neither Macdonald nor Cartier, nor later Laurier, practised politics with the crucial objective of establishing a national democratic state. Indeed, within their framework national politics, when stripped of pretentious rhetoric, was a holding action where the centre, be it Ottawa or Bay Street – that is, the English majority, industry, and finance – kept the nation 'together' by keeping it apart. For them, as well as for those who followed their example (particularly King), leading the country meant playing off French against English, east against west, labour against business. It is this tradition of opportunism, backed up by the threat of physical and military intervention from the central authority, that has been given the name of Canadian pragmatism.

Conventional politics that have a vested interest in accentuating differences, fear the possibility of the parts combining and amount to a rearguard holding action, describe the purpose of the political nationalism of Canada's bourgeoisie. With this mode of politics they have addressed themselves to three critical problems – Quebec, western regional demands, and class politics.

Quebec: Bi-National Nationalism

Quebec has always been threatened by the prospect of national politics. At a bare minimum a nationalist programme had to guarantee French Canada, not merely its inherent language and religious rights, but something more substantive: a political structure and a cultural-economic future of survival in a two-nation state. The eastern bourgeoisie never subscribed to the idea of an equal Quebec. In their eyes the very proposal negated the *raison d'être* of an English-controlled federal state. There was one Ottawa, not two as Quebec required as the only adequate guarantee of its political rights. Without unqualified recognition of its equal status, national politics would play up Quebec's minority status in a majoritarian political system. A nationalism which told Quebec that it was simply one of many strengthened the French-Canadian belief that Confederation was to be equated with the term, 'the Second Conquest'. Its experience with the realities of federal politics taught the lesson that constitutional guarantees were no protection against the in-

nationalism to work in this manner – home rule rather than national independence. Macdonald's statement, "a British subject I was born and a British subject I will die," was more than idle boasting; it was a statement of Canadian political economy. In this sentence he defined the horizon of Canadian nationalists. Later nationalists of the St. Laurent era have been forced to change only one word, "American," putting into practice Pearson's directive to roll with the imperial punch.

fluence wielded by flagwaving Orange legions and Tory men of empire. The confrontation over the public schools question, the scandalous Riel affair, and the two instances of national conscription left no doubt in the mind of French Canada that the national interest of Quebec would always be subordinate to the one-nation interest of English Canada. These events supplied the evidence that, if two peoples had created Canada, only one of those peoples was being served by its political direction.

It is no surprise in these circumstances that even the most reactionary excesses of survival practised by the church and by Duplessis had the support of many in Quebec. Their man of the iron cross stood between them and engulfment. French Canadians were somewhat justified in claiming that Duplessis' policies were no worse than the Anglo-Saxon racism which called French Canada "the cockroach in the kitchen of Canada"[6] and which federal politicians used to win votes in Ontario and the West.

The nationalist offering vis-à-vis Quebec was tantamount to treating French Canada as a hostage. This attitude on the part of the bourgeoisie has always been grounded in the political fear that the need for French-English co-existence (as they understood it) might one day end. It was the eventuality of an ascendant Quebec, more popularly known as 'Québec libre', which gave purpose to the efforts of French-Canadian federalists, Ottawa nationalists, religious interests, and English industrialists to secure Quebec by opposing and isolating its national consciousness as a nation in and for itself. By isolating Quebec with threats and promises, the bourgeoisie created – so it seemed to them – an unassailable situation. In part, that is why Liberals in the time of Laurier and King, with the assistance of a *vendu* class from French Canada, seized upon the opportunity of selling the lie to Quebec that, by confining itself to a ghetto within its borders and in the Liberal party, its political future was assured.[7]

The national self-destructiveness of this act gave the Liberal party power in Parliament, the myth of national unity, and a nationalist following deriving its support from the mutual religious fears and racial suspicions of the English- and French-Canadian masses.* The tactic of separating Quebec politically from the rest of Canada, which the Liberal party achieved, ended the possibility of an authentic French-English state.

The West: National Regionalism

The West has had reasons to fear eastern nationalism. It paid for the cost of industrialization in Ontario out of the huge surpluses it sent east.[8] Little time elapsed before it discovered that it was not regarded as an equal profit-sharing partner in the plans of eastern capitalism. As the branch plant of a distant metropolis, it was charged more for all basic necessities and received proportionately the minimum for its agricultural efforts. The national economic policies of the Liberal and Con-

*It is standard fare for every Liberal and Conservative government to condemn strenuously rightist nationalist appeals and to dissociate their nationalism from them. Indeed, the professional historians who record the innumerable crises of national leaders give us example upon example of every Liberal prime minister who in the nick of time has averted national calamity by turning back the evils of a scarring nationalism. Those Conservative leaders – Meighen, Borden, Diefenbaker – who missed their cue, supposedly failed to wave the magic wand of mature national reason in time and brought the country to the edge. Exeunt the villains. Enter stage centre, the hero – Canadian liberalism. The melodrama picks up as each national figure gives his five-minute confessional on – right, you guessed it – the evils of nationalism. Laurier, King, Pearson, Trudeau win the day. It has never struck Canadian historians such as Ramsay Cook that the most proficient in this five-and-dime display of political soul-bearing are also the most

servative parties relieved neither its indebtedness to eastern capital nor its enforced dependency on federal whim. In an attempt to break away from its precast role as the hinterland of the Canadian economy, it revolted against the monetary grip of the banks, the corrupt practices of the railways, and the restrictions of the tariff. The combination of populism, agricultural collectivism, and anti-capitalism created third-party politics.

In the 1920's the revolt of the West was a great event in Canadian history. Having its roots in three decades of resentment, it challenged the monopoly practices of an unrepresentative, corrupt, two-party system. The national regionalism of the CCF radicals created an alternative to the colonial policies of Ottawa. Its strength lay initially in its political character. It was a mass movement committed to democratizing radically the class structure of a capitalist society. By itself populism could and did threaten the finance-nationalism of the centre, but it could not and did not seize power nationally. The West, in choosing the parliamentary road, redefined its politics and adopted a strategy which the east understood better and was more skilful at – coalition politics.

The bourgeoisie traditionally played the middle against the peripheral parts; and the West quickly learned that this strategy was reversible, with the parts theoretically combining against the centre, Ottawa. What had made King and Laurier apt at manipulating the 'middle game' could not, however, work so easily for western farm labour interests. They had to gamble (a) that they could combine with other regional and provincial groups against the eastern-based bourgeoisie, or (b) that they could disrupt the coalition that King and his company had built. But as the price of entry into coalition the Progressives had to abandon their most valuable instrument – a mass democratic political movement. In leaving by the wayside the force which had propelled regional nationalism into a national stratagem for the parliamentary world of social democratic politics, the West stripped itself of its power. The essential point that King knew better than the West was that national regionalism had appeal as a mass movement, but had much less attraction as just another regionalism. If, in fact, regionalism could be played up to the point where either he or it could bury its anti-capitalist message, the national regionalism of the West would exhaust itself fighting the rival provincialisms which King himself had encouraged. As the man in the centre, ultimately he had more leverage in derailing the regional nationalism of the West by sidetracking it on non-radical issues – the issue of bourgeois nationalism. The farm-labour alliance came to believe that it owed its first loyalty, not to its class, but to the colonial institutions and the national-imperial economy which kept the West powerless.

If expediency and necessity bring together national factions, historically coalition has not led to national consolidation and the more important objective of redistributing the economic and political power of the bourgeoisie. In the case of the West, coalition proved politically acceptable because it perpetuated the illusion that a well-timed squawk on national matters somehow lessened the costs of being a branch plant of eastern interests. On the other hand, the failure of coalition confirmed the worst suspicions of the West that nationalist appeals and national centrist politics were not to be trusted. The experience it

apt in their deployment of nationalism as a force of disunity. This contradiction is ignored. Lacking an analysis, the Canadian historian expects us to believe, as he does, that the nationalism which played a critical role in precipitating one crisis after another is somehow a pragmatic moderate nationalism of liberal realists. This act performed by the liberal leaders of disowning their frequent use of national force and authority as exceptionalism gives them greater leverage in employing their power against anyone who steps out of line. It is not too crude conceptually to reduce this strategy to blatant political opportunism.

learned first hand from the King, St. Laurent, and Pearson governments was that the national ruling coalition of Liberals did not offer a national spectrum of economic and political advantage equal to or greater than what the West on its own could win for itself by supporting the spoils system of national politics. Hence, bourgeois nationalism both as a cause and as a programme aroused all the innate political and economic suspicions that existed nationally.

Class and Nationalism

The defeat of the West and the retreat of Quebec played a decisive role in the nationalist ambitions of the bourgeoisie. As long as both these 'nationalisms' were contained, the only other force which could and did oppose the internal and external policies of the bourgeoisie was the Canadian working class.

The nationalism of the bourgeoisie grew out of their needs as industrial employers and as governors of the political state of Canada. To the extent that the bourgeoisie proclaimed their nationalist intentions, they used nationalism to win the support of the masses for their economic programme of industrialization and for their parliamentary programmes. Macdonald, Laurier, and King consciously understood the power of this strategy. Unless the bourgeoisie had the loyalty of the working man, even the most tentative plan for a national economy would fail. If, for economic reasons, they saw the benefits of using nationalist appeals to mobilize the masses, they saw also the danger of giving the Canadian people a feeling for working class politics and, more important, a mechanism for class consciousness. The danger of a national economic policy and a programme for industrial development lay in the fact that, while the bourgeoisie sought to bring the working class into national politics in directly appealing to it, they made the working class conscious of its class interest and its place in a capitalist order.

For the bourgeoisie to sell their nationalist ideas to the working class was problematic. On the one hand, they were not interested in allying the Canadian workers on an anti-imperial basis. The bourgeoisie did not see the contradiction between their nationalism and the political economy of their capitalism. The two coalesced, because in the nineteenth and twentieth centuries the unity between the one and the other was premised on the belief that Canada could come of age inside the British and American empires, retaining the imperial capital ties in a colonial-national structure. On the other hand, the nationalist plans of the bourgeoisie were rooted in capitalist anti-labour policies. In the national drive for canals and railways in the 1850's, the bourgeoisie used the state repeatedly against striking workers. The pattern of sending in the militia to control workers and to ensure a passive low-paid work force became established governmental policy at the same time as industrial capitalism came to Canada. Workers quickly learned that "in this setting, notions about the atomistic market as the governor of labour matters were pushed aside in favor of a system of state intervention. 'Labour relations' . . . meant troops and mounted police to 'overawe' the labourers, government spies to learn their intentions, and priests paid by the government and stationed among the labourers to teach them meekness. Here was a full programme of intervention, immediately on behalf of the contractors, basically to promote economy for the state. . . ."[9]

If, for economic reasons, the bourgeoisie required a disciplined, cohesive work force, politically they took measures to destroy the potential power of this class as a leading national force.* It was Mackenzie King in his capacity as deputy minis-

---

*"Parties are not, as their philosophers claim, servants of the state cooperating in its service; their real desire is the mastery of the state

ter of labour who devised the first national labour policy at the turn of the century. "He consistently advocated legislation directed to strengthening the state's power to investigate labour disputes, to compel arbitration and conciliation and by this device to blunt the ultimate weapon possessed by the wage-earners, i.e. *their power to withhold labour*. . . . his policies, as he himself subsequently admitted, had the effect of preventing workers from cooperating together to employ their social power."[10] But neither Laurier nor King was successful in the larger aim of preventing the rise of a Canadian trade union movement.

The emergence of an organized labour movement created a dual threat to the Canadian bourgeoisie. Canadian labour was both a force for national unity and a class enemy. But labour's fight against federal nationalism did not make labour anti-nationalist after the fashion of bourgeoisie nationalism, which defended the colonialism of Canadian dependency. Labour's target was the Canadian state in the hands of the national bourgeoisie. Hence, for labour the national struggle was a class struggle, and working class politics an anti-capitalist pro-Canadian position.[11] For both communist and non-communist unions in the 1930's to link the national and class question together was a logical step politically. Significantly, however, militant labour fought the policies of the bourgeoisie only from an anti-capitalist position. Their class analysis of Canadian capitalism singled out what they regarded as the central feature of the political economy of Canada. The fact of imperialism was either regarded as a secondary question or ignored altogether. Labour did not see the need for a national-democratic independence movement, based on the needs of the working class. In concentrating their efforts on only one-half of Canada's historical situation, the Canadian left failed to understand the colonial character of Canadian capitalism. This error blinded the left to the reality of continental capitalism – that the American capital interests were more imperialistic than the British in Canada.[12]

The left concluded erroneously that Canadian capitalism and the class struggle in Canada were different in degree but not in kind from the anti-capitalist struggle of labour in the United States and Britain. Therefore, at the bidding of the communists and other radical progressives, the Canadian trade union movement was handed over to the CIO and the Canadian Workers Unity League was disbanded.

The subsequent events are well known. Canadian and American liberal democrats combined to expel the left-wing socialists from positions of leadership in Canadian industrial unions. Canadian trade unions turned their attention to reformist unionism, ultimately settling for a 'very junior partnership' in the corporate economy – continental co-existence with capitalism. The effective isolation of Canadian communist trade union officials from the majority of Canadian workers destroyed any possibility of a viable anti-capitalist Canadian working-class party. Had both the communists and social democrats understood the exceptionalism of the political economy of Canadian capitalism, they would never have turned over Canadian workers to an imperialist trade union movement.

Politically this move meant that effective control of Canadian trade unions lay with the internationals and their local 'Canadian' branch-plant representatives. Since 1945 the leadership of the Canadian trade unions has indicated the totality of its commitment to liberal ideas by promoting an American political consciousness for Canadian workers: opposition to Canadian unions for Canadian workers. The continentalization of the Canadian trade union movement gave the bourgeoisie a clear

field politically. Labour did not contest the direction of bourgeois nationalism, and after the 1950's, represented by the Canadian Labour Congress, it was neither nationalist nor anti-capitalist. It openly supported the economic policy of the bourgeoisie in defending the capital interests of American business. This policy was an integral part of the metropolitan programme of the 'internationals' – acceptance of American capitalism at home and protection of America's imperial presence abroad.*

Nationalism is both an instrument of class rule and an integral part of the class consciousness of the Canadian working people. Even bourgeois nationalism opens the door to class consciousness. The Canadian bourgeoisie could not control nationalism as a political force, because nationalism is by definition a political programme which creates a mass movement. An economic nationalism which mobilizes workers, farmers, students, and intellectuals is taken over by these groups to advance class demands against the ruling class and against the foreign exploitation of the country's economy. This 'class' nationalism opposes the national philosophy of the bourgeoisie. Significantly, Canadian labour failed to link its class demands to the national question. Its analysis passed over the most salient feature of Canadian capitalism, that without imperial investments and the support of the British and American bourgeoisie, national capitalism in Canada would not survive. In terms of strategy labour did not understand capitalism and imperialism as inseparable realities any more than they recognized that an anti-imperialist movement is a precondition to building a socialist Canada.

An Anti-Imperialist Nationalism

The bourgeoisie are well versed as to their situation. The strategy of keeping Canada together by keeping it apart is rooted in the liberal reality of power that accepts imperialism as the bread-and-butter of its politics. Nationalism and the national consciousness are extensions of the liberal order of things, recording the mirror images of how the bourgeoisie have been able to govern Canada. For them there is no contradiction between imperial demands and national survival. Their national programmes reflect a simple design – making Canadian resources cheap and accessible to British and American capitalists. This eagerness to please and profit has an historical explanation.

The survival and prosperity of this class depends on using the nation for its own advancement in the capitalist world. But the Canadian bourgeoisie have never sat at the high table as an industrial bourgeoisie in their own right. A colonial bourgeoisie gains admittance to the club for its weakness, not its strength. It reveals itself, according to Fanon, "as incapable of giving birth to an authentic bourgeois society with all the economic and industrial consequences which this entails. From the beginning the national bourgeoisie directs its efforts towards activities of the intermediary type. The basis of its strength is found in its aptitude for trade and small business enterprises, and in securing commissions. It is not its money that works, but its business acumen. It does not go in for investments and it cannot achieve that accumulation of capital necessary to the birth and blossoming of an authentic bourgeoisie."[13] The bourgeoisie does not ask for protection; it is protected by the metropolitan authority. Arm and arm with the real power, it plays the part which has been assigned to it. Fanon writes, "They guess that

---

and the brooking of no opposition or rivalship." Dafoe, *Laurier*, p. 43-4. Ostensibly his subject matter is the career of Laurier. However, this book is one of the few examples of class analysis of Canadian politics by a member of Canada's bourgeoisie.

*The breaking of the Canadian Seamen's Union strike, 1947-48, by an alliance of the federal government, social democratic trade union leadership, and Washington illustrates how far to the right the Canadian trade union movement had travelled.

the present situation will not last indefinitely but they intend to make the most of it. Such exploitation and such contempt for the state, however, inevitably gives rise to discontent among the mass of the people."[14]

The bourgeoisie accept the responsibility for legitimizing the political and economic costs of imperialization as their part of the arrangement. They pacify the people and defuse the internal situation, so that each year the economic surplus produced by the people will be shipped to the imperial centre without interruption. The reliability and ultimate status of the bourgeoisie hinge on their performing this critical function.

For the past one hundred years Canada has acted as the safety-deposit box for British and American investments. One can only describe Canada as the hidden colony of two empires, quietly absorbing huge amounts of capital – investments which paid enormous dividends to both imperialist powers. In 1914 Canada accounted for 23 per cent of all US direct investment; in 1964 it totalled 31 per cent. By 1969 the American 'trust' in Canada (both direct and portfolio) had jumped to over $20 billion. "Foreigners hold more than half the total assets of our 400 largest corporations. Non-residents, at last report, control 97 per cent of our automobile industry, 97 per cent of rubber, 78 per cent of chemicals, and 77 per cent of electrical apparatus. The mining and smelting industry is 59 per cent foreign-controlled; the petroleum and natural gas industry 74 per cent. Outside interests control at least 60 per cent of manufacturing."[15]

In protecting the massive inflows of American funds, the Canadian bourgeoisie realized their historic mission as an intermediary. As a consequence the governing bourgeoisie are content with a national consciousness of a people without their own history and who have refused to use the available historical forces to create a national economy and a national culture. Owing their primary commitment to foreign benefactors, they put the needs of capital before the needs of the Canadian people. Their anti-national behaviour is a "desirable and necessary" condition of their well-being as a class. The Canadian semi-sovereign state originated with the class policies of a bourgeoisie incapable of independent thought and independent action. The national bourgeoisie "follows the Western bourgeoisie along its path of negation and decadence without ever having emulated it in its first stages of exploration and invention ... We need not think that it is jumping ahead; it is in fact beginning at the end. It is already senile before it has come to know the petulance, the fearlessness or the will to succeed of youth."[16]

There is no mystery about the behaviour of the bourgeoisie in Canada. They are opposed to a political economy of independence. For them, the nation-state is an obstacle to the complete absorption of Canada into the North American empire. For Canadian liberals national sovereignty is an irrelevant and obsolete concept.* In order to promote and protect imperialism it has been necessary to dismantle the cultural and political institutions of Canada. With dependency comes disintegration.

Bourgeois nationalism is a spent force in Canada. The Canadian people are indifferent to it and the bourgeoisie themselves

*St. Laurent, Pearson, and Trudeau speak only about the evils of nationalism. All three are obsessed with internationalism, believing that if all states turned internationalist, the majority of the world's problems would disappear. When these men speak of internationalism, their remarks are prefaced with the unspoken adjectival phrase, 'American Cold War internationalism.' If Canada's example is to be followed, one would expect the Canadian government to call upon such 'narrowly nationalist' countries such as North Vietnam and the Provisional Revolutionary Government of South Vietnam to abandon their struggle for independence and accept the 'good neighbour' policy of the United States in Asia! To the extent that Canada has a foreign policy, it is to hand out the pathetic advice, "Be like us, follow the imperial leader."

have no faith in it. What remains powerful and alive in the national consciousness is the force of sentimental nationalism. It expresses the discontent and the general anxiety of the Canadian people with their future of living in an advanced capitalist and advanced colonial state.

The English-Canadian people are just beginning to recognize that Canada is a semi-autonomous region of the continent. They realize too that a dependent capitalist region is economically depressed. This is reflected concretely in the inability of Canadian capitalism to solve a range of problems; housing, inflation, lack of new jobs, loss of foreign markets, regional poverty, national planning, student unrest, and US control of the economy. Canadian capitalism is passing through a period of extreme vulnerability.

The strength of Canadian capitalism is its power to suppress its own contradictions. However, the more Americanized Canada becomes, the more disruptive are the effects of the contradictions. Soon enough, Ottawa's role will be to defend openly the advanced colonialism it has imposed on the Canadian people – with no intention of doing anything about it.

Sentimental nationalism is not a revolutionary force, because it does not isolate and crystallize the economic contradictions of capitalism. But it does create the conditions out of which will evolve a revolutionary nationalism – namely, anti-imperialism, which provides the only alternative to the policies of the Canadian bourgeoisie. An anti-imperialist struggle is the only way to break through the tight circle of Canadian history. Anti-imperialism, anti-capitalism and Canadian independence are an inseparable unity.

Analysis leads to strategy. Ideas require testing in practice. The central political issues facing the people of Canada are the historic role of the bourgeoisie in selling the country out and the Americanization of all aspects of Canadian life. These problems must be investigated and discussed throughout Canadian society: by trade union members in their locals, by students in universities, by public employees in government, by individuals in cultural institutions, and by sympathetic businessmen. There should be people's committees to investigate, document, then fight American imperialism in Canada.

NOTES
1. *The Fur Trade in Canada* (rev. ed., Toronto, 1956); *Essays in Canadian Economic History*, collected and published posthumously, M.Q. Innis, ed. (Toronto, 1956). I have analysed this key aspect of Innis' thought in "Harold Innis: Canadian Nationalist," *Journal of Canadian Studies*, May 1969.
2. *The Empire of the St. Lawrence* (Toronto, 1956).
3. *The North American Assault on the Canadian Forest* (Toronto, 1938).
4. (Toronto, 1965).
5. See Donald Creighton, *John A. Macdonald: The Old Chieftain* (Toronto, 1955), chap. III, "Fish and Diplomacy." J. W. Dafoe in *Laurier: A Study in Canadian Politics* (paperback ed., Toronto, 1963), chap. III demonstrates Laurier's commitment to an imperial market. The Abbott plan of 1947 is basically an imperial scheme and a continuation of the national-imperial policy of Macdonald.
6. H. S. Ferns and B. Ostry, *The Age of Mackenzie King* (London, 1955) p. 239.
7. See Pierre Elliott Trudeau, "Some Obstacles to Democracy in Quebec," *Canadian Journal of Economics and Political Science*, August 1958; Roger Graham, *Arthur Meighen*, I (Toronto, 1960); and J. W. Pickersgill, *The Mackenzie King Record*, I, 1939-44 (Toronto, 1960). The latter two books record incidents in which the Liberal party used racist appeals to win votes in Quebec and then turned its racism to double advantage outside Quebec by campaigning against Quebec on the same issue.
8. This point is frequently overlooked because political historians do not avail themselves of all sources of evidence, particularly the writing of Canadian political economists. See H. A. Innis, *A History of the Canadian Pacific Railway* (London, 1923), and G. Myers, *History of Canadian Wealth* (Chicago, 1914); as examples of classics that have

been overlooked. Another more recent example is H. C. Pentland's study of the Canadian political economy as it relates to labour, "Labour and the Development of Industrial Capitalism," an unpublished Toronto PHD thesis. It is a brilliant examination of the creation of the Canadian proletariat.

9. Pentland, "Labour and the Development of Industrial Capitalism," p. 409.

10. Ferns and Ostry, *The Age of Mackenzie King*, p. 65. Italics added.

11. See Tim Buck, *Our Fight for Canada: Selected Writings, 1923-1959* (Toronto, 1959), esp. chaps. 1 and 2, "The Idea of Labour and Democratic Unity" and "The People against the Monopolies." See also Gad Horowitz, *Canadian Labour in Politics* (Toronto, 1968).

12. It is perplexing in reading Harold Innis' writings in the 1930s and 1940s on the political economy of Canada and on the theme of American imperialism in this country to realize that his work went apparently unnoticed by the Canadian left. See his *Essays in Canadian Economic History*, particularly, "Economic Trends in Canadian-American Relations" (1938), "Recent Developments in the Canadian Economy" (1941), and "The Canadian Mining Industry" (1941).

13. F. Fanon, "Pitfalls of National Consciousness," in *The Wretched of the Earth* (New York, 1965), p. 144.

14. *Ibid.*, p. 140.

15. *Toronto Daily Star*, Oct. 17, 1969. A historical perspective on US foreign investment is given in the tables below:

INDUSTRY	1926	1957
PERCENTAGE OWNED BY ALL NON-RESIDENTS		
Manufacturing	38	50
Petroleum and natural gas	—	64
Mining and smelting	37	56
Railroads	55	30
Other utilities	32	15
Total of above industries and merchandizing	37	35
PERCENTAGE OWNED BY US RESIDENTS		
Manufacturing	30	39
Petroleum and natural gas	—	58
Mining and smelting	28	46
Railroads	15	11
Other utilities	23	12
Total of above industries and merchandizing	19	27

Foreign Long-Term Capital Invested in Canada, Direct and Portfolio

Type	1926 $ billions	1926 Per cent	1957 $ billions	1957 Per cent
ALL COUNTRIES				
Direct	1.8	30	10.1	68
Portfolio	4.0	66	6.5	37
Miscellaneous	.3	4	.9	5
Total	6.0	100	17.5	100
UNITED STATES				
Direct	1.4	44	8.5	64
Portfolio	1.7	53	4.3	33
Miscellaneous	.1	3	.5	3
Total	3.2	100	13.3	100

Geographic Distribution of US Direct Investment, 1897-1964

	1924 $ billions	1924 Per cent	1958 $ billions	1958 Per cent	1964 $ billions	1964 Per cent
Europe	.9	17	4.4	16	12.1	27
Canada	1.1	20	8.9	32	13.8	31
Latin America	2.8	52	12.7	43	10.3	23
Other	.6	11	1.1	9	8.1	19
Total	5.4	100	27.1	100	44.3	100

Sources: Kari Levitt, "Canada: Economic Dependence and Political Disintegration," *New World Quarterly*, vol, IV, no. 2, and Hugh G.J. Aitken, *American Capital and Canadian Resources* (Cambridge, Mass., 1961), pp. 68-9.

16. Fanon, *The Wretched of the Earth*, pp. 124-5.

3. Religion as a Source of Perpetuation of Ethnic Identity

David Millett/*University of Ottawa*

It is instructive to read this essay in conjunction with the preceding one. There, Drache was concerned with the political function of ethnic separatism, principally the French-English division, and the political values that supported it. Here, Millett examines the entire ethnic kaleidoscope and the ways in which the organized church has functioned to keep Canadians apart by fostering the survival of ethnic groups. "The most obvious perpetuator of old traditions and prejudices," he says, "is the ethnic church." *As the belief system that supports this institution becomes attenuated, he concludes, ethnic divisiveness will give way to the common sharing of common concerns in a "pan-Canadian identity."*

Reprinted by permission of the author. The thesis is to be published in 1972, by the University of Ottawa Press, as *L'Evolution de la Religion au Canada, 1871-1961* or a similar title.

This paper is based on one main observation, which occurs repeatedly as one studies various ethnic groups in Canada – that of all the institutions supporting the survival of distinctive cultures, the church is usually the strongest and the most active. I would like first to document that the churches are ethnically diverse. I will then examine whether this diversity is simply a reflection of Canadian society, or is also cultivated by them. Finally, I wish to examine what the decline of religion in Canada means for the future of ethnic diversity.

I

The Documentation of Diversity

It is not my intention to document in great detail all the cases where religious organizations support ethnic differences, so I will confine myself to some census material, to information from the annual reports of certain churches, and a small survey I carried out in connection with a doctoral thesis.

If we first take language differences as an indicator of diversity, we will find that the variety of languages of worship in Canada is truly amazing. In 1968, when I conducted a survey of languages of worship, I found that Roman Catholics worshipped in 21 languages, the United Church of Canada in 14, the Anglicans in 12, the Presbyterians in 5, the Lutherans in 9, and the Baptists in 13. Orthodox churches usually worship in their own tongues, with the exception of the Syrians of certain parishes. Altogether I found 118 Roman Catholic parishes worshipping in languages other than English or French, and 502 Protestant congregations worshipping in languages other than English, in the above-mentioned denominations. To these must of course be added hundreds of Orthodox, Mennonite, Hutterite, Doukhobor, and other parishes and congregations.

Notwithstanding the diversity of languages available, each of the major denominations of Christianity in this country, as well as the major non-Christian religions, displays a heavy concentration of people claiming the same national origin, the same language, or both. Roman Catholicism, for instance, ranged from 63.6% to 68.8% French, and 15.5% to 17.3% British, in the period 1931-1961. The last time a breakdown of the British was made, in 1941, they were 52.4% Irish, 28.0% English, 19.1% Scottish, and 0.5% 'Other'. This is why I consider it legitimate to speak of the French and Irish wings of the Catholic church. Even with the heavy immigration of German and Italian Catholics after World War II, their combined force in 1961, was less than that of the Irish (if we assume that half the British were still Irish).

To take another example, the United Church of Canada is essentially British in origin, though its Britishness has steadily declined from 88.4% in 1931 to 77.8% in 1961. Within its British origins, it was 49.5% English, 27.8% Scottish, and 21.3% Irish, in 1941, the last date for which such a breakdown is available.

In the Orthodox Church, the Ukrainians steadily increased their dominance from 54.1% in 1931 to 64.5% in 1951, but began to be challenged by the Greeks and Romanians in the 1950's. By 1961 Ukrainians constituted only 49.7% of the Orthodox, while the combined force of Romanians, Yugoslavs, and Greeks was 30.6%.[1]

Figures on the origins of Jews are complicated by the fact that 'Jewish' was offered as an ethnic origin as well as a religion until 1961. But this response was increasingly rejected by Canadian Jews. It was given by 99.8% of respondents in 1931, but dropped to 66.3% by 1961, and will not be used in 1971. The 1961 figures suggest the composition of Canadian Jewry, with 11.7% Polish, 9.2% Russian, 2.0% Hungarian, 1.6% Austrian, 0.8% German, and 2.7% British, to indicate the main Ashkenazic, German, and Sephardic components. It seems likely, then, that East European (Ashkenazic) origins are heavily dominant.

All the above information has been aimed at making two points: first, that an immense number of languages are employed in religious institutions; and second, that linguistically-defined or origin-defined denominations or parishes permit the survival of a great many ethnic groups. Churches appear to be more ethnically diverse than schools, political movements, or any other major Canadian institution.

II

Is This Diversity Intentional?

Our key question is "Does Canada's diversity make the churches diverse, or do the churches try to keep Canada diverse?" An argument can certainly be made that churches are a repository of diversity by default; that is, other institutions which normally would be diverse are denied this possibility by Canadian law. The public and separate school systems, the courts, and the political systems operate only in the official languages of the country, except in individual cases where this is clearly impossible. The language of work is nearly always English or French. This leaves the churches, the family, and certain recreational institutions as the only places where people seeking those of their own race, national origin or language can gather and feel at ease. And to feel 'at ease', in this case, means primarily to feel that one's language, attitudes, and references to other times and places are understood.

One of the functions of the identifiably ethnic parish or congregation is precisely to make its members 'feel at ease' in this sense. It provides them with words of understanding and familiar rituals which, at least once a week, free the faithful from the tension of speaking another language or of being continually misunderstood, and from the isolation of knowing that one's deepest convictions are not shared by anyone else at work, or at school, or on the street.

Once having set up such an environment, church authorities feel they must maintain it, certainly through a sense of responsibility to those they describe as 'the faithful', but also because it is in their own bureaucratic self-interest. One is easily tempted to count heads at the end of each year and to interpret an increase as strictly the work of the Holy Spirit. Conversely, a decrease must be interpreted as the work of forces contrary to the Holy Spirit, such as forced assimilation by a majority group, or yielding to the temptation to assimilate on the part of the faithful.

Once this line of thought is indulged in, it is very easy for the preservation of ethnic identity to become the *first* priority of an ethnic church, and for strictly religious considerations to be used as *justifications* of ethnic survival. The church then begins to attract primarily those interested in ethnic survival and to alienate those with genuine religious convictions. And the church becomes a *generator* and guardian of ethnic diversity rather than simply reflecting the diversity of the Canadian population. It takes under its wing those national associations, cultural groups, and mutual aid societies which are not strong enough to survive on their own, and sponsors language courses, dancing classes, and political activities.

All this happens to different degrees, and with varying effectiveness, depending on the size of the ethnic population, how many generations it has been in Canada, how regular the flow of immigrants is, and whether a whole church is involved (the Orthodox case) or only an ethnic parish of an English-language or French-language sponsoring church.

The result of this is the hyphenated Canadian, who identifies himself by religion and language (French-Jew, English-Catholic, French-Protestant), or by religion and national origin (Ukrainian-Orthodox, German-Catholic, Scotch-Presbyterian, Swedish-Lutheran).

III

The Future of Religion and Ethnic Diversity

In 1961 Canadians affiliated themselves with 9 principal religious bodies,[2] comprising 94% of the Canadian population. All of these are growing more slowly than the national population, and complaining of a decline in religiosity. I do not propose to enter a discussion of theological reasons for this decline, but simply to suggest that there are also some other reasons which are related to problems of ethnic identity.

The generation of Canadians which has grown up since the advent of television has had an opportunity never before available to experience visually the events and the people of all parts of the country. This experience has tended to break down their regionalism as Maritimers, Central Canadians, Westerners and Coast-dwellers, and at the same time separated them from older people who still think in regional terms. Internationally, television has brought them into visual contact with many countries of the world, no longer confining them to English-speaking Commonwealth countries, as the CBC radio programmes tended to do in the past. Canada, in their eyes, thus becomes less and less a child of Britain, and more and more a self-determining country with a truly international approach to the world. The fact that Canada is less Britain-oriented externally helps destroy the myth that it is essentially British internally. But whereas, for the older generations, the destruction of the British myth leads to the notion of a mosaic, the young people have a different experience. Not being raised with a British myth, they define themselves and the country as simply Canadian. Their definition of themselves is based on the country *as it is*, and not on a lot of other countries which have sent people to live here. Thus they oppose or ignore any institution which seems to perpetuate old traditions, including prejudices brought from other lands.

The most obvious perpetuator of old traditions and prejudices is the ethnic church. As we have seen, *all* major denominations in Canada are ethnically identifiable, and this is reinforced by parish traditions.[3] Churches are also the repository of dying languages, spoken by increasingly elderly people, and directed by increasingly elderly clergy, as recruitment to seminaries and theological colleges drops drastically from year to year. To the young Canadian, then, churches are institutions for old people with old languages and old prejudices which divide people on a very petty basis. For him there are much more serious kinds of division to be overcome, such as rich and poor, rural and urban, Indian and white, and French and English, and independence versus American domination. The Church, far from uniting Canadians under God, divides them into Protestant, Catholic, Orthodox, and Jew, so that they are even discouraged from marrying one another.

If the best of our many ethnic traditions are to be preserved, then, they must be removed from the churches and located in other institutions which are more acceptable to young people, and divorced from the old battles and prejudices which are so often used to justify them. They must be shown to be relevant to the present, in the context of a pan-Canadian identity expressed in two official languages. They must also be shown to be of practical use internationally.[4] People under thirty years of age will no longer study Ukrainian because their father is Ukrainian; they will only do so if the Ukrainian language is shown to be useful to them *in* Canada, *now*, as Canadians, and in Canada's relations to the rest of the world.

Those languages and sub-cultures which will survive will probably be those whose countries of origin are most important on the world scene, and they will survive because our school systems will begin to point out their importance for *all* Canadians, rather than simply for those whose families come from this or that country, and attend an ethnic church.

NOTES
1. This last figure also includes the category 'Other Europeans'. The analogous figure for these in 1931 constituted only 1.6% of all Orthodox; presumably they are mainly Bulgarians.
2. In order of size, these were: Roman Catholic, 8,342,828; United Church of Canada 3,664,008; Anglican 2,409,068; Presbyterian 818,558; Lutheran 662,744; Baptist 593,553; Jewish 254,368; Orthodox 239,766; Greek Catholic 189,653. The total is 17,174,544 out of a national population of 18,238,247.
3. As recently as 1962 I attended a Saint Andrew's Day banquet at a United Church in Montreal, where the guest speaker gave a tongue-in-cheek explanation of "Why the Scots are God's chosen people."
4. I find it rather unfortunate, for example, that with some 70,000 persons of Chinese origin in Canada, we should send still another elderly Anglo-Saxon abroad as Ambassador, however acceptable his credentials.

---

4. Accounting for the Connections: Canada's Changing Political and Economic Realms

B.Y. Card/*University of Alberta*

Written from a staunchly liberal utilitarian viewpoint, this brief excerpt from a longer work on Trends and Change in Canadian Society *makes explicit the normative structure that gives meaning and at least some order to our institutions.*

Reprinted from *Trends and Change in Canadian Society* by B.Y. Card, by permission of the author and The Macmillan Company of Canada Limited. ©1968.

How important to Canada's future are the games and leagues of games we call 'political' and 'economic'? What major strategies are involved in them? Attention is focused on trends and goals that disclose issues and problems which confront Canadians now and will continue to do so in the foreseeable future. The political realm includes all the processes, political parties, and legislative, administrative, or judicial bodies related to government. The economic realm includes all the processes and agencies concerned with the production, distribution, and consumption of goods and services. Two overlapping sectors make up the economic realm – the public sector, in which government departments, bureaus, councils, and Crown corporations are the important agents, and the private sector, in which non-government corporations and individual entrepreneurs are the main agents. The importance of these two realms, first from the perspective of a young Canadian and then from the point of view of a group of young Japanese, will now be considered.

Let us begin with the case of a hypothetical, but in many ways representative, young person of eighteen years of age. While this person could be male or female, we arbitrarily choose a male and just as arbitrarily a situation of a half-hour duration. Our 'case' is now lying in bed enjoying a sound sleep and most probably pleasant dreams, most of which he would never associate with government and only rarely with the economy, especially in any abstract way. Now let us take him from his world of slumber into the 'real' world. However, this will be done in a way that deliberately mixes his 'real' world of consciousness and concrete experiences with specific references to government and the economy. While the 'real' world of youthful experience provides the substance for dreams of both day and night, the realization of dreams and aspirations involves seeing clearly the connections between the ordinary activities of living and the great collective games abstractly referred to as 'political' and 'economic'.

We consider our 'case' as he leaves his home and goes to work. In the left-hand column the 'real' experiences of his immediate situation are outlined. In the right-hand column some of the connections between these 'real' experiences and the underlying, frequently taken-for-granted games conducted in the realms of government and economy are indicated.

'Real' Experiences of George on a Saturday	*Connections of these Experiences with Government and the Economy*
1. The direct rays of the fall sun have just begun to shine through the window of the bedroom, where George has been peacefully sleeping in the comfort and security of the family home.	1. Window space, house design, and construction quality are regulated by a government building code. The house, built by a private construction firm, was financed by a federally arranged and controlled mortgage. The family security is partly a product of national diplomacy and defence, municipal policing, and risk-sharing by insurance arrangements.
2. George is oblivious to all his surroundings until the alarm-clock rings. He jumps out of bed and dresses hurriedly.	2. The alarm-clock is a federally taxed machine that measures federally regulated time. His bed, clothes, and clock, all subject to federal tax, came to him from factories by way of wholesalers and retailers, all organized and controlled according to governmental laws and regulations. His name, 'George', was registered with the government at his birth, and provides him a legal status throughout his life.
3. Since he is in a hurry, George spends as little time as possible in the bathroom before going to breakfast.	3. His functional bathroom, the product of a series of plumbing inventions (produced, distributed, and installed by 'the economy'), makes use of the abundant and inexpensive running water supplied and purified by a technical branch of municipal government.
4. His appetite is excellent, partly because of his strenuous efforts the evenings before playing football for the senior school team, on which he is the offensive team's quarterback.	4. His instruction in football, as well as the facilities, coaching services, and supply of opposing teams to play with, are all related to schools, which are government-controlled and supported agencies for socializing Canadian youth.
5. Hungrily George devours cereal, toast, bacon, and eggs, washing them down with orange juice and milk, while vaguely remembering that these are the things his coach recommends, his mother cooks, and his father pays for.	5. The food items were produced and distributed by economic agencies according to government standards and regulations. The government also played a part in developing better livestock, such as hens, cows, and hogs, and in educating farmers to improve constantly the quantity and quality of their livestock. His coach's instructions were recommended by government health agencies, while the legal status and responsibilities of his father and mother were assigned to them by provincial law at their marriage.
6. At the conclusion of the meal, he puts on the jacket and hat he wears to the service station where he works on Saturdays in order to earn enough for the old car he wants to buy or for taking some kind of training after high school. He has not decided yet.	6. The service station is a small organization operating according to municipal by-laws, dispensing gasoline and oil, discovered, produced, and distributed by a large corporation, and taxed by a provincial government. The car he wants is also the product of a large corporation, while his further training is a provision of the government.
7. As he is about to leave, his father and sister enter the room. "Well, George," his father says, "the radio sportscast this morning said your team played an outstanding game yesterday." His sister remarks: "You should have seen the game, Dad. George was simply great."	7. The sportscast is the product of private and public cooperation in radio broadcasting. The presence of his father at home on Saturday is traceable to work regulations agreed to by union, government, and company officials.

In this case study we have emphasized the broad base of materials, services, regulation, and co-ordination that the Canadian combination of government and economy provides. This base, which has a material side as well as a non-material side of laws, codes, rules, and standards, is frequently taken for granted in the course of everyday living. Without it, social life in Canada would be impossible. With it, social life tends to be orderly, predictable, and relatively secure for most Canadians. This over-all result is the consequence of many different kinds of economic and political games and the ways these games are played. Some of these games and the ways they are played result in social inequalities that handicap our country. At the same time, we depend on our economic and political games to help change handicapping conditions. As we have noted, the realization of individual Canadian dreams, hopes, and aspirations, as well as the satisfactions and prestige which Canadians might enjoy collectively as a nation depend on them.

What are the components of national prestige? We turn here to the opinions of a group of Japanese high school and university students for two reasons. The first is that they present an 'outside' view worth considering. The second is that, to our knowledge, no group of Canadians have been asked the same questions and had their answers published. The Japanese students were asked to rank eight factors contributing to national prestige, using a technique known as 'paired comparisons', in which each factor was compared one at a time with every other factor. The researchers then constructed a scale of factors, in which the relative importance of each factor, as perceived by the students as a group, is indicated by a numerical number or 'weight'. The 3 highest ranking factors and their weights were: a nation's economy – 7.10; a nation's internal government – 5.32; and a nation's international relations – 5.16. The next 2 factors were perceived as of intermediate importance – a nation's cultural and scientific accomplishments – 4.62; and its physical geography and resources – 4.14. The final factors were a nation's national character – 3.84; its military strength – 3.77; a people's attitude towards their nation – 2.30.[1] Canadians may not agree entirely with this ordering and weighting of national prestige factors. However, concern with the contribution of the economy and government to Canada's prestige in today's competitive world is implicit, if not always explicit in much of Canadian thinking.

What main strategies are involved in Canadian political and economic games? For example, are the strategies of the games George and his family are involved in as taxpayers, workers and users of goods and services the same as the strategies of games having as their goal the raising of Canada's prestige among the nations? As we see the matter, there are three kinds of strategies involved in Canada's changing political and economic realms.[2] Each kind is important, and is briefly outlined and explained below.

1. Strategies to produce order and ensure the maintenance of existing or agreed-upon patterns of doing things. Games with these strategies have as their object orderly relationships, predictability, and the fulfilment of contracts and mutual expectations. Players in such games say in essence. "If I do this for you, then you will do that for me." These order-producing strategies call for the limiting or minimizing of lines of action or the things that a person or group could do. Further, the few lines of action that are agreed upon are governed by many criteria that define, clarify, and indicate how the actions are to be performed and under what conditions. For instance, George's family agree to pay a water and light bill every month and in return expect to have uninterrupted water and light service. Or George agrees to work on Saturdays at the service station (limiting his alternative lines of action), while the service station proprietor agrees to pay him so much for his services. George has many criteria for what constitutes a good job

and the proprietor many criteria for what a good employee should be. If each does his part and the performances come up to expected standards, the over-all result is order and predictability. The agreed-upon objectives of each will likely be reached since George and his employer are committed to fulfilling their mutual obligations. The games of most government agencies and of most businesses, since they involve both employers and employees, public servants and citizens, clients and customers, have order, continuity, and predictability as basic strategies.

2. Strategies appropriate to contests, competitions, and conflicts.[3] The second set of strategies may have a rational goal for one group of contestants, but is not agreed upon by opponents. For instance, George's football team has the rational goal of winning its next game, but since this goal cannot be shared with or agreed upon by the other team, it will have to be achieved in a contest. Contests or competition strategies are appropriate where the aim is achievement, solving a problem, or gaining greater prestige or power. The outcome is less predictable than in the 'games' or activities leading to order and fulfilment of contracts or obligations. In contest strategies it is important to maximize the lines of action, to increase the possible ways of doing things, and to minimize those established criteria that might limit action. The saying 'all is fair in love and war' illustrates the notion that in a contest (or conflict) the contestant wishes as few limitations on his action or goal achievement as possible. In George's football league there are just enough rules (criteria) to protect the players and to keep the contest predictable and within bounds, but the large part of the fun and challenge comes from the attempts of each side to increase its lines of action, while making sure that the opposing side has as few alternatives as possible. In Canada's political and economic realms, many of the games are based on contest or competition strategies, which, if carried out according to agreed-upon rules, have many of the qualities of conventional sports – for example, party politics, election campaigns, parliamentary debates, the creation and promotion of companies, the development of markets for commodities or services through advertizing, and some bargaining procedures used by management and by labour unions prior to entering upon wage agreements. While the conduct of these games may produce some disarray as campaigners, parliamentarians, companies, and unions engage in contests, the end result for the whole society is a kind of changing order, a roughly predictable adaptability. On the other hand, when a player or group of players involved in these competitive games has as an ultimate goal only increased power, then the achievement of limited goals is but a stepping-stone to the achievement of bigger goals that could result in a monopoly of political or economic power or of both. In situations where there is an absence of adequate rules, where rules are not followed, or where there is no restraining competition, a power monopoly can be reached that much easier by persons or groups for whom this is a goal. While contest strategies are indispensable parts of the games Canadians are engaged in, one of the greatest challenges they face is evolving domestic and international situations favouring 'fair' contests, in which persons or groups whose aim is ultimate power can be effectively restrained. This involves creating such situations. For this, the next kind of strategy is vital.

3. Strategies favouring creativity and the augmentation and enrichment of group relationships and of individuals as 'selves'. Strategies of this nature are characterized by the availability of many lines of action and also many criteria for judging and evaluating action. In this set of strategies 'feed-back' or continuing dialogue is of the essence. An example of a game with creativity as its ultimate goal might be George's football team meeting with the coach after a game to talk about the last game and evolve some new plays. In such a game the relative official positions and ages of coach and players are not too important.

Their 'social distance' is reduced as each contributes ideas and passes judgement on the ideas expressed. If this game continues successfully the team and coach come up with some new plays or tactics for the next 'official' game; at the same time, each person may feel that these new plays or tactics are in part his because of his contribution to the process of creating them. This tendency of the individual to identify himself with a new product of creative effort and with the other persons who are involved in the effort leads to what we have called the augmentation and enrichment of group relations and of individual 'selves'. Creativity strategies also contribute potentially to strategies designed for order and predictability and to strategies of contests. For example, when the coach is giving instructions to George's team just before their next 'official' game, he will probably commit players better to limited lines of action if his instructions are based on what the group creatively decided. In addition, the fun of competition is enhanced on the playing field as the team knowingly tests the plays that they have had a part in creating. If the plays hold up in competition the team's satisfaction may be enhanced, and if not, reduced. In either case, the chances are that in the long run individual self-development, team morale, individual competence, and team performance will be enhanced by continuing creativity. Some industrial research has shown this to be the case among workers, where the creativity gains were in directions not anticipated by managers and scientists operating with predictability, efficiency, and contest strategies.[4]

In the Canadian political and economic realms, there have been, traditionally, relatively few formally patterned and openly tolerated games having as their ultimate goals creativity and the augmentation of group relations and individual 'selves'. However, in party caucuses, committee and board rooms, back offices and laboratories, and in the informal exchanges of ideas and techniques in the course of performing assigned tasks or in leisure time, there probably has been considerable continuing creativity. One of the recent trends in Canada's political and economic realms is more overt recognition of creativity strategies. This trend is reflected in government-sponsored programmes in community development and preventive welfare, and in such agencies as the Company of Young Canadians and the Canada Council. It is also reflected in the broadening emphasis on and the allotment of greater resources to industrial and business research, in the expansion of personnel-development programmes within companies, and in the greater participation of private economic agencies in nation-wide policy-making through such organizations as the Economic Council of Canada. *As Canadian political and economic games that have traditionally emphasized strategies leading to order, conformity, efficiency, and competitive achievement are redeveloped to include strategies leading to creativity and to group and 'self' augmentation, the quality and vitality of Canadian society may be genuinely advanced. . . .*

NOTES

1. Michiya Chimbori *et al.*, 'Measuring a Nation's Prestige', *The American Journal of Sociology*, LXIX, No. 1 (July 1963), pp. 63-8.
2. The three kinds of strategy mentioned here are the present writer's versions of three theoretical models of social action presented to the Western Association of Sociology and Anthropology Meetings at Banff, Alberta, February 1964, by Professor Edward J. Abramson and Mrs. Jane Abramson of Saskatoon. The Abramsons' theoretical formulation has application to human behaviour generally. Its application to the political and economic realms using the 'games' approach is a special use of a general theory.
3. In the Abramsons' theory this set of strategies is called the game or strategy model. Since we have used the concept of games in a broad way to include all purposeful social behaviour, we have identified this model simply as a contest, competition, or conflict set of strategies.
4. This was essentially the conclusion reached by George C. Homans, *The Human Group* (New York: Harcourt, Bracé and Company, 1950), pp. 48-155, in his analysis of the now famous study of the Bank Wiring Observation Room of the Western Electric Company's Hawthorne Plant at Chicago. For a report of the original study, see F. J. Roethlisberger and W. J. Dickson, *Management and the Worker* (Cambridge: Harvard University Press, 1939).

5. The Eskimo Pantheon and Social Organization

Rémi Savard/*Université Laval*

The intricate intertwining of a people's mythology and religious belief system with the social organization necessitated by the limitations of its physical environment are sensitively analyzed in this study of Eskimo divinities. The symbolic dimension of culture, it is suggested, is functional in maintaining the group's continued existence in the face of a hostile nature.

A society spends its time shaping out of its self its social functions and sometimes its mission, an ideal and simple concept, which it changes and renders more complex all the time.[1]

From the beginning, ethnography devoted to the Eskimos recognized the importance of three religious figures: Lunar-Man, the Woman-From-Below, and the Air (or the

Reprinted from *The Canadian Review of Sociology and Anthropology*, 4:2 (1967), by permission of the author and the publisher. Translated by Marion E. Meyer, Queen's University.

Temperature). In the Spirit-of-the-Air, Thalibtzer saw the survival of a very ancient preshamanistic phase, but he considered the two others to be recent 'divinities' related to shamanism.[2] Whatever the suggested chronological sequence may be, we believe that his historical classification of the three great Eskimo master-spirits is based upon objective group characteristics. It is these characteristics, which we propose to study in the present article.

It is a fact that the Spirit-of-the-Air is far less well defined than the other two. We know of no ritual development connected with it, except for vague incantations designed to produce good weather, or else to arouse a tempest to annoy the enemy. In the Central Arctic, this spirit acquires its most precise definition. There, one finds a little myth of origins which contains the following characteristics: the divinity's sex is male; he has an intermittent rapport with the sun; he plays a supervisory role with respect to taboos related to the menstrual cycle and abortions; he is sometimes called PINGA (*the one from above*).[3] We shall see, further on, that these traits identify him as Lunar-Man. Moving across Eskimo territory, one finds that Lunar-Man and the Woman-From-Below are much better known, but the importance of the first is inversely proportional to the importance of the Spirit-of-the-Air. Thus, besides the divinity from below, which is explicit among the great majority of the groups, one sometimes finds Lunar-Man and sometimes the divinity of the Air. The variations occurring in this trinity could thus be construed as a divine couple in which the female partner alone would be constant.

Version A		*Version B*
a^1 lunar god	atmospheric god	b^1
a^2 goddess from below	goddess from below	b^2

Because of the importance of ancient migratory movements and of the great mobility of Eskimo groups during pre-historic and historic periods, the three divinities are known nearly all across the territory. Couple B, however, is mainly found in the Central Arctic (among Copper Eskimo, Netsilik and Cariboo), while couple A is encountered at the extremities of the territory (Greenland and Alaska).[4] The situation is, however, less clear in Alaska because of numerous super-imposed cultural currents. At the border, dividing the Central Arctic and Greenland, one can find a case half way between A and B, where it is difficult to decide whether a^1 or b^1 predominates. This is true for both the Iglulik Eskimo and the Polar Eskimo of the North–West of Greenland. One of the first observers of the latter group wrote: "The moon is still called ANNINGAK among them, but through the endeavours of the Danish missionaries to get rid of all words which are connected with the original superstitions, this name has been nearly superseded in the south by KAIMUT; it is sometimes called PINGA in the north."[5] ANNINGAK and PINGA, respectively, are the names of the divinities a^1 and b^1. This being established, the Eskimo pantheon seems to take the form of a binary opposition with differentiated values which could be defined as follows:

<u>Above</u>
<u>Below</u>

Because of the fleeting character of the atmospheric divinity, we shall here examine Version A of this pantheon.

Lunar-Man is designated by the expression ANINGA, the possessive form of the kinship term describing the following relationships: brother older than female ego or female ego's brother, depending on the regions. In everyday language, the moon will be designated by the term TATQEQ, the etymology of which appears to send us back to the notion of visual perception.[6] As for the goddess of below, she is called NERRIVIK (*the place where food is found*), TAKANAKAPHALUK (*the terrible one from below*), NULIAJUK (*the one refusing marriage*), UINI-GUMISUITUNG (*the one who didn't want a husband*), AVIL-OQ (?), SEDNA (apparently a locative meaning the *one from below*), ARNAKAPHALUK (*the terrible woman*).

The general economy of the myth of the emerging lunar divinity presents itself in the following way: at the starting point, we are in the presence of two young siblings whose sex is not yet specified and who have a relationship betraying a certain ambiguity between sexual and alimentary activities. The continuation of the account leads us to see the progressive acquisition, by each one of the siblings, of a sexual specificity different from each other, which involves an increasingly well defined, and previously undifferentiated, distinction between alimentary and sexual activities. Once he acquires these natural functions, the boy suggests to his sister that they commit incest, which the young sister refuses.

By this act, she introduces a differentiation of a new type, i.e. between permissible partners and forbidden partners. The myth ends with the transformation of the boy and his sister into Lunar-Man and Sun-Girl respectively. The latter, however, plays a very minor role at the heart of the Eskimo pantheon.[7]

To avoid becoming too theoretical, it may be useful to become familiar with two important sequences of this account. At the beginning, the adolescent boy living with his young sister and mother (or their grandmother, depending on the version) is blind. One day, a polar bear appears at the outskirts of the camp, and the woman suggests to her son that they combine their efforts in an attempt to fell it. He bends the bow and she aims. Later on, she refuses to admit that the animal has been mortally wounded, and thus deprives him of what is considered the rite of passage of the adolescent Eskimo: the killing of his first polar bear.[8] During the meal that follows, the girl, unknown to her mother, drops several pieces of bear meat inside her garment. As she had taken the precaution to gird herself, this food accumulates to the height of her breasts, "upon her naked flesh" according to the original text of the Polar Eskimos. Then, escaping her mother's supervision, she brings food to her beloved brother. Without knowing it, the latter, thus transgresses against the taboo forbidding a young Eskimo to eat of the meat of his first kill. For, to demonstrate properly the fact that he has now become a producer, he is obliged to distribute the whole of his game among his residence companions. At the end of the tale when the same individual, cured of his blindness, attempts to commit incest with his young sister, the latter cuts off her breasts and throws them to him saying: "Since you love me so much, eat this, which is of me!" Thus she evokes the period when her older brother (ANINGA) then blind (TATQEQ) fed upon forbidden meat hidden precisely on the naked breasts of his sister.[9]

The goddess from below, representing the other pole of the pantheon, is at first introduced as one of those arrogant girls who despise "suitors from the village." To her misfortune, she prefers to marry a passing stranger who claims to be rich and powerful. In fact, during their living together, it transpires that he is a Bird-Man, having but a perforated tent for shelter and often wanting even a minimum of food. During the absence of this monstrous spouse, the father and the brothers of the woman come to take her back. They arrive by *umiak*, the ancient craft made of skin, capable of holding from 30 to 40 people, Without delay, the Bird-Man starts to pursue them and raises a tempest intended to sink the boat. To save his people, the father decides to throw his daughter into the sea. When she clings to the sides of the umiak, he cuts off her limbs, which are turned into different species of marine mammals.

Eskimos often confuse this account with the one of the Daughter and the Dog. Here the spouse is a canine. His wife gives birth to humans, man-dogs and sometimes different species of sea mammals. The daughter and the dog live on an island; the father-in-law of the latter comes regularly to bring food to the couple and his grandchildren. For these people, the rules of residence are usually matrilocal during the first years of marriage. During this time, the son-in-law hunts for the group of his spouse. In the above context, the girl is not only taken away, but the father pushes the ridicule to the point of providing the couple with food.[10]

The connection between the woman and the food, so often noticed by observers, allows us to perceive here what appears to be its true semantic value. To eat any meat from one's first kill, is much like marrying one's own sister. The prohibition attached to the rite of passage emphasizes the importance of circulating the product of the hunt. It thus evokes another prohibition – that of incest, whose purpose is to insure the circulation of women among exogamous units. On the other hand, if a group has had a wife stolen, it is tantamount to having had food stolen. The association of woman with food, which appears clearly in this context, is one of position vis-à-vis man. In both cases, circulation is based on the principle of reciprocity which Malinowski observed in the North-East of New Guinea, which Mauss saw as the basis of all social life, and from which Lévi-Strauss derived diverse concrete implications for different matrimonial systems. Culture thus establishes a cycle of reciprocity so as to ensure the survival of the group and, consequently, the survival of the individual. The indispensable condition for such reciprocity, the whole lunar myth proclaims this, is *discontinuity*; the original mythical chaos gives way to a discontinued universe on the biological as well as on the social level. More precisely, we could say that this narrative represents the creation of social distance in an arborescent form. The diverse levels of ramification could be read as follows: since there are different sexes and since sexual activities are different from alimentary activities, it follows that there must be permissible partners and foods on the one hand and forbidden ones, on the other hand.

To convince oneself that the fault of the future goddess is of the same type as is the fault of Lunar-Man, it is enough to remember that the prohibition of incest is only the negative aspect of a positive rule of defining the spouse. To marry one's sister is, for a boy the same as refusing marriage is for a girl. In both cases the group is deprived of a spouse. Thus, if the two myths have different starting points, they nevertheless converge towards the same problem, which is the one of reciprocity perceived in alimentary and sexual terms. ANINGA first deprived the group of food then deprived it of a spouse. The goddess's husband, on the other hand, first seized a woman of the group in order, eventually, to exploit the group for food. In either case, a crime against reciprocity is committed. The myth of the emerging goddess thus picks up and completes the myth of ANINGA. The origin of the two divinities points to its connection with techniques of group maintenance which is what anthropologists call culture. While the lunar narrative establishes an equivalence between cannibalism (eating of the breasts) and incest, the narrative of the goddess, at least as in the account of the young girl and the dog, connects cannibalism (grandfather eaten up by his descendents) and marriage outside the circle in which exchanges take place. Thus, in their own way, these thoughts express the formal complementarity between crimes against exogamy and crimes against endogamy.

We would, however, not feel justified to define such a religious message as a simple reflection of the social reality or even of the social norms. This pantheon then uses the social organization to illustrate the symbolic dimension of culture. In proportion to the continuance of the group in the world, the symbolic dimension of culture provides significance for nature; it does so by chopping up and redistributing those natural realities, food and women, so inequitably distributed at the beginning. Thus the sacred, by which religion has frequently been defined, appears often attached to an attitude of veneration towards a specific type of language which culture uses as a form of self-reflection. In it, culture discovers itself in the form of *rules* and symbolized by discontinuity; it opposes itself to the original and natural chaos which it perceives as continuity (capitalization of spouses and food resulting from the confusion of permissible and non-permissible entities).

Eskimo pre-history destined Version A to be better preserved. Does the diffused character of Version B, as Thalbitzer thought, stem from the antiquity of the Spirit-of-the-Air? If so, one might hypothesize that the latter long ago formed a couple with the spouse of the dog. It would be easy to demonstrate that the latter and the Goddess-of-Below belong to the same semantic field, the field of 'international relations', while the divinities of above (PINGA and ANINGA) send us back to the problems of internal government. Thus it seems to us that the chronological question should be taken up again in terms of the modification of the binary structure under the effects of numerous events which marked the life of these ancient Northern people.

May we therefore conclude these remarks about the Eskimo pantheon by attempting to consider them within the framework of the old dichotomy: magic-religion. In their *Esquisse d'une théorie générale de la magie*, with respect to religion, Hubert and Mauss defined the dichotomy as follows: "we call (rites and magic)...all that which does not belong to an organized cult, a private ritual, a secret, a mystery, or anything tending towards prohibited rituals."[11] Their description of the different types of magic agents and acts can be summarized by the expression *social marginality*. It is in this that magic is different from religion, which can always be located at the center of collective life itself. But it is perhaps their analysis of a model of magical representation which constitutes the most interesting point for our purpose. Investigating further the laws of magic suggested by Frazer, they reduced the law of *similarity* and *contrast* to *contiguity* which they described as follows:

"...individuals and things are bound together into a theoretically limitless number of congenial associates. The chain they constitute is so dense, the continuity is such, that to obtain any planned effect, it is immaterial whether one acts upon one or the other of the links."[12]

The notion of *continuity* thus emerges from these thoughts of Mauss and Hubert. They emphasize it themselves when writing further on: "...the world is conceived as a single animal, whose parts, regardless of distance, are connected among themselves in an inevitable manner. Everything looks alike and everything is in contact. This sort of magic pantheon gives a synthesized representation of our different laws."[13] Finally, exploring this concept of *continuity* more deeply, the authors are led to the concept of *nature*. "Nature is by definition what can be found at the same time in the whole and in its parts. In other words, it is the basis of the law of contiguity; it is also that which can be found in all the members of the same species and thus lays the foundation for the law of similarity. Finally, it is that which allows a thing to act upon another thing, opposed, but of the same species, and thus becomes the basis for the law of opposites."[14]

Having first defined magic and religion as the two poles of the same continuum, the authors succeed in demonstrating a connection between *magic, continuity* and *nature*. As for us, starting with Eskimo data, we were able to establish a relation between *religion, discontinuity* and *culture*. The correlation between these two chains could possibly give us the general framework of collective representations. Religion suggests that to obtain an artificial homogeneity analogous to the natural homogeneity, as used by magic, i.e. to arrive at an equitable distribution of scarce goods among diverse social segments, a rule of reciprocity is needed, which forbids the individual certain goods and prescribes others. Thus, *primitive* religions already dealt, in their own language, with problems which our modern political ideologies are still attempting to resolve. Magicians of old on the other hand, on confronting nature, took an approach which made possible technological and scientific development on which we so much pride ourselves.

NOTES

1. G. Dumézin, *Mitra-Varuna. Essai sur deux représentations Indo-Européenes de la Souverainetée.* 5 ème édition (Paris, 1948).

2. W. Thalbitzer, *The Ammassalik Eskimo.* Contributions to the Ethnology of the East Greenland Natives. Second Half-Volume, Meddelelser om Gronland, Bd. 40 (Copenhagen, 1941), pp. 582-3. To describe the traditional religion of several Siberian groups certain Russian ethnologists had the habit of speaking of two successive waves: *animism and shamanism*. As apparent from the term, the first approach endowed each natural element with a sort of master spirit. Later on shamanism introduced an intermediary between the spirits and the people (the shaman) which the authors in question had perhaps the tendency to define too much by his pranks (M. G. Levin and L. P. Potapov, eds. *The Peoples of Siberia*, Chicago, 1964). For other Russian specialists, the first period was rather one of totemism. (H. N.

Michael, *Studies in Siberian Shamanism*, Toronto, 1963).

3. Rasmussen, *The Netsilik Eskimo: Social Life and Spiritual Culture*. Report of the Fifth Thule Expedition (1921-1923), VIII, 1-2 (Copenhagen, 1931), pp. 229ff.

4. Broadcasting of myths and legends actually tends to accentuate the process of diffusion and homogenization.

5. Capt. Ed. Sabine, *An Account of the Esquimaux who inhabit the West Coast of Greenland, above the latitude 76°* (Portland Place, 1819), p. 86.

6. For further discussion of this question, see R. Savard, *Mythologie Esquimaude, Analyse de Textes Nord-Groenlandais*, Centre d'Etudes Nordiques, Travaux Divers, No. 14, Université Laval (Québec, 1966), p. 105.

7. Among the Udegeys of Siberia the sun is also a young girl courted by the moon. (S.V. Ivanov, A.V. Smolyak, M.G. Levin, "The Udegeys", in Levin and Potapov, *The Peoples of Siberia*, p. 743). With the Evenks, the sun is female, (G. M. Vasilevich, "Early Concepts about the Universe among the Evenks (Materials)", in Michael, *Studies in Siberian Shamanism*, p. 52.

8. The motive of *The Deceived Blind Man* is frequent in North America, its distribution among the Eskimos goes from Alaska to Greenland. In one of our recent works we pointed to ten versions (R. Savard, *Mythologie Esquimaude*, p. 127). Boas in his comparative Tsimshian mythology mentions thirteen Indian versions: Tsimshian, Rivers Inlet, Kwakiutl, Kaigani, Masset, Chilcotin, Carrier, Tlingit, Loucheux, Hare, Assiniboin, Osage, Arapaho, etc. F. Boas, *Tsimshian Mythology*, Thirty-first annual report of the Bureau of American Ethnology, 1909-1910. (Washington, 1916), p. 825 ff. Among the Eskimo, the blind man is always a young adolescent, among the Indians, he is an old man. In the first case the cure is followed by promotion to a state of virility; in the second case, the old man rejuvenates.

9. For a study in greater detail of the variance of this account, see Savard, *Mythologie Esquimaude*.

10. The motive of the marriage of the girl and the dog reminds us of the North American heritage. All Eskimo groups know this story. We have discovered versions among the Arapaho of Oklahoma (A.S. Kroeber, and G.A. Dorsey, *Traditions of the Arapaho*, Publications of the Field Columbian Museum, Anthropological Series, V, 1903, pp. 205 - 226), among the Osage of the same American State (G.A. Dorsey, *Tradition of the Osage*. Publications of the Field Columbian Museum, Anthropological Series, IX, 1904, pp. 31-32), among the Flancs-de-chiens of Great Slave Lake in Canada (E. Petitot, *Traditions Indiennes du Canada Nord-Ouest: Textes originaux et traduction littérale*, Calençon 1888, pp. 469-474), among an Indian group of Vancouver (F. Boas, *Race, Language and Culture*, New York, 1959, p. 440).

11. M. Mauss and H. Hubert, "Esquisse d'une théorie générale de la magie" in Marcel Mauss, *Sociologie et Anthropologie* (Paris, 1950), pp. 1-141.

12. *Ibid.*, p. 58.

13. *Ibid.*, p. 66.

14. *Ibid.*

Private Control of Public Space

Private Control of Public Space

In his essay in Section Two, John O'Neill argues that in modern, one-dimensional society the public has become so subordinated to the private,.individual sensibilities so privatized as to not know, or not care, that we are confronted with "the paradox that society may be free without individuals being free." He concluded his essay with a plea for the generation of a genuine public consciousness "in which men share common assumptions about their moral and physical environment and exercise them in a concern for truth of speech and beauty of form in public places."

The selections in this section deal with ostensibly public space which is in fact private because control is in the hands of a small, closed group. To the extent that this group is able to impose its definitions of the public good on the society, as for example in the case of Smallwood's Newfoundland, through its management of the information media and its monopoly on distribution of

rewards, then the privatization of the public is total. However, absolute control is never able to control absolutely. Accomodations are made, whether from the need for a special form of expertise that is either not available or is in short supply in the controlling group, or from the desire to give the appearance of responsiveness, or as a carefully calculated strategy to strengthen the private group's control. In the process old claims are modified and new ones are made which can eventuate either in a new private group gaining control – the circulation of the elites – or possibly in the transformation to genuinely public space. Alternatively, those denied access may accumulate sufficient power through organization as to openly expose and challenge the hitherto unrecognized belief system that legitimated the private hegemony. Examples in the present revolutionary climate are numerous.

1.   The Quebec 'Family' That Controls Canada

Peter Desbarats/*Ottawa Editor, Toronto Star*

This piece brings together several themes that have been developed in earlier selections. Though he does not use the concept, Desbarats is talking about a network in the sense in which Stebbins defined it as a "psychological predisposition to respond." The members of the Quebec 'family' do not constitute a group in the sociological meaning of that term but, the argument is, the range of options open to them is conditioned by predispositions that arise from this intricate but loose web of affiliation. Lacking specific information about the actual decision-making process surrounding the events he is concerned with, all that can be said is that the author has traced the necessary condition for such predispositions. But this is not sufficient. To validate the claim we require evidence that actions and decisions were in fact influenced by position in the network and this, of course, is difficult to uncover. Nevertheless, Desbarats' argument that the October 1970 crisis was managed as a 'private' affair is intriguing and suggestive of the importance of networks as a parameter in the private control of public space.

Political life in Canada in the Trudeau era has succumbed rapidly to the domination of a small, exclusive, emotional and somewhat old-fashioned Quebec *family*.

The process started at the beginning of the Quiet Revolution in 1960, when it became evident that rapid political and social changes in Quebec would have a determining effect on the future of Canada. It reached a peak during the October Crisis of 1970. With French-speaking Quebeckers in commanding positions in Ottawa, Quebec City and Montreal, as well as in the revolutionary movement which challenged their authority, the crisis was constructed, manipulated and resolved virtually without reference to English-speaking Canada.

During the crisis, English-speaking Canadians were utterly dependent on the *family* (as good a term as any for Quebec's dominant élite). Their information about the crisis came only from sources within the *family*. It was interpreted by members of the *family*. The key political decisions were taken within the *family*.

Reprinted from *Saturday Night* 86:3 (1971), by permission of the author and the publisher.

Frightened by the *family*'s description of insurrection in progress, most English-speaking Canadians simply abdicated their political function. It was a case of – all power to the *family*. The small number of English-speaking Canadians who held out, who refused to take everything on trust, were (and still are) rendered ineffective by their isolation from *family* affairs and the fact that their natural informants and allies in Quebec are themselves members of the *family*.

The out-of-it feeling that was shared by all English-speaking Canadians during the crisis had little to do with the usual problems of language or lack of knowledge about politics in Quebec. It was due to the fact that the crisis was largely a *family* affair involving many Quebeckers who had known each other closely for years. Relations among these protagonists, and between them and many of their radical opponents, were personal and complex.

An understanding of these family relationships in Quebec, or at least an awareness of their existence, is basic to an understanding of how Canada is governed today.

As an English-speaking Quebecker who has lived and worked outside Quebec, I know that this awareness isn't part of English Canada's political consciousness. The concept of a unified national élite is difficult for many English-speaking Canadians to grasp because there is nothing like it in their own experience.

Anyone who has ever tried to operate a national organization or business in Canada has quickly discovered that English-speaking Canada is composed of a number of isolated city states. Each city has its own ruling hierarchy or *family* whose power, except in the case of a few extraordinary individuals, is non-transferable. Influence within the Vancouver *family*, for instance, has little value in Edmonton, less in Winnipeg and probably none at all in Halifax. Even within the same professional strata – journalism, to use a personal example – the isolation of the city states provides for only the sketchiest contacts between English-speaking Canadians of similar interests. The *family* of each city state is served, to a great extent, by its own businessmen, professional class and local intelligentsia.

In the national administration at Ottawa, these individual *families* contribute to the central power structure in a complex fashion. Every party and every government is a constantly shifting network of alliances based on common regional interests, economic concerns, social and ethnic backgrounds, education, idealism and many other factors – at least as far as English-speaking Canadians are concerned.

Unlike English Canada, French Canada is a unified society. Excluding the sparsely populated northern reaches of the province, it covers a relatively small geographic area. It has only one metropolis and one political capital. Quebec City is, like Ottawa, not a great deal more than the place where the government happens to be. Everything else is in Montreal – the brains and muscle of French Canada. It is a very small world, largely undisturbed by immigration, where everyone knows everyone else to an astonishing degree. In fact, it would be quite possible to take a Vancouverite and, by conducting him on a careful tour of art gallery previews, book launchings, concerts and intellectual, commercial and political assemblies, introduce him in a single Montreal winter season to virtually everyone of importance in the Quebec *family*.

It is this unified 'nation' that confronts, in Ottawa, the loose alliance of city states known as English Canada. But that's only a superficial description. To understand a little of what it really means, it's necessary to examine a few of the main nerve clusters which run through Quebec's power structure and to follow up some of the individual strands.

The vivisection is easier than usual at the moment because important incisions and cross-sections have been performed recently by Quebeckers. The fact that this has been done for political reasons within the Quebec *family* doesn't lessen its usefulness for English Canadians.

It hardly matters where one starts. Every strand leads, sooner or later, to every other. A typical incision would be the current *Cité Libre* revelations exploited for their own purposes by supporters of Pierre Vallières, the revolutionary ideologist who spent most of the past four years in prison and whose book, *The White Niggers of America* is being published in translation in Toronto this spring. As everyone now knows, Vallières worked closely with Pierre Trudeau in the early 1960's on a small but influential magazine called *Cité Libre*. Vallières and his friends are using this information today to imply that Trudeau has abandoned Quebec while his more radical former associates have kept the true faith. But for English-speaking Canadians outside Quebec, it is revealing simply to establish the fact that the two men are not, to one another, faceless enemies but relatively close former associates who, if they were to meet on some imaginary non-political planet, would probably greet one another and talk over old times. The importance of this is that when Trudeau enacts legislation which puts Vallières in prison, he is not doing it to a statistic. The decision involves emotion.

This is true of other members of the Quebec *family* in Ottawa. Secretary of State Gérard Pelletier, for instance, was a co-founder of *Cité Libre* with Trudeau and was also Vallières' editor at the Montreal daily *La Presse*. Another influential figure at *Cité Libre* – just to illustrate how complex the strands become as soon as you start to examine them – was publisher Jacques Hébert, the man who was appointed as a kind of ombudsman to investigate the treatment of Vallières and others arrested following the proclamation of the War Measures Act.

One of Vallières' cellmates this winter was the colourful Michel Chartrand, head of the Montreal council of the Quebec-based Confederation of National Trade Unions. In an article about her imprisoned husband in the January issue of the radical Montreal magazine *Last Post*, Simone Chartrand recalled that "it was in 1940, outside my office at Palestre Nationale of the Jeunesse Etudiante Catholique, that I first met Michel . . . I was standing in the hallway with Alexandrine Leduc, who is now the wife of Gérard Pelletier . . . " It was Pelletier who, as a reporter for the Montreal daily *Le Devoir*,

persuaded Michel Chartrand to involve himself in the landmark strike at Asbestos. It took only two days for Chartrand to wind up in jail – the first of many detentions – after a dramatic courtroom performance.

Mme. Chartrand also recalled a meeting in the home of Thérèse Casgrain, appointed to the Senate last year by the Trudeau administration, when Trudeau, Pelletier, Maurice Sauvé (a former Liberal Forestry Minister in Ottawa) and Chartrand were invited to join the CCF party. Chartrand was the only one who took up the challenge. He contested two elections for the CCF and tried without success to persuade Trudeau to become leader of the CCF in Quebec.

Strand upon strand . . . Simone Chartrand shared an office at the headquarters of Jeunesse Etudiante Catholique in 1940 with one of the men primarily responsible, thirty years later, for the law that placed her husband in prison in 1970 – Gérard Pelletier. The third occupant was a young lawyer called Daniel Johnson, Union Nationale Premier of Quebec at the time of his death in 1968. Simone herself was the daughter of a judge, a former Liberal member of the Quebec legislature under the corrupt Taschereau regime. She is the granddaughter of a judge and her only brother is a judge. This winter, Michel Chartrand taunted the judge presiding over his case with reminders of the judge's unsuccessful career as a Liberal politician. A bit of *family* gossip.

Strand upon strand . . . in 1942, Chartrand was an active worker in the anti-conscription *Ligue pour la Défense du Canada* alongside the late André Laurendeau, proposer and co-chairman of the Royal Commission on Bilingualism and Biculturalism; Gérard Filion, industrialist and former director of *Le Devoir*; and Marc Carrière, now president of Dupuy Frères, a large Montreal department store. In the spring of 1942, Chartrand was the campaign organizer for the League's candidate in a Montreal by-election: Jean Drapeau.

Strand upon strand . . . in the 1950's, Jean Marchand, head of the Canadian Catholic Confederation of Labour, now Minister of Regional Expansion in the Trudeau cabinet, tried to oust Chartrand from the union on two occasions. In one of them, the arbitrator who ruled in favour of Chartrand and against Marchand was Pierre Trudeau.

Strand upon strand . . . Jean-Louis Gagnon was editor of the Liberal party's weekly newspaper *La Reforme* in the 1950's when Trudeau was organizing opposition to Duplessis and Liberal candidates such as Paul Gérin-Lajoie were being swatted down by the Union Nationale machine. Gagnon is now head of Information Canada while Gérin-Lajoie is directing Canada's foreign aid programme in Ottawa.

The game is endless. But this is probably enough to indicate that if you trace the career of an average member of the Quebec *family*, sooner or later you will intersect the careers of virtually every other member. The whole system in interlocked. Turn one cog and they all move. Or, to use another analogy: stimulate a single nerve end and the entire system is aware of it.

The triumph or failure, pleasure or pain of any member of the *family* is shared, to some extent by all.

It isn't a phenomenon to denounce. It's a fact of life, a product of Canadian history. But English-speaking Canadians should be fully aware of it, because old rivalries, animosities and spoiled friendships within the *family* are not *family* affairs pure and simple. They affect everyone in Canada.

English Canada should understand that when Prime Minister Trudeau enacts a law that puts Michel Chartrand in prison, he is doing violence to part of his own background. When Jean Marchand lashes out at extremists in Quebec, he isn't merely expounding political philosophy. He is talking about individuals who are known to every member of the *family* and, in some cases, belong to it.

Members of the *family* now in power in Ottawa, would like

Canadians to believe that they can understand and control *family* affairs. But the other side of that coin is their emotional involvement – a characteristic that doesn't usually lead to sound political decisions. It would be wise if English-speaking Canadians didn't accustom themselves too quickly to deferring automatically to the insiders' judgement of events in Quebec, particularly when their own interests are at stake.

One other thing worth noting is that the *family* phenomenon is partly a hangover from the old regime in French Canada when education was limited to a secular and religious élite. The restrictions were still evident in the 1940's when Trudeau's generation was passing through the seminaries, collèges classiques and universities. Now the Quiet Revolution has vastly expanded Quebec's system of higher education and, more recently, started to decentralize it. The various worlds within Quebec – cultural, political and commercial – are becoming too large and specialized for individuals to maintain *family*-type connections with everyone. It is unlikely that the *family*, in another few decades, will be as cohesive as it is today.

---

2. Ethnic Penetration Into Toronto's Elite Structure

Merrijoy Kelner/*University of Toronto*

The core elite that Professor Kelner identifies as being at the apex of the Toronto power structure represents the epitome of private space: its boundaries are tightly closed rendering it impervious to penetration by outsiders and, by definition, the locus of control rests firmly within the group. The strategic elites she identifies represent a less pure type of private space. Though relatively inaccessible, outsiders are admitted if they possess needed skills and other qualifications deemed sufficiently appropriate as to not pollute the purity of the group too much. Alternatively, those formerly excluded from elite status may be able to create their own in those interstitial areas where private space has not been already preempted earlier by others. Such groups are in the process of making their claims and establishing their boundaries. How much control they will be able or will be allowed to assume remains open-ended.

We are reminded in this essay, too, of the utility of the territorial concept for space analysis. Consider, for instance, the bureaucracy or the private club as examples of 'home territories' which limit interaction and so function to reinforce closure. The place of the private school in socializing recruits into the elite is to be noted here, as well as the negative function of the ethnic church and other ethnic organizations in maintaining distance and separateness.

The elite concept has been interpreted in many different and often contradictory ways. One widely accepted usage focuses exclusively on the power held by elite groups (Mills, 1956). Another, somewhat related view stresses the functional importance of elites to society at large (Keller, 1963). A third view emphasizes the rewards that accrue to elites (Lasswell, 1958). Frequently overlooked by investigators of elite status is the element of *prestige*, that is, the social recognition and respect accorded to an individual by others who have power and have themselves already achieved high status.

In the course of a recent study of the ethnic composition of elite groups in the Toronto community, it became apparent that further refinement should incorporate considerations of *both* power and prestige, as well as functional importance to

Reprinted from the *Canadian Review of Sociology and Anthropology*, 7:2 (1970), by permission of the author and the publisher. Based on a paper presented at the Annual Meeting of the Canadian Sociology and Anthropology Association, York University, June, 1969.

society.

For the purpose of the study, two distinct levels of elite status were delineated. The bottom level of the elite structure was seen to consist of persons who have achieved key functional roles in Canadian society. This level, which includes labor leaders, corporation presidents, cabinet ministers, and the like, was defined as the level of *strategic* elites, following Keller's classification. Members of strategic elites qualify for inclusion in these groups on the basis of their achievements, since it is their functional contributions to the society which are the crucial consideration.

The upper level of the elite structure, a much smaller group, was restricted to persons who not only filled key functional roles, but were also accorded high social status in the community. This select group, found at the apex of the elite structure, was defined as a *core* elite.

Members of the core elite form a socially homogeneous group which is distinct from, and superior to, the strategic elites from which it is drawn. It is, in short, more elite than other elites. High social-class position in itself is not a sufficient qualification for core elite status; it must be combined with the power and wealth that accompany functional leadership. The essential point here is that, unless members of strategic elites can use their power and wealth to win acceptance from the social leaders in the community, they will be relegated to the fringes of the elite structure, and can never win admission to the core elite.

Utilizing the conception of two distinct levels of elite status, a study was completed which analyzes the extent and methods of non-Anglo-Saxon penetration into Toronto's elite structure.[1] The primary aim of the study was to explore further Porter's conclusion that elite positions in Canadian society are held almost exclusively by Anglo-Saxons (Porter, 1965) by reference to developments in the Toronto community in the last two decades.

The city of Toronto provides an excellent setting for this kind of research problem: in 1961 close to 40 per cent of its population was foreign born and indications are that this proportion has increased even further in subsequent years. The swift pace of development, together with the large influx of European immigrants, have transformed the social character of the Toronto community since the conclusion of World War II. The presence of so many people of various ethnic origins in a rapidly expanding urban centre has served to release new forces. The pace of technological development and the thrust of industrial expansion have brought new opportunities for advancement. It was postulated that these changes have resulted in alterations in recruitment patterns to elite positions and a weakening of the Anglo-Saxon monopoly of elite status, as access to positions of power and prestige widens and increases.

Data and Methods

Data for the study were acquired in a variety of ways. Detailed interviews were conducted with a representative group of 55 Torontonians occupying important positions in Canadian life. Informal discussions were held with a variety of informants, such as editors of daily newspapers and journalists writing for magazines of local interest. Listings of the boards of directors and top officials of leading companies and institutions were compiled and analysed.

Daily reading of the three Toronto newspapers for a period of two years, plus close attention to local magazines and journals, also provided useful source material. In addition, census figures for Metro Toronto, information concerning the immigration patterns of ethnic groups, old newspaper files, and the biographies of established Toronto families (Gillen, 1965; Wilkinson, 1956; Eaton, 1956; Harkness, 1963; Wilson, 1965) all contributed pertinent data.

Boundaries for the study were drawn with a view to encompassing a broad structure of power and prestige, while still limiting the number of people to be considered. The requirement for inclusion was that members of the study population live and work within the confines of Metro Toronto. No limits were placed on the scope of their influence and reputation, which frequently extended to the international scene.

Following the positional model used by Porter, Mills, and others, elite groups residing in the Toronto community were identified for each major institutional sphere. Such an approach assumes that elite groups consist of those who occupy key positions in major institutional hierarchies. It has been suggested that formal position does not necessarily imply that an individual actually exercises the influence conferred upon him by that position. He may, on occasion, be merely a figurehead for the real, if invisible, power behind the throne. Nevertheless, formal position at the top of a major institutional order is, in itself, an important social phenomenon, one which also has the advantage of providing systematic, codifiable, and verifiable facts.

Use of the positional approach in this study followed closely the pattern established by Porter in *The Vertical Mosaic*. A corporate elite, a labour elite, a political elite, a civil service elite, a communications elite, and an academic elite were delineated. All these groups clearly fit into the category of strategic elites, as defined above. Members of these groups were initially identified in the following way: (1) *The corporate elite* consisted of those residents of Toronto who were listed as directors of the 100 largest Canadian companies.[2] Added to this group were the Toronto-based directors of the major Canadian holding companies, such as the Argus Corporation, Power Corporation of Canada, and George Weston Limited. (2) *The labour elite* consisted of those residents of Toronto who were senior officials of the largest unions, plus those holding executive positions with organizations like the Ontario Federation of Labour, the Toronto Labour Council, and the Canadian Labour Congress. (3) *The political elite* consisted of all Toronto residents who had, since the inception of the study, served as members of the federal cabinet, the provincial cabinet, and the Metropolitan Council, plus all supreme court judges residing in the city. (4) *The civil service elite* consisted of senior provincial and municipal civil servants living in the Toronto area. (5) *The communications elite* consisted of the Toronto-based owners and directors of the major newspapers, book publishing firms, television networks, and radio stations. (6) *The academic elite* consisted of Toronto residents who had been elected by their peers as fellows of the Royal Society of Canada, an exclusive and self-selecting group of academic leaders which includes representatives from all disciplines of higher learning.

The total listings for each group were examined, in order to establish the ethnic backgrounds of those included. All those whose names did not appear to be clearly Anglo-Saxon in origin were followed up in biographical sources such as *Who's Who in Canada* (1967). In addition, personal interviews were conducted with other leaders in the field in order to obtain additional information regarding the ethnic origins of those included in the study population. This was necessary because names alone can be misleading as a guide to ethnicity, particularly since non-Anglo-Saxon names are often discarded along the road to leadership positions.

The aim of this systematic analysis was to assess the extent to which non-Anglo-Saxons have risen to functionally important positions during the past twenty years. It became evident that although non-Anglo-Saxon representation in elite groups has definitely increased since 1948, in no major institutional field has it reached the same level as non-Anglo-Saxon representation in the total community.

Findings

Investigation disclosed that the proportion of non-Anglo-Saxon corporate leaders living in Toronto is still very small, approximately 7 per cent.[3] The 100 largest corporations listed only about 20 non-Anglo-Saxon businessmen among 325 Toronto-based directors, and only one of the 20 had multiple directorships in the leading corporations. None of Canada's major holding companies included non-Anglo-Saxons on their boards.

The labour elite was more receptive to non-Anglo-Saxons than the corporate. Approximately 21 per cent of the labour elite in Toronto were not of Anglo-Saxon origin. The data also indicated that labour leadership at the local level was easier for non-Anglo-Saxons to achieve than at the national level, where few had succeeded in reaching executive positions.

In the political sphere, 19 per cent of those in elite positions were non-Anglo-Saxons. Three of the 32 judges of the supreme court of Ontario were of non-Anglo-Saxon origin, as were two of the six provincial cabinet ministers residing in Toronto, and several of those involved in the municipal political structure. Again, non-Anglo-Saxon penetration into elite positions is shown to be easier to effect at the local level than at the national level; Toronto had no non-Anglo-Saxon federal cabinet ministers representing it at the time of this study, in spite of the ethnic diversity of its population.

The civil service was less receptive to non-Anglo-Saxons at the top levels than some other fields; approximately 10 per cent of its upper-echelon jobs were held by people of non-Anglo-Saxon origin, and these were clustered mainly in the research branch. Only two non-Anglo-Saxon names appeared on the list of over 40 Toronto-based deputy ministers and assistant deputy ministers, while about 25 non-Anglo-Saxons were occupying positions as division or branch heads, out of a total of approximately 229 persons. At the municipal level, two of the 19 senior officials were of non-Anglo-Saxon origin.

Owners and directors of the mass media were still overwhelmingly Anglo-Saxon. All the major book publishers were Anglo-Saxon, as were their boards of directors. Some inroads had been made into top positions in newspaper publishing, however; one of the three daily newspapers had two men of non-Anglo-Saxon origins on its executive committee and another included a prominent non-Anglo-Saxon on its board of directors. One of the two major television networks had a non-Anglo-Saxon director, as did two local radio stations. These men represent only about five per cent of the total list of owners and directors of the media, however.

Non-Anglo-Saxon members of the academic elite, i.e., Fellows of the Royal Society, included approximately 19 per cent of the total list of Fellows living in the Toronto area. It is significant that a higher proportion of these came from the humanities and social sciences division than from the science division.

When Porter's model for identifying members of the elite was applied to the community of Toronto, there was clear indication that in no major institutional field had the proportion of non-Anglo-Saxons in the elite reached the same level as the non-Anglo-Saxon population in the community as a whole. However, comparisons with the ethnic composition of the elite structure 20 years earlier revealed that, in every case where comparable figures were available, non-Anglo-Saxon representation had increased considerably.

An Alternative Model

The Porter model emphasizes the importance of power and institutional position in determining elite status, but does not include considerations of prestige. For example, Porter deliberately excludes members of the Senate from the political elite on the basis that they have no real power. If, however, the concept of prestige enters into the definition of elite status, then senators must be included in the political elite. Warner, Baltzell, Hunter, and others have demonstrated that an individual's reputation in his community plays an important role in locating him in the social stratification hierarchy (Baltzell, 1964; Warner, 1949; Hunter, 1953). However, it is not always the people who hold top-level positions who acquire reputations for influence and achievement in their chosen fields. Just as different personalities realize the power potential of their positions in different ways, so certain individuals exert a significant influence on their society without the underpinnings of formal position to bolster their elite status. A reputation for outstanding accomplishment in a particular field can often bring membership in an elite group, even though the individual involved holds no position on any board of directors or executive committee. Writers and artists, in particular, base their claims to elite status on these kinds of considerations. The leadership group of each institutional sphere mentioned above was redefined utilizing the concept of prestige in conjunction with the concept of power, and the ethnic composition of elite groups was reassessed.

In this second overview, attention was also directed to the dynamic processes taking place in the community. In order to avoid a static approach to the issue of elite status, analysis focused not only on those who have arrived at the top, but also on those currently moving up from the middle levels of leadership.

Findings

This kind of perspective revealed new patterns, established within the past few years, which will eventually have a significant impact on the ethnic constitution of the strategic elites. For example, new trust companies and savings and loans associations have recently been formed or taken over by non-Anglo-Saxons. These newer financial institutions have not yet achieved the stature of the older, established corporations, *i.e.*,

they are not included in the listing of leading financial companies, but they have already helped to facilitate the participation of non-Anglo-Saxon businessmen in ventures which might otherwise never have been funded. Other developments also point to gradual non-Anglo-Saxon penetration into important corporate roles. By 1969 two Jews had been admitted to the Toronto Stock Exchange, formerly an exclusive bastion of Anglo-Saxon power.

Real estate development in Toronto, which has enjoyed tremendous growth since the end of World War II, is a form of enterprise which has become vitally important to non-Anglo-Saxons as a way up the commercial ladder. The building business has offered fresh opportunities to many who found more established commercial fields, like banking and insurance, closed to them. It is a high-risk field which requires little equity to operate on a small scale. By borrowing from the banks on the basis of pledging their own personal worth, and by skilfully manipulating payments to the trades, many small-scale non-Anglo-Saxon builders, particularly Jews and Italians, dramatically widened the scope of their activities, moving from building a few houses to developing complete subdivisions and apartment complexes.

Similarly in other institutional spheres, non-Anglo-Saxons have been moving up toward positions of power and prestige. In the labour field, for example, the large number of Italian labourers has been reflected in the recent inclusion of Italians in the leadership of local trade unions. In the political field, non-Anglo-Saxons have been putting themselves forward as political candidates in increasing numbers. At present, 8 of the city's 22 federal members of Parliament and 7 of the 29 provincial members are of non-Anglo-Saxon origin. The first Jewish senator appointed in Canada also resides in Toronto.

Since the end of World War II, the proportion of non-Anglo-Saxon university professors has increased markedly, particularly in developing fields like the social sciences. Analysis of the ethnic composition of the faculty in the sociology department at the University of Toronto over the past 30 years clearly illustrates the changing patterns of recruitment. During the 1938-1939 university session, the four staff members were all Anglo-Saxons. Ten years later, the faculty consisted of five members, one of whom was non-Anglo-Saxon. During the next 10-year period, the department expanded rapidly, and by the 1967-1968 session, it had developed a faculty of 29 people, 11 of whom were non-Anglo-Saxons. Clearly, the rapid rate of growth imposed an urgent need for qualified personnel, and considerations like ethnic origin became increasingly irrelevant.

At the leadership level, changes in ethnic composition have been slower. More non-Anglo-Saxons have achieved top-level academic posts at York University, which, being newer, had to fill a large number of positions in a short space of time. Approximately 9 of the 20 departmental chairmen at York University were of non-Anglo-Saxon origin, while only one of the 19 chairmen of departments at the University of Toronto was not Anglo-Saxon.

The major thrust of upward mobility has taken place in the interstitial, innovative fields, which had no entrenched aristocracy in control, and in those fields which require a high degree of technical specialization. Some of the most dynamic spheres include mining, entertainment, construction, and psychoanalysis.

The rate of increase in the proportions of non-Anglo-Saxons admitted to strategic elites has not been uniform for all ethnic groups. To date, Jews have been more successful than other non-Anglo-Saxons in reaching leadership positions in major institutional hierarchies, due primarily to their urban background, high educational level, and a generally longer period of acculturation to Canadian society. Variations were also found in the types of routes to elite status that were followed by members of different ethnic groups. The cultural sphere, for example, has drawn a significant proportion of its leadership from the Jewish group, while the labour movement is currently attracting Italians and Ukrainians to its top-ranking positions. A wide variety of non-Anglo-Saxon groups is currently represented in the research and planning branches of the civil service.

Analysis of the avenues of ascent followed by members of strategic elites reveals that in contrast to Anglo-Saxons, who rise within the bureaucratic structure, non-Anglo-Saxons typically achieve prominence outside it, through more individualistic and higher-risk paths. In other words, upward mobility is achieved by Anglo-Saxons through established, stable, corporate entities, while non-Anglo-Saxons have to achieve status as individual entrepreneurs.

In a society which is becoming more and more bureaucratically structured, this differential pattern of upward mobility has significant implications for non-Anglo-Saxons. The bureaucratization of contemporary society has been recognized by many social analysts (see, for example, Bensman and Rosenberg, 1963:269). Today, every major occupation is increasingly organized and bureaucratized. Concurrently, opportunities for individual entrepreneurs to rise to positions of power and prestige are disappearing. Enterprise today requires large capital investments, and this requirement brings with it the necessity for large corporate structures. Thus, it appears that the individualistic, high-risk avenues to elite status that have typically served the ambitious non-Anglo-Saxon, are becoming less and less available to him. In the future, we can expect that non-Anglo-Saxons will increasingly have to make their ascent to elite positions *within* the bureaucratic structure; an accommodation which may well lead to considerable inter-group conflict. The usual pattern is to start one's own small business and to build it up into an important corporate structure, at which time it is customary to add some Anglo-Saxon names to the board of directors, to ensure legitimation.

The Social Elite

Omitted from the Porter study was consideration of leaders in several other major institutional fields, such as the celebrity elite, the cultural elite, the social elite, and the professional elite. The inclusion of prestige as an element of elite status raises the issue of the ethnic origins of social leaders. Social leaders are those who decide who shall be included in the membership of the 'best' clubs and who shall be invited to the most exclusive social gatherings. Their position is based on their upper-class status, which derives from a composite of many factors, including old family prestige and a particular life style.

Analysis demonstrated that the social leadership of the Toronto community is still almost exclusively Anglo-Saxon. The city's high-status social clubs do not welcome non-Anglo-Saxon members either by expressed policy or by long-standing custom. The purpose of these clubs is to limit social interaction to the 'right' people, the people 'one knows', and these are rarely members of non-Anglo-Saxon groups. Detailed interviews with high-status respondents revealed that Anglo-Saxon leaders rarely make close friends among people of other ethnic groups. Social relations between upperclass Anglo-Saxons and others in the community were found to be categorical and formal in nature, and restricted almost entirely to public occasions.

This social exclusion has important repercussions for the hierarchical structure of the society. Social restrictions have the effect of containing power and prestige within a select circle, even though this may not be the primary motive for exclusion. Membership in the leading men's clubs, for example, is a tacit

prerequisite for advancement to top positions in many fields, particularly in the professions and in large corporations. It is in the relaxed club setting that many major decisions are made, and it is through the camaraderie of the club atmosphere that younger men are recognized and selected for future leadership roles. Personal relations are cemented in common social experiences and those who are excluded from them are at a serious disadvantage in their attempts to reach and maintain top positions.

It is important to note, however, that there are powerful forces within the various non-Anglo-Saxon groups which also act to limit social interaction. Their leaders encourage them to maintain a distinctive identity, and, in doing so, they discourage them from close social relations with members of the general community, thus imposing serious limitations upon the degree of upward mobility that can be achieved.

Exclusion from intimate social interaction with the Anglo-Saxon upper class imposes certain practical limitations on advancement into key functional positions, that is, into membership in strategic elites, in the ways suggested above. Such exclusion is also a crucial factor in restricting the entry of non-Anglo-Saxons into the small inner circle designated here as the core elite. This elite nucleus, whose members combine leadership roles in major institutional spheres with high social status, is the most powerful and prestigious group in the community, and it is this group which has proven almost impervious to non-Anglo-Saxon penetration.

Conclusion

The results of this study indicate that the growing need for skilled specialists and executive talent, occasioned by the increasing complexity of management and the constant development of new techniques, combined with the influx of New Canadians into the society, has resulted in freer access to membership in Toronto's strategic elites. Positions of power and prestige have become more accessible to qualified non-Anglo-Saxons as ascriptive criteria have become less important in recruitment.

This democratization process has been shown, however, to have definite limitations, contrary to Keller's thesis that, as industrialization creates large and more complex societies, ruling classes or core elites (as they are described here) will disappear and be replaced by strategic elites. The elite nucleus is still very much in evidence and is still almost completely reserved for upper-class Anglo-Saxons. In short, the shift from criteria based on ascription to those based on achievement is far from complete.

Within their own groups, the non-Anglo-Saxon members of strategic elites occupy positions of high social status and limit their friendships to others of their own socio-economic class. They encourage their children to marry within the upper stratum of their group, in much the same way as the Anglo-Saxons. It is within the community at large that a lack of congruity exists between their wealth and power on the one hand, and their social status on the other, and it is this discrepancy which prevents non-Anglo-Saxon members of strategic elites from entering the core elite and, thus, from achieving the highest levels of power and prestige.

On the basis of this study it seems clear that a dual-level conception of elite status can be usefully applied to research in this area. Application to other settings is now required for its further refinement and development.

NOTES AND BIBLIOGRAPHY
1. In this study, the designation Anglo-Saxon includes members of the English, Scots, Welsh, and Irish groups.

2. The 100 largest Canadian companies (in terms of assets, profits, and sales) were determined by a survey reported in *The Financial Post*, August 13, 1966. The directors were identified through *The Directory of Directors* (Toronto: 1966).

3. These figures should be regarded as approximations only, due to the difficulties involved in assessing ethnic origins.

Baltzell, E. D. *The Protestant Establishment*. New York: Random House, 1964.

Bensman, J. and B. Rosenberg *Mass, Class and Bureaucracy*. Englewood Cliffs: Prentice-Hall, 1963.

Eaton, F. M. *Memory's Wall*. Toronto: Clarke Irwin, 1956.

The *Financial Post, The Directory of Directors*. Toronto: MacLean-Hunter Limited, 1966.

Gillen, M. *The Masseys*. Toronto: Ryerson Press, 1965.

Harkness, R. *J. E. Atkinson of the Star*. Toronto: University of Toronto Press, 1963.

Hunter, F. *Community Power Structure*. Chapel Hill: University of North Carolina Press, 1952.

Keller, S. *Beyond the Ruling Class*. New York: Random House, 1963.

Lasswell, H. *Politics: Who Gets What, When, How*. Cleveland: The World Publishing Co., 1958.

Mills, C. W. *The Power Elite*. New York: Oxford University Press, 1956.

Porter, J. *The Vertical Mosaic*. Toronto: University of Toronto Press, 1965.

Warner, W. L. *Social Class in America*. Chicago: Science Research Associates, 1949.

Who's Who in Canada, 1966-68, Toronto: International Press Limited, 1967.

Wilkinson, A. *Lions in the Way*. Toronto: Macmillan, 1956.

Wilson, A. *John Northway*. Toronto: Burns and MacEachern, 1965.

---

3. Patronage and Paternalism: Politics in Newfoundland

George Perlin/*Queen's University*

Several ideas developed in earlier selections in this volume are brought together in this essay, which provides an intriguing case study of the creation of a proto-public realm from what was hitherto a few well-separated private domains. The picture that is drawn of pre-Confederation Newfoundland is one of a small economic elite maintaining tight control over its private space, the denominational churches each with its own staunchly defended territory, and spatially as well as socially isolated nuclear family units. The task of bringing together these separated units and of invading the private domains of the mercantile aristocracy and the entrenched churches was a formidable one. Making this invasion the central axiom in his political ideology and employing it to arouse the consciousness of those who until then had been excluded, Smallwood was able to mobilize the support he needed to come to power. Having weakened, though not eliminated, these earlier private domains he managed to create his own much larger, much more extensive, and hence much more powerful private realm. The transformation to a genuinely public domain is not yet complete.

Studies of voting behaviour commonly conceptualize the mobilization of electoral support in terms of individual responses to the competitive manipulation of symbols of party, personality, and policy.[1] This model emphasises the importance of the stimulus provided by images conveyed during the period of the election campaign – through personal canvasses, the distribution of pamphlets, public meetings, and advertizing in the mass media. The individual voter is believed to assimilate these images within the frame of an established set of dispositions acquired through his political socialization, past personal experiences, and current group associations. His decision is presumed to reflect the effects of the stimuli of the symbols manipulated in the campaign as mediated by these established dispositions.[2] The development of diffuse affect for parties is held to provide the main element of constancy in responses from election to election. Many voters are believed to establish a sense of identi-

Published for the first time in this collection.

fication with a party, a psychological attachment which affords them a permanent screen through which to sort out the conflicting messages projected during the campaign.[3]

Whatever its validity in other contexts this model does not adequately describe the mobilization of electoral support in Newfoundland. Historically the dominant factor in the Newfoundland context has been the use of public resources to make personal allocations or allocations which can be perceived in personal terms, in return for the delivery of votes. This system has taken two forms. In the first, which may be characterized as patronage politics, allocations are made through a multi-tiered structure of patron-client relationships; in the second, which I shall call paternalistic politics, the structural linkages of the patronage system do not exist or exist only in part, but the cultural dispositions associated with them are still apparent.[4]

The conditions which fostered the development of these systems are rooted in Newfoundland's historical economic reliance upon the fishery and the distinctive way in which the fishery influenced Newfoundland society.

Until the past two decades, the fishery was the predominant source of employment in the Newfoundland economy. As recently as 1935, it accounted for nearly half the male working force and it is still the largest single employer.[5] This central role of the fishing industry had three social consequences of political importance: the credit mechanism, by which the industry operated, created relationships of dependence analogous to feudalism; the working class endured a subsistent livelihood of poverty and insecurity; and the vast part of the population was scattered in tiny isolated coastal settlements.

The organization of the industry had developed a distinctive indigenous form:

> ... from the days when the country first came to be permanently settled until the middle of the nineteenth century, the organization of the fisheries was largely feudal. The merchants or exporters who established themselves in St. John's and other centres employed a number of fishermen to catch fish for them. These fishermen did not receive wages but were provided by the merchants, in return for their services during the fishing season, with sufficient food-stuffs and oth-

er necessities to maintain themselves and their families in tolerable comfort throughout the year. The merchants were shop-keepers or store-keepers as well as exporters of fish. In addition, the fishermen were supplied by the merchants with such gear, equipment and provisions as might be required to enable them to conduct their fishing operations. It was the practice of each merchant to support his own fishermen in bad times as well as good. Money did not change hands; indeed, it could have been said with truth, only a few years ago, that there were families in Newfoundland who had never seen money in their lives. Under this system, very similar to the old truck system in England, large fortunes were made by the merchants; the fishermen, though saved from the danger of destitution were little more than serfs with no hope of becoming independent.

Vicious as was this system, it was not nearly so destructive as that which developed from it. As the population increased, the old feudal practices were gradually modified. The obligation to· support the fishermen in bad times, the only virtue of the former system, became the duty, not of the merchants, but of the State. It was obvious that the fishermen could not conduct the fishery from their own resources, and the custom grew up under which each fisherman went to the merchant in the spring and obtained from him, on credit, supplies of equipment and food to enable him and his family to live, not for the whole year, but during the three or four months of the fishing season. At the end of the season, the fisherman returned to the merchant with his catch of fish, dried and cured, to set off against his account. The price of fish was fixed by merchants, as also was the price of the provisions, etc., supplied to the fishermen and his family in the spring. In cases where fish were valued according to quality, the quality of the fish tendered by the fisherman was determined by a 'culler' or valuer who himself was the employee of the merchant. In good years, a balance was left to the fisherman after deduction of the debt due to the merchant; this balance was paid to him in cash. In bad years, the value of the fish tendered by the fisherman was not sufficient to pay for his supplies and he, therefore, remained in debt to the merchant. The balance available to him in good years was often such as to leave him with no margin after he had provided for himself and his family for the rest of the year, and the same process was, therefore, repeated in the following spring. In bad years, there was no balance at all and while in some cases, which were considered specially deserving, merchants continued to make advances of debt to be repaid during the ensuing year, the majority had no resource to fall back upon and, in default of other employment, were compelled to turn to the Government for relief.[6]

While the risks for those who supplied the credit were great, it was the fisherman who was most profoundly affected by this system. Chained by his obligations to his creditors, he had no independent choice either in the purchase of any goods he might require or in the sale of his products.

Much of what he required the outport resident scraped from his immediate environment.

Subsistence or household production supplied the outport household with a major part of its consumption needs; this included a variety of vegetables and animal, forest, and marine products. In addition, the outporters produced part of their needs for clothes, especially knit-wear, and built their own houses, stages, and wharves. . . . [7]

Even with the diversification of the economy which began at the turn of the twentieth century, the condition of the substantial part of the population remained at best on the fringe of poverty. The precarious nature of outport existence was brought forcefully home during the Depression when unemployment soared to take in half the labour force, and the unemployed were compelled to live on able-bodied relief of six cents a day. As late as 1945, although the War had brought a massive injection of new capital and a major diversion of labour into the construction and service industries, per capita personal income remained at or below the subsistence level. Using the 1961-based Canadian estimate, re-defined in contemporary dollars, for the average family in Newfoundland in 1945, income was one-third less than that which would have constituted the 'poverty line' in Canada.[8]

The family, of economic necessity, had the central role in outport life, the co-operation of all members of the household being essential to production. In some cases economic co-operation was confined to the nuclear family;[9] in others it involved extended kin relations.[10]

There were few secondary groups. To the extent that they existed, they were usually associated with the church, as formal religion was an important part of outport culture. The depth of feeling it generated is to be measured by the intensity of inter-denominational conflict in the nineteenth century when organized gangs of Catholics and Protestants fought each other in the name of their separate faiths.[11] There has been widespread affinity for evangelical religion which has continued to re-assert itself in successive waves of desertions from established sects to new more radical groups entering the community.

The commitment to religion was a significant factor in politics. The religious conflicts of the nineteenth century had only been resolved by the adoption of a system of denominational representation in the distribution of both cabinet appointments and legislative candidacies.[12] This practice helped legitimate political structures, but it also contributed to the perpetuation of sectarian cleavage. Sectarianism received further support from the denominational system of education which permitted the churches to run the schools with public funds.

Isolation was a fact of over-riding importance. In 1945, 68 per cent of the population still lived in settlements with fewer than 1,000 residents.[13] In all there were nearly 1,300 small communities distributed along the 6,000 mile coast. Except for participants in the Labrador fishery who lived on the northeast coast, few fishermen (and rarely their families), ever travelled beyond their own inlet or bay.

News travelled by word of mouth or by the peculiar system of the log book. This log, in every telegraph office, was kept up daily by the postmaster or telegraph operator, who received news bulletins from St. John's, the highlights of which were written, abbreviated in longhand. The book with its page or two of the news of the day, would then be put out for the public to look through.[14]

Isolation re-enforced parochialism in the small outport and increased dependence upon local elites. Priests and clergymen, the merchants, and sometimes an unusually successful fisherman, provided leadership at the local level. Their authority was of broad compass – for two reasons. Firstly, there was no local government and the representatives of external authority, the police and the magistrates, could make only infrequent visits. Secondly, local elites were usually the only members of the community who were educated and who had regular contacts with the outside; thus they were relied upon to mediate in most external transactions. They would be called·upon to attend to such matters as the drafting of wills and deeds and to deal with strangers who came to the community or with representations which had to be made to government.

Deference characterized formal responses to elites. The merchant and his sons would be referred to as "Mr. George" or

"Mr. Bill" and there was a myth about the paternalistic concern of the merchants for the working class, typically characterized by this comment by a merchant explaining why he couldn't accept a union in his fish plant.

I'm not anti-union . . . I just think that in certain circumstances unions are not practical, and this is one of them: isolated outports in Newfoundland. *You haven't the local leadership to run them intelligently, with all due respect to the people – I'm very fond of them.*[15] [emphasis mine]

Upward social mobility was rarely possible at the local level, the only avenue being a sufficient run of good seasons to permit the fisherman to build a schooner and enter trade himself. Inter-generational mobility became a possibility as the educational system developed, but the schools, where they existed, were primitive; few teachers were properly trained, and the pressure of family need was likely to compel most children to leave school after completing only the primary grades. There was no compulsory school attendance age until the 1930's and it was then set at fourteen.

For the greater part of the population dependent upon the fishery, the future held little prospect. They were tied in perpetual debt to a local merchant who, in turn, was usually tied to one of the larger mercantile firms in St. John's.

Economic power was concentrated in these family-held enterprises in the capital. A mercantile aristocracy, begun with the settlement of the first resident merchants in the early nineteenth century, had secured itself upon the foundation of the credit system. Conscious or unconscious inter-marriage, and the laws of inheritance, permitted it to preserve its power and build a life-style of affluence and privilege remote from the realities of outport life.

In the last decade of the nineteenth century and the first decade of the twentieth century, a new element began to challenge this oligarchy. Availing themselves of the government's more active role in the economy which had begun with the development of the tran-insular railroad in 1898, and displaying few scruples in matters of conflict of interest, some of the lesser merchants and professionals used political careers or relationships with politicians to compel a broadening of the economic leadership.[16]

The use of public office to seek personal advantage was paralleled by the use of public funds to build political support. To the extent that it was possible, the general revenues of government were allocated for those policies which could be perceived in terms of personal benefits:

The Government was looked upon as the universal provider, and it was thought to be the duty of the Member for the constituency to see that there was an ever-increasing flow of public money.[17]

The Assembly member in outport districts stood in the role of patron:

As there was no local government, he was expected to fulfill the functions of a Mayor and of every department of public authority. In addition, he was the guardian of local interests, the counsellor and friend of every voter in the constituency and their mouthpiece in the Legislature of the country. Finally, under the peculiar system of administration adopted in Newfoundland, he was not only the liaison between the people and Government but the channel through which the money voted for public purposes within the constituency was allocated and spent.[18]

Public employment was his to offer, from administrative positions within the civil service to manual labour on local works.

In the case of the executive staff, post-election changes are commonly of a sweeping character with effects which manifest themselves in every corner of the Island. In such cases, the main consideration is the good will of the Member for the district concerned. Post Office and Railway employees, Customs Officials, Relieving Officers, Fishery and Timber Inspectors and Wardens, members of the Fire Control Staff, Lighthouse Keepers, and even Stipendiary Magistrates: all are liable to sudden dismissal, however competent their work, as the result of a change of Government.[19]

The partial accounts available characterize the mode of allocation as patronage. The Assembly member dealt with a network of key men who occupied elite roles at the local level. Local elites were effectively brokers of blocs of votes who, from their strategic roles within the community, could bargain for personal material rewards or for community benefits which would enhance their own personal prestige.

The low salience of party was manifest both in the ease with which the coalitions in St. John's could reconstruct themselves in new party forms and in the absence of any effective local party organization.

S.J.R. Noel's description of the shifting of party loyalties in the period from July, 1923, through June, 1924, when no fewer than five cabinets were founded on different party bases gives some sense of the instability of party structures.[20] Between 1904 and 1932 government and opposition legislative coalitions appeared under 10 different party names. Yet the main *dramatis personae* remained more or less the same.

Party organization appeared in most of the outport districts in 1900, but it did not endure for long. To the extent that it did persist, it was in the form of a nominal adjunct to patron-client relationships.[21]

A radical change in the political history of Newfoundland occurred in 1934 when electoral politics were suspended and the Dominion was placed under the administration of a Commission appointed by the British Government – a solution imposed when the government was unable to cope with the financial stresses of the Depression. The Commission effected a number of important administrative reforms and initiated social service programmes which had the effect of ameliorating some of the worst conditions in the outports, but none of the Commission's efforts to broaden the economic base came to fruition. Some diversification had been effected by newsprint and mineral developments in the first quarter of the century but there was no further change of significance until military investment during World War II produced a substantial redeployment of the labour force into the construction and service industries. In 1946 further economic diversification seemed unlikely. Employment on the American bases and in the mining, newsprint, secondary manufacturing and service industries was levelling off and there was a movement in the labour force back to the fishery.[22] Britain had done as much as it wanted or could for Newfoundland and was anxious to rid itself of its responsibilities there.

The electoral hiatus of the Commission period ended not with a return to elective government, but with the calling of a National Convention to recommend to the British Government alternatives on the future constitutional status of the former Dominion which could be placed before the electorate in a referendum. The election of the Convention in 1946 attracted the interest of less than half the eligible voting population, which is not surprising since the Convention had no authority to make policy. Candidates did not seek election as representatives of parties and issues were ill-defined.

But the foundations of a party system soon began to emerge within the Convention. J.R. Smallwood, and a small band of outport delegates, organized to press the case for union with Canada, while a group, largely made up of representatives of the mercantile and professional classes from St. John's advocated a return to independent Dominion status. Smallwood and his supporters formed the Confederate Association; their opponents divided into two groups, the Responsible Government League and the party of Economic Union with the United States. In the constitutional referendum of 1948, Confederation won by a small margin.[23]

There appear to have been three main reasons for the Confederate victory. Firstly, Confederation, through the application to Newfoundland of the more comprehensive and far more generous Canadian social security programme, promised immediate alleviation of the worst aspects of outport life. Secondly, the case for Union was presented not just as a set of specific policy proposals but as the core of an ideology offering the promise of the radical change of the whole society. Framed as a challenge of the 'toiling masses' to the power of the 'Water Street gang', this ideology played not just upon whatever class antagonism there may have been but also upon the resentment of the exploited outport periphery for the exploiting urban centre, St. John's. Finally, there was the leadership of Mr. Smallwood. He was a superior political strategist and tactician who had a keen appreciation of the political culture of the outports. But more than that, as a broadcaster of considerable skill and a brilliantly persuasive platform speaker, he gave the movement a populist leader with whom its modernizing ideology could be symbolically identified.

In 1949, as leader of the victorious Confederates, Mr. Smallwood was invited to become Premier of the interim administration which would be required until a provincial election could be held. From this position he set about the organization of the Newfoundland Liberal party, basing it upon the Confederate Association, but securing recruits as well from the two groups which had opposed Union. The remnants of these groups formed themselves into the Newfoundland Progressive Conservative party.

The decisive factors in shaping the system of support mobilization which emerged in 1949 were the impact of the Canadian social security programme and the developing mystique of Mr. Smallwood's leadership. The Premier, as the prophet of Confederation, was seen as the patron who had bestowed family allowances, more generous old age pensions, and unemployment insurance benefits.

The people were only fishermen and they were in the low income group... The Canadian government... says that if you have under $3,000 income you live on the poverty line. There's no one here... that made anything like that fishing. Once they had seen that the Premier had these securities available... they voted (for him)... I (know of) an old lady (who) said to a PC man in the district "If I voted PC, I'd lose my old age pension." They voted Liberal because the Liberals gave them the social security.[24]

The traditional political culture[25] of outport Newfoundland encouraged the people of the outports to see government and the Premier in a paternalistic role. Attitudes of deference and dependence had characterized the relationship with local elites and had provided the foundation for the pre-Commission patronage system. What distinguished the earlier system from the new one was the changed role of the intermediaries. A number of factors – notably the Commission's strengthening of local administration, the infusion of cash into the economy, increased labour mobility, and improvements in communications – had had the effect of undermining the strategic importance of the traditional local elites. And, Mr. Smallwood had established a personal identification with the outport working class

which he perpetuated by his skillful use of radio and the device of being accessible to anyone who wished to see or talk to him.

At home Smallwood answered his own telephone, whether the caller was a plumber or the Prime Minister of Canada. Anyone could see him at any hour of the day or night. An interview with the Premier was a happening. Visitors crowded into the corridor outside his ground-floor office at Canada House. If the wait happened to be too long, as it usually was, they were welcome to drop into the kitchen and brew a pot of tea.[26]

The net effect of these changes was to eliminate for the most part the intervening brokerage role. What resulted is the system I have chosen to call paternalistic politics. The Premier became a kind of super-patron, distributing government resources to individual clients and client communities which awarded him their votes. His conception of his role was made clear in an address he made in Ferryland during the 1949 federal campaign.

I don't need you. I've been elected. But you need me. I'm sitting on top of the public chest and not one red cent will come out of it for Ferryland unless Greg Power is elected. Unless you vote for my man, you'll be out in the cold for the next five years... Those settlements which vote against Greg Power will get nothing – absolutely nothing.[27]

The full consequences of the enforcement of such a threat were unimaginable in 1949. The pursuit of a policy of economic modernization and efforts to raise the quality of public services in Newfoundland to Canadian standards were to result in capital expenditures on new construction in the next 20 years of an estimated $3,000,000,000.[28] Annual expenditures by the provincial government, in that period, rose from just over $35,000,000 to nearly $350,000,000. New schools, new roads, electricity generating plants, water systems, and other public works all contributed not only to the fulfillment of developmental goals, but also to the maintenance of Liberal support. Mr. Smallwood could claim credit for it all in a general sense, as the man who had led Newfoundland into Confederation but as Premier, he could also legitimately claim to be responsible for most of the programmes in a specific way. His was the authoritative voice in resource allocation. When the Liberals held office in Ottawa, this was probably as true of federal spending in Newfoundland as of provincial, particularly during the Pearson years of minority governments, when Newfoundland's seven seats would be an important factor in the federal balance of power. Private expenditures could also be influenced by Mr. Smallwood. All of the companies engaged in natural resource development benefited from lenient concession agreements and some of them had been helped with government loans or guarantees. Hundreds of other enterprises existed largely because of their accounts with the provincial government or because they had received direct or indirect government assistance. Minimally, private indebtedness to the government gave the Premier a powerful voice in company hiring policies. If the Commission had stamped out the more egregious uses of civil service appointments for political purposes, there was now a far larger reservoir of jobs from the private sector to be distributed.

The distribution of jobs, the allocation of public work expenditures, the location of new enterprises, and improvements in public assistance programmes altogether afforded Premier Smallwood a virtually limitless political resource. He was at the centre of power and the resource was in a very real sense personally his.

The Liberal party had almost no structural existence beyond Smallwood's immediate associates, the legislative caucus and the party organization in St. John's. Thus local elites in the outports, although they no longer could fulfill a brokerage function, still had political uses.

With varying degrees of instrumental involvement, they served as key men for the provincial leadership. In many cases the relationship was purely symbolic, the politician maintaining a visible connection with opinion leaders in the community for the purpose, if none other, of preventing their alienation. Since there was no party organization in the outports, key men might also be asked to undertake organizational tasks. These could encompass activities associated with vote mobilization on polling day where it was necessary, helping the candidate with the logistics of his campaign, or simply acting as chairman for the candidate's local meeting. In most cases key men performed a communications function. They informed the politician of community priorities and served to channel personal and community demands.

In seeking their representatives, politicians sought to establish relationships "with anybody who had power – a clergyman, a leading merchant, any progressive businessman, a school principal, or, if there was a council, the mayor."[29] Usually this meant the traditional community leaders: the clergyman, the leading merchant or a successful fisherman.

For the key man the rewards were generally symbolic:

> You protect their position. People come to them and ask for help. They *can* help, if they persuade you. You are bolstering them, helping them to maintain their status in the community.[30]

But not all demands were channeled through the key men. In fact, a majority of those concerned with personal problems were made directly to the politician. The local member (MHA) could expect a constant flow of mail, 40 or 50 pieces a week from a district of 5,000 voters, asking him to mediate with some government department or looking for a job.

Except in the case of members with long personal associations with their districts, the primary loyalty of key men was not to the MHA but to Premier Smallwood. Thus the MHA was usually more or less dependent upon the Premier. In a critical sense the Premier's power in relation to the MHA's was absolute, for, in the absence of formal party organization, candidate selection was the personal prerogative of the party leader. He might feel obliged to consult with community leaders before selecting a candidate, but the final decision was always his. His decisive role was symbolically affirmed by the avoidance of any pretense of constituency selection. The names of candidates were always announced in press releases from the Premier's office. Members who did not satisfy Mr. Smallwood's expectation were premptorily dropped; the few rebels who thought they could challenge Mr. Smallwood by resigning to run as candidates of the opposition were without success.[31]

In 22 years the Smallwood government has won 6 successive provincial elections. Its support has been firmly based in the outports where, with the exception of 1949, it has never lost more than one district in any election and it has never had less than 75 per cent of the popular vote.

But it has been a paradox of Mr. Smallwood's position that the development goals he has pursued would eventually strike at the system which has kept him in power. Inevitably, the conditions which sustained paternalistic politics would be changed. Ironically, within a year of Mr. Smallwood's greatest victory, the election of 1966, it was apparent that the effectiveness of paternalistic politics was weakening.

For one thing, the population of the outports was rapidly declining. While there was still a slight balance in favour of the outports, the population in communities of 1,000 and less was now only 54 percent of the total[32] and more than 300 of the smaller and more isolated outports had been abandoned,[33] partly under the auspices of a government re-settlement programme. In addition, the enormous improvements in the quality of public services, substantial increases in personal incomes, and exposure through television[34] to the images of the affluent life style of urban middle class North America, had created a constant pressure toward the raising of personal and community expectations. But as expectations had risen, the government's ability to satisfy them had declined. There were three reasons.

Firstly, the expansion of public services, which had already taken place, had not only required a vast increase in the province's borrowings but had also placed increasing demands upon current account revenues. Of total current account revenues in 1969-70, only 46 per cent could be derived from provincial sources.[35] The rest came from the federal government under tax and cost-sharing agreements. Since the provincial tax base had been pretty well stretched to its tolerable limits, any further major expansion in current account expenditures would have to be supported by transfers from Ottawa. Further improvements in the public services in the absence of major federal support would have to be marginal.

Secondly, the kinds of demands now being made required much larger expenditures.

> In this district there was nothing there in the beginning. Now they have roads, and telephones, and electricity. We've done about all we can. The things that are left are things like paving and water and sewer systems. You can't blame them for wanting to have proper plumbing or to get rid of the dust. But these are big problems. They take big money.[36]

Thirdly, the emphasis on the modernization programme, formerly divided between improvements in the quality of public services and economic development, now had to be placed more and more on economic development. Premier Smallwood made this quite explicit in his campaign for re-election as party leader in 1969:

> I could list a number of other things that need to be done but I might as well confess that most of my strength, energy, time, ability, and enthusiasm will be poured into the supreme task:
> Getting new industries;
> Getting employment for our people;
> Getting cash wages for our bread-winners.[37]

The term remaining to paternalistic politics in Newfoundland is obviously short. What is likely to take its place? We might predict that to the extent that the effective outputs of government, necessary to satisfy expectations of paternalism, cannot be made or are restricted, the political support base will become unstable. In this situation Newfoundland would be exposed to what I call promissory politics, a style of politics in which the only effective support mobilization technique is to promise to provide demanded outputs to a degree which the resources of the system are quite incapable of producing. Promissory politics is characterized by frequent alternations in office as each party successively demonstrates its inability to honour its commitments.

The legitimacy of the competitive party system is threatened by promissory politics. As each of the parties shows that it is unable to satisfy the expectations of members of the support base, that base is likely to become progressively narrowed. Alternative forms of political action may seem increasingly appropriate. Another danger in promissory politics is that the political leaders will compete with each other in using the resources that are available to make allocations to try to demonstrate their credibility at the cost of effective mobilization for the purpose of further development.

An alternative to the development of promissory politics is the establishment of a stable competitive party politics in which support is mobilized in the manner described at the outset of this paper. Premier Smallwood's strategy has been to look to this kind of solution. In the summer of 1968, partly in response to a challenge from within the party,[38] and to the defeat of six of the seven Liberal MPs in the June federal election,[39] he undertook to try to institutionalize his leadership in a strong party which would provide both a symbol of continuity and the organizational resources needed to exploit that symbol. By the summer of 1969, district associations had been established in every constituency and a provincial party organization had been created.

It is doubtful that this strategy can be successful unless there is a significant change in the political culture of the outports. The persistence of non-participant dispositions in outport Newfoundland and their migration through population shifts to the urban areas is an obstacle to the establishment of this kind of politics. On the other hand, the emergence of an aggressive new fishermen's union and the fairly rapid recent growth in trade union membership generally constitute behavioural evidence that these traditional dispositions may be changing.[40] A thorough analysis of the political culture of both the urban areas and the outports and an evaluation of the significance for the political culture of the accelerated structural change of the past twenty-two years will be needed before this problem can be explored further.

NOTES

1. Cf. Angus Campbell, et. al. *The American Voter* (New York: 1960), and Bernard Berelson, et al. *Voting* (Chicago: 1954).

2. It is argued that the effect of the campaign is to tend to activate the voter's established dispositions, rather than to change them. For example, Berelson and his collaborators concluded that, "Under the increased pressures of a campaign, people have an increased tendency toward consistency, in all relevant aspects." *Ibid.*, p. 285.

3. Campbell, et al. *op. cit.* discuss the electoral responses of the voter in terms of his party identification, issue orientation, and candidate orientation. In their studies in the United States they have found that party identification is consistently the most accurate indicator of likely voting choice. Cf. Campbell et al. *op. cit.*, chapters 4, 6, 7, and 19.

4. The term patronage has acquired a wide variety of uses. I use it to refer to well-defined structural relationships based upon some form of exchange. A patronage relationship, I suggest, will embrace client attitudes of dependence and deference. It is the persistence of these attitudes which fosters paternalistic politics. But I do not want to imply that paternalistic politics can only develop from a decaying patronage system. Clearly, the postulated cultural requisites of paternalistic politics may exist independently of the prior presence or absence of a patronage system. At this point I simply want to note the distinction between patronage politics and paternalistic politics. I shall be dealing more explicitly with the model in papers I am preparing for the collection, *Community Aspects of Political Development*, A.P. Cohen and Cato Wadel, eds., forthcoming.

5. Cf. *Census of Newfoundland, 1935*; *Report of the Royal Commission on the Economic State and Prospects of Newfoundland and Labrador* (St. John's: 1967), and *Newfoundland and Labrador Historical Statistics*, Vol. I, 1 (St. John's: 1970).

6. Lord Amulree, C.A. MacGrath, W.E. Stavert, *Newfoundland Royal Commission Report*, 1933, Sections 213 and 214.

7. Cato Wadel, "Marginal Adaptations and Modernization in Newfoundland," Institute of Social and Economic Research, (Memorial University of Newfoundland, St. John's: 1969), p. 11.

8. J.R. Podoluk, *Incomes of Canadians*, Dominion Bureau of Statistics Monograph, 1968, discussed a "poverty line" differentiating "low income" families. Podoluk defined a family as "low income" if it was obliged to devote 70 per cent or more of its income to life-support necessities. To apply this standard to Newfoundland in the immediate pre-Confederation period, Podoluk's estimate of the poverty line income for a family of four, based on 1961 data, was re-calculated in 1949 dollars, by comparing the D.B.S. cost of living index for 1961 and 1949. The choice of family size was dictated by the fact that the average family in Newfoundland in the 1945 Census consisted of 4.4 persons. 1949 dollars were used because 1949 was the closest year for which the appropriate figures were available. The Canadian "poverty line" for a family of four in 1949 was estimated at $1,921 on pre-tax income and the average Newfoundland family was estimated to have an income at the time of the Census of $1,068. It seems redundant to observe that these are very crude estimates.

9. Cf. inter alia, James C. Farris, *Cat Harbour, A Newfoundland Fishing Settlement*. Institute of Social and Economic Research, Memorial University of Newfoundland, St. Johns, p. 117.

10. Wadel, *op. cit.*, p. 13

11. Gertrude E. Gunn, *The Political History of Newfoundland, 1832-1864* (Toronto: 1966).

12. *Ibid.*

13. *Census of Newfoundland 1945*, calculated from Table 16, p. 53.

14. S. J. Colman, "Social Changes Since Confederation", in R. J. McAllister, ed., *Newfoundland and Labrador, The First Fifteen Years of Confederation*, St. John's, Newfoundland, p. 9.

15. Spencer Lake, Managing Director of Burgeo Fish Industries, as reported in the *St. John's Telegram*, November 6, 1970

16. My father, Albert Perlin, who has been an active commentator on Newfoundland affairs both as a journalist and popular historian for more than fifty years, has been an invaluable source of information about the class structure and politics of the pre-Commission period.

17. Amulree, et al., *op. cit.*, Section 220.

18. *Ibid.*

19. *Ibid.*

20. S.J.R. Noel, *The Politics of Newfoundland* (Toronto: 1971).

21. In general there was little that organization could accomplish. "During the election the candidate would get some man of stature in the community to take him to call and to be chairman for his public meeting. There wasn't much else to the campaign. There would be a lot of talk, but it wouldn't be organized." This description of a local campaign in the 1920's, given to me in one of my interviews in 1970, seems to have general application.

22. Fisheries reports published by the Commission of Government for 1946, 1947, and 1948 show an increase of about 10 per cent in the fisheries labour force.

23. There were actually two referenda. In the first there were three choices: Confederation, Responsible Government and an extension of rule by Commission. When no majority was established, the choice of continued Commission government, which had been supported by only 14 per cent of the electorate, was eliminated and a second referendum conducted. Confederation received 52.2 per cent of the votes cast.

24. Interview with a merchant in a settlement on the South Coast of Newfoundland conducted as part of a study of the attitudes of the 'key man' of MHA's in six provincial districts.

25. The traditional political culture has been characterized as embracing attitudes of deference toward and dependence upon elites and non-participant orientations toward any form of political activism. Cf. Anthony P. Cohen, "The Managers of Myth: A Study of Elite Conflict and Political Development in a Newfoundland Community", paper presented to the Colloquium *Community Aspects of Political Development With Specific Reference to Newfoundland*, Memorial University, March, 1971.

26. Richard Gwyn, *Smallwood, The Unlikely Revolutionary*, (Toronto:1968), p. 137.

27. *Ibid.*, pp. 125-126.

28. Estimated by projection from Newfoundland and Labrador Historical Statistics, *op. cit.*, Table p. 2

29. Interview with a member of the House of Assembly from a northeast coast district, August, 1970.

30. *Ibid.*

31. Only two got to the stage of actually running. Neither saved his nomination deposit. Others who left Mr. Smallwood with similar intentions were soon deterred by their sampling of opinion.

32. *Newfoundland and Labrador Historical Statistics, op. cit.*. Table A-11.

33. Estimates based upon data in D.R. Matthews, *Communities in Transition, A Study of Government-Initiated Migration in Rural Newfoundland*, Ph.D. dissertation (University of Minnesota:1970).
34. Seventy-two per cent of Newfoundland households were estimated by the *Newfoundland Bulletin* of April, 1969, to have televisions.
35. *Newfoundland and Labrador Historical Statistics, op. cit.*Table 6.
36. MHA interview, north-east coast district, 1970.
37. J.R. Smallwood, *To You With Affection From Joey* (St. John's: 1969), pp. 9-10.
38. John Crosbie, Minister of Health, and Clyde Wells, Minister Without Portfolio, resigned from the cabinet in May, 1968, in protest of bridge financing arrangements for the construction of an oil refinery. Crosbie, who quickly assumed leadership of the internal opposition to the Premier, accused Smallwood of autocratic rule of the cabinet, the caucus, and the party. In 1969 he ran against Smallwood for the leadership of the party and then, having been defeated, sat in the legislature as an Independent Liberal. In the Spring of 1971 he joined the Conservative party. Wells sat as an Independent Liberal with Crosbie and then resigned from the Legislature.
39. In every previous federal election, the Liberals had won all five of the outport seats and on three occasions they won both St. John's seats as well. The Premier, until 1968, had had the leading role in federal Liberal campaigns in Newfoundland, including even the selection of candidates. The loss of the six seats in 1968 was widely interpreted as a personal defeat for Smallwood. In fact, reportedly under pressure, he had not taken his usual prominent role in the campaign and data from a survey I conducted in August, 1968, show him running well ahead of the Liberal party in favourable appraisals. There is one qualification in the survey data: among former Liberals who reported voting Conservative in 1968, dislike of the Premier was a frequently cited reason for changing.
40. Until 1968, trade union membership remained fairly constant at about the 24,000 figure. Exact figures are not yet available, but there has been a very rapid and substantial increase in the past two years. Recruitment among fishermen and fish plant workers alone has added several thousand new union members.

4. The Toronto Social Planning Council and the United Community Fund

Howard Buchbinder/*Praxis*

This article traces a number of events which have happened in Toronto concerning the Metropolitan Social Planning Council and the United Community Fund. These events record an attempt by a number of citizens to get involved in changing the direction and structure of these agencies.

The process whereby the private social agency structure has moved away from the problems of poverty and inequality has been both forced and reinforced by the United Community Fund which raises and disperses the majority of funds which support the private agency service delivery system. If any agency could serve to point up this dynamic, it would be one having social planning as its focus. Instead, the Toronto Social Planning Council has dutifully coordinated existing services for the United Community Fund.

The recognition of this situation by some citizens led to an effort to challenge it via the Board of Directors of the Social Planning Council. What has happened to date is recounted here.

Part I

It is often with a sense of shock and disbelief that the social worker faces a group of angry clients, banded together and demanding certain rights. Caught between the patterns of the bureaucracies they represent and the growing anger of those to whom they dispense services, social workers are feeling a very real squeeze. The growth of welfare rights movements and other such groups provides a counter pressure to the oppressive tactics of the public bureaucracies. As the pressure mounts, social and welfare workers tend to represent the management with greater vigour and react to the recipients with increasing and open hostility. The demand for steel bars, bullet proof glass and protective policemen by the workers in the Hamilton, Ontario welfare office is an appropriate example.

Reprinted from *Praxis Notes*, 1:1 (1971), by permission of the author.

Public Agencies

Most of this growing pressure has been focused on what are known as the public agencies. These are service-dispensing agencies that are publicly supported and are primarily involved in administering income maintenance (money payments), job finding and compensatory (workmen's compensation) functions. The consumers of such services (a new euphemism to replace 'recipients') are generally those who are out of the work force, whether temporarily or permanently. The programs are governed by legislation and represent large bureaucracies. The staffs are often minimally trained, underpaid and suffer oppressive conditions in their workplace.

The increasing pressure of group action is brought on by growing evidence of the nature of such agencies as they begin to break down under the strain of mounting social and economic casualties, casualties far beyond their actual or potential capacity for providing aid. As economic conditions worsen and as the glaring contradictions of the social order become more apparent people grow restive, and then angry. There is little question that as the welfare rolls increase, the resultant skyrocketing costs demand that higher and higher proportions of funds available go directly into payments, further exacerbating the problems of service delivery. Thus, a casualty-oriented system which, by the very nature of its operation tends to keep people in positions of dependency, begins to break down under the increasing stress of decaying economic conditions and escalating client indignation and action.

Private Sector

At the same time there exists another sector in the social welfare apparatus. This is the private or voluntary sector. Having its roots in the early charity movements it began by providing aid to those in the underclasses. However with the development of public programs (both welfare and social insurance) this private sector began to assume that it was the role of the government to deal with indigents. The years of the great depression in North America saw a shift of these charity movements away from helping the poor towards other types of aid.

The great influence of Freudian thought in the post World War I era reverberated throughout the developing behavioural and social sciences and aided the private social welfare sector in its move away from the poor. What had been charity societies began more and more to deal with problems of personal adjustment and what were seen as intra-psychically-motivated problems in functioning.

The expanding social work profession followed this direction and turned from an action-oriented, reform-minded group into a professionalized inner-directed vocation. Over the years two major developments appeared as a result of this process. The agencies in the private sector disengaged from the poor, while the flow of professionally-trained social workers was channelled almost exclusively into the private agency sector.[1]

Ancillary Agencies

The development of the ancillary and support agencies in this private sector reflect this. For example, in Toronto, the Associated Charities was formed in 1888. Its concern was "primarily the prevention of fraudulent applications for financial aid".[2] It was a clearing house for those citizens who offered financial aid and those who were requesting it. This organization led to the formation, in 1919, of the Council of Federations, a structure to provide co-ordination of the activities of the auxiliary agencies which were emerging from what had begun as gifts of charity from individuals.

In addition to co-ordination, the problem of financial support for these developing private agencies was of increasing concern. As a result, a group called the Federated Charities was formed in 1919 to raise funds for its member organizations. "In 1943 the United Welfare Fund took over this function on behalf of its 18 agencies. Its name was eventually changed to the Community Chest."[3] The successor to the United Welfare Fund (later, the Community Chest) was the United Community Fund which took over in 1956.

Thus two functions were delineated with the growth of the private agency sector. The fund raising responsibility was transferred from individual donors to the United Welfare Fund to the Community Chest to the present United Community Fund (UCF). Co-ordination was transferred from the Associated Charities (1888) – to the present Social Planning Council (SPC).

Private Agency Service and Public Need

At first agitation by low-income social welfare clients was seen by professional social workers as not related to them. They very carefully made the distinction between themselves and the public sector indicating the fact that most of those people being called social workers were in point of fact, untrained. Since their own agencies were disengaging themselves from anything to do with poor people and since social work education was heavily influenced by an intra-psychically-oriented-individual-treatment approach, workers in the private agency sector felt insulated from such disturbances.

The donors in the community, on the other hand, were led to believe that the contributions which they gave to the United Community Fund were used via its member agencies to aid in the alleviation of poverty and its disastrous effects on people. Stories in newspapers during campaign time would relate to the "hundred neediest cases."

Financial control in the hands of the centralized UCF, planning and co-ordination in the hands of the SPC, – private agencies disengaging from the poor and serving middle class communities. Professionalization of social work in the private agencies and the growing anger of the poor at the bureaucrats and bureaucracy of the public agencies, all set the background for the Saga of the Social Planning Council in Toronto.

Goals of the SPC

The present Social Planning Council of Metropolitan Toronto was founded in 1956. Its goals were democratic membership (1), co-ordination and planning (2,3,5) and action (4):

1. A membership as inclusive as possible, embracing all organizations, groups and individuals concerned about health and welfare.

2. A re-organization that would provide a medium through which community organizations could council together.

3. A strong research, fact-finding department.

4. A Council not only responsive to change, but one vigorous and dynamic enough to guide and direct change.

5. An area council network to enable those people living in particular geographical areas to study and plan for their own communities. [4]

Twelve years later Wilson Head, then an associate executive director, summed up its function as follows:

Basically . . . we're still operating as a welfare council. We're relating to the needs of the agencies and not to the needs of the people. We shouldn't be chained to these agencies. [5]

Democratic Membership

It was as a result of such criticism from members of the staff that the SPC began to take a look at itself. At the annual meeting in 1969 a welfare recipient was nominated to the Board. This nomination was a result of protest from the floor about the composition of the nominees to the Board of Directors, – a board composed primarily of business men, lawyers, labour leaders, and doctors. The nominee from the floor was elected only after one of the official slate of nominees resigned in her favour as there was no procedure in the by-laws for nomination from the floor or for that matter in any way other than via the nominating committee, which was appointed by the incumbent Board of Directors.

Co-ordination and Action

The growing struggle within and about the Social Planning Council focused into two views: one advocating a traditional co-ordination of agency services (primarily serving a middle class constituency); the other advocated making the SPC relevant to what was happening in the community. In the Social Planning Council's report for 1969 the president of the Board of Directors, Harry L. Wolfson, stated his position:

The future course of activity for the council is difficult to determine. It has been, and still is, the subject of numerous discussions and critical examination. Some would argue that the Council should devote itself to militant social action. Perhaps such action is becoming a feature of the modern scene but the key question arises as to whether such a role is the most appropriate task for the SPC. Particularly is it questionable if one bears in mind the need for the council to function as a social planning body for the entire community. It may indeed well be that other organizations should engage in social action, and that the SPC should concentrate, in the main, on the research and planning of our complex social development structure. For, unless the Council performs such essential and constructive tasks, the indispensable social services could deteriorate into chaos; and should such an unfortunate calamity befall us, those who are in constant need of help would be the first to suffer . . .

The position is stated as a dichotomy between planning and action. The logic is: The involvement of the SPC in action will lead to the deterioration of 'indispensable social services' thereby causing the needy to suffer. The assumption that the agencies co-ordinated by Social Planning Council relate to the needs of exploited and oppressed people (who suffer poverty and inequity) is false. The allegation that the SPC has played a role which has kept the social services from 'deteriorating into chaos' is a blatant overstatement of its function of co-ordination. To discredit social action as a goal of the SPC is to remove the SPC even more from the community (needy or otherwise) than it is presently and to deny its responsibility to be responsive to change.

Responsiveness to Change
During the past year and a half the Social Planning Council and the United Fund have felt a growing pressure to change from within and without.

In the fall of 1968 rumblings began to emanate from within the staff of the Social Planning Council. These rumblings of dissatisfaction were with the role of the Council or, to be more specific, its lack of role with people in the community and its continued involvement with agency structures that were not meeting needs in large sectors of the community.

A series of newspaper articles printed in April of 1969 raised the issues publicly and presented the positions of Board members regarding the role of the SPC.

> Board members frown when asked if they like the social action ideas of some of their staff members. It's the sort of thing that's never been done and the very words 'participatory democracy' seem to conjure up images of placarded demonstration marches and sit-ins.[6]

In actuality the demands of the staff were hardly as the reaction of the board would have one believe. An article by two of the principals of the staff at the time clearly outlines the point of view which had so agitated a number of the directors.

> In the public market place, social planning holds a respectable but precarious position. It is assumed that it brings dollars and programs together in a manner that gets translated into cost benefit for the community. It is frequently used as a mechanism for self examination, or more precisely, self assurance. It is the kind of formula which accentuates citizen efforts at budgeting time or when new government programs loom on the horizon. The meaning, in short, is whatever word users of the moment say it is.[7]

Basic Alternatives
The authors outline three basic alternatives which the SPC can choose in response to community demands. Each of the alternatives presented has definite structural implications for the agency. The first alternative presented was that of system maintenance. This approach is:

> now exercised by a majority of community welfare or social planning councils throughout Canada.... Structurally the operation of such a council exhibits a vertical separation between board and staff, with the influence of staff on policy being minimal and the influence of the board dominant.[8]

It was the feeling that the Toronto SPC was engaged in a system maintenance approach that began to stir up the very mild ferment within the staff and subsequently, the community. Certainly the Board-staff structures and relationships also fit the patterns of the system maintenance model.

The second alternative presented by Drover and Head was that of system change. This approach would:

> focus less on services or standards of existing programs and more on the redistribution of resources for meeting needs both financial and social. Program goals are shifted from co-ordination to a primary interest in institutional, organizational and policy changes....
> This approach relies more heavily than the first on consumer and disadvantaged groups or activist citizen bodies. The important feature is that there is less reliance on consensus....
> structurally, this approach calls for a more diversified Board of Directors with less reliance upon business groups and financial interests and greater representation from the liberal academic community and recipients of services...[9]

Although the article quoted above puts forward a third alternative approach, that of 'policy promotion', it would seem that the general pressure within the Social Planning Council was to reconsider the 'system maintenance' approach and possibly opt for the 'system change' approach. The planning manifestations of these two approaches would be allocative (the distribution of funds for existing welfare services) and additive (advancing new goals but unwilling to accept structures imposed by the funding process).[10]

Resistance to Change
The proposal which would move the Social Planning Council in a system change direction with a new planning thrust was greeted with great resistance by many on the Board of Directors. In fact when the director of the Council at the time resigned to go to Vancouver, Wilson Head, then associate director, was passed over for the position. He was a coauthor of the article quoted above and one of the principal exponents of change within the Social Planning Council staff. The message from the President of the Board of Directors which appeared in the Council report for 1969 gives clear indication of the apparent position of the majority of the Board.[11]

Additionally, it can be noted that the method for perpetuating the Board of Directors was highly controlled. The nominations committee, a creature primarily of the Board of Directors, nominated the total slate; the annual meeting rubber stamped the 'approved slate'. In fact there was no provision for any other arrangement under the constitution.

The first chink in this wall of undemocratic procedure was effected in a very minor way when Suzanne Polgar, a welfare recipient and active member of the Just Society Movement was nominated to the Board at the 1969 annual meeting. A new by-law passed by the Board during 1969 opened the option for nominations from the general membership in addition to those nominees put forward by the nominating committee. It was during this year that the initial pressure for change from without began to emerge. Along with the internal pressure, it exploded at the 1970 annual meeting of the Social Planning Council. The response of the SPC Board and its executive director to these processes discredit their claim that they were a Council "responsive to change."

External Pressure
It is difficult to pin-point all of the threads of discontent which merged in the action concerning the Metropolitan Toronto Social Planning Council. It is clear that there are increasing numbers of social workers and others concerned with social welfare issues who are most disturbed over the non-responsive role being played by that establishment. In Toronto this concern was given a somewhat organized expression during the earlier period in the development of the Just Society Movement

(JSM). The JSM was primarily a movement of low income citizens involved in action for change in the areas of welfare, housing, etc. As the movement began to grow a number of 'professionals' were attracted to its ranks.

These 'professionals' were primarily either social workers or social work students. There were also some teachers, government officials, and others. In order to deal with the problems of a grass roots, low-income organization being inundated by professionals two forms of membership were established. Poor people were 'active members' which implied voting status; 'professionals' were 'associate members' who had non-voting status.

Although the professionals (this is obviously not an accurate description but is utilized here since it is the term which has come into general usage for the non-poor participants in poor people's organizations) had initially involved themselves as supporters of a low-income group it soon became clear that they were most interested in working for change in those institutions with which they were closely associated – social welfare institutions.

Statement to the OAPSW
In the fall of 1969 a number of people from this group appeared at a meeting of the Ontario Association of Professional Social Workers (OAPSW) in Toronto. They presented a statement to the organization which said in part:

Professional Social Work developed to rescue the casualties which occur in modern technological-industrial societies. The alleviation of suffering and the redress of injustices were always prime factors in attracting people to the field of social work.

We are witnesses to a process in which the institutional structures of social work are becoming obstacles to these goals. Increasingly, social workers are employed as bureaucrats, as agents for social control. They are, in spite of themselves, adversaries rather than advocates for the poor, the oppressed, the outsider. Some agencies are becoming irrelevant to the human needs existing in the community.

This process must not go on. The social worker must serve the people who need help, he must be the force who will stand for human dignity, equality and justice against the economic and bureaucratic machineries.

In the midst of technical-social revolution, it is not enough to provide band-aids to the victims. A human revolution is needed in order to control the institutions for human purposes, for the security of families, for the creativity of the individual, for the well-being of all.[12]

It was felt that the social work organization had become a protector of the social work status quo, that it had retreated into professionalism and had followed the same direction as the private agency sector, away from the poor and the oppressed sectors of the community.

This group, which had emerged from the Just Society Movement, decided to present this statement in order to make its presence known to the social work community and to take a first step in actively beginning to work for change in this area.

The Ontario Welfare Council and the UCF
The second event which helped to move this process along occurred in October 1969 and focused on the role of the United Community Fund. In July, 1969 the chairman of the committee for national organizations of the United Community Fund in Toronto sent a letter to the president of the Ontario Welfare Council in which he indicated that a special review of the Council would be undertaken. The Ontario Welfare Council's management, programme and finances were to be the subject

of this review and the basic question to be answered was whether or not the Ontario Welfare Council was an appropriate agency for continued support from the UCF.

In May, 1969 the Ontario Welfare Council had held its annual meeting at Hart House on the University of Toronto campus. The Council had invited both young people and poor people to participate in the meeting and two youths and two poor people were elected to the Board of Directors at this meeting. This represented a departure from the traditional 'rubber stamp' annual meeting so characteristic of groups sponsored by the United Community Fund. The Toronto Globe and Mail of October 3, 1969 reported that this represented a 'shakeup' as nothing like this had ever happened before. The nominations and election of the youth and poor people took place from the floor in most democratic fashion.

Two months following this annual meeting the letter from the UCF to the OWC concerning the review was sent. However the letter indicated that "action with regard to the recommended review is delayed pending . . . an analysis of the results of the difficult 1969 Ontario Welfare Council annual meeting."[13] It was the feeling of the Just Society Associates group that the United Community Fund did not want its constituent agencies to allow poor people to be freely and democratically involved on decision-making boards. The UCF response to that possibility was the threat of a review.[14]

A press conference was held by the social work group in October, 1969 at which time these facts were presented to the public.[15] By so doing the question of the role of the United Community Fund as a control agent vis-à-vis the voluntary (private) social agency structure was placed before the community. The press release concluded:

We are social workers and interested citizens committed to the idea of human betterment. We have been and in many cases are affiliated with the social agency structure that is in great part supported by the United Appeal drive. We have long been caught in the dilemma of speaking out and thereby endangering our jobs or running the risk of a 'reexamination' by the Fund; or, representing the interests of those people who rely on us for services and those many people whom we are unable to serve. We want a public accounting from the United Appeal. We feel it is urgent that the kind of undemocratic, totalitarian control which they are attempting to exercise over the Ontario Welfare Council under the guise of 'normal procedures' be responded to publicly. We intend to go to the social work community and the social agencies to gather even more support than we now have. This is an issue for the total community.[16]

Responses
The UCF denied the charges which were made and the case ostensibly rested there. However the thrust that was developing did not rest. It had moved from the presentation to the professional social work organization to the role of the UCF as a control agent which was unrepresentative of the community in terms of its Board structure.

In general the response of the social work institutions was to focus on the nature of the group of people raising the issues. The identification with the Just Society Movement was dwelt on and various descriptions, 'militant, radical, activist', were applied. There was no attempt on the part of any of these institutions to examine themselves. If anything, it was to strike back.

Following the United Fund-Ontario Welfare Council episode interest was stimulated and people began to attend the meetings of UCF allocations committees. What happened at these meetings was another example of the rigidity and suspicion with which the UCF responded to any public attempt to inquire into their operations. A request was made to the United Community Fund for a list of the times and places of its allocation committee meetings.[17] This request was denied on the basis that the meetings of these committees were not open to the public. They were finally made available when the group indicated they were ready to sit-in the office until they were made available.

The same kind of secrecy occurred when observers at some of the allocations committee meetings attempted to tape record them. They were told that this was not allowed and the reasons given were that "tape recorders are biased", "only the press has the legitimate right to record", "confidentiality would be violated" (this apparently referred to making agency salary levels public) and so on. At each step along the way structures which appeal to the community for funds seemed to be inaccessible for community scrutiny.

These then are the activities which began to mobilize concerns which grew out of much of the history and direction of the private social welfare sector which had disengaged itself from the poor and the centers of growing community concerns. The existence of the Just Society Movement provided a framework in which these concerns could be mobilized. In truth it would be more accurate to state that the Just Society Movement served as a launching platform for this group of professionals. In looking back one can reflect on the irony of the situation in which a poor people's action group provided, in effect, the stimulus and sanction to move for change to a group who had long seen themselves as experts in the understanding of social processes.

It was at this point that the Metropolitan Toronto Social Planning Council entered the picture.

The state of the Social Planning Council was well expressed in a letter from Dr. John Crispo, the Board nominee who had stepped down in order that Suzanne Polgar could be nominated and elected during the 1969 annual meeting.

> The Social Planning Council of Metropolitan Toronto continues to languish in its safe and comfortable pew. Except for several disillusioned and disenchanted Board members and a few thoroughly frustrated staff members, the organization seems to fumble along much as it has done for years.
> ... What condemns the Council almost out of hand is its studied avoidance of any active role in social reform. It is, as I have said so many times before, a status quo plus organization that reinforces the so-called establishment when blatant social injustices must be alleviated lest they set in motion forces leading to fundamental reform.
> ... If there is any hope, it lies in the undercurrent of discontent which exists among many of those associated with the Council. Perhaps this combined concern and pressure can begin to move the Council in the right direction....[18]

System Maintenance and Social Control
We have earlier discussed some of the historical background in the development and direction of the public and private social agency structures and the role of planning councils and the United Fund organization on the private or voluntary service delivery systems. The move of the private sector away from the poor and in the direction of 'personal adjustment' was a reflection of the move of the social and behavioural sciences to more and more of a maintenance position.

> The social sciences are parts of culture, and it so happens that they are carried forward predominately by college and university professors, who are in turn hired by business men trustees. The stake of these last in the status quo is great... The social scientist finds himself caught, therefore, between

the rival demands for straight, incisive, and if need be, radically divergent thinking and the growingly insistent demand that his thinking shall not be subversive.... Putting one's head in the horse's mouth to operate on a sore tooth has manifest disadvantages.[19]

Cloward stated:

> It is characteristic of human societies that social problems of various kinds are defined as resulting, not from institutional inadequacies but from the presumed moral, social and psychological defects of the people implicated in these problems.... Such definitions ... tend to preserve the institutional status quo.[20]

It is understandable that with the increasingly exposed contradictions of the social order (i.e. affluence and poverty, abundance and scarcity, inflation and unemployment, etc.) the social control role of the social agency structure has become more apparent. The fact that a Social Planning Council involves itself in co-ordination of existing structures and is subservient to the United Community Fund makes the beginning of a process of change in the direction of social and community needs virtually impossible. The functional role of the social welfare structures to rationalize the present system of exploitation and inequality becomes more and more apparent to people who suffer most from the inequalities. Finally the younger and less socialized social workers begin to perceive the great contradictions between professional ethics and actual functions which do not lead to individual expression, self determination and the like (contrary to what they were taught).

This growing consciousness, which was certainly not unique to Toronto, initially motivated the involvement of the Just Society Associates. The practical experience with the United Community Fund and the professional social work organization further reinforced this consciousness. It was from this soil that the decision to get involved in the processes of the Social Planning Council grew. A somewhat similar process was occurring within the Council itself (although this process should in no way be overestimated).

1970 Annual Meeting
Thus, at the beginning of 1970 an attempt began to sign up members to the SPC with the aim of running candidates for the Board of Directors at the annual meeting which was to be held in March. Contrary to subsequent press reports the initial group of Just Society Associates was a very loosely-knit group. As interest in the coming Social Planning Council annual meeting augmented, more and more people attended discussions and meetings.

The position of what came to be known as the 'reform' group was clearly stated in a position paper distributed by them:

> The purpose of the Social Planning Council is, supposedly, to identify basic social problems and to propose solutions for them. Yet it has carefully avoided even those issues raised at the Senate Committee on Poverty hearings. It deals only with non-conflict, non-controversial questions.
> The problem is that the Social Planning Council as a creature of the United Appeal, a self-proclaimed 'givers' organization, responds primarily to the established agencies, and the Council's commitment is clearly on the side of the status quo....
> We are members of the Social Planning Council and as candidates of its Board of Directors will not contribute our energies to the perpetuation of a fraud. We will contribute our energies, however, to an organization with a serious

commitment to the poor and to other oppressed people. The 'poverty problem', the 'problem of alienated youth' and 'the trouble with welfare recipients' as viewed from the corporate Board rooms do not interest us. We are interested in social change not social control." [21]

The above statement was signed by thirty-four nominees to the Board of Directors. Twenty-six of the thirty-four were nominees from the general membership of the Social Planning Council.[22] The other eight signers of the statement were from among the forty-five nominees put forward by the nominating committee.

Although the annual meeting was scheduled to take place from 10 am to 4 pm on March 18, 1970 there were only two hours allocated for the actual business part of the meeting. The time allocation was obviously based on the experience of previous years. The major items of business had to do with the nominations and elections and the passage of new by-laws referring to the composition of the nominating committee and procedures for nominations.

The business part of the annual meeting got only as far as the report of the nominating committee when it exploded. There were eighty-two nominees for election to the Board of Directors. Forty-five had been nominated by the nominating committee, thirty-seven had been nominated from the membership under the terms of 'By-Law Number 8'.[23]

Upon entering the meeting the members of the corporation (SPC members) had registered and had been given ballots. Each ballot had a number on it which corresponded to a name which had been recorded next to a number identical to that on the ballot. Thus, the ballots were not secret. The marker of each ballot could be identified.

The ballot sheet for election to the Board of Directors contained the list of the eighty-two nominees. However, there were various designations placed next to a number of names. Some names had one asterisk next to them. This indicated those recommended by the nominating committee. Other names had two asterisks next to them. The explanation at the bottom of the ballot read as follows:

These nominees represent Area Councils, municipal authorities and other organizations whose nominees customarily have been elected as directors and who have been nominated by the nominating committee.

This procedure was challenged in that it represented a very biased presentation of the nominees which was heavily weighted in favour of the candidates put forward by the nominating committee. It was therefore biased against candidates nominated directly from the membership.

The chairman ruled against the challenge and the argument began. As the meeting progressed it became clear that there was no way to hold a proper election under the Social Planning Council's own by-laws. The procedures which had been set up were sloppy, biased and poorly managed. Another example of this was the distribution of ballots. Each member of the Council received a ballot. In addition, there are organizational memberships to the SPC. Each organization was entitled to two votes. Thus it was possible under the procedures that were in force at the meeting for one person to receive up to three ballots, one as an individual and two as a representative of a constituent organization. One participant at the meeting who had received three ballots doodled on one of the ballots and received another one merely for the asking. When she stood up at the meeting, waving her ballots, to explain to the group what had happened it was as the proverbial straw that broke the camel's back. There was really no way to proceed.[24]

The meeting voted to recess and elected a committee of seven people, three from the membership, three from the board and a chairman who would set up workable procedures during the succeeding few weeks so that the annual meeting could be reconvened. The meeting was reconvened on May 12, 1970. (The original meeting was held on March 18.) The elections were duly held and the Board of Directors was elected. Forty-three of the directors elected were from the official slate presented by the nominating committee; two were elected from those nominated directly by the membership. A total of ten of the directors were signers of the statement presented earlier in this article and formed what came to be known as the 'reform group'.

What had begun from a group of 'professionals' affiliated with the Just Society Movement grew into a process which included hundreds of people. The participants represented many groups and individuals, all with concerns about the operation of the social welfare system. It had spread far beyond the project of one group or movement.

UCF Forum

It is important to include in this narrative some information concerning another related development. It overlapped the events of the Social Planning Council although its origins were different. This was a public forum which was held on May 21, 1970 to provide an opportunity for Toronto citizens to question the staff and administration of the United Community Fund as to their activities and operations.

This action emerged from a small group of people who came together early in 1970 to talk about the possibility of holding some kind of public meeting to make people aware of the fact that the Senate Committee on Poverty would be coming to Toronto. The group felt that they wanted to do something concerning questions of poverty and such an idea seemed like a good beginning.

The initial group consisted of a minister, two active members of the Association of Women Electors, an active member of the Liberal Party and a social worker. The discussions of poverty and need moved to a discussion of agency services. What emerged was a good deal of concern over how agencies were relating to questions of poverty and increasing grass roots community activity and how the funding process affected the direction of services and ultimately what was done about poverty and inequality.

From these discussions thoughts were crystallized and the group concluded that it could make a vital contribution by attempting to open up to the community the workings of the United Community Fund. Although the fund held an annual meeting each year and ran an extensive campaign in its pursuit of funds it was not directly accessible to community interest. In fact there was a general feeling that the UCF needed to make itself more directly accessible and accountable to the community at large.

Ad-Hoc Committee

Out of this group an ad-hoc citizens' committee was formed with Rev. Clifford Elliott, a United Church clergyman as chairman. On March 23, 1970 a letter was circulated asking for support from community groups as sponsors of the proposed forum. The letter clearly stated the rationale and purposes of the meeting. It read in part as follows:

In recent years, however, a number of citizens have expressed the desire to re-examine the goals and operations of UCF to make sure that it does, in fact, meet the needs of our community in our day. The following are some of the questions being asked:
1. Do the present services best meet changing community needs? Do we need to re-evaluate the services provided by

the seventy-eight member agencies?

2. Do we need to question the rule that prohibits funding an agency until it has existed for three years? Does this rule discourage grass roots efforts?

3. Is it possible that the private agencies are losing touch with the poor?

4. Is there some way in which the UCF could be in closer touch with the community as it assesses its functioning. . . .

The UCF agreed to participate with the ad-hoc committee in planning the format of the meeting and a series of planning meetings were held with representatives of the fund. The meeting was scheduled for May 21, 1970. Although the ad-hoc committee had been interested in an open public forum with some representatives of the UCF staff and Board to answer questions the UCF people wanted to have a very large number of 'experts' there to answer questions. At one of the planning meetings the number of agency people which the Fund wanted to have present as 'resource people' reached about 300 in a hall which would accommodate about 600.

Memo From the UCF

It was later discovered that on May 13 a confidential memo of 30 pages went out to all executive directors of United Fund agencies. This memo was on United Community Fund stationery from N. A. Millington of the UCF staff. In addition to enclosing the press release for the meeting and a copy of the seating plan of the auditorium, the memo requested four representatives from each of the 78 member agencies, a total of 312 people or half the capacity of the hall. "The hall seats 600 people. If you and your President, plus two other volunteers (recipients of service?) can plan to be present, your agency's interest will be well served. . . ."[25]

Also included was a list of twenty-nine questions that might be asked at the upcoming meeting. By itself this could have been interpreted as a guideline. However, in addition to the twenty-nine questions, twenty-nine answers were provided. When one remembers that this memo was circulated to agency executives one must wonder about the degree of control which the UCF apparently desired to exercise. A look at some of the questions and answers in this confidential memo is of interest. Among them were:

8. Some of the agencies are supposed to be serving the poor and the poorer areas of Metro – can these be identified?
A. Yes, the poor can be identified. If they want to, we can probably name them, but of course our records are confidential. All the Family Service organizations, for example have most of their cases with the economically deprived.
10. Why do so many of the social workers act in such a smug, and complacent manner when the needs of the poor and needy are so urgent?
A. I don't know. I don't know many who do. You might ask why are the 'poor' so difficult to deal with.

In retrospect it seems to this writer that the most important thing about this meeting is that it was held. It appeared that the UCF had succeeded in 'packing' the meeting with agency executives and social workers. At the same time many questions were raised concerning the Fund and another step was taken in the processes which had begun to develop in the community vis-à-vis two important segments of the voluntary or private social agency structure – the United Community Fund and the Social Planning Council of Metropolitan Toronto.

Part II

The Board of Directors elected at the 1970 annual meeting has probably met more often and spent more time on SPC affairs than any previous Board in the history of the SPC. Yet in spite of such activity only a minority of the membership was consistently attendant. One Board member did an informal survey regarding attendance at Board meetings and found that if one were to drop Board members from membership after three consecutive absences from meetings there would be twenty-seven fewer members at this writing.

The Board of Directors and Policy Direction

Board meetings were long, and often tedious. Most issues of business brought to the Board concerning the operations, contact, and negotiations of the SPC were questioned at great length, often to the consternation of the Executive Director who saw this kind of lengthy questioning as a block to his efficiency and that of the staff. There was a constant tension in this area: a good deal of this kind of questioning often seemed to me to be initiated by the 'reform' group, while at the same time, there was an opposite push for 'expediting' matters more quickly. The Board did not act as a 'rubber stamp' for the Executive Director. Nevertheless, there was great resistance on the part of the majority of Board members to deal directly with issues of substance. When such issues emerged the ensuing discussion was almost always of a procedural nature – how should it be disposed of without the Board having to confront it directly. Generally, this discussion would be resolved by creating a committee of one sort or another. A review of the process of development of seemingly new policy governing the role of the Social Planning Council will serve to illustrate what directions the Board actually took in response to the changes demanded by many SPC members.

Earlier in this article the platform of the 'reform' candidates at the 1970 meeting was quoted at length. This position was strongly supportive of accountability to a wider constituency, democratization of procedures, radically restructuring the SPC and a belief in "an organization with a serious commitment to the poor and to other oppressed people." It called for hiring social animators and community organizers and making the changes necessary within the SPC in order to do this.

The Cowley Report

As a result of this position a committee on policy was sanctioned by the president of the Board to formulate a statement outlining the direction in which the SPC should go. This committee was composed of five members, all of whom were supporters of the 'reform' platform. The report of the committee was presented to the Board on September 24, 1970 (it came to be known as the Cowley Report). It posed a distinct departure from the concept of planning as a co-ordination of existing resources:

A second approach would be to take those steps necessary to legitimize the Social Planning Council as the recognized planning body. . .

However since the real base for legitimization would lie with the majority of people affected, the Council staff would need to develop considerable contact at the grass roots level. . .

Although most people are concerned about the issues, the problems and the trends facing their communities, they do not have effective methods of transmitting their concerns. The SPC could become an effective mechanism for receiving and channeling these concerns. . . .

The Social Planning Council could in effect become the focal point for working with community groups on social issues.

In order to establish a broad base of effective grass roots organizations representing all segments of the community, it would undoubtedly be necessary to divert most of the present staff to this function. . . .

If the SPC were to take this course, its present relationship to the United Community Fund would change in nature . . . The Social Planning Council would undoubtedly wish to maintain a close working relationship with the United Fund, but many of the present relationships and responsibilities would need to be dropped because of the proposed new emphasis on the broader issues of social planning.

Although this may sound like a rather ambitious change in direction, it could probably be accomplished with the combined support of all the members of the Board and numerous grass roots organizations[26]. . . .

This report suggested a way for the SPC to become a channel for community concerns by diverting most of the staff to community work and changing its relationship with the United Community Fund. It provided a way for beginning to expand the role of the SPC from the old tradition of co-ordination and allocative planning towards an active sense of and involvement in ongoing community processes.

The Board of Directors chose not to discuss this proposal at any Board meeting. Rather, a decision was delayed by referral to an August committee called the 'President's Committee on Policy', on which only the chairman of the original committee was placed.

Thus rather than meeting the substantive issue head-on the majority of the Board of Directors opted for a procedural, bureaucratic response. It was obvious that this question of policy direction was the major issue before the council as a result of both the annual meeting and also prior staff dissatisfaction. By diverting it to yet another committee, open discussion was avoided by the Board from September, 1970 until February, 1971.

General Membership Meetings
The second factor relevant to discussion of the role of the President's Committee involves two meetings of the general membership of the SPC, the first held in October and the second in December, 1970. A motion had been passed at the 1970 annual meeting calling for a public meeting in September at which time the Board of Directors could report back to the membership. This was very much in keeping with the desire to open up the corporation to the community.

There was a struggle at Board meetings around the scheduling of this public meeting. Originally, the meeting was delayed because the work on the new constitution was not completed. As the date kept getting pushed back a number of Board members insisted on having a public meeting even if it was of an informal nature in order that the membership could be involved in discussion about ongoing issues.

The October meeting was an informal meeting which could not conduct official business. At that time the Cowley Report was discussed. The second public meeting was held on December 16, 1970. It was an official membership meeting. Notification of the meeting was provided to the membership in accordance with the provisions of the constitution. At this meeting a motion was passed which stated:

That our direction be that of social development and social change achieved through working and providing a voice for citizens at the local (grass roots) level, generally by (i) organizing or working with low or no income groups, such as the working poor, pensioners, the unemployed etc. (ii) working with agencies and rate-payers groups etc.

That the Metropolitan Toronto Social Planning Council provide the necessary components of staff research and finances to carry out the new direction.

In essence this motion gave the official sanction of the membership to the Cowley Report. The membership meeting was a legally called and duly constituted meeting of the corporation at which a quorum was present. The SPC Board did not act on the policy passed by the membership meeting. Instead this policy decision was referred to the President's Committee on Policy.

From the time of the annual meeting in 1970 until February, 1971 there was no open discussion at the Board of Directors on the policy direction of the SPC. The fact the one committee reported and two membership meetings were held on the subject of policy do not serve to change this at all. All pressures were responded to in terms of waiting for the report of the President's Committee. Thus we see how the committee structure was used by the majority of members on the Board to avoid responding directly to the membership's concerns.

The President's Committee Report on Policy
When the President's Committee on Policy finally reported much was made of the consensus they had achieved in the committee. This was used to pressure for as little open discussion as possible. The argument suggested that the Board was now facing approval of a policy report which had been worked over and debated for months in committee. Therefore there was no need for extended substantive debate before the Board as a whole. It is accurate to state that a majority of the Board of Directors approved this position. It is therefore also accurate to state that a majority of the members of this present Board of Directors do not support the direction of the Cowley Report or the resolution of December 16. The policy statement passed by the Board in February, 1971 is at great variance with these alternate positions.

In essence the policy reaffirms the services which have been part of the "Council's operation for many years". The policy focuses on the crucial issue of community action and citizen's groups by stating:

The emergence however, in recent months of new types of organizations and the growing strength of existing groups and federations . . . as vital and increasingly large and organized part of the community presents a new and growing demand to which the SPC must respond. Therefore, the SPC will provide within its priorities, professional consultative services to such groups . . . . Such assistance will normally be complementary to the work of other organizations and will usually include research components.

In providing consultative and planning assistance to such organizations and groups, the SPC will not necessarily be associated with actions such groups choose to take or with statements they choose to make.

The activities recommended are those which are congruent with the democratic process and within the legal framework of our society. It is, of course, not appropriate for the SPC to engage in any action which is illegal or politically partisan, or which may seriously or permanently alienate large segments of the community as a whole or those bodies which are responsible for and empowered to bring about effective and necessary change.[27]

It is obvious from even the most cursory reading that the statement does absolutely nothing about social animation or direct community organization. It talks about "consultative and planning assistance" and then sets as criteria for activities a list of things which can only be determined in the most subjective manner. The only clearly distinguishable criterion refers to "within the legal framework".

The policy statement also indulges in the use of a committee to achieve, it seems, a delaying function similar to that served by the President's Committee on Policy. It establishes

> a standing Board/staff committee on policies composed of at least three Board members and three staff members. This committee will:
>
> 1. assess long range policies and short range programs in the light of experience and changing conditions:
>
> 2. recommend to the Board adaptations or revisions of policies and/or programs in the light of this assessment;
>
> 3. recommend to the Board a system of priorities for implementation of programs and policies.
>
> 4. assess requests for activities and recommend to the Board what actions should be taken.[28]

The United Community Fund and SPC Policy Changes

The United Community Fund involved itself in this policy process in a way which seems very similar to its action in July 1969 regarding the Ontario Welfare Council.[29] About six weeks after the December membership meeting at which the policy resolution concerning the SPC and the community was passed, a registered letter was sent (February 1, 1971) from W. Grant Ross, President of the UCF to F. C. Buckley, President of the Social Planning Council of Metropolitan Toronto.[30] The letter indicated that the SPC should proceed with a "self analysis and report in writing on or before April 15 on how your organization measures up to the criteria used in the admission of a new organization to the Fund." The purpose of this self-analysis, was to assist the review committee to determine if the SPC continued to meet the standards of admission to the UCF. Certainly there was much speculation that the timing of the demand for a 'self-analysis' indicated a 'subtle' attempt at control which seemed to be so characteristic of the UCF.

On March 3, 1971, Frank Buckley replied with a letter and enclosed a copy of the Policy Statement of the Social Planning Council adopted by the Board of Directors on February 24, 1971. Several days later Mr. Ross was quoted in the press as indicating that the report had "cleared the air" as far as the intentions of the SPC were concerned.

This discussion of the policy process during the past year illustrates the kinds of problems encountered when trying to change the direction of the Social Planning Council (or any other similar agency). In essence the outcome of this process produces a policy statement which mildly talks about community involvement but sets up all kinds of constraints which are presented under the guise of statements about 'democratic process' or 'alienating large segments of the community'. Rather than posing guidelines within which to function they allow for subjective decisions about what is appropriate in a rhetoric geared to raise anxiety about all kinds of implied undemocratic, illegal and destructive happenings.

It must be clear that a change of direction as indicated by both the Cowley Report and the policy passed by the membership in December (and given some lip service in the final policy passed by the Board) involves reordering priorities and restructuring staff functions. Yet this last policy document deals with the problem by stating:

> If it is not possible immediately to acquire additional staff for this or other needed services the process of relieving professional staff of activities which can be carried out by non-professional or para-professional staff should be accelerated.

It is clear that there is no intention to reorder priorities or restructure the staff to move in a new direction. Any move in a community direction will be initiated only if *all* the present functions can be maintained. This is the kind of new policy direction which the Board of Directors has developed.

It would also seem that the relationship with the United Community Fund remains exactly as it was. The *timeliness* of the request for a self-analysis and the acceptance by the Fund of the policy statement as part of that self-analysis must be seen as a continuation of the kind of exercise of control which raises increasing criticism about the operation and function of the United Community Fund.

It is clear that the value of this past year has been to dramatize how structures like the Metropolitan Toronto Social Planning Council actually work. It sharpens the focus for the coming annual meeting.

The discussions now going on in various places throughout the country and the continent regarding popular control, community control and other such concepts are directly related to the struggle for change and the development of the forms for change. These answers cannot emerge from the Metropolitan Toronto Social Planning Council alone. If, however, the present structure of the Council remains static and if the underlying analysis of its function remains static, then new participants with a bent towards reform will not be enough. The struggle for changing the structure and focus of such agencies from that of tension managers and system maintainers to active agents for change can only be attempted through a basic institutional strategy.

NOTES

1. See R. A. Cloward and I. Epstein, "Private Social Welfare Disengagement from the Poor: the Case of the Family Adjustment Agencies" in Zald, ed., *Social Welfare Institutions* , (N.Y., 1965), p. 623. This book includes an extensive bibliography.
2. SPC Report for 1969, Toronto: 1970.
3. ibid.
4. ibid.
5. "Social Council Wants to Cut Agency Umbilical Cord and Help People", *by Loren Lind, Toronto Globe and Mail*, April 16, 1969.
6. ibid.
7. Grover & Head, "Social Planning and the Councils", *Canadian Welfare*, Jan.-Feb., 1970, p. 12.
8. ibid., p. 12.
9. ibid., p. 12.
10. ibid., p. 13.
11. op. cit., SPC Report for 1969.
12. Interestingly enough, the guest speaker at the meeting at which the quoted brief was presented was the new director of the Social Planning Council, John Frei. His appearance at this meeting was by way of his introduction to the Toronto Social Work community. The brief was presented following Dr. Frei's speech. It was significant that he then took it upon himself to answer the presentation although the brief was addressed to the membership of the OAPSW. The dialogue that ensued was almost totally between the presenters of the brief and Dr. Frei. The membership of this social work organization did not participate in the discussion either then or subsequently.
13. Letter to Mr. Winslow Benson, President, Ontario Welfare Council from Arthur J. Langley, Chairman, Committee for National Organizations, United Community Fund, dated July 31, 1969.
14. It is interesting to note that in March 1971 the UCF decided that the Toronto SPC should do a self review as a result of the apparent policy direction focussing in the direction of social change and community group support. More on this later in the article.
15. From press release of October, 1969.
16. ibid.
17. The allocations committees are voluntary groups which consider agency requests for funds.
18. Published in *Council Comment*, newsletter of the SPC of Metro Toronto, Vol. 10, No. 2, Feb. 1970.
19. Robert Lind, *Knowledge for What?* Grove Press Inc., N.Y. 1939.
20. op. cit., Cloward and Epstein, p. 637.
21. This paper, entitled "How are you Going to Vote" was distributed

to members of the SPC and signed by 34 candidates to the Board of Directors. It will be possible to use this statement as a basis for evaluating what the Board of Directors has accomplished since the 1970 annual meeting.

22. It is interesting to note that the membership of the SPC about doubled in number during the period prior to the annual meeting. There was a great deal of interest.

23. This was the by-law which had been passed by the Board during the year concerning the nominating committee and the procedure for nominations. It had to be ratified by the annual meeting.

24. Although the meeting collapsed under the weight of its own inability to provide fair, unbiased and efficient procedures and was recessed at the vote of the overwhelming majority of those present, there were those like Mayor True Davidson of East York who chose to represent

what had occurred as a "takeover" by "anarchists".

25. Letter from N. A. Millington, Director, Allocations and Agency Relations UCF.

26. From the report of the Committee on Policy presented to the Board of Directors on September 24, 1970.

27. SPC Statement of Policy, approved by the Board of Directors February 24, 1971.

28. ibid.

29. See part 1-iv of this article.

30. W. Grant Ross is also a member of the Board of Directors of the Social Planning Council as are seven other directors of the United Community Fund. His letter was sent and received before the discussion and approval of the Report of the President's Committee on Policy.

---

5. Leadership Conventions in Canada: the Forms and Substance of Participatory Politics

J. Lele, G. Perlin and H. Thorburn/*Queen's University*

One of the sustaining myths of liberal-democratic society is that if, in many of our day-to-day situations, we find that public space is dominated by private interests, at least in our politics we are allowed to choose who will govern us. Since it came into existence with Aristotle and Plato, political sociology has demonstrated that even here we have little choice. Decisions on who will be our leaders are taken by people whom we do not elect and who have appointed themselves as our guardians. As this analysis of Liberal and Progressive Conservative conventions shows, this is as true of Canada as anywhere else. Such an essay suggests two questions. The sociological one is why? The political one is double-barrelled: "Do we accept such a state of affairs and, if not, what alternatives do we have?" Some illustrations of attempts at creating alternatives are provided in Section Seven.

The Progressive Conservative leadership convention of 1967 and the Liberal leadership convention of 1968 have both been represented as important events in the progress toward a more open and 'participatory' party politics in Canada. This view focusses upon the democratic forms of the convention electoral process, emphasizing the election of constituency delegates, the efficacy of the secret ballot in freeing delegates from exposure to manipulative pressures, and the openness and genuine competitiveness of the convention campaign in which candidates seek to win votes by exposing their personalities and views, not just to the delegates during the convention, but to the electorate at large in elaborate pre-convention campaigns.

We challenge this argument on three grounds. Firstly, delegates to the two conventions were predominantly representative of the most privileged groups in Canadian society; secondly, convention rules continued to afford a position of advantage to the elite within the parties; and thirdly, up to the actual act of balloting, opportunities for widespread manipulation existed and were availed of.

In this paper we will seek to demonstrate these three points with some of the evidence we have gathered in a substantial study of the two conventions. Our research has consisted of a

Published for the first time in this collection.

mail survey which yielded completed questionnaires from over fifty per cent of the delegates to the conventions, personal interviews with some 120 senior party members and key informants and an analysis of documents related to the conventions. The main thrust of our argument is that despite differences in the specific circumstances affecting the two major parties and despite the institutional mechanisms which seem to facilitate open conventions, participation is narrowly circumscribed and elite control in terms of processes leading to the final outcome, and hence, over that outcome itself, is still quite substantial. To the extent that leadership conventions are considered to be (along with policy conventions and constituency nominating meetings) major institutional mechanisms through which mass participation is achieved, our research raises considerable doubt about the effectiveness of mass participation in Canadian parties.

The Background

The Progressive Conservative Convention of 1967 was the climax to a bitter four-year fight over the leadership of John Diefenbaker. Diefenbaker, having led the Conservatives to power in 1957, became an increasingly controversial figure within the Party. After the defeat of his government in 1963, restiveness with his leadership, previously confined largely to the Cabinet, spread to the extra-parliamentary party and produced a succession of attempts to force him out. In 1966 Dalton Camp, President of the National Progressive Conservative Association, made a cross-country tour seeking support for a re-appraisal of the leadership. His campaign succeeded in winning from the 1966 annual meeting of the Association a resolution ordering that the National Executive call a leadership convention before the end of 1967.

The Convention met in September, and after five ballots, chose Robert Stanfield, the Premier of Nova Scotia. Stanfield's major opponents were Diefenbaker, who withdrew after three ballots, Duff Roblin, the Premier of Manitoba, and six former members of the federal cabinet, E.D. Fulton, George Hees, Alvin Hamilton, Wallace McCutcheon, Donald Fleming and

Michael Starr.

The Liberal Convention of 1968 was held under less controversial circumstances. Lester Pearson who had served as leader since 1958 and as Prime Minister since 1963, announced in December 1967 that he wished to retire. Accordingly, a Convention was called for April, 1968. Pierre Elliott Trudeau, Pearson's Justice Minister, won on the fourth ballot, defeating six cabinet colleagues, Robert Winters, John Turner, Paul Hellyer, Paul Martin, J. J. Greene, and Allan MacEachen, and a former Quebec minister, Eric Kierans. Another candidate, Mitchell Sharp, then Minister of Finance, withdrew before the Convention to support Trudeau.

TABLE 1: Income, Occupation, and Education of Delegates Compared to Canadian Population As A Whole

	Percent of Liberals	Percent of Conservatives	Percent of All Canadians
Income			
Over $20,000	25.2	26.5	1.1[1]
$15,000 - $19,999	15.5	16.6	1.2
$10,000 - $14,999	25.6	23.0	5.0
$ 5,000 - $ 9,999	23.1	22.5	32.8
$ 4,999 or less	7.6	7.8	59.6
No response	3.0	3.8	
Occupation			
Professional	38.1	36.7	9.2[2]
Owners, Managers, Executives	20.7	22.3	11.5
Sales	10.4	9.9	5.7
Clerical and Other White Collar	4.1	3.1	12.8
Skilled Labour	3.0	3.4	26.9
Unskilled Labour	0.5	0.8	13.8
Farmers	4.8	5.3	8.6
Widows, Pensioned and Retired	3.1	4.7	10.9
Unclassified[3]	16.0	12.0	
No response	2.8	2.4	
Education			
At Least One University Degree	43.1	42.6	5.5[4]
Non-Degree University	13.0	10.5	3.5
Post-High School, Non-University	7.8	8.8	2.7
High School or Less	34.4	36.6	88.6
No response	1.7	1.4	
	(N= 1,201)	(N= 1,091)	

[1] Data for Canada have been compiled from *Taxation Statistics*, 1970 Edition, a publication of the Department of National Revenue, reporting on the taxation year 1968.
[2] Data for Canada compiled from John Meisel in 1968 all Canada sample of 2,767 cases.
[3] This category includes housewives and students who did not provide the occupation of the main wage earner, and some very minor groups, for example, delegates who called themselves simply "politicians".
[4] Data for Canada compiled from John Meisel's 1968 sample of 2,767 cases.

Delegates: Socio-Economic Base

Delegates to the two conventions were drawn from a strikingly narrow socio-economic base. Two-thirds of them had incomes of $10,000 or more a year, although this income group constitutes less than 8 per cent of the Canadian population as a whole. 40 per cent earned $15,000 or more compared to less than 3 per cent of the total population and 25 per cent earned

$20,000 or more compared to 1 per cent of the total population. Looked at from the other end of the scale, although nearly 60 per cent of all Canadians have incomes less than $5,000 a year, delegates in this income group constituted less than 8 per cent of the total delegate body.

The occupational distribution of the delegate samples reflects this bias. Nearly 60 per cent were drawn from professional or executive occupations, although these groups constitute a good deal less than 20 per cent of the total population. Manual labourers were particularly seriously discriminated against. Only about 3 per cent of the delegates came from skilled labourers and less than 1 per cent were unskilled labourers. Farmers were also under-represented, accounting for only about 5 per cent of the delegate samples as compared to close to 10 per cent of the population at large.

Not surprisingly, the delegates collectively had attained significantly higher levels of education than the general population. Over 60 per cent had some post-high school education and 42 per cent had at least one university degree.

Available data suggest that the proportion of the general population with some post-high school training is not much in excess of 12 per cent and the proportion with at least one university degree does not exceed 5.5 per cent.

These collective characteristics of the delegates are consistent with our expectations. The major study of American convention delegates revealed a similar bias and investigations of political participation have repeatedly shown that the degree of political activism varies directly with socio-economic status. We shall have something to say about the reasons for this later; our main point at this stage is to deal with the claim that the convention·process effects broad participation. It is perfectly clear from these data that it does not. In short, if the openness of these conventions is to be judged by their effectiveness in providing proximate representation to the main body of interests reflected in Canadian society, they must be appraised to have failed.

Rule-Making For The Conventions

Our second point is that the convention rules provide a position of advantage to party elites. Historically, as Senator Richard Stanbury, President of the Liberal Federation of Canada, has pointed out this was the accepted practice.

Up until 1958, "the Party was a Cabinet-run party, with Cabinet Ministers having complete responsibility for organization, policy and finance. Conventions during that period were made up of delegates who were generally named by the leaders or their local agents, so that the results of the conventions generally depended upon sub-alliances of leaders at the conventions."[1] In 1965 the party gave itself a new constitution and formulated the rules for regulating conventions. Within the context of this constitution, Stanbury claims that since 1968, the Federation has become substantially participatory and democratic. But the party constitution clearly shows that a substantial role is still retained for elites[2] at conventions. As ex-officio delegates, major officers of federal and provincial party associations, women's organizations and university clubs, along with members of Parliament, the Senate and provincial legislatures are assured status at all conventions. In 1968 these ex-officio delegates continued to constitute some 35 per cent of the total membership of the Convention. In addition, ex-officio delegates enjoy an advantage because of their continuous and more intense participation in party affairs, a fact which prompted the Hull Federal Liberal Association to move an amendment to the Constitution (in 1968) which reads in part: "Whereas, the number of ex-officio delegates is too numerous compared to elected delegates; whereas, certain federal districts have a very large membership; it is proposed that the number of elected delegates be 20 per federal electoral district . . . "[3]

While the Liberals wrote the rules for convention representation into their constitution, the Conservatives had a greater opportunity for manipulation at the elite level because the calling and administration of conventions is left entirely by the party's constitution to the National Executive. Accordingly, members of the elite who sat on the Executive were empowered to set the time and place for the convention, to establish rules for its conduct, to decide how delegates would be apportioned, and to adjudicate the credentials of delegates.

The Executive, acting through the authority of the Convention Committee, therefore, had the specific power to define the scope of mass participation in the convention. Following the precedents of every other convention in the party's history,[4] it used this power to protect the position of the elite by creating a widely defined category of ex-officio delegates, and a category of elite-appointed delegates-at-large. The ex-officio delegates constituted some 26 per cent and delegates-at-large approximately 23 per cent of the total membership of the Convention. Thus, elected delegates made up only 51 per cent.

This tempering of party democracy encountered little opposition within the Convention Committee. No one questioned or apparently thought to question the creation of ex-officio delegates,[5] while such discussion as there was of delegates-at-large focussed mainly upon their method of selection.

The appointment of delegates-at-large is certainly not unique in the tradition of Canadian leadership conventions. They have been widely used at American national party conventions where, as David, Goldman and Bain observe, they "often represent a special form of patronage and recognition . . . (and) provide leaders who can represent (state delegations) in negotiations with other delegations, convention managers, and candidates."[6] Key informants said they had a similar role in the structure of the Conservative Convention. Fund-raisers, substantial contributors to the party, and very active members

without official positions could be assured of participation as delegates-at-large. In addition, such appointments were used to find positions on the convention floor for key members of candidates' organizations.[7]

The presence of large numbers of ex-officio delegates or delegates-at-large does not in itself constitute evidence of elite control of the convention outcome. We assume that if they do seek such control, the party elite will take an active and direct role in the leadership conflict. On this basis our data support the conclusion not only that the elite sought control but also that at the level of candidate decision-making they were fairly successful in achieving it. Not only were ex-officio delegates and, in the Conservative party, delegates-at-large more likely than constituency delegates to be members of candidate organizations, they also constituted majorities in the organizations of the major candidates.

A major factor contributing to elite control of major candidate organizations was the relative homogeneity of their socio-economic status vis-à-vis the rest of Canadian society. They tended to have higher incomes, higher education and most of them lived in large urban centres. Given the exclusiveness of the conventions, the difference between the party elite and the rest of the delegates is not striking but it is enough to demonstrate their relative higher status (See Table 3). Thus we find that young professionals or executives with higher incomes and urban residence from among the party elite dominated the candidate organizations or became major activists in the campaigns. A simple check of the key informants who were active in candidate organizations shows that a very large percentage of them lived in the Toronto-Montreal-Ottawa area. At least fifty per cent of them in each party were lawyers. They formed a socio-economically homogeneous group with very high level of interaction across candidate organizations. Nearly all of them had some contact with other key members of candidate organizations in the past and a majority of them had had such contacts frequently.

TABLE 2: Percentages of Constituency Delegates, Ex-Officio Delegates and Delegates-at-Large Who Were Members of Candidate Organizations, Supporters of Candidates, and Neutrals

	Liberal Party			Progressive Conservative Party			
	Percent of Ex-Officio Delegates		Percent of Constituency Delegates	Percent of Ex-Officio Delegates		Percent of Delegates-at-Large	Percent of Constituency Delegates
	National[2]	All[3]		National[4]	All[5]		
Organization Members[1]	53	43	34	39	33	36	21
Candidate Supporters	34	40	47	44	47	39	48
Neutrals	13	17	19	17	20	25	31

[1] Delegates were classified as organization members if they reported that they had held an official position in a candidate's organization. They were classified as supporters, if they said they had tried to persuade other delegates to vote for a candidate.

[2] The category national ex-officio delegates included only members of the National Executives of the Senior, Women's, Young Liberal and Canadian University Liberal Federations, members of Parliament, defeated candidates, senators, privy councillors members of the Federation standing committee and leaders of provincial Liberal parties.

[3] Including MLAs, Members of Provincial Executives and Defeated Provincial Candidates.

[4] The category national ex-officio delegates included only members of the National Executives of the National Association, the Young Progressive Conservatives, the PC Women's Association and the Progressive Conservative Student Federation, members of parliament, senators and privy councillors.

[5] Including members of provincial legislatures.

TABLE 3 Percentages of Delegates Differentiated As Ex-Officio Delegates, Delegates-at-Large, and Constituency Delegates, Having Selected Social Characteristics

	Liberal Party		Progressive Conservative Party		
	Percentage of Ex-Officio[1] Delegates	Percentage of Constituency Delegates	Percentage of Ex-Officio[2] Delegates	Percentage of Delegates-at-Large	Percent of Constituency Delegates
Sex					
Male	87[3]	83	91[3]	86	78
Female	13	17	9	13	20
	(N= 350)	(N= 783)	(N= 223)	(N= 247)	(N= 562)
Residence Now					
Farm	5	6	5	3	4
Under 1,000	6	11	12	3	8
1,000 - 9,999	15	23	18	11	20
10,000 - 99,999	24	26	22	18	26
100,000 - 249,999	14	8	14	16	8
Over 250,000	36	25	28	44	24
	(N= 335)	(N= 744)	(N= 212)	(N= 247)	(N= 562)
Age					
Under 20	8	3	2	8	1
21 - 25	19	5	5	16	6
26 - 30	9	11	5	12	11
31 - 40	17	26	15	20	22
41 - 50	23	29	27	19	28
51 - 60	14	18	29	10	17
61 - 70	7	6	14	10	9
Over 70	3	2	4	4	4
	(N= 354)	(N= 791)	(N= 223)	(N= 247)	(N= 562)
Occupation[4]					
Professional	39	38	44	41	35
Owners, Managers, Exec.	22	26	23	26	25
Politicians	9	1	9	0	1
Sales	9	13	7	11	12
Clerical	3	6	2	2	4
Skilled Labour	6	5	2	5	5
Farmers	6	7	7	3	7
Armed Services	1	1	1	0	1
Widows or Retired	4	3	2	6	5
Unskilled	1	1	0	2	2
		(N= 773)		(N= 247)	(N= 562)
Income[5]					
$20,000 or more	30	24	7	43	19
$15,000 - $19,999	18	15	12	32	17
$10,000 - $14,999	24	28	23	14	25
$ 5,000 - $ 9,999	20	26	20	7	27
$ 4,999 or less	8	8	38	0	8
	(N= 349)	(N= 783)	(N= 221)	(N= 193)	(N= 548)
Education[5]					
Post-Graduate	8	6	17	11	7
Degree	42	34	39	46	27
University, No Degree	19	11	7	2	8
Post-High But Non-Univ.	7	9	9	14	11
Grades 12 - 13	14	17	14	7	20
Grades 9 - 11	8	18	11	9	19
Grade 8 or less	2	6	4	5	7
	(N= 355)	(N= 791)	(N= 221)	(N= 193)	(N= 548)

[1] This category includes members of the National and Provincial Executives of the Senior, Women's, Young Liberal and Canadian University Liberal Federations, leaders of provincial Liberal parties, and members of the Federation standing committee, CULF local and regional representatives, members of legislatures and defeated candidates, members of Parliament, privy councillors, senators and defeated candidates.

[2] This category includes members of the National Executives of the Progressive Conservative Association, the Young Progressive Conservatives, the Progressive Conservative Women's Federation, and the PCSF, members of legislatures, nominated candidates, members of Parliament, privy councillors and senators.

[3] For clarity, figures have been rounded to the nearest whole number. For this reason and because of the omission of non-responses, they do not add to exactly 100 per cent.

[4] 'Students' and 'housewives' were reclassified for the purposes of this Table according, respectively, to the occupations of their fathers and husbands.

[5] For the purpose of calculating income and educational distributions, students were excluded on the ground their lack of income (or low income) and incomplete education would distort assessments of the significance of these relationships among other members of the sample.

Constituency Delegations: Elite Manipulation

The guarantee of an independent mass voice in the convention was presumed to be afforded by the election of a majority of the delegates at meetings in constituencies. In fact, the extent to which this purpose was fulfilled varied from constituency to constituency because the rules under which the elections were conducted exposed them to manipulation.

The sole criterion for participation in a constituency election in the case of the Conservatives was the possession of a party membership card. These were supposed to have been purchased for a dollar, but often were available free. There was no other prerequisite, not even a minimal length of membership. Thus new voters could be marshalled even as a meeting was in progress.

In some ridings, candidate organizations took advantage of this situation to ensure the election of committed delegates. But none of the candidates had the organizational resources to attempt this practice on a national scale.

In the Liberal case, the qualifications for participation in constituency elections varied from riding to riding. Some required at least ninety days of party membership, while in others there was no minimum condition of any sort. Despite this difference, attempts by candidate organizations to stack constituency meetings actually appear to have been more widespread in the Liberal Party. As one of the organizers for Hellyer put it:

> The general technique was to study the rules and to figure out how to get round them ... One came to expect this sort of thing (the stacking of constituency meetings) in politics and we didn't get too shocked about it.

Evidence from key informants suggests that successful efforts to manipulate constituency elections in this way were made by every major candidate's organization.

Some candidates were in a position to elect very large blocs of constituency delegates. In the Progressive Conservative Party the two best in a position to do this were the provincial premiers. But most of the delegates had been chosen by the time they had declared their candidacies. In Nova Scotia this made little difference because of the absence of independent federal organization. Federal constituency associations there were essentially nominal groups constituted, when the situation demanded, by members of the provincial party. Thus delegates could be expected to be responsive to the wishes of the provincial leadership. Premier Roblin's influence at the constituency level was more limited because federal constituency organization in Manitoba was largely independent of the provincial party. The contrast is apparent in first ballot results, Stanfield winning virtually all of the constituency votes from Nova Scotia and Roblin winning barely half those from Manitoba.

Although there was no Premier among the Liberal candidates, there were two provinces in which candidates were in a position to influence a large number of constituency elections: Quebec and Nova Scotia. Quebec constituencies were part of a separate Quebec federal party which was controlled by the Trudeau forces, and Trudeau and his principal lieutenant, Jean Marchand, the Minister of Manpower, were in a position to apply a variety of pressures to Quebec constituencies. As Minister of Justice, Trudeau had direct charge of what is probably the most important patronage department, but more than that, Prime Minister Pearson had accorded Trudeau and Marchand what amounted to a determinative voice in most decisions affecting Quebec. In Nova Scotia, the provincial party was weak; thus MacEachen, as the federal minister, was in command of the only source of patronage available to Nova Scotian Liberals. The significance of the influence of Trudeau in Quebec and MacEachen in Nova Scotia is reflected in their success in winning substantial majorities of the constituency delegates from their respective provinces on the first ballot.

With one exception, there is little evidence that any other leader in either party tried to create a large bloc of votes which could be used for brokerage purposes. The exception was Premier Smallwood of Newfoundland. Smallwood's organizers observed the rules for constituency elections only in form, the delegates being chosen by the Premier. At the Convention when Smallwood tried to deliver the Newfoundland delegation to Trudeau, some delegates rebelled, but the Premier was largely successful, eighty per cent of his province's delegation supporting Trudeau on the first ballot.

The evidence is insufficient to permit accurate measurement of genuinely open constituency elections. But the main point is clear. The election of constituency delegates could be and was in a number of cases, which we have been able to identify, an ineffective instrument of popular control.

Whatever the forms of the conventions and whatever the myths they professed, major candidates in both parties adopted strategies which assumed that blocs of votes could be controlled and exchanged. The test of this assumption came when some of the candidates defeated on preliminary ballots attempted to transfer their votes to one of the remaining candidates. At the Conservative Convention, McCutcheon, Hees and Fulton all sought to deliver their remaining support to Stanfield while at the Liberal Convention, MacEachen and Greene sought to deliver their remaining support to Trudeau and Hellyer to deliver his remaining support to Winters.

Had there been a direct relationship of loyalty between the delegates and the candidates these efforts to transfer votes should have been successful.

As Tables 4 and 5 show, if such designations of the candidates attempting to direct their supporters had been used to predict delegate behaviour on the subsequent ballot, the probability of an accurate prediction would have been reasonably good in only two cases: among Fulton voters at the Conservative Convention and among Hellyer voters at the Liberal Convention. In the other cases, delegates did not behave in any pattern characteristically different from that of delegates supporting candidates who made no attempt to transfer their votes.

We have shown that the party elite, either as members of candidate organizations or as supporters of candidates tried to manipulate the delegates in favour of the candidates of their choice. These intermediaries became active at the time of conventions for a variety of reasons. It is not necessary to assume that their interests will coincide with the candidates whom they supported and who were attempting to transfer votes. In fact the best way to conceptualize the support structure around the candidate is in terms of a pyramid of linkages. At the apex of the pyramid are the members of the candidate's official organization; linked to each of them at the next level are 'supporters' who have no official status but have volunteered or been persuaded to take a minimal activist role. Linked to the 'supporters' at the bottom of the pyramid, are the 'neutral' delegates who have been persuaded to vote for the candidate, but are not involved in any other way. An intermediary may be placed at either the second or the third level and it need not be assumed that the interests of the intermediary and the defeated candidate will coincide. The intermediary may have a primary loyalty to another group or he may assess the beneficial behaviour for him to be different from the beneficial behaviour for the candidate. The delegate may owe his loyalty to an intermediary and it is from this intermediary that he will take direction.

Take the Hees case for instance. The Quebec delegates supporting Hees were under pressure from Union Nationale organizers to vote for Roblin. In the event, these Quebec delegates did support Roblin, while the other Hees delegates tended to support Stanfield, as Hees had directed.

TABLE 4: Voting Behaviour on Immediately Succeeding Ballot of Conservative Convention Delegates Supporting Candidates Dropped or Withdrawing on Preliminary Ballots

Delegates Who Had Been Supporters Of	Ballot Dropped	Candidate To Whom Delegates Directed	Percentage Who Voted For		
			Roblin	Stanfield	Other
McCutcheon	2	Stanfield (N= 39) ⟶	18.0	41.0	41.0
Hees	3	Stanfield (N= 81) ⟶	34.1	42.0	24.0
Fulton	4	Stanfield (N=154) ⟶	29.0	64.3	6.7
Diefenbaker	3	None (N= 54) ⟶	34.0	26.0	40.0
Hamilton	4	None (N= 59) ⟶	51.0	37.0	12.0
Fleming	2	None (N= 50) ⟶	22.0	32.0	46.0
Starr	1	None (N= 19) ⟶	21.1	10.5	68.4

TABLE 5: Voting Behaviour on Immediately Succeeding Ballot of Liberal Convention Delegates Supporting Candidates Dropped or Withdrawing on Preliminary Ballots

Delegates Who Had Been Supporters Of	Ballot Dropped	Candidate To Whom Delegates Directed	Percentage Who Voted For			
			Trudeau	Turner	Winters	Other
Greene	3	Trudeau (N- 14)[1] ⟶	35.7	7.1	50.0	7.1
MacEachen[2]	2	Trudeau (N- 70) ⟶	47.1	17.1	28.6	8.2
Hellyer	3	Winters (N-156) ⟶	23.1	7.1	69.2	—
Martin	1	None (N-111) ⟶	20.7	16.2	35.1	28.0
Kierans	1	None (N- 48) ⟶	52.1	16.7	12.5	18.7

[1]Greene's support had substantially eroded before he decided to withdraw. Thus there were only 14 delegates in our sample who were still with him when he finally withdrew.

[2]MacEachen's name was not officially withdrawn until ballot three, because of the late delivery of his formal statement of withdrawal to the convention chairman. Since delegates had been informed, at the end of ballot two, of his decision to support Trudeau, however, we have chosen this ballot for the test.

Obviously the space available to us does not permit us to explore the full implications of this problem here. The problem of looking for bloc voting in response to cues is a complex one. It will be explored in greater detail, using much more complicated tests, in later publications.

Summary

In summary, we hold that there are at least three reasons for raising doubts about the claim that the leadership conventions are indicative of the progress towards a more open and participatory politics in Canada. While the secret ballot protects the rights of each delegate's independent choice, it does not free him from exposure to manipulative pressures before he exercises that right. Our data indicate that opportunities existed for such manipulation and that efforts to manipulate delegates were made by all major candidate organizations. Our evidence suggests that even with the secret ballot some groups of dele-

gates did act in bloc. We have also been able to show that the party elite protected its position at the convention through manipulation of convention rules. Both in terms of numbers and activism they were able to dominate the conventions.

These two findings gain further significance in the context of our third point that the delegates to these conventions come almost exclusively from the most privileged groups within Canadian society. In response to this point, it may be argued that it simply reflects the basic cultural context of the Canadian political system. Lack of political participation by lower status groups may thus be explained by the cultural factors of their lower sense of political efficacy, lower sense of satisfaction with the outputs of governments and lower affect for the symbols of the system. It may be argued that within the limited context of the conventions there is very little that political parties can do to encourage greater participation by these groups. These cultural factors are closely linked to the structural factor of control over economic resources. Defenders of the claims of the parties may even argue that the parties made substantial efforts to overcome the problem by offering travel subsidies to the delegates. But these subsidies met only a portion of the delegate's expenses. As one key informant put it, even with the subsidies, "for a fisherman from New Brunswick the cost of attending the (Progressive Conservative) Convention could amount to a month's wages."

If the parties are sincere in their claims to want to open their decision-making processes, they must obviously make far more radical reforms in their organization and modus operandi.

NOTES

1. Stanbury, R. J., *Liberal Party of Canada*, (mimeo June 15, 1969) (emphasis in the original) p. 3.
2. We use the term 'elite' to refer simply to those who hold power. Operationally, we define the elite in a party to embrace those who hold party office or those who hold public office as a consequence of their party role. It may be argued that the operational definition excludes the 'power-holders' who have no formal organizational role. In the context within which this paper is set such 'power-holders', meaning financiers and providers of similar resources, could affect the outcome of the conventions only through the operationally defined elites. We feel, further, that if there did exist such 'power-holders' their role was irrelevant, except through differential resources of different candidates, to the argument of this paper.
3. Liberal Federation of Canada, *Constitutional Amendments*, p. 20.
4. A thorough exposition of organization and procedure at earlier conventions is presented in Ruth M. Bell, *Conservative Party National Conventions 1927-1956*, unpublished M.A. thesis, Carleton University, 1965.
5. Flora MacDonald, whose memorandum on the practice of past conventions was the basis for the delegate apportionment proposals made to the Committee, says the suggestion that there should not be ex-officio delegates, to her knowledge, was never considered. Miss MacDonald and other key informants who were asked about this point took the position that there were certain members of the party who, by virtue of the importance of their positions or the nature of their service, were entitled to an assured place at the Convention.
6. Paul T. David, Ralph M. Goldman, and Richard C. Bain, *The Politics of National Party Conventions*, Washington, 1960, p. 194.
7. For example, Fulton's campaign manager, Lowell Murray, was appointed as a delegate-at-large from Ontario, although, except for the fact of living in Ottawa, he was not directly involved with the Ontario party.

Private Experience and Attempts at Redefining Public Relationships

The Use of Force

Please don't believe
The use of force
Is how we change the social course;
The use of force
You surely know
Is how we keep the status quo.

John K. Rooke

Private Experience and Attempts at Redefining Public Relationships

In earlier sections of the book we have instanced cases of public and private definitions of space as well as the various difficulties attending the actual uses of the space available. The final two sections are concerned with continuing crises in the ways that different groups make sense of social relationships as well as the changing structural features that affect people's perceptions of relationships. This section is concerned entirely with attempts to create new bases for relationships. Zentner's essay is primarily about the ways that changes in public policy seem to precipitate crises in the life-styles of Indians. The summary by Ann Charney of Pierre Vallières' book and the excerpt from the book itself suggest the ways that a personal life-history in French Canada led to the rejection of the entire set of values and relations that operate not only in Canada but throughout North America. Krista Maeots and Caroline Brown in different ways suggest how student protest, pacifism and radical socialism emerged both out of the daily experiences of the participants and out of the examples of other societies. Krista Maeots also suggests the problems of actually developing any political strategy on which the groups could agree. Latowsky and Kelner outline the ideology behind the establishment of communes and a youth counter-culture. These essays are purely suggestive of the many ways that people attempt to redefine relationships. On radical redefinitions examples may also be found in Women's Liberation, the emergence of the CCF in Saskatchewan, or in the growth of movements protesting against pollution and the destruction of the environment. Alternatively, there might be essays on various forms of fundamentalist Christianity and the Edmund Burke Society. The dramatic growth of movements concerned with Canadian national autonomy (such as the Committee for an Independent Canada) are further examples of sections of the population responding to changes which affect their life-styles or attempting to induce changes to produce different life-styles.

It is not the purpose of this book to evaluate these movements. The task for sociologists is to understand how they arise, which types of people support them, what views they have about society and what strategies they develop against the society they wish to change. It is also important to try to assess how important they are, which really means assessing what strength they have in influence and how other sections of society respond to their growth. There are various attempts by sociologists to put such movements in context. The most important introductions are probably:

N. J. Smelser, *Theory of Collective Behaviour*, Free Press, 1963

Roger Brown, *Social Psychology*, Chapter 9, Free Press, 1966

Stan Cohen (Ed.), *Images of Deviance*, Penguin, 1971

Alfred Willener, *The Action-Image of Society*, Tavistock, 1970

E. J. Hobsbawm, *Primitive Rebels*, University of Manchester Press, 1956

I. The Impending Identity Crisis Among Native Peoples

Henry Zentner /*University of Calgary*

Not all a group's spatial boundaries are imposed from outside. As we noted in Smith's essay on household ecology and as we see once again in this selection, many of the boundaries are set up by the group itself from within, as a deliberate distancing technique to maintain the group's own separate and intrinsic identity. Nor do all attempts to change those boundaries come from within, as this essay makes plain. The boundaries that demarcate the Indians' social space are cultural and socio-historical as well as legal and economic. The breaking down of these latter, it is feared, will mean an invasion of cultural boundaries as well with some very real consequences for personal identity.

We have commented before on the role of property in defining private space. Eschewing ownership, the Athabascan Indian has a perception of social space quite different from that of the North American white. He has no public space, in the sense we have used that term in this volume, and his private space is limited, essentially, to the nuclear family. In this almost total absence of social space, public or private, the Athabascan experience is one of an intensely personal privatism.

It is most instructive to read this essay in conjuction with the one by Latowsky and Kelner on youth.

Reprinted from *Prairie Perspectives*, edited by David P. Gagan, by permission of Holt, Rinehart and Winston of Canada Limited. © 1970.

The recent announcement by the Government of Canada of its new Indian policy would appear to pose the most serious threat to their identity yet faced by native peoples. The explicit aim of the new policy is to bring about a shift from the ostensibly unequal status with which native peoples are currently faced to a state of full and complete equality with all other Canadians. "This Government," the statement alleges, "believes in equality. It believes that all men and women have equal rights. It is determined that all shall be treated fairly and that no one shall be shut out of Canadian life, and especially that no one shall be shut out because of his race."[1] Further, "The Indian people . . . are entitled to an equality which preserves and enriches Indian identity and distinction; an equality which stresses Indian participation in its (i.e., the policy's) creation and which manifests itself in all aspects of Indian life."[2] And finally, "True equality presupposes that the Indian people have the right to full and equal participation in the cultural, social, economic and political life of Canada."[3]

The concrete steps which this objective requires are given as follows: "The government believes that the framework within which individual Indians and bands could achieve full participation requires: (1) that the legislative and constitutional bases of discrimination be removed; (2) that there be positive recognition by everyone of the unique contribution of Indian culture to Canadian life; (3) that services come through the same channels and from the same government agencies for all Canadians; (4)

that those who are furthest behind be helped most; (5) that lawful obligations be recognized; and (6) that control of Indian lands be transferred to the Indian people."[4] The Government's White Paper goes on to say that some of the proposed changes could take place quickly, while others would take longer. It is expected, for example, that within five years the Department of Indian Affairs and Northern Development would cease to operate in the field of Indian Affairs and that new laws would be in effect and existing programs would have been devolved by that time. The Indian lands would require special attention for some continuing period of time and the process of transferring control to the Indian people would be under continuous review.

This new policy, then, allegedly promises all Indian people a new and ostensibly equal opportunity to expand and develop their identity within the framework of a Canadian society. This society offers them the rewards and responsibilities of participation, the benefits of involvement, and the pride of belonging. It is evident therefore that in the name of equality the Government is determined that in future the Indian will be compelled to do to and for himself what the Government has historically done to and for him. And it is in this proposal that there inheres the threat to native culture and identity.

The Government's policy appears to rest upon a number of assumptions. It assumes, first of all, that Indians constitute a unitary and undifferentiated category of the Canadian population. It overlooks the fact that there is a wide spectrum of linguistic, ethnic and cultural differences which distinguishes native peoples from one another. It also overlooks the fact that at the time of initial contact with Europeans as well as at the time that reservation status was imposed upon them, some of the native peoples were far more technologically and organizationally advanced than were others. The members of the Iroquois Confederacy, for example, were horticulturalists and had developed advanced politico-military organizational linkages among themselves. Others, such as the Kwakiutl, Salish and Haida on the Pacific coast, were 'ocean farmers' and enjoyed considerable wealth and internal social and occupational differentiation. Still others, such as the Blackfoot, Assinaboia, and Cree located in the Plains region, were hunters and gatherers with far less advanced social and political organization. Yet a blanket policy is to be uniformly applied to all Indians without regard to these cultural and historical differences.

The new policy further assumes that the issue of equality turns solely on existing legal, administrative and economic barriers. It assumes that despite a century or more of wardship status on the part of reservation Indians, with its associated lack of control over their own affairs and the absence of skills in the management of them, all that is lacking at the present time is opportunity. Given opportunity, so the Government's thinking seems to run, the Indian will forthwith seize the initiative which has for so long been denied him and henceforth manage his affairs with vigor and dispatch, as would any other member of Canadian society. At best this view would appear to rest upon an altogether unwarranted optimism concerning native skills and motivations; at worst, it would appear to involve a desperate attempt to solve 'the white man's problem' without regard to the problem as native peoples see it.

What the new policy appears to overlook, indeed assumes out of existence, is that with all due respect to native differences in ethnicity, culture and historical experience, the Indian is not a Euro-Canadian; that however advanced his state of assimilation, his mentality has been and continues to be moulded by a very different cultural and historical tradition: that the values he holds and the goals which he seeks to realize in his life and his society are at many points in radical conflict with those of his fellow Canadians; and, finally, that the sense of a separate and distinct identity which he may not be able to define, but which he seeks to maintain and to extend is often felt to be contingent upon *not* doing the very things which the new policy will in effect compel him to do. Viewed from this perspective, then, the crucial issue appears as one of motivation rather than opportunity. Were the Indian 'properly motivated' all, no doubt, would be well. But that he has not in the past been so motivated seems beyond question; that he is now we may reasonably doubt.

For notwithstanding the well-intentioned and often heroic efforts of missionaries and the less frequently well-intentioned efforts of both private and governmental agencies of various kinds and over varying periods of time, many of these native peoples continue to evidence *an apparent inability* to comprehend and to accept the values, the technology and the organizational forms of their conquerors. Rather, in the eyes of their critics they continue to be imbued with a mystical concept of destiny. They lack an appreciation of the importance of time. They have only limited confidence in their knowledge and techniques with which to meet the environment. They seek to apprehend truth by means of affective rather than cognitive and empirical criteria. They are profligate with money and fail to understand its less immediately obvious economic utility and social functions. Their lack of foresight and co-ordinated planning allegedly borders on laziness and improvidence. They are likewise charged with being devoid of logic and rationality in their approach to life and its problems. Finally, while it is conceded that they are prone to share freely with others such material objects as food, clothing and shelter, they evidence a spiritual individuality and a moral indifference to the welfare of others. In brief, the critics of native peoples make the opposite assumption to that of the Government of Canada, namely, that in view of their apparent intransigence, ignorance, superstition, laziness, improvidence and lack of personal initiative, native people *cannot* be assimilated.

From the perspective of the social scientist the views of both the Government and the critics of native peoples appear too simplistic. As noted above, the former rests its case on an assumed lack of opportunity, whereas the latter, by implication, argues from the premise of an innate lack of skills and capacity. Again, the former overestimates while the latter underestimates the changes which have already taken place in native cultures and behavior patterns – a consequence of the wardship status which the Canadian Government has imposed upon them. But significantly both points of view fail to take cognizance of the fact that the motivation of behavior in native societies, as in any society, is predicated upon a more or less unique perception and definition of the experiential world which its members share. This patterned totality has been termed a society's world-view. And it is a society's world-view which provides the substantive content of its members' mentality. So too this world-view constitutes the bedrock in which is anchored the intuitive sense they have of a unique identity.

Viewed analytically, a society's world-view may be regarded as an amalgam of a number of inter-related components, including; (1) a cosmogony, i.e., a set of beliefs concerning the origin and destiny of man, society, nature and the supernatural; (2) a set of ethical precepts concerning the morally imperative relationships between man, society, nature and the supernatural; and (3) a set of idealized conceptions concerning desirable standards of conduct and behavior. In the interest of convenience, however, it may be sufficient if we think of these categories as corresponding to what in more common parlance have been termed mythology, values, and a social ethic, respectively. Since Max Weber's classic description of what he termed the Protestant Ethic, the notion of specific types of social ethics has been more widely adopted.[5] The present essay follows in this same tradition. In an attempt to illuminate the motivational structure which hypothetically continues to characterize, albeit in varying degree, many native cultures in the Plains region, there follows an anlysis of what can be termed the Pre-Neolithic Ethic. Implied in this conception is the notion that the mythology and values of hunting and gathering peoples give rise to a radically different form of the ideal character structure endorsed by the members of such societies. Although the specific ethnographic data to be analyzed derive from reports on certain Athabascan-speaking peoples of the Canadian North, it is suggested that the observations which follow may, with modifications, have application to peoples in the Plains region whose culture was historically grounded in a hunting and gathering economy and whose religious beliefs were animistic in type.[6]

The Mythological Tradition

Among the Athabascan-speaking peoples of the Canadian North the economy is highly individuated. In the typical case the area occupied by the society simply *exists*, rather than being 'owned,' and is available for use to any individual on the basis of need. Although there is present the custom of sharing material resources, each man is expected to provide for himself and his immediate dependents the necessary food and raw materials essential to survival. And indeed, in a hunting and gathering type of economy, more than this is all but impossible. Thus there is neither occupational specialization nor private property involving land.

In respect of their social organization, the culture emphasizes and the economy compels grouping into nuclear family units, with close affective ties existing only between the members of this constricted social entity. Political organization is non-existent. Outside the bounds of the nuclear family, leadership and authority are almost totally lacking. This is despite the fact that given individuals may acquire differential prestige on the basis of skill in warfare, hunting or healing. Such social distinction, however, carries with it no power to command, nor any obligation to obey. Each family unit remains a law unto itself, as it were. The head of such a unit is compelled to rely upon his own resources, to provide for and protect its members as best he can, and to seek directly from nature supernatural power, authority and sanctions for his behavior.

The mythology of these peoples is highly correlated with their economic and social conditions and has as its distinguishing feature the pre-eminent place in human experience ascribed to nature. Nature appears to be the pervasive force, the governing principle, and the abiding condition in which man and society are constituted. Nature, moreover, is seen as extremely complex and mysterious, as suffused and animated by powerful supernatural forces, and as capricious and dominant over man. Good and evil remain undifferentiated and are seen to randomly pervade nature in all its manifestations. In consequence, it is the better part of wisdom for man to subordinate himself, to blend with nature, and to constitute himself an analogue to the forces which inhere in her. It is this belief that inspires the quest for supernatural power in the form of a guardian spirit. This spirit reveals the requisite knowledge by which the otherwise mysterious and capricious forces inherent in nature can be brought under a measure of control.

Ethnographic reports allege that contact with the supernatural commonly occurs during the course of a dream or a vision. Most accounts tell of the appearance of an apparition. On first appearance it is manifest in human form. In the 'dialogue' which ensues between the supplicant and the apparition, the latter talks with him, giving him a song or a formula for the achievement of some given purpose. As it is leaving it turns into a plant or animal. The supplicant thereupon knows what plant or animal has blessed him and what skin, bone, feathers or whatnot he needs to acquire to place in his sacred medicine bundle. The awesome mystery and power of nature, and the weakness, the dependence, and ephemeral nature of man and society are consequently strongly reinforced in his mind and his experience.

Having experienced contact with the supernatural forces in such an intensely personal and emotional manner, the individual enters into a life-long relationship of dependence with his guardian spirit upon whom he thereafter relies for assistance, guidance, and protection. Indeed, the possession of such a spiritual guardian is, for the native, tantamount to having achieved salvation in a sense which is altogether analogous to that of the Christian tradition. In being so favoured he has met and been joined with the supernatural. But in this there inheres an important distinction. Salvation for the native takes place near the beginning of adult life, whereas for the adherent of the Christian tradition salvation occurs only after death, if at all. The former spends his life in complete confidence that he has achieved it, the latter is engaged in a life-long attempt to prepare himself for its eventual realization. And this, as will be evident later, gives the native a temporal orientation markedly different from that of his counterpart in modern society.

Grounded as it thus is in private and subjective experience, the acquisition of power becomes a self-fulfilling prophecy. Since the individual feels he has power, he behaves as though he had it. What begins as a wish becomes transmuted into a reality. In the eyes of others the supernatural basis of an individual's power as well as its validity can be determined only in pragmatic terms. If the claimant accomplishes what he set out to do, his success serves as *prima facie* evidence of the validity of his claim.

It is not without significance, however, that such pragmatic evidence of power inspires both envy and fear in others. An individual is envied because his presumed powers make him effective in hunting or healing. The fear of him arises out of the possibility that such power might result in the use of superior physical force or in the form of sorcery and witchcraft against other members of the society. But since all members of society are in quest of such power and many succeed in acquiring it in one degree or another, the net effect is to render every man a potentially dangerous enemy of every other. Thus, if the hand of both nature and society are equally turned against him, the individual stands alone in a potentially hostile environment. Under such conditions, the stance that he must adopt toward it and the logic and rationality which he must employ in adapting to it, will be grounded in the tutelary relationship which the individual has with his own unique spirit guardian. And since under these same conditions concepts of logic and rationality are highly individuated and discretely held by members of the society, the range and scope of collective action which can be undertaken in the economic, religious and political spheres of native life are necessarily extremely restricted. The pre-requisite values essential to the motivation of organizational behavior are simply lacking. And it is to an examination of these in some detail that the present analysis must now turn.

Value Commitments

Students of value systems in modern societies have cited a considerable number of dominant value themes. Robin M. Williams, Jr., for example, in his analysis of American society has cited a total of fifteen dominant values.[7] Included are the following: (1) individualism; (2) democracy; (3) freedom; (4) equality; (5) humanitarianism; (6) activity and work; (7) efficiency and practicality; (8) science and secular rationality; (9)

achievement and success; (10) material comfort; (11) progress; (12) external conformity; (13) nationalism-patriotism; (14) racism and group superiority; and (15) moral orientation. It seems reasonable to assume that with possible variations in degree this same value profile is equally characteristic of Canadian society. But significantly, it is the difference in the degree to which different segments of Canadian society endorse and enact these respective values and the variant mythological traditions associated with such differential endorsements that concern us in the present context.

Viewed analytically, it is apparent that this value profile can be broken up into a number of clusters which closely correspond to the institutional spheres in which they are predominantly given expression. Individualism, democracy, freedom, equality and humanitarianism, for example, would appear to find expression primarily in the political sphere. Alternatively, activity and work, efficiency and practicality, science and secular rationality, achievement and success, and progress tend to be given expression largely in the economic sphere. The remainder would appear to be more diffuse in their expression, being manifest in all spheres of behavior. In the interest of brevity, therefore, this latter cluster will be excluded from the analysis which follows and the focus of attention will be upon the two clusters identified earlier as being associated with the political and economic spheres, respectively. If we now attempt to relate these two value clusters to the property conceptions and temporal orientations held by the native peoples in purview, the interplay between their mythological tradition and the degree of endorsement of them will become apparent.

Respecting the cluster of values associated with the political sphere, namely, individualism, democracy, freedom, equality, and humanitarianism, it is perhaps not without significance that native peoples are never subjected to censure for the lack of endorsement of these values. And this for good reason inasmuch as these are among the values which are present in their cultures. Not only are they uniformly held by members of native societies, but their endorsement of them is dogmatic and absolute. The reason is not far to seek. The fears and anxieties associated with their conception of the supernatural and the dangers associated with the possession of supernatural power conduce to an intensely motivated antipathy toward the invasion of another's privacy, toward authority, toward hierarchy, and toward coercion and manipulation of others. At the same time humanitarian sharing of material wealth is likewise predicated upon the fear of another's magical powers which might be exercised if such mutuality in respect of material things is not forthcoming. Accordingly, the respect which is paid to the individual borders on the absolute.

With regard to that cluster of values associated with the economic sphere, namely, activity and work, efficiency and practicality, science and secular rationality, achievement and success, and progress, the situation is quite otherwise. The endorsement of these values presupposes the existence of private property, an occupationally differentiated society, a predisposition toward a rational-empirical as opposed to a magical-intuitive mode of acquiring knowledge, and a temporal orientation to the future rather than the present. In all of these respects the native societies in purview are grossly lacking. Indeed, these economic values are the very antitheses of the political values which they so dogmatically hold.

For as we have seen, the physical space occupied by these natives is a collectively held area which all are free to use according to their needs and for such periods of time as may be required. In native eyes this space and the objects which exist in it are like themselves a part of a larger undifferentiated unity in nature from which none can be separated. Accordingly, the native comes to identify uniformly with the physical space controlled by the society, rather than with particular parts of it which happen to be associated with his own uniquely personal interests. Given these property concepts as well as the extremely limited technological potential of the societies in question, the question of space appropriated for private and alternative uses logically cannot arise. The things which the native counts as his private property are his names, his songs, his dances, his weapons, his medicines, and his spirit guardian. These are his to use in his quest for differential prestige and in terms of which he measures his achievement and success. But his achievement and success arise out of his capacity to manipulate nature. His exploits do not embrace his fellow man.

The native's temporal orientation likewise militates against an endorsement of these same values. For as has been noted the act of achieving salvation, of acquiring supernatural power with which to manipulate nature, typically occurs at the onset of adult life. Moreover, the substantive content of this experience serves only to reinforce the individual's identification of himself as part and parcel of nature. Accordingly, in both his highly individuated spiritual life as well as in his economic life, he remains obsessed by the rhythms of nature. And these are endlessly cyclical in nature. Unlike his modern counterpart, he does not see life extending forward in a linear fashion to some anticipated ultimate climax in which he will achieve salvation. For him this climactic event has already occurred in the past and its meaning and significance is immediately and intimately linked with the cyclical rhythms of nature. Lacking as he does a written record of the past as well as an idealized temporal future, his orientation remains linked to the present – a present which has its genesis in a vague and ill-defined past and which links to an equally vague and ill-defined future. Time is not something to be treasured and conserved. Rather, it is something to be consumed. Accordingly, time in the abstract sense has little meaning for the native. Its value can be realized only in terms of the opportunities which it presents for the satisfaction of minimal physical needs essential to survival. There simply are no alternative uses to which time can be devoted.[8]

In the light of these considerations it is scarcely suprising to find that activity and work are not conceived as leading to enhanced status either in this world or the next. For given the lack of occupational specialization, they may eventuate in gaining a modicum of differential prestige, but one's status will remain unaltered. And since this possibility remains closed to the individual, there is no motivational basis upon which to rest deferment of gratifications in the present in return for future rewards in some greater degree. Achievements and success, therefore, beyond the bounds of physical survival, are largely without meaning to the native.

Efficiency and practicality as valued ends likewise have comparatively little meaning in the eyes of native peoples. Neither do science and secular rationality since they are without linkages to other dominant values held. For as we have seen, the native cultures in purview emphasized passive adjustment to the environment as opposed to active mastery. In place of precise empirical observation and measurement the native cultures emphasized continuous revelation through the medium of the guardian spirit. And since knowledge was to be apprehended by means of affective rather than cognitive criteria, the emphasis was placed upon feeling, intuition, mysticism and fate as against observation, measurement, planning, foresight and reason. Planning and foresight can have meaning only as the planner can assume that he is able to predict and to anticipate the probable consequences of current action in the prospective future. This implies knowledge and an understanding of nature which native societies, given their inadequately developed science and technology, simply lack. And in the absence of any significant development of these several economic values, there was no place for any meaningful concept of progress.

The Pre-Neolithic Ethic

The ideal character structure elaborated in the societies in purview, then centered on the concept of a man who, through a dream or a vision, has acquired supernatural power from nature; who by virtue of having such power has achieved certain practical skills, courage and resourcefulness in hunting or healing; who shares freely with others the material benefits accruing to him as a consequence of such powers and skills; who is intensely concerned with his own spiritual welfare and who respects the spiritual individuality of others; who avoids manipulating others and resists being manipulated by them; who is sensitive to the qualitative and emotional aspects of life and experience; and who above all, is attuned to the mystery and power of nature, who is aware of her and in harmony with her. This, then, is the Pre-Neolithic Ethic which is current among the native peoples of the Canadian North.

The question that now concerns us is the extent to which this ethic continues to manifest itself in the behavior of native peoples who have been cut off from their traditional hunting and gathering economy and have become partially assimilated to the culture of the dominant society. No definitive answer to this question can be given at the present time. Nevertheless, there is much presumptive evidence to suggest that it continues to persist, albeit in modified and attenuated form.[9] Its mythological underpinnings have no doubt been weakened, where they have not been displaced, as a consequence of educational influences and cultural borrowing, most particularly among the younger generation. But having once been institutionalized, it continues to persist in a secularized form in much the same way that the Protestant Ethic continues as a secularized pattern in Canadian society, despite its current divorcement from Calvinistic theology.

Notwithstanding the noisy clamor emanating from the advocates of 'Red Power,' native societies in the Plains region continue to evidence high levels of social pathology and a lack of effective social control over individual behavior. Individualism, freedom, democracy, equality and humanitarianism continue to be dogmatically adhered to. The widespread tendency to accept a subsistence pattern based upon public assistance suggests that the traditional emphasis upon sharing of material wealth remains essentially unaltered, despite its current manifestation at the collective level in the relations between the band as a whole and the Government. Alternatively, work, efficiency, rationality, achievement and progress as valued ends have been given but limited adoption. Individualism is still highly respected and authority, hierarchy, planning, punctuality and the manipulation, whether of other individuals or the society as a whole, continue to be eschewed. The fact that all meaningful political authority and decision-making power has been in the hands of the Government and its agents throughout the period of reservation status has done little to alter these continuing cultural propensities.

But presumably the Government's new policy is going to change all this with a single stroke. Native societies will henceforth be charged with the responsibility for the management of their own affairs, with achieving equality, and with preserving and extending their unique identities. To the extent that the values, motivations and skills requisite to this task are lacking, native societies face the challenge of acquiring them overnight as it were. And assuming that this challenge can somehow be effectively met and native societies do move forward to a position of equality, what implications would this state of affairs have for the preservation and extension of their respective identities?

Quite clearly, if native peoples are to meet the challenge of managing their own affairs, the requisite motivations and skills will have to be taken over from the culture of the dominant society. They will have to adopt the principles of authority, hierarchy, planning, punctuality, and above all, manipulative techniques and practices. All this implies that the values currently placed on individualism, democracy, freedom, equality, and humanitarianism will have to be compromised and relativized. In other words, they will have to take on the attitudes, values and practices which are at present current in the dominant society. And having done this, what besides a hollow illusion can possibly remain of their cherished sense of unique identity?

Some might point to language, others to art and crafts, still others to religious songs, dances and ceremonies. But without the mythology, the values and the Ethic which such things express and in terms of which they alone become meaningful, who will there be to sustain and perpetuate them? Will they not in the end survive only as museum pieces and as cultural curios? The history of majority-minority cultural relations leaves little room for optimism on this point. To the extent that native peoples are brought to a state of genuine equality, they will of necessity be abandoning the very things that make them different. And as these things are surrendered, so will the sense of unique identity be lost. In their continuing search for a meaningful balance between equality and identity, then, native peoples would be wise to make haste slowly. For in so doing they will not only optimize the social costs and benefits accruing to them as a consequence of modernization, but they will also reaffirm the continuing validity of Canada's historic attachment to a policy of ethnic and cultural pluralism – a policy on which the present Government of Canada appears, in this instance at any rate, to have declared a moratorium.

NOTES

1. Jean Chrétien, *Statement of the Government of Canada on Indian Policy,*1969 (Ottawa: Queen's Printer, 1969)p.6.
2. *Ibid.*
3. *Ibid.*
4. *Ibid.*
5. See, for example, Richard T. LaPiere, *The Freudian Ethic* (New York: Duell, Sloan and Pearce, 1959).
6. A general discussion of these practices among Plains Indians appears in Ruth Benedict, *Patterns of Culture* (New York: The New American Library, 1934). The present analysis, however, is based upon a number of sources which are listed below as a guide to further reading. See Cornelius B. Osgood, *The Ethnography of the Great Bear Lake Indians* (Ottawa: National Museum of Canada, Bulletin No. 70, 1931); Diamond Jenness, *The Sekani Indians of British Columbia* (Ottawa: National Museum of Canada, Bulletin No. 84, 1937); Diamond Jenness, *The Sarcee Indians of Alberta* (Ottawa: National Museum of Canada, Bulletin No. 90, 1938); John J. Honigmann, *Ethnography and Acculturation of the Fort Nelson Slave* (Yale University Publications in Anthropology, No. 33, New Haven: Yale University Press, 1946); John J. Honigmann, *Culture and Ethos of Kaska Society* (Yale University Publications in Anthropology, No. 40, New Haven: Yale University Press, 1949); John J. Honigmann, *The Kaska Indians: An Ethnographic Reconstruction* (Yale University Publications in Anthropology, New Haven: Yale University Press, 1954); June Helm MacNeish, "Contemporary Folk Beliefs of a Slave Indian Band," *Journal of American Folklore,* 67 (1954), pp. 185-98; June Helm MacNeish, "Leadership Among the Northeastern Athabascans," *Anthropologia,* O.S.II (1956), pp. 131-63; and J. MacNeish, *The Lynx Point People: The Dynamics of a Northern Athabaskan Band* (Ottawa: National Museum of Canada, Bulletin No. 176, 1961).
7. Robin M. Williams, Jr., American Society: *A Sociological Interpretation* (New York: Alfred A. Knopf, 1951).
8. For a more extensive analysis of the relationship between temporal and spatial phenomena, see Henry Zentner, "The Social Time-Space Relationship: A Theoretical Formulation," *Sociological Inquiry,* XXXVI (Winter, 1966), 61-79. State College, 1967), *passim*
9. See Arthur K. Davis, *et al., A Northern Dilemma: Reference Papers,* Vols. I and II (Bellingham, Washington: Western Washington State College, 1967), *passim.*

2. Personal Experience and the Redefinition of Power Relationships

Pierre Vallières/*Revolutionary*

This passionate statement from a revolutionary for whom the bourgeois utilitarian economy with its intense espousal of individualism both as a justification and a moral value has meant the denial, to the individual, of any personal space and, to the group, access to public space. This selection is the last chapter of Vallières' book White Niggers of America.

Because of the insights it gives us into the man and into the revolutionary cause he espouses, we add here a review of White Niggers *by Ann Charney that appeared in* The Canadian Forum.

The publication of an English version of Pierre Vallières' book, Nègres blancs d'Amérique, *is an important and welcome event. Coming as it does after the recent Quebec crisis, this book may do more to explain it, than the entire flood of analysis and interpretation that has been flowing at us from all directions.*

The analysis we find here is not tailored to the event; the book was written three years before the crisis, and it will be read with interest when most of the books written by experts of the moment have been forgotten.

Unlike these other works, White Niggers of America *is written from the inside, its point of view is that of the active participant, its description of social conditions (and the effect of these conditions on the people who are formed by them) has its source in first hand experience. Very early in the book Vallières warns us of this perspective: "The ideas expressed lay no claim to the objectivity of a neutral person: they are biased and political." At the same time he reminds us that "objectivity too is an ideology – the ideology of the status quo."*

Yet it is unfair to speak of this book only in terms of the crisis and related political events. Its attraction is much broader. It is one of those rare works which manages somehow, through one individual's experience to capture the spirit of a particular generation. Prepared as one is by the public image of Vallières – Marxist, revolutionary, fanatic, prisoner – the great surprise that comes in reading this book is that in spite of all that separates us from him, those of us who grew up in Montreal during the fifties and early sixties recognize parts of our own past in this book.

White Niggers of America *is in fact two books: the autobiography of Pierre Vallières, and a political treatise. In the latter he traces, in one section, the historical development of the people he calls "white niggers". In another section he discusses and rejects the various ideologies that have preoccupied him in his attempts to cope with the world around him. In a last part he describes his conception of the ideal state and the conditions essential to its creation.*

Large chunks of philosophy and personal meditation mingle with the narrative of a life. As a result, there is little unity of tone or emphasis throughout the book. It is not a literary work as such, written in leisure, with sufficient time for corrections, revisions, consultations with editors.

The Introduction is reprinted from *The Canadian Forum*, (April-May 1971) by permission of the author and the publisher.

Reprinted from *White Niggers of America*, by Pierre Vallières, by permission of The Canadian Publishers, McClelland and Stewart Limited, Toronto. © 1971.

In the original French version, the uneven quality of the book does not detract from the powerful emotional force that it exerts. The English translation, while faithful and adequate, loses much of this impact. The narrative has lost its tone of fatality, it seems flat and ordinary.

Its form is determined to a large extent by the conditions in which it was written; it is a book written in prison, by someone who through imposed solitude and self-imposed analysis, discovers many things about himself and his world. He tries to get them all out and into one book because he is uncertain when and if he will be permitted to express himself again, or to have contact with his fellow men.

Vallières subtitled his book "the precocious autobiography of a Quebec terrorist". The English edition has dropped the subtitle, unfortunately I feel, since it indicated the emphasis Vallières chose to give the book.

It is in the autobiography rather than in the polemical parts, that the book acquires its hold over the reader. The theoretical sections are a much less effective argument for his political position than the straightforward description of his own early years, the childhood and adolescence of someone who was "vanquished from birth."

Pierre Vallières' life began in 1938, in the east-end French ghetto of Montreal. His father worked as an unskilled labourer for the Angus Company, from the age of 14 until his death at 53. His mother was an embittered, joyless woman, who tried as much as possible to immobilize Pierre and his father from all but the most essential activity, so as to protect them from danger.

From the moment Pierre is old enough to leave the flat, he begins to revolt against his mother's hopelessness and her passive acceptance of her lot. At this age the revolt takes the form of getting away from her and into the streets – a world of violence, teen-age gangs, and games of daring that often ended in serious injury.

At the end of the second world war, his family realizes a long standing dream: a house of their own in the suburbs, on the South Shore of Montreal, with a bit of land where the children can play in the fresh air. In their case, this most classic of North American dreams becomes in reality a nightmare.

The house is a three room wooden shack, covered with brick paper. There are no paved roads or sidewalks, no sewers, no water supply. The children play in a permanent dust cloud, the air is filled with the stench of open trench sewers, water is collected from rainfall and the rest must be bought from the adjoining community, a middle-class neighbourhood that has no scruples about selling its water to its poorer neighbours, while it erects a fence to keep them off its well tended streets.

This miserable community of shacks and people who for the most part live at the extreme limits of endurance, is lorded over by the grocer, who exploits his monopoly to the hilt, two pious spinsters who run the post office, and the local priest. The two ladies and the priest establish a school for the local children. Here Pierre finds himself treated as a savage, who is expected to show constant gratitude to the benevolent missionaries who educate him in the moral and religious principles dear to their hearts. Any other kind of learning, books, libraries, all are non-existent. "We learned about boredom," Pierre tells us, "while listening to the songs of angels."

Throughout his early years in this community, that was to become Ville Jacques Cartier, Pierre's hatred and revolt continue to grow. His mother loses all control over him. His father, sapped by his work, his wife's pessimism, the dissipation of his dream, turns into a ghost-like figure, who sleeps and works and has little to say in between.

Growing up in the midst of adults beaten by life, and those who exploit this weakness for their profit, Pierre meets, for the first time, a man who has come into the community to help. Pierre remembers Dr. Jacques Ferron with affection and tells us that the doctor's quiet devotion to the people had much to do with his eventual commitment.

At the end of elementary school he must make a choice about the future. Thirteen years old, he defies his mother who wants him to study English and bookkeeping so that he may become an office worker, a position that is at the apex of her ambition for her son. Instead, he opts for a classical college which would permit him to enter university.

As a poor boy, the only way he can continue his studies is to pretend a calling for the priesthood. Once again he is expected to show constant piety, gratitude, and humility for the privilege of being educated.

The level of teaching is as inadequate as that which he has always known. For the first time, however, his world extends beyond misery and hopelessness. New friends, from middle class homes, introduce him to the civilized world of books, ideas, and conversation.

At the same time, the situation at home becomes increasingly intolerable, as his mother continues her pressure to make him abandon his studies and do something 'useful'. Exhausted by these daily confrontations, he must also struggle with himself, as his mind seesaws between his desire to change that which is most offensive in his world, and the pessimism in which he was nurtured. This is the period when existentialism has a strong attraction for him and the world around him appears like "an immense cemetery of dead soldiers, men who fought without reason, a war created by others."

Finally he can no longer contain all these struggles in himself. "Actions not sermons" he screams at his teachers. "All priests will be exploiters, cowards, as long as I will not see them helping the Quebec workers, farmers, and students to burn their churches, their seminaries, their presbyteries, their Cadillacs and all the rest." With this outbreak he discards the role he has played until now. Much to the surprise of his teachers, the model student, always at the head of the class, turns against them and leaves the school.

During the next period, Vallières works as a clerk for the brokerage house of Beaubien & Co. Here he discovers that white collar workers are also part of the "cheap labour market, and that they are even more alienated than factory workers or even farmers." In the evening he writes novels which he shows to a few friends and then destroys.

Slowly he finds his way into the intellectual, artistic, French community in Montreal. Spiritually he remains as troubled as ever. Instead of helping his people, as his childhood idol, Dr. Ferron, continues to do, he is an uncomfortable stranger in his own neighbourhood, even in his family. The cafés and art galleries, however, are not his world either. He is equally disenchanted with his old friends from college who are content to sit and talk and remain 'revolutionaries in slippers.'

At this point the poet Gaston Miron becomes his friend and teacher. Vallières credits him as being instrumental in his moving away from philosophical and literary preoccupations to a practical, political commitment. Under his influence he begins to write political essays. The first of these is published in Le Devoir, *in 1957, entitled* The fear to live, *and it touches on his own struggles to shed his cerebral preoccupations for the 'real life.'*

He continues to be obsessed by feelings of guilt and treachery towards the class he was born into. At the same time he is tortured by his inability to do anything for them. In his desperation he makes an attempt at the priesthood, which, after one year of study, he abandons forever.

He returns to his friends, his writing. This is the time just after the death of Duplessis and the beginning of the first thaw in Quebec life which will eventually lead to the 'quiet revolution,' separatism, and the reexamination of all institutions and traditional values of old Quebec. Vallières, inspired by the new freedom, contributes regularly to Cite Libre, *then under the directorship of Pelletier and Trudeau. A special issue of the magazine, on separatism, leads to a crisis between Vallières and Trudeau. Vallières feels that Trudeau has taken advantage of some confidences that he, naively, trusted him with. He finds Trudeau dogmatic about his magazine and unconcerned with the feelings and opinions of his staff and contributors. Disgusted with the intellectual milieu, Vallières, in 1962, sails for Europe.*

He arrives in France, a land of which he has dreamt so often, to find it a sad, abused place, torn apart by its war with Algeria. He finds work as a labourer and his political education continues. It doesn't take long for him to realize that France will never be his country. The only cure for his alienation, is to return to Quebec. A few days after his return in the spring of 1963, the monument to General Wolfe is pulled down in Quebec. The land 'of silence and endless winters' is changing.

On Pelletier's invitation he becomes a journalist for La Presse. *Here, he tells us, his political education completes itself. A subsequent failure as editor of* Cité Libre *to change it into a journal of combat for Quebec workers, cures him forever of the temptations of the intellectual world. From now on, he has nothing but scorn for philosophical or intellectual commitment, in the European tradition of Merleau-Ponty, Camus and Sartre. He turns to the writings of revolutionaries, men of action, and he finds the inspiration he seeks in the revolutionary movements of his own continent. This new direction climaxes in his adherence to the Front for the Liberation of Quebec.*

In 1966 he is arrested, with Charles Gagnon in front of the United Nations while they are demonstrating on behalf of the FLQ and those of its members in Quebec prisons. After four months in the Manhattan House of Detention, where most of this book was written, they are deported to Montreal. He is tried, after waiting in prison one year for his trial, and condemned to life imprisonment for involuntary homicide, on the charge of having contributed to a death by bombing through "his writings, his words, his attitudes, etc." He obtains a second trial which results in a sentence of two and a half years. Released on bail, while waiting for an appeal to be heard, he is again arrested under the War Measures Act and at the time of writing remains in prison.

Most recently, on March 11th, five of the original charges against Vallières, dating from 1966, which have not yet come to trial, and for which he has spent almost four years in prison, were dropped by the Crown. They were replaced by ten new charges of incitement to murder and kidnapping.

Whatever we think of Pierre Vallières' political beliefs, we can not, after reading this book, dismiss him comfortably as a mere fanatic, opportunist, or criminal. The impression he leaves us with is of a man of high intelligence, extreme sensitivity, who has a great empathy for the intolerable conditions in which many people live, even if he could have easily escaped these conditions in his adult life. Above all there is an impression of utter honesty, whose symptoms, as in Vallières' case, are perpetual self-doubt and constant questioning of all those conditions which appear as given to most people. In the epilogue, which has been dropped from the English edition, Vallières, after his most impassioned declaration of faith, returns to the question that always haunts him: "Am I right or wrong? Is this the best solution?"

Many readers will rediscover in this book, as I have done, the familiar landscape of Montreal in the fifties and early sixties. A place of separate, ethnic ghettos, narrow, provincial morality, frozen in time, where so many people lived out their lives in hopelessness and indifference. Its young, like the adolescent Vallières, dreamt of escape, of other worlds, only to find that Montreal had marked them forever with an unwelcome nostalgia that prevented any other place from being 'theirs'.

Much of the world that formed Pierre Vallières and others like him has disappeared. Yet, many of its least attractive features persist into our own time. If anything, this book leaves one wondering how much of his world is worth preserving. The bitter price of our acquiescence to it is eloquently documented in the book itself as well as in the life Pierre Vallières has chosen as his own.

The conditions under which we live were created by men who lived before us. These conditions (from the relations of production and property to the organization of leisure, education, and culture) can be transformed or destroyed, and other conditions of life that are better, more human, can be created by the power of united men and collectivities (the men and collectivities of *today*) in order to serve other ends than those served by the existing conditions of life.

In the present state of things, these conditions of life constitute an essentially economic organization in the service of a minority. Upon this organization, whose principal end is the search for and accumulation of maximum profits – of money – by means of the exploitation of the labor of the immense majority of human beings, depend political life, intellectual life, education, religious life, and even artistic life, to the extent that these various spheres of human activity are controlled, monopolized, and directed by the ruling minority, in accordance with its economic class interests.

In this world, every individual is supposed to have complete freedom to do as he likes. But in fact, this freedom belongs only to those who have the money to take advantage of it and to *realize* it in their personal activities. Freedom exists only for the dominant minority. The vast majority of individuals are enslaved to work and to conditions of existence over which they have no control, which give them no real power of decision or right to enjoy the wealth produced, and which deprive them of the ownership of their means of production and, consequently, of the concrete freedom to satisfy their true needs – their own needs, and not those of the capitalist market. For the vast majority who live under these conditions – the conditions of present capitalist society – freedom is nothing more than a word, a hoax. The members of the minority can afford to have a *personal* life. The others, the mass of men, have no chance, no right, no concrete possibility of achieving this personal life within the conditions of existence of society today. In order to 'assert themselves as individuals,'[1] they must abolish their present conditions of life, which are also those of the whole society. They will achieve this only through the practical, collective

action of a total revolution,[2] which will not only overthrow the capitalist state but at the same time abolish everything that for centuries has perverted and poisoned social relations, life in society: private ownership of the means of production and exchange, the accumulation and concentration of capital in the hands of a few, the commodity categories, the market economy, exchange based on the 'law of value',[3] and even money itself. It is a question, in short, of 'de-capitalizing' social relations and replacing the present forced cooperation (which profits only a few) by a social solidarity that gives every individual the means of developing his faculties, of concretely realizing his personal freedom. Isolated individuals are contingent, dependent upon the demands of competition, labor, etc., upon the conditions of life created by the bourgeoisie to serve its class interests. The bourgeoisie extols individualism because that individualism subjugates each of us to its economic, political, and ideological power, because that individualism alienates each of us and makes the bourgeoisie invulnerable. It is to the extent that we join together in solidarity that we will free ourselves from all our alienations and that each of us will become more of a *person*.

In the so-called free world we know at present, concrete personal freedom exists only for individuals who succeed in developing themselves within the (small) ruling class and under the conditions created, desired, and maintained by that class. In the so-called independent nations the same conditions of existence often remain, because the economic bases of the division of society into classes and of the exploitation of man by man have not been abolished by the 'accession to independence of this or that colony.'

Only a revolution carried out by the majority of the men in a given collectivity can lay the basis for a true, radical transformation of the conditions of existence of the majority in that collectivity (which can just as easily be the entire world as a country or group of countries).

1

Our ideal, the ideal of the Front de Libération du Québec, is based neither on the opportunistic pragmatism of the capitalist parties, nor on the obsession with 'revolutionary inevitabilities' *(sic!)* of the parties that call themselves Communist.

Our ideal is based solely on what is human, on men, on their activities, their capacity to produce and create, to destroy and recreate, to transform, to unmake and remake, etc. . . .

If there is a certain determinism in history,[4] even within the framework of the universal relativity discovered by Einstein, and notwithstanding (perhaps) Werner Heisenberg's 'principle of the indetermination of matter,'[5] this 'determinism', in my opinion, cannot consist of an *"autonomous, necessary, and natural (determined) development of the productive forces,"* a *natural* development that would deliver whole centuries of humanity up to Chance or Necessity.

I believe, rather, that the development of the 'productive forces' is an essentially human activity and that man himself is without doubt the most important 'productive force' of all. Of course, the men of each generation, each collectivity, each class, and each social category "act on material bases and within material conditions and limits that are *determined*," as Marx and Engels declare; but I understand this word 'determined' in the sense of 'particular', of *particular* material conditions and limits which are partly independent of the will of men but are also, in part, produced, created, or at least accepted by them . . . and which they can therefore change themselves.*[6]

* The question of the interpretation of the word 'determined,' as used here by Marx and Engels, arises only in the French translation from the German. Vallières quotes the French version as "agissent sur des bases

These material conditions of existence of individuals and collectivities – both the conditions which they find ready-made (those that were created by preceding generations) and the conditions which arise out of their own activity (those that are imposed on them by the oppressing class or created on their own initiative, through union activities or revolutionary activities, for example) – are not, and have never been, the necessary product (in the sense of absolute necessity) of an 'autonomous' development of non-human forces of production. They are essentially the product of the activity and struggles of men. And that is why revolutions are possible.

If today we say that the 'proletarian' revolution is possible and that it has even become necessary, it is because we believe there are limits to the exploitation which the workers have been enduring for centuries, exploitation to which they are subjected by other men who are organized economically, politically, and socially to make as much profit as possible from the labor of the majority.

We believe that these limits, this multiform, multiracial, and multinational oppression, must today be left behind, that it must be dynamited all the more violently because scientific and technical progress provides the contemporary masses – at least *can* immediately provide them – with the means of becoming conscious, through a daily experience of exploitation that is opposed to (and contrasted with) the wealth of the 'free world' as displayed by the mass media; the means, I say, of becoming conscious of the many disparities and injustices of the present system. But neither the mass media nor electronic machines nor even big-business-style unions are going to rise up in place of the exploited, or even give the exploited the opportunity, the intellectual means, the finances, and the arms necessary for the victory of a popular uprising. No. It is men who are going to accomplish this work... no matter what the level of development of nuclear energy in their country or in the world!

The consciousness of injustice exalted to a system calls for revolutionary action, for radical changes in the relations of production and property and in social relations in general. But this action cannot spring automatically out of mere awareness of injustice. It must be organized – intellectually, morally, politically, and militarily – into a really revolutionary force, that is, a force which is at the same time militarily effective; psychologically, intellectually and economically de-alienating; democratic; and, morally, founded on solidarity, equality, justice, and honesty.

Such a revolution cannot be accomplished without war, without violence. For the established Order will try to the end to wipe it out in blood. Such a revolution, therefore, means the organization of an anti-capitalist, anti-imperialist, and anti-colonialist war that can end only with the victory or defeat of the working class. Now if we make war, it is in order to win it, and not in order to be martyred in vain in the name of freedom. That is why if there can be no revolution without war, there can be no victorious war without technique.[7]

Every combat technique requires a discipline, an ensemble of means capable of giving maximum effectiveness to fighting units of collectivities. In the age of imperialism, in which we are living (whether we like it or not), there can be no social transformation without a popular revolution, nor any popular revolution without a technique and a discipline conceived for the people and adapted to their means and capacities (present or potential).

et dans des conditions et limites matérielles *déterminées*." The English translation of the same passage uses the word 'definite,' thus confirming Vallières' understanding of '*déterminées*' in the sense of "particular": "... individuals ... as they are ... active under definite material limits, presuppositions and conditions independent of their will." (*The German Ideology*, New York, International Publishers, 1939, p. 13). (Trans.)

Left to the spontaneity of their revolts, which must always be begun over again, the people possess no military strength because they do not see clearly and their class consciousness remains on the level of an *instinct*. That is what the anarchists (who have hearts of gold) always forget. Popular violence does not automatically lead to the overthrow of the established Order, and it can even be an additional factor of political alienation – for whole generations of individuals. The overthrow of the established Order, and the collective de-alienation of the working class that must accompany it, is a problem of conscious and collective organization of the people.

2

The foregoing already shows clearly that our ideal of a society has nothing to do with the electoral programs of the traditional parties. Our program is nothing more nor less than a complete transformation of society and of the men who compose it. It is total revolution.

The political programs of the capitalist parties (Conservative or Liberal, Republican or Democrat) claim to be 'pragmatic'. This pragmatism is nothing but political opportunism which dares not speak its true name. It is determined by 'circumstances', that is, fundamentally, solely by the economic interests of the ruling class or classes.

As for the political programs of the so-called Left parties (traditional Communist, Labor, Socialist, Social Democratic, etc.), most of the time they are based on the same pragmatism but with slight differences, the most important of which is the belief that the revolution will someday come about of its own accord, through electoralism, unionism, and state capitalism. The parties of the Left are forced by their revolutionary past to periodically revive the 'future revolution' and the obsession with economic inevitabilities (as Malraux would say) – failing which, these Leftists would find nothing original to put into their programs.

History demonstrates that revolutionaries (including those of the FLQ) are not wrong in thinking that the emancipation of the workers will be achieved by the workers themselves.

The important thing, for the revolutionaries of the whole world as for those of Quebec, is not to expect the revolution to come from the *natural* and so-called *autonomous* development of the productive forces, but to organize immediately the spontaneous violence which in various ways (from workers' strikes to student demonstrations to juvenile delinquency) springs from the profound and cruel frustrations generated by the present organization of society.

The spontaneous and increasingly fierce violence of the people, in particular of the farmers, workers, and youth, is the response called for (and obtained) by the violence that has been systematically practiced for centuries by the minority ruling classes.

This violence can only increase with the consciousness which entire masses have today that they are being unjustly deprived of the ownership of *their* means of production, as well as of the wealth produced, culture, etc., and that they are being maintained in slavery in the name of democracy, the democracy of free enterprise and the exploitation of man by man.

The essential thing is to prevent this justified violence from periodically getting bogged down in despair or from strangling itself in the collective self-destruction that the fascists know so well how to organize, at the opportune moment, for the great benefit of the Democrats: high finance, the great multinational corporations, the bourgeoisie, and the Church. And the only way to avoid such a misfortune (which is always possible) is for the revolutionaries to organize the people's violence into a progressive force *before* the fascists (who never sleep) take control of it in order first to poison it and then to crush it. And this must be done on an international scale as well as in each country.

Besides, these days there are no more national problems. Santo Domingo, Vietnam, German neo-Nazism, etc., following upon hundreds of similar events, are proof of that.

Revolutionary violence is not, strictly speaking, *ideological*. I mean by 'ideological' or 'ideologized' violence, a violence based on absolute principles, on the unconscious or the irrational, on the negation of reality, etc., such as fascist, racist, and anti-Semitic violence. Revolutionary violence is nothing but the organized and conscious violence of a people, a class, a national or multinational collectivity that has chosen to confront, combat, and overcome the violence – it too, organized and conscious – of the established Order that is crushing it.

This popular, organized, and conscious violence is based on the needs, aspirations, and *rights* of the majority of men. It is demanded every day by the age-old negation of those needs, aspirations, and rights by a minority of thieves, exploiters, and murderers whose economic, political, military, and legal strength (Capital, the State, the Army, Justice) has been built, over the centuries, on the pitiless oppression of billions of men.

This violence does not force individuals and masses into irrational actions, by means of immoral propaganda, as does Nazi violence, which has no scruples about exploiting the instinct for murder that dwells in all the oppressed. In the foregoing account I have repeatedly emphasized the savage hatred that inhabits humiliated men, a hatred without any definite object. Fascism bases its irrational violence on this strong frustration and on the ignorance in which the mass of humanity is deliberately maintained by the classes in power. Fascism liberates hatred the better to destroy the working class.

Revolutionaries, on the contrary, organize the people's violence into a conscious and *independent* force. Fascism, it must be remembered, is also corporatist: in the end it always encourages the collaboration of classes to the advantage of capital and the bourgeoisie. In working to develop a conscious and independent popular force, revolutionaries organize – out of the natural violence of farmers, workers, petty white-collar workers, students, and young people which constitutes the raw material of every revolution – the de-alienation of the masses. In short, a victorious popular revolution is a successful collective psychoanalysis. And by victory I mean here much more than the mere taking of power. The taking of power is only the first in a long series of collective activities that must transform every sector of human life from top to bottom. I shall return to this later.

Any psychoanalysis (individual or collective) is frightening. And that is a normal reflex. For an 'honest ' psychoanalysis soon proposes acts for us to perform, acts that radically contradict our old habits of behaving and thinking. As Freud has demonstrated, the more resistance and anxiety is provoked in the 'patient' (the individual or collectivity) by an act to be performed, the more that act is *necessary*. To de-alienate oneself is not a romantic enterprise.... Only dishonest demagogues can promise the masses happiness the way Santa Claus, at Eaton's, promises the children toys.

Revolution is frightening to the masses, who nevertheless spontaneously desire it. For revolution makes its demands. But at the same time, violence attracts the masses, fascinates them as ritual dances fascinate certain so-called primitive collectivities. The oppressed masses ask nothing better than to have *someone* give them the opportunity and means of 'unloading' all the frustration, hate, and poison that present society has built up in them. That *someone*, unfortunately, is often fascism. And compared with the Nazi machine, the 'authority of the people', my dear Vadeboncoeur, is a little thing indeed!

The big problem is that the fascists have the capital in the beginning while we, *in the beginning*, have only right, justice .. and poverty. But the fascists rarely give their lives for the people. They do nothing out of solidarity, without a material objective. They break strikes and shoot the workers who want to take possession of the factories. They are on the side of the police and the judges. But unfortunately, the people often realize this too late.... And then, once again, resignation, submission, and shame win out over violence and the desire for liberation.

All this is not simple, nor can it always be physically 'controlled'. In time of crisis, theory is a very small weapon. It is *before* the crisis that it is necessary to see clearly and to organize the foundations of a popular revolution. One must always bear in mind that the economic, political, and social crises that encourage the development of an authentically popular revolution are the very ones that at the same time encourage the emergence of fascism. And the ruling classes always have recourse to fascism when they are seized with panic. Because in time of crisis, fascism is their best instrument of combat and repression. When the crisis is over, the fascists become 'democrats', 'liberals', 'Christian socialists'.... Illusory democracy can begin to exploit the people again in a climate of 'social peace'!

3

In the twentieth century fascism has been the permanent temptation of the French-Canadian petty bourgeoisie of Quebec. In the climate of social ferment that is shaking Quebec today, that fact cannot but arouse certain anxieties, even if an important faction of the new petty bourgeoisie calls itself 'socialist' and even if the young intellectuals of Quebec, unlike those of Greenwich Village in New York, do not draw swastikas on the walls and write "Bomb Hanoi Now!" all over the place. In 1965 we saw with what enthusiasm a thousand students of the University of Montreal burned an issue of the 'socialist' *Quartier Latin*, and with what alacrity Judge Laganière contratulated them on this courageous and Christian gesture!

The presence of fascist elements within the separatist movement is also very disturbing, for we all know that fascism is the art of transforming, sublimating, and then crushing popular discontent in the name of a false 'national renaissance' which is only the renaissance of the most frustrated elements of the petty bourgeoisie, that is, of a tiny minority. Quebec separatism in itself is an excellent thing, and I support it 100 percent. But that does not mean that I close my eyes. And I am not unaware of the fact that the Québécois separatists do not all pursue the same objective, that they do not all defend the same interests. Unfortunately for those who advocate a States-General of French Canada, a "dialogue among all parties and all classes in the nation" such as Maître Jacques-Yvan Morin desires[8] can only be a fraud. There might be unanimity on the 'unsuitability of the present structures', but certainly not on the new structures to be set up. I notice that the advocates of a States-General mainly attack the present political structures and do not really call into question the most fundamental structures, the economic ones. To be sure, their objective seems to be the 'economic independence of Quebec', since Monsieur Marchand himself, chairman of the Council for Economic Expansion, affirms that it is "impossible for Quebec to become economically independent without conquering political independence as a *preliminary*." I underline the word *preliminary*, because that is precisely where the fascist temptation lies: first achieve unanimity on this preliminary, and after that we'll see. See what, *after that*? The factories turned over to the workers, or the unions turned into corporations?

I believe there is only one way to escape the fascist temptation: to organize the majority – that is, the workers, farmers, white-collar workers, progressive intellectuals, students, young people, and clear-thinking petty bourgeois – into a revolutionary force that is openly and radically anti-capitalist, anti-imperialist, and anti-colonialist. It is a question of siding with ninety percent of the population against the ten percent who want to seize the opportunity offered them today to increase their domination over the 'ignorant' and by so doing augment the profits and privileges associated with that domination.

I admit that the Sarto Marchands of Quebec do not appear, at first glance, to be fascists. But it will not take long for them to become fascists if Ottawa persists in its present attitude. And since Quebec is a rich country, Washington might manufacture itself a little Tshombe, a little Ky, or a little Balaguer to prevent our country from 'toppling' into the enemy camp. The fascists have a very good press in Washington, notwithstanding the monumental hypocrisy of the kings of the White House.

Only a long experience of revolutionary struggle, requiring an ever higher level of consciousness and responsibility, can enable the oppressed and humiliated masses to escape fascism, to escape the magic of a fanatical nationalism manufactured to serve the needs of a minority of individuals who are seeking a greater measure of economic and political power.[9]

Those who now speak to the masses, taking care not to tell them the whole truth and, above all, preaching nonviolence, electoralism, etc., are imposters who are preparing the way not for revolution but for counter-revolution.[10] "Is it possible that fascism will one day sweep Quebec?" you ask. Yes, it is possible, even after the 'quiet revolution'. For the 'quiet revolution' has also awakened *that* . . .

We are disgusted with 350 years of being bargained over by 'indigenous' and foreign capitalists. This time we are demanding *everything*, independence and economic power included. And if, in order to get that, we have to confront L.B.J.'s Marines, weapons in hand, well, we will take up arms against the Marines, we will follow the example of the Vietnamese people. Then you will have no choice but to go out into the street with us and *follow us* . . . or else seek refuge, comfort, and B-52's in Washington, as General Ky and his clique of traitors are doing. As a number of cliques of traitors did before them. As you yourselves may do tomorrow, you who today demand equality or independence.[11]

4

This revolution that Quebec needs – as do all the countries that are enslaved by capitalism and colonial imperialism – implies nothing more nor less than the disappearance of capitalism itself. That means transformations that are even more profound than those required by the nationalization of foreign capital. It is a question, in fact, of abolishing capital itself, the basis of present society.

Present society, you know as well as I do, rests on what the specialists call a 'market economy', that is, an economy in which the real decisions affecting the whole collectivity, workers as well as non-workers, are made by a handful of financiers (in scholarly language: 'individual economic agents') in accordance with their personal economic interests: the accumulation of constantly increasing profits. This capitalist economy exploits the majority of men by means of a labor market in which the workers (the real producers of wealth), deprived by force of the ownership of their means of production, are compelled to sell their labor (when there happens to be a demand for slaves!) in order to obtain from the system that exploits them the minimum which they and their families must have to subsist, that is, to consume (and so 'reimburse' the system) the products which the capitalists, through advertising, force them to buy at the highest possible price.

In short, a minority of financiers has monopolized the means of production and has organized human labor and society in general (relations of production, relations of exchange, and social relations) in such a way as to appropriate for itself, in the name of allegedly free competition and an illusory equality of individuals, the greatest possible share of the wealth produced by the daily labor of the majority of mankind. These financiers and their army of ideologists call this 'democracy'. The workers call it organized slavery.

We want to replace this economy based on the exploitation of the majority of mankind not only by a new economy but by a new society, in which the category 'economy' will not have the same content it does now. We want to replace it with a society in which the producers (the workers) collectively own and administer their means of production and create, organize, and plan their relations of production and the distribution of their products in accordance with ultimate goals that they choose themselves, for the satisfaction of their true needs, in the framework of an absolute equality of rights, opportunities, and benefits.

In this 'economy', this new society, there will be no more 'free competition', that is, no more capital market and labor market, no more accumulation and concentration of the collective wealth in the hands of a few individuals who are the strongest and richest, no more exploitation of the workers, the immense majority of mankind, by a handful of men who accumulate profits. Rather, there will be an egalitarian (and not totalitarian) social structure without non-workers, without exploiters, and without parasites. A society without classes, therefore, and as soon as possible without a state. For in the last analysis, capitalism is determined, developed, maintained, and periodically renewed, rejuvenated, programmed, etc., by the strongest social class (today the bourgeoisie of big business, of the American or Soviet type), to whom the state belongs and who profit to the maximum from the class nature of present-day society (a nature which, throughout history, successive ruling classes have arbitrarily defined as inalienable). It is this class nature of society and of its legal form, the state (whether it be of the American, British, French, or Soviet type), which the workers and young people – all the progressives of the twentieth century – must destroy. For otherwise how can we make sure that a 'new ruling class' will not be built into a state in which equality would be as much a myth as the 'democratic freedom of individuals' is in the present system?*

Only an egalitarian social structure can make it concretely possible for the workers to actively participate and enjoy to the full the products of their activity, which is free and yet disciplined. It is not merely a question of 'permitting' from above (from the heights of some supreme 'presidium') the free circulation of suggestions, proposals, and criticisms 'at the base,' but of a great deal more. It is a question of setting up, through this egalitarian social structure and by a collective effort, the machinery of a concrete and effective democracy, a democracy for all that will enable the workers and the entire society to make the fullest possible use of the potentialities not only of the economy but of the whole range of human activity and the energies at work in the known universe, energies which men have unlimited power to control and use for human ends, for progress, happiness, and the satisfaction of needs known and as yet unknown.

It is understood that the concrete, local, particular forms of such a structure (which in my opinion can exist securely only on a continental or even world scale – for economic and politi-

---

* The phrase 'new ruling class' refers to the French title of the book by Milovan Djilas that appeared in English as *The New Class* (1957). (Trans.)

cal reasons that I shall explain below) may have many accidental 'variations', good in themselves (or rather, immaterial to the foundations of the structure), according to the specific historical development of the different countries, nationalities, minorities, or 'races.' But these 'variations' only give local color to the essential thing: the establishment of an egalitarian social structure, of a classless society.

In order for this society to exist and endure, three sorts of conditions must be realized, conditions which we shall now sum up as clearly as it is possible to do within the narrow framework of this essay.

They are: first, economic; second, administrative and political; third, subjective and intellectual.

(1) Economic conditions. These conditions, which are fundamental, can be summed up in the disappearance of the following: the commodity categories; calculation in terms of 'value' (which expresses itself through the price system and whose purpose or utility is not, as certain persons affirm, to express the labor time required for the production of the various products or goods, but to accumulate as much profit as possible); money; the system of national accounting connected with the capitalist commodity categories; and the financial and credit system.

The functioning of the commodity categories and the utilization, by a bureaucracy of technocrats, of the law of value make no sense in an economy that calls itself 'socialized.' For that is wanting to socialize the economy without de-capitalizing it. That is putting a new coat of paint on an old automobile. It is being satisfied with an economic revolution in name only. At most, it is making private-enterprise capitalism evolve toward state capitalism. It is leaving in place, as if they were vital to humanity, the roots of the accumulation and concentration of capital and of ever increasing profits in the hands of new social categories, new ruling classes which, by means of their state and of their exclusive control of economic decisions, plans, etc., will not be slow to monopolize in their own interests, as the new class in power, the so-called revolutionized use of the law of value and the commodity categories. The great (American) multinational corporations have socialized 'their' economy too, have planned wages, prices, investments, etc. The USSR of 1967 has become the biggest trust in the world,[12] the corporation with the most widespread activities. General Motors is beginning to court it for an amicable Soviet-American agreement over the heads of the workers, whose conditions of existence have not been fundamentally changed by the revolution of 1917 and who are now faced with having to prepare the overthrow of a new bourgeoisie, less feudal than that of 1917 but more clever and hypocritical. A bourgeoisie which I would call a 'state bourgeoisie'. A bourgeoisie which plays a prudent game in Asia and asks the American and European capitalists to come help it 'reform' its system of planning and reintroduce into the Soviet economy the notions of profit and free competition, so that the USSR may become the number one imperialist power of the year 1980, and the Brezhnev-Kosygin clique the Rockefellers of the year 2000! Is that really what Lenin was prophesying when he naively said that "With socialism (appearing) at every window of contemporary capitalism," it was an "infantile disorder of communism" to refuse any compromise with that system? Today one can say that capitalism is reappearing at every window of Russian and East European socialism. That is what the pragmatism of revolutionary phraseology leads to, once it is in power.

Our ideal is not to turn out a new edition of the 'realism' of the Lenins, Stalins, and Kosygins. Because today that 'realism' has shown itself for what it is. And decidedly, after fifty years of Soviet history, it appears that out of the popular insurrections of 1917 the Russians have made a bourgeois revolution, a revolution that has had recourse to planning (like postwar

France) in order to concentrate – massively, and as quickly as possible – the capital and talent inherited from the old regime on the building of a basic industry and a state capable of 'competing' with the United States. And after fifty years of unparalleled privations imposed on the workers, General Motors and Ford are finding in the USSR and Eastern Europe a market all ready to receive American cars assembled in Moscow. It is Saint-Bruno (SOMA) on a gigantic scale, and Kosygin is the Gérard Filion of the Soviet Union's 'quiet revolution', of peaceful coexistence and cooperation with American fascism!*

All that because after October 1917 they accepted as a 'necessary' and 'temporary survival' the use of commodity categories in the economy. From Bolshevism they quickly passed to planned reformism, and from that to state capitalism. That is what the *autonomous* development of capitalist forces of production leads to!

The Soviets have not understood that the 'law of value' is not a law of nature but a man-made thing, and that the commodity categories and everything connected with them (money, the financial system, credit, the price system, etc.) are man-made things and not natural forces like light, nuclear energy, and so forth. If man is capable today of converting matter into energy and one element into another, how can one deny that he has the capacity not only to 'revise' the law of value but to challenge it?

The 'Marxist' economists, in their libraries crammed with statistical tables, try to "determine the objective conditions for the withering away of the commodity categories."[13] But when they pose this fundamental problem, they forget to put it back in the context of the modes of activity that have been generated by the development of capitalism and the bourgeoisie. They abstractly isolate the commodity categories from the capitalist social structure and its class nature. That is why they forget to pose the problem in the concrete domain where it is located.

First of all, there can be no 'withering away' of the commodity categories unless there also is a 'withering away' of the system of which they are an integral part and in which they serve as an instrument for achieving economic goals set by men – by the classes that have created and constantly perfected that system. To pose the problem of the withering away of the commodity categories is to pose the problem of the withering away of capitalist society itself. Now, can capitalist society 'wither away'? To be sure, it is frustrating for the majority of men. To be sure, it is incapable of adequately meeting the vital needs of hundreds of millions of men. But can this society 'wither away' like a man growing old who, *in spite of himself*, withers away and dies? For my part, I believe that capitalist society can only be *overthrown*. It cannot wither away by itself, any more than the bourgeois class can commit suicide. Only practical action, a revolutionary movement, can sweep away the old society and at the same time the commodity categories, the law of value, etc. There remains to be determined the total content of this revolution, which I shall attempt to do further on in this chapter.

But the essential thing for the moment is to remember that the commodity categories and the law of value, which have been created by men through their activities, can be abolished by men through new activities that are called 'revolutionary', in the sense that they radically change the social relations (of production, exchange, etc.) established by preceding generations or, more precisely, by the ruling classes of those genera-

---

*The Sociéte de montage automobile (SOMA) is a Quebec state enterprise that assembles Renaults and Peugeots from parts bought from the French firms. Its plant was set up in Saint-Bruno, near Montreal, when Gérard Filion was both vice-president of the company and mayor of the town. (Trans.)

tions. It is impossible to imagine that an egalitarian social structure can emerge from the planning of *capitalist* relations of production and exchange, which have been created precisely for the accumulation of capital – of wealth – in the hands of a ruling minority which alone is favored by the system. The planning of capital investments, prices and wages, various types of production, etc., can exist only under state capitalism. In an egalitarian social structure, all that remains is the planning of *distribution* (and not 'exchange' in the capitalist sense of the term) of the goods produced by men to satisfy their needs. That planning is done on a basis of equality for all, an equality which can only be achieved through a long experience of solidarity in the struggle men are compelled to wage to rid themselves of the system that oppresses them economically, politically, militarily, legally, religiously, and ideologically.

The truth of this statement rests on the assumption that two other economic conditions have been realized in the revolutionary movement which has abolished, in this or that part of the world, the traditional commodity relations that are based on monetary exchange and are therefore 'capitalizable'. (Which no revolution, to my knowledge, has yet accomplished.)

These two conditions are:

(1) (a) An identity, as nearly perfect as possible, between the 'juridical subjects' (those who possess the effective *right* to order the means of production and work out new relations of ownership, production, and distribution of products) and the 'economic subjects' (those who are *capable*, practically, of managing these activities). This identity cannot be achieved so long as the different centers for the appropriation of the means of production and the centers for the appropriation of the political and technical powers of distribution remain independent, separate, or opposed, dealing with antagonistic interests (real or artificial).[14]

(b) Absolute economic independence from foreign capitalist markets, should any still exist at the time when an 'economy without capital' can appear.[15] For any extension of the distribution of goods to capitalist markets or any penetration of a de-capitalized economy by foreign capital would soon reduce to nothingness the fundamental objectives of the revolution.

These two conditions, complementary to and inseparable from the preceding ones, bring me to the 'administrative and political' conditions for the establishment, by the majority itself, of an egalitarian society (2), and to the 'subjective and intellectual' conditions for the realization of this human ideal which at first glance appears utopian (3).

The conditions described in (2) and (3) are as important as those enumerated in (1) and are part of what might be called the ensemble of objective conditions for a total revolution. Such a revolution cannot result from a *natural* development (natural in the sense of being independent of the will of individuals and groups) of blind and autonomous forces of production, but solely from a long process of human – that is, conscious and responsible – activities, collective activities of sufficient duration and depth to replace traditional individualism by an effective solidarity. For solidarity is the only foundation on which it is possible to build a truly egalitarian social structure, a social structure which is free for all, fraternal and cooperative and within which each individual can become more of a person, as I said above.

(2) *Administrative and political conditions*. It is an illusion to think one can build an egalitarian social structure while retaining the political categories and the administrative modes of functioning inherited from the development of capitalism by the bourgeoisie. For such a structure must be, can only be, built *collectively*.

The abolition of free competition, of the commodity categories, and of the accumulation of capital through the exploitation of man by man must coincide with the abolition of the traditional state, in which personal freedom is reduced to the 'right' to *enjoy*, within the limits of one's individual fortune and the conditions of existence of one's class, certain very limited powers that are subordinated to the interests of the 'objective power' the system set up by this or that ruling class.

Even in a state in which opinion and criticism were freely expressed, an egalitarian social structure could only be a myth unless the 'national' and then the 'multinational' collectivities possessed the instruments enabling them to command the state, with full knowledge of all the facts – that is, to *govern themselves*, directly, without going through the intermediary of a state 'detached' from the conditions of everyday life.

These instruments are: management of the processes of production and distribution of goods, control of planning (the coordination, in the interest of all, of central and local managements) and control of the division of functions among individuals and groups, and power to set human goals independent of the requirements of the old market economy. This last implies the power to orient policy in the direction of the common interest, the collective and individual interest, which is for every man to assert himself as a person (in present society, a privilege reserved for those who hold economic and military power, the 'state-as-arbitrator' being only a screen to disguise that power).

In order for there to be an egalitarian social structure, the division between the 'base' and the 'presidium', if you will, must disappear. The difference between the 'mass' and the 'elite', and even the distinction between the 'people' and the 'party-as-guide', must disappear. Furthermore, so-called democratic centralism must give way, on the economic level as on the political level, to democracy itself.

It is therefore necessary that it be materially impossible in this structure for individuals or groups of individuals to enjoy political power, economic power, etc., at the expense of other men. The abolition of capital and the replacement of capitalist relations of exchange – which function through a 'price system' that is arbitrarily based on a supposed calculation of man-hours necessary but that deliberately departs as much as it pleases from the levels allegedly fixed by that socially necessary labor, so as to ensure maximum profits for the ruling class! – the replacement of these relations by true relations of distribution based on the needs of each and all (of which I spoke in (1) above) render the exploitation of man by man if not impossible, at least unprofitable. But these new relations of production and distribution must be disciplined (for otherwise you have anarchy) by an administrative and political structure that makes the traditional state obsolete. This structure should make it possible both to decentralize the real decisions and to centralize the information enabling each social group to coordinate freely with the others (which are cooperative and no longer competitive) the allocation or utilization of available resources with a view to obtaining the maximum yield from those resources (material and intellectual) for the greatest benefit of all.

How can that be achieved? By the socialization of modern technology, which is the perfect instrument for the *unification* of the process of appropriation by men of nature (energy, mineral wealth, etc.) and the process of reproduction and transformation of those resources by the *same* men – a unification, at both the local and the international levels, necessitated by the creation of an egalitarian society.

Modern technology makes it possible both to calculate the maximum yield of resources, wherever they are located, and to disseminate the information to the decision-making units scattered over one or several territories. It gives everyone – it *ought* to give everyone – increasingly exact scientific knowledge of the potentialities of external nature and of man himself (who is also a part of 'nature', of the universe). Bringing men face to face, so to speak, with the true knowledge of their capacities, it also gives them the technical means of fulfilling those capacities and of planning them in accordance with one or more of the collective, social objectives that have been freely chosen by men united in a single effort at progress. Which presupposes that *beforehand* these men have learned to unite and to utilize, with maximum efficiency and for their real benefit, all the possibilities of modern technology, which are now monopolized by the same individuals who control capital, the state, the law, etc. And that in turn presupposes that these men have taken possession of technology, which is not accessible to them now but which they are in an objective position to make the basis of their emancipation from enslavement (in all its forms: economic, political, moral, religious, cultural).

This leads me to the 'subjective and intellectual conditions' for building this egalitarian social structure which constitutes 'our ideal' and which – allow me to emphasize it again – presupposes a violent and total revolution.

(3) *Subjective and intellectual conditions.* These conditions are required by our ideal of a society itself, which must be achieved by de-alienated men who have learned to rid themselves of everything that now blocks their individual and collective development: ignorance of modern science and technique; enslavement to routine; the habit of abdicating; individualism; the psychological frustrations that harden man, blind him, or gradually destroy him; the absence of a highly developed, lucid, organized class consciousness; a weak sense of responsibility; ignorance of the possibilities opened up by active solidarity; lack of confidence in the success of a popular revolution and even in the prospect that it will soon be launched; the many disappointments accumulated over decades of betrayals by the unions and compromises by the socialists; fear of overt action; lack of self-confidence; etc., etc.

Man is the principal productive force and the only natural power capable of giving to the ensemble of known and used productive forces a particular goal and a particular organization (which may be changed from one generation to another). He must therefore make the effort to transform himself in order to be really in a position, as Marx and Engels say, to sweep away, by revolution, "all the rottenness of the old system and to become *fit* to build society on new foundations," fit to organize an egalitarian social structure, without non-workers, without exploiters, and without parasites – a society without classes, whose primary social objective is to make it concretely possible for *all* men to assert themselves as individuals without exploiting one another, as they are now forced to do by the conditions of existence created by capitalism.

That is why the subjective and intellectual conditions are the ones it is most important to bring about, for without them nothing can be done. In order to realize these conditions, the revolutionaries of the twentieth century must make use of social techniques: group psychology, 'social animation,'* the development of creativity by the 'gratuitous' exercise of the arts and of writing, the development of manual skill by the practice of domestic mechanics (repair of household objects whose workings, although very simple, are too often not understood), reading, and reflection based on everyday life and current events, both local and international.[16]

The most profound alienation is no doubt the one expressed in the common remark we have all made at one time or another: "I wonder what the world is coming to . . . I honestly don't know where we're heading."

This spontaneous expression of 'disorientation' reveals to

what an extent *we are not free*, in this world that is supposed to be ours.

In the age of interplanetary travel and nuclear energy, we are like primitive people lost in a universe of mysteries.

We do not understand a thousandth part of the contemporary scientific discoveries whose practical applications serve as instruments of domination and exploitation for the capitalist bourgeoisie, which alone possesses the knowledge, the men, and the technology necessary to apply those discoveries to its own ends or interests. Because it alone monopolizes the money that is the cement of present-day society, it can 'buy' the scientists, their discoveries, and the technical instruments for using them practically. It thus possesses increasingly perfected means not only of reinforcing its domination and its system of exploitation, but of *justifying* them 'scientifically', through magazines, reviews, newspapers, radio and television broadcasts, and courses in the *collèges* and universities, whose real function is not to socialize scientific knowledge but to pervert that knowledge and make it work for the ruling classes by transforming it into an ideology justifying the status quo. For pure science – that is, science that is consistent – can only demonstrate that the universe (and therefore human history) is subject to a 'natural' process (which also governs human activity) of continual revolutions. To be sure, it is virtually impossible for the contemporary ruling classes to *freeze* the 'relativist' and 'dialectical' science of the twentieth century into a rigid, monolithic system of knowledge like that of the Middle Ages. Therefore the policy of the bourgeoisie today is to pretend that capitalist society is in perpetual revolution and is capable of resolving all the contradictions and problems raised by contemporary scientists and thinkers. 'Progressive conservatism', in other words![†]

Nevertheless, the social failures of the system (unemployment, war, poverty, economic insecurity, etc.) give the lie to this official optimism and to the opportunistic relativism of the 'science' pages – or broadcasts – of the capitalist press. And in order to crush the practical reactions produced by social injustice, unemployment, racism, war, etc., capitalism must have recourse – on the 'politics and ideology' pages of that same press – to *necessity*, just as the ruling classes did in the Middle Ages. And it is not long before necessity, which is also supposed to be 'scientific' (even though it is nonsense from the point of view of authentic science), is transformed into a police state, as soon as the economic interests of the big bourgeoisie begin to be challenged by the 'ignorant' masses. Then the police and the army quickly supplant science as the justification for the social status quo. A reactionary ideology comes to the assistance of the police state, and the law takes responsibility for imposing on the malcontents a forced respect for necessity! Einstein is sacrificed to Hitler. Engels to Stalin. Curie to Laval.

But between the oppressed people and the 'liberal-totalitarian' big bourgeoisie, there is a petty bourgeoisie which is caught in a dilemma. It cannot really understand Einstein, and it cannot 'swallow' the philosophy of Hitler. Applied fascism (although consistent with the conventional ideas that fill the petty bourgeoisie's 'acquired' or 'consumed' knowledge of the universe) constipates it. It feels sick. It has *nausea.* And – fortunately for capitalism – it takes refuge in irrationalism, either passive or willful (according to circumstances and tastes). The neutralism of individual cowardice becomes 'lucid' existentialism, 'being and nothingness', a room with no exit, that is comfortable in spite of the smell given off by the corpses of the millions of men who are crushed and incinerated – 'scientifically' – by the fascist panic. The smell finally makes them sick, these gentlemen who want to remain 'free' in a universe of barbarism. They begin to shout and ask the fascists to go home. They

---

*In French-Canadian radical movements, 'social animation' is a group sensitization process led by trained group leaders whose purpose is to help people relate to each other and understand social and political issues. Ideally, the group reaches a consensus on analysis and strategy and formulates actions accordingly. (Trans.)

† The name of the conservative party in Canada is the Progressive Conservative Party. (Trans.)

become engaged! But their 'ethics of ambiguity' forbids them to take sides openly and clearly with the workers against the bourgeois, just as their 'lucidity' forbids them to take sides openly with Hitler and his irrationalism, stained as it is with the blood of millions of men.‡   Bloody irrationalism has given them gooseflesh and a guilty conscience. That disturbs their 'clear ideas' about the ambiguity of (petty-bourgeois) human behavior! They give their support to a new liberal and pseudo-democratic government, and their 'engagement' finally boils down to demanding that the state provide 'social peace' without the stench of incinerated corpses, and restore to them the individual freedom momentarily compromised by the necessity of 'resisting' fascism, which has decidedly gone too far: Nietzsche did not expect all *that* of the Führer! 'Beyond good and evil', the absurd once again becomes the quiet philosophy of the melancholy petty bourgeoisie, still caught in the same dilemma, while the big bourgeoisie, re-established on the solid base of capital after a good paying war, entrusts to the 'scientism' of the charlatans of *Planète* and similar publications the 'historic' task of repeating the same old pack of nonsense in a new and currently fashionable vocabulary. A whole collection of digests comes along to supplement this 'scientific information' that is served up to men who are starved for knowledge but have slim pocketbooks, few tools of learning, and scanty leisure!

Thus we daily consume a pseudo-science the way we consume the bread made by Weston, not in order to nourish ourselves but in order to make profits for those who exploit even the most elementary needs of man.

The existentialist 'superstructure' (Christian, nihilistic, neutralist, sadistic, Marxist, etc. – something for every taste, so to speak!) has its 'popular' counterpart in the mass of sentimental romances, detective stories, pornography, scandalous gossip, tales of sadism, gangsterism, and violence, war adventures and murder stories that fill a considerable number of publications and radio and television broadcasts. Plunged into this irrational merchandise with which we are daily inundated by the mass media – the property of the businessmen – we are taught, under pressure, to accept the absurd, to despise existence, we are trained in delinquency and the amoral individualism of the 'struggle for life', and by this means are deflected from our political and revolutionary tasks.

Contemporary science, from psychoanalysis to sociology, while unmasking these processes of an alienation directed and scientifically programmed by the bourgeoisie, lets itself be used like a commodity, and the scientists offer only scant and feeble resistance to the utilization of their discoveries about man for anti-human purposes. When it is 'honest', science is too expensive and remains inaccessible to the majority of men, who cannot afford psychoanalysis or prolonged studies at the universities and great technical institutes. Since science is not truly socialized, in spite of the fact that present-day technology makes such socialization objectively feasible, the businessmen, who are the kings of our democracy, go unchallenged as they plan and socialize stupidity.

And how can one defend himself against this cunning debasement of the mind when one does not possess the intellectual means to combat it? Intellectual means which, in our society, depend on our economic and political power. Power which is nil for the majority of men. Power which is daily negated in the name of free competition, the most widespread and effective myth of the nineteenth and twentieth centuries.

It is one of the most important tasks of contemporary revo-

‡ The reference to the 'ethics of ambiguity' is an allusion to Simone de Beauvoir's book *Pour une morale de l'ambiguité* (1947), which has appeared in English (translated by Bernard Frechtman) under the title *The Ethics of Ambiguity*. (Trans.)

lutionaries to give the farmers, workers, students, and young people the means of freeing themselves from intellectual debasement; and this must be done by perfecting a process of conscious integration of the masses in the collective revolutionary struggle, whose duration may be long and whose end may be very difficult to foresee, but which must begin today. Which, in fact, has already been going on for over a century, starting with the first revolts of the English and French workers of Europe in the early nineteenth century and continuing up to the present Vietnamese revolution, which the Americans are desperately trying to destroy with weapons that in quantity and sophistication go beyond everything we have yet seen in the history of wars and class struggles.

This arduous collective task has *already* been undertaken wherever a serious, clear-sighted effort is being made to teach the masses to think about the world and history, starting not with the abstract creations that the ruling classes have invented to alienate them but with the very conditions of their existence, with life as they have experienced it.

Beginning with the techniques of 'social animation', films, and simple conversations about everyday realities, revolutionaries must teach the masses to produce by themselves, so to speak, the science that has hitherto been reserved for specialists. Otherwise, science will never be socialized and man will never be de-alienated. Because the socialization of scientific knowledge, understood in its continual evolution (its dialectical movement of affirmation and negation of contradictions) and assimilated in its reality, is a fundamental condition for the de-alienation of the majority of humankind and for the achievement of what one might metaphorically call the transition of humanity from prehistory to history.

In order for this transition to take place, science must not be dissolved into a new kind of witchcraft sold in the form of 'products of the mind' that have been emptied of content and offer the deceived consumers only a collection of hollow phrases without practical implications. Science must cease to be enslaved to the capitalist bourgeoisie's accumulation of profits and carry out at last its true function of liberating all men from the so-called objective powers which presently oppress them, but which can cease to exist as blind and oppressive necessities if they are 'possessed' through knowledge and utilized through technology for determined goals and interests. This role, which has hitherto been reserved for the richest (from all points of view) faction of the bourgeoisie, must become the daily activity of humanity, for that is the real and constantly renewed content of what we call human freedom. This freedom must become the practical exercise of all men, and in order for that to happen, it must cease to be the privilege of a minority exploiting the majority.

In short, the number one objective of the total revolution is to give all men the opportunity and the means to acquire knowledge, to understand the discoveries of the scientists, and to use them intelligently and effectively and, in addition, to participate in their turn in scientific research, the perfecting of technology and the exploration and enjoyment of the universe, which belongs to all men . . . and not just to the bourgeois.

It is only by means of this concrete, *conscious* freedom that humanity will be able to fulfill itself, leaving behind the frustrations that make it the slave of international capitalism, and turning to account the many 'forces of nature' which influence its behavior and which it does not yet use for its liberation, because it is just beginning to learn about them, through contemporary biology and physics in particular. And the beginning, or apprenticeship, of this freedom coincides with the beginning, or apprenticeship, of revolutionary action.

For man can acquire the power to determine his activities advisedly – that is, he can acquire true freedom – only by means of a practical, collective, radical revolution, which no Messiah can bring about for him.

5

This ideal – which is also a product of our social activity, of our evolution – seems very far off, vague, even theoretical. But like any ideal, like any objective, it is a working tool, a hypothesis, a hope born of the felt need to *realize* it. And far from being an obstacle to our immediate daily activities, it is indispensable to them, as light is which will in turn give birth to other dreams in the generations that follow us.

Nothing has begun with us and nothing will end with us, unless it be our individual existence. And even if some day individuals succeed in overcoming death, that will only be the beginning of a new era, a new history, also made of 'revolutions'. Will there come a day when life can evolve without death?

Now I've launched into some pretty profound reflections, into questions which neither you nor I can answer, but which remain. I should like to get rid of all these questions. But it seems to me that if I did, I would quickly change into an apathetic clod, moved at most, from time to time, by transitory adventures, superficial and soon forgotten.

My dreams are 'measureless', and yet I am an ordinary man, I think. I cannot 'live my life' without working to make the revolution, and it seems to me that it is pretty much the same for you. It is not a question of playing at being heroes – besides, who can do that, in the era of the atomic bomb and the agonizing war in Vietnam? – but of getting *together* to build a new world in which ordinary men, like you and me, will no longer be the niggers of the millionaires, the warmongers, and the preachers of passivity, but will be free at last to subject the world to their 'whims': love, scientific curiosity, creation . . . in solidarity and equality, in modesty and pride.

NOTES

1. This is not the expression of a personalist but of Marx and Engels. Cf. *The German Ideology*, New York, International Publishers, 1939, p. 78.
2. We shall see below everything that is implied by the expression 'total revolution'.
3. A little further on we shall take up briefly these difficult questions, whose solution is of *vital* importance to the success or failure of the total, completely human revolution carried out by and for man, which constitutes 'our ideal'.
4. My comrade Charles Gagnon has undertaken a critique of Marxist historical determinism. This critique, which is still in the embryonic stage, already contains many positive aspects that are capable of completely renewing Marxism, or rather, I believe, of making it disappear as an independent, self-sufficient system of thought. In the hands of the commissars of the Soviet and Western Communist parties (in the East no less than in the West), Marxism – alas! – has become an ideology enslaved to the economic and political interests of a new bourgeoisie whose instrument of economic domination is state capitalism. Marx, Engels, and Lenin are in part responsible for this state of affairs, which is called 'revisionism'. But only in part. The positive aspect of their critique of philosophical idealism and of illusory capitalist democracy deserves to be better known and studied in greater depth. But their vision of the world, it must be remembered, dates from more than a century ago. And Marx and Engels never read – could not read – Freud, Lévi-Strauss, Einstein, Heisenberg, and the great contemporary physicists, biologists, psychoanalysts, structuralists, sociologists, anthropologists, and psychologists. But the 'Marxists' of today do not have the excuse of being unaware of the giant strides made by contemporary science.

I am personally very grateful to my friend Charles Gagnon for having introduced a certain dose of 'relativism' into my Marxism (which to me was at first an instrument of struggle rather than an object of research). I hope that notwithstanding the very hard conditions of prison life, Charles will be able to pursue his research and someday give us the benefit of the results of his arduous labor.

I think that in these days, taking into account the present results obtained by science, one should speak of 'historical relativism', that is, of a determined relativism (cf. Einstein), perceived, conceived, and reconceived, and applied concretely, through individual or collective acts, by the men of each particular historical period.

This 'historical relativism', which to me is an intuition rather than a system of thought and a clear vision of reality, seems to me to leave man his full measure of freedom, the freedom given him by his nature as a conscious, acting, social being, capable today of converting matter into energy and so on.
5. This principle can be crudely summed up as follows: the more precisely the speed of an electron is measured, the less certainly can its position as a particle within an atom be determined.
6. Because that which is determined is not necessarily determining.
7. What I mean here by 'technique' and 'discipline' goes far beyond the meaning usually given those words by professional military men. Thus, the study of the pure sciences can be as much a part of revolutionary technique, as I understand that term, as the study of the handling of weapons, of purely military strategy and the tactics of guerrilla warfare.
8. See *Dimanche-Matin*, Montreal, September 18, 1966, p. 4.
9. I condemn here only the nationalism of the exploiters and not that of the exploited, the poor, the humiliated.
10. Whether they are aware of it or not makes no difference.
11. A very important struggle is going on at present within the RIN between the Left and the Right of this separatist party. The RIN's support of the Lachute strikers in 1966 suggests that the Left is in power right now, but only by a slim majority. If the influx of young people into the RIN continues to increase, the Left will probably be strengthened. But a movement to the right remains possible, and a 'grand coalition' of the RIN, the RN, and the National Union would be enough to place Quebec under the yoke of an out-and-out fascist government.

One thing troubles me: that the RIN hesitates to take a position radically opposing the war in Vietnam and American imperialism, which nonetheless controls 80 percent of the country this party wants to 'liberate'.

It is up to the rank and file of the RIN to orient their party in the right direction while there is yet time. Pierre Bourgault seems to me to be a little too wavering. That may be because he has no solid base of support either on the Left or on the Right. And is he himself sure on whose support he wants to base his policy?
12. Primarily in so far as basic industry is concerned. In the other sectors of the economy socialized production coexists with cooperative and individual production; especially in the consumer-goods sector, where the USSR is calling more and more on foreign capitalist corporations.
13. Cf. Charles Bettelheim, *Planification et croissance accélérée*, Paris, François Maspero, 1964, p. 25.
14. This somewhat difficult, but precise, vocabulary is borrowed from Bettelheim.
15. For my part, I believe that in order to achieve what Marx calls "a community of free individuals, carrying on their work with the means of production in common, in which the labour-power of all the different individuals is consciously applied as the combined labour power of the community" (quoted by Engels in *Herr Eugen Dühring's Revolution in Science* [*Anti-Dühring*], trans. Emile Burns, New York, International Publishers, p. 149), there must be a multinational revolutionary movement capable of definitively crushing imperialism. And unlike Marx, I do not believe that such an overthrow has anything in common with an imaginary 'withering away' that is tied to the very development of capitalist production, as death is tied to human life, with, as Marx puts it, "the inexorability of a law of Nature" (*Anti-Dühring*, p. 152). I do not believe in inexorability. I believe in revolution.
16. All that, of course, in addition to agitation, propaganda, political action both legal and illegal, etc., etc.

3. Some Problems in the Redefinition of Activism: The Rise and Fall of SUPA

Krista Maeots/*Free-lance Journalist*

This essay might have been titled "Radicals in Search of a Cause." Written from the inside, it is a case study of a disparate, loosely bounded and loosely bonded collectivity of individuals searching for a cause to unite them into a viable group. From the perspective of spatial analysis the study is interesting because this is not a group seeking to preserve its already existing private space, as in the first selection in this section, nor an excluded group seeking to enlarge its public space as in the second. Rather, it portrays a rather inchoate attempt at redefinition of the public goals.

In the mid-sixties in Canada, thousands of young people were inspired by the involvement of American youth in black civil rights agitation, community organizing, university protest and cultural experimentation. They became convinced that the Americans were the vanguard of an international youth revolt against the bureaucratization, centralization and manipulation characteristic of the authority structures of modern industrial societies. The Canadian youth movement became an enthusiastic support group for the American New Left, celebrating its achievements, publicizing its ideas in Canada and emulating its activities. This supportive and, ultimately, dependent relationship was sustained by the belief that youth radicalism would transcend all national boundaries and would ultimately form the basis for a world-wide revolution in human relations.

The Canadian student left, despite its avowed international orientation was decidedly singular in its sources of inspiration during the two major periods of its early organizational history. Prior to the emergence of the American movement in 1962-63, Canadian students were attracted by the radical organizing models of the British peace movement. The first student protests in the 1960's were based on the ideas and techniques of the British Campaign for Nuclear Disarmament. The Canadian Combined Universities Campaign for Nuclear Disarmament was founded in November 1959. Its formation was influenced by students returning from studies in Britain. CUCND mobilization achieved momentum in its response to the Diefenbaker government's Bomarc announcement. In the months that followed, numerous petitions were circulated and meetings and demonstrations were held to protest against the acceptance of nuclear warheads. Independent peace groups were organized in several cities, the first members being left of centre or Marxist in orientation. There was a high proportion of red diaper babies (children whose parents had been involved in communist party activities during the 1930's and 40's). This period in the development of the movement was characterized by attempts to pressure the government for change. Agitation was carried out through educational programs, the publication of a quarterly journal and the preparation of briefs.

The movement was rapidly taken over by non-Marxist socialists and less ideological pacifists and Quakers. Most of the newer members were middle class university students who joined in the reaction to the cold war crises. There was a short period of lull following the test ban treaty of 1963 and the

The essay is a revised version of a term paper done in the spring of 1967 for a sociology course at Queen's University. Published for the first time in this collection.

acceptance of nuclear arms for Canada by the Pearson Government, and then debate focussed on the broader issues of Canada's commitment to NATO, and the general theory and practice of nonviolence. Eventually, CUCND members came to the conclusion that there was no future in Canada at that time for a single-issue peace movement, and their attention turned to the social structures and attitudes supporting military policies. This transition was aided by the efforts of American radicals to extend their organizing activities into Canada. By 1964, members of SDS (Students for a Democratic Society) were mapping out plans for the liberation of Canadian Indians and paying regular visits 'up north'. The CUCND period of Canadian student left politics, came to an end at a conference in Regina in '64, and the Student Union for Peace Action, SUPA, was launched with a draft statement consisting of five points:

The need to challenge the Nation-State System; non-alignment (as a transitional stage between the nation-state and world peace); student syndicalism (whereby students begin to organize people with social problems into 'people's unions'); the relationship between social issues and problems of war and peace and the importance that SUPA reflect its ends and values in its means (thus the importance of using non-violent direct action).[1]

The Regina conference was influenced by ideas emerging from the publication of a document known as the Port Huron Statement by the Students for a Democratic Society in the United States. The Port Huron Statement harkened back to a traditional strain of American liberalism based on a populist individualism that was profoundly anti-intellectual and that in essence denied the importance of class struggle. SDS simply challenged America to live up to its rhetoric. The students' demand for 'participatory democracy' was, in effect, a demand that the United States fulfill the promises of its constitution and its revolution. Participatory democracy as a concept did not transcend liberal pluralism. It relied on a belief that, if all individuals 'had a say' in decision-making, a natural harmony among all people would reveal itself. The concept did not admit to the existence of class contradictions as a basic dynamic in economic, social and political events.

Equally in keeping with the American left liberal tradition was SDS's rejection of structure in organization. It is no accident that a movement that found inspiration in Henry David Thoreau's treatise on civil disobedience did not take easily to notions of building an alternative political party or of establishing a coherent mass organization of the left. Instead, the American New Left singled out minority groups and extremely poverty-stricken segments of the population as primary agents of change, and attempted to organize these groups on a pragmatic basis around their everyday needs with no overall program for achieving a fundamental redistribution of political and economic power. Unaware of or scornful of the socialist tradition in their own country, American radicals were unable to perceive the necessity of evolving a political program that could engage the working class as a whole in revolutionary change. Such difficulties were to be expected in a largely middle class movement operating in a social context in which the labour movement seemed irrevocably committed to business unionism and to the policies of the American Empire, and in a country where the blacks were the most significant force in conflict with the system.

The middle class composition of the youth movement in Canada lent itself to the importation of American New Left ideas and to the generation of similar ideas in the Canadian context. For many in the Canadian middle class, the American left liberal tradition was their tradition also, and they experienced no difficulty in responding to it in the same way as did their American counterparts. Their protests and projects were a northern extension of activities south of the border.

The summer projects that followed the 1964 founding conference of SUPA were almost all community organizing efforts. Students invaded Doukhobor and Métis communities in British Columbia and Saskatchewan, and slums in Kingston and Halifax. The Comox project of 1965, carrying on in the tradition of projects in North Bay and La Macaza the previous year, was the last of the peace organizing efforts in towns with nuclear installations. Members of the movement now focussed on broader issues of poverty and discrimination, with the ideological justification that all social issues were interrelated and somehow connected to the problem of maintaining peace.

A Selma demonstration in Toronto in 1965 attracted hundreds of university students who sympathized with the plight of the American Blacks, and SNCC (Student Non-Violent Coordinating Committee) and SDS members crossed the border frequently to drum up support in Canada. Inevitably, the Canadian students "got all hung-up about the Canadian Indians. It was the closest thing we had to the American Negroes."[2] The students also got hung-up on the Métis, the Halifax blacks, the Doukhobors and the poverty-stricken. The Canadian movement borrowed ideas and tactics from its American counterparts with little discrimination. It was easily seduced by civil rights and C. Wright Mills, and sworn into action by the perplexing vows of 'participatory democracy', and 'community organizing'.

During its first summer, the movement also set up a Vietnam research project in Montreal, and a school for social theory (patterned on the ideas of the American free university movement) in Toronto.

In the fall of 1965, about ninety people met at Ste. Calixte to evaluate their summer's work and make plans for the following months. The conference became known shortly afterwards as 'the false high', but participants still referred to it in a tone of near reverence.

We were all new to the movement . . . we really felt involved in the revolution . . .

There was a mystique about the leaders; some of them were experienced radicals from the United States . . .

There was a real communal feeling there; I've never seen anything like it since . . .

It fit in with a feeling we had . . . I had always felt suspicious about the power plays; it was good to know I was right, and there were people around who knew the Truth . . .

It clicked, people there loved each other[3] . . .

Ste. Calixte was almost a religious conference. It had its high priests and its true believers, its oaths, symbols and sense of common mission. There were calls for renunciation of the old life ("We were guilty about going back to school.") and for dedication to the new. It was a real 'high', but it did not last for long. Those who went out to serve the cause on the campus and in the field were soon disillusioned. Personality conflicts arose among project members, the SUPA office offered little support, and the sense of community was lost. One of the worst problems identified was the lack of guidelines for organizing.

We didn't know what made us different from ordinary

social workers. We were supposed to be intellectuals activating the masses, but where do you begin?   —Joan Newman, Kingston Community Project

We approached the situation with an idealized picture of the Indian ('someone whose whole culture rejects what is hollow about Middle Class America'), what we were going to do ('just learning and making friendly contacts') and what students could or would do ('this was a long term project'). In some sense most of these things are true, but they are only half the story and in a number of communities today we are just white men who came and dabbled and went away again.   —Liora Proctor, Neestow Project

The Neestow Project lasted for three summers, then finally succumbed to outside pressures and internal strains and confusions. The Kingston Community Project continued for a longer stretch of time, but in a different form and with a different spirit that increasingly dissociated it from the original movement.

Many SUPA members were totally disillusioned after the twin catastrophes of an unsuccessful conference in Saskatoon in December of 1965 and an unsuccessful Vietnam action in Ottawa in March, 1966. The Saskatoon meeting turned out to be the exact opposite of the 'false high' at Ste. Calixte. The setting was dismal; the members were 'hung-up'; the atmosphere was stifling. The predominant mood was one of self-deprecation.

People expected others to listen to their problems and love them anyway. Pretty soon everyone hated everyone else . . .

There was a horrible sense of failure . . . somehow we had let the movement down, and it was nobody's fault. It was the movement's fault . . .

I'd never seen such a bunch of screwed up people[4] . . .

The Ottawa Vietnam Week action was the last straw for some of the Ste. Calixte crew. It was claimed that decisions had been made in Toronto in an elitist fashion, with little or no consultation of the membership. There was talk of power plays and oligarchies. Just before the conference, George Grant, who was to have been one of the speakers, withdrew because of a conflict with SUPA leadership. Altogether, less than one hundred persons participated in the week's activities. The only thing that 'redeemed' the action was the arrest of the sit-in participants on Parliament Hill on March 7, and the subsequent trial.

A Montreal federal council meeting in November of 1966 saw a crucial confrontation between two diverging parts of the movement: the Toronto group and the Montreal group, each with its own plans for an upcoming membership conference in December. The Montreal conference organizing committee had resigned after the expression of opposition by Ontario SUPA members to their concept of the purpose of the conference, their plans for its format (which included big name speakers and structured meetings) and their arrangements for accommodations. The conflict was portrayed by two Montrealers as a clash between the politicos of Quebec and the personalists of Ontario.

Is it a therapeutic organization or a political organization? . . . An unstructured conference will lead SUPA further into quicksand . . . We want a direction and purpose in Quebec and also I know Saskatchewan and Alberta will agree with this. Our organization will become more politically effective for change as well as more democratic . . . The less structured the organization is the more a few charismatic leaders run the show[5] . . .

If we are only a social club that fulfills the needs of a few so-called radicals, SUPA has no uses. I've always been of the opinion that the raison d'être of the movement was to bring revolution and not to fulfill the needs of a few sensitive but alienated intellectuals[6]. . .

The Toronto people attributed the problems to an irresponsibility on the part of the Montreal conference planners ("Montreal made no effort whatsoever to communicate with the rest of the movement") and to a lack of sensitivity to the needs of the members of SUPA at that stage of its development:

> . . . the primary goal of this conference must be to involve as many people as possible in an event that will tend to bring them closer to hard political activity; and you do not get that involvement by a resolution-passing, document-writing, speech-giving conference[7]. . .

> . . . Perhaps a basic articulation of our differences is that we are more aware of the depth and totality of the restructuring of consciousness that is necessary to make Canadian youth into political activists because there is no general political awareness equivalent to Quebec's to make us optimistic about the spontaneous development of such radical consciousness.[8] . . .

The Toronto group triumphed in Montreal. The membership conference was postponed to the following summer, and the December conference was changed to an education conference, its location changed to Waterloo.

The Waterloo conference at the end of 1966 revealed the existence of tensions in the movement that were already threatening to destroy it. There was a significant confrontation between the CYC (Company of Young Canadians) volunteers who claimed to be radicals and spoke of the 'impending revolution' and skeptical SUPA members who claimed the CYC's were not radicals and could not be revolutionaries, given the context within which they had chosen to work. There were also confrontations between NDP members and SUPA members, and between newer SUPA members and its older defenders. Shortly after the beginning of the conference, a representative of the Nova Scotia project accused the movement leaders of being overly intellectual and obscure, and removed from the practical considerations of the community organizers. The conference was subsequently restructured to discuss the problems of communication between the various sectors of the movement, and the possibilities of mutual support and criticism. A committee was set up to write a political manifesto for the movement, to be discussed and amended at the September membership conference.

The months following the Waterloo conference of December, 1966, witnessed a continuing divergence among the various tendencies in SUPA. In the fall of 1967, SUPA's long-awaited membership conference, which attracted only a small number of people, became the site for the disbanding of the organization and its replacement by a short-lived New Left Committee.

Who then were the members of SUPA, and why did their movement fall apart after such a brief period of time?

The concept of membership in the movement was always quite vague. Estimates of turnover in membership varied from several hundred to several thousand, depending on what criteria were used. There was general agreement, however, that anyone who had subscribed to the Newsletter, attended the conferences or participated in the actions would qualify as a member of SUPA.

The majority of these subscribers and participants were students or recent graduates between the ages of eighteen and twenty-five. Many of them were residents of the Central Canadian provinces, primarily Ontario, although there was always some representation from the Maritimes and the West. Several CYC organizers considered themselves to be members of SUPA or were sympathetic to the movement, and a few organizers with independent projects identified with the movement, although their projects were not associated with SUPA. Members of various groups such as the Student Christian Movement, Kairos and the NDP also related to the movement.

SUPA activists pointed to similarities between Canadian and American radicals, noting that the chief distinguishing characteristic of both groups was a rejection of the middle class milieu in which they were socialized.[9] A sociological study of the backgrounds of student activists in Chicago revealed a number of interesting characteristics, most of which were similar to characteristics frequently attributed to SUPA members.[10] The study compared the backgrounds and families of activists and non-activists, and discovered that activists tended to come from high income families and recent immigrant stock. They were disproportionately Jewish, and less likely to have small town or rural backgrounds. Their fathers were disproportionately professionals, and both fathers and mothers were disproportionately highly educated. Their mothers were more likely to be employed. The students were likely to have higher grades than their non-activist contemporaries, and different values, with less emphasis on career, religion and marriage. There appeared to be a continuity between the activists' values and those of their parents, who were relatively liberal or left in their political attitudes and relatively active in politics.

The movement in Canada attracted relatively intelligent and articulate students, some seeking an integrated critique of their society, others seeking immediate relief for immediate discontents. It had intellectual, psychological, political and sexual attractions for the middle class students who attached themselves to it. Many people appeared to have joined to find a counter community of sorts, a reference group with values more in consonance with their own experience than those of other contemporaries. Some joined to find therapy for their identity problems. Some joined because of social concerns and a desire to act. Others, because they thought that SUPA was the 'best game in town', more exciting and involving than the Conservative Club or Young Peoples. A number of members cited several of the above as their motives for getting involved.

The motives for joining, however, appeared to be different from the reasons for staying or leaving. The movement had a fantastically high rate of turnover in membership after its CUCND days. Only a very few persons remained active in it for more than a year.

One characteristic frequently attributed to the SUPA community by many of its own members was a tendency towards self-righteousness. This phenomenon might be partially explained by the fact that the movement was built on the basis of individual *moral* responses to social hypocrisies and injustices. (It was described by one of its gurus as "an ethical movement in search of an analysis.")[11] The individual moral stance of members was supplemented, to a certain extent, by the historical and sociological ideas of left liberal and Marxist analyses, but the members tended to be wary of the organizational directions implicit in the development of a coherent ideology.

SUPA members generally viewed their social criticisms as outgrowths of their personal moral insights and intuitions. That is probably one reason why some reacted so strongly to discussions of ideology, fearful of the possibility of external imposition of principles and ideas. Although SUPA never did have a coherent ideology, its members subscribed to a broad set of attitudes and ideas that limited the scope of their activities and gave some indication of the bounds of their consensus. They shared a distrust and dislike of the status quo, and of relationships manifesting authoritarianism, manipulation, elitism, dogmatism or hypocrisy. They placed a high value on personal relationships characterized by openness, integrity, and sensitivity. They tended to develop in-group and out-group stereotypes, prizing their own group above others, and looking down on outsiders. Very few spelled out the details of their Good Society, but most had a great faith in the plasticity of human nature and the flexibility of human arrangements.

These ideas and attitudes were not in themselves enough to keep the movement together. The eschewing of ideology and formal structure made it very difficult for people in the movement to organize on a continuing basis, or even to define and expand upon the consensus that existed within the group. SUPA began to develop a split between a militant wing that was to form the basis later of small groups on the left, and a liberal wing that was increasingly attracted to government institutions like the Company of Young Canadians. The CYC and the Travailleurs Etudiants du Quebec were good examples of mechanisms of social control. They were employed by the Establishment to use the skills and talents of potential opponents for piecemeal reforms, strengthening the status quo. The government provided resources to support the young reformers, but it also defined the limits of their reforms. Organizations and institutions such as these drew a fair number of young activists away from the movement. The Company of Young Canadians, for example, had several active SUPA members working within it, serving on its board of directors, recruiting volunteers, community organizing, and setting up its research department. These people helped to create myths about the CYC that attracted others to the organization. Their own justification for their actions was that they were using government resources for revolutionary purposes, and would continue to do so as long as the government would tolerate it.

Those of us who are in the CYC should be providing the revolutionary core for an imminent, impending split between SUPA and the CYC. SUPA is broke; the CYC has money. Use the money of the CYC to organize, educate, politicize the poor, the have-nots, the lumpen-proletariat against the economic structure and the government of the city, the province, the country. Use Pearson's money to organize against Pearson. Use the taxpayers' money to organize against the biggest taxpayers. Use the CYC to destroy the CYC. Only by organizing, in the de-centralized sense of self-organizing, the poor, the dispossessed, the Indians, the Negroes, the poor whites, the poor working classes, the youth, the fucked, can we count on a necessary constituency when the time is ripe for revolution in this country.[12]

The money was too much to resist. SUPA members started a flirtation with the CYC that inevitably destroyed their credibility as radicals and set some of them up as the rip-off artists of their generation. Predictably, the government clamped down on the CYC when its activities became embarrassing, eliminating all volunteer control of the organization and establishing a form of director guardianship to supervise its activities.

Some of the more militant members of SUPA established a new base, for a brief period of time, in the Canadian Union of Students. But the mainstream student union was too fragile an organization to withstand the clash between its radical activists and a student constituency not yet ready for such ideas. CUS soon collapsed and many of the ex-SUPA militants channelled their energies into a myriad of small and fragmented left organizations, centred on or near the major Canadian university campuses.

In its final death pangs, SUPA delivered its members not only into the CYC and CUS, but also into the drug culture, commune communities, the Waffle wing of the New Democratic Party, a multiplicity of new political and social movements (including women's liberation groups), and a variety of mainstream institutions and occupations. Many who were once allies in their discontent with existing social practices and priorities became bitter enemies in their efforts to work out strategies for social change.

The Student Union for Peace Action did not simply fall victim to government cooptation and ideological divergence. It disintegrated also because of rapid changes in the society that surrounded it.

The Vietnam War created a revulsion in Canada against American imperialism. At the same time, the increasing awareness in Canada that the country had become a consumer market and resource base for American corporations heightened the sense of national consciousness and created a milieu in which socialist solutions to worker's problems attracted the interest of growing numbers of people. Canadians began to give up their flirtations with the 'American Dream' in the late sixties as they witnessed the violent expressions of American corporate and political power, both within the United States and abroad. It was becoming apparent that the multi-national monopoly capitalism which had its main base in America was not the liberator, but the oppressor, of mankind.

Within Canada itself, the rise of Quebec nationalism amplified the growing anti-imperialism of young radicals in English Canada and became an important internal focus for Canadian socialists.

The May events of 1968 in France, and other manifestations of a renewed Marxism among young people, contributed to the rebirth of socialist ideas and notions of class politics among young activists in Canada.

As the Canadian radical youth movement became increasingly socialist and anti-imperialist, it began to face up to the problems of corporate control of Canada and the challenges of the Canadian left tradition. The difficulties created by attempts to organize around the left liberalism of American populism were replaced by a new set of problems concerning the relationship of the socialist left with Canadian social democracy and with the country's social democratic labour tradition.

NOTES
1. Harding, Jim. "An Ethical Movement in Search of an Analysis." *Our Generation* 4(1): 22.
2. Interview with SUPA activist Don Roebuck in the spring of 1967.
3. Interviews with SUPA members who had participated in the Ste. Calixte conference. Spring, 1967.
4. Interviews with SUPA members who had participated in the Saskatoon conference. Spring, 1967.
5. From a letter from Alan Marks, Montreal, to Don Roebuck, Toronto, dated October 17, 1966.
6. From a letter from André Cardinal, Montreal, to Tony Hyde, Toronto, dated October 21, 1966.
7. From a letter from Tony Hyde, Toronto, to Alan Marks, Montreal, dated October 19, 1966.
8. From a letter from Heather Dean, Toronto, to Alan Marks, Montreal, dated October 19, 1966.
9. Interviews with activists Don McKelvey and Don Roebuck in the spring of 1967.
10. Flacks, Richard. "The Liberated Generation: An Exploration of the Roots of Social Protest." Working paper No. 1, Youth and Social Change Project, University of Chicago.
11. Harding, Jim. "An Ethical Movement in Search of an Analysis." *Our Generation* 4(1)
12. Folkman, Ted. *SUPA Newsletter* Special Centennial Issue, p. 20.

4. Student Protest in Canada

Caroline Brown

The author of this paper has been active in radical student politics both in her native Saskatchewan and at Queen's University where this paper was written in early 1969. Like the selection which precedes it, this one is concerned with the underlying structural conditions, the interconnected events on the world scene, and the unique experiences of some Canadian students which both contributed to and became the raison d'être for the assault on the universities during the second half of the 1960's.

In the Preface to his remarkable and totally iconoclastic Bomb Culture* *Jeff Nuttall remarks:*

> *To reduce the international student revolt to the meager proportions normally encompassed by their [i.e. the 'established press'] discussion, and to assess the revolt on the basis of its declared* political *intentions is a ready instrument of reduction, a telescope through which the monster can be viewed from the wrong end, picked up with the eyebrow tweezers of cod-sociology and clapped, safely they hope, in the matchbox of some journalistic category.*
>
> *Actually the plain and obvious fact is that . . . young people, under various pretexts, made war on their elders, and their elders made war on them. The war continues.*

This essay was written before the grim events at Sir George Williams University in Montreal shook usually complacent Canadians into realizing just how real that 'war' was.

Within the context of this paper an attempt shall be made to analyse the nature and bases of student protest in Canada, delineating the major streams of thought or influences, and discussing student tactics and strategies as well as analysing the underlying reasons for the current outburst of student unrest. The basic material for this analysis, of necessity, will be drawn from press reports and magazine articles. However, because the media has been charged, by various factions, with having sensationalized, and often misrepresented, the position of student radicals, an attempt has been made wherever possible to examine original statements found in such publications as *Canadian Dimension, Our Generation, Praxis,* and CUS position papers. The overall emphasis will be on protest in English-speaking Canada and on the activism of the Left. Much of the protest in French-speaking Canada is complicated by other issues such as Quebec's desire for self-determination (a topic too broad to explore in this context). And right-wing protest in Canada is a peripheral type of activity, usually manifest by a kind of anti-activism in response to the actions of the Left. Due to limitations on the length of such a paper it will not be possible to analyse the historical pattern of protest in Canada over the last decade, which began with the CUCND in the late fifties and has undergone various changes. Rather, an attempt shall be made to discuss the immediate situation – 'where it's at' now, to use the current jargon.

The underlying reasons most frequently cited by analysts for the current wave of student protest include: the general sense of anomie reflected in society at large; the ramifications of permissive upbringing in children who are now reaching university

* London, MacGibbon & Kee Ltd., 1968

This essay was written in 1969 as a term paper for a political sociology seminar at Queen's University. Published for the first time in this collection.

age, manifest in a reaction against authoritarian institutions; the failure of idealism reflected in a disillusionment with the gradualism of modern methods of change, as well as a disillusionment with electoral politics and with ideology (although some elements in the protest movement are highly idealistic and some intensely ideological); the hypocrisy evident in the gap between reality and the ideal, accompanied by a lack of humanitarian values in a technological society. The changing sociology of the university itself – from a university to a multiversity – combined with its failure to involve students in its decision-making processes, has been advanced as one of the chief reasons. Reams have been written about student protest from these various angles and practically anything one can say at this point is already cliché. Each of these analyses offer partial explanations but without examining individual motivations – which are many and varied – it is impossible to subscribe to any one of them as a total explanation.

Keeping these in mind and turning to the specifics of student protest in Canada, let us develop a framework for our discussion. In doing so, it may be useful for the sake of analysis to look at the categories outlined by Claude Bissell, President of the University of Toronto. In a speech given at Windsor after his return from a year at Harvard, Bissell identified two groups involved in student protest.

> Among students deeply concerned with the role and future of the university, there are two recognizable groups. One is small, made up of fanatically committed members, and therefore, powerful far beyond numbers. In the US its hard core is an organization called Students for a Democratic Society. They draw upon a literature that is philosophically elaborate, but their actions are governed by four simple assumptions: Western society is hopelessly corrupt; the university is part of that society and its principal apologist; the university must, therefore, be destroyed and refashioned; in the work of cleansing destruction, the ends justify the means. Let us call this group the extremists, or, even the saboteurs.
>
> The second group, much larger than the first, although a minority on the campus, believes that the university is central in our society, that it should be the vanguard of reform, and that accordingly, it should be governed in such a way as to reflect the opinions and wishes of those most closely identified with it. These students believe in open discussion, and, in the statement of their views, they are persistent, uncompromising, and immensely self-assured. Let us call this group the activists.[1]

As president of Canada's best university, Bissell's attitudes can be taken as typical of many persons holding the same position, although perhaps he is more liberal than some and has a greater awareness of the realities of student protest than many presidents have. He is viewed by most Canadians, including many radicals, as a humane, liberal administrator attempting to run a reasonably efficient university. He recognizes that the university needs some changes; but is not willing to push ahead fast enough to meet the demands of the more radical elements. His strategy for change in the university is one of compromising to the more moderate element, the political activists, in order to reduce the power of the more militant faction, the saboteurs. By granting the, in his view, legitimate demands of the activists he feels that it is possible to prevent the saboteurs from seizing upon an issue, which is perceived as significant by the activists, and by large numbers of moderates, and escalating it into a confrontation of such proportions that the original provocation is often obscured. An intelligent strategy; but as he confesses some time later when he is on the point of resigning, he often lacks the power to carry it out, being subjected to many pressures from less liberal elements both within and without the university hierarchy.[2] Perhaps his major tactical blunder was in publicizing his strategy so early. Student radicals have studied these pronouncements with some interest and often used them as a point from which to launch their own strategies. The importance of Bissell's analysis to radicals is evidenced by the fact that "A Strategy for Change" was reprinted in *Praxis*, a radical student bulletin.[3]

Using the categories outlined by Bissell, let us first examine the position and the demands of the element known as the political activists. Broadly, this group is concerned with issues such as 'democratizing the university', and creating a more egalitarian and humanistic society. By democratizing the university is meant, not merely the election of individual students to particular governing bodies, but allowing students to have some say in the overall decisions affecting their education. Their objections to the type of representation often proffered by liberal administrators such as Bissell are articulated by Steve Langdon, SAC president at the U of T, in an interview with *Maclean's*.

> Bissell: You mean that the appointment of students to these committees will not be a contribution to this process? [democratization of the university].
> Langdon: Not unless there is a possibility of changing that hierarchical community.
> Bissell: Because students are not powerful enough?
> Langdon: I think it will not happen partly because of the attitude of faculty and administrators. I also don't think the 'powers that be' in society will permit a university to be that kind of radical community. I think the university is too enmeshed in society for that to occur. It's enmeshed in the kind of courses it offers; in the way it socializes students who go through it; in the research work it's doing. Even the University of Toronto does something like $500,000 worth of research for the American military establishment. I think it's because of this position that you can't get changes in universities.[4]

In addition to their objections to the hierarchical structure of the university and its links with business and military establishments, radical students look upon these types of appointments as 'tokenism' with democratic participation being replaced by 'representivity'.

The political activists, however, are more prepared to confront the administrator on his own terms, for example, arguing in favor of the abolition of examinations by quoting from the Macpherson Report. They prefer to engage in confrontations of ideas rather than confrontations of power, and are willing to negotiate with administrators using 'regular channels' as a first step. In the absence of satisfactory results by this method they resort to direct action tactics – demonstrations, strikes, sit-ins, etc. As a rule this group is unwilling to resort to violent means to attain its ends. Steve Langdon says,

> I think the techniques you use in demonstrations should reflect what you're trying to do. If you're trying to set up a non-violent, non-authoritarian structure, you should use non-violent, non-authoritarian means to do it. But I don't consider taking over an administration building violent. I can't accept the sanctity of private property in a university community, the idea that this building belongs to them and I can't go there.[5]

On the whole, the strategies and tactics of this segment incorporate a greater commitment to legal-rational norms than do those of the more militant faction. They frequently act as a pressure group, committed to the rule-of-law; are less cynical about electoral politics (often belonging to either the Liberal Party or the New Democratic Party); and hold elective positions in student governments. In general, they believe that changes within the university towards a greater freedom and democratic participation will ultimately result in changes in the society at large and, at any rate, look to the university as the legitimate area and focus for their protest. As Bissell says they look to the university as central to society and see it as the 'vanguard of reform'.

Concerning the university the demands of this group include: getting rid of examinations; giving students some control over curriculum; abolishing tuition fees; giving students a voice in university planning, including how the university spends its money and the type of research it engages in; as well as a demand from certain sections for student salaries. They engage in such positive activities as the setting up of course unions or counter-courses as alternative structures so that students may see the difference and make a choice. They are also much more interested in experiments in free education such as Rochdale, as are many of the anarchist faction.

Turning to the more militant group, the so-called saboteurs, one finds that they differ from the political activists not only on strategies and tactics, as is popularly assumed, but also on more basic philosophical questions. Large elements of this group are much more intensely ideological than the former group. Unlike the activists they do not consider it relevant or even possible to work with liberals such as Bissell. Their attitude is that liberalism and all of its accrued myths must first be exposed and smashed before one is able to begin talking about the 'democratizing' of society. Witness, for example, their reaction to Bissell's now famous statement "Beyond Clark Kerr lies, not the millenium, but Ronald Regan".

> If students won't listen to Claude Bissell, they can expect a backlash. This is an implicit threat that our President is going to crack down.
> Another way of saying the same thing is that in a conflict the 'liberal' drops his sympathetic smile and shows his authoritarian teeth. When it boils right down to it, even the liberal President is going to get tough to preserve the *status quo*. Beyond Clark Kerr lies, not the millenium, but Thomas Hobbes and *The Leviathan*.[6]

The writings of Marcuse and others have made them acutely aware of the role of dissent within the legal-rational structure of a democratic, pluralistic society and within the liberal's frame of reference. It simply adds another dimension to the liberal's concept of pluralism, and can be accommodated by the process of what Marcuse terms 'repressive tolerance'[7] and what Philip Resnick, in relating to a Canadian context, has termed 'repressive liberalism'.

> Yet Canadian liberalism, is no less repressive than its American counterpart where fundamentals are concerned. It has been fortunate that it has been better able to keep the structural contradictions in Canadian society under control in the 1960's than Imperial America or Gaullist France, but these contradictions exist nonetheless....
> What liberal theorists cannot acknowledge is that pluralism and countervailing power are another name for class power, and that the unequal distribution of power in Canadian society is maintained and enhanced by legitimizing the balance of interests that exists. Liberalism, for example, does not deny labour the right to participate in the allocation of

the economic pie. Liberalism can only welcome the participation of labour as one of the support elements in the capitalist system, even if strikes are the occasional price one must pay for a 'free economy'. . . .

The same is true in other spheres. Liberal administrators in the universities are not blind to the frustration and powerlessness which most students and junior faculty experience. They are more than prepared to provide forums for the release of this pent-up resentment, to discuss university reform and slowly implement low-key changes in the educational system. . . . Why not give the students more of a stake in the capitalist university and turn them from potential dissenters into a support group for the system?[8]

Thus, the argument concerning the liberal is twofold. On the one hand he is seen as stifling protest by ultimately relying upon coercive power and authoritarianism, hence, implicitly denying his own liberal assumptions. Ultimately his power rests upon an appeal to force, which, as the radicals point out, he is prepared to use to buttress his own position. In this instance what the students are really exposing is the impasse of liberalism when faced with a challenge which would ultimately destroy it. Alternately, the argument used is that liberalism neutralizes dissent by absorbing it through the process of what Resnick calls 'repressive liberalism'. Either method of crushing or disposing of dissent is unacceptable to radicals. The former, however, is the position that many radicals prefer to see exposed as it denies legitimacy to the liberal argument on the basis of its own assumptions. And many of their strategies are calculated to force the liberal to expose himself in this way.

All forms of political dissent range along a continuum. The President recognizes the legitimacy of dissent but would like it articulated in a non-political way. How convenient! The "University must be . . . most tender toward dissent", [This is a quote from Bissell (*Star* and *Globe*, April 16, 1968.)] "so long as it does not actually affect the smooth running of the university." By using the word 'politics' as a kind of swear-word and by appealing to the rhetoric of individual rights, students are being persuaded to dissent, if they must, but on no account to reflect that discontent in organized activity intended to change the nature of the social reality which makes them discontented.[9]

The latter part of this statement is the key to the actions of this group. They are determined to "change the nature of the social reality which makes them dissent", and not to be co-opted into dissenting within the mainstream of what they see as an inhumane, unjust society.

What is the "nature of the social reality that makes them dissent"? Perhaps the best statement on this is presented by Stanley Gray, [former] lecturer in the Department of Economics and Political Science at McGill, ex-chairman of Students for a Democratic University (SDU-the Canadian counterpart of the American SDS), and a leader in various student actions at McGill.

At base, they [student radicals] are demanding that the university's educational processes, social commitment and governing institutions conform to human needs rather than the needs of capital, as defined and enforced by those who run the university.

This reaction is natural and inevitable for this generation of students. The multiversity is a bundle of explosive contradictions: it cannot at one and the same time offer students a degree of education and freedom and prevent them from using this freedom and education to critically evaluate the university and challenge the type of existence it forces upon

them. Well-educated people cannot be kept subservient in their primary milieux, and it is no accident that it is the brightest students who fill the ranks of the campus activists.[10] Alienated from the process and the product of their work, students confront a university that is individually stifling, conservative, status-oriented and hierarchical. Desiring to actively participate in developing for themselves a meaningful and integrated education, they're forced into narrow and specialized training routines and find their course work more and more restricted and degraded with the poor and the oppressed and committed to creating a new social order, students see their administrations whoring their universities to the powers-that-be, directly and indirectly serving the interests of capitalism and imperialism.[11]

The ideology of this group and its relative strength is reflected to a large extent in the type of resolutions which were passed at the CUS Congress in Guelph in September, 1968, indicating the truth of Bissell's statement that they are powerful beyond their numbers. Part of their power must, of course, be attributed to the apathy of the majority. The following policy statement reflects the influence of their thinking.

Canadian society is not self-determined: our culture, political and economic lives are dominated by giant American corporations. . . . The needs of this system both for trained personnel and for economically useful knowledge takes precedence over educational aspirations of the students. Students' needs are subordinated to the needs of an economy they do not control.

We realize that American imperialism is not the sole obstacle to Canadian self-determination. Self-determination is obstructed by the authoritarianism and repression inherent in the corporate organization of our society. Canadian corporatism, were it substituted for American, would be as repressive and authoritarian.

No system which does not include democracy and self-determination is acceptable. Inevitably we must commit ourselves to a democratic non-exploitative alternative.[12]

These statements, in addition, reflect the type of Marxist or neo-Marxist thinking of an increasingly significant element of student protesters. As Gray pointed out in his Couchiching address, "Marxism is coming more and more to be the common denominator of all student movements in North America and Western Europe, even so in the New Left SDS in the United States."[13] Claude Bissell, too, remarked on this development: "I was frankly amazed when I returned to Toronto to find that kind of Marxist approach had become fairly respectable among the extremists. A year or two ago you might have found it at the individual level but not among groups."[14]

The kind of Marxism which the more sophisticated elements of this group are talking about is not primarily the economic determinism of the Old Left but a higher stage of Marxism in which man is liberated from his material and economic circumstances, in which economics become superfluous, and one is free to live according to his own wishes. This is the stage which advanced industrial societies such as Canada could be at as a result of the technological revolution; and technology, in the view of these students, should be used for human ends rather than as an instrument of repression. Given this philosophical analysis, many of these students are challenging such traditional values as the work ethic and attitudes regarding private property, which they see as the gods of capitalism. This attitude is reflected in the way they look upon university buildings – as their buildings to be used as they see fit.

The changing outlook from an essentially non-ideological one to one which has much more of an ideological orientation is reflected also in the "Statement of the New Left Committee – Oct. 1967" at the time of the dissolution of SUPA (Student Union for Peace Action). In fact, one of their conclusions in analyzing the failure of SUPA was that despite the rhetoric about a 'radical analysis', it failed to have any ideological underpinnings. It is now referred to as "a naive populism" which was "greatly hampered by its failure to seriously consider Marxist analyses or socialist perspectives and by its isolation from and ignorance of working-class life and institutions."[15] The New Left Committee then adopted the following statement which reflects the attitudes of many involved in student protest.

Ultimately, we look forward to the development in Canada of a mass, democratic, radical movement. The New Left Committee holds that the working-class, both 'blue-collar' and 'white-collar', because of its numbers and its strategic economic role in this society, will play an essential part in the development of any such movement.[16]

Many of these student radicals look upon activities within the university as peripheral to the real concerns. Martin Loney, president-elect of CUS, speaking at the September Congress reflected on this. "When we talk about student power, when we talk about student reform, it isn't a matter of life and death. But to people starving in unaligned third-world countries, imprisoned in Czechoslovakia and dying in Vietnam, social change is of higher intensity. They don't have the luxury of arguing student power."[17]

Other elements, however, also draw upon a Marxian analysis, in an attempt to see themselves as an exploited class. In part this attitude comes from the writings of Paul Goodman who says, "At present in the United States students – middle class youth – are the major exploited class. The labour of intelligent youth is needed, and they are accordingly subjected to tight scheduling, speed-up and other factory exploitative methods. Then it is not surprising they organize their CIO."[18]

In addition to the Marxist faction within the 'saboteur' element, one finds a large number of what might roughly be called latter-day anarchists. In general, their philosophy is anti-authoritarianism, anti-institution, anti-war, and anti-hierarchy. Often their individualism is demonstrated more in the form of protest against the social-sexual mores of the society and they are frequently concerned with creating a completely new life style.

Commitment must take on a new and fresh meaning. A new life style will evolve debunking any established piety – in thought, dress, speech patterns, art forms, social and sexual behavior, even in stimulants. In our life styles the values of spontaneity, experimentation, individual style and free expression must again be celebrated. Our revolutionary times demand no less a revolutionary personal and cultural transformation.[19]

Their view of the university is one of the 'ivory tower' seeking truth in whatever direction it leads. They would no doubt agree with McGuigan when he says, "It is just as unfair for the radical student to impose the mythology of revolution as an outer boundary of questioning on the university as it is for the liberal to throw up his bounds of questioning. I think both of them impose limitations on academic freedom and I, for one, am not willing to accept the limitation of either."[20] They fit into the 'saboteur' element because of their assumptions about the hypocrisy and corruption of Western society and their rejection of its dominant values.

In addition, this faction has as one of its top priorities the building of counter-institutions. "A radical movement cannot wait to change society 'when it comes to power'. It must do so

from the beginning of its existence by building counter-institutions. This includes everything from strengthening and radicalizing the co-operative movement, whether in housing, food purchase, legal and medical aid, insurance and capital borrowing to the creation of new primary, secondary schools and free universities."[21]

And it is most distrustful of electoral politics, seeing voting in elections and involvement in politics as a question of 'management rather than basic policy' at best, and as a meaningless ritualistic act at worst. Because individuals are so far removed from the real centres of power, a sense of alienation and meaninglessness pervades the political arena as well as other areas of society.

Voting as a result becomes an isolated, magic act set apart from the rest of life and ceases to have any political or social meaning except as an instrument by which the *status quo* is conserved. Electoral pageantry serves the same purpose as a circus – the beguilement of the populace. The voter is reduced to voting for dazzling smiles, clean teeth, smooth voices and firm handshakes – playing the role of a shaking puppet manipulated by the party image makers.[22]

Whereas most of the Marxist element would consider it relevant to vote for the NDP at elections, many of the anarchist faction consider the kinds of 'marginal' gains offered by the NDP to be as irrelevant as any other part of the electoral game. In fact, they see it as being worse than irrelevant – a harmful distraction because it succeeds in involving some individuals who could be spending their time more positively in the building of counter-institutions. They maintain that the new radical movement must not "be dependent in the pathetic way the NDP is dependent with its eighteenth century rationalist approach in an irrational system."[23]

This element of the student movement in particular and the New Left in general has been charged with a kind of anti-intellectualism by its conventional critics and with a lack of ideological base by its Marxian critics. Roussopoulos attempts to answer those charges:

The movement is, in a healthy way, against intellectualism although it is not anti-intellectual. It is anti-dogmatic, and anti-sectarian but progressively ideological, understanding the tremendous importance of creating first an existentially committed constitutency.[24]

To the anarchist, university students are seen as only part of this 'existentially committed constituency'. It would also include trade unionists, low-income tenants, welfare recipients, and other elements of the disaffected.

Although these contemporary anarchists fall into the tradition of the classical French anarchists in their emphasis on libertarianism, they do not conform strictly in their emphasis on the 'building of a movement' and on the 'building of counter-institutions.'

In addition to the various Marxian and anarchistic strains within the protest movement, one finds that often in a confrontation situation there will be a group of nihilistic hangers-on, who join the protest with the hope of precipitating violence. Stan Gray in analysing in *Canadian Dimension* the confrontation over the *McGill Daily* labelled this group the 'mindless activists'.

It will be observed that many of the so-called saboteurs, particularly the Marxists, like the political activists, *do* hold elective offices in student government. In most instances they frankly admit that they are doing so only because it gives them a sounding board from which to propagate their ideas and assists them in 'increasing the consciousness of students'. It is certainly not that they see these positions as a medium for basic social change.

Concerning tactics and strategies, the 'saboteur' element is much more disposed to confrontations of power than of ideas. They look upon radical action itself as a great educating force. "People only become radicalized when they're emotionally involved", says Cyril Levitt, editor of *Praxis*. Demonstrations, sit-ins, and strikes are the kinds of experiences where students become involved and have an opportunity to analyze what the university and society are all about. Gerald McGuigan attempts to illustrate in his article "In Search of Issues" that the term 'issue' has a two-dimensional aspect, the practical and the symbolic. And when an issue is escalated into a confrontation you have an education in the radical sense (i.e. a 'leading out' of students from old forms to a new awareness in terms of the old forms) taking place. "Confrontations . . . are intended to be shocks which create, *ipso facto*, a new set of circumstances and which, if the confrontation is properly chosen, cannot be effectively dealt with by the normal operations of the establishment methods of handling change and new situations."[25]

Student activists are increasingly using the word 'praxis' and calling for a uniting of theory and practice. Unlike the Old Left who have been satisfied for the most part with dissenting within the basic framework of the legal-rational norms of a given society, the 'saboteur' demands the right to act upon his theoretical assumptions. And the most effective method of action is a demonstration of power. Peter Warrian says, "What power we have comes from our potential to bring the institution to a stop."[26] But he also notes in his presidential address to the CUS Congress that "This must not only be the year for socking it to the administrators or their buildings, it must be the year also of taking it to the students; we do this knowing that democracy and liberation will not come through the manipulation of the few, but only through the struggle of all."[27]

Other tactics used by protestors include what is called guerrilla theatre, a type of 'politics of the absurd', whereby students use mimicry, tearing up of academic awards, etc. as a method of exposing the ludicrousness of a particular aspect of university life.

Despite the seeming fragmentation of these various groups, they do co-operate on specific actions, although motivated to do so by very different forces. Concerning structure, the obvious observation is that student protest is highly unstructured, operating usually on the basis of *ad hoc* committees, set up to perform specific functions. These *ad hoc* committees are usually required to report back and gain the approval of the whole body before undertaking any action. Final decisions are arrived at by one of two methods – a democratic vote (simple majority) or consensus – often after considerable debate about which method ought to be used. Given the great variety of opinion and ideological outlook of the participants in a co-operative action, the consensus method has frequently proven impossible and has to some extent been abandoned as a means of decision-making in large groups. It is still used quite considerably in reaching decisions within the various factions. Although there is the appearance of democratic participation and decision-making, and everyone is firmly committed to that principle in rhetoric at least, often an actual examination in particular instances will reveal that the various factions have in fact strategized on their own in advance and are organized in such a way as to see that their wills prevail. Sometimes this is done consciously and calculatedly in order to have an issue exposed in a particular light; at other times, what would normally be called lobbying happens quite unconsciously, even accidentally, because the various factions constitute a tightly-knit in-group and their social interactions are hence with other members of the same group. One must, however, observe that manipulation and authoritarianism are not totally absent from these groups.

Concerning leadership, within the factions one finds emergent leaders in most instances. In some instances one individual will clearly have prominence over others; in others, a group may be said to have equal prominence. These leaders are never elected and have no defined bases for their authority. They emerge as leaders for a variety of reasons, which include such things as theoretical sophistication, ability to articulate well, and often personal or charismatic qualities. In co-operative actions where the various factions are united, the choosing of leaders is often more complex. Frequently the principle of collegiality will apply with each faction contributing one person. In most instances these leaders will be elected or at least agreed to by all factions. The reasons for choosing particular individuals are much more calculated than within the groups. A person may be chosen for his ability to articulate the demands of the group, his acceptability to the various factions, (some Marxists, for example, would never be acceptable to the moderates or to the anarchists, while others, representing essentially the same views, would be quite acceptable to both), because of holding an elective position in student government which gives him an air of legitimacy, and sometimes for his moderation, respectability, or public image.

To sum up, student protest in Canada consists of many influences and a variety of factional viewpoints. A clear understanding of the major streams of thought is necessary to an understanding of what is happening. Although certain groups involved in this protest tend to analyse it by calling it a movement, one cannot accept that it is a movement in the strict sociological sense at this time. A movement must have a much greater cohesiveness than is evident in the current situation. A movement must also have more unified ideological underpinnings. That is, the assumption that Western civilization is corrupt, authoritarian, undemocratic, and ought to be refashioned is not enough, especially when one considers the great variety of solutions envisaged by the various factions for its refashioning, to unify the group and have them co-operate sufficiently to succeed in making it into a movement. A movement must also encompass a greater spectrum of the population, and although an attempt has been made to involve groups other than students, these kinds of alliances have not so far been conspicuously successful. Thus, to speak of student protest in Canada, or protest generally, as a movement is to romanticize and gloss over some of the significant factors which prevent it from being a movement.

On the other hand, student unrest in the 1960's is not the same kind of protest as the protest of the 1930's, which came, not so much from students as from other groups, who indeed might be termed exploited. And it was a reaction to an immediate situation, the Depression. Protest today is occurring during a time of affluence and embodies, at best, a fundamental critique of the underlying assumptions and values of Canadian society. Nor, can it be dismissed as cursorily as Northrop Frye, for example, would like to dismiss it. In an article entitled, "Student Protest Has Shallow Roots", he refers to students as an "alienated proletariat" "in the Marxist sense", which he goes on to say is "a group of people excluded from the benefits of society, to which their efforts entitle them."[28] He attacks the analogy which students make in comparing themselves to Negroes and switches the analogy to one of comparing the protest movement to the feminist revolution. And concludes that, "Student representation on university bodies is not difficult to arrange, but I think that, as with the women's vote, it will make very little difference in practice."[29] This is wishful thinking. Whereas one agrees with him that the analogy with Negroes, who have suffered centuries of oppression and injustice, is inapt, in any sense other than the metaphorical; one also feels that he engages in gross oversimplification in the analogy which he chooses. This kind of assessment of student unrest fails to recognize that to large elements within the protest movement, grievances are deep-seated and go much beyond the trivialities – such as library facilities, parking problems, representation on university governing boards – frequently chosen as issues. These are only symbols of a more basic discontent not only with the university but with the values of society in general.

NOTES AND BIBLIOGRAPHY

1. *Toronto Daily Star*, July 4, 1968, p. 7. The full text of this speech outlining a strategy for change in Canadian universities is given here under the headline, "Claude Bissell Presents His Own Plan for Preventing University Riots Here".
2. The kind of pressure to which university presidents are subjected is documented in an article in the *Globe and Mail* (Oct. 12, 1968) when Bissell opened the question of the elimination of the Board of Governors as a part of his plan "to rebuild the government of the U of T and make it more democratic".

As Andrew Szende points out in the *Star* (Dec. 27, 1969) "the job of a university president has been compared to that of a corporation president but there is a big difference. The university president lacks the corporation president's power, yet must assume responsibilities for all decisions taken in the institution."
3. *Praxis*, Vol. 1, Aug., 1968.
4. *Maclean's*, Nov., 1968, pp. 57-58.
5. *Canadian Magazine*, Oct. 26, 1968, p. 6.
6. *Praxis*, Vol. 1, Aug., 1968, p. 6.
7. By the process of "repressive tolerance" the society is capable of absorbing and dissolving seemingly insoluble conflicts and making them part of its nature. Thus, protest becomes part of the established order and the right to protest is defended by the most staunch advocates of the *status quo*. Marcuse explains in some detail how this transformation takes place in the fields of literature and drama in Chapter 3 of *One-Dimensional Man*. He carries his analysis further in "Repressive Tolerance" found in *A Critique of Pure Tolerance*, Boston, Beacon Press, 1965.
8. *Praxis*, Vol. 11, March, 1969, p. 2. Article called "Repressive Liberalism" by Resnick.
9. *Ibid.*, Vol. 1, August, 1968.
10. Although, to my knowledge, there have been no empirical studies done in Canada to document the contention that "it is the brightest students who fill the ranks of the campus activists", one suspects that this may indeed be the case, at least among the leadership group. In the US where such sampling has been done it has demonstrated that student radicals are better than average in academic achievement and higher than average in IQ.

It is also interesting to note in this context that Gray himself has recently received wide publicity, including headlines in the large Canadian dailies, (See "Marxist Gets $5000 Grant from Ottawa", *Star*, Apr. 15, 1969. Also *Globe*.) as well as coverage on the National CBC News for having been awarded a Canada Council fellowship to complete his studies at Oxford. The media, however, have made no attempt to discern the number of other student radicals receiving similar awards.
11. *Op. Cit. Praxis*. "The New Student Radicalism: Is It an American Import?" by Stanley Gray. This is the text of an address given to the Couchiching Conference, Aug. 1, 1968. Also reprinted in *Canadian Dimension*.
12. *Globe and Mail*, Sept. 3, 1968. Also in *University Affairs*, Vol. 10, # 2, p. 16.
13. *Op. Cit*, Gray
14. *Star*, Sept. 14, 1968.
15. McGuigan, Gerald F., *Student Protest* (Methuen Publications, Toronto, 1968.) p. 107
16. *Ibid.*, p. 110
17. *Globe and Mail*, Sept. 4, 1968, p. 3.
18. Quoted in *The Berkeley Student Revolt*, Ed. Seymour M. Lipset and Sheldon S. Wolin, (Anchor Books, N.Y., 1965) p. 208.
19. Roussopoulos, Dimitrios (ed.) *Our Generation*, Vol. 6, # 1 and 2, p. 12.
20. *Op. cit.*, McGuigan, p. 48.
21. *Op. cit.*, *Our Generation*, p. 12.
22. *Ibid.*, p. 9.
23. *Ibid.*, p. 12.
24. *Ibid.*, p. 16.
25. *Op. cit.*, McGuigan, p. 34.
26. *Op cit.*, *Canadian Magazine*, p. 2.
27. *Canadian Dimension*, Vol. 5, No. 6, Sept.-Oct., p. 11. This is the speech in which Warrian is quoted by the media, as having said, "This is the year to sock it to the administrators. Burn down their buildings." He claims not to have departed from the text of his speech and to have been misquoted. In subsequent press reports, he is usually identified by the alleged *ad lib.*, "Burn down their buildings."
28. Star, Sept. 19, 1968. Northrop Frye, "Student Protest Has Shallow Roots".
29. *Ibid.*

Books:

Adelman and Lee (ed.) *The University Game* (Anansi, Toronto, 1968).

Marcuse, Herbert *One-Dimensional Man* (Beacon Press, Boston, 1964).

McGuigan, Gerald F. (Ed.) *Student Protest* (Methuen, Toronto, 1968).

Magazines:

Canadian Dimension, Vol. 5, No. 5, 1968. Vol. 5, No. 6, 1968. Vol. 5, No. 7, 1968.

Canadian Magazine, October 26, 1968.

The Globe Magazine, Dec. 28, 1968.

Maclean's Magazine, November, 1967. November, 1968.

Our Generation, Vol. 3, No. 4: Vol. 4, No. 1. Vol. 5, No. 1.

Praxis, Vol. 1, August, 1968. Vol. 2, March, 1969.

University Affairs, Vol. 10, No. 2, 1968.

Newspapers:

Toronto Daily Star Bissell, Claude "Claude Bissell Presents His Own Plan for Preventing Riots Here", July 4, 1968.

Hartnett, Arthur, "And Now U. of T. President Bissell Tells It Like It Is", Sept. 14, 1968.

Frye, Northrop, "Student Protest Has Shallow Roots", Sept. 19, 1968.

5. Youth: The New Tribal Group

Evelyn Latowsky/*York University*
Merrijoy Kelner/*University of Toronto*

This highly original and imaginative look at what many consider to be the most remarkable and genuine revolution of this revolutionary age adds a new dimension to our discussion of public and private space. In Section Four we looked at established private space and focused on the mechanisms employed by those inside to maintain their purity and their distance as a means of protecting their space from intruders. Here we have an analysis of the creation of private space. With no existing or on going organizational base, emphasis is on life style and radically new values and beliefs to make the boundaries that separate the ins from the outs. These are cultural boundaries which render the principle of inclusion-exclusion even more potent and effective.

Looked at from the societal level, then, the 'tribe' is indeed creator and a holder of private space. However, looked at from within, the 'tribe' exhibits many characteristics of truly public space: the deliberate eschewing of hierarchy reduces social distance among members to the vanishing point; the rejection of private property and the possessive individualism it generates inhibits the members from carving out their own pockets of private space including that afforded by sex, marriage and the nuclear family. But, and most important, we see here a self-conscious attempt to create a truly public consciousness in the full meaning of that concept as enunciated by O'Neill in his essay in Section Two. In such a world the individual strives for the full realization of his self through his total commitment to community and his sincere and selfless love of others.

> Anthropologists go to exotic peoples who practice what are to them strange customs and cultures, even when such exotic peoples are to be found in the next block.[1]

To refer to the exotic subculture emerging among North American Youth as a 'New Tribal Group' is to characterize these young people in their own idiom – the idiom of their dress, their music, their vocabulary, and, most importantly, their special frame of reference. Adult perspectives on contemporary youth culture range all the way from frenzied criticism to vicarious adulation. Common to most approaches is the basic problem that these perspectives are superimposed from the outside. We suggest here, exploration of an alternative orientation stemming from youth itself.

The tribal identification of youth focuses on the values of simplicity, intimacy, freedom and equality, which have long been associated with tribal life. Many young people share a fundamental moral skepticism about the structures of post-technological adult society and are expressing their ideological opposition through a search for the primordial human experience. This search for alternative bases and modes of human relations is leading an increasing number of youth toward the amorphous goal of tribalism. It is important to recognize that while many young people appear to have reached a certain consensus about ultimate values, there is little agreement as to how they can and should be achieved. (What appears to be emerging among contemporary youth is a common tribal ideal, realized quite differently and only partially by diverse bands or

The article is a revised version of a paper presented at The 69th Annual Meeting of The American Anthropological Association in 1970.

'streams' of the movement: hippies, yippies, live-in rock groups, a variety of new leftists, student activists, protesters, and drop-outs, as well as a sprinkling of 'over 30' sympathizers.) This development does not, in our view constitute an attempt to return to primitive tribalism, but rather a forward thrust in the process of human evolution. For youth is seeking not only to rediscover and recreate the essence of the tribal experience, but more importantly, to transcend it.

Our thesis raises two fundamental questions: First, what is the primordial human experience and what does it tell us about human nature? Second, how is the new tribal group attempting to move beyond traditional tribal boundaries, and what does this tell us about human evolution?

Redfield states that the primordial human community (variously defined as 'primitive,' 'folk,' 'native' et al.) is essentially a moral community, in which the technical order is subordinate to the moral order.[2] In such a community, the moral order encompasses the entire cosmos experienced as a unity: a whole, of which man is merely a part. The primordial human experience, says Redfield, is highly personal. Small and isolated human communities are necessarily intimate communities, in which people are known for their individual qualities. Just as men and women are experienced as unique persons, rather than stereotyped roles, so the cosmos is personal and human-like. The relationship of man to non-man (God, nature) like the relationship of man to man, is one of mutual interdependence. Man works with the elements, not against them; he is in harmony with the elements, not in conflict. He does not set out primarily to control or master or exploit, but rather to relate. He feels a moral obligation to maintain the whole of which he is a part.

In short, Redfield presents us with an ideal type – a primordial human community characterized by mutuality and harmony, union between man and man, man and non-man, and between internal (subjective) and external (objective) human experience.[3]

In contrast to this holistic tribal view of man-in-nature, modern, western perspectives are markedly one-dimensional views of man *against* nature. Myths and theories of the evolution of man, his societies and cultures (from Plato to Parsons) tend to stress the 'rational' dimension of man. To the extent that man has evolved from 'primitive' to 'civilized,' it is contended that it has been through the use of homo sapiens' unique rational problem-solving powers and the scientific and technological advances resulting from them. Man, however, does not always behave 'rationally.' Somewhere, lurking in the deep recesses of his psyche are remnants of his animal nature (hidden furies – drives, emotions, instincts, et al.) which interfere with his allegedly 'real' or rational nature. According to the mythology of rationalism, man must learn to suppress, control, sublimate, or somehow disallow expression of these base desires, if he is to realize his true human or rational potential. To the extent that he has become 'civilized', this view holds, he has created a culture which effectively rewards expression of his rational nature and prevents or punishes irrational behaviour.

The question now arises: Why has man, if he is indeed the possessor of such unique problem-solving abilities, made so few inroads on the problems of understanding and living in harmony with his fellow man? The answer, some suggest, lies in the other part of his nature, the irrational or animal part. Thus, many investigators are currently turning back to the point at which instinct theories were abandoned years ago, and are stressing biological, non-rational aspects and explanations of human behaviour.

We are presently informed that man is, by nature, the killer species, the aggressor *par excellence*, the naked ape living in a human zoo in which survival depends not on any special human qualities, but on the same power struggle between males of the species as we find among some of our primate ancestors and relatives.[4]

Further, we are now told that it is in the interest of the survival of the human species for its males to bond together in all male groups. In these groups, it is claimed, men's superior aggressive tendencies, combined with their superior decision-making powers, can be maximally activated, unimpaired by the intrusion of the inferior female of the species and her politically trivial humanistic concerns.[5]

The basic fallacy common to all such arguments lies in their reductionist assumptions about the nature of the human animal. Man's potential for progress, advance, evolution, is assumed to lie in his ability to dominate and control his environment, and his environment always includes other human beings. Man thus emerges, in one way or another, as the archetypical power seeker, whether he seeks power over nature, other animals, other men, or his 'other-half' i.e. the female of the species.

But rational-technological man has clearly failed to ensure the survival of the human species. Because he has denied his humanity, which necessarily involves the integrated expression of his full human potential, he has sown the seeds of his own destruction. We share with Buber, Fromm, Laing, Maslow, et al. the view of human nature which holds that man is a meaning-seeking animal, who insofar as he is not merely rational, but also reasonable, is not satisfied with materialistic things and positivistic facts. Beyond this, he seeks to take account through symbolic means of the trans-empirical values and ultimate mysteries of human existence.

In a world which still tends to view man as essentially a rational animal and therefore subscribes to the grand rational-technocratic imperative, the young are evolving an alternate ethos and life style based on the belief that man, fully self-actualized, is a feeling as well as a thinking being. The affirmation by youth of the emotive or sensual side of man's nature, as evident in the current emphasis on sensory experience (encounter groups, sensitivity training) and the open expression of affective and sexual impulse, is frequently seen by adults in our society as a reversion to animalistic behaviour. In contrast, Erich Fromm, like Maslow, Laing, Roszak et al, considers sensory enrichment an essential component in the development of a fully integrated human personality. Reason, he points out, flows from the blending (harmony) of rational thought and feeling. What is pathological about man today is the splitting, compartmentalization, and lopsided development characteristic of the "naked ape with the computerized brain."[6]

The new tribal culture, sometimes referred to as a counter-culture (Roszak) or contra-culture (Yinger) is based on the assumption by youth that man can realize his full human potential only in a community in which "personal relationships are not only transactional but transexperiential" (Laing). Such a community, it is hoped, would allow its members the necessary personal freedom to transcend the "purely rational-cerebral consciousness" (Roszak) of technocracy and evolve towards a new unity, fusing mind, body and spirit.

Basic to the ideology of the new tribal group is the premise that human beings qua human should be primarily concerned with the total and harmonious development of the self in a context of intimate relationships with like-minded others. Viewed in evolutionary terms, this consciously directed search

by youth for personal wholeness and community signifies a forward thrust: an attempt to transcend both the personal and social limitations of rational technocracy and to realize to the fullest man's uniquely human potential.

There is increasing evidence, not only for the thesis that the emergence of the new tribal group may be an evolutionary breakthrough, but also that it may be necessary for man's survival. Pushing the technocratic imperative to its limits (nuclear war, pollution, and the like) could mean the end of man on earth. Pushing the stimulus overload (rapid change, novelty, and diversity) much further could physiologically and psychologically produce the same result. There appears to be an adaptive range below and above which the individual's ability not only to adapt, but simply to cope, tends to fall apart. When forced beyond the stress limits of our bio-psychological constitution we respond with the erratic behaviour which Toffler suggests is the hallmark of future shock.[7]

In response to technocratic overload, youth are suggesting prerequisites for human survival – smaller, simpler, more highly personal and essentially egalitarian communities – reminiscent of traditional tribal forms.

In the image of the primordial tribe, the new tribal group aspires to the ideal of a closely-knit community of equally valued human beings. On many of the communes and cooperatives initiated by the young, institutionalized hierarchies of power, privilege and prestige are deliberately avoided.[8] Leadership tends to be casual, situational and charismatic; based solely on the qualities of the individual who rises to lead some specific enterprise. Material interests are de-emphasized: people come before things. Within each small tribal community – as in the traditional bands of the tribe – social relationships are highly personalized. Primary value is placed on caring and sharing: people are expected to spread their regard, their rewards and their concern.

In some ways, however, the new tribal group departs sharply from its predecessors. Probably the most important difference is that of social boundaries. The traditional tribe was essentially an ethnic community; a community of people who not only identified as kin, but who clearly distinguished 'their people' from 'others'. Often the name of the tribe meant 'people' or 'human beings,' differentiating its members, as such, from others – outsiders, strangers 'beyond the pale.' Tribal tradition typically included a simple technology, a communal economy and a complex religious system, giving the culture continuity in both space and time.

In contrast, the new tribal group is not an ethnic community in the traditional sense. Their primary bond is a generational one which cuts across existing boundaries of ethnicity, religion, nationality and sex, and creates new categories and distinctions between the new tribe (youth) and the old (establishment). Unlike the older tribal pattern, the culture of the new tribal group is not rooted in custom and tradition; it lacks the historical continuity of its predecessors. Breaking with the past, the new tribal group is not developing isolated structures geared to a particular ecological niche. It emphasizes process rather than structure, and envisions a human community which transcends established socio-cultural and ecological boundaries and is uniquely geared to a world of flux and change.

Strikingly different from its traditional predecessors whose world image extended only to neighbouring tribes, is the global context within which the new tribal group is emerging. On the North American scene, tribal members stem largely from the affluent, well-educated upper middle and middle classes, the privileged sectors of a highly scientific and technological-oriented society, in which the ready availability of mass communication media brings into instantaneous focus a total picture of the global village.[9] For contemporary youth, this means not only that their world view is greatly expanded, but also that their awareness of themselves as responsible members of the world community is stirred to consciousness. They perceive themselves as a privileged few in an over-populated world of poverty, oppression, racism, violence and bitter struggle for survival. Unlike previous tribes, whose closed cultural themes focused exclusively on their own life quest, the new tribal group is able to open their tribal perspectives to others unlike themselves: the underprivileged ethnic and cultural minorities throughout the world.

Rioux suggests that what is emerging among contemporary youth, as a response to the operation of selective pressures of post-technological society, is a process of socio-cultural 'neotenia'. By this term, he means a prolongation of the stage of cultural incompleteness by means of the extension of characteristics previously associated with adolescence, into adulthood.[10] These youthful characteristics – spontaneity, pliability and openness – the very potentialities which enabled man to take the evolutionary lead, favour his survival as an adult in a world characterized by rapid and large-scale social change; a world in which the individual must, throughout his life, remain open to new ideas, new relationships and new experience.

Geared to a world which they see as unstable and unpredictable, youth characteristically seek meaning in the present. In contrast to the future-orientation of our society – with its emphasis on deferred gratification in order to obtain long-range goals and future rewards (salvation, career, material success and the like) the time-orientation of youth, like traditional tribal man, is expressed in the active present tense: in 'tuning in', 'turning on', 'grooving', 'rapping', and 'being'.

Insisting on the right of each individual to express fully his or her unique human potential ('doing your own thing') each new tribal member is ideally guided, not by traditional rules but by a new morality, rooted in a sense of personal responsibility. Youth is convinced that if man is to discover and bring ultimate meaning into a seemingly absurd era, each individual must be free to do it in his own way.

The tribal response to the human need for ultimate meaning is religion. Eliade contends that the primordial and universal religious experience does not necessarily imply a belief in god, gods or ghosts, but refers to man's consciousness of being, meaning and truth in an unknown, chaotic and fearful cosmos.[11] Further, he points out that the whole person, not just the mind (as Lévi-Strauss would have it) is existentially involved in the religious experience.

In the traditional tribe, significant *rites-de-passage* provided opportunities for members to relate as total and integral persons to man and cosmos. In contemporary technocracy, on the other hand, there is a general decline of significant *rites-de-passage*. The modern urban religious institution, Fichter suggests, is like a 'service station' – an impersonal structure, periodically utilized for the routine fulfillment of formal religious requirements.[12] To fill the existential or spiritual void, youth are creating their own *rites-de-passage*; new tribal rituals based on a new global perspective.

At rock festivals, the newly tribalized young gather in gay costumes to openly and publicly celebrate their joyous union with man, nature and cosmos. In the natural setting of park or beach they sing, dance, share food and pot, and make love as each feels moved, without programme or precedent. By the creative synthesis of symbol and ritual drawn from the repertoire of many religions, of mind-expanding drugs, rock music, flashing bulbs, and sexuality viewed as a "polymorphic instrument of immediate communitas," young people attempt to establish total communion with one another.[13] In these new tribal rituals all members seek the visionary imagination and sensuous awareness traditionally considered to be the special gifts of the tribal shaman.

Within the contemporary tribal culture, consciousness-expanding drugs are considered one of the most significant means of developing the holistic human personality and community. The psychedelic revolution, as experienced and expounded by Leary and his followers is based on the simple formula: change the prevailing mode of consciousness and you change the world.

According to the psychedelic mystique, drugs serve to break down psychological and social barriers to communication and to expand personal awareness. The taking of drugs for this purpose can be seen as an effort to utilize the fruits of technocracy (synthetic chemicals) toward humanistic ends: the realization of man's capacity to love, to reason, to create and to enjoy beauty and to extend his concern to others.

Youthful drug users customarily share the experience with intimates. This sharing of heightened experience ("getting high with a little help from your friends") has the effect of cementing tribal bonds among the participants.[14] Under the influence of mind-expanding drugs, they reach out not only to one another, but to a more generalized union with man and nature.

Powerful myths accompany and reinforce these new tribal rites. For example, Timothy Leary, guru of the psychedelic cult, claims that through LSD "it is possible for man to tap into the unbroken wire of evolution."[15] When mind-expanding drugs enable man to reach the highest ('cellular') level of consciousness, Leary insists, man is then in touch with the DNA chain, which goes right back to the origins of life. The mythology urges everyone to trust the evolutionary process and to harness their cellular wisdom to the external world around them. The tribal chant – 'turn on, tune in, and drop out' – is held to be a 'declaration of evolution': obliging tribal man to find the wisdom within, hook it up in a new way, and above all, detach himself from the technological game. Prophets of the psychedelic revolution look forward to the evolution of new human species capable of living in "harmonious interspecies interactions."[16]

As was the case in older tribal communities, music has become an integral part of the sacred rites of the new tribe of youth. Rock music, with its dynamic rhythms, mind-blowing sounds, defiant lyrics and experimental forms, symbolizes the soaring spirit of the new culture. By drawing on a broad range of cultural sources – Eastern tonal scales, country and Western idioms, African rhythms and the language of the ghettos – music promotes a global perspective among youth.

Through the medium of rock music, strangers of widely divergent backgrounds may unite, if only temporarily, in a community based on instant mutuality. As individuals relate to each other immediately and spontaneously, previous in-group, out-group boundaries become increasingly irrelevant.

The same universalistic ethos is reflected in the uninhibited costumes of the young. They adorn themselves with a conglomeration of Indian head bands, Mexican ponchos, oriental prayer beads, Moroccan caftans and rabbinical beards, transcending historical and geographical boundaries.

A striking feature of the new style of dress is the tendency toward unisex. This blurring of distinctions between male and female modes of dress symbolizes the egalitarian emphasis of the new community. Unisex is a visible manifestation of youth's skepticism about the conventional dichotomy between male and female roles and the double standard in sexual morality. The emphasis in personal relationships between the sexes, as between members of the same sex, is on each individual as a whole human being, and upon direct, primary relationships. What is criticized is dominance, exploitation and hypocrisy. What is stressed is personal freedom, mutuality and frankness.

Denied the opportunities for institutionalized pre-marital and sexual exploration and experimentation found among many tribal cultures, youth today are creating their own open life styles in opposition to the restrictive norms of adult society. In the new tribal ideology, sharing and caring, trust and love, are held to be the prerequisites for all sexual relationships, within or outside of the legal institution of marriage.

The growing disaffection of the young with established educational, occupational and political structures is symptomatic of their basic rejection of a bureaucratic, compartmentalized society. They seek a social environment very much like the tribal one, in which decision-making is a communal undertaking and status differentiation is minimal. The impersonal, 'top down' structures so characteristic of contemporary Western society completely contradicts their goals of personal involvement and respect for each individual.

Summary

The new tribal group emerging among today's youth may be providing an answer to the problem of human survival in the global village: smaller, simpler, more highly personal and essentially egalitarian communities. Unlike traditional tribes, young people today are not developing isolated social groupings adapted to a particular ecological niche. Their goal is to create a human community which transcends traditional social and ecological boundaries and is geared to a constantly changing world.

The anti-technocratic, humanistic stance adopted by many of today's youth challenges current socio-scientific assumptions about the nature of man and society. These young people are clearly motivated beyond the mere quest for "materialistic things and positivistic facts."[17] Not only do they question accepted rationalistic goals, they also reject many of the widely used means of achieving these ends. They tend to view as exploitive the whole structure of inequality with its 'power games' and 'ego trips,' manipulation and control of people as things. What is brought into question by the new tribal ideals are the various concepts of man which depict only one part of his nature – what Marcuse calls 'one dimensional man', 'rational man', 'competitive man', 'man as power seeker' and the like. What is suggested is the rich complexity of human nature and the necessity for integration of man's mind, body and spirit. Only in this way, the young believe, can man achieve full self-realization.

On a societal basis, the ideology developed by the young also encourages a broader and more harmonious perspective. Their emphasis is on total and integral relationships between persons, as opposed to compartmentalized role-playing. They stress the value of each unique individual and deny the validity of distinctions based on nationalism, ethnicity, religion, sex et al. A reflection of their global perspective is the enormous and continued mobility of the young. Everywhere today, like tribal nomads, young people are on the move carrying only the basic necessities, their knapsacks on their backs.[18] United with other young people by generational bonds and a common ethos, they seem to be at home wherever they go.

A focus on process rather than program is perhaps the prime characteristic of their new ethos. In a world in which ideologies come and go and radical change is the rule, a comprehensive way of approaching life has become more important for them than any fixed goals, ideologies, programs, or psychological traits.[19] The new tribal life style signifies an attempt to continually expand personal and social horizons in an environment of instant change.

'The movement' among contemporary tribal youth is most commonly defined, analyzed, and/or criticized, as an incipient revolution. It is suggested here, alternatively, that evolution, rather than revolution, may be the more appropriate designation. What is brought into question is our traditional one-dimensional models of human evolution. To fully comprehend contemporary developments among youth the concept of human evolution, like the concept of human nature, must be broadened to extend beyond material survival and to take account of man's search for transcendental meaning – for harmony and fulfillment both within himself and in relation to his external social and natural environment. It is precisely this consciously directed search on the part of the new tribal group which constitutes an evolutionary breakthrough.

NOTES
1. Paul Bohannan. *Social Anthropology*, 1963, p.7.
2. Robert Redfield (1968) *The Primitive World and its Transformations*. New York, Cornell University Press.
3. For a poetic statement of this view, see: Martin Buber (1958) (2nd Ed.) *I and Thou*, N.Y., Charles Scribner's Sons, pp. 18-22.
4. In the forefront of this line of evolutionary argument are: Robert Ardrey (1961) *African Genesis*, London, Collins Press; (1966), *The Territorial Imperative*, New York, Atheneum Press; Desmond Morris (1967), *The Naked Ape*, London, Jonathan Cape; (1969) *The Human Zoo*.
5. Lionel Tiger (1969) *Men in Groups*, London, Thomas Nelson and Sons.
6. Erich Fromm (1968) *The Revolution of Hope*, N.Y., Bantam Books. Similar views are expressed in: A.H. Maslow (1959)"Psychological Data and Value Theory"in *New Knowledge in Human Values*, A.H. Maslow (ed.) Chicago, Henry Regnery Co. pp. 119-31; R. D. Laing (1967) *The Politics of Experience and the Bird of Paradise*, Middlesex, Penguin Books; Theodore Roszak (1969) *The Making of a Counter Culture*, Garden City, N.Y., Anchor Books.
7. Alvin Toffler (1970) *Future Shock*, New York, Random House.
8. Ray Ald (1970) *The Youth Communes*, Tower Publications.
9. Kenneth Keniston (1968) *The Young Radicals*, New York: Harcourt, Brace and World, Inc.
10. Marcel Rioux (1968) " Youth in the Contemporary World and in Quebec," in W. E. Mann (Ed.) *Canada: A Sociological Profile*, Toronto, Copp Clark.
11. Mircea Eliade (1969) *The Quest*, Chicago, University of Chicago University of Chicago Press, Preface.
12. J. H. Fichter (1954) *Social Relations in the Urban Parish*, Chicago, University of Chicago Press, p. 188.
13. Victor Turner (1969) *The Ritual Process*, Chicago, Aldine, pp. 112-13, 138.
14. Erich Goode (1970) *The Marijuana Smokers*, New York: Basic Books Inc. pp. 22-24.
15. Timothy Leary (1970) *The Politics of Ecstasy*, London, Mac-Gibbon and Kee, p. 350.
16. Ibid: p. 221
17. Orrin E. Klapp (1969) *Collective Search for Identity*, New York: Rinehart & Winston, Inc.
18. See for example, *Transient Youth: 70-71*, Ottawa, The Canadian Council on Social Development, 1971, pp. 45-48.
19. For elaboration of this theme see: Kenneth Keniston (1968) *Young Radicals*, N.Y., Harcourt, Brace and World.

Crises of Public Relationships

Crises of Public Relationships

This book has been concerned with three central issues: social relationships, communication and social order. Most of the evidence presented might be crudely summarized in the following way.

Canada is physically a large country with a small, largely urban population in which social relationships are determined by many factors but primarily by: the size and physical characteristics of the country, the economic and demographic distribution of the population, the sequences of immigration and imperial conquest and the consequent importation of economic, political and cultural institutions. Because of the continuing influence of the United States on her economic and cultural institutions, Canada's problems in maintaining her national independence have recently led to the emergence of various movements committed to the redefinition of nationalism. These range from non-party organizations such as the Committee for an Independent Canada (though with terms of operation which mark it unmistakably the voice of a national bourgeoisie), to the socialist definitions of the Waffle wing of the NDP and the Quebec separatism of the Parti Québécoise. But within the overriding contours of economic control and political federalism, Canadians maintain life-styles which differ sharply from each other. In attempting to account for these variations many frameworks have been adopted by sociologists and anthropologists. Most prominent among these has been a structural-functional approach seeing Canada in terms of the modernization of its social, political and economic institutions (see essays by Naegele and Lipset listed below), as a dichotomy between folk and urban societies (most vividly debated by Quebec sociologists – see Rioux and Martin below), and as Arthur K. Davis has recently argued, in terms of the conflict between the capitalist-industrial centre and the rural periphery. All of these are attempts to apply to Canada frameworks developed elsewhere. Lipset and Naegele have, with few conceptual changes, applied to Canada a model which was developed to understand the USA; the folk-urban debate was a direct result of research done in Chicago; and the hinterland-metropolis dichotomy in the formula provided by Davis is in direct succession to the thesis on peasant revolution argued in China by Mao-Tse-Tung and in Africa by Frantz Fanon, though also presented with different ideological connotations as centre-periphery by Daniel Lerner, Edward Shills and David Apter in the USA. The fact that frameworks are foreign does not of course invalidate them: the test is the extent to which they are able to make sense, both of the dominant features of a society and of its variations. All of these frameworks make only partial sense, to a very large extent because they are not able to provide a basis for examining how sectors of Canadian society see themselves or each other. In other words, although they make some sense in understanding social structures, they too easily equate behaviour and values with these structures.

The assumption with which this book began was that there were indeed traditions in Canadian social science which might more fruitfully act as the basis of Canadian sociology than the introduction of foreign models. These traditions were those in political economy (represented in this book by the contributions of Innis, Levitt, Drache and Lockhart), and those in communications research (represented by McLuhan, Savard, Card and Innis again). In the conception of this book an attempt to come to terms with Canadian society must involve an integration of these approaches: the first because it deals with the foundations of power, and the second because it defines ways of looking at how people make sense of the power-constraints and their relationships with each other. In some of the communications writing – notably that of McLuhan – the emphasis seems to be much more on technology as

communication, though as sociologists we not only have to examine technology but human relationships. One thing we have done in this book, therefore, is to put the Canadian communications arguments in the context of a wider sociological debate on spatial analysis which views relationships at once as social structures, as ecology, as communication and as values. People do not talk to each other simply to have conversation (though they may do so), nor do they talk because they can't make films or hypnotise (though that also may be true). They talk as part of a structure of social relationships: to talk is to establish rapport with other people (or to conflict with them). One of the purposes of organizing this book according to definitions of space is to suggest how different kinds of relationships and the assumptions lying behind them affect the ways that people communicate with each other and how people make sense of these relationships and use the different modes of communication. A sociology which built on this framework does not yet exist in Canada (nor indeed in many other countries) so this book is largely suggestive.

For the concluding essays we have included contributions which give an idea of some of the issues which continue to act as indications of the general problems which affect relations within Canada and between Canadians and the rest of the world. Richard Ossenberg's essay summarizes recent developments in Quebec; the authors of "Canada's Colonies" suggest the ways that Canadian economic and political policies in the Caribbean provide a definition for West Indians and Guyanese of the very limited space that they occupy; while Alan Borovoy makes a plea for the redefinitions of public and private rights following from the uses of the War Measures Act in October 1970. Alexander Lockhart's essay on the unemployment of graduates in Canada is an important analysis both of the effects of technological change on social structure and of the ways that economic ideologies affect public policy.

Other topics of importance that might have been included here are the recent attempts at a redefinition of provincial and federal relations and the dominance of Ontario in Canadian economic growth. Also here, and in other sections of the book, we have little or nothing on crime, literary criticism (and Canadian literature might itself have provided most of the illustrative material for Sections Three to Seven) or the sociology of industry and work. Frequently this is because of the absence of written material. In Social Demography we were unable to obtain publisher's permission for some important essays. But the book is long enough already. The contours that have been drawn here should enable any student of the social sciences and humanities to begin to work out the relationships between national and international wholes, the sectors in which we all have to operate, and issues which help to build up our own personal world views. Such an exercise shows that in Canada there is no such thing as 'politics' or 'sociology' or 'economics' or 'anthropology' or 'history'. We are all social scientists concerned with building a meaningful interdisciplinary approach to understanding Canadian society. On this basis we can also begin to decide for ourselves how we can construct a form of social and political action that is relevant to our own life-styles and to the problems of our society.

FURTHER READING:

On Canada:
K. Naegele, "Canadian Society: Some Reflections" and "Further Reflections", in B. Blishen, Jones, Naegele & Porter (Eds.) *Canadian Society: Sociological Perspectives* (2nd Edition) Toronto: Macmillan, 1964, pp 1-19, 497-522.

W. Mann, Ed, *Canada: A Sociological Profile*, Toronto: Copp Clark, 1968, includes the essay by S. M. Lipset, pp 488-498.

Arthur K. Davis, "Canadian Society and History as Hinterland versus Metropolis", in R. Ossenberg (Ed.) *Canadian Society: Pluralism, Change and Conflict*, Scarborough, Ontario: Prentice Hall, 1971, pp. 6-35.

Edmund Carpenter and Marshall McLuhan, *Explorations in Communication*, Boston: Beacon Press, 1960.

M. Rioux and Y. Martin (Eds.),*French-Canadian Society*, Toronto: McClelland and Stewart, 1964.

Wider Perspectives

H. Lefebvre, *Everyday Life in the Modern World*, London: Allen Lane, The Penguin Press, 1971.

P. Green and S. Levinson (Eds.),*Power and Community*, New York: Random House, 1969.

E. Goffman, *Encounters*, Chicago: Bobbs-Merrill 1960.

Edward T. Hall, *The Hidden Dimension*, Garden City, N.Y.:

Doubleday and Co., 1966.

Stanford M. Lyman and Marvin B. Scott, *A Sociology of the Absurd*, New York: Appleton-Century-Crofts, 1970.

Peter M. Berger and Thomas Luckman, *The Social Construction of Reality*, London: Allen Lane, The Penguin Press, 1967.

Richard N. Marsh, *Comparative Sociology*, New York: Harcourt, Brace & World, 1967.

Barrington Moore, Jr., *Social Origins of Dictatorship and Democracy*, Boston: Beacon Press, 1967.

Paul A. Baran, *The Political Economy of Growth*, New York: Monthly Review Press, 1960

C. Wright Mills and H. Gerth, *Character and Social Structure*, New York: Oxford U.P. 1960

1. Social Pluralism in Quebec: Continuity, Change and Conflict

Richard J. Ossenberg/*University of Calgary*

Several essays in this book have dealt with conflicts between cultures and social classes in Canada and three, those by Bergeron, Desbarats and Vallières have dealt explicitly with Quebec in both ethnic and stratification terms. What we have not so far considered, however, is an analysis of Quebec which draws on the very substantial tradition of sociology existing within Quebec and which provides a framework for exploring the changing intergroup relations within the province. Such an analysis is presented by Richard J. Ossenberg in an essay published in 1971. Because we were unable to obtain permission to reprint the entire article,what follows is a summary of the issues raised by Ossenberg with fairly long illustrative quotations.

Most writing in Quebec has tended to ignore divisions and conflicts within the province and has instead emphasized the persistence of cultural homogeneity among French Canadians vis-à-vis English Canadians. Recently, however, a number of studies have discussed social class differences,[1] though without making an attempt to analyse the nature of cultural pluralism in Quebec. Ossenberg argues for an analysis which does three things: provides a "systematic conceptual model of Canada as a plural society," has an historical dimension in its analysis of the development of social institutions and relationships, and employs a comparative framework in the analysis of Canadian pluralism.

Before commencing this analysis he presents a summary of the "major dimensions and profiles of social class differences between French Canadians today."

In the last decade, the most 'visible' social class within French Canada, from the point of view of both academic and popular interest, has been 'the new middle class'. The French Canadian 'new middle class' is both real and, at the same time, a product of the mass media. It is real in the sense that,

especially since World War II, an increasing proportion of French Canadians have entered into the world of white collar occupations, ranging from clerical to academic.[2] The 'new middle class' has been a product of the mass media in the sense that its sympathies toward separatist movements have been identified with the French Canadian population generally, while the anti-separatist sentiments of the majority of French Canadians in lower social class positions have been obscured.

The 'new middle class' of French Canadians has been properly identified as the main thrust behind the contemporary separatist movement.[3] The 'hard-core' of this group is found among the intelligentsia, especially students and faculty at the University of Montreal. But the separatist sentiments are diffusing to French Canadians generally found in the upper level white-collar occupations, especially in the Montreal area – where the clash of economic interests, ethnic differences, and a sense of 'relative-deprivation' are far more pronounced than they are in more static areas such as Quebec city.

This new French Canadian middle class, with some exceptions to be discussed later in this chapter, is relatively isolated from the other two major social class status groups – the old French Canadian elite, and the majority lower class French Canadians.

The relatively small old-elite French Canadians consist of persons generally of long-standing professional status (physicians, lawyers, merchants, chartered accountants, corporate directors, some university professors) some of whom could trace their heritage to their progenitors of the old days of the seigniorial estates. This group also includes members of the higher Catholic clergy who, like their colleagues, shared a somewhat conservative orientation toward the problems of the lower-class French Canadians. As a group, the old-elite French Canadians generally held power within the French Canadian population and received considerable deference from the Anglo Saxon elite. Since the Quiet Revolution of Quebec, which is most frequently traced to the election of Jean Lesage as Provincial Premier in 1962, the old-elite are becoming increasingly marginal, in view of the great advances made, both economically and politically, by members of the 'new middle class'. As pointed out by Clark[4] the French Canadian old-elite are being forced into a position of ambivalence and compromise because of their need for maintaining favourable relations with the Anglo Saxon elite as well as French Canadian clientèle.

Of special interest to my analysis is the relatively large French Canadian lower class (about 50 per cent).[5] This group has experienced a large degree of 'apartheid' from both upper status French Canadian classes, the old-elite, and the new middle class. Meaningful social relations and political rapport between the French Canadian lower classes and members of the upper status groups have been as minimal as that between French and English Canadians generally. It has been the lower class French Canadians who have inhibited, thus far, the growth and influence of the new middle-class-based separatist ideology. The political behaviour of the lower-class French Canadians, generally contradictory to the aspirations of the new middle class, including the 1970 provincial election, has been amply documented.[6] Very recent developments suggest the potential for these historically-based social class differences to become modified, thereby assuring an unprecedented degree of social solidarity among French Canadians generally.[7]

Following this, Ossenberg provides an account of the historical development of class relations in Quebec. This involves the following features.

1. The importance of the fur trade in the seventeenth and early eighteenth centuries which, far from enforcing a rigid feudal regime in New France, provided a fluid social system in which illegal enterprise flourished, extensive cohabitation between French males and Indian females as well as 'marriages of convenience' made the nuclear rather than the lineal family the basis of society, and eroded the power of the Church because of the rapid economic and social changes. In the circumstances the ancien régime was "virtually powerless in exercising social control over the general colonial population by the time of the British Conquest of 1759."[8]

2. When the British took over, and in particular through the medium of the Quebec Act of 1774, they introduced a system of indirect rule similar to that used extensively by the British in other colonies (e.g. in India, Nigeria, Uganda). This meant that they "put back into power members of the French colonial elite, including the Catholic Clergy and seigneurs and, in addition provided them, at least theoretically, with more power than they had ever enjoyed throughout the history of New France."[9]

3. The result of this policy was widespread rebellion in Quebec against the "French authority figures, notably the seigneurs and the clergy." The British policy of indirect rule in Quebec was less successful in the short run than that practiced in other colonies because "the colony of New France had a comparatively high degree of economic and social change and, consequently, no continuous or pervasive leadership structure."[10] It is therefore difficult to accept that French Canadian culture through the nineteenth and early twentieth centuries was as homogeneous as both French and English Canadian scholars have implied (Ossenberg attributes such an analysis to the elitist tradition in Quebec – largely an attempt by the clergy at legitimizing their class positions – and to the influence of consensus models on English-speaking Canadians).

4. During the first half of the twentieth century the collusion of Anglo-French elites continued during periods of American economic penetration and control. The Duplessis régime, which ruled Quebec through the 1940's and 1950's, maintained a pattern of Quebec elites (including the Church) collaborating with the conquerors which had been established by the 1774 Act.

On the other hand the increasing industrialization and urbanization of Quebec produced lower-class movements which, through labour unions, "provided at least a partial organizational basis for economic and political action which had been absent before."[11] Splits within the church placed the heirarchy against some renegade priests, though Archbishop Charbonneau stated in 1949 during the six month long Asbestos Strike, that:

"The working class is a victim of a conspiracy which wishes to crush it, and when there is a conspiracy to crush the working class, it is the duty of the Church to intervene."[12] For his pains Charbonneau was 'banished' to British Columbia.

In conclusion, Ossenberg discusses the past decade in Quebec and assesses the emerging trends.

Emerging Trends: The Future of Double Pluralism in Quebec

During the time of the rapid social changes occurring in the immediate post-war period of Quebec, the basis for Quebec's most visible expression of discontent – separatism – was evolving. The 'new middle class' was being formed through a combination of factors; first, increasing urbanization and industrialization in Quebec 'opened' or 'widened' the middle class white collar, clerical, and administrative categories among French Canadians, thereby somewhat 'softening' the theretofore rigid French Canadian class distinctions. Although the upward social mobility of the French Canadians during that time was not as extensive as that for English-speaking Quebeckers, there can be no doubt that it did occur.[13] Secondly, the educational institutions of Quebec became increasingly secularized and geared to an urban-industrial economy, giving rise to an increasing group of intellectual elite. Through extensive upward mobility and the consequent feeling of 'relative-deprivation' among the French Canadian new middle class – vis-à-vis their English-speaking counterparts – the Quiet Revolution gathered momentum.

The election of Jean Lesage as Provincial Premier in 1962, with his reformist economic policies and 'Quebec pour les Québécois' slogans, reflected the changing social structure of Quebec, especially that of the French Canadian population. The policies of Lesage were directly geared to the newly discovered aspirations, as well as deprivations of the French Canadian middle class.

But even the Quiet Revolution did not escape the influence of the historical French Canadian internal pluralism, especially with respect to social class differences. The economic reforms of the Liberal Lesage government were extensive, including the government takeover of Quebec Hydro, but these reforms were apparently not seen by members of the French Canadian lower classes, either rural or urban, as having any particular relevance to or benefits for them. The Union Nationale, under Premier Daniel Johnson, was re-elected in 1966, largely through the massive support of the French Canadian lower class.

The Quebec provincial elections of 1970, with the Liberals again returning to power under Robert Bourassa, reflected still further changes in the dynamics of French Canadian pluralism. However, the situation then and now is far more complex than ever before. The considerable support for the separatist *Parti Québécois*, which won only 7 seats but received 24 per cent of the popular vote (closer to one-third of the popular vote if the French Canadian voters are considered as a separate grouping), suggested a degree of French Canadian nationalism not realized before. This contemporary nationalism also reflects a softening of the internal social class differences in the French Canadian population, for an analysis of the voting patterns suggests that separatist candidates were elected in four east-Montreal French Canadian lower class ridings; ridings which had been characterized by conservative voting histories. Therefore, it would appear that there is an increasing correspondence between the traditionally divided French Canadian social classes.

With regard to these developments, it would seem that the double pluralism in Quebec is disappearing, and being replaced by a single dualism, based on French Canadian and English-speaking Canadian differences and conflicts. In other words, it would appear that the long-established French Canadian internal differentiations are increasingly being ameliorated by contemporary social and economic factors.

It would seem to me that such an assumption would be somewhat misleading in the face of the pervasiveness of the differences which have divided French Canadians historically. Some of these internal tensions continue to be of relevance to an analysis of the contemporary scene in Quebec. Before discussing these factors, I wish to refer to contemporary conditions which appear to be building a bridge between the French Canadian social classes.

The first factor is that of the massive educational explosion, especially the enormous increase in French Canadians exposed to higher education. Many, if not most, of the French Canadians entering into institutions of higher learning are of lower social-class background. Dofny has estimated that approximately 37 per cent of the French Canadian students attending the University of Montreal are of lower class background, compared to about 17 per cent of English-speaking lower class background at McGill University[14] Moreover, the newly founded but rapidly expanding system of CEGEPS (the equivalent of junior colleges, or university preparation programs) is catering to a predominantly French Canadian student population. The many branches of the University of Quebec are likewise designed essentially for French Canadian students.

Some of the ideological consequences of this French Canadian educational explosion appear obvious. Basically, it would appear that a conversion to new middle class values, including the ideology of separatism, is occurring among these upwardly mobile French Canadian students of lower class origins. There is some evidence that this conversion is taking place. Among the students at the University of Montreal, only the most conservative estimate would figure the pro-separatist sentiment at 90 per cent of the student population. Guindon, through a survey of first year students at *Ecole des Hautes Commerciales de Montréal* figures that 75 per cent of the students demonstrated a clear preference for *Le Parti Québécois*.[15] It would be surprising if the magnitude of this French Canadian student support of new-middle class ideologies was not found also in the CEGEPS and University of Quebec, where staff are mostly graduates of the University of Montreal.

There are other indications of the relationship between the upward social mobility of the French Canadians and the conversion to separatism, thereby softening the middle class – lower class differences. Studies of the 1962 and 1966 provincial elections in Quebec have clearly shown the affinity between French Canadian youth and the separatist ideology.[16] There was shown to be a direct correlation between the percentage of young French Canadians in each of Montreal's 29 electoral districts and the strength of support for separatist candidates. Also, between both election years, the percentage of French Canadians in favour of separatism more than doubled, including almost half of a representative sample of young French Canadians from all income groups. The same studies also found that the more knowledgeable the French Canadian youth was about provincial politics, the more likely he was to support the separatist cause. If this latter finding is applied to the upward educational mobility among increasing numbers of lower class French Canadians, it would appear that conversion to the values of the French Canadian new middle class is very extensive.

Have the increased educational opportunities for French Canadians correlated with increased occupational opportunities? While the exact nature of this relationship is difficult to assess, a recent study by Dofny[17] would indirectly suggest the existence of this relationship. In a comparison of upward social mobility patterns of English-speaking Quebeckers and French Canadians, Dofny found that the previously documented gap between the two groups was decreasing; that, indeed, the French Canadians were experiencing an unprecedented degree of upward occupational mobility. While Dofny attributed this upward mobility to basic structural changes in the Quebec economy, as opposed to the increasing competitive advantages of the French Canadians vis-à-vis the English-speaking Quebeckers, there can be no doubt that an increasing number of French Canadians are experiencing a 'new middle class' way of life and are being at least exposed to, if not converted to, the separatist ideology resident in this group in recent years.

There is, however, evidence of the continuation of French Canadian pluralism, expressed in the historical internal social class differences. Whereas it is true that the proportion of lower class voters who supported *Le Parti Québécois* increased, in comparison to their support for separatist candidates in previous elections, and thereby also apparently conforming to the middle-class pattern, it is also true that the majority of lower class French Canadians were anti-separatist. Expressions of hostility toward separatists and the French Canadian middle class generally, were very extensive during my daily visits to St. Henri, a lower class French Canadian area in Montreal where, over a period of three months in early 1970, I attempted to assess some aspects of social changes occurring there.

During my research visit to Montreal, it also became clear that the view of the French Canadian intelligentsia toward the French Canadian lower class was essentially a patronizing one, and consisted basically of the need to 'politicize' the working and lower social classes; there was, however, little or no sense of social rapport or solidarity with the lower classes.

It is difficult to assess the role that the militant Confederation of National Trade Unions (CNTU) has played in bridging the gap between the French Canadian social classes. On the one hand, the massive support that its membership gave to Lévesque and his *Le Parti Québécois* in the 1970 elections, would suggest that increasing organization among French Canadian workers would increase their sympathies for the aspirations of the new middle class. On the other hand, it has been suggested that most of the new members of the CNTU are affiliated with white collar occupations,[18] thereby making the argument somewhat redundant.

In any event, it does not appear that the CNTU has thus far provided the organizational vehicle for the problems and aspirations of the French Canadian lower classes. Its militant ideological basis, attempting to appeal to both middle and lower classes, is too diffuse and, I believe, too suspect to draw massive support from the lower classes.

What will be the future of internal French Canadian conflicts and their implications for Canadian confederation? The answer depends on social, economic, and political changes within Quebec, and on the reaction of Canadians elsewhere to these changes.

Theoretical Considerations of Alternatives

One of the most penetrating analyses of internal social class conflicts among French Canadians has been provided by Pinard.[19] Pinard suggests that in the evolution of Quebec during the past forty years, the French Canadian lower classes and middle class have acted in contradiction to each other in terms of political behaviour. In some ways, the French Canadian middle classes over this period, including the recently emergent new middle class, have demonstrated more conservatism and self imposed cultural encapsulation, than have the French Canadian lower class who, in generally supporting economic reformist parties (as opposed to parties calling primarily for national unity), have demonstrated their own severe sense of economic deprivation and, coincidentally, suspicion of the French Canadian middle class.

Pinard's analysis is important in terms of the future evolution of Quebec. If a political movement in Quebec combines both the economic concerns predominant in the lower classes – with the aspirations for cultural identity without over-emphasizing either of these components, an ideological merger between lower and middle class French Canadians would appear likely.

Perhaps Guindon's portrayal of Quebec's bureaucratic revolution[20] provides a key to the potential for such a merger to appear. Guindon suggests that the massive bureaucratic expansion of Quebec industry poses a dilemma for French Canadians. On the one hand, increasing participation of French Canadians in occupations associated with large bureaucratic organizations appears inevitable. On the other hand, bilingualism within these corporations is now being encouraged. Therefore, both the sheer impersonality of bureaucracy – its contractual, as opposed to cultural or traditional basis of operation, threaten to emasculate the cultural identity especially of middle class French Canadians. Moreover, and in adding to Guindon's thesis, the exclusive use of the French language within these bureaucratic organizations would be discouraged by the very nature of their associations with enterprise outside of Quebec, thereby further weakening French Canadian cultural identity which could better survive in the context of small-scale and localistic enterprise. Given such structural dilemmas, and their inevitable dilution of cultural traditions, it would appear that convergence between lower class and middle class French Canadians would increase, based essentially on common concerns of economic deprivation instead of cultural identity.

Extensive economic deprivation among French Canadians of all social classes could bring about a merger which would virtually guarantee a separatist government in Quebec within the next decade. On the other hand, the absence of such a sense of economic deprivation among the French Canadians generally would tend to perpetuate the double pluralism of Quebec which in many ways has been the most important factor in the preservation of Canadian confederation.

The reaction of the Federal Government and the English-speaking population to the manifestation of the social, economic, and political problems of the contemporary colony of Quebec will likely influence the interplay of these considerations and determine the fate of Confederation. French Canadians, similar to minority groups throughout the world, have attained temporary high levels of social solidarity and separatist sentiments in reaction to autocratic and symbolically racist policies and behaviour of the central government supported by majority ethnic groups. The use of arbitrary military force in reaction to the anti-conscription sentiments of the French Canadians during both World Wars and against the workers during the Asbestos Strike of 1949 has been typical of the entire history of French-English relations. But this policy has only contributed to the developing spirit of self-determination among French Canadians of all social classes. The use of the War Measures Act in response to the kidnappings and terrorism of the Front de Libération du Québec in October, 1970 can only accelerate the development of the separatist ideology among *lesQuébécois*, for it will remind them of their common heritage as victims of the double pluralism and elitist collusion which has marked their entire history.

NOTES

1. See, in particular, Herbert Guindon, "Two Cultures: An Essay on Nationalism, Class and Ethnic Tension" in Richard H. Leach (Ed), *Contemporary Canada*. Toronto: University of Toronto Press, 1968, pp 33-59; and Maurice Pinard, "One Party Dominance and Third Parties," *Canadian Journal of Economics and Political Science* XXXIII, August 1967, pp 358-73.
2. Jacques Dofny and Muriel Garon-Audy, "Mobilités professionnelles au Québec", *Sociologie et Sociétés*, I, No. 2 (November, 1969), 277-301.
3. Guindon, "Two Cultures", pp. 57-59.
4. S. D. Clark, "The Position of the French-speaking population in the Northern Industrial Community," in R. Ossenberg, Ed., *op. cit.*, pp 62-88.
5. This is a very crude estimate based on my impression of figures presented by de Jocas and Rocher, "Inter-Generation Mobility in the Province of Quebec", *Canadian Journal of Economics and Political Science XXIII*, Feb. 1966, pp. 58-66 and the considerable upward mobility of the French Canadians since the time of this study.
6. For evidence pertaining to this general pattern, but not including the 1970 election, see Pinard, "Working Class Politics", *passim*. Concerning the 1970 elections, analysis of the votes in various social class differentiated ridings indicated the continuation of the traditional differences in party preference, although not as sharply as before.
7. R. Ossenburg, *Op cit.*, pp 107-109.
8. *Ibid.* p. 112.
9. *Ibid.* p. 114.
10. *Ibid.* p. 115.
11. *Ibid.* p. 117.
12. Quoted in Mason Wade, *The French Canadians 1760-1967*, Toronto: Macmillan of Canada, 1968, II pp 1108-1109.
13. See Dofny and Garon-Audy, "Mobilités Professionnelles".
14. Jacques Dofny, *pers. comm.*
15. Hubert Guindon, *pers. comm.*
16. These studies, conducted by Pierre Guimond and Serge Carlos, both graduate students at the University of Montreal at the time, were reported in a number of newspapers, including *The Montreal Star*, July 26, 1966.
17. Dofny and Garon-Audy, "Mobilités Professionnelles".
18. Hubert Guindon, *pers. comm.*
19. Maurice Pinard, "Working Class Politics: An Interpretation of the Quebec Case", *Canadian Review of Sociology and Anthropology* 7:2 (May 1970)
20. Hubert Guindon, "Language, Careers and Formal Organizations", research in progress.

2. Graduate Unemployment and the Myth of Human Capital

Alexander Lockhart/*Canada Council Fellow in England*

One of the dilemmas affecting all students today is the prospect of unemployment. But for students and politicians alike it is difficult to see how such a situation could have arisen: how in a society with a high standard of living and a high premium on skills, those who possess the skills and the education should be denied jobs. In the following essay Alexander Lockhart examines the economic basis of graduate unemployment and explores how economic mythology came to dominate public policy. In many respects he takes some of the themes of this book several steps further. Not only was public space (the Universities) dominated by the demands of a private economic sector, but politicians attempted to justify their policies in language directly borrowed from economists whose task was to legitimize the activities of that sector.

The implications of this analysis are far-reaching. If Lockhart is right we may see the further growth of an educationally privileged sector who, being denied jobs or being placed in jobs not commensurate with their education, become the focus of dissent and radicalism (a development already marked in the USA). In most respects Lockhart provides the economic foundation for understanding the movements described by Maeots, Brown and Latowsky and Kelner in Section Seven. If his analysis of economics is correct, we have further evidence of a public intellectual space being dominated by narrow, private definitions which failed to take account of wider public issues. The importance of a critical public debate on education and economic issues was never more urgent nor more clearly stated than in this essay.

The Problem

In a speech made to a 1969 graduating convocation the Prime Minister of Canada made the following statement:

> In a growing and prosperous country like Canada the social and economic well-being of all its citizens depends on their capacity to respond quickly to technological change and adjust successfully to developments. The key to the future progress and high standard of living is the education of our young people.[1]

This reiteration of conventional wisdom would hardly be noteworthy if it were not for the fact that in the same year the Canadian Department of Manpower's annual survey of job opportunities for university graduates indicated an average decline of around 25 per cent in the number of new job opportunities for recent graduates compared to the previous year.[2] Significantly, this declining trend, which had begun some 5 years earlier for B.A.s, now reached deeply into science graduates at both the first and post-graduate degree levels. At the same time that industrial demand for graduates was plummeting, the annual increase in the supply of graduates flowing from Canadian universities continued at its decade average of 15 per cent.

Given this and other similar employer surveys, one would expect to see the effects reflected in the unemployment statis-

Published for the first time in this collection.

tics. Unfortunately, such statistical sources do not discriminate adequately between types of unemployment, nor do they reveal 'under-employment', a situation where an individual may take grossly underrated work when jobs relevant to his education are not available. However, several campus surveys do provide confirmation of the rapid closure in occupational opportunities faced by those who have recently graduated with university degrees.

For example, a survey of Canada Manpower and campus placement offices by a Vancouver newspaper revealed that in the fall following the 1970 graduation, 20 per cent of the graduates were still unemployed.[3] Unemployment in British Columbia is always high in the fall, but this represents twice the general unemployment. Unfortunately, this kind of crude survey leaves many important questions unanswered: How many of the employed are under-employed? And how many without jobs are voluntarily unemployed?

Another survey[4] conducted by the local branch of Canada Manpower in 1970 of all the graduates of B.C.'s new Simon Fraser University since 1965 goes a long way towards answering these questions. All respondents had been 'out' at least 1 year since graduation. The nature of work or alternatives to work was queried in detail, and opportunity was given for respondents to evaluate their current situation relative to their expectations. A 55 per cent return was achieved: of these, 52 per cent had sought but did not hold full-time jobs; 77 per cent of this un- or under-employed group had adapted to their curtailed opportunities by renewing their student loans and returning to some form of full-time study (not necessarily post-graduate level). For the less than half who did find full-time employment, nearly one-third said "they did not need the degree to get the job." Such a statement strongly suggests that their work was not relevant to their university training, and they thus may be considered objectively as under-employed. The following comments were cited in the report as typical evaluations: "first degree useless", "education useless", "degree a disadvantage", "might as well have only Grade 12".[5]

There may be particularistic factors about Western Canada and there is certainly reason to believe that one of the above mentioned institutions may not be considered typical. But in the context of the national employment surveys, they certainly represent confirming instances. So too does the rather more intensive and methodologically sophisticated survey conducted by the University of Toronto's Graduate Students' Union (GSU).[6] Although the study is limited to recent PhD graduates, it highlights the emerging anomaly by focusing on the plight of those who have realized the ultimate intent of an education system committed to maximizing the production of intellectual expertise.

The GSU study begins by critically reviewing recent university administered studies into graduate unemployment. Here it is persuasively argued that these other studies have papered over the emerging realities through over-simplified methods or distorted samples. Having made a strong case against the methods of others, the GSU's research pays close attention to its own design. Although the final conclusions and recommendations acquire a strong normative line, this bias is not apparent, at least to this observer, in the research design itself.

According to the GSU study, only 55.3 per cent of those doctoral graduates who sought work during 1969 and 1970 found permanent jobs.[7] An unexpected finding was the revelation that the likelihood of finding permanent employment at the PhD level did not increase over the time of active search. Those who found relevant work tended to do so early while those who were bypassed found themselves in a perpetual limbo.[8] This finding would seem to negate the popular explanation that PhD employment is essentially 'frictional', i.e., that it now takes longer to match individuals to the appropriate jobs, but that in the end everyone gets one.

As for the 44.7 per cent who did not find permanent employment, the study provides very clear data on the nature of their enforced alternatives. Post-Doctoral Fellowships (PDFs) were taken up by 40 per cent of this group; another 15 per cent delayed turning in finished dissertations in order to retain their current fellowship grants; 12 per cent kept their teaching assistantships after receiving their PhD; and 20 per cent reported that none of these alternatives was available and they were doing 'nothing'.[9] Since PDFs are almost entirely specific to the natural science disciplines, the exponential growth in the number of PDFs taken up in Canada reflects the decline in opportunities for science doctoral graduates. In 1956 there were 48 science PDFs in Canadian universities; in 1968, 1000; by 1972 the Science Council anticipates 2500.[10]

Although this staying-in-school adaptation to the lack of relevant job opportunities may initially help disguise the unpredicted emergence of a major socio-economic anomaly, it clearly cannot do so for long. It is therefore essential that the sources of the problem be thoroughly researched and analysed to discover whether the situation is temporary or symptomatic of fundamental changes in the economy's opportunity structure.

Supply and Demand: The Historical Dimension

We can begin by analysing some of the more relevant statistics within their historical context. After the Second World War, North America was in the unique position of having survived with its economy not only intact but in an advanced state of technological development. Radically new forces of production had emerged, and thresholds into fundamentally different organizational concepts had been crossed.[11] The speed with which the war effort had precipitated these changes plus the widespread opinion that these innovations promised new levels of peace time affluence prompted many experts to feel concern about the supply of highly skilled manpower available to the new industrial systems.

This concern was reinforced when economic problems plagued the post-war American economy under conditions where traditional economics models predicted high performance. An explanation of this anomaly came with the development of the theory of 'human capital'. The prime hypothesis of this new theoretical construct was that manpower shortages in certain highly educated technological and managerial occupations were producing a 'bottleneck' in the productive union of ordinary labour and capital. Given this interpretation of the problem the rational cure would clearly be to do everything possible to stimulate growth in the production of human capital so as to remove the critical restriction in the economic process.

The theory found instant support, and the United States embarked upon an immense expansion in its higher educational facilities. Thus within a decade of the implementation of this policy, Clark Kerr, then President of the mammoth University of California system, noted that,

Basic to this [economic] transformation is the growth in the 'knowledge industry', which is coming to permeate government and business and to draw into it more and more people raised to higher and higher levels of skill. The production, distribution and consumption of 'knowledge' in all its forms is said to account for 29 per cent of gross national product ... and 'knowledge production' is growing at about twice the rate of the rest of the economy.[12]

Canada, of course, was no more immune to the diffusion of this new theory than it was to the American culture norm which had always viewed public education instrumentally and had justified previous transformations in its structure in terms of changing economic realities. Thus in spite of a comparatively low level of industrial development and technological demand in determining jobs, Canada nevertheless expanded its higher educational participation at a rate far in excess of all other modern industrial societies with the exception of the United States and Russia.[13] As evidence of this, between 1955 and 1965 Canadian universities nearly tripled their output of graduates, although the university-aged population expanded by only 30 per cent.[14]

This growth rate was double that estimated as necessary in 1955, but in spite of this the Economic Council of Canada complained in its 1965 report[15] that in terms of its 'stock' of education in the labour force, Canada was experiencing a widening gap with the US. The Council reflected the views of most Canadian economists when it recommended that Canada do everything possible to close this 'education gap' as the prime means of achieving its due share of future economic prosperity.

Here is an early example of the intellectual colonization which has recently become a controversial subject in Canadian universities. Canada's economy, though dominated by American capital, is not analogous to the American economy. At the time (1965), the principal areas of human capital shortage in the US economy were in aero-space, electronic components, and other industries dependent upon public contract and subsidy which in turn were part of the function of America's role as a world power.

Clearly, Canada has no such potential, as illustrated by the Government's foreclosure of the 'Arrow', all-Canadian fighter aircraft, and the subsequent collapse of the Canadian aircraft industry. To have imported uncritically a theoretical model designed to meet manpower goals that reflected the American reality would thus seem illogical in the extreme.

By contrast, Sweden, a nation similar to Canada in many ways, has pursued independent policy goals which have resulted in a much higher level of industrialization and a much more stable world trading position (and, incidentally, a slightly higher standard of living) than Canada enjoys. But the important point of comparison is the fact that Sweden has achieved all this with only one-half the proportion of university-aged population attending university that Canada had in 1965.[16]

Thus the basic premise of the human capital theory, i.e., that a causal connection exists between national education levels and national prosperity,[17] would seem to fail past certain threshold levels. Indeed, it is much more logically argued that those nations which have exceptionally high levels of higher educational participation are demonstrating the *effects* of affluence which come from other causal factors.

To treat higher education as a form of personal consumption is, of course, a most legitimate option which may well warrant public subsidy as a means of accruing purely cultural benefits. But the human capital philosophy has never viewed education as personal consumption; rather, education has been rationalized economically as public investment aimed at achieving general economic goals.

This 'higher education as economic investment' philosophy has certainly been reflected in the curricular and enrolment characteristics of Canadian universities. Since 1960 graduate schools have expanded at nearly twice the rate of undergraduate enrolment. This imbalance between 'expert' and 'general' education is further demonstrated if the 'Arts' and 'Sciences' dichotomy is applied to the growth statistics of graduate school. In 1970 only 320 Arts Doctorates were awarded by Canadian universities compared with 1020 awarded in Science.[18] These figures reflect the cumulative effect of the disproportionate rates of growth during the 1960's, rates which are continuing unaltered into the 1970's despite a reversal in these trends at the undergraduate level. The projection of these trends, based on present enrolment, indicate that the ratio between Arts and Sciences doctoral production will reach a 1:10 proportionality by 1973.

Thus the case of the science PhDs is particularly significant, not only because of their disproportionate rates of increase, but also because they reflect the anticipated and planned for end-product of an education system which has since the early 1950's stressed the 'value added' aspect of higher degrees and justified the increasingly high costs of post-graduate production in terms of its alleged widespread economic benefit. (A science PhD is currently estimated to cost the taxpayer $144,000.[19])

Such economic benefits are, of course, wholly dependent upon the assumption that industrial demand for this human capital will match or exceed the available supply. The successive annual reports of the Economic Council, Science Council, and other influential agencies continued to stress this demand aspect through the 1960's. How realistic this high demand *assumption* was, is best evaluated by examining the long-term supply and demand trends for scientific research personnel.

Back in 1959, Canadian universities graduated 200 PhDs. This was half the domestic demand, so in accordance with the 'bottleneck' hypothesis, this shortage was blamed for the economic problems of the day, including general unemployment. A decade later in response to the call for human capital, Canadian graduate schools had increased their annual production of PhDs by a factor of six. During the decade, the bottleneck had been removed, and educationalists were congratulating themselves on achieving 'the impossible'. Unfortunately, the anticipated economic miracle that was to automatically accompany the meeting of human capital demands did not occur. On the contrary, serious economic problems persisted, including the Keynesian anomaly of co-existing high rates of unemployment and inflation.

The cause of unemployment, the labour economists assured everyone, was not stagnation but the fact that too many had too little education to qualify for jobs in a modern economy. But by the mid-60's, university graduates began to be noticeably counted amongst the unemployed and still more were complaining of underemployment. Again following the logic of the human capital theory, the advice to these disillusioned graduates was that they should return to university to improve their qualifications through more specialized professional or post-graduate programmes. But how closely did this advice reflect the realities of the occupation market?

Between 1959 and 1969, while the national PhD output increased six-fold, the overall demand barely doubled. More alarming was the fact that the annual rate of demand increase over this decade had shown a steady decline to the point where by 1968 it was stable, that is, not increasing at all.[20]

These are the statistics of hindsight, but it is amazing how unwilling the relevant agencies were to extrapolate the early warning indicators. An over-reliance on human capital theory by both official government and private industrial sources would seem to be the fault.

In 1968 the National Research Council surveyed the principal Canadian (or Canadian-based) industrial research establishments, asking their research directors to forecast anticipated scientific manpower requisites to 1973. The average annual increase forecast was 10 per cent. However, when the Science Council did a follow-up study in April, 1970 of the 30 most research-intensive corporations which together employ 75 per cent of the industrially based scientists, they found that between the years 1968 and 1970 the actual net increase in scientific employment was less than one-sixth of the original estimate.[21]

In view of this unhappy revelation it is not surprising that in 1970 the Science Council reversed its earlier optimism and regretfully concluded that "the performance of industry has been most discouraging...there have been net decreases in the amount of research and development actually performed in [Canadian] industry...."[22] As for the total number of scientists and engineers employed in Canadian industrial research and development, the Council fears that there is an absolute decline. But on the supply side, according to the Council's projections, even if no new doctoral candidates were admitted after 1970, and counting only those already in the pipeline (allowing for normal attrition), the increase in the PhD pool will continue to grow at the annual rate of nearly 12 per cent until at least 1975.

Of course, such a total closure of graduate admissions is hardly likely, although cutbacks are already occurring – the University of Toronto announced cuts in its 1970 graduate admissions of up to 25 per cent. But even this belated response to the supply/demand logic assures that on the basis of the most optimistic demand projections, there will be two to three new PhDs for every available job over the next decade at least.

Under such circumstances, the once cursed 'brain drain' could be seen as a blessing, at least by the job seekers. But with the existence of analogous conditions in the United States and early warning indicators in the United Kingdom, emigration offers little relief.

As a last resort the option of taking a job that is not functionally relevant to one's highly specialized training must also be considered. This adaptation was suggested by the editor of *Physics Today* who recently recommended that newly graduated physics Doctorates seriously consider high school teaching, social work, or other more menial but socially useful jobs.[23]

But such a suggestion does not appear to lead to a viable solution. Aside from the psychic and economic costs involved in acquiring such production oriented and capital dependent skills as becoming a research scientist only to have one's talent 'wither on the vine' for lack of exercise, the available evidence strongly supports the contention that employers do not look favorably upon those who are 'over-qualified'. However, even if this were not the case, such an adaptation by higher degree holders neglects the plight of those with lower degree qualifications, among whom may be counted high school teachers and social workers.

Indeed, the point of focusing on the special case of the recent PhD graduate was to highlight the general situation for graduates at all levels. Although initially denied and later much mystified by official agencies, the reality of graduate unemployment has now permeated public consciousness. Its fundamental cause, however, remains buried in the failure of the human capital imperative.

* * * *

NOTES

1. Quoted in Marjaleena Repo, *I'm a Ph D Who Needs the Ph D?*, Toronto, Graduate Students' Union, University of Toronto, 1970, p. 8.
2. Canada Department of Manpower and Immigration, *Requirements and Average Starting Salaries: University Graduates, 1969*, Queen's Printer, Ottawa, 1970.
3. Reported in feature article, "Are We Over-educated?", *The Vancouver Province*, November 21, 1970, p. 5.

4. W. L. Roberts, *Simon Fraser Alumni Survey*, (Mimeo), SFU Branch, Canada Manpower, Burnaby, B.C., 1970.

5. *Ibid.*, p. 3.

6. Repo, *Op. Cit.*

7. *Ibid.*, p. 36.

8. *Ibid.*, p. 41.

9. *Ibid.*, p. 41.

10. National Research Council of Canada, *Projections of Manpower Resources and Research Funds*, 1968-72, February, 1969, p. 46.

11. Two popular interpretations of these changes may be found in J. K. Galbraith, *The New Industrial State*, Boston, Houghton Mifflin Co., 1967; and J.-J. Servan-Schreiber, *The American Challenge*, New York, Avon, 1969.

12. Clark Kerr, *The Uses of the University*, Cambridge, Harvard University Press, 1963.

13. The relevant data for 1966 measured in terms of the percentage of university aged population in school is as follows: USA – 43%, USSR – 24%, Canada – 22.5%, France – 16%, Japan – 13.5%, Sweden – 11%, Britain – 7%.

14. W. M. Illing and Z. E. Sigmond, *Enrolment in Schools and Universities, 1951-52 to 1975-76*, Economic Council of Canada, Staff Study No. 20, October 1967, p. 47.

15. Economic Council of Canada, *Second Annual Review*, Queen's Printer, Ottawa, pp. 91-92. The relevant parts of this report were reprinted in *Monthly Labor Review*, April, 1966, pp. 377-80.

16. See note 13.

17. The arguments in support of this position have been most cogently put by E. F. Denison, *Sources of Economic Growth in the United States*, New York, Committee for Economic Development, 1962.

18. Repo, *Op. cit.*, p. 5.

19. *The Vancouver Province*, *Op. cit.*

20. Unpublished Science Council of Canada Report. See also press quotes from the "confidential" Science Council report to the Prime Minister in *The Vancouver Province*, June 30, 1969, p. 17.

21. This figure was arrived at by calculating the discrepancy between the anticipated and actual findings. In the study cited there were 40 instead of the 210 originally estimated. "PhDs Piled High and Deep: The Bonneau Report Revisited", unpublished report by the Science Council of Canada, 1970, p. 1.

22. Quoted in *The Vancouver Province*, June 30, 1969, p. 17.

23. R. Hobart Ellis Jr., "Who Finds the Job?" *Physics Today*, June 1969, p. 117.

---

3.   Rebuilding a Free Society

A. Alan Borovoy/*Canadian Civil Liberties Association*

In two earlier essays in this book F. R. Scott and P. E. Trudeau discussed different aspects of Civil Rights. In 1970 Trudeau suspended Civil Rights in Quebec in an attempt to deal with what he declared to be a crisis of public order: his action was supported by F. R. Scott. Alan Borovoy, the General Counsel for the Canadian Civil Liberties Association, took a different view. In this article, written shortly after the use of the War Measures Act, Mr. Borovoy considers the issues raised by the suspension of civil liberties and outlines the legal case for restoring and expanding those liberties.

The wholesale suspension of civil liberties represents our first response to entry upon the age of violence. Soon we shall have to pick up the pieces and make some hard decisions. Once we recognize that our pre-October tranquility is not recoverable within the foreseeable future, how shall we respond? What adjustments are necessary in a society where urban terror may be part of normal life? Shall we answer subsequent provocations with a suspension of civil liberties? Shall we legislate additional police powers and greater restrictions on a more permanent basis? In short, how will Canada cope with the loss of her innocence?

This article will not deal with the propriety of the Government's decision to adopt emergency powers. In other contexts, I have answered this in the negative. Nor will this article deal with the propriety of the Government's *ever* adopting emergency powers. In other contexts, I have answered this in the affirmative.

These issues have already been debated at great length. What we have only begun to address, however, is what will remain after the revocation of these powers. To what extent will we and should we suffer *permanent* invasions of our traditional freedoms? This is now a more vital consideration.

The comments from official quarters seem to be indicating the direction that we might take. The Prime Minister of Canada has warned us about the possibility of police surveillance on the campuses. The Quebec Minister of Justice has made a number of suggestions about the need for compulsory identity cards and even press censorship. The lack of controversy which has greeted these pronouncements reveals a growing willingness on the part of the Canadian public to sustain a more permanent diminution of our traditional freedoms.

On the other hand, the long-term battle against political terrorism may require not a curtailment but an *enlargement* of our fundamental freedoms. The more we reduce the avenues and the protections for non-violent dissent, the more we incur the risk that dissent will become violent. In an era of deeply felt social grievances between ethnic groups, income groups, and age groups there will be inevitable pressure for substantial change. If the groups seeking change do not feel that the law affords them a fair opportunity to advance their cause through non-violent means, greater numbers of them will resort to or at least endorse violent means. The greatest danger is that otherwise responsible citizens will either sympathize with or decline to oppose political violence. Thus, while our society is legitimately concerned with providing short term protections against the threat of violent dissent, it must simultaneously provide long-term avenues for the expression of non-violent dissent.

In a few months, the emergency powers will be revoked. The problem is how to adjust our short and long-term strategies during the period of the new normalcy which will succeed revocation. To what extent will the impending challenges require a change in our legal safeguards?

Police Powers — A Short-Term Response to Terror

What is the case for the post-crisis expansion of police powers? It is one thing to justify additional powers when there is a real state of apprehended insurrection. But when the *Public Order Act* is revoked, even the Government will be admitting then that there will be no imminent insurrectionist peril. Against what peril then will we need greater powers on a permanent basis? Against terror? Bombings? The possibility of future insurrections?

The onus is on those who would invade our liberties to demonstrate the size of the evil to be purged and the need for the means to be used. Fear is no substitute for thought; faith is no substitute for facts. Evidence of danger and analysis of need are the necessary conditions for a reduction in the freedoms of a free society.

Any proposals for expanded police power must take proper cognizance of their regular powers. Even a cursory examination will reveal that regular police powers are far from inconsiderable.

Essentially, police powers divide into two broad categories — secret information-gathering and open intrusions. The first category includes infiltration, intelligence, and surveillance. The second category includes searches, seizures, arrests, and detentions.

How extensive are the normal police powers of open intrusion? Under the Criminal Code a police officer may arrest without warrant anyone who he has reasonable and probable grounds to believe has committed or is about to commit an indictable offence. He may obtain a warrant to enter a place for search and seizure upon demonstrating to a judicial officer reasonable and probable grounds to believe that the premises in question contain evidence of a criminal offence. Where he reasonably believes that dangerous weapons offences are being committed, he may search without warrant persons and places other than dwelling houses. He may enter without warrant virtually any place including a dwelling house, which he has reasonable and probable grounds to believe is harbouring a person whom he is entitled to arrest. In the absence of dire emergency, it is difficult to conceive why the police would need powers of open intrusion beyond these rather substantial ones.

The powers of secret information-gathering are, at present, virtually unlimited. Almost nothing in law prevents the police from infiltrating, spying, bribing, and even engaging in electronic eavesdropping. While a valid case might be made that some of these powers should be curtailed, particularly wire-tapping and electronic eavesdropping, it is impossible to argue for their expansion. What could be urged, of course, is the more skilful *use* of some of these techniques.

When considering the powers of the police, it would be also wise to bear in mind one of the most significant statements that emerged during the course of the crisis. At one stage, Quebec Premier Robart Bourassa warned his constituents that even the assumption of totalitarian powers could not assure the level of security which we desire. Indeed, there may be little short-term protection which is possible against a small hard core of violent fanatics. Paradoxically, while they are not large enough to possess an all-out insurrectionist capacity, they might be relatively invulnerable to the preventive powers of the state. Even though they cannot overthrow the Government, they can inflict substantial havoc through sporadic sniping, bombing, kidnapping, and assassination. All that is required is a small group of fanatics who are willing to die for their cause. Even the totalitarian powers of the Soviet Union, or as we are witnessing, of fascist Spain, are not enough to prevent all the damage within the capability of a small number of committed terrorists.

The great danger arising from some of these terrorist groups is that the threshold of safety we desire may be, for some time,

an unattainable illusion. But in the quest for it, we may, ourselves, erode the very freedoms we seek to protect. We might surrender a substantial amount of liberty without purchasing a desirable amount of security.

In any event, at this point the proponents of expanded permanent police powers have failed to make their case. They have demonstrated neither the magnitude of the perils we face nor the inadequacy of the powers we have. Apart from a clear and present danger of the illegal seizure of Government, why can't we rely on present police power to provide society with a realistic level of adequate protection? Indeed, why can't the skilful use of those powers prevent the emergence of a clear and present danger? Without satisfactory answers, we should brook no further encroachments.

The Right to Dissent — A Long-Term Response to Terror

So much for our short-term strategies. But what of the long-term strategies? Is the right of and opportunity for non-violent dissent sufficiently guaranteed at present? Is the law fair enough to deprive the violent revolutionaries of sizeable constituencies? In my view, the law in these areas has been defective for a long time. It is potentially repressive and inadequately protective of legitimate non-violent dissent. Moreover, in the aftermath of emergency powers, the political climate may now be more conducive than ever to the actual use of the repressive instruments at our disposal. During the recent debates about the invocation of emergency powers, many claims were made that the existing law was adequate to cope with the perceptible threats to public order. In my opinion, the existing substantive law is not only adequate, but it is also excessive. The wisest preparation for the termination of emergency powers may lie in the liberalization of normal powers.

The Importance and the Limits of Free Speech

One of the most vital vehicles for the promotion of social change is freedom of speech. The right of free speech enables us to mobilize the support of others in order to rectify the wrongs for which we seek redress. Unjust governments and unjust policies are not likely to survive in an atmosphere of free public debate. However, although vital and central, freedom of speech is not and cannot be an absolute. There are some circumstances where other values must prevail. One such value is the social peace. No society can countenance the exercise of speech which precipitates a substantial disruption of peace. As Oliver Wendell Holmes wisely counselled us, there can be no freedom of speech to shout "Fire" in a crowded theatre where there is no fire. In a situation of great physical disorder and violence, there is no meaningful enjoyment of anything, including freedom of speech.

Thus the real issue is how to create a sensible balance between the competing claims of free speech and public order. It is my view that the present law is out of balance. It leans too heavily and unnecessarily toward the protection of peace at the expense of speech. In a number of situations the law restricts the right to speak where the threat to the peace is non-existent, minimal, or capable of adequate protection in other ways. The post-crisis era will require, as never before, the quest for a proper balance. To whatever extent we encroach without need on the freedom of speech, we will promote in our midst the support of violence.

It will be helpful to explore some of the present legal provisions which contain restrictions against free speech. Where possible, we should indicate to what extent the restriction is unwarranted and in what direction reform might lie.

Sedition

The sedition offences purport to punish the person who "teaches or advocates . . . the use, without authority of law, of force as a means to accomplish a governmental change within Canada." Not only does the law prohibit an *act* of force aimed at accomplishing a governmental change, but it also prohibits *speech* in support of such force. What we legitimately seek to prevent are acts of violence. The issue is: at what point in the continuum between the thought and the deed is it appropriate for the law to intervene? Speech which is likely to result in violent deeds is sufficiently dangerous to warrant legal intervention. Speech which is not likely to culminate in this way does not warrant such intervention.

The risk which is created in the sedition offences is that mere teaching and advocacy are wide enough and vague enough concepts to encompass the soapbox orator who has no followers and the intellectual theoretician who seeks no followers. A person who expresses the desirability of overthrowing the government by force is not necessarily a threat. A person who intellectually justifies revolution or violence is not necessarily a threat. The threat is the call to action by someone who has followers. The law properly intervenes at the point where speech is likely to precipitate immediate action. Therefore, the sedition sections should prohibit not the mere teaching or advocacy of the violent overthrow of government, but rather the *incitement* to such action. In the politically polarized climate that we have created, we run the risk of punishing the impotent preacher along with the dangerous demagogue. The Criminal Code should be amended to confine the offence of sedition to the incitement of violence against Government in situations where there is a clear and present danger that the incitement will be acted on.

Causing a Disturbance and Unlawful Assembly

In the summer of 1969, a young man was convicted of the offence of "causing a disturbance" for shouting "traitor Trudeau" at a Liberal Party picnic. Why was it an offence to shout nasty slogans at a noisy picnic? Of course, if a person were to shout even messages of brotherhood so as effectively to interfere with the rights of others, such behaviour might be legitimately punishable. For example, there is no need to tolerate such voluminous vocal ventilation at an otherwise orderly meeting or on a residential street at four o'clock in the morning. Moreover, there might be some basis for visiting penal consequences on the person who shouts a sustained barrage of insults and invective at private citizens. But why, if the target is the Prime Minister and other *public* decision-makers in a noisy public place? Shouldn't the law require that their tolerance be higher?

It appears that the disturbance in question was "caused" by the fact that the slogan was so unpopular in that particular milieu that the supporters of the Prime Minister were provoked to a physical attack upon the accused. Clearly, if the accused had shouted "Bravo Trudeau" no disturbance would have been "caused". The gist of this offence seems to be that the utterances of the speaker attracted violence to himself. Some of the old cases dealing with "unlawful assembly" appear also to take a similar line.

Regrettably, the foregoing case may be a valid expression of the present state of the law. In an article dealing with recent amendments to the offence of "causing a disturbance" one eminent legal authority, Dr. Mark MacGuigan made the following comment:

> In my opinion these words change the traditional law . . . and create an offence . . . where someone uses insulting language in or near a public place and a disturbance results,

even without any intention on the part of the speaker to provoke a breach of the peace.

It is not difficult to foresee the infinite possibilities for repression which inhere in this offence. To whatever extent the law remains in its present form, we will be permitting a violent heckler to exercise an effective veto on freedom of speech and assembly. This section should be amended in order to make clear that, in the context of political and social controversy, a person will be punished not for attracting the violence of antagonists to himself, but rather for inciting the violence of his followers against others.

Hate Propaganda

Recently, a new substantive offence has been added to the Criminal Code. In an effort to counteract a slight resurgence of neo-Nazi activity, Parliament has made it illegal to communicate statements which willfully promote hatred against people because of race, religion, and ethnicity. But many useful utterances in a democratic society will promote what could be described, at the very least, as bitter feelings. The dividing line between creative tension and destructive hate will often be very difficult to draw. Moreover, in its present form, the enactment might imperil people who bear no remote resemblance to the Nazi element for which it was intended.

For example, if a French Canadian nationalist were to denounce the English Canadians for the alleged exploitation of French Canada, could it be said that he was willfully promoting 'hatred' of English speaking Canadians? If an Indian were to heap the blame for his poverty upon the white man, could he be said to be willfully promoting 'hatred' for white people? If a Jew were to indict all of Germany for the atrocities of the Nazis, could he be accused of willfully promoting 'hatred' against all Germans?

Whether or not one agrees with the kinds of views which these people express in the foregoing examples, it would be unfair, unwise, and undemocratic to make them illegal. Yet we run the risk that the formulation, "willfully promote hatred", could lead to precisely such results.

Moreover, the defences which are provided in this section may not be adequate to protect many legitimate exercises of free speech. The defence of truth will have very little application in view of the fact that most utterances in the political arena deal with opinion rather than fact. The immunity conferred upon subjects of 'public interest' gives to the courts far too much power to set the framework of democratic political polemics. On the basis of what criteria and in the light of what evidence will the courts determine whether a matter is in the 'public interest'?

In my view, the risk which this enactment creates to the free speech of a wide variety of people is not justified by the evidence of trouble or potential trouble to the victims of hate propaganda. The Cohen Committee itself, which recommended this legislation, admitted that the hate mongering problem in Canada cannot be described "as one of crisis or near crisis proportion". Moreover, the Director of the Ontario Human Rights Commission, one of the most active government bodies in the field of race relations, declared that ". . . . the Canadian public is relatively immune to extremist, anti-semitic and other 'hate' materials."

In view of the minimal risk to the well being of the intended victims of Nazi propaganda and the potential risk to the free speech of those who have no connection with Nazi propaganda, the best course would be the complete repeal of this section.

Scandalizing Contempt of Court

In the spring of 1969, a young student in the Maritimes went to jail for having written in a university student publication that a certain trial was a "mockery of justice" and that the courts were "tools of the corporate elite". The offence? Scandalizing the court and particularly the presiding judge by bringing the court, the judge, and the proceedings in the trial into "public ridicule and contempt".

A few years earlier, a Vancouver newspaper writer was convicted of scandalizing contempt of court for a crusading article which he had written against the use of capital punishment. In the article he described the jury in a particular capital trial as "the people who planned the murder" of the convicted man and the judge as the one who "chose the time and place and caused the victim to suffer the exquisite torture of anticipation".

What social purpose was served by the imposition of criminal punishment for the exercise of such speech? The offence of scandalizing contempt of court was designed to protect the administration of justice. According to the theory, the courts could not function without the respect of the community. Public statements which lowered or tended to lower public esteem for the courts could undermine judicial authority.

In my view, this is a piece of fatuous mythology. What about the administrative tribunals which also dispense important justice? They can claim no analagous protection to their social reputations. Yet no one has seriously suggested that the Municipal Board, the Liquor Control Board, the CRTC, or the Labour Relations Board need such immunity from contemptuous public criticism. Moreover, the United States Supreme Court, which has no comparable power, has sustained much more vicious attacks without diminution of its eminent role in American society.

On the other hand, an atmosphere of vigorous criticism could improve the quality of judicial performance. Moreover, as the courts move increasingly to the centre of our bitterest social controversies, the right of unfettered criticism will provide an important outlet for disaffected litigants.

The mere existence of the power to punish for scandalizing contempt will serve to inhibit critical commentary. Indeed, the layman who wishes to criticize will be unable to determine in advance whether his proposed remarks are likely to be impugned. The lawyer who wishes to advise him intelligently will be forced to err on the side of caution. Regrettably, the cases reveal little consistency as to what kind of statements will constitute contempt. What one judge may find contemptuous, another may consider fair comment. Compare, for example, the statements which were found contemptuous in the foregoing cases with the following:

Mr. Saint Aubyn is reducing the judicial character to the level of a clown.

... Mr. Justice Higgins is, we believe, what is called a political judge, that is he was appointed because he had well served a political party. He, moreover, seems to know his position, and does not mean to allow any reflection on those to whom he may be said to be in debt for his judgeship.

In both of these cases, the courts acquitted the writers of scandalizing contempt of court. On what basis can we say that the remarks in these cases were any less contemptuous than the ones quoted earlier?

It is better that the judges earn respect through the quality of justice which they dispense rather than through the threat of punishment they can impose. The offence of contempt of court could well be preserved to punish rowdy behaviour in the courtroom, violations of court orders, and commentaries outside of court which would prejudice the interests of litigants before the courts. But there is no basis whatever for perpetuating the power to punish out of court commentary that allegedly 'scandalizes' the courts.

A judge injured by malicious and false statements should have no more power to vindicate his interests than what is available to the ordinary citizen – an action for damages.

Defamatory Libel

During the winter of 1969, a young man in British Columbia was convicted of "defamatory libel" for writing an article in an underground newspaper which awarded "the Pontius Pilate certificate" to a Vancouver magistrate. This case resurrected the offence of defamatory libel from the grave of obscurity in which it had been resting for a generation. It inflicts the punishment of the criminal law upon a person for making a statement that is "likely to injure the reputation of any person by exposing him to hatred, contempt, or ridicule". The original rationale for this offence grew out of the danger that "libellous" statements could provoke breaches of the peace. By now, however, the Criminal Code is overflowing with offences which incite or tend to incite breaches of the peace. In this connection consider the following: counselling the commission of an offence, attempting to commit an offence, causing a disturbance, watching and besetting, obstructing, etc. In view of the multiplicity of prohibitions against promoting breaches of the peace, there is very little role for defamatory libel to play in that area. Virtually the only remaining role is the protection of injured reputations. But why should there be *prosecutions* to vindicate reputations? Why does the state have a greater interest in the reputation of 'A' than in the free speech of 'B'? It is one thing for 'A' to launch a civil action for damages in order to redress the libellous statements of 'B'. But it is quite another matter to threaten 'B' with prosecution, conviction, and possible imprisonment. The vindication of personal reputation does not warrant the awesome power of incarceration. This offence constitutes an additional peril to freedom of speech which cannot be justified by an overriding social value.

Parade By-laws

In the fall of 1968, a group of Vietnam War demonstrators sought a parade permit to march down Toronto's busy Yonge Street. Instead, they were offered a permit to march down Bay Street and University Avenue. Unfortunately, on Saturdays, Bay Street and University Avenue are virtually urban deserts. Thus the parade threatened to become not an exercise in free speech but an exercise in free soliloquy.

Where the Criminal Code usually punishes unlawful speech *after* it has occurred, local by-laws can effectively inhibit speech *before* it occurs. Police authorities exert a peculiar power over freedom of speech and assembly. In virtually every major municipality in this country, the chief of police or police commission has been given the power to determine the time and the route of parades and demonstrations. The determination of time and route is no routine act. It can affect the potency of a demonstration.

Consider this example. The Metropolitan Toronto Police Commission has enacted a by-law which prohibits parades and demonstrations on busy streets unless the parade has been occurring annually for ten consecutive years prior to October 1st, 1964. This exception protects the Santa Claus parade. But the Santa Claus parade is one event which does not require a busy street for an audience. Crowds will flock to whatever street might be assigned to this annual ritual.

On the other hand, political protest could be rendered virtually impotent without ready access to a busy street and an available audience. Without a large audience, it might very well lack the newsworthiness even to attract attention from the media. Herein lies the subtlety of our problem. In Canada we don't ban demonstrations, we re-route them.

The Metropolitan Police by-law also provides that exceptions might be made and busy street parade permits might be granted under "unusual circumstances of municipal, provincial or federal importance". But the power to determine what qualifies as an "unusual circumstance" is exercised by the Chairman of the Police Commission and the chief of police.

A little research will uncover a host of "unusual circumstances" in which these police officials have granted the right to parade on Toronto's busy Yonge Street. Among such exceptions was a convention of the racially segregated Fraternal Order of Eagles. Although this group was granted the permit it sought, the Vietnam parade was re-routed from the busy portions of Yonge Street.

The Metro police by-law would appear to provide a most feeble basis for the exercise of so basic a democratic right as freedom of assembly – feeble because of its perennial priority for freedom of traffic over freedom of assembly, feeble because it considers social ritual more important than political protest, and feeble because it delegates the power to make exceptions to police officials. Granted, political protesters cannot be given automatic access to any street at any time. But the crucial power to set out the criteria for determining time and place should be given to an elected body, not to an appointed one.

The crucial power to apply those criteria in particular cases should be given to someone other than a police body. The police interest in a demonstration is an orderly flow of traffic; the demonstrator's interest is a conspicuous event. Often, these interests are in conflict. No law or by-law should make the police umpires of their own ball game. Yet the by-laws of virtually every major municipality in this country give to the police such amazing power. By re-routing and re-scheduling, they can take the life out of protest. The preservation of such power in the hands of the police constitutes an unwarranted impediment to the right of non-violent dissent.

Beyond Freedom of Speech

As important as freedom of speech is, it is not an adequate instrument for promoting social change. Freedom of speech is based upon the questionable proposition that people can be persuaded by rational argument. Unfortunately, this is a fallacious description of human behaviour. A social order which confines social protest to rational debate would load the dice against social change. Pressure, not reason, is the chief instrument of social persuasion. An employer who pays low wages is more likely to be moved by a well-organized strike than by a well-prepared sermon. Politicians hungering for position will respond more to political tension than to logical syllogism.

This is not to advocate the abandonment of reason in our social discourse. It is to recognize its limitations. Granted pressure without reasons is irresponsible, but reason without pressure is ineffectual. Of course, the range of pressure may not include physical violence. Violence is too much and reason is not enough. The proper operation of the democratic processes demands the effective right to exert non-violent and unpleasant pressures.

Social reformers will need to exert these pressures not only against government, but also against other institutions, both public and private. Social change can be effected not only by the decisions of government, but also by the actions of employers, landlords, educators, etc. What our new era will require is

a set of fair ground rules for the waging of inter-citizen and inter-group conflict. The role of the law is to distribute the levers of pressure more equitably among the parties to social conflict. The more advantaged parties use money as their primary instrument of pressure. The less advantaged use their bodies – they can organize pressure groups, create picket lines, conduct boycotts and so on. Unfortunately in to-day's Canada, the ground rules are not working fairly. The instruments of pressure available to the less advantaged are beset with legal impediments.

The Right to Picket

Where the street demonstration is usually addressed to broad issues of public policy, the picket line usually zeroes in on special issues of business policy. Picket lines are set up near business establishments in order to pressure the proprietor to change his policy. The idea is to discourage customer patronage and employee recruitment until improvements are made. The picket line is one of the most potent weapons of non-violent pressure for workers against employers and for buyers against sellers. No nation committed to the rhetoric of democracy would dare to abolish the right to picket for a lawful purpose. We are more ingenious. In most provinces in this country, we don't abolish picket lines, we cut them down. Evidence of violence or disorder on a picket line can produce a court injunction restricting the number of pickets to not more than three or four per gate. What may have begun as a powerful expression of vital grievances will end up looking like a pathetic advertisement for "Eat at Joe's".

The restrictive injunction confines the pickets to rational discussion. The pickets are solemnly reminded that the token picket line has preserved for them the right to disseminate information about their dispute. They are told they don't need large numbers to convey information. True. But how in the world will the mere dissemination of information help the pickets to persuade prospective employees and customers to stay away from the impugned establishment? Self-interest propels people to continue dealing with the proprietor. They go there seeking economic benefit. How can a token picket line compete with that?

Of course, we cannot allow the pickets to employ violence. But it would be unfair to confine them to reason. The picket line which is both justified and effective will exert social pressure on those seeking access to the picketed premises. The idea is to visit the collective contempt of the protesters on those who would cross the picket line. The object is to make the "scab" feel capable of standing up under a worm every time he enters the impugned premises. This is the discomfort which the pickets must inflict in order to offset the benefits which the proprietor can offer.

The reduced picket line necessarily weakens the pickets' ability to heap social pressure upon a person who would enter the impugned premises. A large demonstration carries greater moral weight in our community than does a token one. Token picketing, regardless of the realities, tends to convey an appearance of half-hearted or non-existent support. If the proprietor may attempt to entice people through his doors with economic benefit, why can't the pickets attempt to repel them with social pressure?

The aim should be equality of bargaining power. Clearly, the restrictive injunction unduly favours proprietors against protesters. Social peace and public order are the interests most invariably invoked to justify picket line restrictions. This raises the dubious proposition that because 'X' commits violence on a picket line, 'Y' can be prohibited from picketing. If 'X' commits violence, 'X' should be charged and convicted. But 'Y' should not be denied one of his few effective weapons of non-violent pressure.

In most situations, there is no reason to doubt the ability of the police to protect the public peace even in a setting of large picket line demonstrations. Not long ago, for example, the Montreal police department was credited with having performed magnificently in protecting the peace during the controversial McGill-français march. That was a march of five thousand. The largest picket line is rarely a fraction of that. Only in those rare circumstances where it can be reasonably demonstrated that police power is not sufficient to protect the peace should there be any consideration given to interfering with picket line activity. When we reduce the size, we remove the sting.

The Right to Boycott

Another instrument of non-violent pressure for change is the consumer boycott. This tactic involves the collective withdrawal of financial patronage from an institution whose policies are under attack. Properly organized, the boycott can be a potent weapon. Very few injuries can elicit the response of financial injury. The Negroes of Montgomery, Alabama repealed one hundred years of segregation by collectively depriving the bus company of their customary patronage. The United Farm Workers won collective bargaining rights through a nation-wide boycott of California grapes.

The problem is that a boycott is very difficult to organize. It is an attempt to sell an amorphous mass of people on the legitimacy of a cause. Apart from the economic difficulties in organization, the conduct of a consumer boycott is beset with legal obstacles. Unless they have enormous resources in order to undertake an advertising campaign, the boycotters will probably seek to publicize their appeal at the very places where the products of the impugned establishment are being offered for public sale. Very often this will lead to picket lines in front of retail outlets which are not parties to the central dispute.

The difficulty is that in almost every jurisdiction in this country the proprietor of a picketed establishment in these circumstances could probably secure a court injunction to prohibit *all* of the picketing near his premises. When people involved in a dispute with one party picket the premises of another party, such activity is considered "secondary picketing" and may, therefore, be liable to complete prohibition.

A few years ago a clothing workers' union decided to launch a boycott against their employer's product. Some of the products were being sold at a retail store in a small Ontario community. The union set up a small picket line in front of the store; their signs simply identified the goods in question and declared that they were not union made. There was no attempt to discourage general public patronage of the retail establishment. The proprietor of the store sought and secured a court injunction removing all of the pickets from the vicinity of his premises. The Ontario Court of Appeal declared that "... the right ... to engage in secondary picketing ... must give way to (a business man's) right to trade. ... " Through judicial pronouncement and in some cases legislation, such secondary picketing is prohibitable almost everywhere in Canada. Conceivably, this doctrine might apply even outside the labour context in which it was spawned.

Why is the right of the merchant to trade more holy than the right of the boycotter to engage in secondary picketing? Significantly, the pickets could not *force* the public to boycott the premises or the goods. All they can do is attempt to *persuade* the public to boycott the goods. As long as the objective of the boycott is not unlawful, why shouldn't the public be able to choose for itself between the salesmanship of the proprietor and the appeals of the pickets?

Of course, some boycotts have been and will continue to be inequitable and unreasonable. But, unless their goals are unlawful, it is better to let the consuming public make the decision. The public, not the courts, should decide whether to support the seller or the boycotter and whether the cause is more valuable than the product. Such an approach, at least, maximizes freedom of choice. It enables the less advantaged to compete more equally with the more advantaged. The law should referee the conflict, not determine its outcome.

The Right to Retaliate

Several months ago in a Canadian city, a notice was served on two tenants requiring them to vacate their apartments by the end of the month. Coincidentally, they had just organized a union of tenants and had successfully secured a reduction in rent from a recalcitrant landlord. At the beginning of the 1970 school season, two high school students in a Canadian city were ordered by the Board of Education to transfer to another school. Both of them had been involved in the publication and dissemination throughout their school of a newspaper highly critical of some of their teachers.

Pressure invites retaliation. We cannot deny the recipient of pressure the right to retaliate with pressure. The concern of the law should not be who wins the fight but how the fight is waged. The ground rules must be fair. However, some types of retaliation exceed the limits of fairness. This may occur when one party has the power unilaterally to deny his adversary the necessities of life – job, home, education. Only the superheroic would take such risks. Since society is composed essentially of men rather than of saints, such retaliatory power can render academic our instruments of non-violent pressure.

The instruments of non-violent pressure must enjoy some immunity against excessive retaliation. This will explain some of the changes in our labour relations legislation. At one time employers could punish union membership with loss of employment. Clearly, the existence of the right to join unions became less than meaningful when the employer could so punish its exercise. To-day our labour laws prohibit discrimination for union activity and they empower independent tribunals to reinstate and compensate for such violations.

What we have done to protect employment, we must do for other day-to-day activities. Consider the landlord-tenant relationship. Apartment tenants all over Canada are banding together to exert greater pressure and engage in collective bargaining with their landlords. Of course, they have the legal right to create such organizations. But numbers of landlords have threatened organizers and members with eviction. In some cases, they have even carried out the threat. Tenant union organizers report that scores of people have refused to join because of the fear of retaliatory eviction.

In such a situation, the democratic right to form tenant pressure groups is somewhat illusory. For too many people the loss of home will be too great a price to pay for the exercise of this right. At the very least, legislation should remove from landlords the power to retaliate against tenants simply because they joined tenant organizations. Moreover, we should make available impartial and expeditious machinery with the power to rescind evictions which are held to be retaliatory.

Another example of such power exists in the relationship between students and educational authorities. On campuses and in high schools all over the country, students are challenging the policies of educational authorities. The inequity arises from the fact that in most cases the educational authority has the legal power to suspend and expel. Although this is not the place to set out the limits of permissible pressure for students, it is the place to call for due process in campus conflicts. Since the education authority is an interested party in disputes with rebelling students, it should not have the final say. It should not be empowered unilaterally to deprive a person of his education. The student should be entitled to appeal suspensions and expulsions to impartial and independent adjudication.

Our various instruments of non-violent pressure must not only be permitted, they must also be protected. They cannot effectively co-exist with the unilateral power to deny the necessities of life. At the very least, we should modify the unilateral feature. We should provide impartial adjudication for denial of residence and education as we have for denial of employment.

* * *

The invocation of emergency powers has dangerously polarized Canadian society. The conduct of the crisis has sustained the impresssion that the citizen has no choice except insurrection or repression. Muddle-headed leftists are defending illegitimate violence; right wing yahoos are attacking legitimate non-violence.

The post-crisis survival of Canadian democracy requires the expansion of effective alternatives. The aggrieved and the disaffected must have more viable channels of non-violent expression – in speech, assembly, economic sanction, and organization. One need not side with rebels against authority, labour against management, tenants against landlords, students against educators, or consumers against producers in order to challenge the present law and the present ground rules. One simply needs a sense of fair play and a desire to make democracy work. Which side is right or wrong at any particular time is not the primary concern of the law in this context. The concern of the law here should be that all parties, right or wrong, have the effective opportunity to impress their views on the social consensus.

It is in this direction that we might find an alternative to the unacceptable extremes of the polarized society. The concept of civil liberties was never more relevant.

---

4. Canada's Colonies

Last Post/*Montreal*

Each essay in this section has attacked what we have called the 'sustaining myths' of Canadian society. This last essay is concerned with one of the most cherished of Canadian myths – that Canada is an 'honest broker' in international affairs. With the last few years of diplomatic activity, it is easy to see how this particular myth is maintained. Prime Minister Trudeau has paid visits to many countries as a peace maker – Russia, India, South East Asia and to the Commonwealth Prime Ministers' Conference. Canada recognized China before the Americans did, and made overtures to pacify the Arab-Israeli conflict in the Middle East. None of these diplomatic ventures stand up to much international scrutiny: no European country took Mr. Trudeau's visit to Russia seriously (most did not report it), and (perhaps cruelest of all) the recognition of Red China was taken in Europe as kite-flying on behalf of Washington.

But there is a further and more insidious myth which is directly related to the diplomatic manoeuvres: Canadians recognize themselves as a tolerant multi-racial society. If the essays by Drache, Bergeron, Vallières and Nagler in the sections above suggest that this may not be true, any analysis of Canadian attitudes to Negroes should deepen the doubts. In 1967 Robert Winks published a short book called Canadian-West Indian Union: A Forty Year Minuet *(London: The Athlone Press), which suggested that one of the reasons why the Canadian Government was* not *able to secure the British Caribbean as her share of the booty after World War One was because Canadian parliamentarians were appalled at the idea of* Black *men sitting in Ottawa alongside Whites. In a more recent book,* The Blacks in Canada *(North Carolina: Duke University Press, 1971), Winks has underlined the fundamental racism in Canadian culture. The following essay takes this analysis a step further. In the Caribbean today Guyanese, Trinidadians and Jamaicans are not demonstrating against British and American imperialism but against Canadian. The tragedy for Canada is that many of the*

Reprinted from *The Last Post*, 1: 3 (1970), by permission of the publisher. "The Caribbean: Why They Hate Canada" was researched and written by the Toronto staff of *The Last Post*.

enterprises they most complain against are not owned by Canadians, but by Americans. We are back to the theme of Kari Levitt's essay at the beginning of this book. By the 'silent surrender' of her economic resources to the USA, Canada is not only subject to the viccissitudes of the American economy but also has to take the brunt of foreign attacks on decisions which were ultimately not of her own making. The private space of the multi-national corporations becomes the public face of Canada.

While rich Canadian tourists lolled about the gleaming resorts of the Caribbean islands a few weeks ago, their easy living was shattered by news that did not fit their fantasies of a holiday in paradise: revolution, it seemed, had broken out in Trinidad. Black power 'mobs' were surging through the streets, a large part of the army had mutinied, demonstrators were being shot down in Port-of-Spain, and foreign businesses, very definitely including Canadian businesses, were surrounded by hostile crowds. The troubles of last February, when such sacred cows as the Royal Bank of Canada were stoned and smashed, were starting all over again – only this time, things appeared far more serious.

The governments of the foreign countries that own and control the economies of the West Indies certainly thought things were serious. Canadian External Affairs Minister Mitchell Sharp assured the House of Commons that plans were ready to evacuate Canadian citizens – though he refused to say what the plans were. That any plans were more likely to involve invasion than evacuation was made clear by the United States – frantic as always with fears of another Cuba – which immediately sent a fleet of six ships, including a helicopter carrier with 2,000 Marines, a landing ship dock, a landing ship tank and an amphibious troop-carrying attack vessel. Arms were quickly flown in to the beleaguered government of Prime Minister Eric Williams, the good friend of Canadian, American and British businessmen.

The rich Canadian tourists, whiling away the dregs of winter in an area of the world that Canada in large part dominates, must have felt a little uneasy as they accepted soothing beverages from immaculate Black servants who called them "Mister Peter, please", who giggled at their jokes and who wept as they left (to quote a Jamaican tourist advertisement).

Why, they must have asked, was there such 'ingratitude' – the same sort of 'ingratitude' that Black West Indian students at Sir George Williams University had shown when they helped smash a computer last year – among a people upon whom Canadian business had showered millions of dollars in investments?

The more hard-headed and unscrupulous among them knew the answer. In Trinidad over 15 per cent of the population is unemployed. The figure reaches one-third among youths between 15 and 19, and 27 per cent among those who are 20 to 24. One-fifth of those who are able to find work at all are employed for less than 32 hours a week. And the situation is the same – or worse – in the other islands of the Commonwealth Caribbean.

Canadian investments in Trinidad and throughout the Caribbean do little to help, for they are made not to help but to exploit – employing only few people by using the latest labor-saving machinery, and paying a pittance to those who are permitted to work; enjoying the profitable bounties of tax holidays and other concessions; and after an initial investment, taking more out of the islands than they put in. Although the Gross Domestic Product of the islands increases by 6 per cent a year, this does not help the Black or Indian workers, for what it measures is the increase in the rate of profit of Canadian and other foreign businesses in the area. The bauxite and alumina used in the Canadian aluminum industry come from Jamaica and Guyana, but every dollar's worth of finished aluminum contributes 83 cents to the Gross Domestic Product of Canada, only 17 cents to that of the West Indies.

Canadians at home know little of their country's economic and political power in the West Indies. Yet it is massive and growing. And it is made not to help the poverty-stricken people, but to manipulate them in the interests of businesses and financiers in Montreal and Toronto whose names are household words.

Driving into Nassau from Windsor Field Airport, you can see Canadian money sprinkled along the route like icing on a cake.

You pass the site of a $20 million condominium project by Toronto's Residential Resorts Development, said to be the largest single housing project in the Bahamas. There's the Canadian-owned Nassau Beach Hotel; the home of F. Ronald Graham, late Vancouver sugar millionaire; the home of Oakville contractor Joseph Tomlinson.

You can see the balconied 20-bedroom house where Canada's most famous Bahamian expatriate, Kirkland Lake gold prospector Sir Harry Oakes, was hacked to death in 1943.

Venturing further, you may catch a glimpse of Lyford Cay, E. P. Taylor's millionaires' ghetto, where the average home costs $700,000 and police man the gates. Of 12,000 developable acres on New Providence Island, E. P. Taylor owns 5,000, while another 3,000 are held by Morry Wingold, a Toronto investment broker.

You may spot the Lucayan Beach Hotel, a $12 million investment in opulence and crime that helped bring about the spectacular collapse of the Atlantic Acceptance Corp. in 1965. Toronto mine promoter Lou Chesler lavishly cultivated politicians to extract a gambling concession from the government, with the idea of turning the area into a new Monte Carlo. At least $1 million in 'consultant fees' went to finance minister Sir Stafford Sands, who also held down a chair on the board of the country's largest bank, the Royal Bank of Canada. The resulting casino with its 'Whites only' policy soon fell out of Canadian control and into the hands of American gangland syndicates.

The Bahamas are only the tip of the iceberg of Canadian financial penetration of the Caribbean area, a penetration political as well as economic because of the tight interlocking of government and business elites. The result is a situation that differs little from colonial slavery, in which the source of wealth is foreign and White, the source of labor local and Black.

The release of colonial bonds brought only a more subtle enslavement to North American financial interest, rather than independence. But the people are beginning to see that the idea of harmonious multi-racial societies is sheer nonsense in a social system where a five per cent non-Black minority controls all the country's natural resources in the interests of foreign shareholders.

In Trinidad, thousands marched through the cane fields and a branch of the Bank of London & Montreal was nationalized. In Guyana, the Student Society of the University of Guyana backed a demonstration in front of the Canadian High Commission, a Royal Bank and the Demerara Bauxite Co., an Alcan subsidiary. In Jamaica, the students formed a wall to block Governor General Roland Michener from the campus of their university.

When the revolution comes, Canadians and their $500 million investment will be in the front line of targets.

And Canadian businessmen know it.

Shortly after the takeover of the Sir George Williams computer centre in protest over Canadian racism, a battalion of 850 Canadian troops landed in the mountainous Jamaican interior to conduct a tropical training exercise.

Since then, two more Canadian regiments have practised their counter-insurgency techniques in the Jamaican hills, while island politicians held closed-door talks on 'subversion' and banned Black Power exponents.

Popular ideology has it that the concept of Canadian imperialism is absurd. Few believe Canada covets foreign natural resources because, it is argued, she has plenty of her own.

Yet Canada is deeply involved in the Caribbean, with a web of investment that snakes through banking, insurance, tourism, real estate, minerals and secondary manufacturing. So sensitive about foreign ownership in her own preserve, Canada is blind to its dangers in other economies. This country imposes ownership restrictions on its own banking and mineral resources, while continuing to cloud its monopolization of Caribbean resources behind a smokescreen of 'good corporate citizenship' and 'more jobs'.

These rationalizations conceal more than they reveal. An examination of Canadian capital at work shows that its investments serve to maintain the Caribbean economy in a state of dependence, disintegration and perpetual under-development.

The expansion of Canadian concerns into the preserve of their nearest Commonwealth neighbors is not a recent development. Because of the salt fish and rum trade links between Halifax and Jamaica, the Bank of Nova Scotia was transplanted to Jamaican soil in 1889. By 1910, Canadian banks had sprouted a network branching through Bermuda, Cuba, Mexico, the Bahamas, Puerto Rico and Trinidad.

After building the Canadian Pacific Railway, Tycoon William Van Horne left Canada to lay rails across Cuba and Guatemala, and won notoriety for his ability to extract scandalous concessions from governments. In turn-of-the-century Cuba, he took advantage of Spain's defeat and his influence in US financial circles to start building a trans-island railway before any government had the power to stop him. And in Guatemala, he is reported to have said: "We asked for everything we could think of and we got all we asked for."

Axe-murder victim Sir Harry Oakes took the fortune he had garnered from Kirkland Lake, Ontario gold, and retired to the

Bahamas to escape his taxes. There he developed a country club and bought Nassau's largest hotel, the British Colonial, sinking half a million dollars into redecorating it to match the color of his wife's favorite sweater. He also gave the island an omnibus service but charged the islanders for rides.

Recognizing the area's economic importance, Canadian politicians have been suggesting a political takeover of the Caribbean for the last fifty years. As early as 1919, Prime Minister Sir Robert Borden considered laying claim to the islands as Canadian possessions, on the grounds that Britain owed Canada something for its sacrifices during the First World War. However, Britain wanted the islands' resources for herself and blocked the transfer.

Since then the idea of political occupation of the islands has masqueraded under less offensive names. Millionaire eastern Caribbean developer Ken Patrick of Montreal's Marigot Investments called the West Indies "the right size problem for Canada", and suggested a "monetary and customs union", in which Canada would play senior partner to the smaller islands and provide for their defence and external diplomacy. In return, the junior partners could provide access to a good climate, agricultural products that previously had to be imported from the US, and a tropical terrain in which to train the Canadian Mobile Command (this suggestion antedated the force's actual deployment in Jamaica).

Other proposals have included 'associate statehood' and turning the area into Canada's eleventh province. Senator Paul Martin stated the case very succintly before the Senate Foreign Affairs Committee hearings on the Caribbean when he said: "Britain's withdrawal and the apparent disinclination of the United States to increase its commitment in the area leave a neat geographical sphere of influence where Canadian effort will not be overshadowed."

As for sphere of influence economics, the Canadian banks have contributed more than is commonly realized to setting up Canadian capitalists in their exploitative positions. There is no doubt that the banks encourage the sale of resources to foreign investors rather than the development of a native entrepreneurial class, and also counsel investors to extract superprofits to compensate for risk. The Canadian banks have worked closely with island governments in attracting North American investment through tax incentives and condoning profit repatriation, leaving no money in the island economy except inside the ministers' pockets. The late Robert Winters, when he was trade minister, called the Canadian Caribbean banks "good ambassadors" – the recent stonings of bank windows and rampages through their premises in several Caribbean countries are an indication of the warm feelings they engender in the local population. In Jamaica's tourist centre the native businesses are festering holes, while the Canadian banks, three in one block, are outrageously large, modern and mushrooming. In Kingston, they have even gone drive-in.

The Canadian insurance companies, at least a dozen and in control of 70 per cent of the area's business, are only beginning to yield to the demand to become good corporate citizens. In previous years, they drew complaints even from the tame local governments for taking West Indian savings and investing them in Canadian projects.

Because of the lack of economic integration, foreign investors play off one island against another in their efforts to get the biggest tax concessions for their ventures. A *Financial Post* history of one Canadian West Indian subsidiary shows the results.

The company is Cooper Canada (formerly Cooper-Weeks), a Toronto sporting goods manufacturer. By setting up a Barbados subsidiary, it is allowed to import raw materials and factory equipment duty-free, and enjoys a 10-year tax holiday, followed by a corporate tax rate of 12½%.

Labor, mostly women, can be had at salaries of $9-$12 a week, enabling the company to make a pair of hockey gloves in Barbados for 35 cents, which cost $1.40 in Canadian labor costs. Add on shipping and import duties, and the gloves can still sell on the Canadian market for 25 to 30 per cent below their domestic competitors.

An added bonus, the *Financial Post* reporter points out, is that management can be flown in from Canada until the local government begins to exert pressure. This, despite the fact that Caribbean satellite operations are justified in the name of more jobs for the local population.

"The Barbados government is very hot – some would even say a bit too anxious – to get local talent at the helm."

John Jack Cooper, president of the parent company, is confident that what happened in Trinidad won't happen in Barbados. "I have such great faith in the people of Barbados that I really don't think it can happen here. We just have to take that chance."

What he has faith in is their continued ignorance. For when a company pays trifling wages, no taxes, no duties and exports all its profits as well as its products, what benefits does it offer the economy it lives parasitically off of, using native tax revenue to finance its roads, harbors and other infrastructural conveniences?

Canadian manufacturing concerns that have exploited government-offered tax concessions to relocate in the West Indies include Bata Shoes, Ogilvy Flour, Seagram's Distillery, Hiram Walker Distilleries, Waterman Leather, True-Form Industries, Polly Cello Packing, Dominion-Canadian Timbers, Vachon et Miron, Salada Foods, Moore Business Forms, Forsyth Shirts, Wellinger & Dunn and Imperial Optical.

The new Caribbean Development Bank, to which Canada is one of the major contributors of development funds, is also expected to encourage satellite manufacturing operations – for example, flying down computer components for circuit wiring, then shipping them back for further processing. This kind of enterprise leaves the island none of the value added in later processing, and is highly capital-intensive, making few ripples in the vast idle labor pool.

This is especially true of the bauxite industry which, through Alcan Aluminum Ltd., guarantees only 9,000 jobs in the whole area. In Jamaica, where Alcan contributes 28% of export earnings, it provides only 3,300 jobs, employing 0.05 per cent of the total labor force.

Not that this is the only disadvantage of leasing this vital resource out to foreign developers. Alcan has successfully resisted years of attempts to get a smelter installed in Guyana so that the Caribbean could get its hand on the value added in fabricating – a long ton of dried bauxite is worth $104 after processing into alumina in the Caribbean, as compared to $1837 after smelting and semi-fabricating.

Former Guyana Prime Minister Cheddi Jagan says in his biography that a United Nations study was done, indicating that an aluminum smelter in Guyana could pay for itself out of profits after 10 years. Alcan has never acknowledged this report, and says that it will negotiate with Guyana if power becomes available "at an economic cost." It is unlikely that hydro power in Guyana or nuclear power in Jamaica could ever be competitive with the vast source at Arvida, Que., even though it may be economically feasible.

And when the worried government of Guyana reacted to the upsurge in Caribbean discontent recently by hinting it would like to buy a controlling interest in Demerara Bauxite, Alcan replied flatly that as far as it was concerned, both company and government were bound by the 25-year contract signed in 1958. Sources within the Burnham government admitted that negotiations were expected to last "a long time" before the miracle would come to pass.

Alcan is one of the many examples of American capital operating through a Canadian management base. Formed in 1928 as an offshoot of the Aluminum Co. of America (Alcoa), Alcan has only 34.7 per cent Canadian ownership and is dominated by the American Mellon-Davis interests. President is Nathaniel Davis, whose father Arthur Vining Davis (after whom Arvida, Quebec is named) left an aluminum estate of $400 million.

The Demerara Bauxite Co. in Guyana was first set up by Alcoa in 1916, later becoming an Alcan subsidiary. Aided by government concessions, Demba paid no royalty on bauxite mined on its own lands up until 1947 and only 10 cents per ton on crown lands.

The centre of the industry is Mackenzie, the Guyana town that grew up around the Alcan mines. Until recently, it was a company town in the worst sense of the term, practising an active policy of apartheid. And even today, it is to a large extent a segregated society.

In Mackenzie, Alcan owned the land and the houses, ran the high school and appointed its teachers, governed the recreation centre, the cinema, the swimming pool and the only all-purpose store. It even sponsored the president of the local YMCA. Those who did not live in the town – mainly workers who lived in Wismar on the opposite bank of the Demerera River – had to carry and present passes before they were allowed to land on Mackenzie soil.

Even within Mackenzie there exists effective segregation. The workers live in a depressed, slum area to the north called 'the village'. Staff members live in the plush area of Watooka, with exclusive clubs and social amenities such as a golf club.

Workers can seldom rise in the employment hierarchy, are poorly paid, are at the mercy of the arbitrary power of foremen, and are subject to a severe list of penalties, at the foreman's discretion and without appeal. It is hardly surprising that the workers react with violence (of 32 work stoppages in the period 1962-67, only two were called by the unions) or that theft directed against the company is common and not regarded as in any way dishonest.

A serious target of complaint is the company hospital. Workers say that whatever their ailment they are always given the same treatment: a bottle of unidentified and useless medicine that they have named 'ADT', – 'any damn thing'.

Guyanese who are on the administrative staff are better treated, but even here intolerance is pervasive. The company frowns on any but the slightest contact between staff Guyanese and the workers, and too many trips from the management ghetto of Watooka to the workers' village of Mackenzie is frowned upon. Both Guyanese and white Canadians on staff are nominally paid the same salary – $1,000 a month. But the 'natives' are paid in Guyanese dollars and the foreigners in Canadian dollars – one Canadian dollar is worth $1.63 in Guyanese currency.

Alcan's track record in Jamaica isn't much more impressive. In production since 1952, Alcan offers fewer jobs here than in its smaller Guyana investment and employs only 40 per cent Jamaican management.

After the land is mined out, the company replaces the topsoil for grazing but operates no reforestation program. A *Globe and Mail* journalist reported seeing a 3000-acre pond full of unusable iron oxide sludge and was told that the mud is "a small price to pay for it all".

Alcan owns a total of 48,000 acres of Jamaican land, renting out 20,000 acres not currently in use to 4,500 tenant farmers, and farming 10,000 acres itself. To show that 4 acres of land and leases of less than 7 years aren't insuperable obstacles to being a good farmer, it has started a 'Farmer of the Month' program, as an "example of what small farmers can do if given understanding and the right sort of encouragement."

This investment in farmer training is a strange outgrowth of a company whose main business is aluminum extraction and processing. Even more surprising when you consider what Alcan boss Nathaniel Davis told the Senate hearings when asked why Canadians are more suited to developing the Jamaican bauxite industry than Jamaicans: "We believe basic economic sense should prevail and that these countries should use their resources in areas that they can develop better themselves." If Jamaicans aren't even to control their own farming it's difficult to see what other 'areas' Davis has in mind – if any.

Alcan's thinking seems to be based on concern for an undiversified economy dependent upon a wasting asset. Yet what will help the country more: taking over native land holdings then renting them back, or processing its bauxite output for industrial uses? Davis admits that little or no industrial research is done in Jamaica, an indication that Alcan is not ultimately interested in the contribution of the bauxite industry to modernization of the economy as a whole.

After the Canadian government's recent blocking of the Denison Mines uranium takeover, and limitation of foreign ownership to 33-1/3 per cent how can it condone the operation of wholly-owned mining subsidiaries in other countries?

Besides Alcan, Canada has another 'multi-national corporation' soon to capture a controlling position in another island economy. Ontario-based Falconbridge Nickel Co. (also American-controlled) is developing a $195 million investment in the Dominican Republic, with ferronickel production slated to begin in 1972. The Dominican government has a 9½ per cent equity interest in this investment, which was announced soon after the US Marines invaded the country and stabilized the economic climate for American-Canadian investment.

While Alcan tries to improve the agricultural industry, Canadian investments in tourism help retard its diversification. North American hotels take up good arable land or hold it for speculation then on top of that import most of their foodstuffs, (removing it as a source of livelihood for the islanders). The hotels make heavy demands on the water supply, draining off large amounts for watering lawns and filling swimming pools.

In countries where the land is fertile enough to grow anything, large amounts are spent on food imports, mostly for the hotel industry which tailors its menus to North American tastes. Building materials are also imported, so that at least 40 per cent of tourist profits leave the country as import costs.

The combination of low wage rates and North American room rates ($50-75 a day in season) has attracted large Canadian investments in tourism, mostly in Miami Beach-type hotels. Commonwealth Holiday Inns, for example, currently has two hotels in Antigua and Barbados, three more under construction in St. Lucia, Granada and St. Vincent, and plans on paper for five more in other islands. Toronto Skyline Hotel just opened one in Kingston, Jamaica and has another planned for Ocho Rios.

In view of the large hotel investment, the Canadian government has tried at various times to set up a school for hotel management in the Caribbean, but found itself blocked by inter-island squabbles about its proposed location.

Real estate developers are often guilty of the same crimes. The *Toronto Star* tells the story of a Toronto developer, Ken Eaton, who bought a 200 acre chunk of good agricultural land in tiny Montserrat and divided it into 780 housing subdivisions, with about 80 per cent Canadian residency. As an incentive for locating there, he persuaded the government to lower income tax and abolish death duties for residents. But at the same time, the existence of his housing project required a massive tax outlay for a deep water harbor, roads and shopping facilities.

When told that his housing project was a ghetto, Eaton could not understand what was wrong: "Naturally our standards are higher. We have barbecues on the beach and we cook T-bone steaks. Do you expect the natives to eat the same food?

...In Canada, a truck driver doesn't live in an executive's house."

E.P. Taylor has plans to build a city of 100,000 people next door to Nassau, to include five golf courses, a millionaires' ghetto and at least one resort hotel. His New Providence Development Co. has already generated revenues of $1.1 million without having erected a single building. He profits from the sale of byproducts of the development process – from gravel, to water, to ice cream from the grazing cows.

A *Financial Post* columnist has said that Taylor is probably the most powerful single voice in the Bahamas' economy. He's chairman of the Trust Corp. of the Bahamas, which handles the affairs of 1,000 registered companies; chairman of RoyWest Ltd., a bank consortium which is the main source of the islands' venture capital; and unpaid chairman of the economic council. The F.P. columnist says, "Canadians in fact are Nassau's new colonizers and E.P. Taylor is their prophet."

Canadian aid figures to the Caribbean reached $24 million last year, a relatively small amount but the largest per capita allocation to any underdeveloped area. Like most other aid-giving countries, Canada ties its aid to the purchase of Canadian goods and services, but has lowered the tied factor from 80 to 66-2/3 per cent. This still has the effect, however, of subsidizing exports of domestic manufacturers and making it harder for island governments to complete their priority projects.

Because Canada has no fleet, up to 25 per cent of loans get eaten up by shipping and insurance charges. With all the aid administered through inefficient and corrupt island government bureaucracies, there is incredible waste. A Senate witness told the hearings about a shipment of Canadian school furniture which sat around on Antiguan docks for at least two months before anyone came around to pick it up. By that time, much of it was missing or destroyed.

As a last resort, a partial solution to the grave unemployment problem – a problem Canadian business helps to create – would be to throw open Canada's doors to immigration from the West Indies. Canadian concerns reap gigantic profits from their Caribbean investments, then bring most of the profits back to Canada. If the profits aren't allowed to remain with the people, the people ought at least to be allowed to follow the profits.

Nothing is less likely to happen. Canadian elites remain thoroughly racist in their attitudes. It is true that the new immigration laws passed in 1967 ended gross discrimination through quotas, but they replaced this with a nine-point test in which the most important factor is arranged employment. And what sort of employment is arranged? For most West Indian girls, the best that can be hoped for is a job as a domestic servant. At least 10,000 girls from the Caribbean are now engaged in this refined form of penal servitude in Montreal and Toronto.

Their lot in Canada is seldom easy or happy. More often it is deeply humiliating. Although the families who employ them try to hide their contempt beneath a mask of good manners, the children that the girls have to clean up after are less restrained and reveal the attitudes they have been taught by their parents. To be told bluntly by a five-year old child, "I don't like you because you're Black" is a frequent experience.

And the situation worsens when the girls try to break out of their domestic prisons and get other jobs. Reported one girl after applying for a job: "When I arrived for the interview I was told the job was already filled." Said another who applied for a position as saleslady in a shop in Montreal's rich English suburb of Westmount: "I was told, 'I'm sorry, but in Westmount I couldn't have a colored saleslady.'"

Another time-honored way to enter Canada was through the farm labor program, by which West Indian labor was imported for two to three months to harvest crops on Canadian farms for $1.65 an hour – a rate higher than the Caribbean standard, but lower than Canadians are willing to work for. This year, however, the Canadian government announced a cutback in the program, closing off even that outlet.

Canadian companies with money to invest have been welcomed with open arms by the Caribbean governments, in the hope that industrialization would solve unemployment and other problems, and on the assumption that only foreign investors could provide the capital for industrialization. There have been industrialization drives, long-term tax holidays, customs rebates, free industrial parks, generous government loans and so forth.

But the program, although enormously successful, has defeated itself. Canadian and other foreign capital has poured in – but the benefits have poured back out. The concessions handed out left and right to attract capital mean that the governments get little in the way of tax revenue. By promising investors a cheap supply of labor, the governments have ensured that little money stays in the islands in the form of wages. And Canadian firms by using the latest machinery and organization methods, have employed few workers so that the unemployment pool, far from being drained, continues to swell. Where the area is truly rich in resources, as in the bauxite of Jamaica and Guyana, those resources are stripped from the ground for advanced processing in Canada – and it is the advanced processing that confers the greatest benefits, so that it is Canadians, rather than West Indians who profit.

As the Caribbean governments hand their islands over to foreign business control, they progressively lose the ability to help their people by anything other than drastic means. But, so far, those governments have shown no appetite whatever for drastic measures. On the contrary, they continue to act as willing partners in the growing bondage of their islands to Canadian, American and British businessmen. So helpless have they become that, since the recent uprising in Trinidad, the best solution that the island's politicians have been able to come up with is the reintroduction of the barbaric punishment of flogging as the penalty for civil disorder.

With bankrupt governments now apparently helpless to resist the demands of the Canadian and other investors to whom they have bound themselves, the West Indian peoples are turning to direct action. It is a natural and inevitable response to the greed of foreign investors and the connivance of weak and often corrupt governments. It is the response of a trapped people seeking freedom and justice.

There will be more uprisings in the Caribbean – and there will be more rich Canadian tourists who will find their jolly larks rudely disturbed by the smell of gunfire and the sound of breaking windows, until the day arrives when there will no longer be immaculate Black servants calling the rich Canadians 'Mister Peter, please', giggling at their jokes, and weeping when they leave.